The Revolution in World Politics

The Revolution

Chairman, Committee on International Relations, The University of Chicago

and Research Associate, Center of International Studies, Princeton University

New York and London

in World Politics

Morton A. Kaplan, (Editor)

John Wiley and Sons, Inc.

Contributors

Vernon V. Aspaturian, Pennsylvania State University

Leonard Binder, University of Chicago

Norman Birnbaum, Nuffield College, Oxford University

George I. Blanksten, Northwestern University

Richard A. Falk, Princeton University

Ernst B. Haas, University of California, Berkeley

A. M. Halpern, RAND Corporation

Malcomb Hoag, RAND Corporation

Stanley Hoffmann, Harvard University

Bert F. Hoselitz, University of Chicago

Herman Kahn, Hudson Institute

Morton A. Kaplan, University of Chicago

R. C. Nairn, Yale University

Herbert Passin, Columbia University

Dr. Robert Waelder, The Institute of the
    Philadelphia Association for Psychoanalysis

Immanuel Wallerstein, Columbia University

Ann R. Willner, Harpur College

Charles Wolf, Jr., RAND Corporation

Joseph J. Zasloff, Pittsburgh University

Foreword

By the end of the 1950's it had become clear that, since World War II, the foreign policy of the United States had been exhausting itself in attempting, with decreasing success, to defend an international status quo which was, in many respects, unviable —which, in fact, existed less in the real world than in an image held by American policy–makers of what the world ought to be like. On the whole, American policies were ill-adapted to the world environment within which they were supposed to preserve American security and welfare over the longer run.

To my mind, this deficiency of American foreign policy—or, rather, of the basic strategy which gives direction to the many component policies—results mainly from two clearly related conditions. One is an inadequate analytical grasp of the political, economic, technological, and ideological forces—many of revolutionary impact— which are shaping and reshaping the world that we inherited from past generations. The other, and more fundamental, is the continued traditional preoccupation with essentially domestic, sectional, and local interests, pursued on the implied assumption —which has been only rarely and, in each case, briefly suspended in American his- tory—that these interests can be satisfied, in the future as well as at present, in iso- lation from the rest of the world. This preoccupation marks not only the vast major- ity of the electorate, but also the majority of political and opinion leaders; it is, therefore, forcefully expressed in Congress, which, in its legislative initiatives and responses, is in much closer touch with domestic than with international realities. It is this essential inward-looking perspective of the American people—at a time when the outside world is searchingly looking in on us—which accounts for their insufficient willingness to give matters of foreign policy the unflagging attention, the imagination, the forbearance and tact, the energy, and the financial resources which must be forthcoming if the survival of key American values is to be safe- guarded.

Unless the first deficiency is corrected, United States leaders will find it difficult to see the world as it is, and as it is changing, and to discover the means by which the forces of change can be affected, if often only marginally, in order to make them yield results more in keeping with our long-run interests. But unless the second deficiency is mended, unless our provincial outlook cedes to an abiding commitment to live and act in the larger world, from which no safe retreat is now feasible, the first deficiency will be hard to remedy, for our leaders will feel little incentive to do so; and, even were it remedied, our leaders would be frustrated if, though knowing what should be done, they lacked the freedom of action which only a new and firm commitment on the part of the nation can supply.

This book is meant to be a contribution toward mending the first deficiency. It contains a penetrating analysis of a considerable sample of what Professor Kaplan calls "the universe of discord, of protest, of revolution" which the United States must duly understand and come to terms with; and it suggests some lines of American policy, both political and military, which, properly implemented, should have appreciable success in this strange but—for us as well as everyone else—one and only universe.

What is said about the new and "uncommitted" countries may be unwelcome news and grate harshly on some of our provincial sensibilities. We may no longer regard "neutralism" as immoral, but we are quick to call expressions of it—as, for example, at the Belgrade Conference of September 1961—irresponsible (although it is not clear that the degree of irresponsibility displayed by the uncommitted countries as a group is much below international par). It is just possible that we call them irresponsible because they do not see things our way, and that they respond in kind. But they do represent more than a third of mankind, and the support they could give to the West might be fully as valuable as the support the West is able to lend them.

The military problem aside, it may well be that the United States and the West can get by with an essentially defensive foreign policy, although it would probably have to be one more intelligently accommodating in design to the interests (and foibles) of the uncommitted countries and a great deal more vigorous in execution than has been the case over the past decade. It may turn out, however, that the survival of the West requires a new and outward-thrusting policy which has a strong, even revolutionary, appeal to the nations of the West, to uncommitted countries, and even to populations, if not to their governments. It should be based on the idea of a new world order in which war, at least highly destructive war, has become obsolete, in which all communities—small or large—remain free to find and maintain their own political, economic, and cultural systems, and in which pressing worldwide problems of want are attacked on the basis of a world-wide, though voluntary, marshalling of resources.

The discerning reader will find in *The Revolution in World Politics* many analyses and ideas with an important bearing on this problem. It is for this reason, as well as our related interest in research on revolutions, that the Center of International Studies is pleased to support Professor Kaplan's searching enterprise.

KLAUS KNORR

Princeton
October 1961

Preface

This book grew out of the assignment to the editor by the American Political Science Association of the task of planning the international relations panels for the 1961 national meeting in St. Louis. In an effort to make the panels both interesting and useful to professional political scientists, the editor sought for a topic of both interest and importance. The present topic—the revolution in world politics—was the result of that search. If the papers really were to be useful, they ought to be publishable; from the beginning then, we operated on the assumption that the papers would be published.

However, we desired to have a meeting of the participants at which they could discuss their papers and help each other in suggesting revisions. This would also add to the unity of the project and the esprit of the participants. At this point, the Center of International Studies at Princeton University, through its Director Klaus Knorr, came to our assistance and provided funds for a conference of the writers. This was held in Princeton in June 1961. We broadened the conference to include papers needed to give the book adequate coverage of its subject, but which, because of time and space limitations, would not be presented at the St. Louis meetings. These papers included the two by the editor, the Zasloff and Birnbaum papers, and the Nairn paper. At the suggestion of a reader for John Wiley and Sons, we added a paper on military policy. We chose the paper by Malcolm Hoag which, minus its new last section, appeared in the July 1961 issue of *World Politics*. All other papers were written expressly for this book. However, because of its timeliness, the foreign policy paper was published separately by the Center of International Studies as a policy memorandum. The project in its present form was supported by and is a product of the Center of International Studies at Princeton University.

MORTON A. KAPLAN

August 1962

Acknowledgments

The editor and authors wish to thank the following for permission to use quotations:

Journal of African History (G. Shepperson, "Notes on American Influence on the Emergence of African Nationalism").

Presses Universitaires de France (Jean-Paul Sartre, "Black Orpheus," from *L'Arte negre (Présence africaine)*, No. 10–11 (1951); originally published by the Librairie Gallimard in *Situations III*, 1949.

Princeton University Press (Almond and Coleman, *The Politics of the Developing Areas*).

Midwest Journal of Political Science (T. C. Schelling, "The Retarded Science of International Strategy").

Pantheon Books (Jacob Burckhardt, *Force and Freedom*).

Massachusetts Institute of Technology Center for International Studies (Alexander Dallin, *The Soviet View of the United Nations*).

Permission from Madame Mathilde Mantoux (Etienne Mantoux, *The Carthaginian Peace*, published by Oxford University Press).

Harvard University Press (Hovet, *Bloc Politics in the United Nations*).

Council on Foreign Relations (Gillin, "Some Aspects for Policy" from *Social Change in Latin America Today*, Richard N. Adams et al., published by Harper and Brothers).

Librairie Armand Colin (Stanley Hoffmann, *Organisations Internationales et Pouvoirs politiques des Etats*).

International Organization (C. Hart Schaaf).

Harvard University Press (Frank Knight, *Intelligence and Democratic Action*).

Fleming H. Revell Co. (Alexander Walters, *My Life and Work*).

American Association for the Advancement of Science (C. P. Snow, "The Moral Un-Neutrality of Science").

The National Institute of Social and Behavioral Science (David E. Apter and Carl Rosberg, "Nationalism and Models of Political Change in Africa," published in the Symposia Studies Series, No. 1).

Princeton University Press (Charles Goulston Gillespie, *The Edge of Objectivity*).

Council on Foreign Relations (Felix Houphout-Boigny, "Black Africa and the

French Union," from *Foreign Affairs Quarterly*).
Dodd, Mead & Company (Ann Roe, *The Making of a Scientist*).
Thomas Nelson and Sons Ltd. (*Ghana, The Autobiography of Kwame Nkrumah*).
International Publishers (V. I. Lenin, *Collected Works and Selected Works*).
Carnegie Endowment for International Peace (Lincoln Bloomfield, "Law, Politics and International Disputes," from *International Conciliation*).
Hamish Hamilton Ltd. (Sir Lewis Namier, *Avenues of History*).
Harvard University Press (T. C. Schelling, *The Strategy of Conflict*).
Public Affairs Press (Doris Appel Graber, *Crisis Diplomacy*).

M. A. K.

Introduction

The Revolution in World Politics would be a portentous title for a book were not the word "revolution" quite so overworked. The word cannot keep its strength when applied to changes in automobile designs and clothing styles. Yet, there are portentous and momentous currents abroad in the world that can be described accurately only by the overworked and inexact term "revolution." Perhaps every generation feels that it stands at some revolutionary threshold. Certainly I felt this way once before when, in the 1930's, Fascism posed both an internal and external threat to the dominant democratic ethos. Perhaps those who felt this way were not entirely wrong, for the Fascist powers may have lost their "once in a thousand years" gamble to change the political and social map of the world only by a combination of fortuitous circumstances.

Perhaps the Fascist challenge may be viewed as the spasm that preceded the present tidal wave threatening to engulf us in the surging currents of political change. Our introductory paper by Dr. Waelder traces the source of contemporary developments back to the French Revolution. Certainly there is some truth in this, although others might find its source or sources elsewhere. We could argue indefinitely about the genesis of the present revolutionary crisis in world politics, but we cannot really doubt its actuality if we are to understand or to respond to political reality.

Our writers begin with the assumption that we are living in a revolutionary age. They are not concerned primarily with defining "revolution" in some general sense or with finding the true genesis of the revolution. They are concerned with the present scope of the revolution, with the nature of the demands being made by masses, by elites, or by revolutionary organizations, and with the potentiality of these demands for producing revolutionary change. These are deep and complex questions about which we know much less than is necessary. The state of our knowledge does not permit simple answers—nor does the nature of the subject. Although scholars are already working on such topics selflessly and with surpassing ability, much more requires to be done.

This book divides the revolution into three general categories, although, of course, no simple scheme of this sort really can be maintained. There is the revolution resulting from the entry onto the world stage of a large number of new nations aspiring to modernize themselves. Many of these nations are ex-colonial nations who see themselves as fighters against imperialism. They are conscious antagonists of a system of domestic and international order they regard as bad or immoral. Often they fail to distinguish between those aspects of the order we in the West would agree are bad and should go and those aspects we would consider essential not only to our own security and way of life, but also to that of many of the new nations.

The second aspect of the revolution—or the second revolution—consists of the Communist challenge to the existing social and political order both intranational and international. Two Communist powers, Russia and China, allied by their ideological adherence to Marx-Leninism and, at least, by some common strategic interests, lead an impressive array of satellite nations and allied parties throughout the world in a dedicated effort to subvert existing social and political relations and to replace them by new relations based on authoritative Marxist doctrine.

The third aspect of the revolution might instead be called pre-revolutionary. The democratic powers faced by the challenges from the Communist bloc and the new nations lack both cohesion and conviction. Important elements of their populations are satisfied with what they have but are unwilling to take risks, except perhaps when directly threatened. Other elements of the populations of the Western nations themselves accept much of the revolutionary philosophy. They are discontented and disenchanted. They want change of a Leftist nature. There is no—or very little— dedicated and loyal support for the status quo. In the United States, in particular, the "loyalists," by and large, are themselves revolutionaries who support not existing institutions, but radically changed institutions that never existed in our history and that are inconsistent with our national values. They are nationalists in an age when the nation-state necessarily and inevitably is losing its sovereignty and autonomy. The birch rod in the mailed fist is as much the symptom of disordered retreat from political reality and responsibility as a Bertrand Russell who sees little but plots and insanity in Western governmental policy.

These three sources of discontent or protest give focus to the volume that follows. Those who dislike the categories employed may place all blame on the editor. The writers of the individual chapters worked loyally and ably within the framework provided by the editor, although sufficient freedom was permitted so that each could focus on that aspect of his assignment that interested him most. This increased, somewhat, the inconsistency that must appear in any symposium; but it also, I believe, encouraged more original and thoughtful contributions than would have been likely had the editor provided a detailed outline of items the individual papers were designed to cover.

Contributors were chosen primarily for their ability rather than their agreement on particular interpretations of the revolution, or revolutions, occurring in international politics. The range of opinions extends from Dr. Waelder's stern criticisms of the various protest movements to Mr. Birnbaum's rather sympathetic but incisive portrayal of the British Left. These disagreements are, I think, understandable and desirable. The events to which reference is made are extremely complex; onesidedness is rather difficult to avoid. Interpretations do tend to be highly selective and to ignore important and pertinent aspects of ambiguous reality. Nonetheless, the reader may agree with me that the areas of unplanned agreement among the writers are much more impressive than the areas of disagreement.

This book is not intended to exhaust the subject of international politics or even of important developments central to current international politics. Important constructive developments such as NATO and the Common Market have not been treated, although they figure in the analysis. There are, however, many valuable studies of these new organizational developments.

Even the subjects that are treated are not treated exhaustively. Although developments in the underdeveloped areas are analyzed, such important areas as India do not receive special treatment. It is hoped that the universe of revolutionary discord in new and underdeveloped nations is sampled effectively, and that the reader will understand that the revolutionary demands in these areas cannot be lumped together. They have different antecedents and respond to different requirements.

The papers on world order are designed to explore the setting within which the protest movements are enunciated. These papers may help us to understand the possible consequences of the protests for the development of world politics. The section on responses is intended to explore the policy implications of the revolutionary protests in the present world setting. The papers in this section illustrate the different pressures which different requirements, for instance, economic or military, place upon American policy in an era of revolutionary change. The attempt to reconcile different needs is one of the most difficult tasks that policy-makers face.

It need not be emphasized that this book is exploratory. It does not pretend to definitive analyses or prescriptions. It is designed, however, as an aid to understanding.

Some few words about the individual papers may be in order. Dr. Waelder was assigned what may have been the most difficult task of any of the paperwriters; he was asked to do a general paper on the movement of protest against Western societies. Since the protest movements do not fall into clearly defined categories, this placed a heavy burden upon him. It was exceptionally difficult to perform this task well within the existing space limitations or to qualify assertions in a manner likely to satisfy all. An attempt to do justice to all runs the risk of doing justice to none. It is a tribute to Dr. Waelder that commentators on his paper generally found themselves in broad agreement with him although they may have disagreed on details of exposition. In some ways the crucial paper of the collection, Dr. Waelder's contribution illuminates our understanding of the depth and intensity underlying the protests against our capitalistic and democratic mores and institutions. It is important to recognize that these protests are strongly ideological: In Dr. Waelder's use of that term, they are resistant to correction based upon controlled observation or investigation. Rational argument is useless. The protesters want change desperately and think they care little about what change brings so long as it destroys what is—although of course utopian images pervade the speech of the protest movements. One might, if one wished, draw the conclusion that the only potential remedy is to change the conditions that produce the protest. We cannot preserve the status quo or revert to some imagined golden age.

Mr. Birnbaum's paper makes specific the concentrated longing for change that is fermenting in the territory of our British ally. The British, despite their welfare-state concessions to the advocates of change, have not succeeded in stifling the demands of their radical Left. The British economy is stagnant. The empire dissolves in a myth of impossible and inharmonious commonwealth. Britain retreats querulously to the status of a third-class power. It is not viable in the age of hydrogen missiles and yet is reluctant to engage itself productively in some larger political unit such as the Common Market. Is it wonderful that there is so much apolitical futility in Great Britain? Is it not to be wondered at, on the contrary, that so many Britons—indeed a large majority of the nation—go through the motions of participating constructively and without protest in an outmoded institutional framework that has little relevance to the problems of our age? The resurgence of the Gaitskell leadership of the Labour Party and the present British flirtation with the Common Market are hopeful signs in a different direction, but it is still too early to assess their importance.

We are inclined to view the British political system as stable when contrasted with the French. And yet, Professor Hoffmann's brilliant paper gives us some reason to believe that French society—as it modernizes, divests itself of empire, and enters into a larger European community—may be mitigating, to some extent, the problems that have plagued French political life in the past. France may be in a period of transition and, despite the present travail accentuated by the Algerian problem, may possibly be on a road that, after some other problems are solved, might lead to stability.

The British and French papers deal with protest movements in Western democratic societies. Professor Passin's incisive paper shifts our attention to a non-Western democracy, Japan. In Japan, industrialization is producing a shift of population that may threaten the dominance of the conservative forces to the advantage of a Left that is non-democratic if not anti-democratic. On the other hand, the startling improvement of Japanese economic and social conditions may undercut the hold of the non-democratic Left on the urbanized worker. Thus, two parallel processes of change are occurring in Japan, and the relative rate of change may be highly important in determining whether Japan solves its problems in a democratic manner.

The three preceding papers sampled the nature of the protest movement in developed areas. The succeeding five papers deal with the protest movement in developing areas. Professor Blanksten's paper places Castroism in its Latin American context. This may have disturbing implications for the United States. Cuba may now be a Communist state, even if a peculiarly Latin Communist state. However, the revolution was genuinely indigenous in its origins; was in some sense responsive to the real needs of the nation, if it were to modernize and to produce some modicum of social justice; and may well provide an example for other Latin states, if the United States is unable to find and to implement some other solution for their problems. Defense of the status quo in Latin America is not a policy that can be supported on the basis of rational analysis.

The two important chapters by Leonard Binder explore the internal and external objectives of the Egyptian revolutionary movement which, of course, received strong support elsewhere in the Arab world. No one can read these chapters without being impressed by the depth of the desire to modernize and to retain independence in foreign policy. Moreover, it is distinctly to the interest of the Arab nations to force the rival blocs into a bargaining contest over them, unless the Arabs carry this so far that they set in motion forces undermining the position of the Western bloc. Had this been better realized at the beginning of the Eisenhower administration, some serious mistakes in American foreign policy might have been avoided.

Professor Wallerstein examines the forces of pan-Africanism which inspire the present politics of that continent. It is difficult to deny that a certain amount of racism is involved, but this is only a natural reaction to the history of the area and of the people who spring from it. Stable conservative regimes cannot be expected in Africa. The problems of the young nations of the area and the demands of the young and rising counterelites preclude this. Moreover, as in the Middle East, there is a drive toward some form of overarching political framework. Whether this drive will be frustrated, as it appears to have been in the Middle East, or whether it will be fulfilled, the fact of the aspiration and the consequences of that fact for internal politics, external policy, and intervention by the radical African nations in the affairs of their less radical neighbors will affect African politics for some time to come. American policies that ignore these demands are hardly likely to be effective.

Professor Zasloff's paper on Indochina deals with an area, unlike the preceding papers, where regionalism is weak. Moreover, this area is one where both Chinese and Russian Communist pressure is extensive. The country itself is divided, undeveloped, torn by dissension, and ruled by an authoritarian regime that does not have enthusiastic support from the populace. It is subjected to internal war and guerrilla attack. It is likely to be the next target after Laos of a large Communist push. As such, it furnishes a case study for what later might happen elsewhere in southeast Asia. Conceivably, at some point, Iran and Iraq in the Middle East—or even India or Pakistan, although these are much larger nations—might face similar problems. There is some need, therefore, to understand the nature of the problem if the United States is to be prepared to deal with it.

The fine papers by Professors Aspaturian and Halpern require little comment. They outline the goals of Russian and Chinese foreign policy with respect to both the form of political life in other states and the character of the state system itself. It should be clear from their papers that the policies of the two Communist giants, despite differences, are revolutionary in a sense that American policy cannot be. Change and disruption naturally work to the disadvantage of a nation such as the United States, which desires minimal change in the character of the international political system and prefers the kind of stable world in which ordered reform of inequitable social and political systems can be carried out. This gives the Communist powers an enormous advantage over the United States. Within limits they can afford to be irresponsible and we cannot. And yet we must understand what the goals of the Communist powers are and the means they are willing to employ to achieve those goals, if we are to cope with the challenge they present.

The next section of the book deals with aspects of world order. My paper on bipolarity is designed to apply the "balance of power" and loose bipolar system models as partial explanations of the differences between contemporary international politics and those of an earlier period. The models, however, are not designed to be either directly descriptive or directly predictive. They are equilibrium models designed to explore equilibrium conditions in an abstract sense. That is, they deal only with a restricted set of variables which must be expanded before the models can be used either descriptively or predictively. Even within the framework of the abstract model, the loose bipolar model does not possess great stability. The bulk of the paper is designed to show that a number of quite specific historic factors affect the behavior of nations in ways that make the system even less stable. Were it not for nuclear deterrence, very severe system disturbances might already have occurred. If the uncommitted nations continue to act in ways disruptive of universalistic principles of international order, the equilibrium of the system will remain quite precarious.

Professor Haas' incisive paper on revolutionary nations and the United Nations is designed to explore the stability of the organization as its environment and the goal structure of its members change. He reaches the conclusion that the authority of the organization is increasing but that its legitimacy is not. This is a depressing conclusion for those who believe that international stability depends on an increase both in international authority and in legitimacy; yet, impressive evidence is offered for the view expressed. Professor Falk on the other hand focusses his attention on the normative aspects of international behavior rather than on the organizational. He discovers that the constraints on intervention are not as strong as they were during the "balance of power" period, but he finds some hope for international order in a potential support for universalistic rules.

Herman Kahn's chilling paper on technological change and international order reminds us that time may not work in our favor. Technological developments that are within our reach may make nuclear weapons so cheap that small nations, guerrilla forces, and criminal bands may come to possess them. Kahn concludes that the existing form of international organization cannot endure for long, as it is incapable of preventing a major blowup. But Kahn holds out little hope that we will agree to change the form of international order—at least to the degree that is necessary—short of a major catastrophe.

The last series of papers attempts to explore the responses to the revolutionary developments in international politics that are potentially open to the United States. The incisive paper by Hoselitz and Willner does not overestimate the possible consequences of American support for modernization in the underdeveloped areas, but it sees such a policy as the only one that might succeed. The article by Dr. Wolf explains the use of a novel methodology designed to explore alternative military-aid strategies. Initial employment of this methodology indicates that within certain limits policies that shift funds from military aid to economic support do not lose much, if anything, from the standpoint of the military defensibility of the area involved and do contribute to its political and economic stability.

The Hoag paper is a powerful theoretical treatment of the limits of nuclear deterrence and as such has important implications for American efforts to deter the Soviet Union (and China) both in the central European theater and in various peripheral arenas. The relationship between the nuclear forces and conventional ground forces is explored. It should be clear from this paper that the military component is an important one for meeting the Communist threat. If the right military systems and strategies are chosen, war may be avoided and time gained to meet the Communist threat at other levels of response. If this is not done, non-military policies that satisfy the revolutionary protests may not avail, for the Communist powers may be able to employ military force, or the actual or implied threat thereof, to produce changes in the political environment that forestall any other kinds of effort we might make.

The Nairn paper is an illuminating treatment of a subject that is becoming increasingly important in the world arena, namely, guerrilla warfare. The Communists are making increasingly effective use of this tool in revolutionary areas to embarrass us or to defeat us or our allies. They understand this weapon both practically and theoretically while we remain amateurs. The present paper does much to relieve our amateur status. It tells us much about how to defend against guerrilla warfare but reaches fairly pessimistic conclusions about the ability of the West to use a weapon of this type against the Communists without extensive political reforms in the affected areas.

The final paper on American foreign policy in a revolutionary age attempts to use the other papers to learn how to change American foreign policy to cope with the revolutionary tides. It holds that the United States has failed to distinguish between a stable and an unstable international environment and has often acted as if the nineteenth-century "balance of power" system were still operating. It concludes that the United States must learn to use these revolutionary movements and to direct them into desirable channels, but that they cannot merely be opposed or deplored.

Contents

I. THE MOVEMENT OF PROTEST AND REVOLUTION   *1*

1. Protest and Revolution against Western Societies, 3   *Robert Waelder*

II. PROTEST MOVEMENTS IN DEVELOPED AREAS   *29*

2. Great Britain: The Reactive Revolt,   *Norman Birnbaum*

Part I, 31, and Part II, 45

3. Protest in Modern France, 69   *Stanley Hoffmann*

4. The Stratigraphy of Protest in Japan, 92   *Herbert Passin*

III. REVOLUTIONARY PROTEST MOVEMENTS IN UNDERDEVELOPED AREAS   *111*

5. Fidel Castro and Latin America, 113   *George I. Blanksten*

6. Pan-Africanism as Protest, 137   *Immanuel Wallerstein*

7. Nasserism: The Protest Movement in the Middle East, 152
   Leonard Binder

8. Egypt's Positive Neutrality, 175   *Leonard Binder*

9. Peasant Protest in South Viet Nam, 192   *Joseph J. Zasloff*

IV. THE COMMUNIST CHALLENGE TO THE STATUS QUO IN A REVOLUTIONARY AGE *207*

10. The Challenge of Soviet Foreign Policy, 209 *Vernon Aspaturian*

11. Communist China's Demands on the World, 233 *A. M. Halpern*

V. PROBLEMS OF INTERNATIONAL ORDER IN A REVOLUTIONARY AGE *249*

12. Bipolarity in a Revolutionary Age, 251 *Morton A. Kaplan*

13. Dynamic Environment and Static System: Revolutionary Regimes in the United Nations, 267 *Ernst B. Haas*

14. Revolutionary Nations and the Quality of International Legal Order, 310 *Richard A. Falk*

15. The Arms Race and World Order, 332 *Herman Kahn*

VI. PROBLEMS FOR POLICY IN A REVOLUTIONARY AGE *353*

16. Economic Development, Political Strategies, and American Aid, 355 *Bert F. Hoselitz and Ann R. Willner*

17. Defense and Development in Less-Developed Countries, 381 *Charles Wolf, Jr.*

18. On Stability in Deterrent Races, 388 *Malcolm W. Hoag*

19. Counterguerrilla Warfare in Southeast Asia, 411 *R. C. Nairn*

20. United States Foreign Policy in a Revolutionary Age, 431 *Morton A. Kaplan*

Index 467

I

The Movement of Protest and Revolution

I

1

Protest and Revolution against
Western Societies

Robert Waelder

Since [the French Revolution] has made the impression of striving more for a renovation of mankind than merely for a reform of France, it has kindled a passion such as even the most violent political revolutions have heretofore not been able to produce. It started a proselytizing campaign and brought propaganda into the world. In this way, it eventually assumed a religious character which astonished contemporaries. Even more, it became itself a kind of religion, an imperfect religion, to be sure . . . but one which nonetheless has flooded the world with its fighters, its apostles and its martyrs. . . .

> Alexis de Tocqueville, *L'ancien régime et la révolution.*

At a time . . . when, with the spread of education and communications, the realisation and impatience of suffering [are] visibly and rapidly growing. . . .

> Translated from Jacob Burckhardt, *Weltgeschichtliche Betrachtungen* (1868)
> by James Hastings Nichols (ed.), in *Force and Freedom,* 1943.

Congenitally ordained to prey upon his fellows, interminably tempted and interminably deceived, man . . . is not, at any rate, fitted for happiness by his natural estate: to this day, the whole creation groaneth and travaileth still. There have been times in which this state of affairs was taken more or less for granted. When it appeared that nothing but a conspiracy between privilege and superstition was blocking the way to the infinite perfectibility of the human race, and when the advance of science and the accumulation of wealth promised an endless progress of material welfare, the torrential forces of *temporal* hope broke out. But Time is an infernal ironist; and the invariable rebuffs inflicted upon the appetites, the ambitions and the aspirations of man could not fail to call out in desperate response the full resources of his natural ferocity; for man was not made to stand indefinitely on his hind feet.

> Etienne Mantoux, *The Carthaginian Peace* (Published 1945).

We are living in the fifth act of the French Revolution.

> Felix Somary, *Erinnerungen aus meinem Leben,* 1955.

The modern movements of protest and revolution against traditional Western society can be seen as part of a world-wide revolutionary process that has gone on for almost 200 years exploding first in one place and then in another, interrupted at times by periods of quiet and restoration, gaining momentum, at first slowly and then rapidly, and now encompassing the entire globe. Its main characteristics are

3

a passionate desire for *change*, with little regard for the needs of conservation and consolidation, and impatience with slow, gradual change; a kind of *evangelical* moral *fervor* for the poor, in earthly goods or in spirit; the twin phenomena of protest against the existing intranational and international stratification, in the form of *socialism* and *nationalism,* respectively, with both movements occasionally hostile and occasionally cooperative. *Hatred for* private *property* and for the frankly acquisitive pursuits of men is characteristic of socialism and often of nationalism, too. Everything receives a particular flavor through the *alienation of the intellectuals,* from whose ranks the political leaders of modern times usually come, from their societies.

I The Western Movements

THE PROGRESSIVE BIAS. Modern bias is strongly in favor of change, and it often favors quick and violent change over slow and non-violent evolution. "Progress" always is, and "revolution" usually is, a laudatory term. Even changes that involve no physical violence are called revolutions to give them added prestige; we speak of the urban, the scientific, the industrial revolution, of revolutions in style or taste.

This bias is a relatively new phenomenon. Throughout most of human history, heavy opprobrium was attached to any deviation from the traditional order of things. To be *cupidus rerum novarum* was a serious accusation in ancient Rome. The middle ages held to the concept of a closed world. As late as in the mid-fifteenth century, the humanist Lorenzo Valla still considered "the physician who tries out new and experimental medicines on the sick rather than the time-tested ones to be contemptible," like "the sailor who prefers to hold an uncharted course to one upon which others safely sail their ships and cargoes." Only forty years later, Columbus began his voyage to uncharted sea.

With some interludes of consolidation and restoration, the world has been changing with increasing velocity since, and public opinion has come to identify change with life, conservation with stagnation and death.

But the question of conservation versus innovation need not be a matter of *weltanschauung,* of principle and ideology. Civilization needs conservation, just as the cultivated soil needs it, as a protection against the return of the jungle and against corrosion; there are many historical examples of regression, of the loss of achievements already gained. But in quiet times and, in particular, in times in which living conditions have been steadily improving, people take for granted what they have and do not consider the possibility that it could be in jeopardy.

Equally, civilization needs innovation if it is to fulfill human aspirations. And in modern, industrialized societies, the end, or the mere slowing down, of economic progress would mean a major calamity because a large part of the people depend, directly or indirectly, on the investment sector of the economy. Whether, in any particular case, we should, or should not, embark on innovation, could be decided on an appraisal of the merits of the case, that is, on the chances and probable costs, material and otherwise, of the innovation. There is no basis for any generalized statement about the optimal relation of conservation and innovation and no likelihood that the same formula will apply in all places and at all times.

There is also the question, not of great immediate importance but possibly crucial in the long run, of how long this constant change at a necessarily accelerating pace can be maintained without progressive interference with the balance of nature and without reaching the limits of natural resources or the possibilities of human adjustment to perpetually changing conditions. Previous speculations about the limits of technology, or the limits of mankind, have proved highly premature, but that does not mean that such limits will not eventually make themselves felt.

However that may be, it is interesting to notice that the attitude toward "progress," which is a question of ideology in political and social matters, has been thoroughly de-ideologized in areas in which great advances toward rationality have been made, as in medicine. There was a time when the application, or non-application, of surgery was a matter of principle. Physicians foreswore the use of the knife in the Hippocratic Oath; surgery was practiced by another, not always fully respected, profession. Today the determination of medical treatment is no longer a matter of ideology; physicians are not divided into conservatives, always advocating conservative treatment, and liberals, always in favor of radical treatment. It is universally recognized that surgery is indicated in some cases and contraindicated in others. There is still a place for temperamental differences between doctors, but it is a marginal one. Perhaps there will be a day when the question of conservation and innovation in public affairs will be equally free from ideology, or prejudice, and nobody will profess himself in favor or against innovation just as a matter of principle.

THE EVANGELICAL FERVOR. The Western world has, in the last 200 years, been the scene of a kind of messianic, albeit secular, fervor. It has found expression in many documents and manifestoes, as in the American Declaration of Independence, the French Declaration of the Rights of Man, and others down to the Atlantic Charter and more recent documents. The moral climate that these declarations indicate has led to an improvement in the living conditions of countless common people beyond the boldest hopes of the reformers of earlier generations. But it has also had some other consequences: "Moral fervor," as Michael Polanyi put it, "in our lifetime has outreached itself by its inordinate aspirations and has heaped on mankind the disasters that have befallen us." [1]

The moral demands "outreached" themselves and became "inordinate" when self-criticism, or criticism of one's own government and society, and the attempt at a sympathetic understanding of an opponent's point of view were carried to the point where people could see only the mote in the eye of their own society and never the beam in the eye of its enemies. It is the kind of attitude which Bernard Shaw must have had in mind when he let the tailor Androcles, just about to be thrown into the circus, express his compassion for the poor lions. But although such attitudes make sense in the faithful Christian who is confidently looking forward to eternal life, they are more difficult to understand in their contemporary, secularized version.

The overreaching of moral demands is shown by the fact that no allowance is made by the moralist critics for the pursuit of national interest, including mere self-

[1] *Beyond Nihilism* (London: Cambridge University Press, 1960), p. 1.

preservation. The United States is requested, in her dealings with other nations, to follow what is said to be "the right." She is requested to have complete disregard for the consequences which such a course would have for American interest in a world where not everybody is motivated by such exclusive dedication. Yet, self-preservation and the pursuit of one's interest are common to all living creatures who can neglect them only at their peril. Morality sets definite limits to the degree to which, and to the ways in which, interests may be pursued, and it sets up obligations to others. But a morality which plainly condemns the consideration of interest as such is not compatible with survival.[2]

How moral aspirations can outreach themselves can be seen, for example, in the attitude of extreme liberalism to crime and the criminal. The lawbreaker has from time immemorial been fair game for human sadism; people openly and unashamedly enjoyed watching wilfully produced human agony at public executions. The fact that the victims were criminals, hence, supposedly "got their just deserts," quieted whatever stirrings of conscience the spectators might otherwise have felt. In the last two centuries, the more conspicuous expressions of sadism have gradually been taken out of law and law enforcement—a development for which every humane person will feel grateful.

But the process has been carried further to the point where the lawbreaker appears to be fully exonerated as a victim of circumstance—"more sinned against than sinning"—and society is seen as responsible. The judges, the government, the upper classes, and even the victim himself [3] appear as the real culprits, and the plea of conditioning by circumstance is never entered on their behalf.

[2] American leaders have often encouraged such unreasonable demands by claiming that the United States is guided in crucial decisions by high moral purpose only; e.g., that we resent Castro's attempt to revolutionize Latin America not as a threat to us but because it threatens our Latin neighbors; or that we engage in aid to underdeveloped countries only because we recognize it as a duty. Such claims are believed by no one and resented by all, as moralizing always is. And it seems to produce in people the irresistible urge to debunk these claims by subjecting them to ever more exacting tests until the breaking point has been reached at which the United States can go no further in jeopardizing its vital interests.

The United States should instead assume a more realistic attitude and make more modest moral claims which can be, and have been, lived up to: that, like everybody else, we defend our vital interests but that, in so doing, we always keep a decent respect for the vital interests of others and seek for a formula that combines them both.

It should be added, however, that the neglect of considerations of national interest, characteristic of liberal attitudes to international problems in the United States is not always due to exaggerated moral demands but sometimes merely to the fact that the possibility of a national catastrophe is not realized. The long period of unearned security which the American people have enjoyed because of their geographical remoteness from other centers of power, the balance of power in Eurasia, and the role of sea power—facts which have either disappeared or been downgraded in recent years—have made the people take security for granted; this feeling, together with anti-European resentment and the complacency produced by American successes, had created an atmosphere in which "power politics" was looked upon as something wicked, and the concept of national interest as a fraud.

[3] Shortly after the First World War, a novel by the Austrian writer Franz Werfel was published under the title: Not the Slayer but the Slain One Is Guilty.

The position is logically untenable. If all behavior is determined to the exclusion of all culpability and responsibility, neither the lawbreaker nor society can be called to account; neither exhortation nor condemnation makes any sense whatever. If, on the other hand, there is sense in attaching blame to society for its acts of commission or omission, the same ought to apply to the lawbreaker, too. The fact that, in this modern view, the lawbreaker is treated on the assumption of complete determinism, while society is treated on the assumption of freedom of choice, merely reflects the will to condemn society.

The basis for this paradoxical moral attitude is the belief, first made popular by Rousseau—and quite fundamental to one branch of liberal thought—that man is good by nature, considerate and kindly to his fellow men. If he behaves towards others in a selfish, callous, brutal, or even deliberately cruel manner, such behavior must be due, in its entirety, to environmental influences, perhaps to grave provocation and unbearable pressures to which he was subjected. He would assume, therefore, the kind attitude germane to his nature if these pressures were removed. Hence, if, for example, a man has slain another man, the *cause* must be sought in the environment, in society. And cause is, in human affairs, invariably equated with *guilt*,[4] no matter how much men may fancy themselves to be determinists.

In a social and international context this means that if groups or nations resort to violence, it *must* be due to grievances that all would consider legitimate; and such behavior could be remedied, and could only be remedied, by redressing these grievances. Thus, when the Germans embraced a rabid nationalism thirty years ago, it must have been due, entirely, to injustices from the peace of Versailles. "We must give justice to Germany," exclaimed Ramsay Macdonald in the League of Nations Assembly immediately after Hitler's seizure of power. Even the late Adolf Hitler himself, we hear in a recent re-interpretation of history,[5] never aimed at the domination of Europe by force. He had, in fact, no long-term goals at all but was merely pushed to what he did, step by step, by Western unreasonableness.

Or, if the leaders of the Soviet Union face the West with uncompromising hostility, it *cannot* be due to tenets of Bolshevism which antedate any contact with the West; it *must* be a response to Western unfriendliness. Perhaps it is a response to the brief and half-hearted intervention in the Russian Civil War; perhaps it is due to the more recent American demand (in 1945) to have Argentina included in the United Nations; or perhaps it is a response to suspicions aroused by the appointment, by the British government, of a diplomat of not sufficiently high standing for negotiations in Moscow. Similarly, Castro's relentless hostility to the United States, shown from the day of his ascension to power, *must* be due to a lack of understanding on the part of the United States for the aspirations of the Cuban people for a better life. And if the facts glaringly contradict these assumptions, the facts must be selected and rearranged until they seem to fit—because the basic assumptions *must* be true.

As Polanyi has suggested, the evangelical fervor of Western Liberalism should also

[4] The Greek *aitia*, e.g., that lives in our word, etiology, has the original meaning of guilt; the negative form *anaitios* means "innocent."

[5] A. J. P. Taylor, *The Origins of the Second World War* (London: Hamish Hamilton, 1961).

be seen as a new edition of the ethics of the Gospel (and of prophetic Judaism). The moral prescriptions of the Gospel, the demand to offer the other cheek, with total self-abnegation, can hardly be practiced for any length of time except by people who live under at least partially sheltered conditions—as in monastic orders—so that the harsher necessities of life are performed by others less burdened by scruples or subject to a different code.

It has therefore been suggested that the prescriptions of the Gospels were never meant to govern the daily lives of continuing communities but that they constituted an *Interimsethik,* a set of moral rules for the waiting time, before the final consummation of history and the coming of the Kingdom of God which was then thought to be imminent.

However that may be, the Church interposed herself between man and the text of the Gospels. It was the function of the Roman Church to direct the messianic expectation away from daily life into an afterlife or a very distant future so to preserve a realistic attitude to the world around us. In this way the Church arrived at a synthesis of hope and realism, of the Don Quixote and the Sancho Panza in us— albeit a synthesis heavily weighted towards immobilism. The compromise became untenable once the possibility of secular improvement had been demonstrated.

The decline of the Churches and of any kind of supranaturalism seems to have led to a revival of messianism in its original form: the expectation of a consummation of history, in the immediate future, that will establish the realm of justice and happiness for all men of "good will." [6]

While this, presumably, is the origin of the immense moral fervor for the "disinherited of the earth" in our time, it is an open question in each individual case to what degree fervor is due to genuine moral passions that have been carried to extreme, even suicidal, conclusions, and to what degree it is due to envy of, or spite for, the establishment in one's own society. Both motivations may, in fact, operate in the same person although only the first, idealistic one is likely to appear in a man's conscious self-interpretation. The fact that moral fervor for the oppressed may sometimes be fed by unconscious hatred of the establishment may explain the frequent indifference of the moral critic towards oppression and injustice, however severe, when it is practiced by the enemies of his society.

But despite their self-damaging implications, these attitudes, whatever their origin, would still not constitute any real danger to the vital interests of Western societies were it not for the peculiar present constellation of forces. One school of thought in the messianic tradition, of particular determination and ruthlessness, has in our time succeeded in establishing complete power over the Eurasian heartland (to use Sir Halford Mackinder's excellent expression). Its leaders believe dogmatically in a modern version of Manichaeism according to which their own side represents both

[6] For the messianic social beliefs cp.: J. L. Talmon, *The Origin of Totalitarian Democracy* (New York: Praeger, 1951), 1st ed. *Utopianism and Politics* (London: Conservative Political Center, 1957.) *Political Messianism: The Romantic Phase* (New York: Praeger, 1960). Norman Cohn, *The Pursuit of the Millenium* (London: Secker and Warburg, 1957).

the morally good and the wave of the future, while our way of life is both irredeemably evil and irreversibly decaying. They not only believe that our downfall is preordained by inexorable laws of history, but so far have held it to be their task to carry out, or at least to help along, the "verdict of history." It is for this reason that the moral passions of Western liberals have often become, in effect, though probably not in conscious intent, an aid to an adversary who frankly rejects the very values for the minor infractions of which they are daily castigating Western society.

At the same time when Nebuchadnezzar threatened the existence of the Jewish kingdom, the prophet Jeremiah urged the people not to resist but to accept servitude to Babylon as a divine punishment for their sins. Like him, and other ancient prophets, many contemporary doctrinaire-liberals profess to believe that our peril is due to our sins and would disappear if we would practice strict morality in all our actions. But although the assumption of a relation between sin and misfortune makes sense for the ancient Hebrews, who believed that God punishes His people for their misconduct, it is less understandable in modern liberal atheists or agnostics who do not think that the moral law determines the course of events. But beliefs can endure long after the rationale for holding them has withered away.

In one important point, however, there is a striking difference between Jeremiah and his contemporary successors: Jeremiah was fully aware of what was in store for the people at the hand of their Babylonian masters; many of his contemporary followers tell us that Nebuchadnezzar does not really exist but that he is merely an hallucination of the State Department.

THE STRUGGLE AGAINST THE "ESTABLISHMENT"—DOMESTIC AND INTERNATIONAL. The protest against the status quo appears as protest against the pecking order of our society and the promotion of the demands of the lower strata at the expense of the higher ones. As has been emphasized before, protest that does not come from the lower orders themselves may be due either to identification with, and compassion for, them, or to hatred of the higher ones.

The demands for justice for all men have grown ever stronger in the Western world since the eighteenth century. Justice, at first interpreted as equality of opportunity, is more and more becoming to mean equality of station; and, as Alexis de Tocqueville foresaw, "the hatred that men bear to privilege increases in proportion as privileges become fewer and less considerable, so that democratic passions would seem to burn more fiercely just when they have least fuel . . ." because in a world in which there are no great differences, the still existing inequalities are all the more unacceptable.[7] Thus, the anti-colonial passions in Asia and Africa have become more inflamed at the very time that more than nine-tenths of the Western colonial empires have become emancipated.

Nationalism, on the other hand, creates a feeling of solidarity along ethnic rather than class lines. It was, at times, welded to the political and social revolt as in the French Revolution, whereas at other times the two movements have been bitterly

[7] *Democracy in America,* Vol. 2, Book 4, Chap. 3.

opposed to each other. Nationalism has been universalist as well as parochial, integrative as well as divisive. It was the former when it strove towards the unity of groups conceived as "nations" that had hitherto been divided into smaller traditional, mostly dynastic, political units as the unification of Italy and Germany. It was disintegrative and divisive when it broke up traditional multinational structures such as the Habsburg monarchy, or pursued its national aspirations without regard for the aspirations, or indeed the very existence, of other nations. In the latter aspect of nationalism, naive egotism, an attitude which in individuals or groups precedes moral development, has been elevated to a sacred duty, and the innocent selfishness of the primitive has thus been transformed into an evil of civilization, namely, the use of morality for immoral ends.

Not infrequently, nationalism has begun as an integrative force and has shown the latter characteristics only after it had realized some of its fundamental aspirations; this was the case of the German development from the nationalism of the Liberals of 1848 over the militaristic nationalism of the Treitschke generation (which still paid at least lip service to Christianity), to the paroxysmal nationalism of a Hitler who knew no law except "the interest of the German people." [8]

Nationalism has, therefore, been called a demonic force. There are examples of a nation turning away from nationalism in disillusionment after it has led the nation into disaster (as happened in France and, more recently, in Germany); but there are no examples of a successful appeasement of undefeated nationalism.

Nationalism sometimes sponsors the aspirations of groups at the lower level of the pyramid of power or wealth, and sometimes the aspirations of groups which are relatively high up on an international scale. In the latter case, it has a double face: It is a rebellion against those who occupy the top positions, but it is at the same time oppressive toward the lower echelons. That was the case of nationalism in industrially advanced countries like modern Germany and Japan; they struggled against the "have" nations—above all England and the United States—who, they claimed, had appropriated the best things on earth at a time when the "younger" nations had not yet appeared on the scene. There was either a demand for colonies, as in Germany and Italy, or an attempt to conquer adjacent territories populated by less advanced peoples—the Ukraine, parts of China—with a view to colonizing them and enslaving the inhabitants. This aspect gives nationalism its peculiar and ambiguous character, at once "revolutionary" and "counter-revolutionary."

[8] It is unmistakable, however, that the germs of the later barbarism existed from the beginning. Sir Lewis Namier, e.g., said about Mazzini, whom he called "a man outstanding for spiritual integrity" and "a sincere lover of liberty," ". . . the moral fervor, purity of purpose and religious sincerity which pervade his writings—words of faith and action rather than of thought—were apt to conceal from contemporaries how deficient his teachings were in substance correlated to every-day reality, and what dangerous germs they contained. National self-glorification and claims to moral superiority were of their core: which entails a measure of depreciation of other peoples, and is not conducive to international comity." *Avenues of History* (London: Hamish Hamilton, 1952), p. 29.

The Austrian poet Franz Grillparzer, a somewhat older contemporary of Mazzini, said around 1848 that the development went "from humanitarianism over nationalism into bestialism."

But where nationalism takes hold of a poor and underdeveloped people, as in Latin America at the present time, the national and the social revolution may run parallel for some time as is demonstrated by the Cuban revolution, or by some of Mao Tse-tung's revisions of orthodox Marxist doctrine, allowing for a temporary coalition with the "national bourgeoise." This places the "struggle against imperialism," that is, the international revolution, ahead of the domestic class struggle.

Whether an individual is more attracted by Socialism (which, under present conditions, means Marxist Socialism and, most probably, Communism) or by nationalism, seems to depend on many circumstances—historical, situational, personal. Among them is also the response of the personality to Marxism's and nationalism's basic attitudes toward life, their implicit *weltanschauung:* The latter is expressed most clearly in their respective doctrines regarding determinism and freedom.

Marxism is strongly determinist and sees the world moving along inexorable laws of history. Men may accelerate or smooth the course of events by correct action or delay it and make it harsher by error and futile resistance, but they cannot change necessity. *Fata volentem ducunt, nolentem trahunt.*

Nationalism, on the other hand, is indeterminist; the future belongs to him who seizes it. Different temperaments are attracted or repelled by these two philosophies.

THE ANTI-CAPITALIST BIAS. The impact of the socialist idea has been cataclysmic. Its strength is probably due, in the main, to a combination of an egalitarian moral fervor with a particular, superficially persuasive interpretation of the non-egalitarian realities, namely the doctrine that the businessman acting under the profit motive is a social parasite who fulfills no social function but who has, through the possession of the means of production, interposed himself between the worker and his tools. He has, thus, been able to extract a heavy tribute from the "toilers"—not unlike the medieval robber barons who extracted river tolls from travelling merchants. This interpretation seems convincing to all but the very few who have either personal experience or theoretical training in economic matters.

This means that the problem of economic rationality, that is, the problem of an optimal employment of scarce resources, is little understood. The problem is difficult enough if only one goal is pursued, in which case we usually speak of a question of strategy rather than of economics. However, it receives a new dimension of complexity if there is a multiplicity of goals, each of which can be pursued only at the expense of some others, as in the promotion of general welfare.

It is the justification of a market, or capitalist, economy that it creates a field in which all players are constantly rewarded by an extension, or punished by a contraction, of their operating range, according to the results of their management in terms of consumers' preferences.

It cannot be taken for granted that consumers' preferences should always be the ultimate determinant of action; in fact, virtually everybody agrees that there must be at least some exceptions from the sovereign and irresponsible rule of the consumer (as in the control of the traffic in narcotics or in building and zoning regulations). Furthermore, even if consumers' preferences are accepted as the ultimate frame of reference, it cannot be taken for granted that a market economy is necessarily the only possible, or the best, solution of the problem of economic rationality. The capitalist system can, therefore, become subject to legitimate criticism on either of these two grounds: because it caters to desires which, in the view of the critic, are not worth indulging in, or because its function of selecting the most economic among the possible alternatives of action might possibly be achieved better by some other mechanism.

But capitalism has only extremely rarely been attacked on any such ground. It has been attacked for more than a century not by people who wished to substitute their solution of the problem of economic rationality for the solution of the market, but by people who are unaware of the very existence of the problem. For them the only economic problems are technological; one produces what is needed, it is as simple as that, and except for the engineer's task, the job of management, as Lenin put it, "can be reduced . . . to simple operations of registration, filing and checking." [9]

Unaware of the problem of economic rationality, the Marxists did not understand what hit them (and everyone else) when socialized industries, supposedly freed from the burden of having to produce "surplus value" for the capitalists, did not have that surplus value available for distribution among the wage earners as one had to expect according to the theory. Nor did they later understand how the "exploited" worker in privately owned industry can receive higher wages than his "liberated" opposite number in socialist countries. Even today observers report that leading men in Eastern Germany, looking at the prosperity of Western Germany and West Berlin, do not consider the possibility that something might be wrong with their economic system: The system, they are satisfied, is superior to capitalism, and it must be due to accidental factors such as bottlenecks if the people have not yet reaped the benefits of socialism.[10] Just the same, they are eager to get rid of capitalist Berlin and thereby of the case that visibly contradicts their theories.

It is this inability on the part of most people, including most intellectuals, in particular, to understand the nature of the economic problem that gives the socialist ideology its virtually irresistible appeal. The arguments which the defender of a market economy can put forward are simply beyond the understanding of those who have neither theoretical instruction nor practical experience in economic matters. They are, in any case, suspect of being self-serving if they are advanced by people with vested interests in the preservation of capitalism; and if advanced by others who are conspicuously lacking in such interests, they can be equally discounted as coming from "lackeys" of capitalism.

[9] *State and Revolution*. Coll. Works, Vol. 21.

[10] There is evidence, however, that some economists in Communist countries have become aware of the problem in recent years. Their insight has been acted upon in Yugoslavia through decentralization and the establishment of a market of sorts. There have also been stirrings in this direction among economists in the Soviet Union and particularly in Poland. But they are still viewed with suspicion by the Communist party who fears the impact of any undermining of the labor theory of value. See Gregory Grossman, *Value and Plan* (Berkeley and Los Angeles: University of California Press, 1960).

The problem of economic rationality is often not understood even by men of very high intelligence. We are accustomed to speak of intelligence as though it were a unitary quality which, as much or as little as there is, can be applied with equal success to all areas of reality. Psychometrics, with its I.Q. measurements, has contributed to this conception.

Yet there is much evidence that an individual can operate on a high intellectual level in one area of reality and on a very low one in another. Theoretical intelligence capable of understanding how things are—in itself but a name for a whole group of abilities, each related to a particular area or aspect of reality—is different from economic intelligence that is quick in realizing how available things could be put to best advantage; from political or military intelligence that grasps the value of everything for a struggle for power; from social intelligence that knows how to make friends and influence people; or from the erotic intelligence of a Casanova.

Several types of higher intelligence are rarely found together in the same person. Lenin was one of the greatest, perhaps the greatest, revolutionary strategists of all times. He sensed like nobody else the points of weakness in existing societies and invented strategies for establishing footholds of power, for enlarging them, and for winning and keeping total power. Even his closest collaborators did not fully understand him for a long time. But the same Lenin was unable to grasp the problem of an optimal allocation of resources to competing goals and the dependence of human welfare on a solution of this problem; he thought economic management was a matter of accounting and statistics.

Andrew Carnegie, an economic genius of the first magnitude, had no understanding for matters of power or ideology. When he set up the Carnegie Endowment for International Peace, he wondered what role the Foundation could play once it would have succeeded in abolishing wars. He told his trustees that it would then be their task to decide on what ills the Foundation should focus next.

In the mid-1930's when civilized men were appalled at the prospect of another war, and one that would involve the bombing of civilians, to boot, a prominent English mathematician is reported to have pointed out that, of course, one would not actually drop any bombs, but in dealing with Hitler it might be necessary to behave for a while as though one would. It does not seem to have occurred to this outstanding man that one cannot bluff a determined adversary while putting one's cards on the table.

The failure to understand the problem of rational allocation of resources and its crucial importance for human welfare may also be seen in another light, namely, as the consequence of *utopian* thinking. Human values are in some degree contradictory, that is one can often realize one value only at the expense of another; liberty and equality or, more generally, individual expression and social order, economic progress and security, income and leisure, are examples of such dichotomies. Decision involves a choice in favor of one value against another or, rather, the determination of an optimal point beyond which any further approach toward the realization of one value would cost too dearly in terms of the other. Because of these contradictions among the things which men hold dear, complete human fulfillment is not possible. The utopian mind, however, does not accept this kind of reasoning. The utopian refuses to believe that there could be any inherent limits to human fulfillment; the very suggestion, he suspects, is a ruse to protect special privilege. In the good society, all men can be completely fulfilled in their individual aspirations, and society can yet be harmonious, without conflict; as Marx had put it: The free development of each is the prerequisite of the free development of all.

It is a kind of preordained harmony; the skeptics, of course, think that this is merely another way of saying that one can have one's cake and eat it, too.

If one believes that all human aspirations are in natural harmony with each other and with the interests of society, and of the whole of mankind—a harmony only so far disturbed and impeded by the "class structure"—one will, of course, not believe that decisions involve choices between irreconcilable values; for if one believed the latter, one would not have accepted the former.

But if the problem of rational allocation is not understood, the system of *private enterprise appears to have no raison d'être* but to be *merely* a form of *privilege,* at once immoral and inexpedient.

This belief, somewhat weakened in the West but holding full sway everywhere else, that government operation of the economy is both morally indicated and practically sensible, while business management is both evil and stupid, appears to be the main reason for the fundamental goodwill enjoyed by the Soviet Union and the widespread distrust of the United States. It is for this reason, I submit, that over so large a part of the world, a light view is taken of Communist aggressive moves, while the West is severely castigated for even moderate acts of self-assertion: Communism stands in the minds of countless people for something fundamentally "progressive," while the West stands for an obsolete system of privilege. Without such fundamental aversion, it would be difficult to understand why a large section of world opinion condemns as aggressiveness in the West what it hails as strength in the East and ridicules as weakness in the West what it applauds as manifestation of peaceful intentions in the East.

To the enormous amount of goodwill which the Soviet Union has enjoyed as the land of Socialism must also be attributed the paralysis of American foreign policy at the end of the Second World War. The Soviet Union established her stranglehold over Eastern Central Europe then, at a time when the balance of physical strength greatly favored the United States and effective resistance would have been possible at small risk. But a vigorous policy toward the Soviet Union would have been vetoed by a substantial part of Western public opinion.

THE ALIENATION OF THE INTELLECTUALS. The intellectuals of the West, as a rule, are not fully identified with their societies. They stand aloof, and while they may feel enthusiastic about some "ideal" society, they are often indifferent or hostile to their society as it actually is.[11]

[11] A characteristic example for the attitude of many Western intellectuals appears in a psychological study of scientists; the author, a noted psychologist, points out that "scientists are very good citizens" and declares: "The scientists involved in espionage have been very few, indeed, and misguided as they may have been, they have acted on principle and not for personal gain." Anne Roe, *The Making of a Scientist* (New York: Dodd, Mead & Co., 1952), p. 240. Thus, the author

To some degree, this has been so in all societies in which intellectuals have enjoyed the freedom of expression. Since the days of the Sophists, they have been in the habit of questioning and challenging the values and the assumptions that were taken for granted in their societies. Some intellectuals, on the other hand, have followed the example of that dissident Sophist, Socrates, who used his intellectual powers not only to challenge current beliefs, but also to give the essential values of his civilization a new, presumably better foundation.

Intellect tends to question and thereby to undermine dogma and tradition.[12] The act of understanding, said the historian of science Charles Coulston Gillispie, is an act of alienation.[13] Psychoanalytic theory suggests a kind of primary antagonism of the ego against the id, that is, of the rational, goal-directed part in us against the impulsive and automatic parts. Alienation is an aspect of emancipation. It is the hostility of *Geist* to life of which there has been so much talk in German philosophy.

In principle this is unavoidable. It is rooted in the very nature of freedom because freedom is destructive as well as creative; the very viability of a free society depends on whether or not it can take advantage of the creative energies unleashed by freedom while keeping its destructive aspects within limits.

But this does not explain the degree of the estrangement or the bitterness with which many Western intellectuals look upon the society which has provided them with a degree of personal security and with opportunities of development not enjoyed at any other time or place. Is this a reaction to freedom which, for the inner-directed, vital like air, is deeply frustrating to the other-directed who need guidance? Is it the very consequence of the emancipation from drudgery and of the newly won leisure which makes people ask beyond life's necessities or luxuries for a meaning in life while they are yet not able to find it for themselves? Is it the constant increase in possible fulfillments and the simple fact that in such situations aspirations always grow a little faster than fulfillments? Or is it the attitude of those who have been conditioned in their childhood to expect immediate fulfillment of every wish, who have accordingly failed to acquire any tolerance toward frustration, and who go to pieces, bundles of despair and fury, whenever they meet with even the slightest frustration as is, after all, not forever avoidable? Somewhere along these lines an

is not sure whether she condemns espionage against the United States at all ("misguided as they *may* have been . . .") and, in any case, does not take a grave view of the matter as long as it was done for ideological reasons and not for monetary gain. It would be rash to conclude, however, that intellectuals of liberal persuasion advocate a *general* tolerance for all ideologies, as was done by John Stuart Mill; as a rule, they make no allowances for ideologies of the Right. But the ideologies of the Left are regarded as "idealistic," and action based on them is excused, or only mildly rebuked, whatever its consequences. No question is asked whether these ideologies may not also be fed from emotional sources not necessarily praiseworthy such as, e.g., lust for power or intellectual conceit.

[12] Cp. the following remark by Frank H. Knight: ". . . the 'liberation of the mind' seems to have released a tendency to acute discontent, criticism, fault-finding that was there all along but held in check by the harsh discipline of pre-liberal culture—or possibly new conditions have caused it to develop with astonishing speed as a culture trait." Frank H. Knight, *Intelligence and Democratic Action* (Cambridge: Harvard University Press, 1960), p. 144.

[13] *The Edge of Objectivity* (Princeton: Princeton University Press, 1960), p. 84.

explanation must be sought for a phenomenon like the "angry young men," for the bitter hatred of their society by members of a generation who, perhaps as the first in history, "never ate their bread with tears."

It must be added, however, that the destructive criticism of Western societies comes only rarely from those intellectuals who have special training or experience in the areas which are particularly relevant for socio-political problems; they come rarely from historians, economists, political scientists, professional diplomats, etc.

This, obviously, does not mean that historians, economists, or political scientists are miraculously free from the disintegrative potentialities of the intellect; but it suggests that in the field in which one has sound knowledge and with which one is in constant contact, such potentialities are likely to manifest themselves mostly in the form of *creative* destruction, as a restructuring of the field [14] with creative value. But without such knowledge, the destructiveness of the intellect has full sway.

What then appears as antagonism of the intellectual to his society must, therefore, be attributed not only to the alienation inherent in the life of the intellect, but also to the naive and arrogant confidence of individuals with higher education. They feel competent not only in matters within the areas of their training and experience, but on any subject of public interest—a pretension to which taxi drivers or plumbers are far less prone.

The fact that the intellectuals of the type of Protagoras are the perpetual debunkers of their society would not change the balance of forces in the world if all societies were equally exposed to such pressures. But if this is not the case, if some societies are shielded against the consequences of intellectual skepticism and debunking as is largely the case in present totalitarian societies, the pressures which intellectuals exert where they are in a position to do so may have the effect of influencing the balance of power in favor of those societies in which they are not in such a position—in favor of monolithic Sparta, against free Athens.

II The Anti-Colonial Revolution

THE SETTING OF THE STAGE. "Western culture," said C. C. Gillispie, "is set off from those of Asia, Africa and the world of Antiquity by two fundamental factors. From one of these it emerged: its religious chrysalis was Christianity, investing history with the promise of fulfillment of a sort. The other it produced: the most dynamic, distinctive and influential creation of the Western world is a progressive science of nature. Only there, in the technical realm, indeed, does the favorite Western idea hold any demonstrable meaning." [15]

These two characteristics contain the germs of the history of contact between Western culture and other cultures. The achievements in the *rational* analysis and control of man's environment gave Western culture an easy superiority over other

[14] The expression is taken from M. Wertheimer, *Productive Thinking* (New York: Harper Brothers, 1945).
[15] Charles Coulston Gillispie, *op. cit.*, p. 8.

people's, provoking them, at first, to futile resistance or to surrender—both exemplified in Caesar's story of the two Aedui brothers, Divitiacus and Dumnorix—and later stimulating identification, envy, and emulation. The *moral and metaphysical* beliefs of the West in an ultimate historical consummation, seen in modern times in the picture of continuous progress, on the other hand, manifested itself at first in missionary activities, both by religious and non-religious bodies, to bring the message of Western creeds to alien cultures; soon there were also men who espoused the cause of the natives against Western rulers. To the leaders of non-Western peoples, finally, Western moral beliefs gave the spiritual weapons with which to ask for a redress of their grievances.

TWO TYPES OF GROUP ANTAGONISM. Group antagonisms take different forms according to whether they are directed against more advanced, or against less advanced, groups. "Advancement," in this context, should be understood as advancement in terms of *alloplastic adjustment,* that is, in terms of man's ability to control his environment and to find suitable means for advancing his ends in relation to his environment. It does *not* mean a higher degree of *autoplastic* adjustment (as the ability to bear frustration and suffering with equanimity or the wisdom of an Epicurus, a Buddha, or a Confucius); nor does it mean *moral* superiority. Least of all, of course, can it be taken as superiority in ultimate human values, or superiority before God—matters about which this writer has no knowledge.

Advancement, in the preceding sense, of greater control of the environment implies a lengthening of the road from impulse to action, that is, a larger measure of self-control in significant areas of human behavior. Under conditions of relatively fair competition, it is reflected by a person's place in the social hierarchies of power, wealth, income, and status. The relative advancement of a group in social interaction with other groups is manifested by the proportional participation of the group in the occupational hierarchy, inasmuch as occupations are open to them. A group is more advanced if fewer of its members are engaged in unskilled or semi-skilled labor than would correspond to their number, and if it has more than its proportional share in leading occupations—administration, spiritual leadership, science, education, arts. The Jews, for example, were a more advanced group in medieval Europe or, in modern times, in Central and Eastern Europe and in Arab lands; so were the Greeks and the Armenians in the Turkish Empire; the Jainas in India; the French in Algeria; so are whites in general as compared to Negroes in Africa, America, or Arabia; so is, on the whole, the West in the global community of men.

The antagonism which the more advanced group feels toward the less advanced one, such as the feelings of American Southerners toward the Negro, is quite different from the antagonism of a less advanced group toward a more advanced one, as in the case of the attitude of African Negroes toward the white settler or Algerian Moslems toward European settlers.

The less advanced group is not resented as such by their more advanced neighbors; rather, it is welcome to perform menial labor and, in some cases, has been imported for that very purpose. As long as their members "know their place," there is no opposition against them in the more advanced group; many people of the latter group may even have a personal affection of sorts for them. It is only if the members of the less advanced group step beyond the limits either of the general rules of conduct prevailing in the society, or of the social conventions regulating their social position, that they arouse resentment. In the cases in which the less advanced group is also believed to be closer to savagery and to an unbridled expression of sexuality, they arouse fear and horror, too.

A group that is more advanced than its environment provokes a different kind of antagonism. Its members usually behave with arrogance, and even if they should not do so, the simple fact of their superiority, difficult to hide, is felt as an insult. One then watches them carefully for any signs of weakness, for flaws; once these flaws are found, as needs they will, they are seized upon by the less advanced group and exploited to the full. Anti-American sentiment, and anti-Western sentiment in general, belong to this category; it is remarkable how closely current accusations against the West resemble the accusations against the Jews that run through the history of anti-Semitism.

While outbreaks of violence against backward groups rarely go beyond actions that should "teach them a lesson," so that they may assume again the humble station to which the more advanced group would like to confine them, the hostility against a more advanced group has no built-in limitations and may go all the way to effect their physical elimination.

These easily observable differences have been obfuscated by catch phrases such as "minority groups" (as though the relative place of groups in the pecking order were determined by their quantitative strength) or by pseudo-scientific investigations of prejudice in which the outcome of the research was implicit in the design of the experiments. For example, anti-Semitism and anti-Negro sentiment in the United States have been grouped together as sentiments or prejudices against "minority groups," although they differ radically in motivation and goal. Anti-Semitism has never been willing to tolerate the Jews, even if they were to behave deferentially toward Gentiles and take their meals in the kitchen; and anti-Negro sentiment has never aimed at eliminating the Negroes from the land through expulsion or harsher measures. The analogy to anti-Semitism can be found not in the anti-Negro sentiment of whites but rather in the violent forms of anti-white sentiment among Black Muslims.

Both responses to the phenomenon of difference in development are natural and therefore, in some measure, unavoidable. They represent a conflict of interest which only time can heal through elimination of the developmental difference and which, in the meantime, charity can do much to mitigate. To ideologize this conflict by seeing it in Manichean terms as a struggle between good and evil can only inflame it and may make it insoluble except for the solutions unmitigated violence provides.

CONDITIONS OF REVOLUTION. Thus, in the contact between groups at different levels of development, the more advanced group is motivated by a fear of being pulled down from levels already reached, while the less advanced group reacts to a blow to their pride.

But it does not react on any large scale unless and until the gap between the two groups is narrowed sufficiently so that a comparison between them is possible.

There is still a further step from resentment to action. For a long time the enormous superiority of Western power discouraged any thought of resistance until, in the Second World War, Western prestige was severely damaged through the defeats suffered at the hands of Germany and Japan. A revolutionary situation existed once the sense of grievance was ignited by the hope of success.

Revolutions do not seem to break out where men are most downtrodden, but rather where conditions have begun to improve.[16] As long as the prevailing conditions, no matter how bad, are stable they are taken for granted. Men *adjust* to them as one adjusts to the climate, to incurable disease, or to death. But once the possibility of improvement has been realized, conditions never improve fast enough to keep pace with rising aspirations.

This is closely analogous to a well-known psychiatric phenomenon and may be a manifestation of the same *biological truth*: The danger of suicide in severe depressions is great not at the height of the depression but rather at the time *when the depression has begun to lift*.

But the tremendous momentum which the anti-colonial revolution has gained in recent years is due, above all, to extraneous circumstances: Namely, the Soviet Union, with all her might, has been backing up and encouraging the most radical anti-Western groups anywhere on earth. Under these conditions, a premium has been placed on the most radical revolutionary action.

So far this refers to events in Asia, Africa and Latin America. But the revolution may yet spill over United States boundaries; revolutions of American Negroes, Chinese in Hawaii, or Mexicans in the Southeast will not be out of the question if the Western position further disintegrates.

In a recent article on the social life of baboons,[17] the authors, two biologists, stated: "In troops where the rank order is clearly defined, fighting is rare" and "fighting [*sc.* over a female] may take place if the dominance order is not clearly established among the males." One may say that fighting between humans, individuals and groups, may break out *if power relationships are unclear,* or liable to different interpretations. As long as power relationships are unambiguous, and so interpreted by all, there is likely to be peace. The existing power distribution is the basis for the legal

---

[16] For example, see the following statements by contemporary scholars: ". . . it is not the backward countries which need revolutions. Being backward, Spain had not yet developed those internal strains which made France, with all its enlightenment, a social volcano." H. R. Trevor-Roper, "The Spanish Enlightenment," *Historical Essays* (London: Macmillan, 1957), p. 271.

"Paradoxically as it may seem, colonial nationalism is far less the response to oppression than to the widening horizons opened up by progressive colonial governments." Rupert Emerson, *From Empire to Nation* (Cambridge: Harvard University Press, 1960), p. 45.

[17] S. L. Washburn and I. De Vore, "The Social Life of Baboons," *Scientific American*, Vol. 204, No. 6 (June 1961), p. 70.

order; when the pecking order is not universally recognized, either because power relationships have changed and human thinking has not kept up with the change, or because different people interpret them differently, fighting may break out until a new pecking order has been established and recognized. This will result in a new legal order.

III The Predicament of the West

THE AMERICAN RESPONSE. The anti-colonial revolution has assumed, or tends to assume, an anti-American stance, except in those countries or groups who feel themselves under pressure from the Soviet bloc or from a country or group that enjoys Communist support.

This development should have surprised no one. The United States has been on top of the world politically and economically for quite some time; with only about 7 per cent of the world's population, the United States has close to one-half of the world's capital. Its situation among the nations is comparable to that of the wealthiest landowner in a district where most people are destitute, at a time when the social order is no longer taken for granted.[18]

The new development came as a surprise to many, however, partly because revolutions were thought of as strictly national affairs and were not considered a part of a concerted international action, and partly because it was widely assumed that revolutions were reactions to oppression and injustice. The record of the United States as a neighbor and as a member of the international community, although not entirely spotless, compared very favorably with that of any other nation. Many a nation owes much to American generosity. It was overlooked, however, that there are reasons other than oppression and injustice, in the ordinary sense, as these words are understood in the West, why people may feel bitter against those more fortunately placed, and that they will feel little difficulty in interpreting their resentment and their aspirations, whatever they may be, as manifestations of a demand for justice.

There is tragic irony in the present situation in which the American people find themselves at the receiving end of a world-wide populist revolution, as Americans have seen themselves for generations as the avant garde of such movements against oligarchy-ridden Europe. For a long time this country has been a leader of populist and nationalist revolutions all over the world, busily undermining traditional political structures and the balance of power anywhere on earth in the name of the principle of self-determination until quite recently.[19] All this was with the expectation

---

[18] Despite its wealth, the United States could maintain its role as the leader of populism in the world as long as American borders were wide open to immigration and everybody was invited to share in the advantages of the American situation. But once the immigration laws had set up "no trespassing" signs around the American real estate, the American people became a privileged nation. No amount of public relations artistry can erase this fact from world consciousness.
[19] One fairly recent example: When the Central Powers, Germany and Austria-Hungary, recognized their defeat in October, 1918 and appealed to President Wilson to mediate an armistice

that the emancipation would appease rather than appetize the colonial peoples, and that they would behave with the moderation shown by the American colonists in the late eighteenth century with an emphasis on prosperity rather than on military power—assumptions for which there was no basis whatsoever.

There are many Americans even today who believe that the anti-American turn of the nationalist and populist revolutions in the "underdeveloped" countries was not a necessary phenomenon but merely the consequence of political mistakes which might have been avoided; perhaps the United States had "supported" dictators who were later overthrown, or failed to put pressure on friendly governments in favor of land reform, or failed to help one-crop countries out of their precarious situation by using American financial strength for a stabilization of world market prices of this commodity, etc. We had permitted ourselves, so it has been said, to be lined up on the wrong side, against the "aspirations of the common people," in the role of the Holy Alliance. If, so the arguments runs, Americans only could fearlessly take up again the banner of the populist revolution, all would be well. One wise observer commented on this more than ten years ago: "A people with the highest standard of living in the world tries desperately to remain the leader of the Left." [20] The unsolved contradictions between the needs of self-preservation which urged the greatest possible conservation of the essentials of the old international order of Western dominance, on the one hand, and the ideological bias in favor of revolution, on the other, was, and I submit still is, at the bottom of the ineffectiveness of American foreign policy.

There are four possible reactions to revolution on the part of those who feel threatened by it. It is the *conservative* response to try to stem the revolutionary tide. The *Bonapartist* (or fascist) solution consists in the setting up of a counterrevolutionary totalitarianism which steals some of the revolutionary thunder and uses the same terror methods as the revolution. There is the *me-too* policy of trying to join the revolution and march with its legions, preferably in its spearhead. Finally, one

---

and peace on the basis of his fourteen points, the President requested, as a prerequisite of his mediation, from Germany that "the power of the king of Prussia" be curtailed, and in the case of Austria-Hungary he took the position that it was up to the various national groups of the Monarchy to decide what concessions to their aspirations by the central government would be satisfactory to them. He thus gave *carte blanche* to the nationalist movements in the Monarchy. In this way, Wilson enforced the overthrow of the Hohenzollern monarchy and the dismemberment of the Austro-Hungarian State. This led, in the first case, to the establishment of the unpopular Weimar republic, soon to be overthrown by the disastrous Hitler movement; and, in the second case, to the creation of a power vacuum in Central Europe, soon to suck in, at first, German, and then, Russian, power.

[20] F. Somary, "From Portsmouth to Korea. The Balance Sheet of American Foreign Policy," unpublished memorandum, 1950. Published German translation: *Neue Schweizer Rundschau,* December 29, 1950.

I can see no chance of the United States regaining its former international position except, *perhaps,* if the American people were willing to repeal the immigration laws and to open the country to countless millions of immigrants from Latin America, Asia, and Africa—a move that would play havoc with American standards of living and with the free institutions and the Western character of the nation. If, however, the American people wish to defend these goods, as every nation would, it would be better to acknowledge the realities of the situation.

may attempt to placate the revolutionary forces by inaugurating *reforms,* in the hope of thus weakening the revolutionary élan. These are, of course, marginal types (*Idealtypen*) of political behavior and, in practice, a policy may lie somewhere in between these sharply defined categories and show characteristics of more than one.

The conservative answer is historically represented most brilliantly by Clemens von Metternich; in our days, Winston Churchill tried it within the narrow limits of his power. It is widely asserted today, particularly in this country and in Britain, that such a policy would, in the present world, be doomed to failure. This may well be so, but it is questionable to what degree this assessment is based on a dispassionate analysis of the forces involved and to what degree on the progressive bias, which is part of the protest attitude itself. There are anti-revolutionary forces everywhere in the world, and the current revolution, like every other revolution, cannot go on forever; a point must be reached where people can no longer adjust sufficiently fast to the constantly accelerating pace of events. One can hardly state *a priori* that a policy of digging in, defending crucial positions, and waiting for the next swing of the pendulum to occur is necessarily doomed to failure. But it runs strongly against the progressive stream of Western thinking.

The Bonapartist solution is quite alien to American traditions. But a policy of trying to stay ahead of the revolution has been repeatedly followed by the United States, although the pressures of national interest have made its *consistent* application impossible. The advocates of this policy believe that if the United States sides with Arabs against England, France, and Israel; with Algerian Moslems against France; with Indonesia against the Netherlands; or with African nationalists against Portugal, the African and Asian nationalists will appreciate these American attitudes and will in some way show their appreciation; to the very least, according to this theory, they will be less hostile than they would otherwise have been. Others, however, believe that this is an unwarranted extrapolation of political experience in a democracy from the domestic to the international scene. Only under conditions in which physical violence is effectively excluded, as is the case within a well-established legal order, so these critics think, is the accumulation of goodwill the royal road to power and influence. In international relations, however, particularly in the present conditions of extreme lawlessness in which nearly every nation faces grave perils, goodwill is of limited value. They believe, furthermore, that for Asian, African, and Latin American intellectuals, the United States is the arch imperialist power, not because of what it does but because of what it *is,* namely, it *is* the world's richest capitalist nation. It is believed, too, that manifestations of benevolence are not likely to alter the course of unfriendly nations, except adversely, by convincing them that the United States is already in so desperate straits that it can be abused with impunity; but that unfriendly nations may, nevertheless, at any moment, change over to the Western side if they feel threatened by Communist powers and *if* they believe that the United States can render them effective assistance.

The last answer to the challenge of revolution, finally, that of reformism, has been the main United States policy all during the crisis; support for a liberal policy of reform everywhere has been further emphasized by the present administration.

It is the basic idea of this American policy to try to convince the world that the American "Revolution," rather than the French and Russian Revolutions, holds the message for their present aspirations. It aspires to win a major part of the people of "underdeveloped" countries for a program of meliorism, financed by the United States, in preference over revolution—a repetition of the Roosevelt New Deal on a world scale. Success or failure of this policy is still hidden in the future, but it is clear that it is undertaken under conditions far less auspicious than those under which the New Deal was launched. A rich man of moderate temperament like Franklin Roosevelt was acceptable to the lower income groups of America as their leader, but that does not mean that rich and moderately tempered America will be acceptable as leader to the *descamisados* and African hut dwellers or to the students in Bogota and Rangoon, particularly while the Soviet world offers its full support for more radical alternatives. The United States can only offer help toward an improvement of living conditions, which must needs be slow, at the price of domestic tranquillity. At the same time, the more radical alternative promises, in addition to the immediate confiscation and distribution of accumulated consumers' goods (including durable goods such as luxurious homes or beaches), the excitement of revolution, with ample opportunities for the squaring of old accounts and for sadistic gratifications. While the embourgeoisement of the poor is more satisfactory in the long run, the expropriation of the rich suggests itself to human impatience as so much quicker and easier. It is the ancient cry: *panem et circenses.*

STRENGTH AND WEAKNESS IN THE WESTERN POSITION. The weaknesses of the Western position are patently obvious; they appear to be rooted in the following facts:

1. The contact of the poor with the rich, together with the progressive breakdown of caste barriers, has brought about constant comparison by the poor of their condition with that of the rich, and with it a sense of suffering, resentment, and envy. These sentiments can hardly be appeased by the prospect of slow improvement because, for a great part of the road at least, impatience *increases* as actual differences diminish and the goal is closer in sight.

2. Under these circumstances, utopian ideas seem entirely plausible to all but a few. Their plausibility rests in the failure of most people to understand the economic problem of rational choice, and in the naive belief that all problems can be easily solved once the authorities have set themselves to them. Furthermore, a democratic party is in a poor position to compete with a totalitarian movement because the democratic party cannot make utopian promises with impunity; a totalitarian movement is under no such restraint; it does not have to worry about redeeming its promises, because on the day of their maturing it has long achieved unchallengeable power.

3. Finally, there is, for Americans, an inner difficulty: The current revolutions strive for goals that Americans have traditionally upheld such as the right of self-determination of all nations, large or small, of all groups whose leaders declare them to be nations. Many of the declarations of nationalist leaders today might have been bodily lifted from speeches of American leaders in the past.

In particular, the following beliefs, widely held in this country, tend to weaken it in the present struggle:

(a) The egalitarian illusion: the assumption that all branches of the human family have been equipped with equal genetic endowment, and that actual differences of performance, therefore, can be due only to differences in opportunity; lack of achievement of some is therefore the responsibility of the more successful ones.

(b) The democratic illusion: the belief that self-government is always workable and indeed the best possible government, regardless of the level of education and information, and that there is something sacred about the principle, "one man, one vote," or its present international application: "one sovereign unit, one vote."

(c) The materialist prejudice: the belief that people are always motivated by economic interest and by a correct evaluation of their economic interest, to boot. A revolution in, say, Asia, must therefore be due to a clamor for land reform denied by the American-supported government, or similar conditions; facts at variance with this theory simply cannot be true.

(d) The sentimentalist illusion: the belief that relations between nations are governed not by the demands of self-interest as interpreted by them but by emotions such as likes or dislikes for another people or admiration or disparagement for its domestic achievement.

(e) The rationalist and moralist illusions: the belief that the establishment of law need not have a basis in a community existing in the minds of men and in physical power, but that law can be based on an appeal to conscience alone, and that the social contract can create an effective community.

(f) The distorted view of revolution: the belief that revolution always is made by those at the bottom of the social pyramid and is caused by oppression and injustice of the regime in power. The very fact of the revolution appears then as *prima facie* evidence for the injustice of the regime; [21] and it is felt that unjust rule must eventually lead to revolution.

The fact that a substantial part of articulate public opinion holds some, or all, of these propositions to be true greatly interferes with a realistic evaluation of the situation.

But there is also one point of strength for the West in its competition with Communism for the allegiance of the remainder of mankind: While the West, in the present climate of opinion, appears to be outclassed in the propaganda battle—as was the Habsburg Monarchy in its final struggle for survival in the midst of revolutionary forces, and for similar reasons—there is also one strong card in the Western hand, and much will depend on whether it will be played with skill (as it has hardly been so far). The strength of the Soviets consists in the fact that the Socialist *idea*, which they incarnate, has an enormous appeal to the intellectuals and, to a lesser degree, to the poor; but it is their weakness that the Socialist *reality* is quite unattractive. No

[21] How unreal this assumption is will be seen when we translate it from the vertical, intranational, to the horizontal context, i.e., from the civil to international war: Who would entertain the notion that the fact that one nation has taken up arms against another is sufficient evidence for the justice of its cause?

amount of argument and of good deeds is likely to convince liberal opinion in this country or abroad, or the masses in backward lands who have become aware of the possibility of a better life, that a capitalist country could do any right except by retreating and surrendering; but neither persuasion nor good deeds are necessary to convince, say, the East Germans.

Among men, as well as in animal and plant life, favorable living conditions bring about a proliferation of life, and whatever people may think ideologically, the direction of their migrations indicates the differences of living conditions. Where migration has been possible at all, as in Berlin and Hong Kong, it has been going from socialism to "capitalism."

It is the Western system, not the Soviet and the various other government-operated systems, that has actually worked better for the satisfaction of human needs and of the aspirations of people in their private lives. The strength of Socialism lies in the plausibility of its *arguments* and *promises;* the strength of the West lies in its *actual deliveries.* But the latter take a long time before they tell their story—long, not only because much experience must have accumulated before much inference can be drawn from it, but also because few people will revise satisfactory theories on account of inconvenient facts; most people will not notice such facts or will explain them away in some fashion. Also, governments unfriendly to the West can easily suppress such facts. It therefore takes at least the coming of age of another generation before there is any chance that widely accepted theories might be revised.

THE CRUCIAL PROBLEM IN THE STRUGGLE. The fundamental fact in the struggle between a pluralist society and a totalitarian system is the permanent *reversibility* of every victory of the former and the *irreversibility* of a victory of the latter. Whenever an attempt by totalitarians at seizing power has failed, the totalitarian movement, or the totalitarian countries that back it up, remains in a position to repeat that attempt tomorrow, the day after tomorrow, and forever after. Whenever totalitarians have seized power in a country, the result is irreversible (except for outside intervention such as overthrew Mussolini and Hitler), because totalitarians destroy every focus of possible resistance after a seizure of power. They must set up, as Lenin put it, a government that nobody will ever overthrow. This has been greatly facilitated in more recent times by modern technology, which has made possible an effective monopoly of the tools of coercion and communications such as has not existed for a long time and perhaps has never existed to quite the same degree.[22]

These ground rules put Western societies at a grave disadvantage. Nevertheless,

---

[22] In the eighteenth and nineteenth centuries, the main weapon of regular armies was the rifle; and rifles could be owned and operated by civilians, too. They could be hidden in backyards or smuggled across frontiers. Hence, the advantage of a governmental force over rebellious citizens was narrowed down to the advantages of superior training and discipline; these were real, but not necessarily decisive advantages, and men of courage had a chance against regular security forces. This was, therefore, the age of minute men, barricades, and expanding democracy; it was in this period that the word was coined that one could do everything with bayonets except sit on them. But tanks and bombing planes cannot be hidden under the floor, nor operated without a large visible organization. *Present technology therefore favors absolute State power.*

they need not necessarily lead to catastrophe as long as the likelihood of a totalitarian take-over is as small as one chance in twenty, because the time that would have to pass until a totalitarian take-over became probable is sufficiently long that unforeseen events may upset all calculations. But, if the totalitarian chance is fairly good, perhaps one chance out of three, totalitarian victory becomes very probable within a relatively brief period of time. Eventual victory, by Communism or totalitarian movements allied to it, over most of the "underdeveloped" world appears, therefore, likely, unless the West can effect a change in the ground rules and make a Communist take-over a reversible event.

It may be that Communism, though with its prestige greatly increased, may yet have less easy sailing in many countries than it had in Russia, China, and Cuba, because the middle classes, the peasants, and unionized labor may be less naive as to what is going to happen. But within the reach of Soviet power, effective resistance against a Communist regime already established is nevertheless an inauspicious enterprise, as events in Eastern Germany and Hungary have shown.

It may be different in countries which are not within easy reach of the Red Army and its air transport and which lie in the shadow of Western sea power. The latter has recently been shown as of little effectiveness in the case of a left-handed support for a small force of invading exiles, but it may yet be effective in enforcing a hands-off policy against a foreign, Hungary-style intervention to crush a local uprising. In this way, perhaps, Alfred Thayer Mahan's concept of the influence of sea power upon history may not yet be entirely obsolete. It may be one of the present-day possibilities of sea power and, therefore, one of the chances of the "world island" (Mackinder), which so largely depends on sea power for its survival, to keep revolutionary results reversible within a certain radius from its power center and, thereby, give trial and error a chance to work itself out.

From this point of view, the establishment of Communist States distant from the Soviet center of power contains, in addition to all too obvious dangers for the West, some possibilities for it, too. If conditions are reversible, Communist propaganda might be defeated in a certain area by the only effective argument there is—by a demonstration of Communism in action.

We, therefore, may question whether it is in the best interest of the United States to continue the policy of containment and to try its utmost to deny Communism access to Latin America and Africa. This policy is straining American resources to the utmost; it greatly antagonizes many people in these countries, as people do not like being told by others what they should do in their own best interest, which they prefer to judge for themselves; and it has not been conspicuous for its success of late. One may wonder whether it would not be preferable for the United States to take more of a back seat and, with the exception of the strategically most sensitive spots, to allow events to take their course. Under such circumstances, one must assume that Communist governments will be set up in some countries in these continents (as they probably will be anyhow); but it is also likely that some other countries will pursue a vigorous anti-Communist course and look to the United States for help. The United States would then not be in the thankless role of a proponent of an unpopular policy and an easy prey for blackmail but would be in the strong position of a power whose help is eagerly sought. In this way, a kind of equilibrium may be established in these continents which, though fraught with dangers for the West, may yet be one that can be lived with and upheld with less strain than is incumbent upon the present attempt of holding an umbrella over these continents and all their people—the willing, the disinterested, and the hostile alike. As time passes, Communism may find itself in these transoceanic outposts confronted with difficulties similar to those it faces in Eastern Europe, albeit without the possibility of easy military intervention.

The obstacle against the adoption of such a policy may lie not only in its undeniable perils, but also in the reluctance of the American people to part with universalist moral schemes and to have recourse to the despised strategies of "power politics."

II

Protest Movements in Developed Areas

II

2

Great Britain: The Reactive Revolt[1]

Norman Birnbaum

I

The face of Great Britain in this fall of 1961 has a paradoxical appearance. The octogenarian Bertrand Russell goes to jail, if only for seven days, after violating police regulations during a campaign against nuclear weapons and NATO. One week later, he is followed in the courts by some thirteen hundred demonstrators—most of them rather younger—from among the ten thousand who sat down in Trafalgar Square to continue the protest. The rest of the country, however, seems quiet and even placid—preoccupied with its own affairs. An economic crisis and labour disputes, even a small race riot in the industrial north, do not erase this impression. Britain seems to be a society stable and confident, enjoying what are by contemporary standards an extraordinary amount of freedom and an only slightly less extraordinary quantum of prosperity. The paradox is so striking that many will suppose that it cannot be resolved. The discrepancy between an impassioned minority's gesture of protest at world history and the prosaic insularity of the majority is too great: We have to conclude that, psychologically, minority and majority simply inhabit different worlds.

The paradox can be resolved, but only if we acknowledge that all is not as it seems. The psychological differences at issue ought not to obscure a common characteristic of all contemporary British reactions to politics. *Reactions* is, in fact, the appropriate term. In Britain, conformist and rebel alike are objects and not subjects of history.

The present ineluctable decline of the country's power and influence began but half a generation ago. Many who have experienced it are unwilling to admit that it has occurred—although it affects the consciousness of all Britons, at one or another level. An immediate consequence of this process of decline, of course, is that the scope of meaningful British intervention in world politics has been drastically reduced. This does not imply that British society has been thrown back upon itself.

---

[1] Two treatments of the period immediately preceding this one may be mentioned: C. L. Mowat's excellent historical study, *Britain Between the Wars, 1918–40* (London: Methuen, 1955), and Asa Briggs' remarkable essay in H. Clegg and A. Flanders (eds.), *The System of Industrial Relations in Great Britain* (Oxford: B. Blackwell, 1954). Briggs' account of recent social changes in Britain does consider the very pervasive effects of the war, as well as the influence of the Labour governments of 1945–50 and 1950–51.

The problem, rather, is that the decisions affecting Britain's future are taken by others.

The compulsive rebellion of some, the cramped local perspectives of others and the yawning apathy of most are all responses to this situation. These particular responses, to be sure, are not inevitable. A decline in power may precipitate political convulsions of a major kind; it need not be accompanied by what is, in Britain, a national sense of shock. (The parallel, and contrasting, case of modern France is instructive.) The exigencies of Britain's postwar position do not, however, affect the British in a vacuum; their capacities (and incapacities) have been preformed by some of the more pervasive aspects of modern British social structure.[2] So pervasive, indeed, are the constraints which shape contemporary British political psychology that their analysis is exceedingly difficult. Many intelligent Britons do not view the pressures to which they are subjected as constraints. They tend, instead, to depict their institutions as uniquely perfected devices for maximizing human gratification.[3] On this view, the sociological analysis of British society itself is, if not impious, irrelevant.[4] In no other major Western country (with the possible exception of the German Federal Republic) is social criticism so obviously confined to a segment of the intellectuals.

The prevailing ideological defensiveness is so strong, indeed, that it takes the form of an attack. A series of positive propositions about British society have been promulgated by articulate politicians, professors, serious journalists, and educators.[5] The argument, reproduced here in crude but not quite caricatured terms, is as follows: British society is in possession of tested modes of meeting and inducing social changes. A broad consensus of political values is the basis of an effective national community in which each section of society has *and* knows its place. Alterations in the distribution of rewards, and even more so in the general balance of forces among the different parts of society, are usually the result of immediate and pragmatic agreements. Indeed, pragmatism is the essence of the British method for dealing with social conflict. It would not be an exaggeration to say that the method consists precisely of having none: Each problem is considered in its own terms, and grandiose attempts at large-scale social reconstruction are eschewed. Of course, Britain has social conflicts; which society does not? In Britain, however, these are settled as they

[2] A sociological analysis of contemporary British society as a whole is still lacking. Much can be learned, however, from the systematic treatments given in: G. D. H. Cole, *The Post-War Condition of Britain* (London: Routledge and K. Paul, 1956) and A. M. Carr-Saunders, D. C. Jones, C. A. Moser, *A Survey of Social Conditions in England and Wales as Illuminated by Statistics* (Oxford: Clarendon Press, 1958). One appreciation of the social atmosphere may be had from T. Harrisson *et al., Britain Revisited* (London: V. Gollancz, 1961).

[3] See my essay " 'Empiricism' and British Politics," *Commentary* (February 1961), and "Social Constraints and Academic Freedom," *Universities and Left Review*, No. 5 (1958).

[4] See *Twentieth Century* (May 1960), entitled "The Science of Society" which discusses the position of sociology in Britain—especially the contributions by O. H. MacGregor, D. G. MacRae, E. Shils, and myself.

[5] A few hours spent with the back files of *The Times* or *The Daily Telegraph*—the newspapers read by the elite—will, in this connection, prove instructive. *The Guardian*, published in Manchester, at times exhibits a certain skepticism; it offers, however, no alternative general view of how things in Britain really get done.

come; in no case do they give rise to those ultimate ideological confrontations which have so troubled less fortunate European societies.

Thus, the *homme moyen intellectuel*. The lower apologetics, further, has a higher counterpart: Some of the most distinguished social philosophers in British universities have advanced universal prescriptions for mankind's ills which read like abstract glosses on this interpretation of British society.[6] The arguments for "empiricism," "piecemeal social engineering," and the like, and against a number of imprecisely defined evils ("positive freedom," "sociological holism" and more) clearly imply that modern Britain is a striking instance of a successful experiment in liberal philosophy. With so much energy expended on ideological self-congratulation, it is not surprising that some of Britain's difficulties have recently had less attention than they merit. This distortion of focus, indeed, may well be due to the painful discrepancy between this simple, almost idyllic, image of Britain and a reality that is more complex and less satisfactory.

Contemporary Britain is, whatever its apologists may say, a stagnant society.[7] Its citizens are burdened by a miscellany of mutual grievances which seriously affect their morale, many of which are direct derivatives of the peculiarities of the British class system. What sometimes passes for consensus in Britain is, rather, the artefact of a tenuous balance of opposing forces. (Where there is so much talk of consensus, we are of course entitled to suspect that it may be defective.)

Far from approaching their problems pragmatically, the British manifest a variety of ideological interpretations of their situation—although those who promulgate contrasting or conflicting ideologies are agreed on the pragmatic value of denying that they do so. In these circumstances, domestic revolt (or, more accurately, dissent) has a curiously strident tone: The rebels sense, rightly that they have to shout to be heard at all. The British response to the revolution in the outside world, on the other hand, is for the most part a stubborn refusal to acknowledge that it presents an intractable problem. The resultant combination, aggressive protest on the one hand and complacent self-congratulation on the other, produces precisely that paradoxical appearance with which we began. This is the appropriate point, perhaps, at which to begin looking behind appearances. We may turn to the social setting in which these ideological tendencies have developed.

II

The loss of Empire has affected British political attitudes both directly and indirectly. Not alone administrators and businessmen participated in the control of the Empire; during two world wars (and in the more recent conflicts in Malaya, Kenya,

---

[6] See I. Berlin, *Two Concepts of Liberty* (Oxford: Clarendon Press, 1958) and K. R. Popper, *The Open Society and its Enemies*, Vols. 1 and 2 (London: G. Routledge and Sons, Ltd., 1945). M. Oakeshott, *Political Education* (Cambridge: 1951), takes a different tack—and indeed discourages social criticism to a degree (and in a manner) not found in the other works.

[7] A careful reading of the weeklies, *The Economist* or *The Spectator* for the past few years will show that a nagging awareness of this condition dogs not a few members of Britain's economic and cultural elite. On the left, *The New Statesman*—until recently, at least—had other concerns.

and the Mid-East) hundreds of thousands of ordinary Britons enjoyed what was in effect a colonial situation with respect to Afro-Asian populations. They conveyed their experiences, of course, to their families—a highly effective method of political education. When the Labour Party leadership in 1956 opposed the British government's military intervention in Egypt, it challenged the chauvinistic and imperialistic sentiments of millions of Labour voters in the working class.[8] Many of the latter seemed to intuit, and sympathize with, the psychological components of Sir Anthony Eden's policy. This was conceived not alone as a rational military-political measure, but as a gesture of outraged protest against the seizure of "our" Suez Canal by the "wogs"—a denial of that alteration of forces in the world which was, eventually, to leave the "wogs" in possession of the Canal. The national division over the Suez intervention arrayed, in fact, those still possessed of the middle-class liberal conscience—many of whom were British Socialists—against the majority of the nation.

(To some extent, the racial conflicts that have occurred in Britain in recent years have been encouraged by the transfer of colonialist racial attitudes to the homeland. Hannah Arendt, in her *Origins of Totalitarianism*,[9] argued that the transfer of colonialist attitudes to Europe was itself a pre-condition of Fascism; this suggestion has, unfortunately, not given rise to a precise program of social research in the two countries where it is presently relevant, Britain and France. The influx of tens of thousands of Africans, Asians, and West Indians—with the resultant pressures on housing and the fear of economic competition—has been, in itself, a sufficient stimulus to conflict.[10] But this particular demonstration of the unity of the Commonwealth has been interpreted by many Britons as something of a reversal of the order of nature, as painfully visible proof that the Empire has become something else.)

The indirect consequences of the end of Empire have been no less effective. Those with liberal consciences could celebrate the liberation of India as a triumph of British statesmanship. The rest acquiesced but viewed the abdication of British power in Asia as part of a steady process of decline that was marked by any number of events: the displacement of Britain by the United States as a major world power; the slow domestic economic recovery after the war (underscored by Germany's economic success and its competitiveness in foreign markets); the rise of Soviet power. The style, the articulateness, the self-consciousness of British reactions to these phenomena vary from class to class. The reactions, however, do have a common tone, in which bewilderment, petulance, and resentment are mixed. This external situation, moreover, has compounded with major changes in domestic social structure to produce a general sense of disorientation which has as yet to be replaced by anything else.

It is common to characterize the alterations in the relationship between the social

<hr />

[8] See E. Childers, *The Road to Suez* (London: 1962). The domestic atmosphere in Britain in the late fall and winter of 1956 will not be forgotten by those who experienced it.

[9] H. Arendt, *The Origins of Totalitarianism,* 2nd ed. (New York: Harcourt Brace, 1958), Chaps. 6, 7, and 8.

[10] The latest and one of the most interesting studies of this problem is: R. Glass, *The Newcomers: The West Indians in London* (London: 1960).

classes brought about by the Labour government, 1945–51, as triumphs of Socialism. It must be remembered, however, that British Socialism has for nearly forty years, ever since the beginning of the decline of liberalism and the Liberal Party, mobilized the spiritual energies of an important minority of the middle-class intelligentsia. The leadership it gave to the Labour movement was ameliorative and reformist in temper.[11] The gains registered in the area of social policy in 1945–51 were striking, but they hardly constituted (nor were they intended to constitute) a social revolution of a full-scale sort.[12]

The Welfare State, rather, gave the working class a minimal but guaranteed share in the distribution of the national income.[13] The National Health Service, an enlargement of educational provision, the extension of pre-existing welfare services and benefits (which were not always inconsiderable), food subsidies and a rehousing program were the means of redistribution. The continuation of wartime economic controls, the nationalization of the Bank of England, of the mining, power, transport, and steel industries were measures designed to institutionalize a planned economy. (Interestingly enough, there were no experiments with workers' control in industry and the nationalized industries were deliberately insulated from direct parliamentary control.[14]) It was on this latter front that the Conservative counterattack, when it came in 1951, was mounted; the principle of redistribution through a Welfare State was not at first attacked.[15] Instead, social values were propagated which made redistributive notions seem either inefficient, utopian, or unnecessary, as the ideological context demanded.

The Conservative counterattack, later consolidated in the electoral victories of 1955 and 1959, made very effective use of a number of public discontents with the Labour government. The coincidence of postwar economic difficulties with Labour rule was bad luck. The failure of the government, particularly in its last two years, to develop a positive political appeal was perhaps less accidental. Redistribution had alienated the professional, managerial, and clerical sections of the middle classes. At least initially tolerant of Labour, these groups now tended to view the prospect

---

[11] See Beatrice Webb's autobiographical account of her youth: *My Apprenticeship* (London: Longmans, Green and Co., 1926). The recent memoirs by the Chancellor of the Exchequer in the 1945 Labour Government, Hugh Dalton, contain much that is useful to an appreciation of the mentality of these middle-class socialists; *Call Back Yesterday,* Vols. 1 and 2 (London: F. Muller, 1953–57). (A third volume, on Labour's postwar governments, is scheduled for publication in 1962.)

[12] R. Miliband, *Parliamentary Socialism* (London: 1961) is a critique of Labour's renunciation, explicit and implicit, of the possibilities of revolutionary action. Dr. Miliband is also one of the Labour's Left's most prominent theorists; his work is interesting on this as well as many other, counts.

[13] R. Titmuss, *Essays on the Welfare State* (London: G. Allen and Unwin, 1957) is the authoritative discussion of these postwar changes and their social effects.

[14] See A. Rogow (with the assistance of P. Shore), *The Labour Government and British Industry* (Oxford: B. Blackwell, 1955).

[15] The essays by P. Goldmann and by two Tory ministers, I. MacLeod and E. Powell, in the pamphlet *The Future of the Welfare State* (London: Conservative Political Centre, 1958), are worth reading. They express the view of the younger and more flexible Conservative faction— after seven years of office and while preparing the electoral triumph of 1959.

of a continued Labour government as a threat to their own existence. Redistributive measures, as they affected the tax system, had eliminated some of the differential between themselves and the working class. By 1950 this was interpreted not as a temporary sacrifice but as preliminary to the erosion of their social identity. This anxiety could have been overcome only by a program which appealed to their national sentiments (and activated memories of the 1930's) by emphasizing the need for the modernization of Britain's outmoded social and economic infrastructure. Instead, Labour's program at the beginning of the 50's was curiously bifurcated. The middle-class reformists, tired and without new ideas in domestic policy, demonstrated their sense of "national responsibility" in the sphere of foreign affairs. Rearmament on a very large scale (which, of course, used up the resources that might have been put into a new economic program) was the result. The working-class section of the Labour movement concentrated on the defense of the advantages it had won since 1945. But it was the Conservatives under Churchill who seemed to have unique capacities for "national" leadership, and the defensive strategy adopted by the articulate representatives of the working class could not alter, and may indeed have reinforced, the anti-Labour tendency in the middle classes. The marginal constituencies returned Conservative candidates. A much different social experiment began.[16]

The political techniques of the new British Conservativism are not entirely refined, but they have been more or less successful in electoral terms. The new Conservatives have resisted the demands of the more visceral segment of their party, which hoped for an attack on the Labour movement. Instead, the postwar Conservative governments have allowed the working class a certain share in prosperity—if a share that had to be obtained in the market and not by direct political means. The welfare services have, to a certain extent, been allowed to run down, chiefly through the device of not extending them, of increasing welfare expenditure at a rate less than the rate of increase in national income. Frontal assaults on the Welfare State, again, have been conspicuously absent, although there have been two or three guerrilla raids. The essential means adopted by the Conservatives have been two:

1. A generally unplanned and uncontrolled economic expansion has been encouraged. The long-term adequacy of this policy may be doubted, on the basis of Britain's relatively low *average* annual rate of economic growth, but there have been perceptible spurts of increased popular purchasing power.[17]

2. The mass media have been developed as systematic purveyors of the ideology (or lack of one) appropriate to the new consumer society.[18] As we shall see, this

[16] See R. B. McCallum and A. Readman, *The British General Election of 1945* (London: Oxford University Press, 1947); H. G. Nicholas, *The British General Election of 1950* (London: Macmillan, 1951); D. E. Butler, *The British General Election of 1951* (London: Macmillan, 1952).

[17] A. Shonfield, *British Economic Policy Since the War*, 2nd ed. (London: 1959).

[18] H. H. Wilson, *Pressure Group: The Campaign for Commercial Television in Britain* (London: Secker and Warburg, 1961), shows what importance large sectors of British business (and their allies and spokesmen in the Conservative Party) attached to the introduction of commercial television.

has stimulated protest on the right as well as the left. For the moment, it suffices to observe that the values presented by commercial television and the daily and weekly press, while explicitly apolitical, are implicitly anti-Labour. These include a belief in the propriety and immutability of the prevailing status system, and the endorsement of a style of life which, where it is not centered on personal success, is privatized in the extreme. The mass media seem to be effecting a spiritual homogenization of the British population; awareness of social conflict has been reduced, and a curiously amorphous public ideology has taken its place—as if fewer Britons can identify their own particular interests in a society become ever more opaque.

These techniques are, however, not infallible. The expansive movement of the economy has been checked—as, again, this year—by bouts of restrictionism. The new Conservatives have been unable to mount a coherent economic program. The economic ideology manifested by the more traditional membership of their Party— shopkeepers and small businessmen, small-town professionals, and retired officers— is an obscure conglomerate of instinctive deflationism and self-righteous self-seeking. The pressures exerted on the Conservative leadership in this way are not insuperable, the more so because important sections of British industry regard a rigorous deflationism as absurd.

There are, however, other and equally important economic influences on the Conservatives. The City of London, or more accurately that part of it which deals in international finance, is insistently deflationist. Under these conflicting influences the Conservative Governments have produced an erratic succession of budgets. Tax concessions to the middle classes have been followed by credit restrictions which increased the cost of house purchase; periods of increasing real income for the working class have been interrupted by cuts in the Welfare Services and higher charges for the remaining ones, as well as by substantial patches of unemployment. Briefly put, despite ten years of uninterrupted rule, the Conservatives have not convinced the nation that they are in control of events in the economy, where their successes and failures are most visible.

Similarly, what may be termed the political education undertaken by the mass media has been a considerable, but not an unequivocal, success. However opaque the workings of the new British society, ordinary men and women are able to sense (and not alone in the economic sphere) its impact on their lives. The awareness of social conflict has been reduced, even repressed, but it has not been eliminated. Those brief ten days in the electoral campaign of 1959, when the Labour Party made the running with an attack on what it denounced as "the windfall state," did not overcome the intrinsic advantages enjoyed by the Conservatives. However, they did show that the language of social protest, if spoken with suitable diction, does not find the British entirely deaf.[19] (The coincidence of the election and a sizeable scandal in London property speculation was to Labour's advantage; the discovery by a Conservative newspaper that a rather prominent London Labour politician was an associate of speculative interests was not.)

[19] D. E. Butler, with R. Rose, *The British General Election of 1959* (London: Macmillan, 1960).

Despite the mass media's image of Britain as a society of satisfied consumers, the actual and potential discontents of the populace (particularly in the spheres of education and the status system and with respect to their society's general lack of amenities and dynamism) are very important. They cannot be conjured out of existence. The new British Left at times entertains exaggerated notions of the omnipotence of the mass media which contradict, in interesting fashion, its own belief in the educability of the populace—but this is a point that can be discussed subsequently.[20]

Prosperity has been the chief visible characteristic of Britain for the last half-decade; the uses of prosperity merit examination. For a large section of the working class, the material gains have been very great.[21] Relatively continuous full employment contrasts strikingly with the prewar depression. The National Health Service has broadened the basis of the prewar medical insurance system; a program of rehousing (since stopped, largely, by the Conservatives) has diminished the slum areas, which two decades ago, were among the most pestilential in Europe. Most important, of course, has been the steady amounts of cash which have come to working-class families.

It is true that the workers' market advantages have had to be won and maintained by trade-union pressure, including a number of acrimonious strikes. It is also true that much working-class prosperity is the result of overtime, dual job holding, and multiple family employment. Some claim, indeed, that the working-class share of the national income ceased to increase proportionally early in the current period of Conservative government. Academic economists agree or disagree in terms of their political preferences.

In any case, it is clear that a majority of working-class families have approached or attained some of the material prerogatives of a middle-class existence: reasonable housing, ample diet, the possession of durable goods, paid vacations. Security of employment is lacking, of course, and this is one, but only one, reason for the persistence, indeed the reinforcement, of some of the traditional status distinctions between the British social classes. The objective gains of the working class, finally, have not been accompanied by a subjective sense of full incorporation in the national community. Prosperity has eroded but not eliminated its sense of exclusion.

Not everyone in Britain, any more than in America, is prosperous.[22] There are millions living at or below a marginal rate of subsistence: those on state old-age pensions, the chronically or cyclically unemployed, those with large families and small incomes (family allowances have not been increased to match the rise in the cost of living). Moreover, working-class families with adequate incomes for most purposes are frequently stuck in bad housing; public rehousing is no longer avail-

[20] The essay by Stuart Hall, "Absolute Beginnings," in *Universities and Left Review*, No. 7 (1959), is a sophisticated instance of this *genre*. See also "TV and Broadcasting," *New Left Review*, No. 7 (1961).

[21] Data will be found in Cole and Carr-Saunders et al., *op. cit.*

[22] See the essay by P. Townsend in: N. Mackenzie (ed.), *Conviction* (London: MacGibbon and Kee, 1958).

able, and their own means are insufficient to purchase or rent alternative private housing. This is particularly true of the colored working-class population, and the resultant crowding into already crowded working-class districts is an obvious source of racial conflict.

Prosperity has affected the middle classes unequally. We may begin by noting that the middle classes have in fact profited from the Welfare State, particularly from the National Health Service and the 1944 Education Act.[23] (The majority of the university students who would not have continued their education in the prewar period are from the middle classes.) This has not, of course, precluded a certain middle-class resentment of the Welfare State, caused by high taxes and the obvious if incomplete closure of the gap between working-class and middle-class incomes. But this resentment is also unequal. It appears to be strongest in certain traditional middle-class occupations, both in the lower middle classes (clerks) and in the middle classes proper (among professionals). These groups, particularly their older members, take seriously the classical ideology of "individual responsibility" and "service." [24] The ideology has, in the past, justified considerable inequality and today is used often to legitimate new inequalities—in which advantages are enjoyed by a managerial elite whose ethic contrasts strikingly with the old professional code. Nonetheless, millions of Britons seem to cling to their old values, although what is striking about their resentment is that it is directed downwards, at the working class, and not upwards at those who, by old standards, are merely earning easy money. There is another segment of the middle classes, shopkeepers at the bottom and some businessmen at the top, whose resentment of the Welfare State is not clothed in an old ideology: They simply want more for themselves and see no way of obtaining this other than leaving less to others.

I have intimated that these attitudes are strongest among older members of the middle classes. It is too early to pronounce on the attitudes of their children, but some interesting changes may be taking place. In a number of occupations, with bank employees, for instance, old resistances to trade unionism are slowly dissolving. There is little or no evidence, however, to suggest that the younger members of the middle classes are moving Left. Their attitudes to the working class, to be sure, are frequently less obscurantist and more calculating. They do not, in large numbers, suppose that the workers are workers because of "laziness." The working class, they think, is a good class not to be in. There are three reasons for this change; consideration of them brings us to the new middle classes and their response to prosperity.[25]

Changes in occupational structure have greatly expanded the range of technical,

<hr />

[23] See R. Titmuss, *op. cit.*

[24] Excessively idealized portraits of these groups by two authors who share their ideology will be found in: A. Maude and R. Lewis, *The English Middle Classes* (London: Phoenix House, 1949) and in their *Professional People* (London: Phoenix House, 1952). Both books bespeak much hostility to the Welfare State—and to the working class.

[25] An excellent analytic and historical treatment of some of the older components of this stratum will be found in D. Lockwood, *The Black-Coated Worker* (London: G. Allen and Unwin, 1957). Something may also be learned from M. Young and P. Willmott, *Family and Class in a London Suburb* (London: Routledge and K. Paul, 1960).

semi-professional, and white-collar employment, in both the secondary and tertiary sectors of the economy. Individuals in these posts are usually better educated and less servile than their clerical predecessors in the middle classes. They seem to manifest different attitudes to their work; in any event, the technicians at least evince a certain discrimination between the satisfactions of technical achievement and status gratifications. All the members of this grouping, meanwhile, are openly and unashamedly interested in the things that money can buy; in this respect, they are perhaps among the most "Americanized" elements in British society.

The second factor in this group's response to prosperity is its own somewhat heterogeneous class origins. A sizeable minority in these new middle-class occupations are themselves offspring of working-class families; the rest find themselves in a genuinely ambiguous area, with respect to traditional systems of status allocation, for which neither their parents nor their schools have prepared them. These two factors seem to inhibit the development of hostility to the working class and to promote what appears to be a matter-of-fact attitude to the advantages enjoyed by their own occupations. This relative detachment allows some in the new middle classes to criticize the lack of dynamism of the nation's economic elite, to entertain (vague) suspicions that the society's priorities are wrong. These doubts, however, are confined to a small minority. Opposed to them is an *arrivisme* derived from the entire occupational group's ideological dependence upon Britain's new managerial type, the third component in the response of the new middle classes to prosperity.

Never, in the history of the world's first and, for many generations leading, capitalist society, have businessmen been at the top of the status hierarchy.[26] The familiar processes, not unique to Britain, by which industrial and commercial wealth associated itself with antecedent status systems have, in modern Britain, contributed to a certain genteel inefficiency in the British economy.[27] (This inefficiency may well be a national as well as a class phenomenon, of course: The British worker has long since ceased to be the rival of many of his counterparts elsewhere, and the national imperial nostalgia may account for this shared ineptitude.) This is today most visible, perhaps, in certain key positions in the direction of the economy. Some senior civil servants responsible for economic affairs are proud of their lack of academic training

[26] See R. Clements, *Managers: A Study of their Careers in British Industry* (London: G. Allen and Unwin, 1958) and the impressionistic but convincing sketch by R. Samuel, "The Boss as Hero," *Universities and Left Review*, No. 7 (1959). The essay by P. Shore ("In the Room at the Top") in *Conviction, op. cit.* is also useful.

[27] Among recent British historians, L. E. Woodward and R. C. K. Ensor are not usually thought of either as utilizing a sociological approach or exhibiting much critical detachment toward the British elite. Their volumes in the Oxford History of England series, however, provide data on the development of the elite which are all the more valuable for being presented in so unconscious a fashion. See: L. E. Woodward, *The Age of Reform, 1815–70* (Oxford: 1946) and R. C. K. Ensor, *England, 1870–1914* (Oxford: 1946). Sociological studies of the contemporary elite are practically non-existent. See H. Thomas et al., *The Establishment* (London: A. Blond, 1959) and the special issue of *The Twentieth Century*, "Who Rules Britain?" (October 1957). Biographies are particularly useful sources for the functioning of the British elite. See, for instance, the portrait of the life of a former editor of *The Times*, J. E. Wrench, *Geoffrey Dawson and Our Times* (London: Hutchinson, 1955).

in economics and the social sciences. Finance in the City of London works by convention, by gentleman's agreement, by an implicit set of rules which discourages aggression and innovation. There are other sectors of the economy in which the casualness and inefficiency of managers and staff strike the outsider as slothful. These, of course, are attitudes proper to gentlemen, or those who would be thought such, whatever other causes may be at work.

A new managerial elite, however, has developed in postwar Britain. Its attitudes are different, it works harder, and it values production. It ought not to be thought that Richard Baxter has come to life again: These are new-style entrepreneurs, working through large-scale organizations. It is this group which, through its control of the mass media, is seeking to re-make Britain into a consumer's society something like the managers imagine American to be. There are even persons of this sort in the City of London, although the new managers are generally located elsewhere. Their ostentatious critique of British economic stagnation has combined with certain persistent structural conflicts in the economy (the tension, for instance, between London finance and Midlands industry, which also has a status component).

For immediate purposes, we can say that the diffusion downwards in the society of the new managerial ethic has functioned as a dissolvent of certain ideological rigidities. The new managers do not find it morally reprehensible that working-class families have acquired washing machines; after all, they would like to sell them automobiles. The new economic elite, however, is not able either to assume unquestioned command of the Conservative Party, or to displace more conservative economic interests in the political elite. Its lack of complete success may be due to the ideological resistances the latter have been able to generate, resistances which also blunt the determination of the new managers by inducing many of them to seek recognition by the old ruling class.

I have said that businessmen were never, in Britain, at the very apex of the society; this place was filled by the imperial magnates. The magnates constituted the political-economic directorate of the Empire; they assumed responsibility for the stability of the framework in which ordinary economic activities took place, and they expected and received deference from those concerned only with the latter. In politics, imperial administration, and certain critical economic positions, chiefly in the City and international enterprise, the magnates exercised command of British society.

Amateurs in all but the art of maintaining themselves in power, they were careful not to practice a self-defeating exclusiveness. New men, if they made themselves enough of a nuisance, were admitted to the club. Middle-class servitors in the civil service, the universities and education, the Church, the "responsible" press, were given important responsibilities and rewarded appropriately. (The co-optation of the educated middle class was the easier because the liberal offensive against the ruling class, with time, became attenuated: The latter adopted something of liberalism, and much of the doctrine's substance was taken over and transmuted by the Labour Party, with which many of the intelligentsia were not prepared to make common cause.) In short, the traditional British ruling class managed the Empire with skill and cunning.

What is remarkable is that the entire sequence of events of the last thirty years (depression, the rise of German Fascism, war, the postwar Labour governments, and the loss of Empire and world political power) has not dissolved the group. Its adaptive maneuvers have sometimes been inappropriate and it has exhibited signs of ideological rigidity, which are, in short, the classic symptoms of decay. Yet the imprint it has imposed on all of British culture, perhaps more than the critical economic posts to which it has clung, has enabled it to encapsulate or beat off its divided challengers.

The uniqueness of British society has consisted not least in the fact that it never was a "bourgeois" society of the western European sort. The British fusion of middle-class and upper-class culture is an important component of British political stability. It also, particularly in this century, has tended to empty middle-class culture of its hard and critical elements. Moreover, the combination has effectively excluded the working class from high culture, even through the recent improvement in its material and social fortunes. It is, therefore, to the present situation of British culture that we must turn now.

Much has been written of the "Establishment" in British culture. The "Establishment" takes its name from the Established Church and is commonly supposed to manifest the anti-qualities allegedly associated with the latter: compulsive deference to authority, an unqualified endorsement of the current social order (with an especially hypocritical opprobrium reserved for the latter's critics), and an obsessional revulsion for conflict, change, and new ideas. The recent history of the Established Church, of course, suggests that this is an extremely unfair characterization of it; the description is, perhaps, less inaccurate when applied to some prevalent attitudes in the British cultural elite. What is at issue in recent criticisms of the "Establishment" is the structure of that elite. There is, we are told, a cultural directorate comprising the universities, particularly Oxbridge, the upper reaches of the educational system, the BBC, the "better" newspapers and periodicals, and publishing. Many images of the "Establishment" insist on its political dimensions; it is also supposed to include the senior levels of the Civil Service, the Military, the Conservative Party (some critics of the present Labour Party leadership, indeed, insist that it is too much like a part of the "Establishment"), and the City of London. Nearly all portrayals of the "Establishment" insist that it functions by personal contact; a hint, even a discrete cough, is enough to set in motion the repressive machinery perfected to deal with those who attack the oligarchs. Bound by ties of sympathy and interest, the latter have, in any case, quite definite conventions as to what may and may not be said and done.

It is clear that these images of the "Establishment" are grotesquely simplified; they ignore the conflicts within the British elite. In any case, the term "Establishment" has been used, often, to encompass those aspects of the elite its critics dislike— that is to say, practically all of them. In the sphere of culture, at least, the term "Establishment" can be given a somewhat more limited definition. It applies to all those who defend the moral values, the style of life, and the peculiarly narrow psychological climate of the educated elite in a Britain of defined and enduring class divisions, a fixed world position, and unbroken cultural traditions. Viewed in this way, the "Establishment" is not a power group with an ideology but rather an ideology seeking attachment to a power group: The Britain represented by the values of the "Establishment" no longer exists. The values persist, or rather, their verbal elaboration does. Objectively, this often serves to legitimate interests, practices and groupings alien to the traditional "Establishment." The rhetoric of liberalism accompanies the progress of the British version of the organization man; lessons in the ethic of service are read by tax evaders; the doctrine of public responsibility for mass education justifies a commercial television system of subliminal standards.

The persistence of this set of values which, in its day, put solid ideological ground under the imperial magnates' feet, is an interesting expression of the ambiguity of the present cultural situation in Britain. The fact that these standards have not been forgotten can be interpreted as proof of their educative influence: The new men thrown up by prosperity can claim respectability only in these terms. These values cannot be realized in the actual state of British society. In so far as this is not acknowledged, hypocrisy or cynicism must result from the maintenance of the pretence. The "Establishment," then, is an important negative cultural force: Its promulgation of the values of 1939 hinders a solution to Britain's difficulties in 1961.

The persistence of this ideology has prevented the new men from developing one of their own; it also generates a profound confusion, even malaise, in all sectors of the society. The postwar period has seen a considerable expansion of educational opportunity; offspring of the working class have entered the academic secondary schools in great numbers, and many of them have joined new recruits from the lower and intermediate strata of the middle classes at the universities.[28] Britain never had, and still does not have, a national system of education in the continental manner, nor even in the American one. The universities, the public (that is, private) and the grammar schools were all institutions which provided, rather explicitly, training in a class-specific code of thought and behavior. Now that the universities and grammar schools are heterogeneous in their class composition, their students are (sometimes involuntarily) resistant to this sort of indoctrination. For the moment, however, there seems to be little else to give them.

British higher education has had a marked tendency to produce gentlemen amateurs (the three-year period for a bachelor's degree is short compared to that required for first degree in other European countries). The study of classical languages and literature has had a disproportionate amount of prestige; the natural and social sciences have been relatively neglected. C. P. Snow's remarks on *The Two Cultures*

[28] See D. V. Glass, "Education," in M. Ginsberg (ed.), *Law and Opinion in the 20th Century* (London: Stevens, 1959); J. Floud, A. H. Halsey et al., *Social Class and Educational Opportunity* (London: Heinemann, 1956); *New Left Review,* Special Issue on Education, No. 11 (1961); B. Jackson and D. Marsden, *Education and the Working Class* (London: 1962). D. Potter, *The Glittering Coffin* (London: 1960) is *inter alia* an interesting account of a working class boy's response to Oxford.

evoked much discussion recently because they struck home: The traditional British intellectual from the middle classes or the elite is generally not alone ignorant of science but profoundly unaware of his ignorance.[29] The difficulty is not simply one which can be overcome by investing more capital in the science departments of the universities. The dominant national mode of thought is casual; its unsystematic character is defended as "empirical," but it is curiously unable to deal with the complexities of an advanced industrial culture. Historically, it would appear that the great Victorian intellectuals consumed most of the innovating energies available to the British middle classes; their contemporary descendants are unable to add much to their heritage. It is not surprising, in these circumstances, that a new generation of university students sometimes reacts as if its studies were meaningless.

These are problems which, of course, directly affect but a small percentage of the adult population. The others are left to fend for themselves. The schools which the majority of British children attend usually have the outer paraphernalia of the middle-class schools, such as uniforms and a peculiar hierarchical system of authority by which prefects (elder students) discipline their younger peers. In short, they attempt to induct their pupils into that system of consensus which underlies British "individualism." They do so, however, without any discernible cultural content (the contrast with the Continent or even the United States is striking, in this case), culture being reserved for the middle classes. Attendance at one of these schools is generally interpreted by the children as an indication of the occupational and social fate that awaits them—exclusion from a whole range of opportunities and rewards. That the pupils are not, in this event, highly motivated will surprise no one, although of course there are educators who see evidence for the maintenance of the exclusion in this lack of motivation.

The culture of the educated class, then, has become brittle; in a few years, at most, it may relapse into a self-conscious antiquarian nostalgia. The more aggressive claimants of place in the political elite are *parvenus* unable to make a cultural contribution of their own; they have half assimilated, half degraded, the tradition of their predecessors. The working class, its traditional cultural solidarity reduced to an economic defensiveness, has been left to the mass media. This sketch is unduly schematic; it ignores those traces of vitality which, despite the reactive character of protest in Britain, give some of it a certain connection with the more creative aspects of the national tradition. It is to protest itself that we turn now.

[29] C. P. Snow, "The Two Cultures and the Scientific Revolution," (Cambridge: Cambridge University Press, 1959); see the symposium in *Encounter* (August 1959).

Part Two

Great Britain: The Reactive Revolt

Norman Birnbaum

I

Protest, of course, must eventually take political forms. Recent protest in Britain has been affected by the inner development of British politics in the last decade. Above, I wrote of the spiritual homogenization of the populace by the mass media and of its limits. We may now consider an equivalent phenomenon in the sphere of politics itself. Political homogenization in postwar Britain has this special trait: Sharp conflicts of principle and policy are as likely to divide the two major parties internally as to oppose them to one another. The conflicts between new and old Conservatives, between the moderates of the Labour Party and the Labour Left, have resulted in a largely unintended and generally tacit *rapprochement* between the parties. Unintended and tacit in origins, this *rapprochement* has been reinforced by both parties' leaderships' views of electoral necessity: new Conservatism and moderate socialism have been designed, positively, to attract marginal voters and, negatively, to avoid mobilizing latent class anxieties which might, from each party's standpoint, bring more hostile voters to the polls.

Two principle mechanisms have effected this homogenization. The parties' central organizations have imposed themselves on party congresses and on the local groupings alike. In Parliament, the Cabinet and the Shadow Cabinet (the leadership of the opposition) have imposed themselves on the parliamentarians.[1] It is true that resistance to the parliamentary leadership within Parliament has been much more continuous, overt, and troublesome within the Labour Party; but this resistance has been encapsulated and is now, ten years after the Bevanite revolt, further than ever from assuming command of the Party. Furthermore, the post of Prime Minister has not recently been one of *primus inter pares*. Successive postwar Prime Ministers have exercised extraordinary authority within their own governments. Eden, indeed, with the help of a compliant Foreign Secretary, presented his Cabinet with a *fait accompli* over Suez. The public seems to respond to this concentration and apparent personalization of power. The 1959 election, indeed, had a distinctly "Presidential" atmosphere, with posters of Macmillan and Gaitskell visible everywhere.

The decline of Parliament, the conspicuous absence of striking debate (and the apparent irrelevance of such striking debate as does occur in the course of political

[1] See R. T. McKenzie, *British Political Parties* (London: 1955).

decision) have been remarked upon by a host of commentators. What has escaped discussion, in Britain, are the ways in which this phenomenon is a function of a generally intensified process of bureaucratization in British society.[2] The British simply lack a political vocabulary for dealing with this development which has taken place in the economy, among trade unions, and in the mass media as well as in politics. Britain is, of course, peculiarly liable to what may be termed creeping bureaucratization. The highly developed patterns of consensus in the traditional elite have served the new oligarchs as models; power is exerted discreetly, often hidden from public awareness by an ideology which denies that anything of public concern is in fact happening. Liberalism in Britain, by insisting on the distinction that ought to prevail between the state and society has, by a sort of compulsive irrealism, allowed the fusion of state and society to proceed apace.

In these curious circumstances, three general reactions may be noted:

1. A considerable amount of political disorientation exists. Large numbers of Britons do not seem to know how their present political system works. Where they sense their own ignorance, they do not quite know how to overcome it, but this is, in any event, the minority case. That ignorance, in most instances, is overlaid by another source of disorientation: Many Britons are without consistent standards of political judgment. Much of this stems from political withdrawal; not having any explicit political ends, they are disinterested in political means.

2. The prevalent political withdrawal often takes the form, noted in a number of countries, of privatization. Prosperity, of course, facilitates this response: A sphere has apparently (and, in some cases, actually) emerged in which individuals can do things for themselves and can renounce self-conscious collective action. But privatization has also been observed in non-prosperous societies (as in the Soviet Union). What is at issue, perhaps, is a long-term tendency of modern politics from which Britain is not exempt.

3. The resultant depoliticization of the populace is a political fact of the first importance. It reinforces that popular passivity which is in any case a correlate of bureaucratization, and, despite the persistence of a liberal ideology, increasingly assimilates elections to plebiscites. Those who point to the continued existence of conflicts, or who criticize Britain's social institutions in this atmosphere, threaten not only the civic, but the psychic peace of their fellow citizens. In these circumstances, depoliticization is implicitly but emphatically conservative; a commitment to politics has become either the mark of the political professional or the rebel.[3] It remains, now, to examine Britain's rebels, near-rebels, and pseudo-rebels.

The British Communists, unlike their counterparts in France, Weimar Germany, Italy, and Republican Spain, never attracted a massive working-class following.[4] The

[2] With his usual perspicacity, R. H. S. Crossman has seen something of the problem. See his Fabian Tract, *Socialism and the New Despotism* (London: 1956).
[3] The reactions of a younger group of Leftist thinkers have been set down in E. P. Thompson (ed.), *Out of Apathy* (London: Stevens, 1959).
[4] See H. Pelling, *The British Communist Party* (London: A. and C. Black, 1958) and N. Wood, *Communism and the British Intellectuals* (New York: Columbia University Press, 1959).

Party was, instead, an alliance of working-class militants and members of the intelligentsia. The former worked through the trade unions (in some cases, as members of the shop stewards' movement, against the official trade-union leaders). The latter, in the professions, education, journalism or the arts, were most influential, as we might have expected, in the 1930's; in that period British Communism attracted many of the well-born, and many more of the well-educated, in a revolt against a ruling class which seemed both powerful and callous. Where in Western societies a Marxist party wins the allegiance of the intelligentsia, we may suppose that the privileged are ambivalent about their own privileges. In Britain, this source of middle-class support for the Communists was all the more effective because of the class-specific character of middle-class culture. Joining the Communist Party (or accepting its leadership or collaboration on a range of issues) appealed to many as a mode of enlarging their experience. Furthermore, British Communists often fused a peculiar form of nationalism with revolutionary doctrine: The coming elimination of class antagonisms was to be an act of national self-discovery and re-integration. This theme, in a number of variants, continually recurs in the ideology of the British Left. Socialist internationalism and a devotion to little England (or Welsh or Scots' or Irish nationalism) have coexisted for decades. Working-class recruits often joined the Communist Party because it seemed unrestrainedly militant in its strategic doctrine; whatever tactical concessions it made to the Labour Party, it insisted on the political value of industrial action. Hopes in and illusions about the Soviet Union, for a long time, were approximately equivalent in both sectors of the Party.

The purges of the 30's and the consolidation of Stalinism had the usual effects on some of the intellectuals. This was countered, in the United Kingdom, by the especially intense concern of the intellectuals with the fate of the Spanish Republic (as well as the rise of Fascism in general.) Were the Spanish Communists not defending the Republic and, in these circumstances, was not criticism of the Communist movement a gratuitous contribution to the Right? (It was only much later that Orwell's critique of Stalinism struck home.)

It must also be remembered that, in contradistinction to Franklin Roosevelt's government, the Conservative governments of the 30's were viewed as, until 1939, bent on encouraging European Fascism. Even among those who entertained doubts, therefore, as to whether the 1936 Soviet Constitution had been applied to the letter in the Soviet Union, there were effective inhibitions on a break with the Communist Party. The German-Soviet Non-Aggression Pact of 1939, for many, overcame those inhibitions. But these were difficulties more or less peculiar to the intellectuals, and to other middle class recruits either to the Party itself or to its orbit; the working class militants, by and large, were either less squeamish about Stalinism or treated accounts of it as inventions. (The response of the working class rank and file in France and Italy to the crisis of 1956 was not dissimilar.)

The end of the 30's, then, saw a serious decline in the numbers and influence of the British Communist Party. The Soviet Union's entry into the war, however, reversed this trend. The hard-core militants remained in the Party; the more sensitive of them hoped that the postwar period would bring a relaxation of Stalinist repression. They prepared themselves, however, for their eventual acceptance of Zhdanovism by viewing the German attack on the Soviet Union as a justification of the Stalinist terror that had preceded it. Meanwhile, newer and younger recruits joined the party from the middle classes. Their social and occupational origins were discernibly different from those of their predecessors in the 30's: They were from the intermediate and lower ranges of the middle classes, and they tended to be technicians, scientists, and administrators rather than intellectuals with humanistic interests. They were attracted by an image of Communism as a system which, transferred to Britain, would pulverize its traditional inertia and inefficiencies and give it a newer and higher national unity. In this respect, they were ideologically closer to the working class militants in the Party than their predecessors. This explains something of the Party's cohesion in the postwar years.

The Labour victory of 1945 compelled the British Communists to adopt a policy of critical support of the Labour Government. The number of Communist M.P.'s elected in 1945 was but two; a small group of Labour M.P.'s suspected of being Communists were subsequently dropped by the Labour Party as candidates. The pronounced moderation of the Labour Government's domestic policy gradually altered the policy of critical support to one in which criticism became predominant; the foreign policy decisions which aligned the Labour Government with the United States at the beginnings of the Cold War completed this process.

From the late 40's onwards, the Communist Party was reduced, with respect to the Labour Party, to fishing in its often troubled waters. The domestic effects of the Cold War in Britain were not as striking as they were in the United States. Nothing like McCarthyism developed, although it need not be imagined that known Communists were entirely without occupational difficulties. The chief effect of the Cold War (compounded with the Labour Government's loss of momentum) was to discourage critical political thought. The British Communist Party, therefore, was forced back into a defensive ideological position; new recruits to it were few, although it did attract some who were psychologically repelled by the generally restrictive social climate.

The Twentieth Congress of the CPSU, and the crisis of the Communist movement in 1956 had profound effects on the British Communists. Following Khrushchev's speech, a number of Communist intellectuals began to publish, in opposition to the Central Committee, a journal, *The Reasoner*. Its editors were Edward Thompson and John Saville. Thompson and Saville were never Stalinists; they had, rather, suffered in silence throughout the Stalinist period. Their attack on the leadership of the British Communist Party was interesting particularly for the discrepancy between its objectives and its actual results. Its objectives were nothing less than the conversion of the Party into an independent and critical group of British socialists, exerting pressure from the Left on the Labour Party. *The Reasoner* attracted the support of a number of Communist intellectuals, but in the end, the Party leadership beat off the challenge with little difficulty. The dissidents were either expelled or forced to resign.

The crisis in Poland, in October 1956, and the Hungarian Revolution strengthened the resolution of the intellectuals; the singular conclusion to the period of the

"Hundred Flowers" in China in 1957 finished the process. Dozens of intellectuals left the Party, including some very respectable scholars in the universities. This time, the scientists and technicians were not unaffected. Another loss to the Party, however, was that of a group of working-class activists who went over to the hitherto miniscule British Trotskyite group. It is difficult to say why these men, not numbering more than a few hundred but highly experienced and influential in factory agitation, chose the crisis of 1956 as an occasion for leaving the Party. It can be supposed that they were long restive under Party discipline, and that they had begun to suspect that the Soviet Union was not an unequivocally revolutionary force. The Hungarian repression, and the ideological justification for a break with the Communists supplied by the Party's own intellectuals, allowed them to shift to a pure agitational culture. This, and other losses in the working class and the trade union movement, was apparently evaluated by the Party leadership as more severe than the defection of the intellectuals.

The Trotskyite movement, which received new impetus from the difficulties of the Communists, had always exhibited those centrifugal tendencies which characterize the life of Leftist sects. The new infusion of personnel in 1956 and 1957 allowed some surprised Trotskyite leaders to imagine that, for them, a new period of ideological prosperity was at hand. The adherence to Trotskyism of two or three intellectuals may have contributed to their euphoria. In fact, the intrinsic sectarianism of the movement by 1959 had produced new splits. The ultimate beneficiary of the crisis in the Communist Party was the Labour Party.

Enough has been said in the preceding sections of this essay to suggest that the Labour Party is not now, and in the discernible future will not be, a revolutionary force in British society.[5] Quite apart from the rather obvious difficulty that Britain is not a nation with a revolutionary potential, the Labour Party is and has been a coalition of exceedingly different elements. The (occasional) near-revolutionary impulses manifested by the minority have always been cancelled out by the (persistent) reformism of the majority. On the one occasion when a pre-revolutionary mood swept over the Party and millions of its voters (during the 1926 General Strike),[6] the leadership was ideologically unprepared to give expression to it; in any case, the weight of that particular struggle was born by the trade-union movement. Despite some legacies of syndicalism, the unions were unable, and unwilling, to develop the struggle in a revolutionary direction.

The chief elements in the Labour coalition are the trade unions and a group of middle-class intellectuals. Whereas middle-class voters constitute, in ordinary circumstances, a relatively low proportion of the Labour vote (1945 was something of an exception), the influence of middle-class leaders in the Party, and particularly in the Parliamentary Party, is very great. Attlee and Gaitskell are of upper middle-class origins; despite their alliance with working-class politicians they have retained the personal *habitus* and style of thought of the educated middle class. Their un-

---

[5] See G. D. H. Cole, *British Working-Class Politics, 1832–1914* (London: G. Routledge and Sons, Ltd., 1941), and *A History of the Labour Party from 1914* (London: 1948).

[6] J. Symons, *The General Strike* (London: Cresset Press, 1957).

deviating refusal of an ideological critique of the social structure (disguised as ideological pragmatism), their extreme respect for the rules of the Parliamentary and political game (which the Conservatives, sure of their status as the party of gentlemen, have more consistently violated), and above all, their implicit assumption that a new British social policy could be derived from a middle-class ethic, are evidence of the tenacity of their heritage. This last point requires emphasis: At times it has seemed that the Labour Party's vision of the egalitarian "New Jerusalem" in Britain was one in which all were to be elevated to middle-class standards. In another version of what a socialist Britain might look like, to be sure, a more organic theory predominates: The place provided for the working class is to be made worthier of human beings, access to the elite and intermediate levels of the class structure is to be thrown open, but the class structure, however modified, is to continue.

It well may be asked why the working-class segment of the Labour Party accepts middle-class leadership. The answer is that its attitude is not entirely unambiguous.[7] The trade-union leaders are often, of course, recruited from the sections of the working class most receptive to the cultural pressures of the larger society. The incorporation in the British class struggle of the British class system strikes them as not alone part of the nature of things social but as a positive asset. In fact, the middle class does have the education, the techniques of command and compromise, and the experience lacking to all but the most exceptional of working class leaders. Underlying the trade unionists' acceptance of middle-class political leadership, additionally, is their definition of the market struggle as a limited one. Having renounced syndicalism, they are only logical to seek a political alliance with the more sympathetic sections of the middle classes. There is, however, a powerful, if presently suppressed, countercurrent. The British working class has long been encapsulated in its own peculiar culture, one which emphasized familiar, neighborhood, and class loyalties and which was drastically separated from the higher national culture by idiom, perspective, and a certain bluntness of style. Working-class and middle-class Labour politicians are no less marked by these differences than the rest of their countrymen. The important role in the Parliamentary Party of articulate and sophisticated journalists, lawyers, and university teachers has at times irritated working-class sensitivities.[8]

It is striking, however, that the present intense ideological conflict within the Labour Party can on no account be derived from these differences. The positions taken by the middle-class leadership under Gaitskell are supported by a majority of the trade unionists in the Party. (The most able and important trade-union leaders, incidentally, now exercise their influence outside the Parliamentary Labour Party; the trade-union M.P.'s are not a conspicuously distinguished group.) The leader of the Party's Left, Michael Foot, is from a noted middle-class family. It is true that

---

[7] M. Harrison, *Trade Unions and the Labour Party Since 1945* (London: Allen and Unwin, 1960) and F. Zweig, *The Worker in the Affluent Society* (London: 1961).

[8] On working-class culture, see R. Hoggart, *The Uses of Literacy* (London: Chatto and Windus, 1957); A. Bullock's biography of the late Ernest Bevin [*Life and Times of Ernest Bevin*], Vol. 1 (London: Heinemann, 1960) tells us a good deal about these conflicts within the Labour Party.

Frank Cousins, the General Secretary of the Transport and Generals Workers' Union, supports the Party's Left; but his predecessors in that post supported the Right.

Gaitskell's general line is reasonably coherent, and its major elements may be stated as follows: [9] Capitalism has had its teeth pulled; Democratic Socialists have to deal with opponents vastly different than those of a generation, or even two decades, ago. The outlines of the Welfare State have been accepted by most parties to political debate; the question really is the extent to which the welfare function is to be extended. Wholesale nationalization is very likely to prove inefficient (and in any case is an electoral liability). The workers themselves seem, through their trade unions, to abjure anything like workers' control of industry. Government direction of a mixed economy, and generous expenditure on the Welfare Services (and on national necessities like education, as well as on national amenities like the arts) are to be the mechanisms of socialist politics. The gradual elimination of painful discrepancies in material rewards between the social classes and, above all, the provision of adequate educational opportunity to open careers to talent from all of them will, in time, erode that exaggerated snobbism which still disfigures Britain.

This interpretation of contemporary British society dictates a particular approach to electoral politics. Gaitskell's opponents in the Labour Party, quite unfairly, hold that the reverse order applies, and that the Party leadership's ideological justification of its tactics and strategy is simply intellectual opportunism. If it were simply that, it might well prove less resistant to their attacks on it. In fact, these views constitute a perfectly plausible response to a situation of objectively limited possibilities; it is their adaptation to the situation which makes them so effective. The working class, or important sections of it, is undergoing a process of partial assimilation to a middle-class style of life; an aggressive class emphasis in Labour politics in these circumstances would be inappropriate. Moreover, it would alienate precisely those middle-class voters, in a period of expansion in the tertiary sector of the economy, without whose votes no Labour government is possible.

Precisely the most self-conscious and articulate elements in the working class are

[9] The recent debate on the future of the Labour Party is compounded of a number of elements: differing interpretations of recent changes in British social structure and their political consequences, conflicting views of the sources of popular electoral decision, and divergent conceptions of socialism. The earlier anthology edited by R. H. S. Crossman, *New Fabian Essays* (London: Turnstile Press, 1952), reflects the views of many in the Labour Party at the beginning of a prolonged and unanticipated period of political drought for British Socialism. Many of the tendencies expressed in the subsequent debate can be found, however, *in nuce* in this text. C. A. R. Crosland's *The Future of Socialism* (London: J. Cape, 1956) opened the current phase of the discussion. Two recent contributions represent antithetical views: Crosland's *Can Labour Win?* and Crossman's *Labour in the Affluent Society,* both Fabian tracts published in London in 1960. The reflections on the election written by M. Abrams, R. Rose, and R. Hinden, *Must Labour Lose?* (Harmondsworth: Penguin Books, 1960) appear to be consonant with what a large majority of the Parliamentary Labour Party thinks. See the critique by R. Samuel, "Dr. Abrams and the End of Politics," *New Left Review,* No. 5 (1960). Abrams originally published his views on the 1959 election in *Socialist Commentary,* and from August 1960 a number of issues carried an interesting discussion of the problems he raised. It is interesting that in this debate, John Strachey's very serious text, *Contemporary Capitalism* (London: V. Gollancz, 1956), has gone largely unremarked.

affected by the new prosperity; previously they have been traditional Labour voters. Approximately one-third of the working class usually votes Conservative; pending the conclusion of a number of current inquiries into "The Tory Worker," we can guess that they are among the most economically, intellectually, and psychologically restricted manual workers. Their Toryism well may be a classical case of what Engels termed "false consciousness"—insofar as it is conscious at all. The threat to Labour's traditional working-class vote, clearly, is of a different kind. What, during the 1959 election campaign, Gaitskell termed "a modest programme of social reform" is clearly designed to meet the ideological requirements of those seeking group and individual advancment within the present social structure. That is what the Labour Party's battered Left cannot forgive Gaitskell.

The Left of the Labour Party draws upon a number of traditions: Christian Socialism and pacificism, the militancy of the old Independent Labour Party, the blunt and atheoretic British Marxism of the old Social Democratic Federation. Mostly, however, it seems to draw upon nostalgia—for a period in which all lines were sharply drawn, the enemy was clearly identifiable, and the need for immediate and drastic action was clear.[10] It rejects the recent analysis of British society propagated by the Labour leadership (which found its most cogent expression in Anthony Crosland's *The Future of Socialism*). Behind the newer public-relations techniques of a reformed British capitalism it detects an ancient and unrepentant beast. The burden of its charge against the leadership is that it allows the Conservatives to define the limits of Labour politics; the Labour Left, for instance, does not share Gaitskell's doubts about the constitutional propriety and political efficacy of industrial action for political purposes. The Left enjoys considerable, practically massive, support in the local party organizations. There, the intellectuals (often school teachers and technicians) and trade-union militants to whom an unambiguous vision of political conflict appeals, are relatively independent of those groupings which dominate the Parliamentary Labour Party—in which the Left is a small minority. Once led by the gifted Aneuran Bevan, then deserted by him, this minority is in continual conflict with the Party leadership.

The Party's Left did, recently, twice score on the leadership. After the Party's defeat in 1959, Gaitskell proposed to amend that clause in the Party's Constitution which called for the "common ownership of the means of production, distribution and exchange." The storm that followed in the Party, aligning with the Left many who customarily supported Gaitskell (a certain element of working-class resentment against the middle-class intellectuals in Gaitskell's *entourage* played some part in this), may best be characterized by recalling Kautsky's injunction to Bernstein during an ideological crisis in the German Social Democratic Party: "One doesn't say things like that; one simply does them!"

The Party's present continuity with its socialist traditions having been reaffirmed, Gaitskell was again free in fact to revise them. In 1960, an even more striking success occurred when the Party's annual conference approved a policy of unilateral nuclear disarmament for Britain. The fiction that the Party's parliamentary leadership, or

[10] See the weekly, *Tribune*.

even its executive committee, was subordinate to the conference had publicly to be discarded, but a year later the decision was reversed. The Left, which had temporarily won trade-union support on this issue, lost it when trade-union officialdom reimposed its authority.

In general, however, the Labour Left can claim a considerable, if negative, sort of success. Some members of the Party who rationally agree with the leadership appear, at times, to accept the Left's claims to be sole custodians of the Party's Socialist Conscience. The Left has an embarrassing competence in discovering just those issues on which the leadership's tendency to moderation pushes it either into tacit acceptance of the government's policies or into a somewhat half-hearted opposition. The Left is not so incurably sectarian as to suppose that a Labour government under the present leadership would not differ from a Conservative one. What it does is to create an intra-party atmosphere in which the leadership has been forced onto the ideological defensive; that some element of drive and inner resolution is missing in the party is a proposition with which it is difficult to disagree. (The more intelligent opponents of the Left do not take seriously their own stated view that the Left is responsible for most of the Party's present electoral difficulties.)

The Left's success is, however, strictly negative; neither its parliamentarians, nor those who support it elsewhere in the Party, have been able to develop a political program to oppose Gaitskell's. The Left's demand that the total working-class vote be mobilized by a militant Socialist politics is unrealistic; quite apart from the Tory worker, the remainder of the working class is not at the moment responsive to the political appeals of the 1930's. The Left despite the fact that many of its personnel come from the new middle classes is even more incapable of making contact with this stratum at this stage of its development. It takes such consolation as it can from the fact that Gaitskell himself does not appear to be very effective in this respect either. Given this condition of mutual *stasis,* indeed of frustration, it is not surprising that in a sphere where the differences between party factions do seem more meaningful—foreign affairs—they are intense and bitter.

The Attlee government, from the very beginnings of the Cold War, accepted America's initiatives in policy toward the Soviet Union. The stationing of American nuclear strike forces in the United Kingdom dates from 1950, and the Labour Party leadership has more or less consistently followed the logic of both its decisions to make available the bases and to develop an independent British atomic and thermonuclear arsenal. German rearmament, NATO, the entire chain of alliances and pacts thrown up about the borders of the Soviet Union, have all had official Labour support. The Labour Party opposed the Suez intervention (not least, on grounds that it had no American sanction), but in 1958 it gave only cautious expression to its doubts about the American-British intervention in the Lebanon and Jordan. It is true that the Labour Party has taken a rather different line on the recognition of the Chinese People's Republic, and that it has urged "flexibility" in the approach to the Soviet Union, particularly in the period when Dulles appeared not to have read Stalin's death notice; but in these respects Labour policy has not differed appreciably from that of the Conservatives.

Indeed, the bipartisanship of official Labour foreign policy has at times seemed to constitute a major source of irritation to the Labour Left; the roots of its opposition, however, lie rather deeper. Firstly, the Labour Left finds it exceedingly difficult to participate in the ideological defense of the West. This strikes many in the Labour Party as the extension into foreign policy of that alleged acceptance of the capitalist social system they find so repugnant in the Party's domestic program. The obvious deficiencies in the West's ideological position (the alliance with a number of regimes of dubious democratic credentials, the ambiguous nature of Western Germany's recent conversion to democratic values, and the more unreasoning sorts of anti-Communism manifest in the United States) have been less causes of this attitude than not entirely unwelcome justifications of it. Secondly, the Labour Left is ideologically incapable of a pure form of anti-Soviet politics; many of its supporters conceive of the Soviet Union as an errant socialist state, but a socialist state nonetheless; this attitude, difficult to justify during the rigors of Stalin's last years, has been greatly reinforced by recent developments inside the Soviet Union and the Communist bloc generally. Other attitudes, exhibited by perhaps more members of the Left, constitute a third and more complex source of opposition on foreign policy; these may be imperfectly summarized as the conception of an independent British mission in the world.[11]

For the Labour Left, it is clear, this mission would take the form of some kind of neutralism; Britain would either leave NATO or assume a highly independent role within it. (The closure of, or the imposition of very severe controls upon, American bases is a *sine qua non* of this policy.) Equally important, Britain would strengthen its ties with the Commonwealth nations, not least, those in Africa and Asia. Free to resume social democratic experimentation at home—it is one of the least implausible theses of the Labour Left that the material and psychological requirements of Britain's adherence to NATO have severely restricted opportunities for a Socialist politic in Britain—and linked to the Commonwealth nations by ties both economic and ideological, Britain would once again emerge as an independent force in the world. What is at issue, now, is not the degree of realism or irrealism this conception entails, but the fact that it is a socialist version of what may be termed imperial nostalgia. Britain's neutralist-Socialist mission in the world, upon closer examination, appears to have interesting similarities with the Labour doctrine to which it is opposed: the Party leadership's conception of "responsible" foreign policy. Both, briefly, are derived from the liberal conscience's strenuous notion of the duty of the educated and the privileged in the world, Britain being cast for international purposes not incorrectly as an educated and privileged nation. (We shall see, subsequently, that the ideological similarities between those who would, at any price, renounce British nuclear weapons and some of those who would risk the suicidal implications of retaining them, in so exposed a country, are equally striking.)

On one set of issues, both factions of the Labour Party seem to agree—those connected with the process of decolonization. Important differences on specific questions of tactics and timing (the Party's leadership as we might expect, tends to take a

[11] See the pamphlet by J. Rex, *Britain Without the Bomb, New Left Review* (1960).

more administrative attitude to some of these questions, that is, it is not instinctively suspicious of the police) are discernible. By and large, however, the entire Labour Party favors an accelerated process of decolonization and tends to sympathize with the liberation movements in colonial territories. This has not always been an unequivocal way to win votes: Some years ago Gaitskell found it necessary to repudiate Barbara Castle, a prominent Left M.P., who had publicly intimated that the behavior of British troops in Cyprus was not beyond reproach. On the critical issue of Suez, however, the Party was largely united.

What is striking about the attitude of the Labour Party is not so much its morality as its peculiar moral temper: Much emphasis is placed upon Britain's responsibility for colonial peoples, even though this is a responsibility the colonial peoples would often be pleased to have the British shed. Often enough, and particularly on the Party's Left, a curious idealization of colonial liberation leaders and movements may be noted; it seems extraordinarily difficult, for instance, for any number of Labourites to deal with the fact that in Ghana the opposition finds itself not merely out-numbered in Parliament but in jail. Perhaps this is connected with the fact that the recognition of the omnipresence of one-party regimes in ex-colonial countries might lead to a critical examination of the proposition that Britain has unique ideological goods for export.

The possibility of a new British contribution to socialism has also been a preoccupation of that group known as the British New Left.[12] The European New Left, as a whole, emerged in the late 50's in a fusion of two streams of discontent. Communists, or Communist sympathizers, began to express their criticisms of Stalinism and bureaucracy in Communist society and in the Western Communist parties. This led, quickly enough, to a search for a principled basis of criticism and, often, to a break with the Communist movement.

Some Social Democrats, meanwhile, were mounting an attack on the particular forms of reformism found in the Western European parties; this frequently led them to a reconsideration of Marxism. These two tendencies met, ideologically, in a revival of the problem of *alienation* discussed in Marx's early manuscripts. The revisionist Communists and revolutionary Social Democrats engaged on this intellectual terrain were somewhat surprised to find a good deal of it already occupied by Catholic and Protestant social thinkers seeking to humanize (and socialize) their ethics; the European New Left has in fact been strengthened by the participation of socialists with religious commitments.

This deviation from the socialist traditions, rigidified in the second half of the nineteenth century, is significant; the new Left is a movement which has attracted a new generation, indifferent where not hostile to ossified concepts of socialism. The particular concatenation of events which has produced the New Left has varied from country to country. Everywhere, the crisis of Communism was important. In Italy, it was the major event; there, the movement includes many not only in Nenni's

---

[12] See the journals *Universities and Left Review* and *The New Reasoner* which merged at the end of 1959 in *New Left Review*. The essay by G. Lichtheim on the British new Left in *Soviet Survey*, No. 32 (1960), is a reasonable assessment.

Socialist Party and some Socialist Democrats, but some who have remained in the PCI. In France, the coincidence of the Hungarian Revolution and the Suez intervention affected both the PCF and the SFIO and the new PSU was the eventual result—a party which has also gained a notable convert to socialism in Pierre Mendès-France. In Great Britain, the crisis of the Communist Party was an important but not the dominant event. Rather, the Suez intervention awakened the political interests of a younger generation—anti-colonialism fusing almost immediately with the campaign against nuclear weapons. The younger generation, many of its members "scholarship boys," was also critical of the cultural traditions it was supposed to assimilate in the universities; a concern with cultural questions in a special characteristic of the British New Left.

I have spoken of the New Left as a movement; it would be more accurate to characterize it as a mood—particularly in Britain, where it has not assumed any definite organizational form. Those in the New Left consider it their duty to work inside the Labour Party, where they have effected a tactical alliance with the Bevanite rump led by Michael Foot; the boundaries between the old and new left are sometimes obscure. Indeed, in Britain, all the boundaries are fluid. The work of Richard Titmuss and his associates, a sustained and careful critique of the Welfare State, is generally associated with the New Left; but the Titmuss group were the authors of the Labour Party's new pension plans. The fluidity of the boundaries may well be another instance of the curious absorptive capacities by which British society and culture seem able to encapsulate and assimilate, while degutting, new ideas. The New Left did become fashionable for a while, and has subsequently lost much of its drive and originality; the phenomena are connected.

The publication of two journals, subsequently merged (1959) in the *New Left Review,* constituted the beginning of the New Left in Britain. *The Reasoner,* which became *The New Reasoner* when it changed from mimeographed to printed form and its editors were expelled from the Communist Party, has been mentioned. Its editors, readers, and contributors were generally in their late 30's, at least; it was produced in the industrial north of England, and its editors did have contact with the Labour movement, which is so important in that part of the country; it was, finally, marked by an obsessive insistence on finding new content for Marxist forms of thought. The *Universities and Left Review,* begun by a group of recent Oxford graduates, was much livelier; its readers were younger; it attacked a number of themes not hitherto central to discussion within the Labour Party; and, finally, it was an instant success.

The success of *Universities and Left Review* (edited and distributed in a manner which may charitably be termed improvised, some 8000 of each issue were sold, and its contents were often publicly discussed elsewhere) is not entirely easy to explain. The idiom of the younger generation, of course, was fresh; the concentration on problems of mass and high culture, of the quality of daily life, and the search for a new socialist ethic seemed both new and relevant. What was remarkable about much of this was that it represented an effort, mainly unintended, to admix British socialist thought with American and Continental elements. The emphasis on mass culture owed much to *Dissent,* even if the British problem was set in the context of the prosperity of the British working class. The discussion of a new socialist morality was imported from Paris. The image of British society developed in *ULR* bore a striking resemblance to Wright Mills' portrait of America. This intellectual internationalism, rather exceptional in recent British socialism, may be explained by the cosmopolitan identities of the four original editors of *ULR*—a West Indian, a Canadian Catholic, and two offspring of the Eastern European Jewish immigration of the turn of the century. It is also explained, in part, as a reaction to the provincialism of much instruction in the social sciences in British universities. The simultaneous renewal of certain characteristically British socialist concerns ('Titmuss' inquiries into the material conditions of the nation and the discussion of the working class and national culture by Richard Hoggart and Raymond Williams) [13] seemed to promise a genuine renewal of British socialist thought. The promise has not been fulfilled; it remains to ask why.

The merger of *ULR* with the *New Reasoner* in *New Left Review* in 1959 marked an implicit renunciation of the program of *ULR.* The new journal turned, increasingly, to the daily stuff of politics. The editors and contributors of *The New Reasoner,* liberated from the Communist Party, gradually lost their ideological identity in the old Labour Left. It is rather more surprising that much the same thing happened to the younger *ULR* group. On the colonial problem, foreign policy (the New Left is, of course, neutralist and in favor of British nuclear disarmament), and on domestic social policy the New Left appears to have little to say that is not being said by the old. Its very real intellectual break-through in the sphere of culture (and the related area of education) has not been followed by the development of a program for a new socialist politics.

The *ULR* began, in effect, by asking if a new socialist politics was possible; its lack of success suggests that the question was painfully relevant. The *ULR* and the *New Left Review* have both published interesting inquiries, to be sure, into the structure of the new Britain capitalism; these have not given answers to the problem of inducing a socially critical, much less revolutionary, consciousness in an electorate only too eager to cooperate with its masters. The New Left insists on the manipulability of public opinion, but occasionally drops this theme in favor of an impassioned defense of popular capacities for spiritual growth, despite indoctrination. The contradiction has not been resolved in any practical way. Neither has the promising fusion of continental socialist theory and American social criticism which British Labourism developed. In these circumstances, the energies of the journal's young readers (and of nearly every other homeless member of the British Left) have gone into a movement ostensibly apolitical; the Campaign for Nuclear Disarmament.

The Campaign for Nuclear Disarmament was founded in 1957 by a group of senior London intellectuals, the most prominent of them being Bertrand Russell. The leaders' original conception of the campaign was significantly different from its eventual course. Press statements signed by lists of notables; occasional public meet-

[13] Titmuss, *op. cit.;* Hoggart, *op. cit.;* R. Williams, *Culture and Society* (London: 1957) and *The Long Revolution* (London: 1960).

ings to be addressed by the same notables; the gradual enlightenment of the public; the gradual conversion of the politicians. In short, what we may, with some justice, term the Left-Wing of the elite supposed that the usual methods of elite persuasion were appropriate. They reckoned without the fact that their attack on the manufacture and stockpiling of British nuclear weapons was interpreted by the government and the custodians of "responsible" opinion, including the Labour Party leadership, as beyond the limits of acceptable political debate. The notables of the Campaign were surprised, then, to find that their pronouncements were very largely ignored by the press and the other media of information; insofar as the Campaign was mentioned—not often—it was derided. The politicians and the editors who refused to play the game in the conventional British way did, in fact, sense more about the Campaign than its founders.

The latter insisted on its moral and non-political character. The manufacture and stockpiling of nuclear weapons with a view toward their eventual use was simply evil; the theory of the deterrent, moreover, entailed suicide for Great Britain. To these propositions were joined no political proposals. Some in the campaign initially thought their position compatible with the retention of American nuclear strike bases in Britain; others denied that it entailed a break with NATO; still others talked of a "British example to the world," to be echoed much later in Gaitskell's "non-nuclear club." No particular effort was made to enlist the support of the Labour Left; the trade unions (whose members, after all, produced British nuclear weapons and built nuclear bases) were ignored; a generalized critique of British foreign policy was simply lacking. The appeal to the public was based on conscience and self-interest: The apolitical formulation was supposed to mobilize the reserves of humanitarianism and common sense to be found in all parties. Contrary to the intentions of most of its initiators, however, the Campaign did assume an increasingly political character. It threatened and still threatens the leadership of the Labour Party, and it has introduced into contemporary British politics an ethic and tactics which almost merit the designation, revolutionary.

The initiators of the Campaign made only cursory provision for local organization. They were rather surprised when local groups not only developed at a rapid rate, but demanded a voice in the formulation and execution of Campaign policy. The Campaign, at its local levels, attracted three sorts of support:

1. A good many young people (many of them in their teens, in universities or schools), chiefly from all strata of the middle classes, seemed to find in the Campaign an occasion for expressing the usual discontents with their elders. The peculiar atmosphere of complacency with which the political elite dealt with the problem of nuclear weapons added to their irritation: Many of the young were and are far from complacent about the future of their nation, and complacency on this score struck them as symptomatic of the general incapacities of their parents, teachers, and rulers.[14] It must be emphasized that this youthful recruitment for the Campaign was by no means limited to the politically conscious, although participation in

[14] See Potter, *op. cit.*, for a reasonably typical statement of the views of the younger intellectuals.

the Campaign for many served as a form of political education. Most of the young were apolitical, concerned expressly only with nuclear weapons; their general discontents were by and large unarticulated. Of the politically engaged, Liberals and even a scattering of Conservatives were outnumbered by those with Labour sympathies, but they were not overwhelmingly outnumbered.

2. The Campaign, along with the short-lived Suez protest that preceded it and the continuing movement against colonialism (a formal Anti-Apartheid Campaign has also been organized), mobilized the remnants of the bearers of the liberal conscience among those who cannot be described as young. Many of these Campaigners, as Christians, brought to the Campaign a moral fervor matched only by their consistent refusal to think in political terms. It is this group which means what it says when it proposes a British moral example to the world. It is as convinced of the political efficacy of direct moral utterance as it is of Britain's unique capacity to deliver such utterance.

3. Somewhat later, the Labour Left began to appreciate the potentialities of the campaign. Although many on the Left of the Party endorsed the Campaign from its inception, they tended to think of it as an utopian or unrealistic instrument of politics. The Campaign's activists, most of them exceedingly uninterested in conventional Labour politics, convinced them that they were wrong.

The activists had, first, to convince the leaders of the Campaign itself. Against the latter's premonitions of disaster they pushed through, in 1958, a project for a four day demonstrative march from London to Aldermaston, the British nuclear weapons factory in Berkshire. The march, begun in Trafalgar Square, was mainly composed of the young. Their blue jeans, beards, jazz band and songs attracted derisive comment from the press,—but comment had been attracted. Next year's march, from Aldermaston to London, increased geometrically in size; the one in 1960 was larger, and by 1961 the march had to be split into two divisions, converging upon Trafalgar Square from Aldermaston and from an American NATO airbase in Essex. (This last point is of some interest because, by 1961, the Campaign had begun to formulate a political program.) The marches themselves attracted so much publicity that the CND was able, increasingly, to gain a kind of hearing in the mass media; at any rate, the ability of CND to put nearly 100,000 demonstrators into Trafalgar Square is a measure of the size and determination of the movement.

The activists did not stop with the marches. Sit-downs at rocket bases and in front of government buildings precipitated a split over tactics in CND. Most recently, Bertrand Russell formed his Committee of One Hundred to pursue a policy of civil disobedience; H.M. Government obliged with a massive opportunity for further propaganda by jailing Russell for a week. The "civil disobedience" in question has consisted mainly of deliberate violations of minor police regulations during sit-downs in Trafalgar Square or in front of the Ministry of Defense and the American and Soviet Embassies. There have been efforts, however, to board the American submarine tender and the rocket-equipped submarines based not far from Glasgow. The general public regards these demonstrations with astonishment rather than with hostility or sympathy. There is little doubt, however, that they have enlarged the range of debate about British foreign policy; despite the obvious absence of public sympathy for the demonstrations, these have contributed to a national mood in which the government is unable to take an authentically "strong" line in the current East-West crisis.

During these developments, the Labour Left has seized upon the CND and used it as a very effective weapon of intra-party warfare. The Left has claimed that the youthful and moral energies mobilized by CND can be captured by the Labour Party only if it renounces its current bipartisan foreign policy. The leadership has executed a number of maneuvers under this pressure, one of the last of them being the proposal for a "non-nuclear club." In 1960, however, the Left was able to defeat the leadership and the Party Conference passed a resolution favoring unilateral British nuclear disarmament; the leadership's triumph on this issue in 1961 was accompanied by its defeat on another resolution, which demanded an end to the American nuclear submarine bases in the United Kingdom. Despite the fact that the Labour Party today is not committed by its Conference to unilateral nuclear disarmament for Britain, nuclear disarmament remains an effective focus of many sorts of intra-party discontent.

Moreover, the Labour Left has given CND an increasingly political complexion; it has also been used as a recruiting ground for younger socialists, through the curious argument that only by joining the Labour Party (and campaigning against its leadership) can the young turn it into the kind of movement they now find it not to be. The demonstrations and the recent tactics adopted by the Russell group, in particular, also appeal to the Labour Left. These help, after all, to relieve its electoral and parliamentary frustrations and to create that atmosphere of simple moral struggle which it finds psychologically necessary. For the moment, despite a number of prominent converts among trade union officialdom, the movement against nuclear weapons has made little headway in the working class. It remains an expression of middle-class social protests. In a society organized like Great Britain, this is important enough: Elite and sub-elite recruits disaffected on so critical an issue can be an embarrassment to those in power. As yet, however, the nuclear protest movement in all of its variant forms has not encompassed enough people to pose an immediate threat of political disruption. Its ultimate potentialities (of which its leaders are now more aware) for something approaching revolutionary action ought not to be underestimated.

Finally, it may be well to add a word on the Communist Party's relationship to the nuclear disarmament movement—on which a certain confusion persists in the United States. The Communist at first regarded CND with contempt; this changed to embarrassment as the movement registered its initial successes. Precisely in a situation in which only the broadest and most flexible of tactics could allow it to make contact with any movement outside its own, the leadership of the British C.P. could not transcend its own incurable sectarianism. The psychology of the membership of CND and the movement's loose and haphazard structure made efforts at Communist penetration seem peculiarly unpromising. More important, CND and, more recently, the Committee of One Hundred have failed to distinguish between "imperialist" and "socialist" megatons and have condemned all nuclear weapons with equal energy. The C.P. has been reduced to ambiguous endorsement of the Aldermaston marches and to deploring the nuclear disarmers' tendency to criticize the Soviet Union. There are no Communists in the CND leadership and there is not much evidence of Communist participation at the local level. That the movement, with its attack on Britain's present foreign policy, cannot be entirely unwelcome to the Soviet Government is obvious.

This essay has often, too often, referred to the liberal conscience as surviving in contemporary Britain; what can be said about the recent revival of the Liberal Party itself? The fact that in the 1959 General Election, the total Liberal vote rose appreciably, and that in some constituencies the Liberals displaced Labour in second place on the ballot, suggests that the revival merits attention. The Liberals freely criticize both major parties and have doubtless profited, not least from among the young, from a certain revulsion for the recent political climate. A new generation of Liberal politicians has assumed command of what was a party in an advanced stage of spiritual arteriosclerosis; it is difficult to see what positive policies they will develop in their effort to attain major party status.[15]

For the moment, the Liberals have struck a number of attitudes, and in this respect they are not unlike the New Left—if rather more respectable. The Liberals have criticized the psychological restrictionism and the obsessive inability to innovate which characterizes much of British society. Not being bound to the Labour movement, they have also intimated that it affects the working class and its organizations as well. (Only a very few in the Labour movement, mainly intellectuals like Richard Crossman, Anthony Crosland, and Raymond Williams, have dared to do this.)

But the Liberals seem to lack a total picture of what has brought British society to this condition; furthermore, their image of a changed Britain is expressed in vocabulary which emphasizes its psychological consequences for individuals but says little or nothing about its institutions. The Liberals have drawn heavily upon the new middle class at its lower and intermediate levels; the negative components in the ideology of its supporters have been emphasized. They do not wish to be identified with the working class; they do not accept at face value the Conservatives' claim to be the only possible governors of Britain.

It is a striking indication of the potential disdain for conventional judgments to be found in the new Liberal Party that it very nearly approved a policy of unilateral nuclear disarmament for Britain. Unless concretized in rather a more substantial fashion, however, the potential independence of judgment of the Liberals is likely to evaporate; the social groups it represents are unable to alter British politics by themselves and must seek alliance with the strata above or below. There is no indication that the Liberal Party will be able to enlist either substantial sectors of the working class or, as it might have hoped, the managerial elite. If the liberal conscience is to find a modernized political expression, those interested in the effort are

[15] The leader of the Liberal Party has recently published a tract which is a remarkable exercise in generality. See J. Grimond, *The Liberal Future* (London: 1959).

likely to throw their energies into the intra-party disputes of either the Conservative or Labour coalitions.

The tendencies described above range from Left through center, insofar as the traditional alignment applies to British politics. We may now examine, briefly, the extreme and eccentric Right. These are groups in pseudo-revolt; what interests them is not the defense of fixed interests and positions but the destruction of a world they never made.

The traditional Right-Wing of the Conservative Party does not appear to have grasped what has happened to British and world society; indeed, it may be doubted whether it quite understands its own fate within the Conservative organization. It has a leader with impeccable credentials, Lord Salisbury—but Salisbury, after helping Macmillan to power, became a nuisance and was induced to resign from the Cabinet. He resigned precisely on an issue which troubles the Tory Right, greatly: the nature of Britain's relations to its colonies and ex-colonies.

On balance, the hesitant, but final liquidation of Empire by a Conservative government is incomprehensible to the Party's old guard.[16] It seems to them part of a process which includes inflation, working class prosperity, juvenile delinquency, colored immigration to Britain, American domination, and a general dissolution of all received expectations and standards. To these manifold ills, the Conservative Right cannot even oppose a coherent theory. (The one intellectual in Britain who consistently speaks for it, T. E. Utley, sees fit to spend his time denouncing not Communism or the Welfare State, but the French Revolution. This demonstrable capacity for going to the root of things has at times embarrassed the party of his choice; it is interesting that Utley is no longer an editorialist for *The Times*.)

The Tory Right would like, of course, an attack on the Trade Unions and the working class; it has a *rentier* mentality. Its pleasure at measures of economic restriction has been somewhat diminished by the fact that these tend to affect Conservative voters as well. The government's latest economic policy does indeed call for a restriction in wage increases; it also proposes some form of economic planning. In this, and a number of other questions, the Tory Right has been able to hinder but not block its own party leadership.

The analogy with the Labour Party Left has often been drawn, but it is not entirely satisfactory. It is true that, by and large, the parliamentary representatives of each oppositional faction are older and more inflexible than their party leaders. But the Labour Left is, at least, allied with the younger intellectuals of the Labour movement while the Conservative right is particularly disturbed at the views of those younger Conservative intellectuals who are in the "Bow Group."[17] They fear that these ideologues of the new Conservatism are covert socialists. Insofar as the Tory Right rests on a *rentier* base (retired officers and respectable ladies are very prominent in traditional local Conservative politics), and the Labour Left on an eroding

---

[16] The Party's *avant-garde,* however, understands very well what is happening. See the Bow Group pamphlet, *The New Africa* (London: 1962).

[17] See the Bow Group essays edited by D. Howell and T. Raisin, *Principles in Practise* (London: 1961).

working-class base, the analogy may be maintained. Both seem to speak for declining social strata.

There is this additional and important difference between the two extremes: The Labour Left's ideology is elaborated by intellectuals not directly recruited from the traditional working class. This gives the Labour Left the objective possibility, which it may or may not take, of constructing a political theory which can account for the transformation of that class. The Tory Right has almost no intellectuals; its spokesmen are members of the groups which respond instinctively to its appeal, and their capacity for articulating an appeal to other groups is extremely limited. They can, and do, speak the language of chauvinism and of "little England," which is not peculiar to themselves. (Obsessed by the belief that Britain itself is in immediate danger of internal Bolshevization, they are also resentful of the alliance with a powerful America.) But it is not, by itself, a vocabulary with which an entire election can be fought.

What the Tory Right feels about its own government, a curious and enterprising group known as the League of Empire Loyalists says—and does. The League supposes that a monstrous conspiracy to denude Britain not only of its Empire, but of its very national substance is at work and has no hesitation in pronouncing the present Conservative Government party to the conspiracy. The forcible maintenance of the colonies and the exclusion of colored immigrants from the United Kingdom seem to be the main, if not the only, planks in its platform. The League is a very small group, but it has attracted a certain notoriety by its demonstrative attacks on the government. Its most notable feat, recently, has been the smuggling of two pseudo-bishops into an Anglican Ecumenical conference to protest an invitation to Archbishop Makarios, then leader of the Greek Cypriot campaign for independence. It has also sent commandoes into battle during the numerous recent London street demonstrations against Apartheid and colonialism.

These last battles, few but sharp, also have been joined by the British Fascists, who still exist. Mosley, their aging but brilliant leader, now takes the line that his only fault was "premature anti-Communism." [18] His journal, significantly, is entitled *The European*. Mosley propagates a doctrine of national rennaissance through a new-style authoritarian state; he does not appear to have anything to say that he did not offer (on German and Italian Fascist models) twenty-five years ago. The racialism and anti-Semitism of the movement attract, of course, a number of recruits from the *lumpenproletariat;* the Fascists do carry on agitation in districts where racial conflict is latent. They are, equally, few in number; their few parliamentary candidates recently invariably have done very badly. Although the Fascists may well express the latent racialism and xenophobia of a good many people who ordinarily vote either Conservative or Labour, it is difficult to envisage circumstances in which many will be prepared to follow Mosley onto the streets or vote for him. In this respect he must envy the nuclear disarmers.

This survey of the situation in Britain can conclude with some remarks on what may be termed cultural revolt, or cultural dissent. Much has been heard about Brit-

[18] See C. Cross, *The Fascists in Britain* (London: 1961).

ain's "angry young men," a group of dramatists and novelists who dominated discussion, at least, on the London literary scene during the second half of the recent decade.[19] In fact, the "angry young men" by no means constitute a unified movement with a single aesthetic or social doctrine. Rather, their works, like John Osborne's "Look Back in Anger," or Kingsley Amis' earlier "Lucky Jim," are conspicuous for their negative aspects. They represent a break with the genteel tradition in British literature (a break attempted many times before, it will be recalled) and an attack on the culture of the upper middle class. This last they depict as utterly lacking in vitality, at best empty and at worst a façade behind which brutality and egoism are at work. Some have insisted on a connection between the new literary mood and the alteration in the social composition of the educated brought about by the 1944 Education Act; the hypothesis is plausible. The *dramatis personae* of the new literature are provincials, *parvenus,* gypsies, workers, even Jews from the East End of London; there has emerged a British Jewish theatre which resembles nothing so much as the New York Group Theatre of the early '30's. What has occurred is a certain widening of perspective; the self-depiction of British society has become complicated and more differentiated. Some of this has a socially critical or a socialist content, if a rather vague one; the rest, like the surveys of British life projected on television, does not. It is difficult to avoid the impression, however, that much of the new realism is really a new version of British provincialism.

Certainly, the most profoundly "anti-bourgeois" novels produced recently in Britain have been written by the Oxford philosopher, Iris Murdoch,[20] whose debt to French existentialism is very great. Iris Murdoch's novels lack all direct political or even social commentary; her subjects come from the more esoteric reaches of middle-class society itself. But her message, that all is not as it seems, is profoundly corrosive of British middle-class culture.

Cultural corrosion in the arts, of course, must have some kind of correlate in society itself. Particularly among the young, something has been happening to the British style of life. London is the center of these developments, and they radiate to the provinces at an unequal rate.[21] For the young in the entire range of strata constituting the middle class, the predominant influence has been Continental: Interest in good food, a certain ease of manner lacking in the older generation, and an open interest in sexuality have crossed the Channel.

For working-class youth, the models are American: Mass entertainment has trans-

---

[19] See the symposium edited by T. Maschler, *Declaration* (London: MacGibbon and Kee, 1957). See also the recent study by J. Mander, *The Writer and Commitment* (London: Secker and Warburg, 1961). A particularly effective statement on the class character of British high culture has come recently from a young Briton who, like many, prefers the United States. See M. B. Green, *A Mirror for Anglo-Saxons* (New York: Harper, 1960).

[20] Miss Murdoch's latest novel, *The Severed Head* (London: Chatto and Windus, 1961) is rather far from Socialist realism.

[21] Colin MacInnes' fictionalized account of the London race riots of 1958, *Absolute Beginners* (London: MacGibbon and Kee, 1959), provides a colorful and accurate *montage* of the new culture of central London and of the eagerness of working-class youth to adopt it.

mitted a spectrum of conceptions and values strange to the older working-class generation, with its tight-knit familistic culture and its extremely limited sensuality. Although traditional Dixieland jazz may or may not still be found in New Orleans, it is exceedingly hard to avoid hearing it in the Midlands. These influences have been gladly, even generously, received by the young; what is striking is that they have not been assimilated with indigenous cultural elements, and that these seem to be declining by default.

Here, too, the passive and reactive character of the contemporary British response to social change is evident. Among certain intellectuals, particularly but not exclusively from working-class families, the response has been a curious sentimentalization of the old working-class culture; its traditional solidarity and human solidity have been portrayed as the only possible basis for the development of a future national culture. The pronounced negative components in working-class culture have been ignored (its philistinism and narrowness, for instance); the difficult problem of transcending a middle-class culture, to the external accoutrements of which some of the working class now aspire, has not even been faced.[22]

Although the young experiment in this fashion, and the intellectuals speculate as to how the pieces of a fragmented national culture may be fused, a considerable part of the traditionally cultivated middle class insists that nothing is really wrong. The recent and absurd trial over the publication of an unexpurgated version of Lawrence's *Lady Chatterly's Lover* is a case in point.[23] The prosecution asked the jury if this was fit literature to be placed in the hands of shop girls. The defense paraded an impressive set of witnesses, including a bishop who defended the portrayal of sexual intercourse as sacramental and a large number of university teachers of English who declared that Lawrence's openness about sexuality was puritan in inspiration. The point is not whether these experts were correct, but that they were forced to fight on alien terrain. The maintenance of the fiction that Britain is a Christian country, neatly divided into classes, all of which accept that middle-class moral authority preserved especially in the ancient universities, may be regarded as an historical curiosity. It is also an interesting example of a defense mechanism, of a refusal to come to terms with historical change, which does not allow an optimistic prognosis as to Britain's future.

IV

In conclusion, something may be said about the possible effects of the social and cultural situation sketched above on Britain's foreign policy. In one respect, this is very difficult: Britain is an opaque society, even when undergoing changes which might be expected to render its basic structures more visible. In another respect,

[22] A recent Fabian pamphlet by R. Wollheim has the merit of raising some of these problems: *Socialism and Culture* (London: 1961).
[23] C. H. Rolph (ed.), *The Trial of Lady Chatterley* (London: Penguin Books, 1961).

nothing is easier: The balance of social and cultural forces in contemporary Britain is so exquisite that, barring catastrophe, we can suppose that things will continue as they are.

Internally, a major alteration in political forces can be produced only by prolonged economic crisis accompanied by a material and persistent drop in the national standard of living. (Some of the most radical of British socialists now say that, contrary to their normal image of capitalism, the working class will not be the only class to suffer from a crisis, even if it is the first one to do so.) A depression of this sort will presumably put another Labour Government in office; it will also so reduce its scope for experimentation as to limit it to emergency measures. These measures will be drastic, but they will not necessarily constitute preliminary steps toward a social revolution in Britain. If we may extrapolate from the recent past, a Labour government elected in these circumstances under the present Labour leadership will be careful to establish working relations with important segments of the economic elite. It is probable that a government of this type can institutionalize in Britain the sort of economic planning now found in France, and this with the cooperation of some from the managerial elite. No profound innovations in Britain's international commitments need be looked for from such a regime; the economic crisis will *not* provide incentives to considerable displays of British independence of NATO.

There is, however, a further possibility about which we can only speculate; it lies in the realm of national psychology. A severe economic crisis of this sort must deal a further blow to the self-esteem of the nation, as sensed by millions of ordinary Britons. It is possible that this will accentuate the current British inversion, and that a bout of chauvinism and xenophobia will result, with direct consequences for the position of the colored minority in Britain and indirect consequences for Britain's foreign relationships in general. A certain withdrawal may take place; it is even possible (but not very probable, to be sure) that a domestic swing to the Right may be accompanied by an external *rapprochement* with the Communist bloc.

Britain's entry into the Common Market, at this writing by no means certain, may precipitate just this sort of psychological crisis. It is significant that membership in the Common Market is opposed by the Labour Left and the Tory Right with equal indignation, if with somewhat different arguments. The Labour Left entertains chilling visions of an international capitalist conspiracy to extirpate (hypothetical) advances toward British socialism; it appears to have overlooked the existence of large and militant working-class parties in Belgium, France, and Italy—not to mention German Social Democracy.[24] The Tory Right fears the political implications of a European economic union; Britain's sovereignty is allegedly threatened. Both insist that joining the Market must entail the sacrifice of Britain's unique mission in the world, a mission which it can exercise only through those Commonwealth ties which the Common Market would supposedly weaken. If Britain does enter the Market,

[24] See the pamphlet by M. Barratt-Brown and J. Hughes published by *New Left Review*, "Britain's Crisis and the Common Market" (1961). The Labour center and Right, however, also have their doubts on the Common Market—both Harold Wilson and Douglas Jay are opposed to Britain's entry.

the pound will be almost certainly devalued; Continental competition will have painful effects on the entire British economy. The new Conservatives and the Liberals think that only this shock will revivify Britain; many industrialists and economists, more crudely, anticipate lower wages. The experiment will be just that; its success is not certain, and its failure would have incalculable consequences.

An undercurrent of resentment at the United States, which has urged Britain to enter the Market, is discernible in some recent public discussion in Britain. Indeed, the conception of an independent world role for Britain (in the context of the Commonwealth) is often intended to make Britain independent of the United States. It is at this point, finally, that we may examine the peculiar strains which affect Britain's membership in the anti-Communist alliance led by the United States.

The present British political elite is aware that it rules a small country, extremely vulnerable to nuclear attack. It has long since decided (Suez was both an aberration and a convincing lesson) that it can at best fight delaying actions in colonial areas. The decision to allow South Africa to leave the Commonwealth, and Britain's recent tacit support for the Katanga regime, are not as contradictory as may appear; both are part of a policy of cutting losses. The elite, further, senses that the population of the United Kingdom is tired of war and the threat of war.

The process of depoliticization discussed in this essay also has contributed to a massive public indifference to the more militant forms of anti-Communism; to this must be added a surprising residue of wartime pro-Russian sentiment [25] and the fact that, untroubled by a domestic Communist movement of any importance, the British do not consider themselves ideologically threatened by Communism. The American attitude on this score is held by millions of Britons to be a sign of either political immaturity or political pathology. Further, the elite aspires (or pretends) to a higher form of political wisdom and supposes that it can transmit this to its American allies; this almost invariably takes the form of urging patience and restraint in situations of crisis. Briefly put, the British commitment to the anti-Communist alliance is more ambiguous than is commonly supposed. It is true that Britain has placed nuclear strike bases at America's disposal; it is increasingly clear that the British elite assumes that the Americans can always be persuaded not to force matters to the point where they must be used.

So much for the Conservatives; what about the Labour movement? The strength of Gaitskell's own commitment to the American alliance need not be doubted. At times, it has seemed somewhat stronger than that of H.M. Foreign Office. It may be suggested, however, that the vehemence of Gaitskell's view, and that of the Party faction he represents, is directly proportional to their awareness of the unreliability, on this issue, of the Labour movement as a whole. In general we may suppose that the more acute the international crisis, the more likely are the centrifugal tendencies in the Labour movement to be activated.

The specific circumstances of particular crises will, of course, vary. The frankness with which almost the entire range of British opinion has declared that Britain is

[25] The extremely enthusiastic reception given the first Soviet space pilot, Major Gagarin, when he visited Britain in 1961, was partly a response to the Berlin crisis.

unwilling to fight on Berlin suggests that no foreseeable confrontation of the two super-powers will result in the sort of partisan consensus that would allow a British government to take the country to war. It can be urged that, with American bases in Britain, British assent is not indispensable. To this it must be said that between five minutes to midnight and midnight even, or especially, Conservative Government may prove capable of very decisive action on this score.

There is one final reason for accepting this line of argument. It is that the movement for nuclear disarmament does not do so. Its leaders and followers are convinced that the Conservative Government and the present Labour leadership would in fact, to use the official phrase, "honour their commitments." In these circumstances, pressure from this movement not to participate in American military moves can only increase. Labour official policy is not immune from yet another and perhaps more enduring reversal.

The movement for nuclear disarmament, despite its inner confusion, hesitations, and consummate amateurishness (perhaps because of the latter) has succeeded where all other postwar social protest in Britain has failed. It has focussed a variety of discontents on one issue and fused an heterogeneous set of supporters into a body which refuses to accept the British political consensus. Many members of the movement believe that nuclear weapons symbolize the ultimate pathology of a society to which they are opposed; many find nothing wrong with the society that the elimination of nuclear weapons cannot cure.

The coexistence in the same movement of these divergent types of motivation may be an indication of a potential weakness; for the moment, it is effectively a strength. The capacity of the movement to put thousands onto the London streets, a capacity which in a moment of acute crisis will surely be exploited, is the most astonishing feature of the current British political scene. This quasi-revolutionary development is, in the last analysis, also a reaction to the nation's changed position in the world. A moralizing politics of conscience originally enabled the British middle class to master the imperial and industrial power at the nation's disposal. It is not the least of ironies that with that power drastically reduced, the politics of conscience now emerges as a radical critique of conventional politics. The revolt, however, remains a reactive one.

[26] See the very perceptive account of Britain's current *malaise* by George Lichtheim, "The British Way of Life and the Common Market," *Commentary* (October 1961). See also, the valuable essay by S. M. Lipset, "The British Voter," published in two parts in *The New Leader* (November 7 and 21, 1960).

3

Protest in Modern France

Stanley Hoffmann

There is a double paradox involved in writing an essay on protest in France that is to be included among pieces devoted to "the revolution in world politics." In the first place, there is no such thing as a contemporary French protest *movement*: There is a multiplicity of French protests, and they certainly did not begin to appear after the Second World War: They have deep roots and, so to speak, ancient *lettres de noblesse*. Secondly, the framework for this book seems to frown on most of the present forces for change and to describe them largely as destructive; to anyone familiar with French culture, such an attitude is singularly unappealing. As Raymond Aron remarked, Americans tend to believe that man fulfills himself when he adjusts to society and cooperates with it as a good citizen who does not challenge its basic values. Frenchmen, on the contrary, think that man is himself only when he rebels and says no to all the conventions or established beliefs that threaten his personality. Here we find the key to our subject: In France, protest is the norm. This essay is an attempt to show how intimately the types and the style of protest in France are tied to the structure of French society and France's political system. After a brief description of such types and style, I shall present an explanation in those terms and illustrate it with the particularly interesting example of the protest of the intellectuals. Finally, I will ask to what extent present social and political changes are likely to affect the pattern of French protests.

I

There are few nations in which protest movements have been, on the one hand, so frequent and so diverse in their origins, channels, and purposes, and so similar, on the other hand, in their manifestations.

WHO? There are times in French history when every social group and political organization seems to be protesting against the status quo; in other periods, protest originates from a clearly limited sector of society or of the political scene. If we take a long-term view of France since the collapse of the Second Empire in 1870 and establish a chart of the principle protest movements, their universality will be striking.

If we look at *society* as a whole, we find such movements everywhere:

1. There are protest movements originating among the groups situated at the bottom of the social hierarchy, aimed at those groups exerting the various powers of command in society. Thus, there have been movements among the workers (the revolutionary syndicalism of the early CGT), the peasants (the Dorgères movement of the 1930's and the wave of 1961), the shopkeepers and artisans (Poujadism), the small businessmen (in the 30's they joined massively Right-Wing leagues or parties; after the war and in its early years Gingembre's Confédération des Petites et Moyennes Entreprises was a vociferous protest organization).

2. There are protest movements originating also within the ruling groups.[1] Some appear within the political class, which has to be subdivided in turn into its civilian branch and its military branch; we find protest movements against the domestic status quo or France's international position in the form of political parties such as the PSF or PPF before the war, the RPF after the war, the PSU today, the Communist Party since its creation; we also find spectacular expressions of protest in the French army during the Algerian war. Within the groups which exercise economic power, protest during the period of the Popular Front amounted to a sabotage of the Front's economic and financial policies. The third element of the ruling groups "spiritual" power is composed of the Church hierarchy and of the intellectuals; the Church was a powerful force of protest in the early years of the Third Republic and again at the time of the separation of Church and State; as for the intellectuals, at least some groups among them—at times all of them—have been sharply critical of political and social affairs.

3. Protest movements are sometimes organized (by political parties, interest groups, or conspiratorial groups), sometimes not. In the latter case, they have appeared either as sudden explosions (the Commune of Paris in 1871, the sitdown strikes of 1936, the abortive *putsch* of April 1961), or as hasty rallies from various points of the horizon around a leader (Boulangisme), or as the expression of similar attitudes held by men acting within their professions (bankers and businessmen, writers and journalists).

If we take a closer look at the *political system,* we find that the universality of protest transcends all the distinctions made by specialists of political science.

1. Gabriel Almond[2] has commented on the "poor boundary maintenance between the society and the political system in France"; he has emphasized in particular the lack of a clear separation between the functions of interest groups and those of political parties. The interpenetration of those two types of bodies appears in two instances: Some men carry their protest against the status quo into a party as well as into an interest group (in the 30's Communists on the Left; many businessmen and veterans on the Right). There also have been many protest alliances between such bodies: Thus, the 30's were marked by the alliance of Left-Wing parties and

[1] The classification used here was proposed by Raymond Aron in his lectures, *Le développement de la société industrielle et la stratification sociale* (Paris: 1957), pp. 94 ff.

[2] In his introduction to: Gabriel A. Almond and James S. Coleman (eds.), *The Politics of Developing Areas* (Princeton: Princeton University Press, 1960), pp. 37–38.

the labor-union movement against the Fascist threat and by the conglomeration of Right-Wing leagues, parties, veterans' groups, and taxpayers' movements against the Popular Front. The protest movement against EDC in 1953–54 was an even stranger alliance of parties, businessmen, labor unionists, and intellectuals of Left and Right. In 1960–61, opposition to the Algerian war was led by a coalition of essentially non-Communist Left-Wing groups composed of unions, a small party (the PSU), the National Students Union, study groups (the Club Jean Moulin), and intellectuals.

2. Within the sphere of political parties, we find two structures particularly adapted to the expression of protest: the small ideological sect, usually dominated by intellectuals, which buys intellectual rigidity and purity at the cost of isolation, and the authoritarian league, which tries to enlist masses of people in quasi-military fashion behind much more ambiguous objectives.

3. Within the sphere of interest groups, we find that protest affects all the types of "interest articulation" distinguished by Almond. It affects institutional interest groups, such as the army or the Church; non-associational groups, such as occasional, usually short-lived, study groups which criticize the status quo and try to propose alternatives; associational interest groups such as the peasants' organizations, the French labor movement, with its long history of resistance to any form of cooperation with business, or the Fédération Nationale Catholique founded in 1924 in protest against new anti-clerical measures; and anomic groups breaking into the political system from society, such as Dorgères' and Poujade's movements.

4. The issues which gave rise to protest have been of all sorts; some have been social issues concerning the status of given groups within French society; some have been national issues concerning the role of France in the world and the policy to be followed by the country toward other nations. This was, after all, the original issue around which resistance movements were formed; it was the issue in the battle over the European Defense Community and, today, in the protest movement of extreme-Right elements against de Gaulle's Algerian policy. National issues were very heavily at stake in the Poujade movement and in the protest of the Right against the Popular Front. There have also been constitutional issues concerning the institutions which the nations ought to adopt (they were at the root of Boulangism and of the RPF). Finally, philosophical issues were at the heart of the intellectuals' protest against Republican ideology around 1900, of the intellectuals' protest against France's stagnation around 1930, or of the protest of the defenders of the lay-state tradition today. Intellectual protest movements, such as that of the "Left-Wing progressive intellectuals" so brilliantly denounced by Raymond Aron,[3] or that of the intellectuals opposed to the Algerian war, usually develop around a mixture of all such issues.

HOW? It might appear that I am lumping under the heading of protest all kinds of expressions of discontent which have little in common. However, it seems that whatever the social milieu in which they originated, whatever the channels they used or created, and whatever the issues involved, those movements have acted in a common style. French protest is marked by three closely related features:

[3] See his *Opium of the Intellectuals* (New York: 1958).

A Fundamentally Destructive Character. Of course, any protest is first of all a refusal to accept a certain situation: In this respect Poujadists or the intellectuals who signed the "Manifesto of the 121," recognizing the right of young men to disobey the draft in the Algerian war, are not different from American Populists or British unilateralists. However, the style of protest differs according to whether this original refusal is followed by something or it is not. What characterizes almost all French protest movements is their refusal to cooperate with "the enemy" (that is, the group responsible for the measure or state of affairs against which the protest is lodged) in order to produce the desired change.

At best (if this is the right word), the protest movement will advocate the revolutionary substitution of a new order of things for the present one: This was the case of the French labor movement at the turn of the century or of the French Communist Party in its early, militant years. In a milder and more confused way, this was also what the intellectual neutralists of the late 40's and early 50's hoped to achieve, as they very often associated a foreign policy of non-alignment with drastic social reforms in France (cp. *L'Observateur* and *Esprit* in that period). In an equally confused but much more violent way, this seems to be the case of the terrorist organizations and army conspiracies which fight de Gaulle's Algerian policy.

At worst, and more frequently, the protest movement will simply try to sabotage public policy and practice a most negative "politique du pire," with the hope that it will lead to the collapse of the group or regime against which the movement fights. France's small authoritarian leagues, Maurras' Action Française in the 30's (when any hope of ever setting up Maurras' mythical monarchy was quite dead), and Doriot's PPF behaved in this fashion. So did, twenty years later, those anti-EDC leaders who were opposed to any form of German rearmament despite France's allies' obvious determination to achieve some sort of rearmament. It was, of course, even more true of Poujade's attitude, but it was also the line of the more impassioned leaders of the RPF, and today some of the more bitter supporters of Mendès-France do not hesitate, in their protest against the Fifth Republic, to preach a similar gospel. The relations between business and labor in the late 30's were marked by the same intransigence: Labor, with its long tradition of class distrust, refused any concession which would have allowed a less disastrously rigid enforcement of the 40-hour week, and business, protesting against the legislation imposed by the State, did its best to sabotage its application. The behavior of some elements of the French army ever since de Gaulle announced his policy of self-determination for Algeria shows a similar inclination to oppose and to block official policy in the absence of any realistic alternative. French protest is the rejection of reform; its purpose is not so much to redress a wrong as to punish the wrong-doer.

"Totalism." What I refer to here, is the ideological dimension adopted by practically any protest movement. It expresses its hostility in terms which go much beyond the immediate occasion of the protest and which challenge or involve the very foundations of the social order, the political order, or both. In the 30's, conservative criticism of the Third Republic for its inefficiency and its corruption tended to develop

into a general questioning of democracy and of industrial society; the groups which demonstrated against the regime on February 6, 1934, were influenced by Maurras' counterrevolutionary ideology, just as Marxism, in a more or less diluted form, colors many of the attacks on the Algerian war and the Fifth Republic today: They broaden into a general assault on French and foreign capitalism. Nor did the proponents of appeasement in the 30's use mere *ad hoc* arguments: They either presented a spirited and radical defense of pacifism; or developed an over-all attack on France's foreign policy and on her allies. The nationalists of the 50's did not protest only against France's colonial retreats and her minor role in NATO, they often spoke as if there existed a universal conspiracy to humiliate her—a conspiracy in which Communist inspiration, Arab hostility and Anglo-Saxon malevolence all played a part (cp. *L'Aurore,* and many RPF, Poujadist, and other Right-Wing speeches or writings, in particular Soustelle's). A shopkeeper's rebellion against harsher measures of tax control rapidly became a call for resistance against French decadence in the world and for the summoning of a new States General. The Dreyfus case, with its succession of Left-Wing protest at first, and Right-Wing protest after the victory of the Left, is the best example of the degree to which the scope of a debate may become universal. A long if grudging practice of "reformism" has not succeeded in erasing the basic hostility of the labor movement to a *syndicalisme de gestion,* which would imply not so much the abandonment of its grievances, as the explicit recognition of the "capitalist" order of society.

One of the consequences of this "total" attitude is, of course, to reinforce the intransigence which results from the negative character of the protest. Another consequence is that protest battles are waged in moral terms: The moralism so characteristic of French intellectuals pervades all French protest movements; they argue not about interests but about principles; they appeal to notions of good and evil or to traditional values.

Defeatism. Defeatism is a more surprising feature. Nevertheless, there is a strand of despair about the possibility of ever succeeding. It is as if the very leaders of the protesting group knew all along that their role consisted simply in expressing that sonorous "no" without which man remains unfinished, rather than achieving whatever goal they had in mind—as though they expected that however far their protest might carry them (for instance, even into power!), nothing much would really be changed at the end. The gesture thus matters more than the outcome.

We could find such an attitude among French syndicalists, whose fate it has been to fall from the dream of a "total reconstruction" of society into the reality of mere permanent protest: Militancy has declined, and protest talk or action, such as the vote for the most extreme party or union on election day, is all that remains of the hope of collective liberation.[4] What carried Poujade's followers across France was not so much the expectation of reversing the trend toward industrialization, as the

---

[4] The best study remains Val Lorwin's *The French Labor Movement* (Cambridge: Harvard University Press, 1954).

exhilarating adventure which interrupted the drabness of everyday life.[5] The men who raised barricades in Algiers in January 1960, and some of the leaders of the April 1961 *putsch,* such as General Challe, were staging a *baroud d' honneur* against de Gaulle rather than expecting to reverse his policy: The trials of the spring and summer of 1961 revealed that many officers rallied to Challe even though they doubted that his attempt could get very far. Defeatism colored the protest of Péguy, Sorel, Barrès, and, later, Drieu la Rochelle, against the mediocrity in which they saw France ensconced; Sartre has recently confessed his own sense of failure.[6]

A certain lack of conviction about one's chances of success and a grudging recognition of the status quo's strength contribute to the explanation of the brittleness of most of the protest movements. Some of their members always get discouraged earlier than others and exchange their original revolt for submission or apathy. What ends most French protest movements is the absorption of many of the rebels into the system and the disappearance of the others. Such absorption is sometimes resentful, as in the case of the workers; sometimes uneasy, as in the case of some of the early neutralists who have become more or less resigned to France's choice of the Atlantic alliance; or, it is sometimes surprisingly smooth, as in the case of M. Debré's attitude toward NATO, or in the cases of many once-rebellious political leaders who are won over by the "games, poisons and delights" of the system.[7] Whichever it is, the system wins. One may ask whether protest movements fail because their leaders do not really believe in their success, or whether they lose faith because of the record of past failures. It is, of course, a combination of the two: Protest movements both arise and fail because of the system's very structure and style.

II

Both the universality and the style of French protest result from the nature of French society and of France's political system.[8]

AN EXPLANATION. The nature of French *society,* as it existed from the Revolution until very recently, created the conditions for many of the types of protest.

1. Society rested on a consensus which included the upper bourgeoisie, the lower middle classes (composed both of independent operators and of civil servants or

---

[5] See the author's *Le mouvement Poujade* (Paris: A. Colin, 1956).

[6] In his preface to Paul Nizan, *Aden Arabie* (Paris: 1960).

[7] For instance: from extreme Left to Right in cases such as Millerand, Briand, Laval; from extreme Right to Center in the case of many Poujadist deputies or Gaullist leaders under the Fourth Republic. Albert Camus's bitter play, *l'Etat de Siège,* is a lively allegorical treatment of the whole theme of protest and failure, with the return, at the end, of the politicians who had fled when the Plague struck.

[8] I have elaborated on these points in my piece on "The Effects of World War II on French Society and Politics," *French Historical Studies,* Vol. 2, No. 1 (Spring 1961), and in a chapter of a forthcoming collective book on postwar France, to be published under the auspices of the Harvard Center for International Affairs.

employees), as well as the peasants. This consensus around what I have elsewhere called the stalemate society tended to preserve largely pre-industrial values and attitudes and to dilute or delay industrialization. Now this consensus excluded the industrial proletariat and created a major psychological barrier between the workers and the rest of the population. In particular, a bourgeoisie, whose attitude toward industrial enterprise and economic rationality never had much resemblance to the ideal type described by Professor Waelder in his chapter, insisted both on applying to the workers' "bourgeois" standards of social ascent (*enrichissez-vous*) and on treating the workers according to the degree of loyalty shown by them toward their employers—one of the many aspects of the feudal hangover among the bourgeoisie. The *social* distance (that is, differences in income, education, way of life) between the workers and the bourgeois may have been less than in England, but the *intellectual* distance (mutual acceptance and behavior) was greater, especially since it was increased by the contrast between the bourgeois' treatment of the workers and the bourgeois' community of values with mystical glorification of, and legal protection of, the peasants. The result was that the workers could not but adopt an attitude of protest against the established order and dream of revolution or revenge.[9] But the very numerical inferiority of the workers made their dream a rather hopeless one: Here we find the roots of negativism, "totalism," and defeatism in working-class movements.

2. The consensus among the other groups, which rested on a common resistance to the machine age and on an unwritten agreement to keep the middle classes as large as possible, was of such a nature that it could be threatened by two kinds of external disruption. On the one hand, any severe economic depression, reducing the national income, would increase tensions among groups fighting for its distribution and create particularly strong protest movements among those who were most severely hit by falling prices. Hence, the rebellion of Western France's peasants and the protest of the small businessmen and shopkeepers during the 30's, for they were not as well sheltered from the depression as the big enterprises which benefited from various ententes or government contracts. On the other hand, any period of rapid industrialization, accompanied by the elimination of, or increased hardships for, marginal independent producers or shopkeepers, would provoke those victims of economic progress into complaining of betrayal by the state, which failed to safeguard their way of life: This was what happened in the case of Poujadism. Thus we may conclude that the very nature of French society created one structural protest, that of the industrial workers, and latent protests, whose explosion depended on what French economists call *la conjoncture.*

Other forms of protest can be explained by the nature of the French *political system.*

1. The fundamental factor here is the permanent split in French political thought since the Revolution, or rather a double split. On the one hand, there is the opposition of those Frenchmen who have remained faithful to counterrevolutionary ideas to

[9] See Hadley Cantril, *The Politics of Despair.*

those who have accepted the principle of government based on consent. On the other hand, there is the division among the latter, between the Liberals who fear that any system of government in which the "will of the people" is not carefully filtered and diluted will upset the stalemate society to which they are attached above all; the Democrats, who are also attached to it but whose social conservatism is less fearful and whose respect for traditional elites is nil; and finally, the social reformers who reject the formula of the stalemate society altogether.

Two consequences of this basic split are important for our subject. First, the believers in counterrevolutionary dogmas have been permanently reduced to the condition of a sniping protest group; for more than forty years, this was the fate and the role of Maurras' Action Française: bitter denunciation of all the institutions and men of the regime, coming out of an intellectually well-staffed but politically limited ghetto. To the extent to which the Republic has been militantly opposed to counterrevolutionary ideas, and the Church wedded to them, Catholics have been obliged to create protest movements of their own. Second, although the "ideological" formula of the Third and Fourth Republics was on the Left (an alliance between all the "heirs of the Revolution"), its "social" basis was the stalemate society. Consequently, extreme-Left political parties found themselves either in part (Socialists, until 1936) or totally (Communists) in the position of protest groups: Although the SFIO, following Jaurès' line, accepted the political institutions of the regime as legitimate, it refused to participate in the government for over thirty years or to vote the military budget in peace time.

2. Not only because of the split in French political thought, but also as an effect of the instability of regimes in the nineteenth century, of the electoral laws and parliamentary rules of the Third Republic, and of France's economic and social complexity, France developed a party system both multiple and heterogeneous. Those very divisions of the French political scene, and its resulting incapacity at forging stable coalitions, have condemned the political system to "immobilism" at important times. Consequently, any group which felt that action was vital has tended to organize a protest movement in order to break the deadlock. Immobilism was less damaging and, subsequently, protest less frequent, as long as the function of the state was essentially ideological. But when, in the 30's, the impact of the world outside began to upset both France's economic and social balance and her role in the world, the load carried by the political system became too heavy for her multi-party parliamentary regime. The explosive issue of what de Gaulle calls *le rang* has provoked, as a result of the regime's fumblings and failures, reactions directed both against the outside world and against the weakness of the government. This was the case, for instance, when France's Right protested against practically the whole universe, in addition to the regime, after the Sakhiet bombing incident which preceded the fall of the Fourth Republic; the same thing had happened on a larger scale when both the Left and the Right attacked Blum's dead-center compromise policy of nonintervention in the Spanish Civil War.

This is why it seems, at times, that all organizations are engaged in an orgy of protest: They pull a paralyzed state in different directions, hit at one another over it, and recriminate against it for its passivity. Thus, the protest groups appear altogether as a consequence of the non-pragmatic, non-reformist quality of a fragmented political system, as the only alternative to complete stagnation, but also as a contribution to the system's weakness. Legal reform being blocked, the first task of the protest movement is, inevitably, to attack the political system for its paralysis. The negative character of the protest makes the prospect of reform even more distant, for it throws the regime on the defensive (leagues in the 30's; RPF and anti-EDC rallies under the Fourth Republic; protests by peasants, parliamentarians, unions, and intellectuals under the Fifth Republic). It also makes France's adjustment to change in the world more difficult. Two vicious circles are thereby created: First, the division of opinion regarding France's role in international affairs, which explains why the political system has so repeatedly mishandled the issue, is perpetuated by this very indecisiveness on top; second, the spectacle of a political system paralyzed by the "game" which its members play according to their individual calculations produces its opposite—protests in the form of rabidly ideological groups which prefer the vacuum of pure principles to the villainy of unprincipled power. The alternative to gradual reform is the concatenation of stagnation and protest.

The peculiarities of French protest result not only from the nature of the social consensus and of political divisions, but also from features which can be found *both in the society and in the polity.*

1. Fragmentation is the first feature of French protest. Until recently, the inability of the French to create effective voluntary associations was as great as when Tocqueville lamented about it. Few interests were organized; the membership of business and labor unions, as well as parties, remained small; the economy was splintered into a myriad of small landowners, small businessmen, small shopkeepers; the working class was dispersed among countless enterprises; the multiparty system was extraordinarily complex. Consequently, the French body politic lacked adequate institutional channels for the expresssion and redress of grievances. Such fragmentation explains, first, the frequency and diversity of protest movements: They are both a substitute for the creation of, and the demonstration of, the failure to create stable, broadly based channels. Second, the defeatism I have mentioned results in part from the impossibility of mobilizing a large section of the population for common, positive goals over a long period of time.

2. The second, and crucial, characteristic has been studied admirably by Michel Crozier: [10] It is the style of authority which defines human relations both in society and in political life. The French style of authority rules out participation. Instead of solving conflicts in cooperation and through compromises, individuals and groups refer those conflicts to a higher, central authority which will thus be held responsible for the outcome. The result of this attitude is centralization (within business or bureaucratic organizations as well as within the political system as a whole) and the preservation of the individual's capacity to protest. The range of the individual's

[10] See his articles: "La France, terre de commandement," in *Esprit* (December 1957), pp. 779–98, and "Le citoyen," *ibid.* (February 1961), pp. 193–211.

attitudes goes from apathy to resistance, with distrust coloring the whole spectrum. The lack of participation means that decisions will be made by a small number of men (the bureaucrats and the representatives in the case of the political system); centralization means that those men will carefully try to preserve their privilege of making decisions alone; permanent distrust and latent resistance below mean that the subjects will try to limit this privilege by surrounding the decision-makers' competence with legal restrictions and themselves with vested rights; it also means that they will protest as soon as they think that arbitrariness has broken out on top. This description fits the behavior of businessmen or unionists who prefer to leave the settlement of labor problems to the government. It also fits the model of political behavior proposed by Alain: The citizen is not a militant; he wants to be left alone; he abandons decisions to elites he distrusts and leaves the task of supervising those elites to representatives whom he also distrusts.

We have seen, above, that many protest movements result from the paralysis of the political system; we see now that protest can indeed be aimed either at the failure of higher authority to take the decisions which are referred to it, *or,* on the contrary, at decisions made by higher authority which seem to invade vested rights. This explains both why such movements are destructive, for many of them are initiatives against the exercise of initiative by others, and why there is, within them, a streak of defeatism. They are revolts against a central authority which is expected to have the final say, because ultimate responsibility for decisions has been entrusted to it: It is rebellion within an established pattern, not revolution against it. Consequently, as in the case of the "additional protocols" to EDC, or of the 1961 cabinet measures in favor of the peasants, the central authority, in order to preserve its position, usually *grants* (*octroi*) some concessions to the protest movements on its own initiative; it is at that point that rebellion often ebbs away: Harmony is restored without cooperation, by flexibility on top and acquiescence at the bottom. Thus, by an intriguing paradox, protest succeeds to the extent to which it contained a kernel of specific grievances but fails to the extent to which it was a broader challenge of the decision-makers.[11]

3. The roots of both this style of authority and fragmentation are deep indeed: As Crozier, Laurence Wylie, and Jesse R. Pitts [12] have shown, they are in the school system which "tends to produce autonomous, independent and critical individuals rather than participating and responsible citizens." [13]

[11] The gradual absorption of the prewar PSF and postwar RPF into the parliamentary system could be analyzed as the result of such a process. The Daladier cabinet, to a large extent, followed a policy of "La Rocque-ism without La Rocque," just as many of the cabinets of the Fourth Republic, in their anti-Communism and economic program, followed a line of "Guallism (RPF-style) without de Gaulle," and the nationalist Mollet government of 1956 can be taxed with Poujadism without Poujade.

[12] See Laurence Wylie's admirable study, *Village in the Vaucluse* (Cambridge: Harvard University Press, 1957), and Jesse R. Pitts' provocative unpublished Harvard dissertation, "The Bourgeois Family and French Economic Retardation" (1958).

[13] Crozier, *op. cit.,* in *Esprit* (February 1961), p. 210.

This school system leaves little initiative to the child: Elders teach him the world, starting with general principles. The competitive system increases the pressure on him. He is taught, while in school, no civics or economics, but he is encouraged to sharpen his personality by using his critical faculties in scientific, literary, and psychological subjects. The result is an individual endowed with general principles untested by practical experience and with little or no ability to organize or participate in teamwork. He has learned both to accept superior authority in his social or public life and to escape from it in his inner life. As for expressing protest, all he disposes of are peer groups which, in Pitts' words, are mere delinquent communities: defensive protest groups against school and family pressures, recognized by neither and consequently brittle and semi-clandestine. We can understand why so many rebellious adolescents later become most conformist citizens, and why protest movements will tend to be "total," destructive, and defeatist altogether. The roots are in the national culture. The circle is hard to break.

We may consequently ask whether the kind of protest we have described, far from being "dysfunctional" or subversive to the social order, does not, on the contrary, play a vital *role* in saving the individual from becoming a mere cog in society and the French body politic from the Scylla of violent conflict and the Charybdis of oppression.

For the stalemate society, with all its weaknesses, has been the broadest form of consensus conceivable in France, and the immobilist political system has at least preserved the underlying society and made possible the peaceful coexistence of incompatible parties and schools of thought. Such a society, such a polity, engendered protest movements for the reasons we have given; but they have absorbed them as well. Indeed, the merit of the Third Republic and even of the Fourth, before 1958, was that it tamed one protest movement after another. In a nation such as France, there is more than cynicism in Renan's statement that the aim of politics should not be to solve issues but to wait until they are exhausted, and more than wit in Robert de Jouvenel's maxim that stagnation is the only form of faithfulness to one's principles. For there have been only two ways of keeping the nation together: One may be called the institutionalization of political stalemate; the other is Richelieu's formula of a strait jacket to contain a divided and fickle nation.

Both political systems, it must be stressed, depend on centralization for their success. The former perpetuates distrust between the leaders and the led, as well as the social tensions inherent in French society and, therefore, breeds protest movements; but precisely, it is the only one which allows their free expression. The protest movement is both the safety valve of a society divided by deep conflicts and the traditional French form of democracy. Indeed, the very division of opinion, which has prevented any party from ever getting all of its program carried out, and the very nature of society, more interested in preventing abuses than in allowing the exercise of state power, have turned every vote into a protest vote and every party into a protest group. It is a protest against the status quo or against those who threaten

it.[14] When the goal is to checkmate the opponent, not to reach a compromise with him, the game of politics resembles the strategy of deterrence.

AN ILLUSTRATION. As an example of the kind of mechanism I have described, I want to take the case of the French intellectuals; for it is among them that the tradition of protest is most ancient; it begins with the eighteenth century, long before the appearance of the modern proletariat. It is among them that the effects of the social and political circumstances analyzed above are most interesting to observe.

What we find is the persistence of a *style of action* which Tocqueville has admirably, if unkindly, studied in a chapter of *The Old Regime and the Revolution*. This style has marked three important "intellectual crises" in the twentieth century: around 1900, around 1930, and at the time of the liberation.

1. Its first characteristic is the ideological bent of the protest: Political discontent is wrapped in metaphysics. The intellectual revolt against the ideology of the Third Republic took the form of a reaction against the categorical imperative, against scientism, and the "sclerosis of rationalism," for the rehabilitation of mobility, activism, and faith behind the banner of Bergson. The ferment of the 30's, which was largely aimed at the political and social flaws of an immobilist regime and of a poorly organized and badly run capitalist economy, was often couched in the language of "personalist" philosophy, which proposed to create "a new man," no longer the social atom of liberalism but a person rooted in various living communities. Marxism provided much of the inspiration of liberation thought, and even existentialist philosophy has tried to come to terms with it.

This bent is both a form of what I have called totalism, earlier, and the product of a conviction that there are general laws or principles which govern human affairs whose discovery and enforcement would make the difference between chaos and order.[15] It is this aspect of Marxism which has contributed most to its success in France, especially in the 30's and 40's, when the acceleration of history, as Daniel Halévy has called it, destroyed all previous certitudes and seemed to require a new compass. Claude Bourdet, certainly not an orthodox Marxist, recently wrote about the "fundamental principles of politico-economic analysis applicable to all societies." But intellectuals of the Right, such as Maurras, also liked to believe in laws of political science capable of preventing social decay and national decadence. A corollary of this belief in general principles is the search for universality, the conviction that whatever protest is made concerns not only France, but mankind. It includes the passionate interest for, or belief in, "waves of the future" or streams

---

[14] I would argue that the Radical party's skill was its capacity of being both an indispensable party of government (or rather occupation of power) and a protest party, according to Alain's precepts. The Independents of the Fourth (and Fifth) Republics have been playing a similar role.
[15] Even sophisticated intellectuals like Maurice Duverger have a tendency to look for such universal laws: His last book, *De la dictature* (Paris: R. Julliard, 1961), with its sweeping generalizations, is a perfect, if depressing, example.

of history. This explains why foreign examples, considered to be representative of such trends, are studied and proposed as models, lest France remain left on the shore or swimming against the tide. Both the belief in a key to the universe and the passion for universality can be traced to the nature of French education.

2. A second characteristic is a deep moralism. "The political convictions of French writers are only moral attitudes." [16] Both the protest of 1900 and that of 1930 were revolts against mediocrity, against a civilization in which virtue and heroism seemed to have no place (in this respect, many of France's intellectual Fascists were merely disciples of Barrès', without any hope left about the possibility of saving France and with the conviction that Fascism represented the new wave of the future). The intellectuals of the liberation often started with a moral meditation about the difficulty of human relations in the century of "the cold," and about the universal presence of death as the Emperor of the twentieth century. What followed was both a denunciation of all "miserable consolers"—imbeciles, cowards, or stinkers—and a common desire to transcend nihilism.

Such moralism has, as a consequence, a sharp polarization between Left and Right: On the Left, the old quest for justice, the protest against inequality at home (that is, for the proletariat) and abroad (for oppressed colonial peoples) [17] has dominated the French university. Here again, Marxism has found the ground ready for it, because it presented itself not only in its scientist aspect, but also as the continuation of the old moral fight for human liberation. It thus stilled the thirst for a secular religion which Carl Becker had found already among Enlightenment philosophers. On the Right, which has dominated the academies, much theorizing and anti-Republican writing has been the result of a burning moral fear of decadence. Today's Left-Wing intellectual protest against the Algerian war and Right-Wing protest against "softness" in waging the war reflect such polarization.

Another consequence has been the tendency to substitute prophetism, or the search for scapegoats (such as the United States, symbol of the "cold," of the mechanization of life, of commercialism, or of capitalist inequity), or the mere attachment to abstract principles, for the quest of accommodation or political solutions. But the inevitable outcome of such a divorce from the world of action has been some form of defeatism: the conscious or unconscious selection of Antigone's attitude as that of the true intellectual, the clinging to slogans and rituals,[18] or the final withdrawal from "engagement" altogether. No believer in a "mystique" can fail to notice some day the abyss between "mystique" and "politique." On the whole, French intellectuals (Sartre included, despite his denial) have been rebels rather than revo-

[16] Maurice Merleau-Ponty, quoted by René Rémond, "Les Intellectuels et La Politique," *Révue Française de Science Politique*, Vol. IX, No. 4, p. 867.

[17] Concern for underdeveloped peoples has become the principle subject of French Left-Wing intellectuals: a fascinating mixture of generosity, a quest for a new universalism despite France's relative decline, and an expression of *mauvaise conscience*.

[18] For instance, the slogan, long repeated by Sartre, that since the Communist Party represents the proletariat, and the proletariat is the "universal class" or the carrier of *le sens de l'histoire*, the intellectual should support the Communists.

lutionaries,[19] aghast at the sacrifice of purity which revolution entails, and, therefore, all too often condemned to fall from rebellious fervor to futility.

3. A third characteristic has been, and remains, the conviction of French intellectuals that they play the role of the conscience of society and that they are not mere specialists who may well be entitled to respect in their different spheres of expertise but whose views on public affairs deserve no greater attention than those of any other citizen. Crozier has denounced a "will of separation" in French intellectual fashions which preserves the distance between the intelligentsia and the rest of society and thus partakes of that determination to preserve one's vested rights so characteristic of France's style of authority. In a searching analysis, a distinguished French intellectual has recently recognized that even Left-Wing anti-Americanism contained a heavy dose of elitist dislike for a mass democracy in which such a distance is not acknowledged.[20]

These were already the features of the French intellectuals in the eighteenth century, but they no longer can be explained by the *causes* which Tocqueville suggested: In the eighteenth century there was an imposed separation between the world of the intellectuals, who were kept "quite out of touch with practical politics," and the world of power, which tolerated no participation. In this political vacuum around the centers of power, the writers were able to become the guides of public opinion. But ever since the Revolution, the intellectuals have had direct and massive access to politics and can no longer be exonerated by a reference to their forced ignorance of practice. Nevertheless, the symptoms of "protest intellectualism," which appeared at the time of this divorce, have survived it. Tocqueville himself recognized that this was already true under the Revolution, whose excesses he explains precisely by the fact that it was led by intellectuals whose contempt for facts, desire to reconstruct the whole universe, and literary phraseology became the very marks of the Revolution. However, ever since, French intellectuals have merged with representatives of numerous other groups within the political class (Jaurès and Léon Blum became the heads of a workers' party). Nevertheless the features are still here, and the leadership of opinion by the intellectuals has not been challenged. What explains such permanence?

1. The answer has to be found, first, in the nature of French society. The importance of the role of the intellectual is the product of a society in which specialization was seen as a narrowing of the mind, not a deepening of knowledge; in which, consequently, *la culture générale,* whose cement is literature, was the necessary condition for access to top positions. This was a society in which politics was seen as the supreme activity of the spirit and in which entry into intellectual or quasi-intellectual professions was, for centuries, the privileged method of social ascent, favored by an aristocracy whose values put intellectual achievement far above material success.

[19] See the "great debate" between Sartre and Camus after the publication of *The Rebel* and *Les Temps Modernes* (Summer 1952). The hero of Sartre's last play, *Les Sequestrés d'Altona,* is a typical rebel.
[20] J. M. Domenach, "Le modèle américain," Vol. 3, *Esprit* (October 1960).

Such a privileged position was both an honor and a risk: In times of purges, it was the intellectuals who were hit hardest, precisely because their pretense at being the conscience of society was taken seriously.

At the same time, the gradual, if slow, evolution of society from one still dominated by such values (which the bourgeoisie had adopted even before the Revolution) to one far closer to other Western industrial societies has contributed to increase the "protest" content of French thought. The intellectuals of the Left resented the growing importance of money and the effects of their own dependence on the market. They denounced those nations which seemed to them most advanced on the road to such corruption—first England, then Germany, later the United States. They looked forward to a society in which the fundamental values would be those of intellectual as well as manual labor.[21] The intellectuals of the Right rejected industrial society and mechanization altogether; they looked back to a society inspired by rural and aristocratic values and dominated by notables—including the intelligentsia.

2. But the protest of the intellectuals had a second reason as well: the nature of the political system. The four-way split of French thought did not only divide intellectuals and political classes: It condemned the former to be almost constantly frustrated by the conflicts or impotence of the latter.

When a political regime was established on too narrow a basis (for instance, the two monarchies of 1815–48 and the Vichy regime after the initial period of unanimity), the divorce between politics and the intellectuals reappeared in a way quite comparable to that of the Old Regime. The intellectuals supporting the regime tended to become uncompromising doctrinaires, the intellectuals in opposition attacked it with the same abstract intransigence as that shown by the *philosophes*. The result was massive protest and an intellectual civil war.

When a political regime rested on a much broader basis, it could be one of two things. It could be a "savior" or a strong-man regime, such as that of Napoléon III, in which case, the bulk of the intellectuals would protest soon enough against the restrictions to public freedoms; it could be a democratic but "immobilist" regime, and the intellectuals would soon be frustrated again.

Intellectual protest was bred by the inevitable divorce between a political system which could function only by avoiding too neat a polarization and an intelligentsia which always tended toward extreme positions.[22] The intellectuals would have to choose between becoming the mere justifiers of the status quo or dissenters of the Left or Right protesting against the paralysis of the regime—or, if they did not choose, they could become both dissenters and justifiers, like Alain!

Three consequences would flow from such an unhappy state of affairs. First,

[21] French Marxists are very often the heirs of positivism; they see in Communism the achievement of a scientific society led by benevolent and knowledgeable representatives of temporal power—the organizers of work, and spiritual power—the intelligentsia.

[22] One can see how uncomfortable the position of the intellectuals would be: dissatisfied with pluralist, representative regimes because of immobilism, they are even more hostile to "strong-man" regimes, because of the atmosphere of forced or fake unanimity. "Unhappy consciousness" indeed!

both being split among themselves and often opposed to the politicians in power, the intellectuals would inevitably become intransigent moralists: The absence of an intellectual consensus explains the extraordinary prevalence of moralist thinking over utilitarian arguments. Second, the relations between the intellectuals and the public would oscillate from almost complete alienation—when the country was in a mood for a savior and the intellectuals were, on the whole, in opposition (this is again the case since 1958)—to relative harmony when the polarization of the intellectuals between Left and Right corresponded to a similar deep split of opinion (1900, 1936). Third, the relations between the intellectuals and the parties are almost always bad, except in brief periods of "dawn"—at the foundation time of a regime, before disillusionment sets in. After that, the intellectuals begin to snipe at the compromises and maneuvers of political strategy and, particularly, at those intellectuals who, having become party leaders, seem to be the very symbols of betrayal, in a world *"où l'action n'est pas la soeur du rêve."* [23]

3. A third reason for the protest of the intellectuals has been, ever since the turn of the century and with increasing importance since the 30's, the decline of France's role in the world. To men who believed with almost equal fervor in the universality of France and civilization, such decline could not but provoke a rash of complaints either against the very trend of history, denounced as a return to barbarism, or against the men in power, blamed for letting France fall back in the race. And thus it has seemed as if, seeing France unflatteringly reflected in foreign eyes, French intellectuals had either wanted to repudiate alien testimonies altogether, or else angrily urged their compatriots to adopt the apparently more successful doctrines which had swept over and pushed ahead Fascist Italy, Nazi Germany, or Soviet Russia.

Thus, protest was no longer due, as in the eighteenth century, to a lack of political participation by intellectuals. It came from the frustrations which a fragmented political system imposed on a divided intelligentsia: The very immobility of the system fostered impatience in every tendency and seemed to leave its chance to every utopia. It is not surprising that if to "play the game" of politics, or to accept society as it was (with its class and group tensions), meant resignation to perpetual discord or gradual decadence, so many intellectuals would decide that only through rebellion could grandeur, solidarity, and fraternity be found again. "I revolt, therefore we are," wrote Camus. Alas, this hope turned out to be in vain in almost every case.

The Resistance period has become a powerful and nostalgic myth because this was the one protest movement which seemed to restore unity and harmony, not only among most of the intellectuals, but between them, the parties, and the people —within the Great Alliance of the Winners. However, it was, once more, a negative kind of union, and the apparent triumph of the movement in 1944 came shortly before its disintegration.

[23] See, for instance, Colette Audry's subtle hatchet job on Léon Blum, *Léon Blum ou la politique du juste* (Paris: 1955); Maurras was not any kinder to Right-Wing politicians. Mendès-France has been treated much more respectfully, as a kind of tragic hero, because he had refused the usual deals and half-measures. (Indeed, *Le Canard Enchaîné* once called his cabinet—which it supported—not really a government but the opposition in power!)

III

The future of protest in France deserves some exploration. Since protest movements are the product of a certain kind of society and polity, it would seem that the transformation of the latter would bring about changes among the former. The trouble is that if French society has indeed been undergoing a revolution, and the political system has been shaken up too, the political scene remains in dubious shape, and the connections between economic and social change and political behavior are anything but direct.

SYMPTOMS OF CHANGE. The decisive event in the gradual liquidation of the stalemate society since 1945 is that France is becoming industrialized.

The stalemate *society* required the following structures or institutions: first, a limited State whose only role was to preserve the equilibrium between the various groups—a protector, not a manager; second, a hierarchical society with a large peasant reservoir, careful social distances between the various strata among the consensus groups, and the maintenance of as many independent operators as possible; third, a clear-cut separation between the workers and the other elements of the population. All those elements are in the process of disappearing.

1. The State plays a leading role in the French economy; this role has been more or less grudgingly accepted by all groups in French society: The Poujadist revolt, the less-noisy sniping by small business groups, and some of the protests by peasant organizations have seemed to challenge this extension of state activities, because public policies tended toward the elimination of marginal producers in all this areas. But, on the whole, the attitudes of even those forces have evolved in recent years from a heroic and pointless refusal to change, to a much greater willingness to adapt, and, indeed, to expect that the State would dutifully direct and subsidize their adaptation.

2. As a consequence of both state planning and the impressive conversion of French business to the ethics of modernization (productivity and expansion), the fragmentation of the economy and of society is beginning to disappear: The village is less of a self-contained unit; the family is less tight; the differences between ranks and statuses crumble; and a more uniform way of life emerges. As a result, the peasant basis of society shrinks more and more, and the new growing middle classes are predominantly salaried. The new society which emerges appears as less cramped than the old one; its driving force seems to be economic rationality, rather than the social rationality of a bourgeoisie reluctant to accept the challenge of social mobility and economic growth. In this society, interests are far more effectively organized than they ever were before. Channels for the orderly expression of grievances are now available.

3. The working class is gradually integrated into the nation: in part because the opposition in values and in the ways of life is less complete, in part because the greater specialization of industrial labor has, at the same time, fragmented the

proletariat as a class and integrated a major portion of it in the firms. Consequently, the worker finds himself less segregated from the rest of society, less unwilling to cooperate with men who in turn behave toward him as if a common interest in prosperity rather than an insurmountable abyss might exist. The *prestance idéale* of the proletariat might lose, but its material lot benefits from the change. As a sociologist has put it, it is the end of the trilogy "family enterprise, shopkeeper, revolutionary syndicalism." [24] The workers would still be vividly concerned with specific reforms but would gradually lose interest in criticism *de principe* (for instance, in challenging the principle of private property): This would imply a change from an attitude of permanent protest to a much more conservative and consensual one.

There are signs of change in the political sphere also.

1. The counterrevolutionary extreme-Right is practically dead. The fatal blow which the Vichy fiasco dealt to the plausibility of its doctrines, the liquidation of the stalemate society, and the extension of the State's role have relegated Maurrasian dogmas to the scholars' museum and to the politicians' cemetery.

2. The divisions between the other main schools of traditional French thought are being blurred both by the growth of Christian Democracy and by the changes in society and in the role of the State. Many of the old issues which have given rise to protest movements of the Left and Right are on the road to extinction. The pace and character of industrialization renders largely obsolete the extreme-Left's protest against France's previously "frozen" capitalism. The Socialists long ago ceased to behave like a party of protest, and the Communists, who of course still do, are highly embarrassed in attempting to give a "correct" analysis of the changes in French society. The issue of *laïcité* still produces a corporative protest among public school-teachers; but it is no longer a national issue.

3. A gradual adjustment to the outside world has brought about a surprising amount of consensus and silence where tumult and turmoil reigned just a few years ago. The neutralists' protests against the Western alliance are mere whispers, nationalist complaints about the role of France in NATO are more tame, and the enemy camps of European supra-nationalists and anti-Europeans appear to have exterminated each other, to the advantage of practical and gradual "Europeans."

Finally, there are signs of change in the *intelligentsia* as well.

1. Polarization seems to have decreased. The attraction of Communism and of Marxist orthodoxy has fallen: Many Left-Wing intellectuals discovered that "Marxism had become the myth of the Left-Wing intellectuals" and was an excuse for ignoring "the entire sociological and historical reality in which they live." [25] The disillusioned and self-critical ex-Communist intellectual has become a familiar actor on the

[24] Jesse R. Pitts, "Adieu à la France de papa," *La Caravelle,* Cambridge, Mass. (Autumn 1959).
[25] Edgar Morin, "Intellectuels: critique du mythe et mythe de la critique," *Arguments,* Vol. 4, No. 20 (4ème trimestre 1960), p. 38. See also the change of *Esprit*'s line under J. M. Domenach as announced in the issue of November 1957.

French literary scene. At the other pole, many intellectuals of the Right have lapsed into pure futility, and it is only the evolution of the Algerian war which has re-injected militancy into some of them. One symptom of this lowering of tension is the decline of anti-Americanism—that form of protest against the modern Western world which had so long been shared by both extremes. Another symptom was the sudden attraction of Mendès-France, the champion of pragmatic politics, for so many intellectuals.

2. The evolution of French society also threatens the pre-eminence of the intellectuals and their role as guides of public opinion. In a society where the number of specialized tasks is multiplied, where individuals perform more and more sharply differentiated functions and belong to a broad range of organizations and communities, the appeal of the "specialist of general culture" and of his style of intransigent abstract argument falls off. In such a society, politics is no longer considered the supreme activity of the mind. The new forms of mass culture include audio-visual techniques, which tend to reduce the importance of literary modes of expression.[26] The narrowing of the gap between the various schools of thought also tend to make the shrill moralism of traditional intellectual protest less palatable.

The question which is thus raised is whether industrial society is not going, in France as much as elsewhere, to usher in a world in which private concerns will divert the citizen from political activity. Since, in France, protest was ideological, won't "the end of ideology" mean the inherent end of protest?

REASONS FOR CONTINUITY. There are, however, very serious reasons for doubting that we are anywhere near such a fundamental mutation in French public life.[27] Some of the most essential *causes* of French protest are still with us.

1. Changes in society have been extensive but not complete. In the first place, even though fragmentation may have decreased, the French style of authority has not changed yet. Crozier's description remains correct. As he points out, this style is singularly unadapted to an industrial society in which social distances are narrowed, the sphere of individual independence shrinks due to the growth of social activities, and organizational units are both large and obliged to cooperate. There is a time lag here: The patterns of behavior remain behind the new structures. As long as secondary and higher education, with their elitist and individualistic bent, remain a bottleneck, this lag is likely not only to perpetuate the behavior just described, but also to sharpen tensions between innovators and traditionalists, between the new and old types of social relations.

In the second place, a similar time lag affects the relations between the workers and the rest of the population (particularly the employers). There is a *détente* which corresponds to the change in structures and in values on both sides, but old reflexes and attitudes have not been driven out. The workers' sense of injustice persists, the

[26] See the remarks of Jean Duvignaud, "L'intervention des intellectuels dans la vie publique," *Arguments*, pp. 45–46.
[27] I have elaborated more fully the following remarks in "Observations sur la crise politique française," *Archives européennes de sociologie,* Vol. 1, No. 2 (1960), pp. 303–20.

industrial proletariat remains inadequately organized, and it is housing which serves as a bottleneck here. Consequently, again, old tensions are still present, and new ones stem from the coexistence of traditional and recent values.[28]

Third, the very process of modernization provokes protests from all the groups which are either being eliminated or benefiting from economic progress less rapidly than other groups. These are protests which any period of fast development will produce anywhere, but, as the peasants' movement of 1961 has shown, they are particularly spectacular whenever the political system fails to meet such grievances adequately.

2. This is what has been happening in France, for the response of the political system to changes in society has been extremely limited. The structures of French political life are in a state of chaos, and the style of French policies has not been transformed. The Gaullist State is not a sign of, or force for, change: It is both an exception from and a confirmation of a traditional pattern. It is an exception, because it is a "mon-archical" regime in which, nevertheless, public freedoms and the institutions of representative government are preserved. It is a confirmation, because despite its attempt at establishing a new synthesis of French political traditions, it is in fact just one more form of what Nicholas Wahl has called the administrative tradition.[29] Underneath the regime, the political foundations of protest movements have not been destroyed—on the contrary, they remain alive.

In the first place, even though the articulation of interest may be more effective than in the past, nothing has happened so far to create more responsible political parties. The old ones are still here; of the two new parties since 1958, one (the UNR) is hardly likely to survive General de Gaulle and has already been affected by the withdrawal of a protest group which rails against "abandon" in Algeria; the other (the PSU) is a typically intellectual protest movement, marked by swift evolution toward an ideological and intransigent indictment of the regime and of society altogether: Here Marxist phraseology becomes, once more, a substitute for realistic analysis. Consequently, the public's mixture of apathy and distrust toward the parties continues. At the same time, if the voters' choice remains limited to those parties, then, barring a drastic constitutional reform, the old political patterns of representative government are likely to re-emerge. For instance, a far less revolted working class will persist in voting for a party of protest such as the Communist Party, whose behavior has been quite aptly described by Duverger as a "Poujadism of the Left."

In the second place, inadequate though they may have been, and although, as we have seen, their frequent deadlocks led to protest movements, France's parties and parliamentarians served as transmission belts between the public and the rulers—ministers or bureaucrats. Today, such intermediaries have been reduced to frustration and ridicule by the regime's almost systematic humiliation of Parliament. Consequently, the government often fails to notice in time the discontent which brews,

[28] See the remarks by Serge Moscovici in his monograph, *Reconversion industrielle et changements sociaux* (Paris: 1961), pp. 311–12.
[29] In S. H. Beer and A. Ulam, *Patterns of Government* (New York: Random House, 1958), Chap. 16 ff.

so to speak, in rotating sections of the population. Furthermore, the parliamentarians themselves tend to behave as a protest group, adding their voices to those of the other dissenters. Thus, protest becomes a substitute for the old intermediaries, after having often been a result of their divisions. Moreover, especially on the Algerian issue, the regime's extreme caution, its quest for unanimity, and its preference for mystifying magic over decisive surgery have produced effects quite comparable to those of previous parliamentarian *immobilisme*—that is, an orgy of protest from both extremes, each one finding in the course of events a vindication of its views and an indictment of the regime. The fact that one of those protesting groups includes a sizable part of the army has proved to be particularly dangerous for the political system.

Third, even though some of the old issues may be dying, and although there may be neither *"crise de structure"* nor *"crise de légitimité,"* in Duverger's words, one of the obstacles to radical constitutional change is precisely the absence of any consensus on the institutions—an issue which is almost bound to lead to new ideological clashes and new protest movements. The army revolt of April 1961 and the trials which followed have revealed to what extent the legitimacy of the institutions is judged to be merely conditional and depends on the substance of the policies which the regime pursues. This is not the only area in which we find that the old style of political argument has survived; every new issue in recent years—from German rearmament to decolonization—has been dealt with in the same ideological spirit, through the same mixture of obstinacy and stalemate, the same pattern of reluctance to compromise and addiction to protest, and with the same attachment to myths instead of reality as in the past.

In recent years, the most important, that is, hard-fought, of the new issues have been those which the painful process of France's adjustment to the postwar world has raised. Although, as we have seen, such adjustment has been achieved in many areas, the way in which decolonization has been handled, and particularly the endless and poisonous Algerian conflict, has weakened France's institutions, perpetuated a sense of humiliation and, consequently, has kept protests both against France's regimes and against the outside world alive and raised them to an increasingly higher pitch.

It well may be that, if the Algerian issue is settled, no new one may be of sufficient importance again to shake the political system, which would be faced essentially with technical problems of resource allocation. However, we should not forget—and the peasants' protests of 1961 have reminded us—that the mark of France's political style is precisely its capacity to turn even minor issues into intellectual or ideological civil wars. For there is an autonomy of the political system which perpetuates divisions and attitudes even after the old social bases have disappeared. Protest movements emerge always either in reaction to authoritarian efforts at overcoming such obstacles, or in reaction against the impotence of a regime which reflects such conflicts too faithfully.

3. The relations between society and polity are a third cause of worry. For three obstacles to participation may find themselves combined, perpetuating thereby that very style of authority which is responsible for protest movements. The first is the

traditional kind of apathy produced by a political system which breeds, among citizens, a sense of alienation, a feeling of impotence due to their inability to influence the policy-makers. The second is the new indifference toward public affairs instilled in the bulk of population by a mass culture devoid of political content and by the "professionalization" of the citizen's life. The third obstacle would concern those leaders in every group or organization of industrial society whose functions, even though they are not public ones, are nevertheless political in the larger sense of the word. Since most collective "private" activities affect, or partake of, public policy, those new notables, far more numerous and diverse than the old, would be thoroughly frustrated and dissatisfied if no way were found to coordinate their aims and acts and to channel their grievances within the political system.[30]

In each of these three cases, it is the liaison between society and polity which is at stake. To the extent to which the state has become the motor of society—and no amount of "technocracy" in government can eliminate the need for political choices —the urgency of participation and of an effective liaison has increased. Two sets of measures appear both indispensable and still distant. The first is decentralization; without it, groups in society will continue to rely on and look to the centralized bureaucracy: The vicious circle of non-participation at the bottom and protest against arbitrariness or inaction at the top will persist. The second is the appearance of a new political class, "notables," drawn largely from among the leaders of collective private organizations—but also from the strata below—and willing to serve, not merely within those organizations, or as representatives of those bodies' interests accredited to government organs, but within parties and Parliament. Unfortunately nobody has any recipe.[31]

4. As long as those various problems have received no solution, intellectuals will continue to protest. They will continue, in part, because not all of them are resigned to the demise of the intellectuals' pre-eminence *qua* intellectuals and to their replacement by experts in industrial society (hence the resistance of many of them to changes in education which would seal the fate of *culture générale*); in part because no political regime likely to emerge from the present limbo will satisfy all of them; in part because their hostility to France's parties remains thorough, whether they criticize, as in the past, those parties' lack of backbone, or whether they denounce, in a sudden thirst for pragmatism, the ideological rigidity and sterility of parties that try to be "pure";[32] in part, finally, because France's adjustment to the world continues to raise those very moral issues which, so often before, have provoked French intellectuals into protests against one another, against the government's policy, or against the outside world. They remain the issues of justice versus the national interest or survival versus decadence.

In this respect, the Algerian drama has been, by its very complexity, more divisive

---

[30] There are excellent remarks on this point in: Joseph Rovan, *Une idée neuve: la démocratie* (Paris: Editions du Seuil, 1961).
[31] See, for instance, the rather lame conclusion of the otherwise interesting and sound study by Jean Meynaud and Alain Lancelot, *La participation des Français à la politique* (Paris: 1961).
[32] See, for instance, the very critical attitude of the Club Jean Moulin (a study group of civil servants and intellectuals) toward political parties in its publications.

and agonizing for French intellectuals than even the Dreyfus case: The alignments may have been less clear, but the battles have not been less fierce. If the political system, under both the Fourth and the Fifth Republics, has tended to lapse into impotence or ambiguity over this issue, it is from among the intellectuals that the most searching debates, the most passionate denunciations—either of tortures or of "defeatism"—and the most daring analyses have come, as the names of Camus, P. H. Simon, Jules Roy, Jeanson, Domenach, Aron, Mus, or Bayet, Thierry-Maulnier, Girardet, etc.—indicate. The great tradition continues.

Thus we may conclude that the disappearance of the pattern of French protest movements would require some monumental changes. The first would be a transformation of the political system, such that the citizens would no longer feel left out of the game of their representatives or of the decisions of their Chief of State—in other words, an end of the oscillation from the inefficient oligarchy of representative government to the more efficient but even more exclusive regime of a savior. The second would be a broad enough consensus on essential domestic and foreign policy matters to relieve the intelligentsia of its permanent frustration. The third, and most important, would be a change in the style of authority both in society and in politics, such that the individual would become capable of reaching compromises, by direct cooperation with others, and of joining pragmatic political parties. Nothing is more important in this connection than a reform of education; it has begun, although in fragmentary fashion. In particular, a change in the centuries-old style of secondary education would have deep, if only gradual, effects on the style of authority.

Protest movements have flourished because the French have felt so little responsibility for the decisions of the men "in power": It was easy to rebel against "them," whenever one was hurt by "them." But they have flourished also because Frenchmen never felt in agreement with the decisions of "power": The lack of political consensus aggravated and justified that avoidance of participation which France's social structure and style of social relations engendered. The two problems can only be solved together.[33] It is only when every group feels that it has really participated in collective decisions that the French citizen will cease to "oscillate between revolt and apathy and to find it difficult to adopt responsible attitudes";[34] but it is only when those groups no longer deem their values and beliefs to be incompatible that participation will be possible without damage. Should such a stage be reached, there would still be intellectuals for whom eternal vigilance, dissent, and protest will remain a duty, as the only alternative to conformism. But we are still far from the day when French society will be so homogeneous, France's role in the world so clearly marked, and political democracy so well organized, that protest against the tyranny of the majority will be unnecessary moral hygiene. For the time being, it is still the safety valve of conflicts and the substitute for an effective polity.

[33] Joseph Rovan (*op. cit.*) makes the mistake, in the second part of his book, of building a purely formalistic scheme of participation in the purest French "legalist" tradition, without any reference to political divisions. It is a bloodless scheme of institutions, based on the hypothesis of consensus and on a genuine *escamotage* of politics in the sense of conflicts; hence the author's mixture of annoyance with, embarrassment toward, and underestimation of, political parties. It is a fine pluralist construction for what Louis Hartz calls a liberal society—not for France, at least not yet.
[34] *Esprit* (February 1961), p. 206.

4

The Stratigraphy of Protest in Japan

Herbert Passin

The massive demonstrations of May and June 1960 which forced the resignation of the Kishi Cabinet and the cancellation of President Eisenhower's trip to Japan alarmed Americans as much as they elated the Chinese Communists. The complacent American view of Japan as a sturdy conservative force loyally allied to the United States through a wise and benevolent Occupation and generous economic aid was rudely shattered. Since the outbreaks came at a time when student unrest was overthrowing governments in South Korea and Turkey—also allies—it was natural that many Americans should see in them Communist-inspired plots and a Japan in the grip of a "revolutionary situation." But if these interpreters were wrong—and it has taken a great deal of soul-searching for informed opinion to understand fully what happened [1]—they were no less wrong than the Chinese Communists, who read the situation in much the same way. After a two-week trip to Japan in August 1960, Liu Ning-i, Chairman of the All-China Federation of Trade Unions, reported jubilantly that the revolutionary situation in Japan was well advanced. "The Japanese people's future is full of brightness and hope," he wrote.

But even if we discount the over-pessimism of naive American opinion and the over-optimism of the Chinese communists, it is apparent that there are powerful revolutionary forces on the loose in Japan. To say this, however, is not to say that Japan is on the verge of a revolution. The existence of revolutionary sentiment alone is not sufficient to bring about a revolution. Revolution depends on the crystallization of the sentiment into appropriate organizational forms, around appropriate issues, and based on the extent to which conservative forces are able to maintain their self-confidence and vigor. In Japan, the revolutionary forces are still far from having won-over or neutralized the majority of public sentiment, and the conservative forces still show every sign of vitality, ability, determination, and confidence. But the incidents surrounding the May-June events have revealed several important things. First, disaffection and alienation with the status quo are widespread, particularly among students, labor, and intellectuals. Second, the fabric of consensus is seriously

[1] See, e.g., E. O. Reischauer, "The Broken Dialogue with Japan," *Foreign Affairs* (October 1960); Reischauer, "Some Thoughts on Japanese Democracy," *Japan Quarterly* (January–March 1961); "Japanese Intellectuals Discuss American-Japanese Relations" (Introduction by Robert Scalapino), special issue of *Far Eastern Survey* (October 1960); "Japan Today" (Introduction by Ivan Morris), *New Leader,* Section 2 (November 28, 1960).

torn, politics is sharply polarized. Third, American policy is deeply implicated in internal political issues; this deep involvement intensifies Japan's susceptibility to the polarization of the Cold War.

I

The external signs of the "radicalization" of Japan are quite clear. Since the end of the war there has been a steady increase in the "progressive" vote. Moreover, within this "progressive" vote, the balance has shifted steadily toward the Left. In 1952 and 1953, the Right Socialists within the Japan Socialist Party (JSP) were able to command a bare majority of the total Socialist vote.[2] However, in the elections of autumn 1960, the JSP, which is predominantly "Left" today,[3] alone won 27 per cent of the national vote, while the Right Socialists, who split from the JSP in late 1959 to form their own Democratic Socialist Party (DSP), received only 8.7 per cent.[4] At the present time, the total "progressive" vote (including the Communists, Socialists, and Democratic Socialists) tallies about 39 per cent.

The composition of the vote is equally revealing. The progressives base themselves primarily on the urban youth, the educated classes, and the organized working class. Public-opinion polls and voting surveys show a consistently higher "progres-

[2] In 1952, of the total Socialist vote, which tallied 21.3 per cent of the national vote, the Right accounted for 11.5 per cent and the Left for 9.8 per cent; with this proportion, the Right won 57 seats in the Diet to the Left's 54. In 1953, the total Socialist vote rose to 26 per cent, the Right accounting for about 14 per cent and the Left for about 13; however, this time, the Left, with a slightly smaller vote, won 72 seats to the Right's 66.

[3] The Party has undergone two major Right-Left splits since the end of the war. The 1952 split was finally repaired in 1955, in time for the national elections of that year, but another split took place in late 1959. The most recent split, however, has divided the Right-Wing, the Nishio faction having left the Party to form the Democratic Socialist Party and the Kawakami faction having remained within the Party, with Mr. Kawakami himself, in an evident effort to prevent his followers from joining the Nishio exodus, elected Party Chairman. A good account of these developments will be found in David C. S. Sissons: "Recent Developments in Japan's Socialist Movement" (in two parts), *Far Eastern Survey,* Vol. 29, No. 3 (March 1960), and Vol. 29, No. 6 (June 1960).

[4] Since the Kawakami faction of the JSP shares approximately the same ideological position as the newly-formed DSP, a more accurate picture of the "Right socialist" vote in the country would include the votes cast for the Kawakami faction, which comes to approximately 4.5 per cent of the national vote (about 17 per cent of the JSP vote). This would suggest a little over 13 per cent of the electorate voting a Right-socialist position, and about 22.5 per cent voting Left socialist (the total JSP vote minus the Kawakami votes).

At the time of the Party split in late 1959, the distribution of Diet seats was as follows:

JSP   (Kawakami faction)   128 (35)
DSP   37

After the 1960 elections, the distribution was as follows:

JSP   (Kawakami faction)   145 (28)
DSP   17

sive" vote in urban areas than in the countryside (and also in the larger cities than in the small cities and towns), in lower age groups than in higher age groups, in higher educational levels than in lower, and among workers than among non-workers (also among organized workers than among unorganized workers, and among big-city workers than among small-city and town workers). The conservative vote is characteristically strongest in the countryside, among older age groups, and among farmers and small-business elements.

Many qualifications would have to be placed on the significance of this vote. Certainly not all of it, even for the Left Socialists, is "revolutionary" in character. Much of it is more correctly a "protest" vote that reflects support for the Socialists on particular issues and distrust of the professional conservative politicians. But it certainly shows that the arena of discontent, within which revolutionary ideas have their play, has been growing.

If these trends continue in a straight line for the next decade or so, it is clear that at some point in the foreseeable future, the progressive vote, now almost 40 per cent, should pass the 50 per cent mark, bringing the Socialists to power. Projections of the inner trends lead to similar conclusions. The rural population is declining rapidly, the urban population rising. The level of education continues to rise year by year. The majority of youth entering the voting ranks for the first time vote Left; as they move up the age scale, and as the older age groups retire from the scene, there should be an increasingly "radicalization" of each age group.

The question, then, is whether these trends will in fact continue to their apparent conclusion, or whether there might not be other forces or new developments in the making that could cut them short. It often happens that a protest movement waxes at the very moment the conditions that brought it into being disappear. This, I suspect, may very well be what is happening in Japan today. In a more general way, the question is: How much revolutionary discontent can a modern industrial society accommodate and under what conditions? In early 1946, a Cabinet Minister, scheduled to be purged within a few days, offered me the following prediction. "We will become, I think, a country like France or Italy. Our Left will go to one-fourth or even one-third of the population. As long as it remains at that level, I think we shall be able to live with it, just as France and Italy can." "And if it goes beyond?" I asked. "That," he said "is what I don't know." Fifteen years later, Japan has reached the Minister's peril point, the so-called "one-third barrier," as the Socialists themselves characterize it. Whether we judge it to have penetrated significantly beyond depends upon how we evaluate the Right-Socialist vote, which includes the 8.7 per cent who voted for the DSP as well as the 4.5 per cent who voted for the Right-Wing Kawakami faction of the JSP.[5] The suspicion that the "one-third barrier" may be a natural limit has haunted the Socialists for some time, and it underlies the debates between Right and Left over whether the Party is to be a "class party," a "mass party," or a "people's" party, that is, capable of appealing to elements outside of the working class. In the perennial debates over this issue, the experiences of European Socialist

[5] In the 1960 elections, the "progressive vote," which tallied 38.8 per cent, was distributed as follows:

parties, such as the British Labour Party and the German Social-Democratic Party, weigh heavily in the minds of the moderates. The most recent version of this dispute revolves around the concept, most strongly identified with the new General Secretary, Mr. Eda Saburo, the successor to the assassinated Mr. Asanuma, of the "structural revolution." Although the term has been taken from some debates within the Italian Communist Party—which makes it more palatable to the extreme Left—it seems to represent a search for a pragmatic, nuanceé responsible opposition to replace the negative politics of all-out opposition. It is a politics of "continuing the dialogue." The party may not be able to hold to this policy, under pressure from its own left, but it is a significant experiment.

II

Whatever the ultimate fate of this experiment, Japanese politics today remains sharply polarized. The gap between Right and Left is deep and principled, and the area of consensus is extremely limited. As in any country where politics is so ideological, compromise is difficult, and all issues tend to take on a total character. Unions strike for higher wages with the slogans of "Down with the Government," "Yankees Go Home," "Protect the Constitution," "Recognize Communist China," "Hands Off Cuba," and "Reject the Japanese-American Security Treaty." Whatever the starting point of the protest—higher prices, the encroachment of American bases on farmland, or the building of experimental rocket bases—it quickly trips off the same range of issues, as if they formed a seamless web. No issue stands alone, to be dealt with piecemeal and *ad hoc,* but is part of a matrix of issues, interdependent and mutually reinforcing. Each "struggle," then, as the Japanese progressives term it, quickly becomes generalized into a major confrontation of very much the same elements: intellectuals, students, and unionists on the one side, and whatever com-

Party (and Faction)		% of national vote
JSP		27.2
Left factions *	22.7	
Kawakami faction	4.5	⎤ 13.2 "right
DSP	8.7	⎦ socialists"
Japan Communist Party		2.9
TOTAL	38.8	

* Including the Suzuki, Nomizo, Wada, Rōnō, and Matsumoto factions, plus a small number of uncommitted Diet members.

If the DSP vote is considered firmly part of the progressive vote, then the progressives have indeed gone well beyond one-third. However, if the DSP vote is considered largely a "centrist" vote, then the "progressive" vote falls to 30.1 per cent. If, in addition, we consider the 4.5 per cent of the votes cast for Kawakami-faction candidates as, by and large, also "centrist," then the hard-core "progressive" votes—of Left Socialists and Communists—falls to 25.6 per cent, and the "Right-Socialist" vote (for the DSP and the Kawakami faction) rises to 13.2 per cent. This figure shows a remarkable stability for the Right-Socialist sentiment in the country: In 1952, it was about 12 per cent; in 1953 and 1955, about 14 per cent. The big growth in the Socialist vote has been on the Left, from 10 per cent in 1952 to about 23 per cent in 1960.

bination of status quo forces happens to emerge on the other side. Peasant demonstrations against, say, the extension of American airbase runways or the installation of Japanese rocket-testing bases are often joined by students—not always to the peasants' liking, it may be added. Striking workers find themselves joined by student pickets, or even by other "progressive" elements, such as intellectuals, "defenders of peace," and "defenders of the Constitution," offering physical, financial, and moral support. Similarly, the May–June 1960 demonstrations began with the students but were soon joined by unionists and intellectuals.

This quality of all-out, uncompromising struggle is the most disturbing feature of the political climate of Japan today. "If you think the dialogue between Japan and America is in danger," one of Japan's leading public figures recently said to me, "let me tell you that the dialogue between Left and Right here in Japan is in even more danger. It is becoming harder every day to bring them into the same room, much less to have a real discussion." Therefore, although the normal procedures of parliamentary government prevail in the great bulk of ordinary matters, they increasingly are being abandoned when the great issues, over which public opinion divides sharply, come up. The tactics of "struggle," of "direct action," and of extra-parliamentary pressure begin to replace those of negotiation, compromise, and discussion. Not only is the work of the Diet seriously impeded, but the refusal to accept its authority and the resort to mass pressure and violent parliamentary filibustering bring the institution of parliamentary democracy itself into disrepute.

There are no doubt many people, worried by this growing polarization of national politics, who would favor a politics of the center. But their continuing failure is itself a mark of the profundity of the polarization. The main attempt, the Socialist-Democratic coalition governments of 1947–48, first under Socialist Katayama and then under conservative Democrat Ashida, collapsed with such an éclat as to bring the very notion of a centralist government into disrepute. In the elections that followed immediately, in 1949, the Communists went from their normal 3 per cent to 10 per cent of the national vote and 35 seats in the Diet.[6] Since then there has been, particularly on the Left, a steady weakening of the moderate forces, if not absolutely, then at least relatively. In five years, the organized Right Socialists have declined from a high point of about 14 per cent of the national vote (a slight majority of the combined Socialist vote of 27 per cent) and 66 members of the Diet in 1955, to under 9 per cent of the national vote (as against over 27 per cent [7] for the Left Socialists) and only 17 seats in 1960. On the conservative side, the factions favorable to a politics of the center have so far been constrained by the requirements of party unity.

What we find, therefore, is that the mainstream of Japan is divided sharply into two social-political combinations: the progressives, based largely on organized

[6] But in the following elections in 1952, the Communist vote plummeted once again to 2.7 per cent with no seats in the Diet. It is clear that a great part of the Left-Socialist vote, discontented with the politics of coalition, went to the Communists in 1949 and returned "home" when the danger of coalition was over.

[7] See the qualification to this argument in footnote 5, pp. 94–95.

workers, intellectuals,[8] and students, and the conservatives, based largely on business-men, the middle classes, and the peasantry.

Many observers would add a third, the ultra-Right, but I, for the present time, see it on the periphery, rather than in the center. The traditional sources of Right-Wing strength—the military and peasant discontent, especially as it was refracted through the Army—no longer exist. The virulent ultra-nationalism which fed it has been, as well, too thoroughly discredited as a comprehensive ideology; the patriotic component, even in its extreme form, has been, to a large extent, absorbed by the neo-nationalism of the progressives. In the light of Japanese history it would be foolhardy to argue that the ultra-Right presents no menace at all, but this is still on the margins of society. The crackpots and toughs of the ultra-Right can create trouble through direct action and terrorism, and they can create a mood of general willingness to resort to violence and extra-parliamentary methods. The unleashing of terrorism on the Right can also stimulate a reactive terrorism and violence on the Left, a cycle already visible during the May-June riots. So far, however, a large, moderate public, remembering the terrorism of the late '30's all too well, has reacted so strongly against violence, whether of the Left or of the Right, that this cycle has not yet been able to run a full course.[9] What is much more serious for the time being is that the presence of an ultra-Right, however insignificant, stirs historical memories, still very much alive, which may very well interfere with the normalization of Japanese politics. A Left that sees ultra-Rightism behind every conservative move is much less inclined to compromise and accept the adjustive mechanisms of parliamen-tary democracy than one that takes conservative measures at face value and opposes them on their inherent merits. I am not unmindful of the fact that under certain conditions a genuine revival of an ultra-Right, although certainly not of the massive proportions of the prewar period, is conceivable. But this is not Japan's immediate problem.

The social-political combinations I have suggested also require certain qualifica-tions as well as, perhaps, a more dynamic estimate of the potential of each group. Not all workers, nor even all organized workers, support the progressive side. Moreover, although the peasantry, transformed by the American land reforms and buoyed up both by a continuing high level of prosperity and a stable improvement of its economic and political position, in relation to the urban sector, is certainly in no revolutionary mood, one can conceive of many conditions in which this might change. For the moment, however, the peasantry gives its main support to the con-servatives, and the government and the conservatives, in their turn, cultivate it carefully by devoted attention to its problems.

[8] By this term, I would include—following a recent suggestion by Professor T. Takahashi of Tokyo University—the "minor intellectuals"—school teachers, higher technicians, higher civil servants, and white-collar workers.

[9] The sharp decline of the Communist vote in 1952 resulted, at least in part, from strong public revulsion against the Party's "fire-bottle" tactics of the early part of the year. Since that time, the Party has carried on a systematic campaign to transform itself into a "peaceful" and "lovable" Party.

III

It seems to me useful to see the modern forms of protest and alienation in Japan as deriving from four principal strata of national experience. The first of these is the "reactive nationalism"—to use Rostow's useful term—that lay at the heart of much of the Meiji Restoration movement. The need to "prove" herself to and against the West, the struggle for recognition and equality, the constant tension of tradition and modernity, the search for a stable identity capable of synthesizing the conflicting elements, are problems essentially similar to those of the new states today. The second is the class-conflict stage of modern industrial society, classically described by Engels in his *Conditions of the Working Classes in England in 1844*. With the maturing industrialization of Japan and the formation of a modern working class, the same kinds of revolutionary protest developed as in Western Europe and the United States of, say, the 1930's. The third element derives from the humiliation of Japan's defeat and the complete destruction of the authority of the old order. The consequence has been a deep secular movement, strongly reminiscent of the tensions of the Meiji Era, to restore national self-respect and self-direction—what a colleague and I have elsewhere called "the search for identity." [10] Therefore, although Japan was herself a powerful and ruthless empire, it has been possible for many Japanese to indulge themselves in an orgy of self-pity as victims of imperialism, as a colonial or "semi-colonial" dependent people struggling for independence and liberation. The fourth layer is typical modern discontent with mass society, protest against aimlessness, rootlessness, vulgarity, commercialism, declining standards, and boredom.

One would expect that such diverse layers would normally have their own different style and direction. Before the war, for example, the class-struggle sentiment was strongly anti-nationalist, and the nationalist sentiment normally went to the support of the militarists. Today, however, we find all these layers strongly intertwined and reinforcing each other. The postwar socialist movement has fallen heir to a nationalist resurgence, with which it cannot always be entirely at ease, particularly in the case of the prewar leaders. To be sure there is the rationalization that nationalism is "progressive" and "revolutionary" in the period of struggle for national independence, but a Suzuki Mōsaburo cannot intone the slogans of "racial" or "national unity" with the same conviction as an old-style fire-eating nationalist of prewar days. The intellectual's contempt for the "mambo-boy," which he may formulate in terms of "American influence" or of "capitalist decadence," echoes the prewar ultra-nationalist's complaints and the late Meiji "Japanist" laments that Japan is "losing her soul." And we can surely detect the echo of the *samurai* contempt for the merchant classes and private egotism in the intellectual's anti-capitalism and anti-commercialism.

Two situations bring the different elements together: first, the complete destruc-

[10] J. W. Bennett, H. Passin, R. McKnight, *In Search of Identity* (Minneapolis: University of Minnesota Press, 1958).

tion of the prestige and moral authority of the old order—of the military, the war leaders, the weak and corrupt politicians, the compliant businessmen, the police, and the official ideologists; second, the continuing presence of the United States, which provides a convenient focus for the polarization of all discontent.

We find, therefore, that the modern protest in Japan has a dual character: In part it is similar to types of protest well known in the Western advanced countries—anti-capitalism, the workers' struggle, anti-traditionalism, liberalism, etc., from an early phase, and the tensions of the mass society at a later stage; in part it has the tone of an under-developed country—assertive nationalism and occasionally even racialism, the feeling of a struggle for "true" national independence, and great hyper-sensitivity.

IV

Before we examine the historical stratigraphy of protest in Japan, let us look at the problem from a slightly different angle. Every protest movement, whether it develops into a full revolutionary movement or not, is a protest against a particular status quo. This status quo includes the dominant social consensus, the ruling political coalition, and the dominant ideology. In a country like Japan, we would also have to add the prevailing balance of modernity and tradition. Each combination, each formula, as it were, includes some forces and excludes others, represents some and excludes others, satisfies some and arouses protest in others. It will be useful to identify, in a general way, just what combination a particular form of protest, rebelliousness, or revolutionary mood is directed against.

Modern Japan's first coalition of triumphant junior *samurai* and court nobles started out with several enormous advantages: the *élan* of revolutionary victory and powerful support of the legitimacy conferred upon it by the Imperial Throne. Yet it quickly evoked a protest from two sides. The conservative *samurai* protest, symbolized by Saigo Takamori, against over-Westernization and insufficient nationalism, was finally subdued only by large-scale military action. On the other hand, the excluded *samurai* and the small rural industrialists and landlords, who had no share in the new government, mounted a protest movement around the slogans of "people's rights" (*minken*) and "representative government" that eventually forced a reluctant regime to adopt a constitution and to establish a representative assembly. It was, to be sure, a strictly controlled system, and the autocratic oligarchy still held the power cards, but it was, nevertheless, the entering wedge for an evolution not anticipated by the Meiji leaders.

The new power balance of the oligarchy, as the center of power, and the military (a potential competitor), in the wings, still only gave minimal concessions to the upper-class rural and urban elements represented by the political parties. It certainly gave none at all to the mass of the peasantry or to the just-emerging working classes. Yet firm and forehanded as the oligarchy tried to be, it had not reckoned fully with the power of the new forces it had created by modernization and education. The new middle class, businessmen, and educated classes, brought up in the new schools and exposed to a strong dose of Western ideas, were not content to be permanently excluded from a share in the government. Expressing themselves mainly through the political parties, they pushed constantly for an enlargement of the franchise and greater power for the representative as against the autocratic element in the state. Their ultimate goal, if clearly formulated, would have been a fully responsible system of cabinet government, that is, a cabinet formed by the majority party of the elected assembly and responsible to it. Lower-class protest was, of course, firmly repressed.

The end of the First World War found a vastly changed Japan with a new central coalition. For the first time, business was accepted as a full partner with the political parties and the bureaucracy, the heir of the oligarchy of forty years before. But enlarged as this coalition was, it still aroused the bitter and violent protest of both the new progressive element—the working class, which was enfranchised only in 1925, the Westernized liberals, the students, and the intellectuals—and of the conservative traditionalists, now represented primarily by the armed forces. In the struggle, which was a bitter one indeed, the party-business-bureaucracy regime was able to restrain the progressive forces, but with the May 15, 1932 and the February 26, 1936 incidents, it fell before the forces of militant nationalism. From this time on, a new power coalition dominated the Japanese scene, with the military as its center and the support of a fully compliant bureaucracy and a now-chastened business class. It was only defeat in the war that finally destroyed it.

REACTIVE NATIONALISM. It is sometimes forgotten, now that Japan is such an old "new state," that she too began her modern career under the strong fear of Western domination. The earliest Western treaties with Japan imposed humiliating conditions, such as extraterritoriality and tariff control, that were completely thrown off only after Japan had proved that she was "worthy" of equal treatment by defeating China and Russia in war. Therefore, although Japan was never a colony, she shared the same feeling of inferiority toward the West as the colonial countries. A sensitive Japanese could not but feel the disparity between Western power and Japanese weakness. However he might regard his traditional values and institutions as superior, this meant, in an effective sense, inferiority, at least in those matters that enter into the balance-sheet of national strength. It was necessary to overcome this inferiority as quickly as possible and to draw level with the West.

The leading elements of the anti-Tokugawa coalition, the younger *samurai* of the western and southern fiefs, were motivated, therefore, not so much by abstract ideological considerations as by the practical need for Japan to strengthen herself against Western pressure. This meant two things above all: the creation of a strong, efficient, centralized modern-state apparatus and the building of industrial-military power. All the reforms flowed from these two requirements: the ending of feudalism and its class system, industrialization and modern economic methods, a modern conscript army, and a modern educational system. In developing its new institutions,

Japan looked to the West for suitable models. In other words, she had to westernize herself in order to resist the West.

But this creates a dilemma which still remains to plague the Japanese, perhaps as much today as ever before now that Japan has gone through another "colonial" period of Occupation by a foreign power: how to be Western and yet remain Japanese. The problem was already adumbrated as early as the late eighteenth and early nineteenth centuries by the so-called "Dutch scholars" (the students of Western learning through the medium of the Dutch language). Laboriously piecing out their picture of Western power, they arrived at the formula "Western science, but Eastern morals." With suitable modifications for geography, this formula has continued to echo down through the years as each new nation enters the orbit of modernization —in the form of the Indian spirit, or of pan-Arabism, or of the African personality. The extreme alternatives were: to retain the traditional structure intact, but to beef it up with Western arms and power (if it could have been conceived in the late nineteenth century, perhaps giving every *samurai* an atom bomb would have been included) or to replace the traditional system completely by some version of a generic Western society, even to the elimination of the Japanese language by English and the introduction of Christianity. No conceivable balance, therefore, was capable of satisfying all internal opinion. Even the minimal adjustments of the central Meiji leadership brought the conservative *samurai,* as early as the 1870's, into violent protest and finally into the climactic revolt of Saigo Takamori, which required the full military weight of the new regime to be put down.

How fragile any existing balance was may be seen in the rapid alternations of Westernization and reaction. Since 1868, Japan has gone through three such cycles. The early "Western fever" of the 1860's and 1870's was followed by the conservative reaction of the late 1880's which continued right down to the First World War. This period saw the formulation of the Meiji Constitution, the Emperor's Rescript on Education, the development of the Emperor myth, and the rise of "Japanism." The new wave of Westernism and liberalism after the First World War was followed in its turn by the victory of ultra-nationalist militarism. And the new Western fever, or perhaps more accurately the "American fever," of the early Occupation period has been followed by a strong nationalist reaction, this time under the leadership of the left and the "progressive" forces.

THE WORKING CLASS [11] AND MODERN INDUSTRIAL SOCIETY. *The Left.* The rapid industrialization of Japan created both a working class and its typical discontents. It also created a powerful tradition of working-class alienation from "the system." In spite of certain unique elements arising from special historical conditions and Japan's cultural background, the essential picture is familiar to us from the experi-

---

[11] For a good account of the labor movement, the reader is directed to the writings of Solomon Levine, particularly his *Industrial Relations in Postwar Japan* (Urbana: University of Illinois Press, 1958); James Abegglen, particularly his *The Japanese Factory* (Glencoe: The Free Press, 1958); and Benjamin Martin.

ence of the working class in the West. The Japanese working class, torn from the sustaining warmth of the organic peasant communities of the countryside, was severely exploited by a particularly arrogant and narrow-minded management, well aware of the trade advantages of a low-paid labor force in a modern industrial economy. From their very first appearance on the scene, the workers were kept under strict control, either by paternalism or outright repression.

Moreover, the working class was politically disenfranchised for the first sixty years of the New Japan. Its acceptance into full citizenship in political society has been a grudging process. The liberal Kato-Shidehara Cabinet enacted full manhood suffrage, free of tax qualifications, in 1925. Characteristically it balanced this liberal measure by immediately passing a strengthened Peace Preservation Law to prevent the "overthrow of the Emperor system" and of the system of private property.

The workers' movements, therefore, found themselves, from the very start, ranged against the status quo, and anti-status quo ideologies, from anarchism to socialism and even Christian socialism. These movements made their appearance as early as the beginning of the twentieth century.[12] When the labor movement began to reveal its modern shape after the First World War, neither of the two central power coalitions of the 1920's and 1930's—the businessman-bureaucrat-politician combination of the early period and the military-bureaucrat combination of the end of the period—could accommodate it. The working-class movement, therefore, particularly after the First World War, could not help but be anti-status quo and revolutionary. The Peace Preservation Law, thought control, and the growing suppression of radicalism, liberalism, and nonconformism drove it further to the Left. Although the repression was largely effective, particularly in the late 1930's, once it was lifted after the war by the American Occupation, the power of this tradition became apparent immediately. The postwar leadership and ideologies brought to the fore were those most strongly opposed to the prewar regime, which meant Leftists, socialists, and Marxists. From that time on, a vastly expanded labor movement has maintained this strong Leftist and class-struggle bias, with its corollary orientation toward political, rather than purely economic, action.

To some extent the rigors of control and repression were moderated by the projection of traditional paternalistic concepts into modern industry.[13] But this has always been a two-edged sword. Insofar as this paternalism gave genuine benefits, particularly to workers of limited horizons, fresh from rural backgrounds, working in small enterprises, it did create a version of the happy family working harmoniously for the common interest. But once these three essential conditions no longer obtain, the system of paternalism becomes irksome to the workers, a further restraint on their full development. As the benefits, such as sick care, job guarantees, unemployment insurance, pensions, etc., become increasingly available through the imper-

[12] See Cecil Uehara, *Leftwing Social Movements in Japan. An Annotated Bibliography* (Tokyo: Tuttle, 1959).

[13] A good account of the institutions of paternalism may be found in several articles by Iwao Ishino and John Bennett as well as in Levine, *op. cit.,* and Abegglen, *op. cit.,* and Bennett and Ishino, *The Social Anthropology of Paternalism in Japan* (Minneapolis: University of Minnesota Press—forthcoming).

sonal mechanisms of the state, the need for the traditional system declines. The personal relation of employer and worker in a small enterprise is replaced by the impersonal imperatives of modern large-scale enterprise. At the same time, the rise in the level of education, the growing individuation, and the "demonstration effect" of the way of life of the upper classes, have altered the worker's willingness to continue in the position of a dependent and filial child of a benevolent father-boss.[14]

The high class consciousness, which characterizes much of the organized labor movement, is no new thing in Japan. It was, to be sure, stimulated by the course of the struggle and by the ideological outlook of the leadership. But it was already present in ample measure throughout society as a whole. Although Japan had left feudalism behind, it carried over the strong class bias of Tokugawa society, the disposition to see people in terms of class, and the sense of strong hierarchical barriers between superiors and inferiors. This class consciousness, along with the sense of alienation from the status quo, particularly among the Leftist-dominated organized workers, has led to what I should like to call the "institutionalization" of the trade-union movement as a part of working-class life. The workers have never been particularly responsive to the "proletarian literature" of the 1920's and 1930's, nor to their far less-numerous postwar counterparts, but the unions have succeeded since the war, in creating, to some extent, an area of "working-class culture." A wide range of social and cultural activities of organized workers are channelled through the union movement, in parallel, as it were, to similar activities in the non-trade-union world. The enormous variety of sports associations, singing clubs, women's auxiliaries, outings, and educational activities can take up much of the worker's leisure time. An interesting example is the Workers' Musical League (*Ro-on*), which provides music at low cost to workers. Through its large-scale booking of concert halls, musical organizations, and musicians, it has by now become an important factor in concert management and in musical life. The alliance of Left intellectuals with organized workers, already apparent in the 1920's, is similarly strengthened by union educational activities, which provide an outlet—as well as, sometimes, a source of income—to many professors, writers, and journalists. And, since "power goes with money," even in proletarian organizations, the dependence of the Japan Socialist Party on the financial support of the unions makes it more responsive to political pressures from the Leftist unions than vice versa.

Apart from ideology and politics, one structural feature of the labor movement strongly reinforces its political orientation: its large proportion of government workers. The Japan Teachers' Union, with about 600,000 members, is both the largest union in Japan and one of the most political. In *Sohyo* (General Council of

[14] Benjamin Martin, "Japanese Mining Labor: The Miike Strike," *Far Eastern Survey*, Vol. 30 (February 1961), p. 27, gives an extremely interesting example: "In the years immediately following the war the newly established Miike union was relatively docile and made little trouble for the management. The changing times did not seem to have outwardly affected labor-management relations but the customary arrogance of the mine executives, previously never challenged by the semi-literate miners of the old days, created an increasing sense of irritation among workers who were often as well educated as their superiors."

Trade Unions), the largest and most Left of Japan's labor bodies (claimed membership: about 3,400,000), approximately two-thirds of the members are government workers, either "public employees" or employees of government corporations, such as the national railways and communications. This means that in an important sense their "class enemy" is government itself, rather than private individuals or corporations, so that labor-management issues can only be negotiated with the political authority. Their interest in the composition of government, the orientation of the Cabinet, and the allocation of priorities in the national budget makes them very political.

If I have emphasized the forces making for organized dissent in the working class, I do not wish to leave the impression that this is the whole picture. Certainly the organized working class is largely dominated by a Leftist anti-status quo leadership and ideology. But the organized labor movement, numbering some 6.5 to 7 million members, is only about 25 per cent of the total non-agricultural labor force of over 26 millions. Moreover, the most Leftist of the unions, *Sohyo,* constitutes slightly less than half of the total union membership, and not all of this can be counted upon as absolutely obedient to the initiatives of the leadership. The leadership of the rival federation, the *Zenro,* along with the smaller associated *Sodomei,* is much more moderate.

The Right. But there was, in the interwar years, a powerful Rightist dissent from the liberal capitalist version of industrial society as well. For the fanatic partisans of the "Showa Restoration," intent on a new version of "Western science and Eastern morals," the balance of tradition and modernity was tilted the wrong way. The true national polity (*kokutai*) they wished to establish was not conceivable in the corruption, divisiveness, and egotism of the existing order. Their targets, therefore, became the corrupt political parties, with their unseemly squabbling, partisan spirit, bribery, and indifference to the national interest; the selfish capitalists, who had already earned their undying hatred by a greater concern for profits and low taxes than for the needs of the military; liberalism; Western influence; and internationalism. The military contempt for capitalism was reinforced by an important structural feature of the Japanese army. The majority of recruits were from the peasantry, and many of the junior officers were themselves of peasant or small-landowner stock. The normal conservative peasant distrust of the corrupt Westernized cities was exacerbated by the agrarian depression. Since the peasants had virtually no other channels or protest, it was the junior officers, extremely sensitive to the problems of the countryside and the worries of their troops, who undertook to express them.

Lt. Colonel Aizawa Saburo, for example, on trial for the murder in 1935 of General Nagata, chief of the Military Affairs Bureau, explained his motive as follows: "When I thought of these things (the sad fate of the country, the impoverishment of the peasants, the official scandals, and the weakness of foreign policy), I could not merely pass the time giving military training to my regiment." The junior officer Goto Akinori explained his part in the May 15, 1932, incident in similar terms:

. . . The impoverishment of the agricultural villages is the cause of grave concern for thoughtful persons. It is extremely dangerous that while soldiers from the villages expose themselves to death at the front they should have to worry about their starving families . . . In utter disregard of the poverty-stricken farmers the fabulously rich continue their pursuit of private gain. Meanwhile the children of the farmers are so poor they must go to school in the morning without breakfast . . . To let a day go by without doing something is to endanger the army one day longer, was my thought. . . .

Thus, while the working-class and liberal protest was coming increasingly under Marxist, socialist, and liberal influence, the Rightist anti-capitalist protest was finding its ideologists in Kita Ikki, Gondo Seikyo, and Okawa Shumei, with their notions of "socialism under the Emperor," "agrarian socialism," and "revolutionary imperial socialism." It is, therefore, not surprising that the militarist and ultra-nationalist terrorists of the 1930's invariably numbered the representatives of the "plutocracy" among their victims, along with the politicians and the other "evil advisers" who were "misleading the Emperor."

DEFEAT AND OCCUPATION. Japan's crushing defeat in the war has been as traumatic an experience as the intrusion of the West in the late nineteenth century, and it has re-opened many of the same dilemmas, however modern their dress. The difference is that now the balance of forces has changed. The authority and legitimacy of the old order were destroyed, and the hitherto suppressed progressive forces were released into the mainstream of national life.

The collapse of the old order implicated not only the military and the ultra-nationalists, but everything that appeared to be associated with it: the older generation, the compliant politicians and businessmen, the family system, and "Japanese tradition" itself.[15] The result was, in the words of Takeyama Michio, that "the Japanese jumped to the conclusion that historic Japan in its entirety was wrong, and there followed a period of bitter self-rejection and self-indictment."[16] Moreover, however bad the old system may have been, it had given meaning and purpose to life, a way of seeing the world, and an opportunity for service and sacrifice to a larger cause. The search for a new ideology and a new synthesis inevitably brought many people to Marxism, which had already been a powerful force among the progressives of the '20's and the '30's, since it was the only fully elaborated system of thought that was both comprehensive and not discredited by the past. It appealed to the purely intellectual need for systematic understanding, and it appealed to the need for purpose and self-sacrifice. Western liberalism was too tepid, neither comprehensive nor demanding enough; and later, as we shall see, it was compromised by its association with "capitalism" and with the United States. For many people searching for something pure, uncontaminated by the war and the hated past, the Communists had a special appeal; as the principal victims and opponents of the militarists, they were virtually the only uncompromised political

[15] Indicative of this outlook is the title of a study by one of Japan's leading sociologists, Professor Kawashima Takeyoshi, *The Family System as Ideology.*
[16] Takeyama Michio, "Tradition and Japanese Youth," *Japan Quarterly* (July–September 1960).

force, if only for the reason that all of their leaders were either in jail or in exile. Tsurumi Shunsuke, a leading young intellectual, himself American-educated, has explained this very brilliantly in a fascinating account of why he supports the Japan Communist Party even though he is not a Marxist. The recent revival of religious sects, which have mushroomed all over Japan, undoubtedly represents another form of search for synthesis. Significantly the religious resurgence has not gone into the traditional channels of Shintoism, Buddhism, or even Christianity, but into deviant and newly established messianic religions.

At the same time that the discredited conservative forces were being held back by purges and the disfavor of the Occupation, the progressive forces were being given their head. A tremendous outburst of "democratic" energies, along with the continuing American reforms, touched almost every sector of Japanese life. In the first period of the Occupation, this force was strongly identified with the United States, and the ensuing Americanization of Japan began to take on epidemic proportions. But the early enthusiasm, particularly of the intellectuals, soon gave way to an inevitable reaction. What was unfortunate was that this wholly expectable nationalist reaction coincided with an apparently new direction in American policy, to some extent a result of the cold war. The liberals felt deeply betrayed; America's reactionary "reverse course," as they termed it, was forcing them to defend the American reforms not only against the conservatives, but against the Americans themselves.

Another important development has been the emergence of a powerful streak of nihilism, particularly among the youth. The rapid changes, the confusions, the "transvaluation of values," and the discrediting of the old authority without its replacement by a new, have created what the Japanese themselves refer to as a "spiritual void." Nor is this entirely new. Nihilism has long had a deep appeal to modern Japanese, as we can see in the undiminished popularity of Dostoevsky,[17] for example, or in such important Japanese novelists as Akutagawa Ryunosuke and Dazai Osamu. Characteristically, it has been non-political and anti-traditional, asserting the priority of individual judgment over social convention and judgment. Therefore, eroticism, both as a pure, primary experience and as a form of Sade's criticism of civil society, plays an important role. The *erogro* (erotic and grotesque) literature of the 1920's has been succeeded by the postwar eroticism and hedonism of Tamura Taijiro, whose *Nikutai no Mon* (*The Gates of the Flesh*) opened the movement, and Ishihara Shinichiro, its greatest hero. Ishihara's *Taiyozoku* (*Tribe of the Sun*), which rapidly became a runaway best-seller, gave the movement its form and even its name. Japan's *taiyozoku* now take their place as the counterpart of the angry young men, the *stilyagi,* and the beatniks of other countries.

But although it considers itself non-political, its anti-conventional hedonism cannot fail to be implicitly political. As an all-out rejection of "the system," it

[17] Russian literature has had, in some ways, a greater appeal to modern Japanese intellectuals than that of any other country. Already in the early and middle Meiji period, the great Russians of the nineteenth century were well known, and the nihilism of Vera Zasulich, Bakunin, and Dostoievsky was as popular as the idealistic anarchism of Kropotkin and Tolstoy.

implies its own politics of dissent against tradition, custom, authority, political leadership, and the status quo. Nor should this be too surprising when we reflect that England's angry young men are probably well represented in the unilateralist movement and that America's beatniks once seemed to find in Fidel Castro their "existentialist hero." The nihilism will, therefore, lead either to an unresolved despair, which will continuously corrode authority, or to the search for a resolution which, under present conditions, is most likely to mean the acceptance of a "revolutionary" —that is, an anti-status quo—authority. This streak is found among the leaders of the student Zengakuren, particularly among those who are so revolutionary that they cannot even accept the authority of the Japanese Communist Party and must regard the Soviet Union and Communist China as already too reactionary for them.[18]

The complicating element in the postwar situation is the position of the United States. The United States has managed, by its massive presence, to become bound up with the profoundest divisions within the country on both internal and external questions. It is identified with the anti-progressive side on virtually all the important and symbolic issues in the country: rearmament, the revival of the power of the military, the restoration of the police power, the revision of the Constitution, the strengthening of the conservative elements, the reversal of the Occupation reforms, and the absence of formal diplomatic relations with Communist China. Its presence is a continuing affront to a reviving nationalist sentiment. If we were to formulate the standard view of the Japanese progressives, it would run somewhat as follows: "fascist and imperialist United States, the home of monopoly capitalism, is supporting Japan's conservatives, backed by Japan's own monopoly capitalists, in power in order to keep the country in a state of economic and political dependence so that she can continue to use the military bases as a springboard for aggression." The maintenance of American bases, the Japanese-American Security Treaty, and continued economic dependence upon the United States reinstate deep memories of the "unequal treaties" of Meiji times. In the words of Asanuma Inejiro, the recently-assassinated General Secretary of the Japan Socialist Party, ". . . we must struggle for peace and independence, and carry on the struggle for the return of Okinawa to Japan, the struggle for restoration of normal relations with Communist China and the struggle against nuclear bombs. We must combine all these struggles into one struggle for revision of the unequal Security Pact and connect this struggle with the struggle for the people's welfare." [19]

The status quo, then, against which Japanese discontent directs itself, is, symbolically, the Japanese-American alliance. This may, I think, explain something about the intensity of the May-June demonstrations against the Security Treaty, as well as about the peculiar intensity of Japanese feelings on the recognition of Communist China, now one of the central issues in Japanese politics. For many, China

[18] See the extremely illuminating article by Lewis Feuer, "A Talk with Zengakuren," *The New Leader* (May 1, 1961).
[19] Preface to "Decisions at the Regular Convention of the Japan Socialist Party, 1957"; quoted in Nakamura Kikuo, "Party Politics," *New Leader*, Section 2 [Supplement entitled "Japan Today"] (November 28, 1960).

has become the symbol of "true national independence" and of Japan's right to self-direction. Since America has been the principal obstacle to the restoration of normal relations, the assertion of friendship to China offers the added thrill of thumbing one's nose at America. That successive conservative governments, regularly re-elected by almost two-thirds of the electorate, continue a policy of non-recognition is put down to mere supine obedience to America. The result is that the "China Boom," which swept the country from 1953 onwards, has taken on the character of an emotional crusade, and Japanese visitors to the mainland now outnumber those of any other nationality. Not all, even among the progressives, would be prepared to agree with the extreme proposition, frequently formulated by Japanese visitors to China in joint statements with their Chinese hosts, that "the United States is the common enemy of the Chinese and the Japanese people," but the logic of it is hard to resist.

In the new version of the old game of "how can I be both Japanese and Western," the cards are cut in a different way. Before the war, to be anti-traditional meant to be somehow "un-Japanese." But today, thanks to the United States and to the contempt for the old order, one can be both anti-traditional and 100-per cent Japanese. It is the conservatives, America's allies, who have to prove that they are not the "catspaw of foreign imperialism"—even if only "objectively." Raymond Aron has somewhere commented on the "Americanized Japanese who detest their American teachers."

THE "MASS SOCIETY." Let us now return to the question of whether the political trend will continue long enough to bring the progressives into office. Sixteen years after the end of the war, the kind of internal situation assumed by this extrapolation probably can be accepted no longer. Japan's remarkable sustained rate of economic growth,[20] perhaps the highest in the world, has brought her a long way into the era of mass abundance, mass society, and mass culture. It is true that the Japanese economy still remains extremely vulnerable, but so far the continuing prosperity has brought about far-reaching changes. The standard of living has been rising continuously, the surplus rural population is being absorbed so rapidly that a farm and small-town labor shortage is beginning to make its appearance, agricultural production has been increasing despite the predictions of experts that it was impossible, the wage gap between large and small enterprise has been narrowing, and—*mirabile dictu*—even mechanization has been growing on the tiny farms experts adjudged too small for mechanization.[21] The outward consequences of these changes are all too evident. My own personal impression on visiting Japan early in 1960, after an absence of some two and a half years, was that everybody I knew had gained one

[20] Between 1947 and 1952 the average annual growth rate was 11.5 per cent; between 1953 and 1959, 8.3 per cent. From April 1959 to March 1960, the growth rate reached the extraordinary figure of 17 per cent, while mining and manufacturing production increased 29 per cent over fiscal year 1958.

[21] To cite two brief examples: between 1933 and 1958, the number of hand tractors in use went up from 1,000 to 337,800 and threshing machines from 67,000 to 2,343,400. The current figures would undoubtedly show another important increase. See Fukushima Yoichi, "Agricultural Technology," *Japan Quarterly* (July–September 1960).

inch in girth. The rate of ownership of the standard gadgets of the mass consumption society—television, radio, washing machines, refrigerators, transistor radios, cameras, modern kitchen equipment—now compares favorably with that of Western Europe. Automobile ownership has already reached the middle classes solidly, and there seems no reason to doubt that within a measurable period it will be as common among the working classes as in Western Europe. In short, Japan is now beginning to savor the dubious blessings of advanced industrial society in its high-consumption phase: economic abundance and the insoluble traffic jams of Ginza and Marunouchi; universal literacy along with soap operas and comic books; air-conditioning and suburbia. It is still too early to assess all of the consequences of these structural changes: the *embourgeoisement* of the working classes, particularly of the organized workers; the growth of the *sarariman* (salaryman), Japan's version of the middle class salariate and white-collar element; the absolute decline of the labor force in the primary production sectors (farming, fishery, and forestry), along with stability in the secondary sectors (manufacturing) and a vast increase in the tertiary sectors; a general narrowing of the gap in outlook and standards among the classes; the terrible overcrowding of the cities; a growing shift in agriculture to mechanization and capital-intensive production (dairying, poultry, meat, and specialty crops).

There are other changes in the offing whose effects we are not yet in a position to estimate. Educated unemployment, for example, has been an endemic feature of Japanese life since the 1920's. Although the supply-demand situation has fluctuated, Japanese university graduates retain a sharp memory of the fear of joblessness. The Occupation-sponsored reform of the educational system, which raised the university population almost ten times to its present high of over 700,000 students, only intensified the insecurity, coming as it did in the midst of the postwar economic confusion. But the last few years have seen a radical change; in some categories, available jobs now far exceed the number of candidates. What will happen to student radicalism after several years without fear of unemployment? And what happens to the radical student, even today, we might ask, once he has found a job with a steady future and with some scope for growth? In some cases there is a rapid subsidance of radical feelings, perhaps even a growing identification with the "establishment"; in others, a new form of dissatisfaction, not unknown in the West, a groping for meaning, adventure, and purpose. The generation of students educated entirely in the schools reformed by the American Occupation is just beginning to enter the universities. They come with a completely different background and outlook from the *après-guerre* students who have until now dominated the scene. With no personal experience of the war, free of the traditional ethics of subservience and self-effacement, encouraged to express their individuality, they are bound to be different from the embittered, disillusioned postwar students who could still their self-doubts, self-hatred, and insecurity only through radicalism and Marxism. Many of them may still see in Marxism the synthesis of their needs for meaning, purpose, and self-definition; others may start out on new paths in their new, affluent society. Suffice it to say, in some respect recent Western experience will be a better guide to what is happening than the immediate Japanese past.

The observer cannot fail to be struck by the enormous gap between these new developments—the "objective situation," as the socialists would call it—and the awareness of it, particularly on the Left. The Leftist slogans, which seem much more appropriate to the depressed 1930's, or even, in certain ways, to the extreme nationalist phase of some colonial movement, strike one as strangely out of tune with the developing reality. Many Leftists have had the greatest difficulty in accepting the evidence of growth before their very eyes. As late as five years ago, a leading academic economist offered the challenging thesis that Japan needed a crash program to achieve a sustained growth of 4 per cent; that very year, the actual growth rate was over 8 per cent. Japan's most distinguished and senior agricultural economist recently acknowledged to me that even in his wildest moments he could not have anticipated the changes. "In fact," he said, "I can still hardly believe them. If anybody tells you that five years ago he could have predicted this, then he is lying." The implications of the new situation are just beginning to percolate into the consciousness of Japanese intellectual life. Increasingly we find discussions of the "new middle class," or even of the "new intellectuals"; and the problem of rei-ja (the Japanese pronunciation of the word "leisure"—a new and very popular word in the Japanese vocabulary) has become a major issue in the mass media, eliciting much the same range of comments on mass society and mass culture that we are so familiar with in Europe and America. In a sense, what we are seeing is a race between the trend line, based upon an earlier set of conditions, and the new situation: Which will arrive first, the projection of the trend to 50 per cent plus one, or a full awareness of the new situation?

III

Revolutionary Protest Movements in Underdeveloped Areas

III

5

Fidel Castro and Latin America

George I. Blanksten

An old Latin American political axiom has it that "every 'ism' is a somebody-ism." Putting the matter that way of course exaggerates the situation. Nevertheless, "somebody-ist" movements abound in Latin America. Paraguay has its *franquismo*, supported by the admirers of General Rafael Franco;[1] Brazil had its *querimismo*;[2] Ecuador its *velasquismo*, based on the followers of President José María Velasco Ibarra; Uruguay its *batllismo*, founded by President José Batlle y Ordóñez; and Argentina its *peronismo*. Cuba today has its *fidelismo*, with which this paper is concerned.

The *curriculum vitae* of *fidelismo* is readily provided. It began in 1947, when Fidel Castro Ruz, then a twenty-one-year old Cuban law student, took part in an invasion of the Dominican Republic in an unsuccessful attempt to overthrow the government of Generalissimo Rafael Leónidas Trujillo Molina. The following year found Fidel Castro in Colombia, where he took part in the *bogotazo*, the tumultuous rioting which began at Bogotá during the Ninth International Conference of American States. In 1952, Dr. Castro, during the course of his legal practice in Cuba, filed a brief with the Court of Constitutional Guarantees asking that body to declare unconstitutional the government of General Fulgencio Batista y Zaldivar, who had resumed power by a *coup d'état* in March of that year. When the court rejected Castro's legal plea, he turned to revolutionary activity against the Batista regime. On July 26, 1953—*fidelismo* is known officially as the 26th of July Movement— Castro led an unsuccessful attack on a military post at Santiago, in eastern Cuba. Imprisoned for this act, he was freed through an amnesty in 1955. He then left Cuba to spend almost two years in exile, principally in Mexico, preparing for his major contest with Batista. In December 1956, Castro and a small band of guerilla invaders landed in eastern Cuba. During the following two years the island was gripped by civil war, with Fidel Castro acquiring legendary stature as the guerilla leader of the rebels. Batista at length fell from power on January 1, 1959. *Fidelismo* then took up the reins of government. The last lines of this *curriculum vitae* remained to be written at the time this paper was prepared.

No doubt, much of *fidelismo* is peculiar to Castro, and much is indigenous to

---

[1] Not connected with Spain's Generalissimo Francisco Franco.
[2] Literally, "we-wantism," a popular abbreviation of the "We want Vargas" movement launched in 1945.

Cuba. Yet, a substantial sector of the movement remains generalizable as a part of the revolution of our time. For the purpose of analysis of *fidelismo* in that context, it is helpful to examine the four major components of the movement. These components—let us call them the keys to *fidelismo*—are the historic political instability of Cuba, the political contrast between metropolitan Havana and the remainder of the island, the domestic, social, and economic changes in Cuba, and problems in the country's relations with the United States.

These keys are discussed below. They are also important to the politics of other Latin American nations and help to place the Castro revolution in context as a hemispheric phenomenon. None of this is intended to deny the totalitarian elements in the particular Cuban revolution—or the close relationship between Castro, Communism, and the Soviet Union. The totalitarian element, in particular, may provide Castroism with organizational means to discourage counterrevolutionary movements or *coups d'états*. Yet, these aspects of the Cuban problem have been much discussed to the neglect of the indigenous factors that helped to create the Castro movement and that help to give *fidelismo* hemispheric-wide appeal. To equate the appeal of Castroism with Communism, or even with totalitarianism, is to make as great a mistake as to ignore the Communist or totalitarian aspects of the present Cuban regime. To understand the indigenous factors, an analysis of their components is necessary. It is to their systematic examination that we now turn. Attention is also extended, where relevant, to these components as they function in the general Latin American context.

I

Cuba's historic political instability stands first among the four major keys to *fidelismo*. Political instability may be regarded as a condition characterized by frequent so-called "revolution" and recurrent dictatorship, much of it short-lived. Far from being peculiar to Cuba, political instability, thus defined, is a general Latin American characteristic. Each of its elements—frequent so-called "revolution" and chronic dictatorship—is worth consideration, from the twin standpoints of Latin America as a whole and Cuba in particular.

The American nations are famous for their "revolutions." Indeed, the Brazilian Emperor Dom Pedro II is said to have remarked, when he visited the Philadelphia Exposition in 1876, that many of the Latin American countries had more revolutions per minute than the machines he saw on display at the exposition. However, few words are more loosely and promiscuously used in the Americas than "revolution." An amazing array of dissimilar and unrelated occurrences go by this name in the Western Hemisphere. The Wars of Independence have been so dubbed, as well as minor changes in government, the promulgation of new constitutions, and political violence of almost any variety. Actually, true revolution—that is, a basic change in the political system or a recasting of the social order—is surprisingly infrequent in

Hispanic America. But "typical revolutions"—changes in government brought about by other than constitutional means, usually not accompanied by fundamental changes in the social or political order—are constantly recurring. Violence, or the threat of it, is often present in such movements. Their frequency is a major Latin American political problem. "Since the turn of the present century," a student of this phenomenon has observed, "the governments of the nations to the south have been overthrown . . . seventy-six times. . . . Revolutions are still the order of the day. . . . Bolivia, for example, has had violent changes of government in 1920, 1930, 1934, 1936, 1937, 1943, 1946, and 1952." [3] Thus far during the twentieth century, on the bare mathematics of the matter, the average Latin American state has experienced four so-called "revolutions."

In this regard, Cuba is fairly typical of Hispanic America. Among the most recent of the states in the area to achieve national independence, Cuba has undergone somewhat more than the average number of "revolutions" since the island's national political career was launched in 1901. A violent uprising against the government of President Tómas Estrada Palma in 1906 brought military intervention by the United States, then acting under the Platt Amendment.[4] After the departure of the "North American" armed forces in 1909, the constitutional order was not again interrupted until General Gerardo Machado assumed the presidency in 1925. In a *coup d'état* three years later, Machado prolonged his period in power and intensified his dictatorship. Two "revolutions" occurred in 1933. The first overthrew Machado and installed Dr. Carlos Manuel de Cespedes as provisional president. The second, led by Batista, then an army sergeant, unseated Cespedes. Batista remained in power until the election of 1944, following which he went into voluntary exile in the United States. In a *coup d'état* in 1952, Batista overthrew the government of President Carlos Prío Socarrás to return to power. And it was this second Batista regime that Castro's "revolution" ousted in 1959. Measured against the general Latin American average, this Cuban record is a little—but not much—more than par for the course.

Involved in the problem of political instability, in addition to the frequency of so-called "revolution," is the phenomenon of recurrent dictatorship. While the situation is continually changing, it is generally true that at any given moment at least a half-dozen Latin American countries are governed by dictatorship, normally military in orientation. The reasons for this are many and deep-seated. Among them is the authoritarian political tradition the Spanish Empire imposed upon its American colonies. Itself historically governed by divine-right monarchy, Spain left a tradition of strong government in the Western Hemisphere. Indeed, this tradition was so marked that many of the nineteenth-century leaders of the movements for Latin

[3] Austin F. Macdonald, *Latin-American Politics and Government,* 2nd ed. (New York: Thomas Y. Crowell Co., 1954), pp. 11–12. See also Russell H. Fitzgibbon, "Revolutions: Western Hemisphere," *The South Atlantic Quarterly,* Vol. 55, No. 3 (July 1956), pp. 263–79; and George I. Blanksten, "Revolutions," in Harold E. Davis (ed.), *Government and Politics in Latin America* (New York: The Ronald Press, 1958), pp. 119–46.
[4] The controversial Platt Amendment is discussed on pp. 128–133, to follow.

American independence believed that monarchy should be retained as the newly independent states' form of government. In conformity with this reasoning, monarchies were in fact attempted in the nineteenth century in Mexico, Brazil, and Haiti. Even those who advocated the establishment of republican systems in Latin America were convinced that they should be strongly authoritarian. In preparing the draft of Bolivia's first constitution, "The Liberator" Simón Bolívar produced an instrument providing for a president with not only lifelong tenure, but also the authority to choose his own successor.

The President of the Republic becomes in our Constitution the sun, which, firm in the center, gives life to the universe [Bolívar wrote]. I have never been an enemy of monarchy, as far as general principles are concerned; on the contrary, I consider monarchies essential for the respectability and well-being of new nations. . . . The new states of America . . . need kings with the name of presidents.[5]

In seeking the keys to *fidelismo,* it is worth emphasizing that Cuba received much more than the average Hispanic-American dose of this Spanish tradition of political authoritarianism. Not only was Cuba one of the first places in the Western Hemisphere where Spanish colonial power was established, but it is also worth remembering that this island was the last place in the Americas to be freed from that power. Christopher Columbus, the celebrated Admiral of the Ocean Sea himself, visited Cuba during his second voyage in 1493. Spanish colonial government was established there shortly after, and remained in the island for four centuries. Cuba's history as a Spanish colony stands in marked contrast to that of, say, Argentina, where the Spanish Viceroyalty of the United Provinces of the La Plata River was not established until 1776, lasting only until the independence movement which began in 1810.[6] Not only did Cuba endure a longer history of Spanish colonial rule than any other American colony, but also the military and authoritarian orientation of that rule was heavier in the island than elsewhere in Hispanic America. During the colonial period, Cuba served as a military and supply base, first for the Spanish conquest and later for the government of the New World. Spain conquered Mexico from Cuba, and moved from the island to other parts of the Americas as well. No other part of Latin America has endured a longer or more heavily military tradition of political authoritarianism than has Cuba.

Since the achievement of Cuban independence, this tradition has been reflected in the recurrence of military dictatorship in the island's government. Among the most celebrated of the country's dictatorships was that presided over from 1925 until 1933 by General Gerardo Machado. His regime has been regarded as "one of the cruelest that Latin America has ever seen. Machado . . . ruthlessly oppressed his opponents, frequently by means of torture and murder. The . . . life of the

---

[5] Quoted in Blanksten, "Caudillismo in Northwestern South America," *The South Atlantic Quarterly,* Vol. 51, No. 4 (October 1952), pp. 498–99.

[6] Also worth contrasting with Cuba were the following colonial vice-royalties, with the dates of both their founding and the beginnings of the successful independence movements: New Spain (Mexico), 1535, 1821; New Castille (Peru), 1542, 1821; and New Granada (Colombia, Ecuador, Venezuela, and Panama), 1717, 1809.

republic was paralyzed." [7] Shortly after the fall of Machado, Sergeant Fulgencio Batista rose to national power, promoting himself to colonel during the process. Although Batista's first period in power, which lasted until 1944, bore many of the characteristics of dictatorship, the regime was mild as compared with Machado's, and a number of constitutional reforms were put into effect. These made possible the election of 1944, which ushered in an eight-year period of civilian constitutional government. During this time the presidency was occupied by Dr. Ramón Grau San Martín (1944–48) and Dr. Carlos Prío Socarrás (1948–52). Batista's second regime (1952–58), unlike his first, was a rigid dictatorship sufficiently ruthless to lead many Cubans to compare it with the Machado period. Castro overthrew this dictatorship. In establishing another, he presided over a continuation of, rather than a departure from, a four-century-old tradition of military authoritarianism. It was this consideration that gave point in 1959 to the widely-told joke to the effect that when the bearded Castro was secretly shaved he turned out to be Batista.

Cuba's historic political instability thus stands as a first key to *fidelismo*. A number of the movement's basic characteristics derive from this tradition. The most obvious of these is that *fidelismo*, like a number of previous Cuban regimes, has embraced the continuation of government through dictatorship. Few lists of *fidelista* objectives have assigned significant priority to the restoration of constitutional government in the country. The holding of elections, while mentioned as a possibility early in the Castro regime, eventually lost its place among *fidelista* intentions. The Cuban press, censored by Batista and a number of his predecessors, continued in censorship during the Castro regime. Radio, television, the theater, and other mass-communication media were likewise controlled. While civil and political liberties were not much less curtailed by Castro than by many of the previous governments, neither were the liberties permitted by him in any way significant in contrast to the policies of Machado or of Batista's second regime.

As a military dictatorship, the Castro regime illustrated a curious phase in the evolution of Cuban militarism. Beyond providing a defense system for the community, the Cuban army has long performed domestic political functions. The frequency with which military officers have assumed the presidency of the republic has already been noted. High-ranking army officers have historically been important politicians, and the military influence has provided a species of backdrop for politics. In view of the fact that the significance of militarism in Latin-American politics has long been recognized, it is a curious circumstance that social scientists have only recently begun to turn their attention to this problem. Early studies indicate that the process of political clique-formation among army officers, correlations between military rank and the class systems, and relationships between military rank and political orientation offer potential insight into many aspects of Latin-American politics. In a number of the countries, for example, general officers tend to lead conservative political movements, while a significant radicalism recruits its political leadership from the group of military ranks bounded at the top by colonel and at the bottom by captain. Additional studies of these matters are sorely needed to test

[7] Miguel Jorrín, *Governments of Latin America* (New York: D. Van Nostrand Co., 1953), p. 276.

such hypotheses which are occupying interesting places in the as yet small and pioneering literature on the armed forces of Latin America.[8]

In any case, the story of Machado, Batista, and Castro suggests a curious direction in the evolution of Cuban militarism. Machado's military regime was dominated by general officers who exercized a conservative influence on national politics. Batista was a sergeant at the time of his first uprising in 1933. Securing the aid of junior army officers, his movement effectively liquidated the officer class which had ruled Cuba before and during the Machado regime. Batista's military government differed from his predecessors' in that it was based upon a lower-ranking officer group. The latent political coalition between the large landowners and the military command was markedly weakened in Cuba after 1933. While the first Batista government was of course a military regime, it was a lower-ranking group that exercised political power then than had been the case in earlier governments. After the election of 1944, Batista maintained his contact with the junior army officers. When he made his *coup d'état* in 1952, he confided that "I did it with captains and lieutenants." [9]

As Batista's revolution of 1933 was a military purge, so, too, in a sense, was Castro's revolution. Shortly after Castro came to power in 1959, his firing squads embarked upon a sensationally wholesale program of executing military men who had served Batista's government. Much has been written about these executions. Castro called them, and the trials that preceded most of them, "revolutionary justice." His enemies pointed to the executions as additional evidence of the ruthless dictatorship of *fidelismo*. It may not be amiss to suggest that they constituted a new military purge in a country historically governed by its armed forces. It has been estimated that 557 men were executed by Castro's firing squads during the first few months of 1959. With very few exceptions, these had been soldiers and policemen of the Batista government. Again the question of military rank becomes significant. The overwhelming majority of the executed were junior officers and men holding non-commissioned ranks. Also prominent among the victims were army conscripts who had been assigned to firing squads. Of the 557 executions, the most widely publicized was that of Captain Jesús Sosa Blanco. Among his distinctions was the fact that he was the highest-ranking of the military people put to death at that time. Batista's "captains and lieutenants" were liquidated.

Fidel Castro's popular militia thereupon filled the military vacuum. The basic significance of this pattern of the evolution of Cuban militarism remained unclear at the time this paper was written. There appears to be a perhaps ironic democratization of the military, in the sense that its politically influential center of gravity has moved to progressively lower military ranks. Cuba remained under military rule, to be sure; but the progression from Machado's generals through Batista's junior

[8] See Edwin Lieuwen, *Arms and Politics in Latin America* (New York: Published for the Council on Foreign Relations by Frederick A. Praeger, 1960), *passim;* and Robert J. Alexander, "The Army in Politics," in Davis, *op. cit.,* pp. 147–65.

[9] Stanley R. Ross, "Some Observations on Military Coups in the Caribbean," in A. Curtis Wilgus (ed.), *The Caribbean: Its Political Problems* (Gainesville: University of Florida Press, 1956), pp. 112–13.

officers to Castro's popular militia appears to reflect a broadening of the base of the country's militarism.

Cuba's historic political instability has also been reflected by remarkable difficulty in achieving political institutionalization, and this too throws light on the nature of *fidelismo*. Cuban opposition parties have been in the habit of accusing the groups in power of violating the country's written constitutions. These have indeed been violated, but traditional instability lies at the heart of the problem at least as much as does any personal skulduggery of men in public office. Since independence, Cuba has had two major written constitutions. Neither ever achieved genuine institutionalization. The first, promulgated in 1901, was violated in 1906, 1928, 1933 (twice), 1934, and in 1937. The second, a Batista instrument proclaimed in 1940, not only has been violated at least as often as the first, but also will probably never actually function in Cuba. Theoretically, the Constitution of 1940 provides for a variation of parliamentary government, with the president of the republic functioning as a species of figurehead, while major authority is to be exercised by a prime minister and his cabinet.

Batista found the parliamentary system, foreign to Cuban traditions and practices, to be the answer to a dictator's prayer. Serving as the "figurehead" president under the Constitution of 1940, he pursued the practice of obtaining the prime minister's and cabinet ministers' signed but undated resignations at the time he appointed them to office. When it suited his purposes, President Batista dated the resignations and delivered them to the press. Even during the eight-year constitutional period, from 1944 to 1952, the parliamentary system did not take genuine institutional hold. Because he declared that he expected the prime minister to exercise more power than he would himself, President Ramón Grau San Martín was berated by the Cuban press as a weakling unfit to hold national public office. Throughout the constitutional period, prime ministers generally entertained the political ambition of becoming president, a pattern contrary to the spirit of the parliamentary system. Batista again lived comfortably with his constitution when he returned to power in 1952. Castro's use of the parliamentary idea has been but a minor variation of Batista's. Theoretically, Castro has been prime minister, to be sure, and his presidents, powerless figureheads; but neither prime minister nor president—not to mention a parliament! —has been elected. The record is clear that constitutional government has yet to take root in Cuba, and that the Constitutions of 1901 and 1940 have both failed to establish a viable institutional framework.[10]

Civilian political parties have not had much more success in achieving stable institutionalization on the island. During the first generation of national independence, the Liberal Party enjoyed something of stability, but this was damaged by its support of Machado. The Cuban Revolutionary (*Auténtico*) Party emerged from the revolution of 1933 and endured to support the administrations of Presidents Grau and Prío. Leftist participation has been provided by the Party of the Cuban

[10] See Fitzgibbon, "Constitutional Development in Latin America: A Synthesis," *American Political Science Review*, Vol. 34 (June 1945), pp. 500–522; and William S. Stakes, "The Cuban Parliamentary System in Action, 1940–1947," *Journal of Politics* (April 1949), pp. 335–64.

People and the Communist Party. But civilian political parties, whether of the Right or of the Left, have exhibited a remarkable instability and a chronic incapacity to work with, and otherwise relate to, each other. *Fidelismo* clearly demonstrates this condition of the parties. Numerous attempts have been made to relate civilian political parties to the Castro government but all have failed. This has also been true of the opposition—it is more accurate to say "oppositions"—to Castro. Here too it has been virtually impossible for the parties to join together in a stable fashion in pursuit of a common cause.

Furthermore, the country's political instability has tended to intensify *personalismo* in Cuba and, with it, a popular tendency to respond to charismatic leadership. *Personalismo* may be regarded as the custom of following or opposing a political leader on the basis of his personality rather than on ideological grounds. Many students of Latin American politics have found this to be a widespread tendency in the area. Pierson and Gil, for example, point to "the high value placed on the individual and personal leadership," promoting "a disposition to vote for the man rather than the party or the platform." [11] Another student has said: "From earliest days the Latin Americans . . . have always been more interested in their public men than in their public policies. They have tended to follow colorful leaders, to the subordination of issues. . . . A picturesque demagogue is virtually assured a large following." [12] Expanded *personalismo* has increased the tendency of charismatic leaders to rise to national power in Cuba. Convinced that he is the only figure on the scene who can "save the country," the charismatic leader feels an "inner call." He is recognized by his followers as a "natural" leader of men. They "do not obey him by virtue of tradition or statute, but because they believe in him," Max Weber has pointed out. He governs through a species of divine right, but "his divine mission must 'prove' itself in that those who faithfully surrender to him must fare well. If they do not fare well, he is obviously not the master sent by the gods." [13]

Personalismo is clearly central in *fidelismo,* and Fidel Castro is one of Latin America's leading case studies in charismatic leadership. Two implications of this are significant. First, his role is defined by his charismatic hold on his followers, rather than by an institutional or constitutional position he might hold. Secondly, the magic of charisma is not easily transferable—Fidel Castro, and Fidel alone, heads *fidelismo.* From time to time during the course of his regime, rumors arose to the effect that he was about to be displaced by one or more of his associates as leader of his movement. Prominently mentioned as candidates for this leadership were his younger brother, Raul Castro, *fidelismo's* military commander; Major Ernesto ("Che") Guevara, chief of the National Bank of Cuba ("Che's" National Bank); and Antonio Núñez Jiménez, head of the National Institute of Agrarian

[11] William W. Pierson and Federico G. Gil, *Governments of Latin America* (New York: McGraw-Hill Book Co., 1957), p. 31.
[12] Macdonald, *op. cit.,* p. 2.
[13] Max Weber (H. H. Gerth and C. Wright Mills, tr.), *From Max Weber: Essays in Sociology* (New York: Oxford University Press, 1946), pp. 79, 249.

Reform (INRA). It seemed likely, however, that none of these figures would be able to inherit Fidel's charismatic hold on his movement. It has been said that

> Fidel is the most charismatic figure produced by Latin America, at least in this century. . . . Castro's domination of Cuban events is virtually unique. . . . The history of Cuba in the last two or three years is the biography of Fidel.[14]

The island's historic political instability, then, stands as a first of the major keys to the nature of *fidelismo*. As such, this consideration points to the Castro revolution as one more upheaval in a country with more than the average Latin American predilection for "revolutions," and to the *fidelista* dictatorship as one more strong government in a culture historically given to political authoritarianism. As a military dictatorship, the Castro regime appears to have encouraged further democratization of the political role of the armed forces, as evidenced by the emergence of a popular militia on the ruins of Machado- and Batista-style armies. The place of political instability in *fidelismo* is further attested to in the lack of institutionalization which has characterized the movement. This has been reflected in the absence of constitutionalism, in the inability of civilian political parties to relate to Castro, and in the heavily charismatic, rather than institutional, leadership which has given *fidelismo* much of its course and character.

II

A second significant key to the nature of the movement is to be found in the striking political contrast between metropolitan Havana and the rest of Cuba. Again, it may be helpful to compare the island with the remainder of Latin America. Throughout the area—indeed, in most underdeveloped areas [15]—sharp contrasts and conflicts characterize the relationships between urban centers and rural communities. These relationships appear to be a function of the process of economic development in two significant ways. First, urban centers in the developing areas serve as nuclei of commercialization and the beginnings of industrialization, as centers of "modernization" or "Westernization," and as focal points of secularization. In contrast, the rural areas live in a landed or agricultural, rather than commercial or industrializing, economy and tend to be more "backward," traditional, religious, and superstitious. In the underdeveloped areas, illiteracy rates are sharply higher in rural than in urban communities, and standards of living differ dramatically, being much higher in the cities than in their hinterlands.

Second, underdeveloped areas are theaters of rapid social and economic change. A major facet of this change is urbanization, the movement of people from the

[14] Fitzgibbon, "The Revolution Next Door: Cuba," *Annals of the American Academy of Political and Social Science,* Vol. 334 (March 1961), pp. 113–22, especially pp. 114, 116–17.
[15] See Gabriel A. Almond and James S. Coleman (eds.), *The Politics of the Developing Areas* (Princeton; Princeton University Press, 1960), especially pp. 455–531.

rural areas to the cities. This trend, intensified by the tendency of European immigrants to locate in the major cities of Latin America, has been one of the area's major social phenomena of the twentieth century. There is no Hispanic-American country in which there has been a trend away from urbanization; everywhere the impressive fact has been the movement toward the city, the swelling of urban populations. This trend has given rise to what is sometimes referred to as the problem of *la cabeza de Goliat* (Goliath's head), characterizing a country in which a giant urban head rests upon a dwarflike rural body. In Latin America this situation is by no means peculiar to Cuba. It is acute in a number of other countries, such as Uruguay, where more than half of the national population lives in the metropolitan area of Montevideo; Argentina, where a little more than one-fourth of the people are located in Greater Buenos Aires; and Venezuela, where approximately 20 per cent of the population lives in Caracas.

If the Cuban case is viewed in this perspective, a number of significant propositions emerge. In the first place, the island is no mere case study in *la cabeza de Goliat*. Rather, Cuba exhibits an exaggerated caricature of the problem. Fifty-three per cent—more than one-half—of the total national population is urban residing principally *in one city*—the metropolitan area of Havana! Far from being representative of the cultural life of the rest of the island, Havana—secularized, commercialized, "Westernized," sophisticated, and "modern"—stands not only as the metropolis of the Caribbean, but also, ranking with New York, Chicago, Buenos Aires, and Mexico City, as one of the major metropolitan centers of the Western Hemisphere.

Moreover, Havana has stood historically in a position of political opposition to the rest of the island. In the Americas, it has been pointed out, "Hispanic culture has always been strongly urbanized." [16] Throughout the imperial period, Spain treated its American colonies as a collection of cities, setting the pattern for the deep division separating urban from rural life. The seat of governmental power in colonial times, Havana provided "the chief centers of political activity of the upper classes and, indeed, the only community levels upon which they—rather than the home government in Europe—could exercise power." [17] Traditionally the headquarters of elite groups, in contemporary times Havana has come to be the home of those political groups which gained in strength as the island's economic development proceeded. Especially important among these groups were organized labor, the urbanized "middle sectors"—identified as "politically ambitious middle groups" active in commerce and developing industry [18]—and other newly emerging industrializing and entrepreneurial groups. Caught in the economic development of Cuba, these Havana-based interests frequently pursued courses opposed to the desires of rural sectors, feeding the historic fires of rural-urban conflict.

Against this background, *fidelismo* took shape as a rural movement at war against Havana interests. During his years as the leader of the rebels against Batista, Fidel

[16] William S. Stokes, *Latin-American Politics* (New York: Thomas Y. Crowell Co., 1959), p. 502.
[17] Blanksten, "Problems of Local Government in the Caribbean," in Wilgus, *op. cit.*, p. 226.
[18] John J. Johnson, *Political Change in Latin America: The Emergence of the Middle Sectors* (Stanford: Stanford University Press, 1958), p. vii and *passim*.

Castro led rural Cuba in its historic, and now open, war against Havana. Castro's image as the champion of the back country grew after December 1956, when he set up rebel headquarters in the rural Sierra Maestra. The back country's enemies of Havana flocked to him in an intensely indigenous nationalism. Suffering real and imagined hardships at the cruel hands of the metropolis, the rural fraternity of the disadvantaged provided *fidelismo* with an agrarian popular base.

Thus, a second key to *fidelismo*. In a very real sense, Castro's rise to power was the triumph of rural Cuba over Havana. The imprisoned metropolis saw its interests crushed by Fidel. The industrializing "middle sectors" fell prey to the back country, and Cuba's economic development, insofar as it had depended upon urban leadership, was significantly retarded.[19] Seen as a rural victory over the metropolis, *fidelismo* was curiously reminiscent of the regime of General Juan Manuel Rosas which had ruled Argentina more than a century before. It, too, was a triumph of the "interior" over the urban capital, of the intensely indigenous over the secular.

III

Domestic Cuban social and economic conditions cannot be ignored as a major key to *fidelismo*. The island, like most underdeveloped areas, is a theater of remarkably rapid change. In combination with the country's historic political instability, this pattern of social and economic transformation has influenced the nature of *fidelismo* in two ways. The first is a matter of public morality. The second gives Castro's movement something of the flavor of the agrarian-populistic or *Aprista* parties common in a number of Hispanic-American countries.

The problem of public morality is widespread in the Latin American political culture in a form often difficult for "North Americans" to understand. In many of the countries, including Cuba, politicians and government officials are generally distrusted and popularly assumed to be guilty of a wide variety of forms of graft and corruption. Most Latin Americans are cynical about equating ordinary morality with politics, and *la mordida* (the "bite") is generally expected in the discharge of governmental functions. "They tell you that I am stealing your money," a Latin American officeholder is said to have told a public rally. "Who would you rather have steal your money than me?"

It is important to distinguish the charge or expectation of corruption from the question of the extent to which it takes place in fact. Much more is known about the former than the latter. Mass media in most of the Latin American countries indulge in the belief that their governments, or many of their officials, are corrupt. The public acceptance of this belief is widespread. On the other hand, it is as difficult to substantiate as it is to disprove such accusations, and little is objectively known of the extent to which they are justified. This writer's guess—and it is only that—

[19] John J. Johnson, "The Political Role of the Latin-American Middle Sectors," *Annals of the American Academy of Political and Social Science,* Vol. 334 (March 1961), pp. 20–29.

is that graft and corruption in fact do occur in Latin America, but probably not on as large a scale as is popularly believed.

In any case, pre-Castro Cuba was characterized by the typical Latin-American situation in this regard. Government officials were generally believed to be corrupt and were often pictured in the press as enriching themselves at public expense. A few illustrations of this Cuban pattern might be mentioned here. During the administration of President Ramón Grau San Martín (1944–48), one of the more celebrated Havana sights visited by guided tours was a huge diamond set in the floor of the *Capitolio,* the building in which the Cuban Congress met. In 1947, the diamond was stolen, and the Havana press rose to the mystery-solving challenge with considerable zest. Many of the papers declared that it was inevitable that the diamond would be stolen, simply because it had been placed in the building where the national legislature, composed of Cuba's leading thieves, met. Some argued that President Grau himself was the culprit; many who disagreed pointed out that he could steal more without leaving the presidential office. Three years after the expiration of his term, Grau was formally charged with having misappropriated one hundred and seventy-four million dollars; the ultimate indictment was for forty million, "mainly because valuable evidence was apparently stolen by gunmen from a public office." [20] Many exiled Cuban ex-presidents have been reported as living handsomely because of self-enrichment at public expense while in office. Among the leading recent instances of this is Dr. Carlos Prío Socarrás, Grau's successor (1948–52) in the presidency. Both of Batista's regimes were similarly characterized by charges and expectations of corruption. With the expansion of the "North American" tourist trade during his time, luxurious gambling casinos and other entertainment centers, publicly supposed to be centers of dishonesty and immorality, flourished in Havana.

One significant side of *fidelismo* is its role as a crusade for public morality. Castro's movement has been a species of political puritanism, curiously Spartan-like in character. An amazing variety of charges and accusations has been hurled against the Castro regime, to be sure; but graft and corruption are significantly absent among them. Virtually no looting was engaged in during the tumultuous first days after the fall of Batista; money taken from the raided gambling casinos lay virtually untouched in the streets. *Fidelismo* has moved, often in naive ways, against gambling and other activities assumed to be corrupt, and the administrative morality of the Castro government seems strangely out of place in a Cuba grown cynical in such matters.

The following news story offers some insight into the stern and humorless extremes achieved in *fidelismo's* war against *la mordida:*

> Premier Fidel Castro has decided to revise the rules of baseball, it was disclosed today.
> Last Sunday, after cutting cane at a nearby sugar mill, Dr. Castro pitched in a sandlot game. But when a runner stole second base on him, the Premier ordered him back to first.
> 'In the revolution,' Dr. Castro said, 'no one can steal—even in baseball.' [21]

[20] R. A. Gómez, *Government and Politics in Latin America* (New York: Random House, 1960), p. 67.
[21] Quoted in *The New Yorker,* March 25, 1961, p. 29.

The face of *fidelismo's* Spartan-like public morality should be neither ignored nor underestimated.

The rural character of *fidelismo*, springing from Cuba's historic rural-urban conflict, has already been noted. From this standpoint, the Castro movement has acquired a substantial agrarian-populistic base and may be regarded as containing some of the elements of an *Aprista* party. Common in Latin America, *Aprista* parties have two distinguishing characteristics. First, they seek far-reaching social and economic changes in rural areas, usually including land reform. Second, they demanded the integration of the rural lower classes into the political process; indeed, *Aprismo* boasts a greater percentage of lower-class adherents than can any other Latin-American political movement. The chief prototype of this class of political party is, of course, the celebrated *Aprista* Party or APRA [22] of Peru. Other *Aprista* parties include the *Acción Democrática* of Venezuela and the National Liberation Party of Costa Rica.[23] In a sense, Mexico's governing PRI [24] is also a party of this type.

Rural conditions in pre-Castro Cuba were by no means the most severe in Latin America. Nevertheless, sufficiently inequitable circumstances to feed an agrarian-populistic revolt certainly existed. Forty-seven per cent of the national population was classified as rural, and 40 per cent of the island's work force was engaged in agriculture. In 1946, 8 per cent of the farmers owned 71.1 per cent of the land while 39 per cent owned only 3.3 per cent of the land. Many of the rural workers were the employees of the more than one hundred fifty sugar mills located throughout the country. Owing to the seasonal production of sugar, there was an average annual unemployment rate of 25 per cent.

The typical Cuban agriculturalist [it has been pointed out] is not a peasant in the usual European sense of the term but rather a landless proletarian who customarily works for wages in groups or gangs under the direction and supervision of others. . . . He has traditionally been the forgotten man of Cuban society. For the most part employed only a few months during the sugar, tobacco, or coffee harvests, he has barely managed to exist the remainder of the year.[25]

Especially during the years when *fidelismo* was a rebel movement in the back country fighting against Batista's Havana, Castro acquired a strong agrarian following increasingly dedicated to rural reforms. The construction of schools and other educational programs, of benefit especially to rural Cuba, acquired significant status among the goals of his movement. Housing and medical programs also found their

[22] After the initial letters of *Alianza Popular Revolucionaria Americana* (American Popular Revolutionary Alliance).

[23] See Harry Kantor, *The Ideology and Program of the Peruvian Aprista Movement* (Berkeley: University of California Press, 1953), *passim;* and Robert J. Alexander, "The Latin-American Aprista Parties," *Political Quarterly*, Vol. 20 (1949), pp. 236–47.

[24] After the initial letters of *Partido Revolucionario Institucional* (Institutional Revolutionary Party).

[25] See Leo Huberman and Paul Sweezy, *Cuba: Anatomy of a Revolution* (New York: Monthly Review Press, 1960), *passim,* especially p. 80.

way into *fidelismo*. So, too, did land reform, and the pattern of land tenure faced significant changes during the Castro regime. Following the promulgation in May 1959 of the agrarian reform law, a government agency, the National Institute of Agrarian Reform (INRA[26]) was established under the leadership of Antonio Núñez Jiménez, to administer Castro's land program. It was estimated that, by mid-1960, INRA, then a gigantic administrative entity, held title to more than one-half the land surface of Cuba.[27] It thus seemed clear that substantial *Aprista*-like rural changes were contemplated by *fidelismo*.

Yet, the relationship of these changes to the economic development of Cuba is at best questionable. This development, properly considered, is not a vague or general umbrella covering all varieties of change. Rather, economic development is the more sharply defined phenomenon of technological innovation, resulting in greater efficiency on the part of the productive arts. A more effective technology draws a higher level of production—that is, a greater gross national product per capita—from a known initial input into an economy.[28]

On the eve of the fall of Batista, Cuba's standard of living, expressed in terms of gross national product per capita, was the third highest in Latin America.[29] To be sure, a degree of perhaps inevitable bias is built into the gross national-product figures. For one thing, international economic comparisons are never easy to make, as a number of significant factors are often difficult to reduce to quantitatively comparable terms. Moreover, translation of gross national-product figures into United States dollars catches aspects of trade relations and foreign exchange rates not entirely relevant to economic development and standards of living. Finally, Cuban national figures are distorted by the problem of *la cabeza de Goliat*—more than half the island's population lives in the metropolitan area of Havana, and other urban centers, where the standard of living is substantially higher than in the rest of the country. For example, 87 per cent of the dwelling units in Havana have electricity, whereas only 9 per cent of the island's rural units are so equipped.[30]

Even after due regard is paid to these statistical pitfalls, pre-Castro Cuba's standard of living remained among the highest in Latin America. It did not seem likely, at the time this paper was written, that national living standards might be expected to rise under *fidelismo*. Indeed, such statistical changes as were in the making in 1961 seemed headed in the other direction. A number of propositions flow from this situation. In the first place, while revolutions and other political phenomena appear to flow from economic growth in the underdeveloped areas,[31] it does not seem possible to make a reasonable case for regarding *fidelismo* as deriving from, or contributing to, Cuba's economic development. The ties, if they exist at all, are

[26] After the initial letters of *Instituto Nacional de Reforma Agraria*.
[27] Fitzgibbon, *op. cit.*, p. 115.
[28] See Blanksten, "The Aspiration for Economic Development," *Annals of the American Academy of Political and Social Science,* Vol. 334 (March 1961), pp. 10–19.
[29] See Table 1, p. 26, below.
[30] Huberman and Sweezy, *op. cit.*, p. 4.
[31] See Almond and Coleman, *op. cit., passim.*

not easy to find between Castro's movement and theories of revolutions of rising expectations or of "take-off" in economic growth.[32] The mainsprings of *fidelismo* must be sought elsewhere in the island's national life.

Table 1 Economic Development in Latin America *

(Rank Order of Countries Based on Gross National Product per Capita)

RANK	COUNTRY	GROSS NATIONAL PRODUCT PER CAPITA (IN U.S. DOLLARS)
1	Argentina	$ 688
2	Venezuela	457
3	*CUBA*	*454*
4	Uruguay	382
5	Panama	382
6	Chile	335
7	Brazil	278
8	Colombia	231
9	Costa Rica	203
10	Mexico	199
11	Dominican Republic	189
12	Guatemala	182
13	Nicaragua	168
14	El Salvador	167
15	Paraguay	166
16	Honduras	134
17	Peru	118
18	Bolivia	109
19	Ecuador	93
20	Haiti	62
For Comparison	United States	2200

* Source: Blanksten, *op. cit.,* pp. 10–19, especially p. 11. See also Davis, *op. cit.,* pp. 50–93, especially pp. 60–71; and Almond and Coleman, *op. cit.,* pp. 455–531.

Moreover, economic development must depend heavily upon emerging industrializing and entrepreneurial groups. These groups—the so-called "middle sectors"— have developed in urban centers in Latin America, especially in Havana. Insofar as it has been an agrarian-populistic movement directed against Havana interests, *fidelismo* has warred against the urban "middle sectors," seriously paralyzing their ability to continue functioning. In this view, the Castro regime can be seen as

[32] The reader may wish to consult the following works by W. W. Rostow: *The Process of Economic Growth* (London: Oxford University Press, 1953); "Trends in the Allocation of Resources in Secular Growth," in Leon H. Dupriez (ed.), *Economic Progress* (Louvain: Institut de Recherches Economiques et Sociales, 1955); "The Take-off into Self-Sustained Growth," *The Economic Journal* (March 1956), pp. 25–48; "The Stages of Economic Growth," *The Economic History Review,* second series, Vol. 12, No. 1 (August 1959), pp. 1–16; and *The Stages of Economic Growth* (New York: Cambridge University Press, 1960).

opposing the country's economic development insofar as technological innovation is central to the growth process.[33]

Domestic Cuban economic and social conditions, then, provide a third key to the Castro movement. As reflected in *fidelismo,* these have taken the forms of a puritanic crusade for the advancement of public morality and agrarian-populistic attempts to improve literacy, housing, medical, and land-tenure conditions in the rural areas. In view of the nature of Havana's economy and Cuba's overall level of economic development, however, it does not seem likely that this aspect of the movement will make a positive contribution to the island's standard of living.

IV

Finally, Cuba's relations with the United States provide a fourth major key to the nature of *fidelismo.* Again, comparisons with the experience of other Latin-American countries might be useful. It is worth noting that, of the twenty states of the area, some are far removed from the "Colossus of the North." Simply in terms of air miles, no European capital, not even Moscow, is farther from the geographic center of the United States than is Buenos Aires, Argentina; and only one European capital, Athens, Greece, is farther from that center than is Brasilia, the new seat of the Brazilian government. On the other hand, the Middle American countries— Mexico, Central America, and the Caribbean islands—are closer to the "Yanquis" and much more subject to their influence. While there have been unhappy periods in the histories of the relations of the United States with most of the Latin-American countries [34]—it is instructive that Brazil is the only one in which a statue of James Monroe has been erected—the Middle American states have felt the influence of the United States much more than have the countries on the continent of South America. Many years ago, for example, a Mexican newspaper observed editorially that the United States "like everything big frightens us, like everything strong seduces us, like everything rich arouses our envy and makes us forget the clay feet of the Anglo-American colossus to focus our attention upon its head of gold." [35] General Porfirio Díaz is said to have complained thus: "Poor Mexico! So far from God; so close to the United States!"

Compared with the rest of Middle America, Cuba is once more a caricature rather than a case study. Indeed, if General Díaz had had a second tear, he might well have shed it for Cuba. Lying less than one hundred miles off the Florida coast, the island has been showered with virtually everything "Yanqui" ranging from the fragments

[33] See Johnson, *Political Change in Latin America: The Emergence of the Middle Sectors, passim;* and Johnson, "The Political Role of the Latin-American Middle Sectors," pp. 20–29, especially pp. 28–29.
[34] See, for example, Graham H. Stuart, *Latin America and the United States,* 5th ed. (New York: Appleton-Century-Crofts, 1955), *passim.*
[35] Quoted in Donald Marquand Dozer, *Are We Good Neighbors?* (Gainesville: University of Florida Press, 1959), p. 2.

of the battleship *Maine* to the debris of a shattered dream launched from Cape Canaveral. The island was first occupied by the armed forces of the United States and then overrun by hordes of vacationing tourists sprawling on Havana's beaches by day and filling its night clubs and gambling casinos by night. "Yanqui" business firms have invested heavily in the Cuban economy and controlled much of it, and the "Colossus of the North" has provided the chief markets for the island's exports.

It was ever thus, throughout Cuba's national history. The United States, of course, played a major military role in the achievement of the island's independence from Spain. Although the first Cuban president Tomás Estrada Palma (1902–09) expressed "the immense gratitude which the people feel towards the American nation," [36] it is worth remembering that Jose Martí, the major national hero of the island's independence, saw the United States as beginning "to bring into the open its latent spirit of aggression." [37] Martí's view of the "Yanquis'" part in the struggle for insular independence is much more widely held among Cubans than Estrada's attitude.

Indeed, the fateful Platt Amendment was to become the major symbol of their image of the United States. Adopted in 1901 by the Congress of the United States as an amendment to an Army appropriation bill, the Platt instrument was later written into Cuba's first constitution and also into a treaty between the Washington and Havana governments in 1904. The "Amendment" provided, among other things, for limitations on Cuba's authority to conduct its own foreign relations and to contract public debts. At the same time, the United States was guaranteed the right to intervene militarily in the island to maintain order there and to hold naval bases in Cuba.[38] The first "Yanqui" military occupation was terminated in 1902. Under the Platt Amendment, however, "North American" armed forces returned four years later to occupy the country until 1909. During the administration of Pres-

[36] Stuart, *op. cit.,* p. 212.

[37] Dozer, *op. cit.,* p. 2.

[38] The Platt Amendment has become so controversial in the relations between the United States and Cuba that the relevant clauses of that instrument deserve quotation in full:

(1) That the Government of Cuba shall never enter into any treaty or other compact with any foreign Power or Powers which will impair or tend to impair the independence of Cuba, nor in any manner authorize or permit any foreign Power or Powers to obtain by colonization or for military or naval purposes, or otherwise, lodgment in or control over any portion of said Island.

(2) That said Government shall not assume or contract any public debt to pay the interest upon which, and to make reasonable sinking-fund provision for discharge of which, the ordinary revenues of the Island, after defraying the current expenses of the Government, shall be inadequate.

(3) That the Government of Cuba consents that the United States may exercise the right to intervene for the preservation of Cuban independence, the maintenance of a government adequate for the protection of life, property, and individual liberty, and for discharging the obligations with respect to Cuba imposed by the Treaty of Paris on the United States, now to be assumed and undertaken by the Government of Cuba.

(4) That all acts of the United States in Cuba during its military occupation thereof are ratified and validated, and all lawful right acquired thereunder shall be maintained and protected.

(5) That the Government of Cuba will execute, and as far as necessary extend, the plans already devised or other plans to be mutually agreed upon, for the sanitation of the cities of the Island to the end that a recurrence of epidemic and infectious diseases may be prevented,

ident Alfredo Zayas (1921–25), the "Amendment" was invoked repeatedly. At length, "North American" President Franklin D. Roosevelt abrogated the Platt Amendment in 1934 as an early step in his administration's Good Neighbor Policy toward Latin America. Provision was made at that time for the retention of the United States naval base at Guantánamo Bay, originally acquired under the "Amendment."

Following the abrogation of the Platt Amendment, United States influence continued in Cuba. As its forms changed, its volume increased. "Yanqui" investments in the island, already valued at $80,000,000 as early as 1901, rose steadily in the following half-century. Most of these investments were connected with the sugar industry, with "North American" firms owning or controlling 54 per cent of the island's sugar mills during the Batista period. United States interests invested heavily in other sectors of Cuba's economy as well, particularly in tobacco, fruit, transportation, docks, electric light and power, telecommunications, banks, luxury hotels, and steamship and air lines. Late in the Batista regime, the island's imports achieved an annual average value of $640,000,000, and exports were valued at $766,000,000. Approximately two-thirds of each of these figures represented trade with the United States.

Under Batista, Cuba—principally Havana—became increasingly attractive as a vacation resort for "Yanqui" tourists. Many, originally oriented toward the pleasures of Miami Beach, seemed suddenly to discover an even more beckoning playground less than an hour away by commercial airline. Crowding into the luxury hotels, night clubs, and gambling casinos of Havana, these fun-seeking vacationers fed a Cuban image of the "Yanqui" as a shallow and insensitive materialist with unlimited amounts of money to devote to amusing himself. This writer once visited a Havana night club whose management had secured the services of Jorge Negrete, then one of Mexico's most well-known popular singers. The Cuban master of ceremonies was obviously moved in announcing his pleasure in being able to introduce the distinguished Mexican artist, about to interpret the music of Mexico he loved most. "No, no!" shouted the "Yanqui"-dominated audience. "No Mexicans! If we wanted Mexican music we would have flown to Mexico! Give us Cubans! *Viva Cuba!*" The celebrated Mexican's chagrin could not have approximated that of his Cuban hosts.

Such continuing "North American" economic, cultural, and social influence in

thereby assuring protection to the people and commerce of Cuba, as well as to the commerce of the Southern ports of the United States and the people residing therein.

(6) That the Isle of Pines shall be omitted from the proposed constitutional boundaries of Cuba, the title thereto left to future adjustments by treaty.

(7) That to enable the United States to maintain the independence of Cuba, and to protect the people thereof, as well as for its own defense, the Government of Cuba will sell or lease to the United States lands necessary for coaling or naval stations at certain specified points, to be agreed upon with the President of the United States.

(8) That by way of further assurance the Government of Cuba will embody the foregoing provisions in a permanent treaty with the United States.

See *United States Statutes at Large,* Vol. 31, p. 897, or *House Document No. 2,* 57th Congress, 1st Session, p. 47. The reader may also wish to consult Raymond L. Buell, "Cuba and the Platt Amendment," *Foreign Policy Reports,* Vol. 5, No. 3 (April 17, 1929) and Stuart, *op. cit.,* pp. 186–230, especially pp. 213–14.

Cuba has given rise on the island to a phenomenon that has been called "Platt-ism." [39] This might be defined as the circumstance that, despite the abrogation of the Platt Amendment more than a generation before the rise of Fidel Castro, Cuba has "continued to experience a significant degree probably of economic and certainly of psychological subordination to the United States." [40] No doubt, "Plattism" is essentially psychological in nature. It is widely believed in Cuba that the Platt Amendment is still in force. While quantitative data on this are not available, it is probably true that the overwhelming majority of the Cubans who have heard of the document have *not* heard that it was abrogated. The heavy economic and other influences of the "Yanquis," and the retention of the United States naval base at Guantánamo Bay are, for most Cubans, more than ample evidence that the Platt Amendment still lives. Legally and technically, it was put to rest in 1934; psycho-logically, it continues to dominate Cubans. This discrepancy is the soul of "Plattism."

And "Plattism" is a major element of *fidelismo,* governing many of its attitudes and policies toward the United States. What to many "North Americans" might appear to be quaintly unrealistic windmill-tilting against a long-dead dragon is to the Cuba of Fidel Castro an urgent, necessary, and just war against a living Platt Amendment. In this context it has been necessary to eliminate "Yanqui" economic influence in the island. "Plattism," no doubt, has motivated much of the nation-alization and expropriation of United States business interests in Cuba in 1960. The same psychological phenomenon strains to do battle at Guantánamo Bay. Such *fidelista* policies would certainly have brought renewed United States military inter-vention in Cuba if the Platt Amendment had still been in force. Such intervention, for the "Plattism" of *fidelismo,* is largely indistinguishable from the anti-Castro Cuban exiles' abortive "Yanqui"-aided invasion of the island in April 1961.

Furthermore, much of the interplay between *fidelismo* and Communism has de-rived its curious course and character from "Plattism." For one thing, it should be noted that the Cuban Communist Party had long been one of the four or five most important Communist organizations in Latin America, lagging behind only those of Brazil, Chile, and perhaps Argentina and Mexico.[41] It has been estimated that the Cuban Communists have from 20,000 to 30,000 members. If that figure seems small to "North Americans" accustomed to thinking in larger numbers, it would be, on a comparable basis, roughly equivalent to a Communist Party with more than 670,000 members in the United States.

Pre-Castro Cuban Communism, however, despite its influence among some of the rural sugar workers, was essentially an urban movement with its strength con-centrated in, and almost restricted to, Havana. In the period before the fall of Batista—that is, when *fidelismo* was essentially a rural movement at war against the urban capital—there was little evidence of Communist association with the 26th

[39] This writer is indebted to Dr. Russell H. Fitzgibbon for the term "Plattism," which was ap-parently first used in his article, "The Revolution Next Door: Cuba," p. 114.
[40] *Ibid.,* p. 114.
[41] See Robert J. Alexander, *Communism in Latin America* (New Brunswick: Rutgers University Press, 1957), *passim.*

of July movement. It is perhaps significant that those of Castro's lieutenants who were then reputed to be Communists, such as Raul Castro, Major Ernesto ("Che") Guevara, and Major Camilo Cienfuegos, acquired this reputation more from their foreign and international associations than from connections with the Havana-based Cuban Communist Party. It was not until *fidelismo* took Havana in 1959 that the island's Communist organization clearly threw its support to the already victorious Castro regime. "The Communists," it has been observed, "mounted the Castro bandwagon so late in its parade to success that their motives should have been suspect for that reason if for no other." [42] Fidel Castro reacted sympathetically to the Communists. Perhaps he would have been something less than human not to have appreciated their vocal, imaginative, and dedicated support and assistance. Furthermore, in the Cuban context, "Plattism" operated to present the *fidelistas* and the Communists with a common enemy, the United States.

The role of "Plattism" has been somewhat less spectacular in Castro's relationships with Cuban Communists than in the case of international Communism. Under *fidelista* leadership, Cuba's relations with the Soviet Union, Communist China, North Korea, and other states with crucial roles in the Soviet bloc have been redefined, sometimes under sensational circumstances. Formal diplomatic relations with these countries have become remarkably cordial. Trade and other economic agreements have been entered into with Soviet-bloc governments in an endeavor to fill the vacuum in the Cuban economy left by the departing "Yanquis." Castro personally attended the session of the United Nations General Assembly at New York in September 1960 as did the Soviets' Nikita Khrushchev, and made a major public spectacle of his endorsement of the Russian leader's opposition to the positions taken by the United States on a number of questions. Planes and tanks manufactured in the Soviet Union, machine guns and other small arms made in Czechoslovakia, and military aid from other Communist countries have flowed to Cuba. The value of these armaments in strengthening Castro's militia was demonstrated with devastating effectiveness by the defeat dealt the anti-*fidelista* invaders in April 1961.

The decisive climax of the Communist question came in December 1961, when Fidel Castro declared in a major address that he was a "Marxist-Leninist." He asserted that he had been so oriented since his student days, but that he had withheld public statements to this effect for fear of alienating anti-Communist Cubans from the *fidelista* revolution. By the end of 1961, Castro asserted, he no longer feared the consequences of such alienation. The complete significance of this declaration remained unclear at the time this chapter was written. Some observers believed that Castro's statement was essentially an attempt to place the Soviet Union under obligation to offer greater aid to the Cuban regime in coping with its mounting domestic problems and the continuing deterioration of its foreign relations, not only with the United States, but also with most of the other American republics. Others saw the move as an attempt to offset the rising strength of "Che" Guevara by creating a "Marxist-Leninist" or Soviet counterweight against Guevara's apparent

[42] Fitzgibbon, *op. cit.,* p. 117.

leaning toward Chinese Communism. In any case, and whatever the explanation, Castro's statement in December 1961 constituted a major step toward the identification of *fidelismo* with Communism.

The place of Communism in *fidelismo* is both crucial and subtle. It seems likely that this role is far more negative than positive, that is, that it is motivated more by rejection of the United States than it is by acceptance of the Soviet system. Insofar as this is true, Castro's posture toward Communism appears to be the consummate expression of "Plattism." It has been noted that the imbalance or discrepancy between the legal extinctness, on the one hand, and, on the other, the psychological persistence of Cuba's subordination to the United States is the essence of "Plattism." There is some possibility that the process of *fidelismo* itself might work out this imbalance. Such a solution cannot be depended on, however, because the road leading in that direction is replete with dangerous pitfalls.

V

In one sense the contribution of *fidelismo* to the revolution of our time is, in the Latin American context, but the donation of one more bottle for the same old wine. Little—indeed, surprisingly little—is new, creative, or original in the Castro movement. At bottom it is essentially the latest synthesis of elements which have been afoot in the Western Hemisphere since the opening years of the twentieth century. Yet this is precisely the appeal of *fidelismo* throughout Latin America. Fidel Castro strikes responsive chords in all countries of the Americas because his movement is composed of old and familiar elements, most of which have long been at large throughout the American republics. *Fidelismo* is more than exportable from Cuba to other Latin American countries. Most of its components were already abroad in the Americas long before Castro seized upon them in Cuba.

Consider, for example, the various keys to *fidelismo*. The first of them, political instability, characterized by frequent so-called "revolution" and dictatorship, is as generally Latin American as it is Cuban. Political authoritarianism, although more deeply rooted historically in the Caribbean islands than elsewhere in the Americas, is by no means peculiar to Cuba. Neither does the island boast a monopoly on military dictatorship in the Western Hemisphere. A study published in 1960 indicated that no fewer than fourteen of the twenty Latin American countries were living with at least as much political militarism as was Cuba.[43] Indeed, approved textbooks used in the military schools of Ecuador did not hesitate to teach that "the last step in a military career is the presidency of the republic." [44] Difficulty in achieving political institutionalization is likewise as generally Hispanic-American as Cuban. Constitutions come and go in the area, where the basic law that lives for more than a quarter of a century is rare indeed. No fewer than eight of the countries have

[43] Lieuwen, *op. cit.*, pp. 154–168.
[44] Quoted in Blanksten, *Ecuador: Constitutions and Caudillos* (Berkeley: University of California Press, 1951), p. 36.

each had ten or more written constitutions, and two of the states, the Dominican Republic and Venezuela, have each had more than twenty.[45] The chronic instability of civilian political parties likewise belongs not merely to Cuba, but also to the entire Latin American world.

In these times, [a Bolivian has written of his own country's parties,] "nothing is simpler than to found a political party. To form a political party only three people and one object are necessary: a president, a vice president, a secretary, and a rubber stamp. The party can get along even without the vice president and the secretary. . . . There have been cases in which the existence of only the rubber stamp has been sufficient.[46]

And Fidel Castro is probably not the last—he is certainly not the first—charismatic spellbinder to thrive on the *personalismo* of a Latin America that has known a Juan Domingo Perón, a Getulio Vargas, a Jorge Eliecer Gaitan, a Rafael Leónidas Trujillo Molina, and a Víctor Raúl Haya de la Torre. "Never before had I heard such a speech," an Ecuadoran legislator once said of one more "man with a mission." "When it was finished, the president and congress were unashamedly in tears, and we stood up and voted unanimously for his bill. . . . I [was] such a fool, such a fool, to vote for his insane measure! . . . I have been mesmerized by experts. . . ."[47] In short, to export the first *fidelista* key to other Latin American countries would be but to dump it on already badly glutted markets.

The second key, *la cabeza de Goliat,* the rural-urban conflict, will spread in Latin America with or without Fidel Castro's assistance. Goliath has already reared his ugly head in Argentina, Paraguay, Uruguay, and Venezuela. Urbanization is apparently the inevitable handmaiden of economic development in the underdeveloped areas. As the growth process proceeds, the ever-widening schism separating the secularized, commercialized, and industrialized urban centers from the traditional and agrarian rural areas will doubtlessly aggravate the conflict, often giving rise to intensely indigenous anti-urban nationalisms. Hear the roar of the rural cannon trained on Goliath in Peru:

[the rural-urban] division is not merely physical. It pervades our entire social and economic life. . . . If it is true that no capital is really representative of the country that it governs, this is more than ever true in the case of Lima. . . . Lima is the center, but it is not central. It was the seat of Spanish colonial power; now it is the seat of the Government. . . . 'They founded it next to the sea, that it might look out toward Spain; ever since it has looked toward the outside world, courting foreigners; it is the sweetheart of the sailors of the seven seas; but it is not ours.[48]

Essentially, the expansion of this conflict is a function of the increasing political modernization of Latin America. To lay this, too, at the door of Fidel Castro would be to give him even more credit than he has claimed for himself.

[45] See Davis, *op. cit.,* pp. 225–51.
[46] Luis Teran Gomez, *Los Partidos Politicos y su Accion Democratica* (La Paz: Editorial La Paz, 1942), pp. 60–61.
[47] Quoted in Blanksten, *op. cit.,* p. 50.
[48] José Carlos Mariátegui, *Siete Ensayos de Interpretación de la Realidad Peruana* (Lima: Biblioteca "Amanta," 1943), p. 153; and Moises Sáenz, *The Peruvian Indian* (Washington: Strategic Index of the Americas, 1944), p. 8.

Fidelismo's third key, internal social and economic conditions, tends to straddle the exportability question. On the one hand, this key contains an element—public morality—which is probably more difficult to export to other Latin-American countries than any other aspect of the Castro movement. Expectations of graft, corruption, and other forms of dishonesty in public office are widespread throughout the area. The diminution of this public immorality in Cuba is likely to be one of the long-range consequences of *fidelismo* in that country. But it is extremely difficult to imagine any circumstance under which the Castro regime could export its Spartan-like puritanism to any other American nation. Even assuming the future rise of *fidelista* power and influence to ridiculously unrealistic proportions, the prospects of the indefinite tenure of *la mordida* seem safe, secure, and generally unthreatened in the other American republics.

On the other hand, the agrarian-populistic nature of the 26th of July movement is substantially exportable to many of the Hispanic-American states which have long been sensitized to problems of land tenure, illiteracy, poor housing, problems of health and sanitation, and generally low standards of living. Throughout Latin America, *Aprista* parties—APRA in Peru, *Acción Democrática* in Venezuela, the National Liberation Party in Costa Rica, and the PRI in Mexico—have preached that reforms in these areas are both necessary and long overdue. It has been noted that this aspect of *fidelismo* is not likely to contribute to the economic development of Cuba. But it is ironic that insofar as this element of the Castro movement makes itself felt in other American countries, reforms promoting their economic development might well be hastened in the states with more receptive standards of living. Throughout the Western Hemisphere, Fidel Castro has come to symbolize "the aspirations of the Latin American commoner for a better life," it has been pointed out.

> That economic and perhaps even social improvement, though certainly not political democratization, can conceivably be achieved . . . has been brought home to the Latin-American man in the street by the vastly improved communications of mid-twentieth century. He is not as devoted to the traditional democracy of the West as are most people in the United States because he has known less of it.[49]

There is, therefore, some likelihood that *fidelismo* might intensify demands, in many of the countries with lower standards of living, for greater speed in social and economic changes expected to promote the growth of the economies involved.

The final key to *fidelismo,* anti-United States sentiment, has, of course, long existed throughout Latin America. Indeed, a close student of such attitudes has reported in a recent study that "the normal state of Latin America is to be hostile to the United States." [50] Historically, this Yankee-phobia has had its ups and downs. At the time of the First World War, a Latin American intellectual told the "North Americans" that

> What you people must get out of your minds . . . is the idea that we . . . want to be like you. We do not—in any respect. . . . We don't want your type of education, your

[49] Fitzgibbon, *op. cit.,* p. 121.
[50] Dozer, *op. cit.,* p. 403.

kind of religion, your commercialized ideas of living. . . . Our civilization is older than yours by centuries. It suits us. Your paternalism, your continual oversight of Latin-American affairs is irritating to us. You assume too much, and the benevolent role fools none of us. . . . Why talk about a unity that does not live? Why keep up all this Pan-American propaganda unless—what we all believe—for your own purposes of exploitation and political dominance? [51]

During the "Good Neighbor Policy" of the administration of the "North American" President Franklin D. Roosevelt, particularly during the years of the Second World War, Latin American attitudes toward the United States were probably abnormally friendly. In the era of the Cold War, however, suspicion and distrust of the "Colossus of the North" have regained much lost ground in the Western Hemisphere.[52]

As a manifestation of renascent Yankeephobia, the "Plattism" of *fidelismo* has had a profound effect in a generally receptive Hispanic America. Although the formal declarations of some governments occasionally express a contrary view, it has been pointed out with considerable insight that "Castro is, to an uncomfortable degree, correct when he implies or states forthrightly that the governments in more than one Latin American state do not really speak for large numbers of those they govern." [53] Throughout the Western Hemisphere, admiration is quick and widespread for regimes that dare to express defiance of the "Yanquis." *Fidelismo* "is definitely a danger to our continued peaceful relations with Latin America," Robert C. Hill, a United States Ambassador to Mexico during the administrations of President Dwight D. Eisenhower, declared in a recent press interview. "They have traditional reasons for hating and fearing us and when one of their own can thumb his nose at us and get away with it, he has their sympathy." [54] This observation has been substantiated by demonstrations throughout the Americas in support of *fidelismo* against the "Yanquis."

The Castro movement thus looms as a formidable component of the revolution of our time. Most, although not all, of its major elements are readily exportable to other Latin American countries, where *fidelismo* has acquired increasing numbers of sympathizers in the Americas. Yet, Cuba's involvement in the Cold War should not feed distorted views of the situation. Support for *fidelismo* should not be equated with Communism. Yankeephobia has achieved dizzying heights in the past in Latin America and, conceivably, might regain them in the future. But the gross error involved in the oversimplification that interprets anti-United States sentiment as Communism should be avoided. It is unlikely that the influence of *fidelismo*, however great, in Latin America could operate to win substantial support there for the Soviet cause should the chips of the Cold War be down.

[51] Mexican diplomat Luis Cabrera, quoted in Frederick L. Schuman, *International Politics*, 2nd ed. (New York: McGraw-Hill Book Co., 1937), p. 347.
[52] This cooling of Latin-American attitudes is painstakingly documented in Dozer, *op. cit., passim*, especially pp. 188–354.
[53] Fitzgibbon, *op. cit.*, p. 121.
[54] Quoted in Chicago *Sun-Times*, April 30, 1961, Section 2, p. 2.

6

Pan-Africanism as Protest

Immanuel Wallerstein

The background of pan-Africanism as a movement of protest is to be found in the European slave trade in Africa. As a consequence of this trade, Africans were sent to the Western Hemisphere, particularly to the United States and the West Indies. The numbers by which African societies, particularly in West Africa, were thus depleted is a moot question.[1] The very least that can be said is that it represented a significant diminution of the population, and, often, its most healthy segments. Furthermore, the slave trade weakened the military strength and social fabric of many African tribes and contributed to the relative ease with which European colonial rule was established virtually throughout the African continent.

The relations of European [2] and African, and hence of white man and black man, became increasingly that of superior to inferior throughout the modern era, both in Africa and elsewhere in the world. By the end of the nineteenth century, this style of relationship became very much imbedded in the psychology of the European and was partially accepted by both African and Western Hemisphere Negroes.

Of course, slaves and persons considered inherently inferior seldom accept fully the eternal legitimacy of their plight. They are even less likely to do so when their status is rendered anomalous, as it was in this case, by the emerging egalitarian norms of European culture. Hence, the century following the French revolution saw the gradual abolition of the slave trade and of the institution of slavery in one European country after another. The slave revolt in Haiti led to the creation, in 1804, of an independent state, of Negro-African cultural inspiration, in the Western Hemisphere. The movement to resettle freed slaves in Africa led to the creation in 1847 of the independent state of Liberia.[3] Until the mid-twentieth century, Haiti,

---

[1] For a recent summary discussion of the extent of the slave-trade, see B. Davidson, *The Lost Cities of Africa* (Boston: Little-Brown, 1959), p. 130 ff. For more detailed accounts, see W. E. B. Du Bois, "The Suppression of the African Slave Trade to the United States of America," *Harvard Historical Studies*, No. 1 (New York: Longmans, Green, 1904), *passim;* Eric Williams, *Capitalism and Slavery* (Chapel Hill: University of North Carolina Press, 1945).

[2] In this essay, "European" will be used to include, unless otherwise specified, North American whites and white settlers in Africa. "African" will, however, refer only to the indigenous population of Africa and is to be distinguished from North American and West Indian Negroes. This is purely a terminological distinction, for convenience.

[3] A similar movement led to the establishment of the British Crown Colony of Sierra Leone in 1808.

137

Liberia, and the ancient kingdom of Ethiopia remained the only independent nations [4] governed by black men which were recognized more or less as official members of the world community of nations.

The ending of slavery in various Western Hemisphere countries did not mean equality of rights for Negroes. Their basic position as subordinates in the social structure was still widely accepted as inevitable and wise. The justification for this subordination rested on an assumption that Negroes were in some manner less intelligent than whites and, hence, incapable of adequately performing tasks requiring higher skills.

One kind of response possible to such an assumption is to argue that such differences as exist are cultural, rather than biological, in origin. If one makes this response, the solution is to speed up the process of education among the Negroes to make them capable of equal accomplishment. This was essentially the response of Frederick Douglass and Booker T. Washington,[5] among others. Another kind of response is to separate the two groups completely, so that the Negroes could establish their own community, achieving that of which they were capable, at their own pace. This was essentially the response of the American Colonization Society,[6] which was responsible for the establishment of freed slaves in Liberia.

What both these responses have in common is that they implicitly accept the assumptions made by those who justify the subordination of Negroes in society, particularly the assumption that the Negro has no cultural accomplishments worthy of note. The evidence for such an assumption was considered to be the absence of any higher civilization, then or further in the past, in black Africa.

At the turn of the twentieth century, a new group of Negro intellectuals appeared on the scene in the Western Hemisphere. They demanded more militance in the struggle to achieve equal rights in their countries. They demanded more militance for the defense of the independence of the three Negro states and for the extension of political rights in African colonies. Above all, they rejected the assumption of the absence of Negro accomplishments in world history. They wanted equality both within the Western world between Negro and white and between Western nations and African nations (in existence or to be created). They wanted this equality not as a reward for successfully learning the ways of European civilization, but as a right

---

[4] Ethiopia, of course, came under Italian rule from 1936–41.

[5] "Education is the sole and only hope of the Negro race in America. Transportation, colonization, and other schemes of misguided enthusiasts, are impracticable and futile." "The Negro's Hope," cited in Booker T. Washington, *Black-Belt Diamonds* (New York: Fortune and Scott, 1898), p. 4. Washington was not the first to advocate this response. The first Negro college graduate in the United States, John Russwurm, received his degree from Bowdoin in 1826. Prior to the Civil War, many Negro leaders, including Frederick Douglass, advocated education as the solution of the Negro problem. Negro schools were established both in the North and in the South even before the Civil War. This was greatly intensified after the Civil War.

[6] "It is not merely with law and prejudice that the free man of colour has here to contend; but with superior knowledge, wealth, and influence, with a deep sense of thraldom to his past and disadvantages of his present condition . . . In Liberia, he exhibits not the semblance, but the reality of freedom. . . ." *Address of the Managers of the American Colonization Society to the People of the United States* (Washington: James C. Dunn, 1832), pp. 3–4.

derived both from the natural dignity of man and from the glorious achievements of African civilization. The fight for the rights of Negroes in North America, the fight for the rights of Africans in Africa, and the revival of Negro interest in African history [7] all began to blend. One of the first fruits of this blend was "pan-Africanism."

In 1900, Henry Sylvester-Williams of Trinidad issued a call for a pan-African conference on behalf of a committee of white and colored Britishers. This meeting was held in London. It seems to be the first use of the term pan-African.[8] The chairman of the conference was an American Negro bishop, Alexander Walters. The Secretary was a young American Negro Ph.D., named W. E. B. Du Bois, who later became one of the leaders of the National Association for the Advancement of Colored People (NAACP). Both Walters and Du Bois had been invited because they were attending the Paris Exposition.[9] The delegates were mainly American and West Indian Negroes and African and white residents of London. The objects of the conference reflected this representation. As stated by Bishop Walters, they were:

First, to bring into closer touch with each other the peoples of African descent throughout the world; second, to inaugurate plans to bring about a more friendly relation between the Caucasian and African races; third, to start a movement looking forward to the securing to all African races living in civilized countries their full rights and to promote their business interests.[10]

What is striking is the emphasis here on the theme of racial equality. This was underlined in Du Bois' famous statement, which is found in the "Address to the Nations of the World," which, as chairman of the Committee on Address, he made in the name of the Conference: "The problem of the twentieth century is the problem of the color line. . . ." [11] The conference was, however, also interested in the protection of African lands in South and West Africa and obtained the promise from Queen Victoria not to "overlook the interests and welfare of the native races." [12]

In North America, in the following years, interest was centered once again on the internal racial situation; 1905 saw the founding of the Niagara Movement, followed by the establishment in 1910 of the NAACP. The pan-African idea lay dormant [13] until Du Bois revived it dramatically at the end of the First World War.

In 1919, Du Bois succeeded, over the opposition of Woodrow Wilson, in conven-

[7] A review of the revival of Negro interest in African history is found in Ulysses Lee, "The ASNLH, The Journal of Negro History, and American Scholarly Interest in Africa," in J. A. Davis (ed.), Africa Seen by American Negroes (Dijon: Présence Africaine, 1958).

[8] Cp. G. Padmore, Pan-Africanism or Communism? (London: Dobson, 1956), p. 118.

[9] Personal communication from W. E. B. Du Bois.

[10] Alexander Walters, My Life and Work (New York: Fleming H. Revell Co., 1917), p. 253.

[11] Ibid., p. 257.

[12] Cp. Padmore, op. cit., pp. 117–18.

[13] From time to time, American Negro interest in Africa would find some expression. In 1896, there was a Conference on Africa held in Atlanta. See J. W. E. Bowen (ed.), Addresses and Proceedings of a Congress on Africa (Atlanta: Gammon Theological Seminary, 1896). In 1911, Booker T. Washington convened the International Conference on the Negro. That same year, Du Bois and Edward Blyden participated in the first Universal Races Congress, in London.

ing the first Pan-African Congress. He did this by securing the support of Blaise Diagne, black deputy from Senegal in the French Parliament, and through Diagne, the acquiescence of Clemenceau. A second Congress was held in London, Paris, and Brussels in 1921; the third in London and Lisbon in 1923; the fourth in New York in 1927. Following the failure to arrange one in Tunis in 1929, there were no further Congresses until after the Second World War.[14] Du Bois played a leading role throughout these Congresses, earning the title "father of pan-Africanism."

The most noteworthy feature of the four Congresses is that they followed directly in the footpaths of the 1900 London Conference. The large majority of the delegates were Western Hemisphere Negroes, as were its leading figures. While reforms in various African countries were sought, and independence was generally accepted as a legitimate objective, the actual demands of the Congresses were limited to insisting on "the right of Africans everywhere to have a voice in their government." [15] Pan-Africanism remains at this stage primarily a protest against racial inequality. Indeed, despite the interest of the Congresses in African questions, there was little African interest in pan-Africanism. Rayford Logan, an American Negro active in the Congresses, has reported:

> Following the third Congress, 1923 [Du Bois] met in Sierra Leone members and promoters of the [National] Congress of [British] West Africa. . . . But there seems to have been little rapport between the Pan-African Congress and the Congress of West Africa.[16]

Not only did pan-Africanism not seem to attract widespread support in Africa, but it ran into great difficulty in the Western Hemisphere, where "one of the most important obstacles to Du Bois' Pan-Africanism resulted from the meteoric rise of Marcus Garvey." [17] Garvey did not appeal to the intellectual and middle-class elements who were the supporters of the NAACP and the pan-African Congresses. His was a "Back to Africa" movement which emphasized mass participation in an

[14] See Padmore, *op. cit.*, Chaps. 7 and 8, for the detailed history. On the French opposition to the Tunis meeting, see W. E. B. Du Bois, *Dusk and Dawn* (New York: Harcourt Brace, 1940), 279–80.

[15] Padmore's summary comment. Cp. *ibid.*, p. 143. Indeed Du Bois stated in 1919 that self-determination could not be applied to "uncivilized peoples." *The World and Africa* (New York: The Viking Press, 1947), p. 8.

Aside from excerpts in Padmore, I have found the full texts of only the Second Pan-African Congress. Cp. appendix to Franck L. Schoell, *La Question des noirs aux Etats-Unis* (Paris: Payot, 1923).

[16] Rayford Logan, "The Historical Aspects of Pan-Africanism, 1900–1945," p. 44, in S. W. Allen, ed., *Pan-Africanism Reconsidered* (Berkeley & Los Angeles: University of California Press, 1962). Du Bois himself asserts that the pan-African idea during the first Congresses was "American rather than African" (*The World and Africa*, p. 242).

The same Third Congress was organized, however, in Lisbon, in collaboration with the *Liga Africana*, a group of Portuguese Africans resident in Lisbon. (Padmore, *op. cit.*, p. 141.) The crucial difference is that the Congress of West Africa was composed largely of persons resident in Africa.

[17] *Ibid.*, p. 14. Padmore also terms Garvey's Black Zionism as "the rival political ideology" to pan-Africanism. *Op. cit.*, p. 89.

ongoing organization. He placed great emphasis on an increasing role for Negro merchants in trade between the West Indies, the United States, and Africa. Garveyism, furthermore, by its use (almost in parody) of European aristocratic costumes and honorifics, and by its inverted racism, was basically assimilationist in its ideology, in that it accepted the European premises of argument and merely reversed the conclusions.

Padmore argues that the difference between Garveyism and pan-Africanism is that

[The latter] was never conceived as a Back to Africa Movement, but rather as a dynamic political philosophy and guide to action for Africans in Africa who were laying the foundations of national organizations.[18]

Despite the fact that it was pan-Africanism, not Garveyism, which laid emphasis on African liberation—an emphasis perhaps exaggerated by Padmore in retrospect in 1956—we have the testimony of Padmore's close friend, President Kwame Nkrumah of Ghana, that it was reading Garvey more than anything else that first inspired his nationalism.[19] Still, Garveyism died and pan-Africanism survived. It did so, despite the opposition of the colonial powers, the Garveyites, and the Communists,[20] largely because it obtained new bases of support after the Second World War, which transformed its emphasis and, hence, its political role. Before discussing the second period of pan-Africanism, however, it would be useful to review what had been occurring in Africa during this same time.

Under the colonial administration in Africa, a class of educated men grew up who were more or less Westernized in their habits and outlooks. This group found the arbitrary occupational limits, the economic and social discriminations, and the inability to participate in government very frustrating, particularly in view of the egalitarian ideals which were preached by many in the metropolitan centers of the colonial empires. Small semi-political groupings of these intellectuals began to come into existence in some parts of Africa. British West Africa has a particularly long history in this regard. Indeed, in some ways, the 1900 London Pan-African Conference was a follow-up to the founding in 1897, in the Gold Coast, of the Aborigines Rights Protection Society and the latter's successful petition to the Queen to protect African land rights. Throughout British Africa such proto-nationalist movements grew up. We might include here such diverse groups as the Kikuyu Central Association in Kenya; the Industrial and Commercial Workers Union and the African National Congress in the Union of South Africa; and the National Congress of British West Africa. In French Africa, there was less leeway for such groups, but political activity started in Senegal and Madagascar, as well as, of course, in North Africa. Even in Portuguese Africa, especially during the liberal era, there were some groups such as the *Liga Africana*. These organizations tended to have two things

---

[18] *Ibid.*, p. 105.
[19] "I think that of all the literature I studied, the book that did more than any other to fire my enthusiasm was *Philosophy and Opinions of Marcus Garvey*, published in 1923." *Ghana: The Autobiography of Kwame Nkrumah* (Edinburgh: Thomas Nelson and Sons, 1957), p. 45.
[20] Cp. Padmore, *op. cit., passim,* especially Chap. 16.

in common. They were groups with limited political effectiveness in Africa, because of the absence of mass support. They were somewhat ambivalent in their political objectives, often not clarifying in their own minds what was the relation between cultural assimilation, extension of political rights, preservation of traditional land rights, and an ultimate goal of independence. Some of these organizations, especially in French and Portuguese Africa, openly avowed assimilation as their goal. Others were more cautious.

Meanwhile, just before, during, and after the Second World War, a new young generation of nationalists began to clarify the alternatives: They rejected assimilation, demanded independence outright, and organized mass movements to secure these ends. This occurred earlier in British West Africa and French North Africa than elsewhere, but it became a mode of organization and of thought that eventually spread everywhere. One of the earliest signs of this new sentiment was found in the fifth Pan-African Congress, organized by Du Bois immediately after the Second World War, in Manchester, England.

The fifth Congress still included many Western Hemisphere Negroes among its leadership: Du Bois, Padmore (Trinidad), and Milliard and Makonnen of British Guiana. But it included as well some African exiles, many of whom have since become political leaders in their countries, notably Kwame Nkrumah and Jomo Kenyatta. These were "exiles" of a different variety from those present at previous Congresses, for these were exiles about to go home. As Shepperson notes:

No nationalism draws its strength from outside sources primarily, though a period of exile—if only in Harlem, Chicago, or a Negro American college—has been a recognized mechanism for the political education of nationalist leaders at least since the 1848 revolutions in Europe.[21]

Both Padmore and Nkrumah remark on the difference of tone of the fifth Congress from previous ones. Padmore attributes this difference to "its plebeian character." [22] Nkrumah accepts this factor of the attendance at the Congress of trade unionists and others who were not "bourgeois Negro reformers." [23] But he adds:

As the preponderance of members attending the Congress were African, its ideology became African nationalism—a revolt by African nationalism against colonialism, racialism and imperialism in Africa—and it adopted Marxian socialism as its philosophy.[24]

Finally he suggests that the main difference is that the delegates were "practical men and men of action." [25] This fifth Congress then marks a break both with the first four Congresses and with Garveyism, since

[21] G. Shepperson, "Notes on Negro American Influence on the Emergence of African Nationalism," *Journal of African History*, Vol. 1, No. 2, 1960, p. 312.
[22] Padmore, *op. cit.*, p. 161.
[23] *Ghana*, p. 53. It must be remembered that the Fifth Congress "was planned to coincide with the second conference of the W.F.T.U. [World Federation of Trade Unions]." Padmore, *op. cit.*, p. 155.
[24] *Ghana*, p. 56 (italics added).
[25] *Loc. cit.*

[Neither was] born of indigenous African consciousness. Garvey's ideology was concerned with *black* nationalism as opposed to *African* nationalism. And it was this 5th Pan-African Congress that provided an outlet for African nationalism and brought about the awakening of Africa's political consciousness.[26]

The fifth Congress is the beginning of the second period of pan-Africanism—its transformation from being primarily a protest movement against racial inequality, largely involving Western Hemisphere Negroes, to being primarily an African movement for the liberation of African colonies from colonial rule. Indeed, by 1960, Rayford Logan would actually define pan-Africanism as "self-government or independence by African nations south of the Sahara." [27] And as a movement for national independence, Du Bois would note that it was in direct conflict with another pan-African movement:

The Pan-African movement which [Jan Smuts] represents is a union of the white rulers of Kenya, Rhodesia and the Union of South Africa, to rule the African continent in the interests of white investors and exploiters.[28]

The goal of pan-Africanism now seemed clear, and the sides were ranged.

Yet, strangely enough, the moment pan-Africanism became outright a movement for national liberation, it faded into the background as an organized movement. However, the West African National Secretariat, whose secretary was Nkrumah, did grow out of the fifth Congress. But, founded in 1946, the Secretariat virtually died out in 1947, with the return of Nkrumah to the Gold Coast.[29] Its formal existence was ended in 1952. Aside from a somewhat abortive pan-African meeting in Kumasi in 1953,[30] there would be no political congress again until 1958.

The nationalist struggle for independence in the various African nations had to be fought under different conditions in each country. It was natural that organizational efforts now took a primarily national form. This was especially true since the theme that was now emphasized was that a successful nationalist revolution was the prerequisite to the achievement of all other objectives: political, economic, and cultural. Nationalism as a protest meant an insistence that self-determination in a nation-state was a universal form to which Africans were entitled and the responsibility for which they were capable of assuming. European conservatives doubted this capability. But African protest was directed as much against the European Left (both Communists and Social Democrats), which often asserted the primacy of the class struggle and argued that the true liberation of the individual lay in changing the economic basis of his existence. African nationalists did not accept that they were any less ready for the nation-state than anyone else. Pan-Africanism insisted that

[26] *Ibid.,* pp. 53–54.

[27] Logan, *op. cit.,* p. 37.

[28] W. E. B. Du Bois, *The World and Africa,* p. 244.

[29] For details, see Padmore, *op. cit.,* pp. 172–74 and *Ghana,* pp. 55–63.

[30] Cp. P. Decraene, "Le Pan-Africanisme" (Paris: *Que sais-je?* No. 847, Presses Universitaires de France, 1959), pp. 26–27. In effect, this was little more than a reunion of Nkrumah and Nnamdi Azikiwe, then president of the National Congress of Nigeria and the Cameroons. There were a few Liberian observers.

there could be no exceptions to this general rule anywhere on the African continent, thus rejecting claims made by many colonial powers that the situation in their empire was somehow special. The pan-African ideal was kept alive in this period by a few nationalist leaders throughout Africa who were planning a possible sixth Pan-African Conference.[31] It was, however, a dormant idea for the moment. They were too preoccupied with their separate struggles, too cut off from each other by space and language, to pursue this ideal more than intermittently. The majority of leaders came to feel that independence first, unity later, was the most promising and effective tactic to follow.

Alongside this somewhat dormant political pan-Africanism, a cultural renaissance was taking place. As political pan-Africanism seemed up to this point to be largely an activity of the English-speaking world (British Caribbean, the United States, Liberia, and British Africa), so the cultural renaissance was at first largely an activity of the French-speaking world (French Africa, French Caribbean and Haiti, Madagascar, and the Belgian Congo). Here too the origins can be traced to the Western Hemisphere. In 1928, Jean Price-Mars of Haiti published an ethnographic work on ancient African civilization, *Ainsi parla l'oncle* . . . , which, though not the first such attempt, had an important effect in French intellectual circles and especially among French Africans and West Indian Negroes.[32] In 1939, Aimé Césaire of Martinique wrote his poem *Cahiers d'un retour au pays natal* in which he first used the term negritude.[33] This term, taken up in a colloquy between Césaire and Léopold-Sédar Senghor, now President of Senegal, became the unifying theme of the African cultural awakening.

Negritude is a protest against the assumption that there is no African cultural heritage worth preserving. It is also a protest against the assumption that the African cultural heritage must be measured in the light of European cultural values. It is, furthermore, a protest against the assumption that Africans are not capable of the *same kind* of cultural achievements as Europeans are. As one can see, these various protests do not all go in the same direction. They may even be said to be somewhat contradictory. The opposing strains are to be found within the movement, sometimes within individuals. Yet, they are held together by the fact that they are all protests against European cultural superiority.

There are perhaps two major themes developed under the name of negritude. One is the argument, of which Senghor is a principal spokesman, that there is some special, unique quality to African culture, some "emotional fervor"[34] which gives it its Negro quality. This quality is not lost when Negroes are transplanted to the Western Hemisphere. It can still be found in their literature, their art, their music,

[31] It is said that the African leaders present at Manchester had pledged each other that the one whose country would first come to independence would convene the Sixth Conference. The honor fell to Nkrumah.

[32] Decraene, *op. cit.*, pp. 16–17.

[33] (Paris: Editions Présence Africaine, reprinted 1956), p. 73.

[34] Cited in J.-P. Sartre, "Black Orpheus," *L'Art nègre* [*Présence Africaine*], Nos. 10–11 (1951), p. 235. For a European analysis which takes the same viewpoint, see Janheinz Jahn, *Muntu: An Outline of Neo-African Culture* (London: Faber and Faber, 1961), especially Chap. 5.

even their philosophy. That this quality is valid, that it is important to preserve and extend it, is what constitutes, for Senghor and many others, the meaning of negritude, of "Negro-African" culture.

There is, however, another emphasis, one which has asserted that negritude is a quality of revolutionary protest, hence in some ways inherently transient. Because the Negro is downtrodden, perhaps the most downtrodden, he produces a vital art, whose vitality reflects its sociological origins. Jean-Paul Sartre's famous analysis of negritude, "Black Orpheus," [35] in effect argues this thesis. Jacques Rabemananjara also argues that:

> The Negro poet remains the man condemned to a permanent crisis of revolt, *insofar* as he has not been delivered of his complex of the colonized and come out of his situation of scorn. . . .[36]

Rabemananjara is a Malagasy poet and statesman and, hence, not a *Negro* African. However, his viewpoint is shared by many Negroes, especially in the Western Hemisphere and the Union of South Africa.[37]

There is a sense in which this latter line of reasoning may be considered more *Africa*-oriented (in the sense of the continent of Africa) and less *Negro*-oriented than the line of reasoning Senghor represents. Negritude as a revolutionary protest can come to terms more easily with Arab Africa, a problem we shall discuss shortly, than negritude as an inherent quality. Still, the distinction is not clear-cut. Though negritude is an assertion of separateness from the world, that is the white world, it is far from isolationist. Negritude as revolutionary protest obviously places itself within a world-wide tradition, a set of universal values. But even for Senghor, cultural isolation is to be rejected:

> So that our negritude may be not a museum piece but rather the effective instrument of a liberation, we must rid it of its dross, of its picturesque qualities and place it within the solidary movement of the contemporary world.[38]

The organizational heart of this African cultural renaissance became a review edited in Paris by Alioune Diop, *Présence Africaine*. Founded in 1947, it received the initial patronage of some of France's most eminent intellectuals (Gide, Camus,

[35] He says: "In fact, Negritude appears as the weak stage of a dialectical progression: the theoretical and practical affirmation of a white supremacy is the thesis; the position of Negritude as antithetical value is the moment of negativity. But this negative moment is not sufficient in itself and the blacks who employ it well know it; they know that it serves to prepare the way for the synthesis or the realization of the human society without racism. Thus Negritude is dedicated to its own destruction, it is passage and not objective, means and not the ultimate goal." *Op. cit.*, p. 245.

[36] "Le poète noir et son peuple," *Présence Africaine*, n.s. 16, Oct.–Nov. 1957, pp. 19–20 (italics added).

[37] There are, of course, some Negro and African intellectuals who reject the idea of negritude altogether, either as a special inherent quality, or a socially-determined revolutionary protest, asserting it to be mysticism or "racism in reverse." See, for example, E. Mphalehle, "The Cult of Negritude," *Encounter*, Vol. 17, No. 3 (March 1960), pp. 50–52.

[38] Cited in Decraene, *op. cit.*, p. 30.

Sartre, Mounier). In 1956, the editors of the review convened the first World Congress of Black Writers and Artists in Paris. Price-Mars was its chairman. The Congress brought together African intellectuals (more French-speaking than English-speaking), Malagasies, North American and West Indian Negroes. Thus, the first major pan-African Congress since 1945 was a cultural rather than a political one. The lines, however, pulled together. Poet and politician overlapped. The men of culture asserted the need for political independence as a prerequisite for effective cultural revival.[39] The Paris Conference, preceded by Bandung, was followed in 1957 by the independence of Ghana, which opened the way for a new political expression of pan-Africanism, indeed a new period in the history of pan-Africanism.

The independence of Ghana had a galvanizing effect on the African continent. Although a small country, Ghana was the first black African country to win its independence from colonial rule.[40] Ghana led the way. It showed that independence could be won, a lesson which had its greatest impact on non-British Africa. Furthermore, Ghana's leader, Kwame Nkrumah, still nourished the pan-African ideals he had worked for in the 1945–47 period. With the independence of his own country secured, Nkrumah began to turn his attention to pan-Africanism.

Pan-Africanism now began to take on two separate, although obviously related, faces: It was both a movement to liberate the remaining colonial areas of Africa and a movement to unite the independent states of Africa into a larger whole. One of the problems was that the process of decolonization, of securing independence, often led to the breakdown of existing colonial entities, the so-called "balkanization" of Africa.[41] The creation of a multiplicity of independent units made even more difficult the achievement of inter-state unity later, because of the vast increase in persons having political interests in opposing unification.

Nevertheless, the move for unity began to show surprising strength. Unity, too, was protest. It was protest against the artificial boundaries created by the colonial powers and the role they played in the final balkanization of Africa during the period of decolonization. It was protest against the continuing political and economic weakness of even independent Africa against the world of Europe. It was protest against the constant assertion by Europeans that African unity was impossible,

[39] Alioune Diop wrote: "The Congress has derived . . . three fundamental truths. . . . This trinity may be schematized as follows:
    1) No people without a culture
    2) No culture without ancestors
    3) No authentic cultural liberation without a prior political liberation."
"Après le congrès," *Présence Africaine*, n.s., Vol. 11 (Décembre 1956—Janvier 1957), p. 4.

[40] In fact, Sudan became independent one year earlier. However, despite its large black population, Sudan is politically dominated by its Arab north and tended to regard itself (and be regarded by others) as a primarily Arab state.

[41] This phrase was originally made famous in Senghor's opposition to the French 1956 *loi-cadre*, which devolved some executive power on the various African territories of France, but not on the two major interterritorial entities, French West Africa and French Equatorial Africa. The phrase has since been taken up widely throughout Africa. See the editorial, "Balkanisation et unité," in *Présence Africaine*, n.s., Vol. 23 (Décembre 1958—Janvier 1959), pp. 3–5.

especially when the argument emphasized ethnic diversity as the barrier, since this argument threatened equally national unity. Many African nationalists tended to make not "independence" but "independence and unity" the goal, arguing that without unity the goals of the anti-colonial struggle were unfulfilled.

Two principal organizations arose to work towards these goals: the Conference of Independent African States and the All-African People's Conference. These two Conferences along with the Congress of Black Writers and Artists [42] formed the three descendants of the Pan-African Congresses. The two political groups differed in that the first was a grouping of independent African states, whereas the second grouped political parties and trade unions in both independent and colonial Africa. Thus far, the Conference of Independent African States has met in Accra in 1958 and Addis Ababa in 1960. The All-African People's Conference has met in Accra in 1958, Tunis in 1960, and Cairo in 1961.

Aside from the important role of Ghana in originally convening both sets of Conferences—in each case the first meeting was in Accra—the most significant fact to notice about them was that Africa, for the first time in the history of pan-Africanism, was defined continentally to include the Arab north as well as Negro Africa. Nor was this lightly or peripherally done. The continental unity of Africa now became a central theme of pan-Africanism.

North Africans had never been invited to attend the original Pan-African Congresses. It is true that Tunis was chosen as the site of a Pan-African Congress in 1929, which was never held because of French opposition. The reason seems largely that Tunis was at least in Africa. It was, thus, better than a European city because it was accessible to delegates [43] in an era before airline travel was common. It is true, furthermore, that the resolutions of the fifth Pan-African Conference included a call for the independence of Algeria, Morocco, and Tunisia.[44] Still, the great emphasis on the question of color and the trans-Atlantic involvement based on race precluded any serious thought of including North Africa. But as pan-Africanism shifted from being primarily a protest against racial inequality to being a movement for national liberation, and then a movement for creating new interstate unity, the interrelation of the struggle of Arab Africa and black Africa became more apparent, especially once the Algerian war of independence became a vital factor in speeding up the decolonization of black Africa.[45]

It might be thought that the logic of cultural pan-Africanism militated against including Arab civilizations in the political scheme. But this neglects the fact that there was at least one way of interpreting negritude—that is, negritude as revolutionary protest—that created no difficulties in this regard. It neglected further the

[42] At its second meeting, this group changed its name to the Congress of Black Men of Culture.
[43] Cf. Padmore, *op. cit.*, p. 143; Du Bois, *op. cit.*, p. 243, on the reasons for choosing Tunis.
[44] Cf. Decraene, *op. cit.*, p. 22. The full text of the resolutions is to be found in G. Padmore (ed.), *History of the Pan-African Congress* (Manchester: Pan-African Federation, n.d., ca., 1947).
[45] Cf. B. Rivlin, "Arab Africa in an Emerging African Community," *Journal of International Affairs*, Vol. 15, No. 1 (1961), 42–51.

fact that cultural history can be reanalyzed in ways more compatible with political visions of the future. And, indeed, a school of historians has begun to argue the links of Negro Africa with ancient Egypt.[46]

Some of the push towards continental pan-Africanism derived from the fact that, at least for the French areas, North African nationalism developed more rapidly and served in some ways as an inspiration to black-African nationalism. Part of it derived from the fact that when, in April 1958, Nkrumah wished to convene a meeting of independent African states, the only existing states were five Arab states and three black African ones (plus the Union of South Africa). Part of the impetus came from the sentiment, separately developed in the Maghreb,[47] and to a lesser extent in Egypt,[48] that the Arab states needed black Africa to reinforce their own positions in their struggle against the European world.

Pan-Africanism as an ideology has come to mean the triptych of national independence, negritude, and continental unity. The three goals, while occasionally detracting one from the other, have managed thus far to be more or less in harmony, precisely because they all represent a form of protest against the white European world. These three objectives find combined expression in the two major policy proposals of the pan-Africanists: neutralism as a foreign policy and the pursuit of "African Socialism" at home. Neutralism is justified as a safeguard of independence, an indispensable tactic in the pursuit of unity, a logical outgrowth of a belief in negritude (for the Soviet Union is part of the European world, and Communism a Western ideology).

The logic of neutralism and of negritude has led to the search for an "African Socialism." Whereas at the time of the fifth Pan-African Congress there was talk of Marxian Socialism as a goal and of the rights of the proletariat, this language has been replaced gradually by an insistence that Africa knew an ancient communal Socialism which could be the basis for a modern Socialist economy,[49] and that the class struggle is not a meaningful concept in contemporary African society.[50]

[46] See the works of Cheikh Anta Diop, passim. See also my article, "The Search for National Identity in West Africa," Présence Africaine, Vols. xxxiv–xxxv, Nos. 6–7 (1960), pp. 17–29 (English ed.).

In fact, such an interpretation has long emotional and historical roots. See, for example, the story told by a Sierra Leone professional man about his childhood schooling shortly after the First World War. "We studied Roman history. . . . I began to develop a sense of depth in my appreciation of time. And also the first stirrings of nationalism. To me the Carthaginians were fellow-Africans." Robert W. Cole, Kossoh Town Boy (Cambridge: University Press, 1960), pp. 175–76.

[47] A reading of the Tunisian paper, Jeune Afrique, the Algerian papers, El Moudjahid and L'Ouvrier Algérien, or the Moroccan papers, Al Istiqlal and L'Avant-Garde will reveal how large a proportion of their space is devoted to black Africa.

[48] Nasser's emphasis on Africa is revealed in Egypt's Liberation (Washington: Public Affairs Press, 1955), pp. 86 and 109–11.

[49] See, for example, the argument of Senghor: "We would learn that we had already realized socialism before the coming of the European." African Socialism (New York: American Society of African Culture, 1959), p. 32.

[50] See, for example, the statement of Sékou Touré, President of Guinea: "If you take up the problem of classes, you will note that there exists in Africa only one and the same class, the class of

"African Socialism" is distinguished from a universal ideology of Socialism, thus serving the cause both of neutralism and of negritude.

Pan-Africanism has become the ideology of the militant wing of African nationalism. There are some leaders who hesitate to commit themselves, even some who are hostile—although almost all pay pan-Africanism the nominal obeisance which indicates its popular appeal. Its oponents can scarcely be said to have evolved a conservative counterideology, but those who resist the claims of the pan-Africanists tend also to be dubious about neutralism and "African Socialism." [51]

The period of de-colonization, especially from 1956 on, was marked by the anomaly that those who were most militant in their demands for independence *and* unity were often forced to choose the dismantling of existing political units in order to speed the path to independence. Thus, the price of independence came to be balkanization. A striking example is the case of Guinea, in 1958, when it opted for independence in the de Gaulle Referendum of 1958 but thereby brought about the definitive breakup of the Federation of French West Africa, a structure which had been under attack for some time. Guinea did so in the belief that not only would its own independence be speeded up, but that of the other West African states as well.[52] Unity was a goal, but it was the uniting of *independent* units that was sought.

Those African nations who were the first to obtain their independence have been the most militant on pan-Africanism. It is easy to understand this. Leaving aside settler areas, where the pace of decolonization has been slower because of the political strength of the settlers, militance in nationalist claims, which had a pan-African orientation, has led to a more rapid achievement of independence. Thus the group of independent states who met in the Conference of Independent African States in 1958 tended to place emphasis on pan-African themes. The African group at the United Nations from 1958 to 1960 reflected this united militance.

In 1960, a series of other countries in Africa received their independence, partially in the wake of the first group. Their path having been relatively smoother, they were less inclined to maintain strong pan-Africanist positions. The first group was determined to achieve or restore the larger unities, whose breakdown or nonexistence they felt to be the result of the maneuvers of the colonial powers during the period of decolonization.

The arrival on the scene of this new group of governments, less oriented to a pan-African ideology, coincided with the Congo crisis of 1960, which temporarily crystallized a division of African governments on pan-Africanism into two groupings, called the Casablanca and Brazzaville groups, named after conferences held

the dispossessed." *Textes des Interviews* (Conakry: République de Guinée, September 1959), No. 3, p. 7.

[51] But there are some important exceptions to this correlation. In 1961, the Moroccan government position was pan-Africanist but lukewarm to socialist slogans. By contrast, the Senegalese government declared itself on the "African path to socialism" but was lukewarm to political pan-African slogans. These "inconsistencies" are largely semantic ones, readily explicable by an analysis of the particular history and politics of each country.

[52] This belief was to be largely confirmed by subsequent events. See my "How Seven States Were Born in Former French West Africa," *Africa Report,* Vol. 6, No. 3 (March 1961).

in the two cities.[53] The membership of the two groups has varied. The Casablanca group, militant pan-Africanists, has at least included Algeria, Ghana, Guinea, Mali, Morocco, and the United Arab Republic. The Brazzaville group has at least included the majority of former French black African states.

It is important to note what has divided the Casablanca and Brazzaville groups. The key issues have been the Congo and Algeria, the Casablanca group having stood for full backing to the Lumumbists in the Congo[54] and the Provisional Government of the Algerian Republic in Algeria. A parallel split has occurred in the trade union over the key issue of whether the African trade unions, who were to form the All-African Trade-Union Federation, would be required to disaffiliate from all other internationals (in effect, from the International Confederation of Free Trade Unions) or not. The Casablanca group stood for disaffiliation.

The strength of "Casablanca" has been the fact that they have incarnated the spirit of pan-Africanism, whose motivating force antedates the particular quarrels of the present, support for which is to be found throughout the continent of Africa. An African government which resists pan-Africanism—and its concomitants, neutralism and African socialism—has an extra burden to bear in the struggle to maintain its power and its popular support.

What then are the prospects of pan-Africanism? Independence has been achieved virtually throughout the African continent. Negritude is prospering. It is unity which seems the hardest goal. The difficulties are real. What militates to some extent in its favor is the remarkable tolerance and eclecticism the pan-African movement has, on the whole, shown thus far. Splits within countries and between countries have seldom been irreversible, and passions have thus far seldom become rancours. Even where rancour might be the greatest, directed outward to the white European world, the very success of African nationalism has served to blunt the anger which gave rise to the protest. Furthermore, the split in the white European world, the Cold War, has thus far served to accelerate the process of decolonization. It may do the same for the process of African unification.

Perhaps the strongest factor pushing towards unity is the sense of incompleteness of the revolution, the unfulfilled protest. This sense of incompleteness is matched by both determination and surprising optimism. The recent statement of Gabriel d'Arboussier, Senegal's Minister of Justice, and original Secretary-General of Africa's largest interterritorial party, the *Rassemblement Démocratique Africain,* may be cited as typical of this optimism:

The union of States of West Africa will come about in the next five years; the year 1965 will see without a doubt the flourishing of a new, bilingual civilization, a civilization

[53] A rapid account of various attempts at federation and larger unities in recent years will be found in my *Africa: The Politics of Independence* (New York: Vintage, 1961), Chap. 6. For a detailed list of the various conferences, see "Regroupements Africains," *Interafrique Presse,* Nos. 292–293 (5–12 Mai 1961), and "La Conférence de Monrovia," *Interafrique Presse,* Nos. 295–296 (26 Mai—2 Juin 1961).

[54] See Robert Good, "Four African Views of the Congo Crisis," *Africa Report,* Vol. 6, No. 6 (June 1961).

composed of the Anglo-Saxon genius, the French genius, the African genius, but to which will perhaps be added new concepts of economic organization coming from the experience of the socialist countries.[55]

Pan-Africanism remains an ideology of the young in Africa today, a protest against the past, a vision of the future. When protests are largely satisfied and visions partly fulfilled, then ideologies slip silently back into the historical shadow. This may be the fate of pan-Africanism.

[55] Speech delivered in Dakar, Senegal, January 18, 1961, reported in *Afrique nouvelle* (Dakar), No. 708 (March 1, 1961), p. 9.

7

Nasserism: The Protest Movement in the Middle East

Leonard Binder

I "Nasserism" and Pan-Arabism

The pan-Arab movement is a protest against three related political situations. The most obvious target of pan-Arab protest is the division of Arabic speaking peoples into a number of independent states. Secondarily, it is a protest against the existing economic and social systems of all the Arab countries and against the political power structure of some. The third protest is against the bipolarization of international power.

The form of Arab nationalism which is characterized by these three protests is sometimes referred to as "Nasserism," with the implications that the policies of the UAR have substantial support beyond the borders of that country and that they are an accurate reflection of pan-Arab ideology. But in equating "Nasserism" or pan-Arabism with the policies of the UAR we may be confusing a diffuse symbol with but one of its concrete manifestations.

The problem rests upon the multiple meanings and usages of the term "Nasserism," and the confusion which results from the failure to probe more deeply behind it. Nevertheless, it may be argued that the truly important thing is the diffuse ideological and social movement of generalized protest known as "Nasserism," rather than the specific policies of the Nasser-led UAR. The concrete policy, however, is the test of what is essential in the ideology. It is the policy rather than the internal logic or philosophical foundation which gives us the meaning of the theory.[1]

The first thing to bear in mind is the fact that "Nasserism" is not used by the Arabs themselves to describe their aspirations. This is a term of Western construction. Arab writers generally ignore the term, but when they do not, they find it objectionable. According to Dr. Abd al-Qadir Hatim, the West talks of "Nasserism" as though Nasser were intent on establishing an empire because they are imperialists and believe that everyone else is too.[2] Al-Rimawi asserts that the whole purpose

[1] For a detailed study based on this view, see my *Religion and Politics in Pakistan* (Berkeley: University of California Press, 1961).
[2] Abd al-Qadir Hatim, *Hawl al-Nazriyyah al-Ishtirakiyyah* [*On the Theory of Socialism*] Kutub Qawmiyyah Series, No. 14 (Cairo, July 1959), p. 8.

of the imperialists, Zionists, and certain Arab-ruling circles may be summed up in the single slogan "the destruction of Nasserism."

But this Nasserism does not refer to a single individual, and does not refer to a specific government such as that of the UAR. It refers clearly and precisely to the national revolutionary force—in its ideological position, its principles, its goals, in whatsoever it has realized by way of victories in the spheres of nationalism, liberation, unity and in the economic and social spheres of life. That slogan is a war cry repeated by the forces of opposition and their stooges in the Arab homeland, a war to destroy the national revolutionary force and the new Arab national movement.[3]

But barely concealed beneath Rimawi's breathless prose is the assertion that "Nasserism," as used by the opponents of Arab nationalism, attempts to isolate President Nasser and the government of the UAR from the Arab people, while what they really oppose are the aspirations and the interests of the people. These aspirations are to be carried to fruition by the government of the UAR.

The birth of the UAR has come to declare, for the first time in modern Arab history, and for hundreds of years, the establishment of a united Arab state in which (a) there is no hostile or basic contradiction, in terms of will or interest, between the people and the government, and (b) in which there is no hostile or fundamental contradiction, in terms of will or interest, between that government and the Arab nation.[4]

The author's apologetic for the policies of the UAR and of President Nasser is directed against the unregenerate Ba'this who have mischievously refused to recognize that the formation of the UAR initiated a new stage in the Arab struggle.[5] According to Hatim, the third stage of Arab nationalism appeared when President Nasser added a philosophy or creed (madhab) to the socio-historical existence of the Arab nation and to the consciousness which gave birth to solidary action in Palestine and Port Said.[6] Nasser did not move directly from the first stage to the third stage because the landmarks of the ideology of the Arab nation were not clear. They are not written on paper as is the Communist Manifesto, but they are written in the hearts of the Arab people.[7]

The argument of these two authors is clear. They hold that the consciousness and aspirations of the whole Arab people, as represented in certain social facts and as evolved in a particular historical process, are concretely manifested in the policies of the United Arab Republic. Hatim does little more than assert this justification, but Rimawi outlines the goals of the Arab national revolutionary movement and attempts to prove that the UAR is objectively capable of realizing these goals—despite his attack on its wisdom and practicality. Hence, those opposing Nasser do not oppose the legitimacy of his leadership, they oppose the Arab national movement.

[3] Abd Allah al Rimawi, al Mantiq al-Thawri [The Revolutionary Logic] (Cairo, 1961), p. 95.
[4] Ibid., pp. 55–56.
[5] Ibid., p. 32. On the Ba'th Party, see the works of Michel Aflaq, and Salah al-Din al-Bitar cited below, and those of Munif al-Razzaz, etc. See also "The Constitution of the Arab Resurrection Socialist Party (Ba'th)," Middle East Journal, Vol. 13, No. 2 (Spring 1959), pp. 195–200.
[6] Hatim, op. cit., pp. 5–7.
[7] Ibid., p. 8.

These opponents number more than a few; they include Bourguiba, the Syrian Nationalists, the Lebanese Confessionalists, the Hashemites, the "Communist-infiltrated" government of Iraq, and the traditional Arab rulers. With so many opponents claiming to speak for the interests of the Arab people, or for parts of them, it is probably not incorrect to assume that there is a good deal of interaction between policy-formation in the UAR and expectations about popular reaction throughout the Arab world. The policy of the UAR, therefore, may be seen as an adaptation of the practical choices of the Egyptian political-military elite to the exigencies of the opinion of the (politically) participant Arab classes.

Even this careful definition of "Nasserism" is none too specific, but it has the merit of suggesting that the policy indicated by that term is dynamic and responsive. It is probably highly personal because of the overwhelming dominance of President Nasser—politically within the UAR and symbolically elsewhere. If nothing succeeds like success then it follows, too, that to some extent the Arab national movement has adapted itself to the policies of the UAR. In other words the two elements of our equation—the policies of the UAR and those things "written in the hearts of the Arab people"—are not equal, but they influence one another in the direction of equality.

In seeking to lead the Arab national movement and to benefit by its support, Nasser may not do as he likes, but he is at the same time under no compulsion to do any specific thing at a specific time. There is no ideological rigidity here, even if Arab nationalism appears less flexible at times than Communism. Up to a limit, a shrewd calculation of gains and losses, rather than a perverse, affective rebellion, is the more appropriate expectation in dealing with the leadership of the UAR.

II Policy and Ideology

The essentially non-ideological character of UAR policy has been proposed, but there is some controversy over this matter. In most writing on Arab politics by Arab writers there is frequent reference to the principles of the revolution and the ideals of the Arab people. In President Nasser's speeches there is also a good deal of emphasis upon the same theme. Of course, a set of principles is not an ideology, but even such principles as may be found do not set narrow limits to the range of policy choices before the government of the UAR. Furthermore, it is a generally well-known feature of contemporary Arab nationalist thought that the national movement lacks an ideology.[8] This does not mean that there are no Arab ideologies, nor that the philosophical foundations and logical derivatives of statements on Arab politics may not be fruitfully investigated. It does mean that there is no widely accepted theory which satisfies the majority of the Arab intelligentsia. From the search for an ideology, it is possible to understand that to be without one is a source of shame

[8] See Rejwan in W. Z. Laqueur, *The Middle East in Transition* (New York, 1958) and H. Z. Nusaibeh, *The Ideas of Arab Nationalism* (Ithaca, 1956).

to many. An official ideology, however, can be a serious embarrassment to a government as well as a welcome support to legitimacy.

The difficulty here is typical of that discovered in studying many areas of Egyptian politics, for the very reason that policy grows and does not spring full blown from the head of Zeus. We have already seen where Hatim propounds the view that only in the last stage, after 1956, did President Nasser provide the Arab movement (né the Egyptian revolution) with an ideology, the source of which was in the hearts of the people. Another minister, Dr. Tharwat Ukasha, presents a similar view and suggests, more specifically, that the idea behind the National Union will be found in the statements and speeches of President Nasser, but that this idea was always present in the hopes of the people and was represented by the Revolutionary Council which laid the plans leading to the admirable state of affairs now existing in Egypt.[9] In his recent introduction to a newer edition of Nasser's *Philosophy of the Revolution,* Kamal al-Din Husain writes that part two of the book answers the two questions: What was the aim of the revolution and what is the way of achieving that aim? [10] The answer to the first question is simple, the revolution sought what every Arab seeks for his homeland. The second question was more difficult, but its answer is primarily to remove the obstacles from the path and give leadership to the lost caravan.

If these semi-official statements follow the same line of according President Nasser ideological leadership, while asserting that he is doing no more than expressing the will of the Arab people, his own statements and many unofficial statements uphold the view that the ideology of the revolutionary movement is still not fixed. The most graphic of these is Nasser's report of the results of his seeking the advice of those "with opinions and expertise."

Every idea we heard had no aim other than to destroy some other one! Had we followed all that we heard we would have killed them all and destroyed all the ideas.[11]

Much later Nasser was to admit openly that the leaders of the revolution had no idea of what to do when they suddenly found themselves in power. They made mistakes, especially in appointing that first civilian cabinet, for they did not appreciate the difference in mentality between themselves and the politicians and administrators whom they appointed.[12] But more pointedly, Nasser has stated that there is no fixed plan for the National Union; progress is to be made by trial and error.[13] At a recent cabinet meeting the President was importuned to consider revising the

[9] Tharwat 'Ukasha, *Itihaduna Falsafah Khalqiyyah* [*Our Union Is a Moral Philosophy*] al-Maktabah al-Thaqafiyyah Series, No. 16, Ministry of Culture and National Guidance, n.d., pp. 3–4. The National Union is the mass popular organization which replaces political parties in the UAR.

[10] Kamal al-Din Husain, "Introduction," in Gamal Abd al-Nasser, *Falsafat al-Thawrah,* n.d., n.p. Introductory insert has no page numbers.

[11] Nasser, *Falsafat al-Thawrah,* pp. 26, 27.

[12] *Nasser's Speeches* (English) (1959), p. 570.

[13] *Ibid.,* p. 315.

system of administration in government-controlled companies to bring it more into line with the ideology of "Arab socialism." His answer was to point out the difficulty and the length of time necessary to study such a project, and he added that the accepted basis of administration in both East and West is efficiency.

These views of Nasser are borne out in most conversations with informed Egyptians. In answer to inquiries about the ideology of the UAR government, an admittedly unfair question,[14] two sorts of answers are forthcoming. Either people say that there is none, or they refer the inquirer to President Nasser's published speeches. If one inquires more specifically about certain policies of the UAR, then the answer is almost invariably that the policy is not rigid, it does not stem from any fixed idea, it will be tested pragmatically and discarded if found wanting.

Of course, opposition nationalist groups may have their favorite ideologians. If you ask Ba'this about the ideology of the Arab national movement, they will no doubt refer to Michel Aflaq and several others. Some of these ideologically inclined pan-Arabists have come over to Nasser's side behind Rimawi; and it is of great interest to note the way in which that ex-Ba'thi has turned the tables on his former comrades in justifying the pragmatism of Nasser against the romanticism of Aflaq. Without mentioning Nasser or Aflaq he asserts that the Arabs must work to construct a theory on the basis of the experiences and successes of the Arab and Afro-Asian peoples. They must ask, he goes on, whether the slogans, policies, and positions of the government of the UAR are a correct expression of the revolutionary aims and of the interest of Arab nationalism. Then they must ask whether there is any fundamental hostile contradiction between the Arab people and that government. (We have already noted where Rimawi answers the latter in the negative.) Rimawi continues: "Those who pretend that a theory already exists are simpletons, and their productions are superficial and confused. The ideology of Arab nationalism is in the process of coming into being, and that process must be encouraged. Every Arab group or party has a part to play in this effort, but the part played by those who experience the realities of the Arab nation will differ from that of the ivory-tower theorist. The latter borrows from old philosophies or from the experience of other countries or strains to point out secondary contradictions and in the end finds himself consciously or unconsciously a tool of either the Communists or the imperialists.[15]

The primary premise has become the identity of the policy of the UAR and the interest of the Arab nation. Once this has been established, building the theory of Arab nationalism becomes a process combining exegesis, justification, and generalization.

Despite the lack of ideological limitation, the policy of the UAR can be shown to be more or less fixed at the present time and to have gone through a sort of rational (in the historic sense) growth. This, no doubt, is due to a gradually

[14] Not entirely unfair, however, for President Nasser has described his country as an exporter of ideology. *Nasser's Speeches* (English) (1959), p. 524.
[15] Rimawi, *op. cit.*, pp. 60–62.

increasing awareness of the attitudes of the broader Arab public, as well as to the effect of international pressures and the blind logic of history which never permits an act to be completely erased from the consciousness of man.

III   Pan-Arabism

The pan-Arab ideal of the Ba'th Party of Syria has become the goal of the UAR, even if not an unequivocal one. The Ba'th called for (and still does) comprehensive Arab unity; that is, for the creation of a single Arab state stretching from the Atlantic to the Persian Gulf. The exact means of achieving this unity and its institutional complement, whether a unitary state or not, is left conveniently open. Nevertheless, as Abdullah Rimawi insists, the formation of the UAR has pointed the way to a possible answer. That answer is the complete merger of Arab states whether neighboring or not.

But the implication of this simple, no-buts-about-it, answer are now clear, for all to see. Given the size, wealth, military power, and demographic composition of the Arab states (with the exclusion of the Maghrib, perhaps), that implication is the domination of Egypt. The fact that even with this implication the idea is very attractive to many Sunni Arab intellectuals is a testimony to the charismatic qualities of President Nasser, as well as to certain other factors. These other factors may be summed up briefly as follows: None of the Eastern Arab states is either homogeneous or large enough to provide, at one and the same time, sufficient bases for Arab nations and sufficient scope for the aspirations of the educated classes.[16] To be a Syrian, Jordanian, or Iraqi has none of the appeal and little of the ideological reality of being an Arab. As for the possibility of an Arab state comprising the Fertile Crescent—Nuri Sa'id's plan or that of the Syrian Nationalists now under attack from Cairo—the statement attributed to Sa'd Zaghlul about the consequences of adding zero and zero together seem to apply.

There are significant differences between the societies and cultures of the Nile Valley and of the Fertile Crescent, but the intellectual classes and their medium of cultural exchange are similar. Furthermore, if Nasser's repeated emphasis upon power, glory, honor, dignity, independence, self-reliance, and, in the special sense of the local idiom, personality, has any meaning, it is because Nasser himself appears to have achieved these, and one can identify with the "champion of Arabism" who was born in a village in upper Egypt. It must take a good deal of forebearance for any Arab to deny himself the vicarious glory of feeling himself to have shared in Nasser's "victories."

For those who seek some more concrete sense of the reasons for the success of "Nasserism" in this pan-Arabist sense, Professor Karl Deutch's analysis of the forma-

[16] This point is elaborated in "Prolegomena to the Comparative Study of Middle East Governments," *APSR*, Vol. 51, No. 3 (1957).

tion of national communities in Europe is applicable here, perhaps even more than in the areas he studied.[17] In line with that analysis, Egypt is the core area, not because of its geographic location, nor because of its surplus wealth, but because of its size, population, stability, relative security, and its intellectual leadership of the Arab world. Egypt does not offer many economic attractions to other Arab areas, and its surplus educated elite is potentially competitive with those from other Arab countries; nevertheless, there is some expectation that Egypt may be able to manage effective economic development.

Despite these tendencies we should beware of overexaggerating the seriousness with which comprehensive Arab unity is advocated outside of Egypt. In many cases, the fate of Syria appears to have given solemn pause to those who have something to lose, although others assume the pro-Nasserist stance as the most acceptable of the Left or radical positions in opposing their own traditional or conservative governments.[18] In still other cases the pro-Nasserist position is to some extent a communal position for Sunni Arabs who are in the minority and who, thereby, may wield the international prestige of the President of the UAR in their domestic battles. The balance of attractions and repulsions cannot be estimated yet for, even if Syrians, and especially Ba'this, found themselves with little policy-making power, Egypt knew that it was being judged in the "Northern Region" and efforts were bent to developing the resources of Syria even to the extent of transferring funds (directly and with moderate fanfare) to the regional budget from Cairo.[19]

Of course, no one explicitly advocates the subordination of all the Arab states to Nasser's leadership, but no other practical course is suggested. Rimawi is outspoken that the UAR has the capability of realizing all the Arab aims, but he does not draw the logical conclusion. The UAR leaders themselves were circumspect about expressing their aspirations even before the Syrian break with the UAR; first, because they were, doubtless, not yet ready to cope with another "region," though they were willing to if necessary; and second because there was no need to be explicit. Hatim vigorously denied that Nasser has imperialist aspirations, and Nasser was careful to point out that the UAR came into being as a result of Syrian initiative. But the facts of the situation were all in favor of the UAR anyway. Its population [before the Syrian rupture] numbered over 26 million to a maximum total of 15 million for the rest of the Fertile Crescent. All that needed to be done was advocate unity, not in any legal sense, but the unity of brothers and the solidarity of the family.[20] When Kassim offered a proposal for federal unity shortly after the Iraqi revolution, Nasser pointed out that there was no hurry: First let Kassim consolidate his revolution, then one could consider ways and means of achieving unity.[21]

[17] K. Deutsch, et al., The Political Community and the North Atlantic Area (Princeton: Princeton University Press, 1957).

[18] In 1957 Aflaq was of the opinion that Rightists and Leftists could cooperate during the anti-imperialist stage of the Arab struggle; Michel Aflaq, Fi Sabil al-Ba'th (Beirut, 1959), p. 220.

[19] Al-Jaridah al-Rasmiyya [Official Gazette] No. 157 (July 14, 1960), p. 1264.

[20] This is 'Ukasha's central theme, op. cit.

[21] Nasser's Speeches (English) (1959), pp. 282–83.

To illustrate the current policy of the UAR on the pan-Arab issue, there is no better or more interesting set of documents than the recent exchange of letters between King Husain of Jordan and President Nasser. Relations between Jordan and the UAR have gone from moderately good, during the Nabulsi period of 1956 and early 1957, to bad, after Nabulsi's dismissal and the landing of British troops during the Lebanese and Iraqi crises of 1958, to slightly better, after the appointment of Majali as Prime Minister, until after the Bhamdun conference when al-Majali was assassinated. Both sides have accused one another of this murder and of worse; and the incident reversed an agreement between the two countries. Then just as suddenly, relations improved after King Husain sent a personal letter to President Nasser. The letters do not cover over the differences between the two rulers, but they constitute a cautious agreement to disagree.

Husain's letter expressed his desire to seek a better future for the Arab nation, "leaving the judgment of the righteousness of intentions and deeds to God, to history and the people. . . . The Arab nation," he wrote, "will never be the property of Husain ibn Talal or of Gamal Abd al-Nasser." Both of them are simply responsible servants of the Arab nation. The dangers and problems facing the Arabs are great; hence, it behooves the Arab leaders to cooperate rather than dispute.

But Husain's main plea was contained in his statement of his belief that the most elementary principles of cooperation and of steadfastness in the face of danger were "the equality of all the sons of our nation in good or bad times, their full equality in their rights and duties, and *non-intervention of some in the affairs of others*." [22]

It need hardly be pointed out that the principle of non-intervention has lost much of its meaning throughout the world today, but nowhere is the definition of an internal affair so anomalous as among the Arab countries. Some Arabs have insisted on the rule of non-intervention in both domestic and foreign affairs, but in Arab politics any statement about Arab nationalism necessarily affects the internal affairs of several sovereign states.[23]

President Nasser's response was in the same non-committal tone, though it was interpreted as a friendly, if frank answer. That letter is an admirable summary of the UAR position. A précis of its relevant sections follows:

The disputes among the Arab states are not superficial, they reflect factual contradictions in the present Arab situation. But Arab solidarity is essential in the face of grave dangers and powerful enemies. True solidarity is needed, not a façade; nor should it be a solidarity which limits the Arab effort or restricts the Arab vanguards . . . We praised you when you dismissed Glubb Pasha, but opposed you when you cooperated with those who sought to isolate Egypt after the Suez attack. There is no doubt that Egypt loses much when Jordan is separated from her, but the loss to Jordan is much greater. We supported every Arab country in its struggle for freedom, the Palestine case was our motive for opposing the Baghdad Pact, it was our motive for purchasing arms from the

[22] *Al-Ahram* (March 31, 1961); *Egyptian Mail* (April 1, 1961) (Italics added).
[23] Muhammad Mustafa al-Sha'bini, *al-Hiyad al-Ijabi* [*Positive Neutrality*], Kitab al-Madfa'iyyah (Cairo, 1960), pp. 72, 95.

Soviet bloc (breaking the arms monopoly) and our stand on Palestine was the reason for the tri-partite armed aggression in 1956.[24] We have borne the major burden of supporting Algeria's struggle for freedom, and we supported the independence of Tunis, Morocco, Sudan, Iraq, Oman, the Arab South,[25] Lebanon and even Jordan. This we do as our duty, for we believe that *our people, as a result of its material and moral potentialities was placed by fate at the head of the Arab struggle and forms its base.* The role of the base is not domination but service.

Domestically we seek democracy, not only in general elections, but participation in a national economic revolution to increase production and achieve equality in distribution. We seek to equalize opportunities and to melt the differences between citizens. We plan to double the national income in ten years. To achieve equitable distribution we have limited land ownership, nationalized the British, French, and Belgian monopolies, the banks and the insurance companies. We have levied progressive taxes and established cooperatives.

We believe in Arab nationalism as a true and genuine current moving toward comprehensive Arab unity. *We are not so much interested in its constitutional form as we are in the will of the Arab people.*

Our policy is a reflection of our existence, an existence against which we cannot rebel. But this does not mean that we wish to impose that policy on other Arab states, for I know that each Arab state is more capable than others in facing its special circumstances and has more right to have the last word regarding those circumstances. There is no doubt that there are things about which we can differ, but let us face those in a spirit of brotherly forgiveness.[26]

The letter, even in its abbreviated form, needs little commentary. Although admitting the special circumstances of Jordan, Nasser claims for the UAR, in a phrase reminiscent of Rimawi, by virtue of its material and moral potentialities, the leadership of the Arab struggle for comprehensive unity. The contradictions which characterize the Arab situation are not explained, but they are strongly hinted at in Nasser's statements on domestic policy and in the section on positive neutrality which was omitted.

The letters show that the UAR prefers to maintain normal relations with its sister Arab states as a basis for achieving its aims. The violent attacks on Husain were quite suddenly switched off at his first overture—an overture which implied no concessions. Husain is surely the weaker of the two, but the UAR prefers to bide its time and to use the tactics of the sun rather than those of the wind in getting the Jordanian king to remove his coat.

Though this represents the present policy of the UAR with regard to pan-Arabism, it was not the original position of the Free Officers when they took power. Ideologically they were, perhaps, not opposed to comprehensive Arab unity, but they had no position on the matter at all. From the little we know of the contents of the manifestoes of the Free Officers group before the 1952 *coup,* it is clear that com-

---

[24] The emphasis on Palestine is a rebuttal to Husain's claim that Jordan bears the brunt of the common Arab struggle.
[25] The Arab South is the current term for Aden and the Aden Protectorate.
[26] *Al-Ahram, loc. cit.* (Italics added.)

prehensive unity was not in their program, though Arab solidarity was mentioned as one of their principles. In the past, Egyptians have not been so sure that they were Arabs, some preferring to see themselves as part of Europe or to draw their nationalist inspiration from Egypt's Pharaonic past.

Some of this controversy has been described in an article by A. G. Chejne, and he comes to the conclusion, despite Egypt's leadership in the formation of the Arab League in 1945, that Egypt was not committed to a vigorous Arab policy until 1954.[27] His conclusion is well sustained by an examination of Nasser's speeches, which do not address themselves importantly to Arab questions until 1955, that is, until the controversy over Iraq's adherence to the Baghdad Pact broke out in full fury. Since that time there have been many references to the imperialists' attempt to convince the Egyptians that they were not Arabs and to foster Pharaonism as a kind of intellectual imperialism.[28]

But an analysis of Nasser's speeches further indicates that comprehensive unity did not loom large in Egyptian policy until after the union of Syria and Egypt, that is to say, until forced upon Egypt by the logic of events themselves. On March 28, 1955 Nasser first stated the six principles of the revolution: (1) ending imperialism, (2) eradicating feudalism, (3) breaking monopolies and the political domination of capital, (4) establishing social justice, (5) creating a powerful national army, and (6) establishing a truly democratic system.[29] As late as June 1, 1956, these same six principles formed the skeleton of a major address.[30] In that speech a vague reference to the progress of Arab nationalism was included in Nasser's discussion of a strong national army and its role in resisting the Baghdad Pact.[31] It appears that Egypt's Arab policy was forced upon it first by fear of the consequences of the Baghdad Pact and later by the apparently unexpected support of the Arab people at the time of the nationalization of the Suez Canal Company.

All the evidence seems to point to the Anglo-Egyptian treaty initialled in August 1954 as the most significant turning point in Egyptian policy, even as the events of March 1954 set up the internal political conditions for that turn. Those earlier events by which Nasser took over from Naguib are well enough known. It is clear that Nasser and his supporters had not yet consolidated their position when they signed the treaty providing for the evacuation of the British troops from the Canal Zone. Nasser's speeches of that period are full of rebuttals against his critics who claimed, apparently, that the new treaty was no better than that of 1936, that it did not provide for immediate evacuation, that some Britishers would remain, that it provided for the return of the British army, that the provision for consultation in case of the threat of aggression was the equivalent of joining a Western defense pact, and that Nasser was a tool of the imperialists. The list of audiences to whom Nasser spoke during these months reads like a catalogue of important interest groups.

[27] Anwar G. Chejne,
[28] E.g., 'Ukasha, op. cit., p. 61.
[29] Nasser's Speeches (Arabic), Vol. 3, p. 679.
[30] Ibid., Vol. 6, pp. 1170 f.
[31] Ibid., p. 1222 f.

There followed speeches to a great many units of the military.[32] The most consistently repeated theme was that Egypt had joined no pact and would not do so.

The date of the attempted assassination of Nasser was the height of the domestic crisis, after which he was able to assert full control. But externally the launching of the Baghdad Pact threatened to isolate Egypt and compel Nasser into an agreement that would endanger his government all over again. The hoped for financial support from the United States in return for agreeing to the terms of the Anglo-Egyptian Treaty began to fade as this new issue arose.

Nasser could not join a Western dominated pact even if he wanted to,[33] and the circumstances prevailing at the end of 1954 determined that the refusal to join defensive pacts with non-Arab states would become a fundamental principle of Egyptian foreign policy. Nasser doubtless felt that he had made the maximum of concessions to Britain and the United States in the treaty—it was in discussing this treaty that he described his action as "realistic" in the sense of compromising. If the first task of any government is to preserve itself, then the first task facing the leaders of the revolutionary government was to prove that the treaty was not a surrender to the West. To prove their sincerity and to fend off great external pressures, they had to oppose extension of the Baghdad Pact to Arab countries. These circumstances led Egypt into Arab politics in the immediate aftermath of the signing of the Anglo-Egyptian Treaty of 1954.

The first major address in which President Nasser appears to have laid special emphasis upon Arab nationalism as opposed to Egyptian nationalism took place on August 12, 1956. There he said:

> Then the voices in the Arab world began to say that it is not the Suez Canal, but the Arab Canal. Arab nationalism began to appear in its best form and clearest meaning. Various kinds of support began to come from Arab kings and presidents and Arab peoples. Arab nationalism began to show its existence and its truth. I read an article on Arab nationalism in a foreign newspaper, and it said, "Arab nationalism became a danger after 1952 and after the writing of the *Philosophy of the Revolution.*" Then I thought we as Arabs must be a single nation. We must fight as for a single cause.[34]

From that time on Nasser's speeches show that pan-Arabism had become one of the major components of Egyptian policy. This turn was doubtless a part of the more general effort to win wide support against a possible armed attack after the nationalization. But after the attack, the response of Arab nationalists outside of Egypt was compelling: Jordan and Iraq were both ripe for revolution and the

[32] These audiences are at best indirect evidence, but they do throw some light on the identity of the groups which the Revolutionary Council considered to be powerful and influential. It appears that a good deal of political thinking went into the "non-constitutional" treaty ratification campaign.
[33] The limitations on Nasser's leadership are suggested in an editorial by Muhammad Hasanain Haikal in *al-Ahram* (January 27, 1961).
[34] *Nasser's Speeches* (Arabic), Vol. 7, p. 1393.

Syrian Ba'this had begun to advocate seriously the union of the two countries.[35] Pan-Arabism might then be called "Nasserism," even more particularly after the Lebanese troubles of 1958.

The moral of these events is easily drawn. The close interrelationship of the three levels of Egyptian policy—Arab policy, domestic policy, and foreign policy—is obvious. The rational intent behind the choices made, and the role of situational factors in narrowing the range of choice, appears to overshadow the role of the still diffuse ideological and psychological factors associated with the broad nationalistic movement. It is the series of policy positions which appear to control the definition of nationalist ideology. Though revolutionary slogans and ideological controversies appear to be matters more of political style and expression within Egypt, they are nevertheless more important where the sense of a national identity is not so secure. Finally and more specifically, it should be borne in mind that two crises, one of internal security at the end of 1954, and one of external security at the end of 1956, were both turning points in Egypt's Arab and foreign policies. For domestic policy, the turning points were in February–March 1954, when Nasser took authority and moved against the still active conservative politicians; and in 1957 when the government suddenly found itself owning a large number of former British and French firms in addition to the Suez Canal Company.

IV Arab Socialism

For many observers, the true nature of the political phenomenon known as "Nasserism" is to be understood in terms of the social change taking place in the Arab countries. Although the full explication of this view is extremely difficult, due to the absence of relevant empirical data and our limited understanding of the operative mechanism which relates social change to political protest and political protest to declared policy, it is nevertheless possible to elaborate on the idea itself. In its simplest form, the social change thesis holds that as a result of Western European pressures—economic, political, and military—on the Ottoman Empire, the traditional structure of Islamic society grew weaker, and new classes, rival elites, were created which challenged the existing distribution of social, economic, and political values. Although this social movement was at first moderate in its demands, its radicalism increased with the increase in the ranks of the new classes and with the increasing awareness of the weakness and economic and technical backwardness of the Islamic countries. From seeking military and bureaucratic reform it moved to demanding a constitutional form of government, then to opposition to foreign influence, to popular sovereignty, to secularism, to land reform, and more recently to socialism. In the Arab countries under the Ottoman Empire, the constitutional

[35] Salah al-Din al-Bitar, al-Siyasah al-Arabiyyah [The Arab Policy] (Beirut, 1960), p. 48, advocated the union of Syria and Egypt as the first step to Arab unity in 1955. Michel Aflaq, Ma'arakat al-Musir al-Wahid [Battle for a Single Destiny] 2nd ed. (Beirut, 1959), pp. 66–85.

phase was followed by demands for independence. These political demands with implications of opposition to the traditional military, the bureaucratic aristocracy, the ulama, the landowners, and to foreign and minority groups were justified by a nationalist ideology.

The hard facts at our disposal are few, but what there are of them indicate that the dominant ideology among the new classes, and especially among the Sunni Arabs of these classes, is pan-Arabism—probably under the leadership of President Nasser. If we proceed further for non-evaluative data to help us understand these things, we may attempt to assess the interests of these classes and compare those interests with the policies of social reform being carried out in the UAR. As we may now expect, these policies have been formed in the crucible of events, having been but vaguely fixed in the minds of the leadership before the revolution. The general direction was there, as part of the explanation of pre-revolutionary reality, but the method of achieving these goals was not at all clear, as Nasser himself has said. When once we have been able to compare these interests and policies, should we find some hiatus between the two, we shall then have some idea of the nature and strength of the ideological residuum.

The two most important of the groups bearing the new nationalist ideology are the military and the bureaucracy. These are not the only ones to have been affected by the changes of the last century and a half. The peasantry has been disturbed by the sometimes amazing growth of its numbers, by changes in tax-farming procedures, by new title-settlement procedures, by the change to cash crops in many places, by new irrigation systems which have relieved the peasant of ownership or control over his water requirements, and by extension of the network of modern transport and mass media to some rural areas. Tribes have been settled, decimated, moved to new areas, have had their traditional leaders removed, and have had their products replaced in the markets. Small merchants and artisans have been weakened by the competition of standardized manufactures and a new class of importers and wholesale dealers; their guilds have been dissolved, the activities of their semireligious organizations have been restricted, their sources of credit have dwindled, and their dependence upon the bureaucracy has increased. The ulama have lost their independence of government and their financial independence, and have lost much influence and prestige at the same time. Whole new classes have come into being in the cities. There is a new and growing industrial labor group; a very large group in the lower services category: hawkers, porters, car-watchers, sweepers, doormen, garbage collectors, and domestics; a much smaller group engaged in finance, foreign trade, and industry; a new group of professionals: doctors, lawyers, accountants, engineers, professors, and economists and, at much lower levels, journalists, teachers, nurses, technicians, and artists.

But the earliest changes, deliberately instituted, were in the military and then in the bureaucracy, as a means of coping with the military pressures exerted from Europe. Efforts to modernize the military are a century and a half old, but the armies of the Middle East still reflect the characteristic dichotomy of modernity and often squalid traditionality which renders every Middle Eastern city incomprehensible to foreigners and an irritant to its middle-class inhabitants. The officer corps, but not the ranks, belongs to the modern middle class, though whenever imperialism held sway, or whenever there were important minorities, the officer corps was not "nationalized" until recent times; and then it was nationalized only where patriarchal forms of government had all but disappeared. (Until 1936, for example, the Egyptian army officer corps was predominantly Turkish, Circassian, or otherwise aristocratic in social origin.) These armies have been expanded, yet not so much as to account for their great influence. Their influence in recent times is not due to their size, but to their modern weapons, to the political impotence of the bulk of the urban classes, to the gradual loss of religious legitimacy by traditional rulers, and to the lack of cohesiveness among middle-class urban groups.

Students are still largely embryonic civil servants, and civil servants of the lower ranks are vestigial students. In these two groups we find the largest part of the urban middle class, especially in the politically dominant capital city. These, together with the far fewer professionals, high and low,[36] create the climate of nationalist opinion; they read, listen, discuss political events, applaud or denounce government policy, and belong to political parties; but rarely do they create a government or bring one down. These are the ones described as educated, cultured, or as belonging to the intelligentsia, and it is the climate of their opinion which has provided the military with an ideology, even though the military was the first to be exposed to Western learning.

Nevertheless revolutionary governments dominated by the military, even when they have learned the extent of their dependence upon the bureaucracy, are not the exponents of bureaucratic interests, but more nearly the exponents of the middle-class ideology which was created to justify those interests. The distinction is important because the justification is made in general nationalist and often socialist terms, in the interest of the inarticulate peasantry and the relatively small class of workers.[37] More emphasis is given to the interests which must be curbed rather than to those which must be benefited. The military, however, does not hesitate to include itself in this conception of the national interest. The six goals of the Egyptian revolution include the creation of a strong national army, along with statements of opposition to imperialism, feudalism, and monopoly capitalism. The other goals of establishing social justice and a truly democratic system are extremely vague in meaning, and

[36] Teachers are civil servants, it should be remembered.
[37] This is true of the Egyptian revolution despite occasional vagueness of expression, e.g. On March 27, 1955 Nasser said that "this revolution arose to represent the middle class, it arose to represent the hope of the majority of this people." His audience was a group of workers. *Nasser's Speeches* (Arabic) Vol. 3, p. 685. The major tendency at the present time follows this theme of lumping all classes together, but there was a significant difference between the attitude of the Revolutionary government in the spring of 1954 and its attitude in the summer of 1955 as judged from *Nasser's Speeches*: see Vol. 2, p. 238 on students; p. 270 on the lawyers syndicate; p. 279 telling the civil servants to think of the peasants; p. 361 on the bad effects of university education before the revolution; compare this with an important speech made on July 22, 1955, Vol. 4, mentioning the benefits bestowed by the Revolution on the writers and the intelligentsia, p. 867; doctors, p. 870; teachers, p. 875; journalists, actors, and movie makers, p. 879; civil servants, p. 880.

we have already noted that the Free Officers were at a loss as to how to achieve these ends when they came into power.

It is by no means easy to reconstruct the desires of the urban middle classes at the time of the revolution, but we may hazard a few generalizations. There can be little doubt that most would as soon have had Farouk go, and no doubt that all except some in the Canal cities wanted the British army to leave Egypt. If we bear in mind that many of the professionals are actually government employees, we may easily conclude that there was a broad consensus that salaries and allowances had to be raised, the cost of living lowered, inflation stopped, the rules for the protection of civil servants expanded and adhered to closely, promotions given regularly according to the book, and political victimization stopped. Low-cost housing was needed, bribery and corruption in the bureaucracy were sources of complaint, and the extension of urban amenities to outlying quarters was demanded. The great influence of the landowning class was felt by many to be the reason for the failure to realize these objectives and for the corruption of parliamentary democracy.

Another general aspiration existed, expressed as the need for industrialization or economic development, but perhaps just as often sensed in the discomfort or insecurity of life in an environment of immense social, economic, and cultural contrast. Doubtless, many feel that they will benefit directly from economic development and the spread of literacy and education; but many benefit at present from the easy availability of cheap menial services. More, however, fall into neither category but are ashamed of the squalor of the metropolis and feel that the economic and social conditions now prevailing do not offord the environment in which a respectable civil servant can live a moderately ostentatious bourgeois existence.

If the foregoing is a fair representation of the demands of the nationalist classes in Cairo, it is not unreasonable to suppose that the Free Officers were well aware of them. They are, after all, sprung from the same classes; [38] their families were spread throughout many occupations, not excluding agriculture. Nor is it true that they had no objectives whatsoever when they took power. The objectives they had were mainly those which had been adumbrated, but not realized, under the monarchy. In many ways the revolution is a more vigorous continuation of pre-revolutionary tendencies.

Not only in international questions and in the issue of British occupation was the position of the Revolutionary Command Council similar to that of the Wafd, but the proposal for the High Dam at Aswan already existed. There had been a number of efforts to restrict landownership and regulate tenancy, most of which had failed. Cooperatives had been established but did not work too well. Various community-development projects for agricultural areas had been started but were not really off the ground. Food subsidies were granted on certain staples to ease the lot of the urban lower classes. Industrialization plans were being worked on. Expenditure on education was increasing yearly, and the right of labor to organize was recognized.

These facts have led some to argue that the revolution was "unnecessary," but a

[38] 'Ukasha, op. cit., p. 23.

great many more feel that landowner domination of parliament and the king constituted formidable roadblocks to progress. The Free Officers swept them out of the way and proceeded as vigorously as they might to realize those projects which were already on the order of the day. The army was, of course, a direct beneficiary of the new regime, and large landowners were hurt, but it is difficult to single out any other group as having been particularly favored or marked for penalization. As the government's domestic policy developed, however, the position of some improved while that of others declined. And, it should be borne in mind, domestic, social, and economic policy is still not fixed.

We have already had some suggestion of the present configuration of the social and economic policy of the UAR in President Nasser's letter to King Husain. No detailed elaboration can be made here, but some additional information may be helpful. Not only have all banks and insurance companies been nationalized, but most large industrial establishments are government controlled and managed through three organizations: the Economic Development Organization, the Nasr Organization, and the Misr Organization. Eighty-two per cent of all non-agricultural investment is currently being made by the "Public Sector." The national income of Egypt was about 1267 million pounds during 1960–61, while the government planned to spend over 700 million pounds in the regular and development budgets. Indirect taxes still account for much more than any other source of revenue for the regular budget, while profits from the Suez Canal and from government-owned companies, especially the nationalized British, French, and now Belgian concerns, contribute to the development budget. As a consequence, development policy is almost entirely a government affair; private investment, except through the purchase of shares of government companies, is no longer encouraged in fact. Even new enterprises requiring as little as 1000 pounds capital must receive the approval of the Ministry of Industries, and all obvious loopholes are stopped up by the usual austerity regulations on imports, building, currency, rents, foreign travel, and prices.

About 10 per cent of Egypt's agricultural land has been redistributed, and paternalistic cooperatives have been established in the villages of these areas, though it is hoped to expand the system to include all agricultural areas. Education and health, community development, agricultural extension, and labor exchange services have all been increased, some more and some less. New labor legislation has given some additional protection to industrial workers. Adequate supplies of staple foods have been assured, and fixed prices generally prevail in the markets.

Still, Egypt's problems are very great. Rural destitution remains the rule. Migration to the big city is unabated. The population continues to increase at a rate sufficient to counterbalance development. The universities turn out more graduates, B.A.'s, M.D.'s social workers, and lawyers than can find employment. The regular service is overstaffed yet continues to hire some new graduates, even while many new functions are being granted to specialized organizations working under their own regulations and hiring the graduates of special institutes, the Faculty of Commerce, or retired Army officers. The professional classes feel the squeeze as austerity is tightened and their clients become more circumspect about fees.

It is clear that the UAR is engaged in a difficult race against time and the birth rate. It has set itself a plan to double the national income in ten years, a plan which is heavily dependent on foreign currency to pay for capital goods, and it hopes to avoid all inflation during that period.

From the foregoing it would appear that the nationalist classes are not much better off economically than they were before. Some peasants are better off, as are some workers, some merchants, small industrialists, contractors, army officers, technical experts, economists, engineers, and apparently a small class of rural dignitaries of moderate land holdings and some of the higher ulama.

The variety of these groups indicates that the benefits they have derived are not the result of a fixed policy of redistribution. The peasants who are better off are those who have received land and who have had their rents reduced. Agricultural policy was one of the major foundations of the legitimization of the revolutionary regime until recently. Labor groups remain closely controlled, but the modest benefits they have received are the direct result of their assistance to Nasser during the crisis of March 1954. The other groups, all of whom are small, have benefited because of the importance of their contribution to the policies of the UAR or because development funds, jobs, or concessions aiming at administrative rationalization have been channelled in their direction.

If the conclusions of our analysis and our method are accepted, it follows that (1) there is a substantial gap between the interests of the nationalist classes and government policies, which is in a small part explained by alienation and in a much larger part explained by interpretations of the government's purposes and expectations, that is, their ideology; and that (2) if government policy has been oriented to the ideology of the nationalist classes, it has not responded in its development to the demands of these classes except in making some minor concessions.

Despite this gap between the expectations of the nationalist classes and the performance of the government, they support the present regime even if not with rabid enthusiasm. In general, the urban lower class believes that the revolution has benefited them by giving them greater dignity and protection, legal and otherwise, against the wealthier classes, the minorities, and foreigners. The government frequently resorts to organizing student and worker demonstrations which do not appear to be taken seriously by the urban middle class; but the latter, in turn, supports Nasser and his foreign policy especially. The nationalist classes, as earlier described, range in their views from complete support of the government and belief in its ability to raise standards of living and to achieve equality to the view that the government's preference for nation-building policies is ruining the country by ruining its educated elite.

The more usual attitude, however, is that the squeeze on the middle classes is justified in order to benefit the less fortunate, but that it is rather unpleasant medicine. Toward internal policy there is much complaining, but usually in a spirit of patriotic sacrifice, resignation, or of good-natured and self-directed laughter. Some are fairly optimistic about the future. Many would like greater political freedom. Surprisingly few, however, draw any conclusions from domestic problems to foreign policy.

These attitudes are no more than evidence of a largely unexpressed ideology. We have already noted that one of the central problems of pan-Arabism, according to its literary exponents, is its lack of an agreed theory. Some, like Aflaq argue that no theory is necessary,[39] others like Rimawi argue that the theory is to be found in the evolving policies of the UAR, but it is likely that many more like Nusaibeh believe that the theory is somewhere out there waiting to be discovered.[40] It is further evident that there is no ideology of social reform separate from Arab nationalism. That is to say, nearly all writers and speechmakers insist that the reform of Arab society is one integral part of the nationalist idea, that social reform is a necessary prelude to the full realization of Arab nationalism, and that (or but) Arab nationalism itself defines the nature of the required social reform or the nature of the genuine Arab society.

The details of this problem are complex, and the literature extensive, so that here we can give only a summary impression of the diffuse idea of the ideal society which apparently prevails among the nationalist classes. Four types of theory come to explain this ideology, and we assume that the authors, in this case, do reflect the sentiments of their public. All four types are concerned with what is called Arab Socialism. The adherents of the first of these we shall call the scientific socialists, the second are the humanists, the third are the Labor Party socialists, and the fourth the pragmatic etatistes.

The scientific socialists use Marxist terminology, are obviously well versed in Communist literature, and are mostly concerned to prove that Marxism does not apply to the Arabs. Most of these writers are Lebanese or Syrians. A good example of one of them is Afif al-Bahansi's *Introduction to Arab Socialism*.[41]

The humanists are not economists but more likely belletrists who find in socialism a reflection of the goodness and charity of the simple human being. As yet I have found only Egyptians writing in this tone, and it would appear that there is a good deal of non-political literature expressed in the same nostalgic, almost banal and romantic manner. 'Abd al-Mon'im al-Sawi's *The Socialism of Our Country* illustrates the point only too well,[42] and the same viewpoint has been expressed by Ihsan 'Abd al-Quddus in various articles in *Rose al-Yusuf*.[43]

The Labor Party socialists are followers of Laski and sometimes graduates of the London School of Economics. The most prominent of this small group is Hatim, who has written only one pamphlet but has sponsored many others and has had translations made of Laski's, G. D. H. Cole's, and Rostow's works.[44] The leading pragmatic etatist is, of course, President Nasser. The Ba'this fall somewhere between the scientific socialists and the humanists.

On the basis of a preliminary examination of this literature, certain important

[39] See "Radical-Reform Nationalism in Syria and Egypt," *The Muslim World* (April, July, 1959).
[40] H. K. Nusaibeh, *op. cit.*
[41] Afif al-Bahansi, *Madkhal ila al-Ishtirakiyyah al-Arabiyyah* (Damascus, 1957) (?).
[42] "Abd al-Mun'im al-Sawi," *Ishtirakiyyat Baladina,* al Maktabah al-Thaqafiyyah Series No. 18, Ministry of Culture (Cairo), n.d.
[43] E.g., *Rose al-Yusuf,* February 13, 20, 27; March 13, 20, 1961.
[44] Hatim is Minister of State in charge of Broadcasting and the Information Service. He is also on the editorial committee of the Ikhtarna Lak series.

common features can be found. Because they appear to reflect popular opinion we shall concentrate our attention upon them to the exclusion of the interesting differences among the exponents of Arab Socialism. All of these tendencies reject the Marxist idea of the class struggle. If there is any conflict among classes it is subordinate to the national struggle against imperialism and foreign capitalism. The Arab socialist ideal is that of cooperation among all classes, or binding the classes together, or reducing the distance between them, or encouraging their mutually responsible interaction.[45]

After rejecting both the Hegelian and Marxian dialectic and Sartre's lack of an absolute ethical purpose, al-Bahansi finds the answer in man's nature: Man has freedom to act as a dynamic being and he has consciousness (wa'i). These two forces work together and their confluence is called conscience (wijdan). The confluence of the individual and the external world is similarly necessary and is called cohesion (ilti'am).[46]

Al-Sawi tells the story of a village boy whose father dies and who discovers in his obligation to his younger brother that fatherhood belongs to all men in their relations to one another, and then learns from the considerateness of his fellow villagers that every man is his brother's keeper.[47]

He began to understand (he was only ten years old) that disputes among the people of our country were but a kind of social supervision over the behavior of the individuals themselves, should they deviate or take a mind to transgress against whatever the society considered good. He began to discover good interpretations for whatever he saw and heard, and all these explanations led him to the conclusion that the society of our country has a powerful awareness, that it does not determine anything which is not right and good.[48]

And again, the village celebration "explained to him the socialism of our country as the most beautiful of possible humanist explanations of socialism, and social justice, and democracy, and cooperation." [49]

Hatim accepts the view, accredited to Strachey, that a broad political organization of all the people is necessary to realize socialism; but in rejecting Marxism he points out that Arab society is not like others, divided into two warring camps, but is made up of homogeneous groups. "Arab society became homogeneous after political parties . . . ceased to exist." [50] Ihsan Abd al-Quddus uses the example of the extended family of the village 'umdah of fifty years ago to demonstrate Arab socialism.[51]

As near as can be judged from our preliminary survey, Arab socialism is a kind

[45] The last view is that of Muhammad Hasanain Haikal. Nasser prefers to speak of closing the gap between classes.
[46] al-Bahansi, op. cit., p. 50.
[47] Al-Sawi, op. cit., pp. 11, 34, et passim.
[48] Ibid., p. 34.
[49] Ibid., p. 58.
[50] Hatim, op. cit., p. 41.
[51] Rose al-Yusuf, February 13, 1961, p. 6.

of emotional extension of the nationalist idea to the problems resulting from the loosening of traditional social ties. As Nasser put it in a recent speech at Damascus University, Arabs must now think of the whole nation as their family and they should enjoy the same privileges and owe the same obligations as they do to their families. The Arab nation is one great *gemeinschaft,* and evidence for this assertion is found in the various traditional *gemeinschaftlich* customs prevalent within families or in village society.[52] Class harmony and mutual responsibility are part of the distinctive Arab character and Arab philosophy.

If Arab Socialism is essentially an atavism, that did not prevent various writers from putting forward specific suggestions for its achievement. Hatim and Bahansi both do this, but the most remarkably portentous suggestions appeared in the Ba'th constitution.[53] In its broad outlines, the government of the UAR has followed the Ba'thi line. To fully grasp the paradox here we must note again that the Ba'this are under a cloud in the UAR, that there is not a shred of evidence that the Ba'th has influenced economic policy in Egypt (as opposed to Syria), and that ex-Ba'thi Rimawi has developed a theory which looks to the pragmatic solutions of the Egyptian government for its inspiration.

The government of the UAR followed the Ba'thi suggestions not because they were Ba'thi suggestions, nor because they represented the most plausible operative interpretation of the national-social ideal, but because, after failing for a long while to find a way out of its economic difficulties, a number of circumstances made them seem the most plausible response to the existing situation and the great pressure for development. Practical difficulties prevented further time-consuming study. The next step was to rationalize the new policy in terms of the prevalent ideology of social reform, and the result is the aim of establishing a Socialist-Cooperative-Democracy.

In his early speeches, Nasser did not use the term socialism. He spoke of the need to advance all classes of the people,[54] then of the need to close the gaps which separated the classes,[55] of the desire to create a society in which the rich will help the poor,[56] and of the government as a government of all classes which looked on Egypt as one big family.[57] The first time that Nasser used the term socialism was on May 19, 1955 after his return from Bandung.[58] He explained it then to mean closing the gap between classes, and shortly thereafter said, "This is the first Id (*al Fitr*) we have assembled together in which our efforts to create a strong socialist society have made some headway." [59] Socialism was to be the method of achieving social justice.[60]

[52] 'Ukasha, *op. cit.,* p. 111.
[53] See note 3.
[54] *Nasser's Speeches* (Arabic), Vol. 1, p. 76.
[55] *Ibid.,* p. 101.
[56] *Ibid.,* p. 150.
[57] *Ibid.,* Vol. 2, p. 424.
[58] *Ibid.,* Vol. 4, p. 743.
[59] *Ibid.,* p. 751.
[60] *Ibid.,* p. 768.

The last explanation of socialism suggests that he had something more definite in mind than merely the cooperation of all classes. This suggestion is further supported by several attacks on capitalism during the same period, changing one of the six principles of the revolution from ending monopolies [61] to ending the rule of capitalism. This emphasis must be contrasted with his earlier speeches immediately after the events of March 1954. At that time he told a number of labor groups that both capital and labor had their rights and that both should cooperate in their mutual interest and in the interest of the nation.[62] Nasser now uses the phrase Socialist-Democratic Cooperative society but, in a variety of ways, as a society without exploitation,[63] and as a society of owners.[64] However, he also has used the term socialism to refer to the "public sector" of the UAR economy.

From an examination of Egyptian economic policy it becomes clear that what began as a vague idea of somehow deriving an ideal society out of the ideological remnants of traditional society has now become a determined effort on the part of the government to direct the economy; to prevent the creation of large and independent concentrations of economic power and to control existing ones; and to rely only on loans, grants, and profits from government enterprises, compulsory and voluntary sales of bonds, and taxes for the development capital which it needs.

This is essentially a development policy, and as yet it has not deeply affected Egyptian social structure or social values. Land reform did affect social structure, though not so much as power structure.

The reason for the lack of a severe social impact from recent development policies is not only due to the time lag in social change and the limited nature of present achievements, it is also due to the paternalistic form which these policies have taken and to the relative compartmentalization of the developing sector. Politically, paternalism has meant recognizing and working through existing social groups and occupational associations, but the more modern associations have been reduced to protective societies capable of pressing for redress of individual grievances, for the most part. The difference between a traditional interest system and a highly bureaucratized and rationalized one is not so great except for the number of groups recognized.

Development policy has not created a really new elite. The revolution itself removed the aristocratic landowning monopoly on all positions of authority, but it did not exclude members of the former elite. The new elite is not comprised of "new" men, it is rather made up of families (not individuals) of substantial middle-class positions within the traditional social structure. These families have some agricultural connections so that the idealization of village life is not all nostalgia, but most members of the family hold government posts in various ministries and many have relatives in the armed services and perhaps even among the ulama. Those who have the best training and/or the best connections, or who have demonstrated both

[61] *Ibid.*, Vol. 3, p. 724.
[62] *Ibid.*, Vol. 2, pp. 242, 244, 257.
[63] *Ibid.* [English] (April–June 1960), p. 115.
[64] *Ibid.*, p. 152.

their loyalty and their ability to get things done, may be co-opted into the outer circle of decision-makers or may become direct beneficiaries of development policy.

Traditional family structure and the values that go with it have not been attacked, instead the educated groups most imbued with these values have been strengthened. It is, therefore, not at all a foregone conclusion that increased national income will accelerate social change. On the other hand, the failure of the development plan may lead to more drastic measures, which will break down further the traditional structures. It is difficult, therefore, to state whether social protest in Egypt is against Europeanization or against traditional Islamic social values.

The compartmentalization of the development effort was not envisioned earlier and is clearly another occasion of the triumph of events over ideals. The original hope for the cooperation of private capital with the government was disappointed first by the unwillingness of foreign capital to invest in Egypt and then by the withholding of the large sums expected from the United States after Nasser had signed the Anglo-Egyptian treaty of 1954. The dispute with the United States over the Baghdad Pact, prolonged by the arms deal with the Soviet Union, was moderated by the promise of assistance in constructing the High Dam, but burst forth with renewed vigor after this promise was withdrawn.

Throughout this period Egypt was getting most of its advice from American experts in attempting to draw up a development plan, but no real plan was completed nor had local capital responded very much to the development needs of Egypt by the time of the Suez invasion. That invasion brought about the nationalization of the British and French firms in Egypt so that in 1957 the government suddenly found itself with the largest industrial establishment in the country. Indeed with the exception of the Misr group, the government then controlled all big industrial establishments.[65] Together with the few earlier government projects, these firms were organized under the Economic Development Organization and a five-year plan was hastily put together for immediate implementation. East European advice was now sought and granted, the National Planning Commission was set up, and as obstacles arose various enterprises were nationalized, as were all major sources of savings and investment funds. The suddenly developing situation of 1957 pointed the way in which planned development might proceed. With its hands partly untied, the government proceeded vigorously along the only path it saw clear and, thus the form of the development policy of the UAR was sealed.

The national plan purports to be a coordinated social and economic plan, but its social aspect is restricted to the provision of funds for welfare services and education. Industrialization and the High Dam are the two biggest aims of the Plan, and no competing demands will be permitted to stand in their way. The impact of these programs on Egyptian society and politics is still anybody's guess—at least one expert does not believe that the labor force will be expanded, though this is one of the government's goals.[66] At any rate the quality and quantity of social change will

[65] The Misr group has now been taken over by the government.
[66] F. Harbison and I. A. Ibrahim, *Human Resources for Egyptian Enterprise* (New York: McGraw-Hill Book Co., 1958), p. 135.

be the result of the direction of the development program rather than development being controlled by an ideological conception of the ideal society.

In the meantime, for the people of Egypt, and especially the nationalist classes, the hiatus between their demands and the ability of the government to supply them is filled by the belief that there is some direct connection between the government's economic policy and their vague social reform aspirations. As one goes up the economic scale, this belief probably becomes weaker; but even where it is weak there is the compensatory feeling of a new dignity and importance for Egyptians and all Arabs on the international political stage.

8

Egypt's Positive Neutrality

Leonard Binder

I The United States and the United Arab Republic

To act with wisdom and moderation and with enlightened self-interest is the antithesis of revolution and extremist protest. It is this sort of behavior that we least expect from the leaders of revolutionary governments, but wisdom and restraint are expected of the developed countries. Lack of restraint can take many forms, as Mossadegh's stubborn refusal to deal with the Anglo-Iranian Oil Company and Nasser's truculent nationalization of the Suez Canal Company. The one approached an infantile suicidalism while the other courted a direct reprisal. But were these acts of irrationality or were they miscalculations? It is evident that Mossadegh was sure that he would break British-American solidarity eventually. He was wrong, not mad. Nasser has said that he weighed the possibility of a British attack, but he decided that there was a 75 per cent improbability of that occurring. Both gambled and lost, though Nasser did not lose much; and for both, the domestic consequences of refusing to gamble probably outweighed even the great risks taken.

In one of the newest and more recondite apologies for the policies of the United Arab Republic and President Nasser's leadership of the pan-Arab movement, those who called for wisdom and realism [1] are described as the indefatigable "stooges of imperialism." The true revolutionary position, the author holds, stands on principle and refuses compromise. Yet, in the aftermath of the treaty arranging for the British evacuation of the Canal Zone, it was President Nasser himself who used that exact term (realism) to describe his motives in agreeing to less than complete, immediate, and unconditional evacuation of Britain's 70,000 troops.[2] There are other examples, too, that help to illustrate the existence of some policy flexibility in the UAR: the agreement with the Sudan on the division of the Nile waters, the resumption of normal relations with Britain (despite the latter's unwillingness to permit the UAR to open consulates where they chose in colonial territories), the acceptance of King

---

[1] Abd Allah al-Rimawi, *al Mantiq al-Thawri* [*The Revolutionary Logic*] (Cairo, 1961), p. 99.
[2] President Gamal Abd al-Nasser, *Khutub wa Tasrihat* [*Speeches and Interviews*]. Published in ten volumes in Arabic by the Editorial Committee of *Ikhtarna Lak* [*We Have Chosen For You*]. Additional volumes published in English by the Information Administration. All at Cairo, without dates. Hereafter to be cited as *Nasser's Speeches* (Arabic or English), Vol. 3 (August 21, 1954), p. 487.

Husain's recent friendly overtures, and even the relatively mild reaction to the implication of the United States in the Cuban rebellion of April 1961.[3]

For the time being, at least, the policy of the government of the UAR cannot be viewed as a closed book, determined *a priori* to take the most extreme and uncompromising position. It still enjoys a range of freedom of action. Understanding the bases of its policy is not a useless academic pursuit, because it may suggest ways in which we can educe more accommodating reactions. This is not to argue, however, that the interests of the United States and those of the UAR are potentially the same, for they are not.

The conflict between the United States and the UAR is one of interests and ideology, but it is not a conflict between rationality and irrationality. Though there may be many relatively constant determinants of foreign policy such as geography, demography, and economy, understanding these factors in their relation to specific situations is always an ideological process. Hence, aside from the normal aspiration of human beings for increased material welfare, other preferences and the choice of means depend upon beliefs about what is good and on the cognitive efforts to find out what is possible. When the neutralist states are accused of irrationality, it is assumed that our view of world affairs is the only correct one, that the irresponsible neutral refuses to recognize the aggressiveness of the Soviet Union and derives a vicarious pleasure out of seeing the culturally haughty and economically superior West get kicked around. This accusation may be correct, but it does not explain UAR policy, nor does it accord with Arab explanations of the policy of positive neutrality.

A plausible explanation is not a justification. Indeed, we are living in a world in which other nations perversely refuse to see things our way because their situation, that is, their interests and objectives, is not ours. Another important aspect of this problem should be borne in mind. The right of national self-determination may be quite acceptable in the abstract but, like all abstract absolutes, becomes a matter of dispute when put into practical application. Even if there is an agreement to apply the principle in a particular case, and often there is not, the boundaries of self-determination are always unclear.

It is a standard assumption in the West that all states are interdependent, and from this assumption certain conclusions about the limits of self-determination are derived. Interdependence is not a constant either, and its implications appear to vary with the postulation of diverse international systems. What is good for a "balance of power" system with a First World War technology may not be good for a bipolar system with a Third World War technology.

But nationalist ideologies do not appear to adjust to the times as easily as do counterideologies. Self-determination is not the only demand of unsatisfied nationalism; equality, too, is insisted upon regardless of the size and power of the state.

[3] *Rose al-Yusuf,* May 1, 1961, p. 13, reported that the UAR Foreign Ministry threatened the United States chargé that his government could not guarantee the safety of the Embassy building and staff during the forthcoming demonstration unless the United States Embassy withheld from publishing its government's views on the Cuban affair.

We may strongly hold that we have special responsibilities by virtue of our size and power, but it is unlikely that Nasser will accept this view any more than King Husain will accept the assertion that the UAR has special responsibilities among the Arab states because of its moral and material circumstances.

Despite the fact that the use of the slogan "positive neutrality" is of relatively recent vintage, the current opposition to nearly all international acts of the United States has roots that go deeper than either Arab policy or the social policy of the United Arab Republic. To take only the most obvious example, we must go back at least to 1941–42 when Britain pressed Egypt to declare war upon the Axis powers. Both Farouk and his Premier Ali Maher temporized, with the result that the British forced Farouk to appoint Nahhas Pasha who did the necessary. Farouk swore that he would never forget that outrage, but it was left to the revolutionary nationalists to carry out his word.

A similar anti-Western reaction followed the refusal of the Western powers to act on Egypt's plea for United Nations intervention in her bid to revise the treaty of 1936 with Britain, on the ground that the circumstances of 1936 (the threat of Italian aggression) had passed. The failure of this initiative as well as the Palestine Resolution of November 29, 1947 were important factors in Egypt's decision not to support the United Nations' action in Korea.

Later, opposition to the West took the special form of opposing the establishment of any joint-defense organization in the Middle East and of preventing other Arab states from joining such a pact at the time the West proposed the establishment of a Middle East Command and later a Middle East Defense Organization. Not only did Egypt demand evacuation before discussing any such pact, but she also initiated the Arab collective security treaty in the Arab League to forestall the Western effort and strengthen her counterclaim that the defense of the area should be the responsibility of the area powers themselves. These events took place before the revolution of July 1952, and to a large extent set limits on the policy choices available to the new regime.

As might be expected, the governments which held office under Farouk from 1942 to 1952 were immobilist. Their position *vis à vis* with the West, and especially Great Britain, was one of withholding support rather than seriously seeking some powerful international counterweight. This generalization holds true despite some short-lived pro-Axis feeling when it was thought that Rommel might sweep into Alexandria from the desert. But, as events demonstrated, Egypt had nothing to offer in return for Western compliance and in desperation turned first to an ill-prepared involvement in the Palestine War and then to guerrilla attacks in the Canal zone.

The attitude which prevailed at the time is nicely put in a brief article written by Salah al-Din al Bitar of the Syrian Ba'th Party in 1950. After discussing the horrors of atomic war, al-Bitar wrote that the bipolar split is to be abhorred quite as much as the domination of a single power. The Arabs are seeking new social and political forms, but they are not finding the answers they want in either the American or the Soviet systems. Moreover Western imperialism divided the

Arab homeland, maintained it in a divided condition, took away Palestine, drove out its people, made it Jewish, and continues in its efforts to make Arab lands Jewish. Thus, the Arab position must reflect an attitude toward the West which is in harmony with the lack of Western justice. It must strengthen the Arab case in the United Nations, so that the smaller nations will be astonished and ask why the Arabs so behave when *they are non-Communist states in the Western sphere.* When they learn the answer, the smaller states will press the United States, United Kingdom, and France to change their duplicitous policies.[4]

There is no evidence here, or in the action of Egyptian governments up to 1955, of attempts to exploit the bipolar division of power by bringing Soviet pressures to bear against the United States. During that period, none of the neutralist states had done anything of the kind except for Yugoslavia. In this special sense, it might be said truly that the United States was the leader of the Free World (or non-Communist world) during the period in question.

In order to change this situation two factors were needed which were not previously present: the first was the willingness of the Soviet Union to accept neutralist overtures, and the second was a revolutionary leader ready to take the double chance of incurring the wrath of the West and getting involved with Russia. Mossadegh had already shown the way, but the Russians were not yet ready.

Nasser made his decision to take the chance after becoming embroiled with the United States over the Baghdad Pact and the refusal of the West to supply him with arms. There was no real precedent on which he would rely or which could help to explain his action. We do know, however, that he had not yet consolidated his hold on Egypt; he has insisted on the decisive importance of the Israeli attack on Gaza in 1955. The precise importance of that attack is still shrouded in the heavy obscurity of the so-called Lavon Affair, so that Israeli motivation is a matter of dispute. Domestically, at any rate, it appears that the attack may have weakened Nasser's efforts to win the confidence of some of the military.[5]

The internal pressure on Nasser may have been compelling in itself, but it is worthy of note that the arms deal with the Soviet Union did not take place until after the Bandung Conference. From Nasser's speeches it is clear that that conference had a profound effect on his thinking. There is no way that we can be sure of the precise nature of this effect, but we can guess that he was impressed by the respectability achieved by Communist China at the conference and perhaps surprised also to see Indonesia thus responding to the creation of SEATO. He was perhaps also impressed by the respectability accorded the term socialism, which he used only after returning from Bandung. Above all he may have been impressed by the size of the gathering, its potentiality for representing "world opinion," and its support for Arab

[4] al-Bitar, *al-Siyasa, al-Arabiyyah* (Beirut, 1960), pp. 23–27.
[5] *Nasser's Speeches* (Arabic) Vol. 3, pp. 686–88. From November 10, 1954 until December 2, 1954, Nasser addressed 12 military groups in the 13 speeches made during the period. Vol. 3, pp. 598–634. In these speeches, Nasser recorded his gratitude for the role played by the Signal Corps officers (p. 598) and the Air Corps (p. 612) during the crisis of the previous February and March.

causes. It may also be noted that the conference followed the first great Western defeat in Indo-China.

Whatever were Nasser's calculations of the risk, he gambled and won. Not only was there no appreciable negative response from the West besides pained surprise, but the United States did not join the Baghdad Pact and no guarantees or substantial arms were given to Israel. Instead, Dulles proposed a plan for a solution of the Arab-Israeli dispute to be financed by the United States, and when that failed to advance matters, the United States reluctantly agreed to assist Egypt in building the High Dam at Aswan on the basis of the advice of the United States Ambassador in Cairo.

The withdrawal of this offer of assistance may be seen as a delayed reaction. Apparently the first American view was that the whole problem was tied up with the Arab-Israeli dispute: no dispute, no need for arms.

But the time for such an approach had passed with the break between the United States and Egypt over the Baghdad Pact. With the wisdom of hindsight it may now be said that substantial economic aid should have followed on the signature of the evacuation treaty. That is what Nasser expected and needed. The dispute with the Israelis was not then a barrier to good American-Egyptian relations; to seek a solution to that dispute in order to improve those relations after they had deteriorated puts the cart before the horse. After this series of errors, the United States reversed itself.

If the Arab-Israeli dispute could not be resolved, it was thought, then perhaps its effects on United States–Egyptian relations could be overcome by really generous economic assistance. But this reasonable approach was not followed through. When Nasser recognized Communist China, however, it appeared decided that he was unalterably opposed to accommodation with the West. It is likely that President Nasser did not appreciate the affect that this act, which had been performed by England, India, and Indonesia, might have during that period of delicate negotiations. But it is an open question as to who was the more perverse and irrational, Dulles or Nasser. Several reports suggest that Dulles seized this and other excuses for doing what he had wanted to do from the beginning anyway. For Nasser it may or may not have been the right price to pay for the sale of 10 million dollars worth of cotton.

From 1954 through the end of the Suez crisis, we may conclude, Nasser was primarily concerned with the domestic security of his regime of moderate revolution. If he were to hold power and have the support of the more radical military, he had to avoid political and military entanglements with the West, increase the social services and the number of available jobs, and build up the army. Doing the best that he could with limited resources, he opposed the Baghdad Pact with pan-Arabism, got the Soviet Union to sell him arms, and used the arms deal to get United States financial support for the High Dam. In this manner was Nasser started on the road to neutralism, but, obviously it was a rather special kind of neutralism. The personal fate of no other neutralist leader was so closely tied to the outcome of his dealings with the great powers. The nullification of the Baghdad Pact was a personal victory.

The arms deal was a personal victory. The withdrawal of the American offer of assistance in building the High Dam was a personal insult, and the successful nationalization of the Suez Canal Company was a personal achievement.

At the end of the Suez crisis, Nasser was no longer under great personal pressure. For domestic purposes, in any case, he had proven that his administrative organization was capable of holding itself together, and the value of his propaganda apparatus externally was established. With the realization of these two achievements, Egypt discovered itself with concrete opportunities to fulfill some of the aspirations only dimly suggested in Nasser's *Philosophy of the Revolution*. We have noted elsewhere the manner in which the nationalization of British and French firms provided the basis for a new economic effort from 1957. We have seen how Nasser's need for Arab allies against the Baghdad Pact and the Arab nationalists' need for leadership combined to present Egypt with a pan-Arab policy.

The early months of 1957, which saw the defeat of the Eisenhower Doctrine, can be singled out as the turning point for Egypt, both domestically and externally. The Ba'th's idea of comprehensive Arab unity suddenly became a realistic possibility as one watched the reaction to the Suez crisis in Jordan, Syria, Lebanon, and Iraq. Moreover, the importance of the fact that both the United States and the Soviet Union had supported Egypt during the crisis, in opposition to their support of the Palestine resolution of 1947, was not lost on Nasser. Hence, it is from this date that we can denote a new purposefulness in the UAR's pursuit of positive neutrality.

For Nasser the new opportunities presented themselves in the form of realizing the dream of a great Arab state stretching from the Ocean to the Gulf, with Egypt playing the role of Prussia and he the role of Bismarck. The investment capital to be derived from the revenues from Arab petroleum and the Middle Eastern and African markets for the expected surplus manufactures of an industrialized Egypt constituted possible solutions for immediate economic problems. Egyptian neutrality changed from a defense against Western pressures to a positive means of achieving those goals by either winning the support of the great powers or excluding them from the Egyptian sphere of interest.

This discussion will now permit us to draw certain conclusions about the various phases through which Egyptian neutrality has passed. At first neutralism was (1) a device to press the West for certain concessions, then it became (2) a means of seeking Afro-Asian support for Egyptian goals, thereafter it was used as (3) a justification for dealing with the Eastern bloc, and most recently has been (4) identified with Arab nationalism and has been used in an effort to exclude Western influence from the Middle East. It was doubtless also used to combat Soviet influence in Syria and Iraq, but it is evident that such gains as the Soviet Union hoped to make in those countries were offset by the expectations of greater gains from supporting Egypt. Hence, it is with Soviet encouragement that the "activist" neutrality of Egypt has developed its newer distinctive characteristics. These characteristics go beyond revolutionary Arab propaganda and include (a) cooperation with the Soviet Union in return for continued Soviet support, (b) an attempt to assert leadership among the Afro-Asian countries, and (c) a moderately successful effort to organize the movement of positive neutrality into a third bloc.

Cooperation with the Soviet bloc takes the form of sustaining the Soviet claims to be the friend of neutrals, to offer aid without strings attached, and to be diligently seeking peaceful coexistence. Nasser's bid for leadership in the Afro-Asian bloc is manifested in the number of Afro-Asian conferences held in Cairo and, most recently, in his speech before the General Assembly of the United Nations in 1960. The effort to organize the neutralist bloc is evidenced in the high degree of cooperation between the United Arab Republic and Yugoslavia, a somewhat lessened enthusiasm for India, the establishment of the Afro-Asian Solidarity Conference, and the follow-up work after the recent Casablanca Conference. The final bit of evidence of growing importance of positive neutralism for pan-Arabism is the growing body of ideological writing on the subject.

An examination of the speeches and press interviews of President Nasser generally supports the outline presented above. His early speeches record his attempts to press the West for concessions. On November 20, 1953 he made his first criticism of the "Free World," that is the United States, for its failure to grant Egypt any development loans in the fourteen months since the revolution.[6] On April 19, 1954 he made a thinly veiled threat that he might seek arms from the Eastern bloc if the West did not comply with his request.[7] On the second anniversary of the revolution he made one of his most revealing statements about Egyptian foreign policy and his grasp of the Cold War situation; he said that this was no longer the age of power politics, but an age in which the great powers were vying for the friendship of the lesser powers. Egypt, he announced, would withhold its friendship from those who did not cooperate with her.[8]

This statement is in accord with the passive nature of Egyptian foreign policy at the time, but Nasser went on to identify Egypt as part of the Afro-Asian bloc and reviewed the strategic and moral foundations which would one day permit Egypt to play a more significant role in world affairs.[9] After initialing the evacuation treaty, Nasser repeated the latter theme, stating that the evacuation would permit Egypt to fulfill its international mission: *Egypt would force the world to recognize its existence.*[10]

Despite these euphoric references to future glories, Nasser withheld from declaring Egypt to be neutral, in fact. Egypt preferred neutrality but was still tied to Britain by the provisions of the Treaty of 1954. Nasser explained that neutrality required power, "the question is shall I wait until the enemy burns my house?" But this ambivalence was quickly revealed when he added that he believed a Third World War unlikely because of the balance of terror.[11] Nasser was attempting to

[6] *Ibid.*, Vol. 1, p. 173.
[7] *Ibid.*, Vol. 2, p. 275.
[8] *Ibid.*, Vol. 1, p. 173.
[9] *Ibid.*, pp. 420–21.
[10] *Ibid.*, p. 477 (Italics added).
[11] *Ibid.*, Vol. 3, p. 493.

justify the arrangement whereby the British might return to Egypt within a period of seven years, while at the same time suggesting that such a return would be unlikely.

After the controversy with the West over the Baghdad Pact had fully emerged, he stated that there was no difference between the East and the West: Egypt wanted no military pacts.[12] Nasser then set out to attend the Bandung meetings, and in speeches in India, Indonesia, back in Cairo, and in Yugoslavia he stressed the attachment of Egypt to the idea of Afro-Asian cooperation to achieve peace. He frequently repeated the ten principles agreed upon at Bandung, most of which refer to the preservation of the independence of small states, their equality, and the importance of the principle of non-intervention.[13] In Yugoslavia he first made the point that Egypt's foreign policy was a reflection of the principles on which the domestic revolution was based.

Despite the strength of this new neutralist tendency, Nasser revealed some hesitation, or at least uncertainty about the reaction of the West, in an interview with a correspondent from the *Daily Herald* after the announcement of the arms deal with Czechoslovakia was made. When asked if Egypt had taken a neutralist position, Nasser answered,

How can we be neutral when we are tied for seven years more by a treaty with Britain about the Suez Canal base. The question is not one of whether we are neutral, but it is a question of not submitting to the control of any foreign power.[14]

Thus independence, rather than neutrality, remained the dominant theme.

II Positive Neutrality

Nasser's first recorded use of the term "positive neutrality" was in September 1956 after the Brioni conference at the height of the Suez controversy. The preferred terminology reflects the ill-repute of the word "neutrality" at the time, and with this simple reference to positive neutrality the words "positive peaceful coexistence" appear four times in the same short interview.[15] The context further shows that Nasser was primarily concerned with justifying his opposition to the Baghdad Pact and his arms deal with the East.

In March 1957, however, Nasser identified Egypt's policy with Arab nationalism and the effort to have all the Arabs maintain the policy of positive neutrality.[16] In December 1957, Nasser declared that, "positive neutrality and non-alignment have appeared in the area, words in which every citizen believes . . . every citizen of the

[12] *Ibid.*, p. 655.
[13] *Ibid.*, pp. 718, 723, 726; Vol. 4, pp. 828, 848–49, 908 f.
[14] *Ibid.*, Vol. 5, p. 1032.
[15] *Ibid.*, Vol. 7, pp. 1449–50.
[16] *Ibid.*, Vol. 8, p. 1572.

Arab area used to call for non-alignment, for positive neutrality. . . ." [17] Nasser was no longer begging for arms or loans, he was threatening to mobilize all the resources of the Middle East for the end he deemed correct for the Arab nation.

If Nasser's speeches reflect the gradual development of Egypt's neutral policy, most of the ideological material is retrospective and can be taken as justification of current UAR policy; but the Ba'this of Syria long preceded Egyptian spokesmen in their firm attachment to neutralism. Each of the authors whose writings have been examined has his own approach and they vary greatly in ability and insight into the problem. The writings are, furthermore, disparate in that they range from books to simple editorials or speeches. One can expect that the number of tracts on positive neutrality will be augmented as the intelligentsia catches up with policy-makers, but for the present we must be content with materials of uneven quality. The only really important effort is that by Clovis Maqsud, but it is original enough to make it a little less useful as a gloss on current policy than the others. As a consequence of these limitations, we have deemed it preferable to deal with all together as they relate to certain common themes.

As we have seen, the major element in the Arab conception of neutralism is neither peace nor international responsibility, but the primacy of national independence, self-determination, and non-intervention. Muhammad Hasanain Haikal holds that the word neutrality first appeared before the revolution as an expression of the struggle for complete independence in a world divided into two blocs.[18] For Rimawi, independence and the refusal to enter the sphere of influence of any bloc is the very definition of positive neutrality.[19] Al-Sha'bini holds that positive neutrality is the only foreign policy which guarantees the realization of all of the "basic motivations of human behavior." He equates the nation with the individual and asserts that both are motivated by a group of needs that are "dynamically organized in a pyramidal form." These are self-preservation and economic requirements, security, peace, freedom and independence and self-esteem.[20] There can be no economic or political "awakening" without independence, so that independence must precede the achievement of self-esteem.[21] He exemplifies the achievement of the last stage by quoting from one of Nasser's speeches about how he threatened to throw George Allen out of his office if he came to deliver a "warning" from Washington.[22] But the implication of this independence is not evenly balanced between the two blocs. Its primary meaning is anti-imperialism in the classical use of that term.[23]

Just about every writer agrees that positive neutrality is the external manifestation of the Arab revolutionary ideal or of the revolutionary policies of Egypt. Haikal explains the development of positive neutrality without the benefit of ideology in this way. Al-Ashmuni writes that peace has a new meaning, it is economic as well as

[17] Ibid., Vol. 10, p. 1804.
[18] Muhammad Hasanain Haikal, Al-Ahram (January 27, 1961).
[19] Rimawi, al-Mantiq al-Thawri (Cairo, 1961), pp. 98, 275.
[20] al-Sha'bini, al-Hiyad al-Ijabi (Cairo, 1960), p. 133.
[21] Ibid., p. 143.
[22] Ibid., pp. 146–49.
[23] Ibid., pp. 47, 102, 134; al-Bitar, op. cit., pp. 68–69, 98.

political. The search for economic development and independence within Egypt had its international expression in the Bandung meetings which spread the ideas of the Egyptian revolution over a great part of the world.[24] Rimawi, Bitar, and Aflaq, all of them Ba'this of one sort or another, agree that positive neutralism is a manifestation of the socialist ideology of Arab nationalism. Rimawi insists that the Arab socialists have a new solution, Bitar and 'Aflaq simply call for the working out of a middle road between capitalism and Communism, but all three see positive neutralism as an answer to the ideological aspects of the bipolar struggle.[25] Maqsud, more consistent than the rest, flatly states that positive neutrality is *not* organically related to the national movement. It did not simply appear overnight either. Its attachment to the Arab movement is a long story including the Palestine defeat, the absence of a modern leadership, the military coups, and later experiences with both East and West.[26]

Maqsud's dissent points up the core of the problem of neutralist ideology for Arab nationalists. Nearly all writers grasp the fact that positive neutrality is a response to bipolarity. As a dependent variable, it is difficult to view it as an inherent element of Arab nationalism; hence, most writers dutifully call positive neutrality a "stage" in the historical development of the Arab movement.[27] But if it is only a stage, is the policy it implies merely a tactical device to realize certain Arab interests? There are really two derivative issues that flow from this question, the first is the moral question of justifying positive neutrality as more than tactical balancing, and the second is the practical consideration of whether or not the policy can achieve the goals claimed for it.

The moral issue is resolved by the questionable assumption that the interests of Arab nationalism accord with the highest moral needs of the world at this time. We have already seen where positive neutralism is held to be the foreign policy which will complete the domestic revolution that offers a new social and political solution to the world; and it is also held that Arab unity [28] can be achieved through positive neutrality and, in more general terms, that neutralism accords with the interest [29] of the Arab people. Far from avoiding moral issues, positive neutrality involves taking a stand on international issues. It hopes to build an international stream which will offer solutions to all problems, reduce the possibility of aggression, and build peace.[30] For Maqsud, the positive aspect of positive neutrality arises when the major bloc exponent which takes the correct stand is rewarded by neutralist support; thus, positive neutrality means no *permanent* commitment to either

[24] Hasan al-Ashmuni, *Duwwal al-Hiyad,* Kutub Qawmiyyah, No. 85 (Cairo, December 20, 1960), pp. 6–7.

[25] Rimawi, *op. cit.,* pp. 19–21, 52; Bitar, *op. cit.,* p. 32; Aflaq, *Ma'arakat al-Musir al-Wahid* (Beirut, 1949), p. 216.

[26] Clovis Maqsud, *Ma'ana al-Hiyad al-Ijabi* [*The Meaning of Positive Neutrality*] (Beirut, 1960), pp. 102 f.

[27] Haikal, *loc. cit.;* Maqsud, *op. cit.,* pp. 7, 101 f.; Aflaq, *op. cit.,* 217.

[28] Sha'bini, *op. cit.,* p. 13; Rimawi, *op. cit.,* p. 34; Maqsud, *op. cit.,* p. 102.

[29] Bitar, *op. cit.,* p. 71; Rimawi, *op. cit.,* pp. 280–81; 'Aflaq, p. 216.

[30] Haikal, *loc. cit.*

bloc but encourages temporary support.[31] Rimawi disagrees with Maqsud's balancing idea and writes instead that positive neutrality does not mean neutrality regarding matters of principle. The Arab approach to international problems is one which stems from their own third way.[32]

All agree, as might be expected, that the goal of positive neutrality is peace. Rimawi alone fails to relate peace to Arab "interests." For him the desire for peace is a matter of pure principles; but the Arabs will not accept peace at any price.[33] Haikal writes that the Arabs need peace in order to develop. 'Aflaq believes that it is not in the Arab interest that either of the major blocs collapse; hence, it is important to work for the lessening of tension between the two and to work toward permitting both to fulfill their promises of freedom and welfare to all peoples. Professor Butros-Ghali carefully distinguishes between positive neutrality and peaceful coexistence; the latter, he writes, is the slogan of those involved in the Cold War and is based on the balance of terror, while the former is idealist and spirtual and is the slogan of the non-industrial, militarily weak states.[34] The aim of the neutralists is to disarm the two armed camps.

Obviously, the sort of peace that is referred to throughout these works is the absence of a thermonuclear war. The point is made quite explicitly by Bitar.[35]

In order to stress the positive moral aspect of their neutrality, these writers take great pains to distinguish positive neutrality from legal neutrality, the Swiss type of neutrality, and the Austrian example of neutralization (to which the Laos problem might be assimilated). All of these are referred to as types of negative neutrality.[36] At worst, such neutral states stand by in isolation hoping that they will not be affected by any hostilities; at best they can act as arbitrators in minor cases. Neutralized states may serve to reduce tension, but the restrictions on their foreign policies would be too great a burden on the nationalist states of Asia and Africa even if Austria and Germany could abide neutralization.[37] Besides, negative neutrality is dependent upon an older type of weapons technology which would permit neutrals to stay clear of hostilities, while positive neutrality is not related to any weapons technology.[38]

This last view of Maqsud is especially surprising since he is the only one who has seriously attempted to relate his discussion of the balancing role of neutrals to the problem of mutual deterrence, and he devotes himself to a refutation of Henry Kissinger's *Nuclear Weapons and Foreign Policy*.[39] Tactical balancing is generally held to be a "negative" policy. Butros-Ghali defines negative neutrality in this manner,

[31] Maqsud, *op. cit.*, pp. 57, 87 f.
[32] Rimawi, *op. cit.*, pp. 277–78.
[33] *Ibid.*, pp. 280–81.
[34] Butros Butros-Ghali, *Dirasat fi al-Siyasah al-Duwwaliyyah* [*Studies in International Relations*] (Cairo, 1961), pp. 35–37.
[35] Bitar, *op. cit.*, p. 67.
[36] Sha'bini, op. cit., pp. 47 f., 59, 63; Maqsud, *op. cit.*, pp. 28 f., 49–59; Haikal, *loc. cit.*
[37] Maqsud, *op. cit.*, pp. 31, 49–51.
[38] *Ibid.*, p. 109.
[39] *Ibid.*, pp. 121 f.

but denies that positive neutrality tends to increase international tension or to exploit the great power conflict—for by definition its aim is peace. The major stage on which the neutrals can act for peace is the United Nations, but their neutrality will not thereby be affected since, in the Security Council, both the United States and the Soviet Union must agree before action is taken. There is no mention of action by the General Assembly, and the very weak argument is rounded out by a supreme contradiction when the author writes that the neutrals are better off in case a hot war starts because then they can choose whichever side will benefit them most, while those who are not neutral will have no choice.[40]

Sha'bini uses the term balancing, but he does not have the same thing in mind. For him positive neutrality is comprised of the positive elements already discussed plus legal neutrality, that is, giving no benefit to either bloc that is not given to both.[41] 'Aflaq, as we have seen, implies that neutralist balancing must aim at preventing either bloc from crushing the other, but he does not indicate how this can be done. Rimawi simply denies outright that positive neutrality is either tactical or strategic.[42]

As against these rather flimsy attempts to discuss positive neutrality in practical terms, Maqsud's little book stands out. His approach throughout is historical and materialistic and has an air of realism about it. He is less concerned with the positive moral aspects of neutrality than its positive political aspects. Where Rimawi's historical dialectic leads him to emphasize support for the United Arab Republic above all else, Maqsud's is bent toward the application of positive neutrality as a practical device for achieving Arab ends. According to Maqsud, positive neutrality is not isolation from, or equally opposing, both blocs, as Nasser would put it, but is supporting each in limited fashion: guaranteeing the West's oil but agreeing to the East's demands that the West withdraw from its foreign bases. This kind of balancing must be directed at finding solutions to problems and reducing tension.

Some pages later, Maqsud turns to a discussion of the sources of influence of positive neutrality, a discussion which throws more light on his concept of balancing. The first source is moral, and it implies mobilizing world public opinion both among the neutrals and within the committed states. The second source arises from the situation of mutual deterrence prevailing between the two blocs. Both bloc leaders tend to be moderate because of the great strain of the balance of terror. The greatest gain which has been realized through their moderation is their willingness to accept the neutrality of certain states.[43] Thus, the United States acted to end the aggression of its secondary bloc members in Egypt in 1956 and Soviet Russia tried to improve Indian-Chinese relations after the Chinese aggression on the Indian border. But when the United States and the Soviet Union met directly, they resorted to conventional warfare, which led to the development of the Kissinger

[40] Butros-Ghali, *op. cit.,* pp. 19–22.
[41] Sha'bini, *op. cit.,* pp. 58–59.
[42] Rimawi, *op. cit.,* p. 275.
[43] Maqsud, *op. cit.,* p. 128.

thesis concerning the possibility of limited nuclear warfare. This notion, writes Maqsud, was based on misinformation about Soviet scientific achievements; hence, the nuclear stand-off still dominates East-West relations.[44]

The neutrals can take advantage of mutual deterrence to extend the area of peace. This is not opportunism, for politics is the art of the possible, and the possible at this stage of international tension lies in taking the initiative in straightening out the difficulties of mankind and harnessing technology to the purposes of peace. To this end the neutrals must: (1) keep the balance by working for disarmament, (2) encourage competitive peaceful coexistence, (3) work to establish an effective supervision over weapons production, (4) strengthen the United Nations, (5) *avoid the making of any kind of an agreement at the summit because* (a) this will reduce the chances *for the neutrals to profit* and (b) it will create hopes that cannot be fulfilled.[45]

It remains for us to complete our juxtaposition of contemporary Arab neutralist theory with the political practice of the UAR by searching for interpretations of two of the more recent policy trends. These trends are efforts to build an organized bloc of neutrals and to win the leadership of the bloc. Most writers are silent on the question of a neutralist bloc. Sha'bini, whose views are about the most innocuous, denied that the goal is a third bloc. The neutralists should achieve their joint ends by strengthening their mutual relations and influencing world public opinion.[46] The aim of positive neutrality is to substitute collective security for bloc alliances and to revive the concept of the just war.[47] And again in discussing the 1956 Brioni meetings of Tito, Nehru, and Nasser, Sha'bini quotes *al-Ahram* as reporting that the Yugoslav authorities were astonished when reporters said that the basis for a new neutralist bloc had been laid, and those authorities declared that the best name for the policies of the three countries was "positive peaceful coexistence" (not neutrality).[48]

The growing attractiveness of the idea of an organized neutralist bloc may be illustrated by the comparison of two statements of Salah al-Din al-Bitar, the first in 1955 just after Nasser's first visit to Yugoslavia and the second in 1957 after the Suez crisis. In 1955 al-Bitar simply reported that Nehru was the leader of the positive neutrals and that he was opposed to the formation of a bloc because he felt it would result in the tightening of the other blocs.[49] In 1957 he called for the unity of all the Arabs who supported non-alignment and neutrality as a basis for unifying all the Arab peoples.[50]

Maqsud's views on the matter are much more in keeping with the policy of the UAR after the Casablanca conference. He denies that the neutrals desire to com-

[44] *Ibid.*, p. 135.
[45] *Ibid.*, p. 137.
[46] Sha'bini, *op. cit.*, p. 60.
[47] *Ibid.*, pp. 58, 100.
[48] *Ibid.*, p. 94.
[49] Bitar, *op. cit.*, p. 66.
[50] *Ibid.*, p. 91.

prise a third nuclear force.[51] Their power is derived from their cooperation and moral influence, but they must be better organized.[52] Later he deplores the fact that the neutrals can take no direct initiative in the two-sided disarmament talks because they are not organized. Needless to say, Soviet insistence upon a three man triumvirate for the United Nations Secretariat, as well as for the disarmament supervision organization, plays right into the hands of those who would organize the neutrals. The question is, after all, which neutrals and how would they be appointed? Would they have to be acceptable to both the United States and the Soviet Union, or would they represent a neutralist bloc?

The fact that there are differences among the neutrals is noticed only by Maqsud. He notes that India refuses to use the term positive neutrality but ascribes this to the unpleasant connotation of the word "neutrality" in English, which is the language of the Indian elite.[53] He implies that there is no important difference between the policies of India and Egypt, though the West has treated them both differently, especially since 1956.[54] There is no essential difference in their policies, nor can any difference be ascribed to the differences in national character. The differences are due to geographical circumstances. India has a secondary strategic position so her neutrality is accepted, while the Arabs are in an area of critically strategic importance. The West will not, therefore, accept the neutrality of the Arabs.[55]

The arguments of those who support Nasser's candidacy for leadership of the neutralist bloc fall into two groups: they claim that Nasser initiated the term or the policy and that he has been its foremost exponent. Ashmuni blandly asserts that the Bandung resolutions reflected Egypt's revolutionary principles, and that Nehru followed in Nasser's footsteps.[56] He finds the origin of positive neutrality at Bandung. Butros-Ghali finds its roots in the Pantcha Sila first recorded in the preamble of the Sino-Indian treaty of 1954.[57] Sha'bini insists that the meaning of positive neutrality has stemmed from the UAR and that it first appeared at the meeting of the Arab heads of state which issued its joint communiqué on February 27, 1957.[58] (The date is significant in view of the conclusion that the UAR altered its policies after the Suez invasion.) Rimawi does not call for the formation of a bloc, nor does he insist on Egypt's leadership of the neutralist bloc, but he does argue that the practical application of positive neutrality is to be found in the policy of the UAR, thus rendering all further theoretical discussion useless.[59]

As limited as they are, these tracts do provide us with some insight into the Arab idea of neutrality. Clearly, the Arabs are not primarily concerned with the Cold

---

[51] There is some confusion here because the Arabic word for force (as in third force) is the same as the word for power (as in nuclear power).

[52] Maqsud, op. cit., p. 98.

[53] Ibid., p. 86.

[54] Ibid., p. 77.

[55] Ibid., pp. 94–95.

[56] Ashmuni, op. cit., pp. 7, 8.

[57] Butros-Ghali, op. cit., p. 6.

[58] Sha'bini, op. cit., p. 91.

[59] Rimawi, op. cit., p. 53.

War and its peaceful demise. They are aware of the destructiveness which will result from a thermonuclear war and agree that a peaceful solution must be sought. However, they do not put agreement between the United States and the Soviet Union above their own aspirations. Positive neutrality means pursuing an independent policy in accord with the Arab national interest, which is further defined in terms of the pan-Arab aspiration and in building Arab Socialism.

Even though tactical balancing is admitted to be immoral, nearly all writers accept it in one form or another. The purpose of balancing is agreed to be peace and ending the Cold War, but this is to be achieved by dissolving the blocs, persuading the great powers to help strengthen the smaller powers, and by the gradual adjustment of the Soviet and American political systems until they meet at some point in the middle. The Arabs tend to disregard the differences between the Eastern and Western blocs except insofar as these two follow diverse but equally misguided ideologies. The Arabs also see the United States as their major opponent in achieving their nationalist goals but acknowledge that the Soviet Union's recognition of Arab neutrality is probably only a tactical device.

There is no evidence that the Arabs believe that irresponsible action on their part can turn the Cold War into a hot war, lose the Cold War for one side, or bring the Soviet Union into the Middle East. In working for their own ends, Arab neutralists are inevitably working for peace in their view. But such typical nationalist logic barely conceals their determination to turn the present international situation to advantage. Finally, these tracts not only sustain our analysis of the UAR's neutrality, they strongly suggest that the UAR will not be tightly bound by ideological considerations in the future any more than in the past. All agree that positive neutrality requires maneuver and flexibility even if not merely self-interested.

III   Responsible Neutrality

Neutralism has become a generic term for the common features of the response of many underdeveloped countries to the bipolarization of international power. But neutralism in this broad sense is only a lowest common denominator. The basic neutralist position is a defensive one, and it is often aimed against Western assumptions or long established positions which could not be borne in the face of domestic extremist opposition. Some neutrals remain in this defensive posture: India, Burma, Ceylon, Iraq, Lebanon, Sudan, Yugoslavia; some modified their defensive posture by seeking limited irredenta and accepting Soviet arms—Indonesia and Morocco are examples; while others find themselves with new opportunities to play important international roles or to increase in power, influence, and territory: Egypt, Ghana, and possibly Cuba seem to fit in here. Some of those who have retained the defensive posture are more worried about aggression or subversion from other neutralist states, and these tend to be "neutralist pro-West." Those who have the most to gain from neutralism, not because of bipolarity, but because of the structure of the subordinate or "area" international systems in which they are located, tend to be "neutralist pro-Soviet" as revisionist states might be expected to be. The latter also tend to be more pragmatic and less idealistic in their foreign policies, if only because they have specific goals; and they are for the same reason more committed to the idea of an organized neutralist bloc which can be counted on to respond in the right way at the right time.

Egypt's neutrality is not a copy of the Indian or Yugoslav policies; it derives special benefits from its position in the Middle East, including its relative lack of exposure to Soviet aggression and the aid policies of the Soviet Union. Another characteristic of the positive neutrality of the UAR is that while its beginning was essentially defensive, it has now become an active means of achieving revisionist ends. The UAR, alone in the Middle East, shares this ability to derive special international benefits from the pursuit of positive neutrality with certain African states. These are the two areas of the most significant "pan-nationalist" movements, and at the present moment the pan-Arab movement appears to be the more vigorous. Hence, the UAR stands to be the gretest beneficiary of the strengthening of positive neutrality in the international arena, unless perhaps the benefits of the Soviet Union prove in the end to be greater.

Egypt and the Soviet Union have not been without their own disputes, witness the union with Syria in 1958 and the Iraqi revolt of the same year. Some hard words were passed at the time, but it would appear that the Soviet Union has decided to let Nasser have his way in the Middle East in return for support elsewhere. If this assumption is correct, then the Soviet Union will not intervene in UAR-Iraqi relations to support Iraq and, as we have seen in Laos, the Berlin issue, and the problem of nuclear testing, the UAR will not lend support to a vigorous neutralist position in Cold-War issues. The Congo issue appears to be an extension of the same sort of arrangement to Africa, with Nkrumah as the major beneficiary.

The United States stands to lose a great deal if the UAR succeeds in achieving its goals by its present methods. We will lose a good many friends whom we still retain and find them replaced by a power committed to hostility towards us. Nasser's pan-Arabism does not now allow for compromise, it calls for the unification of armies, for a common market, and for popular organizations, but not for federal constitutions and political safeguards. Governments which resist these overtures, and even those who withhold their delegates from the numerous pan-Arab meetings held in Cairo, are accused not of disbelief in the ultimate truth of Arab nationalism, but of serving the interests of the United States. Whether we would or not, we are being compelled to play the devil in the piece.

We shall lose more than friends, of course. We shall lose our influence over important petroleum resources, and lose our access to an important strategic area. We shall run the risk of seeing both Turkey and Iran subjected to pressure from the south as well as the north and may well fear the hostile manipulation of the entire neutralist bloc against us.

In the final analysis, it may be this "activist" neutralism of the UAR which most threatens American security. If the outcome of the Cold War depends upon the resolution of a series of Laos-like issues, the new responsibilities of the neutralist states have become manifest. The neutrals might have helped to establish a truly neutral government in Laos, but none was willing to incur the wrath of the Soviet Union. It is apparent that the neutrals cannot get together on a Cold-War issue, their unity is limited to issues between themselves and individual Western powers. Neither is this limitation a perverse psychological reaction to the memory of imperialism; rather, it is due to the loose structure of the Western bloc which permits some members to be flouted while others are courted. If the Russo-Chinese split hardens and China can find the resources, the same game may be played with the Communist bloc.

At one time neutralism was no more than a tactical refusal to side openly with the West. It was a weak form of pressure, at a time when political and economic benefits were expected from the West alone and Western values were tacitly accepted. Our greatest loss in the Cold War has not been territory, but the loss of our unique position as the sole source of both material and ideological assistance to the developing states. Those who have accepted Soviet assistance as a challenge to this Western position, and who have sought to exploit what they too naively believed to be a fixed balance of deterrence, have also accepted the *a priori* political reasoning of neo-Marxism. Like the Soviet Union, these activist neutrals are ambitious revisionist powers with a new sense of their ability to control events. At the present time neither they nor we can say exactly what limits may be set upon the expansion of neutralist power by the nature of the dominant bipolar system—with the result that a series of small changes in the developing areas may destroy the balance of the system rather than relegate both superpowers to impotence, as the exponents of positive neutrality suggest.

It is useless to suppose that we can restore the earlier kind of neutralism, but it is worth noting that our earlier criticism of "negative" neutralism had some ideological impact. Proceeding on the basis of this experience, it appears that we might well take the activist neutralists at their word: If positive neutrality is to be judged pragmatically by its ability to bring the Cold War to a peaceful conclusion, then let us so judge it. *A priori* assumptions about the necessary relationship between this function and the realization of the "interests" of the neutral states may be put to the same tests. For the rest we can only try to use our material resources in such a way as to prove that responsible neutrality and enlightened self-interest do go together.

9

Peasant Protest in South Viet Nam

Joseph J. Zasloff

Viet Nam is still an active participant in the revolutions of our time. Its turbulent history of war, continuous since 1945, has not yet ended. Currently the government of South Viet Nam is struggling for survival against well-organized, strongly sustained guerrilla forces—the Viet Cong—inspired and supported by the Communist Vietminh government of the North, which has made no secret of its goal of crushing the southern government and uniting Viet Nam under its hegemony.

The most important aspect of the struggle, at present, is a contest for the allegiance of the peasantry, the largest single segment of the population. The outcome of this contest many well decide Viet Nam's future political system. Although the peasants are politically unorganized, they constitute both the base and core of Vietnamese society and are, therefore, the medium upon which guerrilla activity is centered. Mao Tse-tung, in outlining his concepts of guerrilla warfare, likens the peasantry to water and the guerrillas to the fish that inhabit it.

The extent to which other politically important groups of the South are willing to support their government will also be strongly influenced by the outcome of the contest. Of these groups, the military and the intellectuals are particularly sensitive to the government's program for confronting guerrilla activity in the countryside, as both groups are aware of the pivotal role of the peasantry.

The effectiveness of Viet Cong activity is intimately connected with the southern peasants' attitude toward President Diem's government: If it is either neutral or hostile, the concomitant may be a toleration or support of the Communist guerrillas that enables them to operate successfully. However, since the peasantry as a group has no organized opposition of its own through which protest against the present government can be expressed, its support or toleration of the Viet Cong does not necessarily imply a proclivity to Communism. The aim of this paper is to explore the relationship of guerrilla activity to peasant discontent and protest.

I Sources of Peasant Discontent

The processes of rapid change which the twentieth century has brought to southeast Asia, largely through the impact of French rule, has severely jolted traditional society, creating stresses which give rise to anxiety and unrest. Urbanization, restratification, secularization, commercialization, and Westernized education have all made their mark in Viet Nam.[1] Peasant hostility to urban rulers is deeply imbedded: Almost automatically, any ruler and his entourage are regarded as alien representatives of the urban elite who are dedicated to altering the peasantry's traditional way of life. At present in Viet Nam, the gap between the style of life and the aspirations of the urban, intellectual ruling group and those of the peasantry is greater than ever.[2] This gap has been an important factor in the inability of southern leadership to win peasant support.

The struggle for independence from France was at first a force unifying the urban intellectuals, the nationalist leaders, with the peasantry who supported the nationalist cause.[3] When the French reimposed colonial rule after the Second World War, nationalist guerrillas, largely Vietminh–directed, utilized peasant sympathy and support in their constant harassment of the French administration. The French discovered that it was virtually impossible to prevent guerrilla activity from having a solid base in the villages; they could control the cities and the areas along main roads during the day, but at night, in the countryside, the Vietminh ruled.[4]

The nationalist struggle against the colonial regime launched the notion, particularly widespread throughout the peasantry, that prosperity and social justice would succeed the exploiting foreign rule.[5] Great disappointments, unfortunately, were in store for the population and, as in many emergent nations, the unity produced by earlier struggle was sorely strained. To begin with, the nation was physically severed at the 17th parallel. Northern refugees inundated the South; political-religious sects vied for local autonomy; diverse political factions conspired to seize power; and the Communists applied violence in their agitation to overthrow the southern regime. Under these conditions, neither democracy nor prosperity resulted. Expectations expanded more rapidly than the ability to satisfy them, and the new regime was faced with a "revolution of rising frustrations." [6] When the French departed, the unifying symbol of the common enemy was eliminated from a society which was otherwise rent by divisive forces, and there was no strong, unifying substitute readily available.

[1] Gabriel A. Almond and James S. Coleman, *The Politics of Developing Areas* (Princeton: Princeton University Press, 1960). The five categories mentioned were selected by the authors in their analysis of the processes of change in developing areas.

[2] For a discussion of the gap between the modernist and traditional elements, see Edward Shils, "Political Development in the New States," *Comparative Studies in Society and History* (April 1960), pp. 265–92.

[3] See Ellen J. Hammer, *The Struggle for Indochina* (Stanford: Stanford University Press, 1954) and *The Struggle for Indochina Continues* (Stanford: Stanford University Press, 1955), for discussion of the nationalist struggle.

[4] For an excellent treatise on nationalism, see Rupert Emerson, *From Empire to Nation* (Cambridge: Harvard University Press, 1960). Also consult Milton Sachs, "Marxism in Viet Nam" in Frank N. Trager and Associates, *Marxism in Southeast Asia: A Study of Four Countries* (Stanford: Stanford University Press, 1959) and J. H. Brimmell, *Communism in Southeast Asia: A Political Analysis* (New York: Oxford University Press, 1959).

[5] See Paul Mus, *Viet Nam: Sociologie d'une guerre* (Paris: Editions du Seuil, 1952).

[6] This term is taken from *The Emerging Nations*. Max F. Millikan and Donald Blackmer (eds.), (Boston: Little, Brown and Company, 1961), p. 41.

Viet Nam is divided into three distinct sections—the North, the Center, and the South (formerly known as Tonkin, Annam, and Cochin-China). Though the sections have actually been unified for a long period and have spoken a common language, differences in dialect, custom, and tradition are sufficiently important to make natives of each section appear somewhat as strangers to each other. Many traits of the Vietnamese regime which succeeded French rule made it still seem alien to the southern peasant. President Diem and his family come from Hué, the former capital of Annam, and many of his key bureaucrats are from the Center also, or from the North. Ruled by Centrist Diem inevitably raised suspicion among the southern peasantry.

Religious factionalism is a further source of estrangement of the Diem regime from the peasantry. The ancestor cult, with roots in Confucianism, Taoism, and Buddhism, is the most widespread religion of the country, and, of the present sects that have developed from them, the Cao Dai and Hoa Hao claim several million adherents. The Catholicism of President Diem and his family fosters resentment, possibly because it is unlike the peasants' religious practices or because it is Western and, perhaps, a reminder of French rule. Whatever the reason for the resentment, identification between the peasantry and the government is made more difficult. Hoa Hao and Cao Dai claim additional and more concerted grievances. When their military organizations were broken up by the Diem government, many of their leaders fled; others were imprisoned or executed. Ostensibly, both sects are now free to practice their religion, but they are forbidden by the government, acting to prevent their possible growth in political strength, to hold meetings or ceremonies which would draw members from wide areas.[7]

So far President Diem has not been able to personify for the peasants the goals of the revolution which could give them the national consciousness needed for obtaining unity. If he could supply such charismatic leadership, he might guide the nation toward modernization despite the many divisive forces. In this respect, Diem's background is a disadvantage. Ho Chi Minh, not Ngo Dinh Diem, was the revered hero, leading the Vietnamese struggle for freedom from the French.[8] In 1933, Diem served as Minister of the Interior in Bao Dai's Cabinet but resigned in protest against French policies after only eight months in office. Relatively withdrawn then from public life, he lived abroad for a number of years, spending part of the time in Catholic seminaries in the United States and Belgium. Diem has a reputation among the intellectuals as an incorruptible opponent of French Colonialism, but he was not known by the broader population as an active participant in the nationalist revolution.

An ascetic bachelor and a pious Catholic, President Diem is aloof in his personal life, and as the son of a prominent mandarin at the Court of Hué, he often exhibits

---

[7] For discussion of the sects, see Bernard B. Fall, "*The Political-Religious Sects of Vietnam,*" *Pacific Affairs,* Vol. 28 (September 1955), pp. 235–53.

[8] See Robert Shaplen, "The Enigma of Ho Chi Minh," *The Reporter,* Vol. 12 (January 27, 1955), pp. 11–19.

traits of a haughty aristocrat. With his rather de Gaulle-like sense of destiny he acts as if he has received a mandate from heaven to lead Viet Nam to unity, security, and even grandeur. He has attempted to project a personal image to unite the masses behind him. Pictures of him are plastered everywhere, even in the most remote mountain village, and banners proclaim the glory of his personal leadership throughout the countryside. The press and radio are daily filled with fulsome praise of his prowess. In recent years, despite his difficulty in overcoming his aloofness, he has circulated widely among the rural populace and this seems to have generated respect, if not enthusiasm, for himself. He has not overcome, however, a widespread impression that his family and entourage are venal; nor has he managed to transcend traditional symbols and become a charismatic leader who can unify the people by inspiring them to substitute national objectives for narrower, factional goals.[9]

The political system which Diem has constructed in his bitter struggle for control depends largely on the members of his family and a few trusted advisors. One of his younger brothers, Ngo Dinh Nhu, is the chief political figure in Saigon. Nhu wields power through the Revolutionary Workers Party (Can Lao), a semi-secret, elite organization which coopts key members throughout the society. When he deems it necessary, he calls upon support from the National Revolutionary Movement (NRM), the official party with mass membership. Both Nhu and his wife were elected to the National Assembly which, with no genuine opposition parties gaining representation, provides only a democratic façade.[10] Madame Nhu is politically active as a leader of the feminist movement; her father was appointed Ambassador to the United States. Since she and Nhu live with Diem in the Presidential Palace, she serves as official hostess and first lady. Madame Nhu has a widespread reputation as a vigorous entrepreneur, able to combine clever business transactions with adroit political manipulation. Diem's youngest brother, Nho Dinh Can, rules Central Viet Nam in an autocratic fashion from his headquarters in Hué. A third brother, Ngo Dinh Luyen, serves as Ambassador to Great Britain, the Benelux countries, and several newly independent African nations. Ngo Dinh Thuc, the eldest of the family who is now a Catholic archbishop in Hué, exercises strong ideological influence on the President.[11] He instituted an academy at Vinh Long, with five of his priests composing the faculty, to teach "Personalism," the official philosophy of the Diem government. Civil servants, army officers, and school teachers are selected to attend Archbishop Thuc's academy in order to spread "Personalist" doctrines.[12]

[9] For discussion of the role of the charismatic leader see Edward B. Shils, "The Concentration and Dispersion of Charisma: Their Bearing on Economic Policy in Underdeveloped Countries," *World Politics,* Vol. 11 (October 1958), pp. 232–255.

[10] Housed in Saigon in a French-built, former opera house, the National Assembly is the subject of an anecdote which reveals its popular reputation. "When the French were here," the story goes, "a tragedy played once a week. Now there is comedy every day."

[11] A fifth brother was executed by the Vietminh in 1946, a fact which intensifies the President's hatred of the Communists.

[12] For discussion of "Personalism" see John C. Donnell, "National Renovation Campaigns in Vietnam," *Pacific Affairs,* Vol. 32, No. 1 (March 1959), pp. 73–88.

In placing his family in positions of major influence, Diem follows a time-honored Oriental practice. In view of the strong family bonds of Vietnamese society, it would, in fact, be unusual if he did not fill key positions with his relatives. Continuing challenges to his rule reinforce his need for officials whose personal loyalty is beyond doubt. Sympathetic observers of Diem's regime justify his nepotism by pointing out that in a country with so narrow an intellectual base, the President's family, well educated and competent, would be considered likely candidates for responsible government posts under any non-Communist regime.[13]

The pattern of a family regime is plainly more offensive to the modernist intellectual group than to the usually traditionalist peasantry. Nevertheless, the fact that the family regime consists of aristocratic Catholics from the alien Center section does nothing to endear the government to the southern peasant and also increases his willingness to believe widespread rumors of corruption in ruling circles.

II Guerrilla Operations and the Peasantry

On May 13, 1959, the ultimate aim of the Vietminh government in the North was made clear by the statement of its central committee that the time had come to "struggle heroically and perseveringly to smash the government of President Diem." [14] One of the main gambits toward this objective is the thesis of the Viet Cong agents that Communism represents the wave of the future and thus best serves the interests of the peasantry. To demonstrate their thesis effectively, they must try to produce concrete evidence that the southern regime is too weak and ineffective to provide proper protection and services to its population.

The moves of the Viet Cong guerrillas to produce the desired evidence have been many and thorough for several years. Village and hamlet chiefs, local police commissioners, youth leaders, members of the security forces—in fact all government functionaries—have been vulnerable to assassination. During 1960, for example, some 4000 officials were killed as a result of Viet Cong activity. This terrorism is discriminating, with victims being carefully selected. Prize targets are unpopular local officials, since their elimination both demonstrates Viet Cong strength and appears to protect the interests of the peasantry. Sometimes all the inhabitants of a village will be assembled at night under Viet Cong orders to witness the execution of such an official, said to be a "traitor" to the "national revolution." Continuously alert to local sentiment, the guerrillas develop coalitions with disgruntled members of the sects and other important village groups in order to mark down additional targets for either death or harassment. The letter to a hamlet official cited below, one of several examined by the writer on a research trip in a southern village in April 1960, shows one method of Viet Cong operation:

[13] For examples, see Wesley Fishel, "Political Realities in Vietnam" *Asian Survey* (April 1961), p. 6 and Joseph Buttinger, *The Smaller Dragon* (New York: Praeger, 1958).
[14] Joseph Alsop, "Warnings Aplenty," *New York Herald Tribune* (April 17, 1961).

Battalion Thong Kiet
Company 256
No. 35/CTQS

Coalition of the Armed Forces
of the Religious Sects Against
Americans and Diem

To: Tam-Anh, Secretary of My-Thanh B Hamlet
My-Thuan Village, Binh Minh District (Vinh Long)

While the situation is critical, the fighting movement of the people becomes stronger and stronger every day. The Americans and Diem oppress the people without pity. They use dictatorship, one religion and a one-family system to govern the country. They are entirely isolated from the people, and their regime is declining at its very roots. The Americans and Diem use barbarian policies. There is no barbarian measure which they have not employed. Their regime is a barbarian and bloody one.

Based on the above situation, the Revolution and the people do not recognize this regime nor the various reactionary organizations of the Americans and Diem. For this reason, the Revolution and the People have recently taken opposition measures at various places, as well as here in My Thuan that you, undoubtedly, have heard of and seen.

Since the day the hamlet chief paid for his crime, you have committed many indecent deeds, sometimes secretly and other times openly. Hiding from the people and bypassing the Revolution, you have stubbornly continued to work for the rebels. To be exact, you recently tied two draft evaders and handed them over to the Americans and Diem, sold family declaration forms, and collected money from the people. At present you have given the hamlet orders to take the names and ages of persons in each family to compel people to work at the agrovilles. You collaborate closely with the hamlet officials, carry out plots against the peace by the Americans and Diem, side with landowners in the fixing of riceland rent, force farmers to pay high rent, and look after rented lands for landowners.

All these actions which are very detrimental to the Revolution and the People prove that you may be the future hamlet chief. It would be very dangerous if you did not repent soon.

We, the commanding staff of Company 256 of Battalion Ly Thuong Kiet wholeheartedly warn you so that you can correct yourself. Resign immediately from your function as secretary and stop collaborating with rebels. If you still stubbornly do so, you will be entirely responsible in front of the Revolution and the People.

War Zone March 29, 1960
BCH Company 256
—Sealed—

Viet Cong tactics, of course, include disruption of administration and retardation of economic development. To this end, the guerrillas cut communications, block roads, blast bridges, and plunder rubber plantations. Attacks are also made on plantations and government installations primarily to gather arms and ammunition, as well as office machines and supplies for propaganda activities. Another tactic, though less frequently employed, is to attack units of the national army. In January 1960, for example, the Viet Cong unleashed a surprise attack on government troops at Tay Ninh, enabling them to capture large quantities of arms and inflict serious casualties before they withdrew to refuge across the Cambodian border. A recently adopted technique is the exertion of economic control over some southern areas. Following the rice harvest, the peasants are required to bring their rice to a common storage point—a "rice bank"—under Viet Cong control. After obtaining a receipt for their rice, they may withdraw quantities necessary to meet their needs.

Combined with all of these activities is an incessant propaganda campaign. The Viet Cong disseminate thousands of leaflets denouncing the Diem government, some printed crudely under field conditions, others prepared with greater care in the North, in Cambodia, or clandestinely in southern towns. In addition, political lectures are given in areas under Communist control and whispering campaigns are carried on at every opportunity.

The Viet Cong guerrillas generate from a variety of sources. Many of those sent from the North include southerners who went to the North in 1954, following the Geneva Accord, and who are now returned to their native regions with instructions to carry out guerrilla activities. Some work their way south through Laos, infiltrating the mountains of the Haut Plateau region to agitate among the non-Vietnamese indigenous mountaineers. A larger number follow the Ho Chi Minh Trail, wandering unchallenged through Cambodia, and slip with ease into the dense jungle and marshes of the southern delta areas, past the long frontiers, which are impossible to patrol effectively. Still others reach the southern coastal regions by sailing the South China Sea from Cambodia in boats which are indistinguishable from the fishing junks plying coastal waters.

It is difficult to estimate what part of the 12,000 to 20,000 guerrillas originate in the North, but it is generally believed that their leaders, working under the general direction of Hanoi, are furnished from there.[15] Arms, ammunition, and supplies are also sent from the North, though here again it is difficult to estimate what proportion of the total originates from this source.[16] Since Laos has tipped farther into Pathet Lao control and large quantities of Soviet Bloc weapons were shipped to Laos during the hostilities, it is reasonable to surmise that a new supply of weapons is being carried into South Viet Nam across Laotian and Cambodian borders.[17]

The Viet Cong draws part of its membership from the southern peasantry. Though most of the Communist forces were removed from the South when the Geneva Accord was signed, a nucleus was left behind to become the core of Viet Cong cadres and to gather new recruits from varying sources. A number of disgruntled adherents of Cao Dai and Hoa Hao have joined the Viet Cong to express their protest against the government. Other southern recruits include social misfits and the usual quota of men lured by opportunities for adventure and violence. Still another source of membership is the segment of the rural population which finds

---

[15] United States Secretary of Defense McNamara testified that two-thirds of the guerrillas were believed to come from the North.

[16] Robert Trumbull, New York *Times* Southeast Asia correspondent has written:
"Some qualified sources doubt the validity of a general impression that the Viet Cong is heavily supplied from communist-ruled North Vietnam. There has been considerable evidence that the communists have not found this necessary on any major scale." "Story of Nguyen Thanh—and of Vietnam," *New York Times Magazine* (July 2, 1961), pp. 8–9.

[17] See "The Hazards Before SEATO," *The Economist* (April 1, 1961), pp. 9–11, and also: Michel Bosquet, "Laos, la part du feu," *L'Express* (30 Mars 1961), pp. 10–11, and Robert Buillain, "Le Gachis Laotien" *Le Monde* (23–29 Mars 1961), three articles.

its dissatisfaction with government retaliatory measures pushed so far that joining in Viet Cong activities seems the only way to express resentment.

The Viet Cong are reported to use a variety of techniques to enlist southern members who might not normally volunteer. In regions where the Viet Cong are in control, participation in guerrilla activities amounts to a draft call. Though such service may be regarded by the "draftees" as an unpleasant duty, social pressures and ultimate sanctions make it seem necessary to undertake the demands that are made. There is some dragooning: During one period, for instance, the Viet Cong kidnapped potential recruits and involved them in subversive activities. Thus implicated, the recruits' fear of punishment by their government, if discovered, allowed them to be virtually blackmailed into continuing their Viet Cong activities. Fear undoubtedly plays a positive role in maintaining Viet Cong membership in the South. Recruits know well that Law 10/59 of the southern government promises severe punishment for Viet Cong crimes, including public administration of the guillotine at the scene of the crime for those convicted of a capital offense. No general amnesty policy, as in Malaya, has been developed by the government. The recruit is caught between two fires: Government policy does not make it easy for him to abandon voluntarily his Viet Cong involvement, and the Viet Cong penalizes defection with death. Reiteration of well-planned propaganda helps the Viet Cong mobilize recruits and support. Constant elaboration of the theme that the Americans have replaced the French as the imperialist power further exploits the discontent of the peasantry with the southern regime and evokes nationalist sentiment. Communism, presented and understood in simplistic terms, seems to some southern peasants to offer greater justice and a better life.

Ironically, the anti–Viet Cong operations of the government have supplied another source of Viet Cong support. When Government troops swoop into an area where guerrilla agents are reported to be, uncommitted and innocent villagers often become targets of the security forces who are unable to distinguish them from the Viet Cong. The guerrillas may well be using the tactic of provoking the government into retaliatory measures which will cause further disaffection of the local population, a stratagem that has proved successful in many underground operations.[18] President Diem has promised severe punishment to any member of his security forces who pillages, rapes, loots, or in any other way acts outside the bounds of military propriety. Such measures, however, are difficult to enforce in the climate of anti-guerrilla jungle warfare. Tensions increase with each attack, and reprisals are often carried out spontaneously, maintaining a vicious circle.[19]

Many peasants are caught between the conflicting pressures of the government and the Viet Cong. Even if a man wishes to be free of Viet Cong demands for food, supplies, and information, both his fear of Communist reprisal and his antipathy

[18] Northern refugees often point out that Communism has a greater appeal in the South than in the Center or North since the South was not subjected to Vietminh control.
[19] See J. K. Zawodny, "Guerrilla Warfare and Subversion as a Means of Political Change," in his paper delivered at the 1961 Annual Meeting of the American Political Science Association (September 6–9, 1961).

toward the government make him unwilling to inform government authorities of the whereabouts of Viet Cong members. When the peasantry will not supply such information, the government's task of flushing out the guerrillas becomes insuperable.

III Guerrilla Activity for the South?

The success of the Viet Cong guerrillas in disrupting normal activity and creating havoc raises the question of initiating reverse activity against the northern regime of Ho Chi Minh. If unfulfilled expectations contribute to the present support of the Viet Cong in the South, it would seem that a greater degree of support would be available if the Diem regime were to agitate in the North. Expectations there have been satisfied even less: Living conditions are poor, and the grounds are increasing for resentment against totalitarian government policies.[20] The regimented wretchedness of the north Vietnamese masses has been pointed out by Joseph Alsop, who advocates southern guerrilla activity in the North:

North Viet Nam, in other words, is a ripe target for precisely the kind of underground assault now being made on South Viet Nam—if anyone had the guts to take the risk of sponsoring and supporting this kind of assault. . . .

You cannot permit an enemy unlimited freedom to hit you whenever and wherever he pleases, while never hitting back yourself, without suffering mortal damage in the end.[21]

Assuming that the northern population offered a susceptible base for subversion, the Diem government would have to find men willing to endure tremendous hardship and constant peril of their lives, just as the Viet Cong and resistance fighters throughout history have done. Fervent belief in a cause or an ideology is an important ingredient in such activity. The leaders of the guerrilla movement in the South have their Communist doctrine to inspire them, and this is reinforced with the nationalist cause that originally motivated activity against the French. No comparable inspiration has developed for the southerners, who refrain from supporting Viet Cong activity, and it seems highly unlikely that President Diem's "Personalism" can provide the southern substitute for Communism as the inspiration for guerrilla leadership. Thus, the availability of enough men in the South who would be willing to carry out sustained guerrilla activity in the North at all matching Viet Cong activity is open to question.

Recruits might be found among refugees from the North, especially among the committed Catholics. Their desire to return to their native regions and their anti-Communism could perhaps provide them with sufficient motivation to lead guerrilla

[20] For a discussion of a North Vietnamese peasant revolt taking place in the province of Nghi An in November 1956, see Brian Crozier, *The Rebels: A Story of Post War Insurrections* (Boston: Beacon Press, 1960), pp. 93–96. In addition, see Bernard B. Fall, "Crisis in North Viet Nam," *Far Eastern Survey*, Vol. 26 (January 1957), pp. 12–15, and, by the same author, *The Viet Minh Regime*, rev. ed. (New York: Institute of Pacific Relations, 1956). A more recent report of northern peasant discontent is contained in *The Washington Post* (August 26, 1961), p. A8.
[21] Joseph Alsop, "The Double Standard," *New York Herald Tribune* (April 19, 1961).

operations and recruit new members from the dissatisfied northern peasantry. It is also conceivable that a southern propaganda campaign picturing the Chinese, the traditional enemy of the Vietnamese, as the new imperialists would arouse sufficient nationalist sentiment in the North to inspire action. However, these are purely tentative notions which may offer opportunity for conjecture but inadequately provide firm ground on which to base a policy.

Assuming that enough guerrillas could be recruited to carry on subversion in the North, the possible results would still need to be carefully weighed by the South. What might appear to be the greatest hope for success—the instigation of a popular revolution in North Viet Nam—could instead turn out to be the disaster of Hungary, with the Communist Chinese playing the role of the Russians. It is certainly not to the interest of the South to provoke an increment of Chinese-Communist control in the North. But if southern guerrilla activity could succeed in harassing the North, it might lead to negotiations whereby each side would agree to cease subversion. Recent news reports suggest that the southern government, supported by American aid, will attempt to inspire guerrilla activity in the North.[22] If such activity could induce the Vietminh to cease its disruptive agitation in the South (although this appears highly unlikely), it would represent a tremendous success.

IV   Impact of Subversion on Governmental Policy

The South Viet Nam government has a great need to design policies that will win popular support, yet continued subversion in the countryside goads it into enacting tighter controls and repressive measures which further disaffect the peasantry. As peasant discontent with the government mounts, so do the possibilities for greater Viet Cong support increase. The bitter challenge of the Communists to the government, the separatist tendencies of the religious sects, and the discontent of the peasantry reinforce the centralist tendencies of the regime and contribute to Diem's belief that power must be wielded by the few he can trust.

The security forces, supplemented by the political and administrative machinery, provide the chief instruments of control. The army contains 150,000 troops, and the government has announced its intention to add 20,000 more. The Civil Guard, a quasi-military organization which supplements the army in the provinces has enlisted over 50,000; the police force, under national control, contains some 8000; and the Sûreté (secret police) is estimated at 7700 members. In addition, local self-defense units, not including the youth corps, which is receiving military training, number more than 45,000. The ratio of security forces to the total population, therefore, might be calculated at one to forty-three.

[22] *Time Magazine,* Vol. 78, No. 5 (August 4, 1961), p. 30, and the following newspaper articles: John G. Norris, "West Defenseless Against 10-Penny Nail," *The Washington Post* (August 20, 1961), p. E3, James Eliot Cross, "Paramilitary Weapon Just 1 Arrow in Quiver," *The Washington Post* (May 21, 1961), p. E1, and Stewart Alsop, "This Guerilla Business," *New York Herald Tribune* (May 3, 1961).

Administration is conducted through a highly centralized bureaucracy, strongly controlled by the Presidency. The ministers who head the administrative departments, outside of a few close to the President's official family, exercise little independent policy-making functions, for their task is one of carrying out the instructions of the President and his inner clique. Governmental programs are framed in Saigon and communicated through the province, the district, and the village. Although the lower echelons may resent the great pressure put on them to fulfill the task imposed by higher headquarters, they are reluctant to communicate any opposition, criticism, or information that would reflect unfavorably on the program desired by higher echelons. In such an administrative environment, governmental programs remain unadapted to peasant desires, while dissatisfaction with and obstruction of the programs mount.

The pattern of local administration in rural areas resembles that in enemy-occupied territory during wartime. Officials operate in garrison-like quarters surrounded by barbed-wire barricades and travel into the countryside only under heavy guard. The posts of province and district chiefs are held primarily by army officers who are inclined to feel that fighting the Communists, rather than the normal routine of administration, is their primary task.

Pervasive controls of the population have been developed. A villager may not leave his village for more than a day without a visa signed by the chief. In some provincial towns citizens are required to display colored balls in front of their lodgings to indicate the number of people present—a control device to aid the police. There are internment camps, now holding an estimated 25,000, to which anyone suspected of subversive activity may be committed by administrative action. Administrators at every echelon employ informers to gather accounts of the Viet Cong. Thus the intelligence networks, though inefficient, are spread throughout the society.[23]

Government authorities expend great effort in their attempts to build positive loyalty among the peasantry. Every gathering is used as an opportunity to pronounce slogans in favor of the government and to denounce the Viet Cong. Rallies are organized frequently to whip up hatred of the North, and village youth have been organized to receive political indoctrination and military instruction. The NRM applies pressure on the peasantry to join in order to claim "grass roots" support. Though attempts to build loyalty are vigorous, they seem to compound discontent, rather than allay it.

An important government effort to deal with subversion in the countryside has been the program of resettling the segment of the peasantry who inhabit the regions of greatest Viet Cong activity. Early in 1959, a plan was inaugurated to regroup certain families into areas where they could be placed under heavy surveillance. Some of the groups to be moved were known as "Viet Cong families"—those whom

[23] An anecdote about the abundant intelligence activities of the government is instructive. The story is told that in the region of Camau, six intelligence networks were paying informers: the army, the civil guard, the Sureté, Can Lao, province chief and district chief. All were receiving their information from one source—a Viet Cong agent.

local authorities believed had sympathy toward the Communists or who were, because they had relatives in the North or in the Viet Cong organization in the South, especially vulnerable to Viet Cong persuasion. These "Viet Cong families" were to be concentrated in agglomeration centers, known in Vietnamese as *khi khu*. Other centers, *khi ap*, were to concentrate families thought to be reliable, patriotic, and loyal to the southern government, who lived in remote areas and were, therefore, difficult to protect from the blandishments and threats of the Viet Cong. Both loyal and Viet Cong families were to be moved to concentrated areas where they would not be in a position to give aid, comfort, or information to the underground.

The plan at once stirred protest. The designation of "Viet Cong families" depended upon the arbitrary judgment of local officials whose basis for action was often no more than their own prejudices. The "loyal families," too, felt wronged in being associated with the "Viet Cong families." Furthermore, the plan was conceived in terms of pure military security without economic and social factors being taken into account. But before the plan was widely put into effect, it gave way to the establishment of "agrovilles."

On July 7, 1959, President Diem announced a program to establish densely populated settlement areas in the countryside. The agrovilles would group the rural populace in settlements bordering on major roads and arteries of communication to facilitate circulation of government security forces among the encampments. A formerly dispersed rural population would thus be concentrated into a living area around which barricades could be constructed, guard posts established, and population movement controlled. It was presumed that bringing people into controlled areas would remove them from susceptibility to Viet Cong tax collection, information gathering, terrorism, and recruitment.

This program, too, roused protest. It mobilized the peasantry to work, without compensation, on ten-day shifts. Neither food nor transportation was provided, and each worker was required to bring his own work implements. Duty at some of the agrovilles carried into the harvest season, preventing the peasant in some cases from bringing in the crop from his own rice fields. Very few families, as might be anticipated, wished to move to the agrovilles. They did not want to leave their traditional homesteads, with their gardens, trees, and surrounding rice fields, and they especially resented being separated from their ancestral tombs beside which they regularly worshipped. The new homes sites were barren, without trees to provide shade from the torrid sun, in an area composed of a vast checkerboard of canals crisscrossing square plots of land on which there was only untended grass and a mud foundation for their huts. Some of the peasants were now required to walk long distances to their rice fields and gardens and could not give them the attention required. Few of the farm animals could be moved to the new plots, as there was no place to house them. The water buffalo, the sturdy draught animals of the monsoon tropics, were particularly not permitted to enter the agrovilles because their weight caused their hooves to sink into the new mud roads.

To most of the families it was repugnant to leave their thatched huts spread out pleasantly along rivers and canals and dwell in concentrated areas under watchful government eyes. Promises that the future would bring them schools, maternity clinics, electricity—city life in the countryside—did not assuage their discontent and objection to being required to purchase land for which they had no desire.

The activity of the Viet Cong against the agrovilles was vituperative. They ordered the inhabitants under their persuasion not to cooperate with the government in the implementation of its program. They burned and sacked the sites under construction whenever possible and threatened government officials responsible for administering the program. The chief of Vinh Long province, in an interview in April 1960, told of the tremendous pressure he was under from Saigon to complete an agroville in his province. Speeding up the work would be his death warrant, he predicted, since making regular trips to the site would make him an easy target for the Viet Cong. Ten days after the interview, he was assassinated. He had gone to the agroville in a convoy accompanied by armed body guards and a heavily fortified jeep. A Viet Cong ambush had laid a roadblock to snare the vehicle upon its return trip. His assistants and guards were isolated and the chief was shot. After receiving a lecture by the assailants, the others were sent scrambling for freedom. It seems evident that the chief was selected as the target because he had primary responsibility for implementing the agroville program in his province.

Two major theories have been forwarded to explain the vigorous, anti-agroville activity of the Viet Cong. One claims that the Viet Cong realized that the agrovilles would, when fully in operation, eliminate the possibility of attacks by ending peasant vulnerability to demands of the underground. The other holds that the Communists were, as usual, exploiting the peasant bitterness and leading their protest. The selection of the province chief, a symbol of the government's agroville program, for assassination might have been designed to identify the Viet Cong as willing to fight for the interests of the people against the tyrants.

The agroville experiment, by stirring up further discontent among the peasants, increased their propensity to protest through support of the Viet Cong. Whether this factor was outbalanced by the increased physical security the agrovilles have provided is open to question.

V   Concluding Observations

For a regime with so precarious a base, the outcome of the attempt of the South Viet Nam government to win the cooperation of the peasantry in its anti-guerrilla struggle is extremely important if it to develop support among other groups. Currently, there is no important segment of Vietnamese society whose strong loyalty the government can claim. Although some 750,000 Catholic refugees from the North provided solid backing for President Diem in the immediate years following the Geneva Accord, they have exhibited mounting dissatisfaction with the government in more recent years. The business and landowning elite are not strongly anti-Diem, but the land reform program and the anti-business bias of his regime do not endear it to them. The bureaucracy, though obedient, is not enthusiastic about the leadership, since recent Vietnamese history has taught functionaries to be adaptable but cautious with their political allegiance.[24]

Vietnamese intellectuals are also disgruntled with the present political system. This group, the most articulate of all the classes in emergent societies, has an importance far outbalancing its relative paucity in number, because it provides the potential leadership. In Viet Nam it is severely critical of the government's narrow base, nepotism, corruption, and repression. The military, with control of the means of violence, has the ability to seize power and, judging from the pattern of *coups* elsewhere in Asia, represents a constant threat to the regime.[25] Although the officer corps does not make its attitude toward the regime easily discernible, there is reason to believe that considerable dissatisfaction exists. The army has a youthful, energetic, progressive group of officers who have received Western-style military training, either under French aegis or, more recently, in United States Service schools. They are strongly nationalist, anti-Communist, and impatient to see their nation develop strength and prestige. Rumors are rampant that promotions are based on personal favoritism, family connections, political affiliation, and membership in the Catholic Church. These rumors, added to the other charges against the regime, tend to demoralize the army. Further grounds for dissatisfaction stem from President Diem's policy of staffing important posts with officers personally loyal to him and shifting their units by direct communication with them, thus ignoring the normal chain of command and sometimes leaving military commanders wondering what has become of their subordinate units.[26]

The army officers and the intellectuals realize that if the peasantry inclines further toward the Vietminh, the nation may well be lost to the Communists. Fear of this fate was a major factor in the thinking of the few officers who undertook the abortive *coup d'état* of November 1960, which some of the most dissatisfied intellectuals joined. Though President Diem was successful in checking their ill-planned *coup,* the conditions which explain its origin have not changed and the danger of similar attempts in the future remains.

A more encouraging aspect of Vietnamese life in recent years has been a steady, if undramatic, amelioration of material living conditions—especially for the peasantry. American aid, covering almost two-thirds of South Viet Nam's current budget expenditures, has contributed significantly to this improvement. The export of rice, the staple ingredient of the Vietnamese diet, has not increased in proportion to the increase in production, suggesting that there has probably been an increase in con-

[24] A civil servant who has served since 1939, by now would have had to adjust to French colonial rule, to a Japanese-controlled Vichy regime, to a Bao Dai government dominated by the Japanese, to rule by the Viet Minh, to the postwar French system, and to the government of President Diem.

[25] For a discussion of the role of the army in southeast Asian politics, see Lucian W. Pye, *Armies in the Process of Political Modernization* (Cambridge: Center for International Studies, MIT, 1959); and Guy J. Pauker, "Southeast Asia as a Problem Area in the Next Decade," *World Politics,* Vol. 11, No. 3 (April 1959), pp. 339–40.

[26] See Stanley Karnow, "Diem Defeats His Own Best Troops," *The Reporter,* Vol. 24 (January 19, 1961), pp. 24–29.

sumption. New canals, irrigation projects, roads, and communication networks have been developed. Consumer items have become readily available. A land-reform program favorable to the peasantry was enacted in 1955, which included provisions for rent reduction, land-tenure security, and transfer—limiting a landowner to one hundred hectares of rice land, plus up to fifteen hectares for each family ancestral cult under his responsibility.[27] In fact, both government policy and Viet Cong operations have together brought about the abolition of absentee landlordism. The government's land-reform process requires the landowner to sell to the government, after which the occupants of the land make the purchase. The Viet Cong, on the other hand, has forbidden the peasantry to cooperate in this program, and in areas where the Viet Cong is powerful, the peasants do not generally pay rent; indeed, the absentee landlord would risk assassination if he attempted to collect it. Ironically, though the standard of living for the southern peasant has improved, it is doubtful that the government has earned recognition commensurate with the achievement, as expectations have probably mounted even higher.

In the foreseeable future, guerrillas in the countryside will continue to be a serious problem for Viet Nam. Because of the difficulty of preventing constant infiltration through the jungle terrain of the long Cambodian and Laotian frontiers, the task of eliminating the stream of new recruits, equipment, and direction from the North seems almost insuperable. Even in Malaya, where the guerrillas did not enjoy these assets, 40,000 well-trained, organized, and equipped Commonwealth troops, together with more than 100,000 police and special constables, fought for over ten years to end the emergency.[28] For Viet Nam, aggressive and flexible military measures are necessary to eliminate the guerrillas, but force alone cannot solve the problem.

The aim of this paper has been to analyze the relationship of peasant discontent to guerrilla activity, not to suggest a policy. If the analysis has validity, a thesis emerges: The cooperation of the peasantry must be won in order to reduce the subversion by the guerrillas. Social and economic measures designed to improve life for the peasantry, important for their own sake to be sure, will help in the contest for their allegiance. Since, however, the development of such measures, by their nature, involves a long time span, they cannot produce the rapid psychological impact that is required for the present emergency. It is primary that before the political leadership can gain the *support* of the peasant, it must first win his *confidence*. The current political leadership has not proven itself adequate to the task of inspiring this necessary confidence. Whether the right political, economic, and social policy can be found and made effective in time remains one of the most significant open questions of the current world crisis.

[27] See J. Price Gittinger, "Progress in South Viet Nam's Agrarian Reform," *Far Eastern Survey,* Vol. 29, No. 1 (January 1960), pp. 1–5.

[28] Lucian W. Pye, *Guerilla Communism in Malaya* (Princeton: Princeton University Press, 1956). Pye concludes his study with a perceptive examination of the need for measures producing political development in the struggle against Communism in Asia.

IV

The Communist Challenge
to the Status Quo in a
Revolutionary Age

10

The Challenge of Soviet Foreign Policy

Vernon V. Aspaturian

It is customary, to the point of triteness, to speak of the multiple revolutions of our age—the Communist, the colonial, and the technological. At the same time, obscured by a fog of platitudes, is the fact that the Soviet Union has maneuvered itself into becoming the main reservoir of power in each case, threatening to channel all the revolutions into a single overpowering torrential surge which will wash out the old social order in favor of a new social system, allegedly ordained by the mandate of history.[1]

The most imposing challenge of Soviet foreign policy in the mid-twentieth century is that it has established a virtual monopoly on revolutionary change, establishing its tempo, guiding its direction, and determined to shape its ultimate configuration. The Bolshevik Revolution of 1917, seen from a perspective of more than four decades, emerges as one of the great watersheds in the drama of human history. The multiple revolutions and transformations of the last four decades have been powerfully shaped and influenced by its ideas and by the power of the Soviet State it brought into being.

In the 1960's, little more than one hundred years after the appearance of the *Communist Manifesto,* Communism is no longer a simple idea—it is a way of life embracing thirteen states, with a population of nearly one billion people, occupying approximately one-third of the earth's total land surface. Within this world are to be found over two hundred different nationalities and ethnic and linguistic groups, most of the races of mankind, numerous cultures, and religions representing every major system in the world, except Hinduism. Furthermore, Communist Parties, large and small, powerful and impotent, are to be found in sixty-eight additional countries on five continents, ranging from minuscule and furtive illegal conspiratorial groups to large mass parties such as those of France, Italy, and Indonesia. All of these parties are inspired by the common ideology of Marxism-Leninism and are dedicated to bringing Communism to their own countries by force, revolution, subversion,

---

[1] The new Program of the Communist Party adopted by the Twenty-Second Party Congress reads: "Socialist revolutions, national liberation and anti-imperialist revolutions, people's democratic revolutions, broad peasants' movements, the struggle of the masses for the overthrow of fascism and other despotic regimes, and general democratic movements against national oppression are all being merged into a single world revolutionary process undermining and destroying capitalism," *Pravda* (July 30, 1961).

conquest, or election, under the protective umbrella of Soviet nuclear and missile capability.

The most significant elements in the progression of Communism from an idea to a potential world civilization are the almost uninterrupted and relentless movement upward and outward and the continuing dynamism it demonstrates in its zeal to supplant all existing ways of life. Only the great universal messianic religions of history, such as Islam and Christianity, have had comparable success in the transmutation of an idea into a social system.

Communism, in forty years, has transformed Russia irrevocably. In the process, the ideas of Communism have also undergone substantial revision and reshaping. The Communism which challenges the world in the mid-twentieth century is not the hypothetical, untried, utopian dream of Marx and Engels but the concrete realities of a new social order, forged in the Soviet Union during the past four decades.

Communism as an ideology of internal change is transformed into an ideology of universal revolution when its norms become effective foreign-policy objectives of the Soviet State. From the very inception of the Soviet state, the ultimate objectives of Soviet foreign policy have been universal and ecumenical in character; even the transformation of the Russian social order was calculatedly designed to provide a concrete model which was to be universalized by the very power capabilities with which it equipped the Soviet state. The concrete social system of the Soviet Union thus becomes transcendentalized as a universalized configurative goal of Soviet foreign policy. Since the growing power of the Soviet state stands prepared to translate this goal into reality, world Communism cannot be dismissed simply as an abstract philosophical goal to be fervently aspired. It is instead a utopian norm, reflecting a concrete social system, elevated to the level of state policy.

I The Revolutionary Character of Soviet Foreign Policy

Soviet foreign policy is authentically revolutionary because its objectives transcend simple territorial expansion, self-defense, or a redistribution of power in its favor; neither is it the simple propagation of an ideology or religious faith. It seeks nothing less than the total annihilation of what it calls the "capitalist-imperialist" system and the residual pre-capitalist social orders which are dependent on it. In their place it seeks to install a new universal ideo-social system, modeled on itself and the Soviet orbit as a whole. Wherever Soviet or Communist power or both have been established, profound and fundamental socio-economic changes have been instituted. They result in the transfer of power from one class to another and the destruction of the economic foundations of power enjoyed by the former paramount or governing classes, through the expropriation and nationalization of land, natural resources, industrial establishments, financial institutions, all media of transportation, communication, and information—all of which become the property of the state; the state, in turn, is reduced to the instrumentality of a new revolutionary power elite. These fundamental changes are considered basic, and they constitute the minimum transformations that must be executed in order to eradicate the old social system and create the foundations for the new.

No matter what internecine heresies may flourish within the Communist orbit, or what schisms may develop, all Communist parties accept these transformations as fundamental and indispensable. How they should be executed and what pattern of reconstruction should be adopted in each case may be a matter of fierce controversy, but the area of ideological consensus remains extraordinarily broad and intense.

With the expansion of the Communist world, the possibilities of schisms and heresies are correspondingly maximized, particularly if separate centers of power crystallize around disputed ideological issues. This will inevitably fragment the Communist movement into a polycentric system—as indeed it has already been so fractured—and to that degree will result in the dilution and corruption of the ideology itself; but it will not necessarily interfere with its continuous advance. The ideological corruption of Communist doctrine and the erosion of the monolithic character of its power are not unmixed blessings for the West. If history is any guide, it surely demonstrates that the universalization of the great religions—Christianity, Islam, and Buddhism—has been accelerated by the corruption and erosion of their doctrinal purity because it enabled them to absorb marginal adherents, who are always more numerous than the true believers.

The proceedings of the Twenty-Second Party Congress have brought to the surface the simmering ideological, personality, and power disputes between the Soviet Union and China—opening interesting opportunities for the West—but for the foreseeable future, the Soviet Union remains the *de facto* power center of the Communist world. Without the Soviet Union, the entire Communist movement could be easily crushed by the overwhelming superiority of the Western world. Just as the United States is the main prop of the Western world, the Soviet Union is the mainstay of the Communist world. Even China recognizes that this condition will persist until she becomes an autonomous nuclear power, in which case both the Soviet Union and the West will be confronted with one of those rare moments in history (which, however, have been all too frequent in the post Second World War era) when a fundamental shift will take place in the power structure of international relations.

Nevertheless, for the present, as the power of the Soviet Union grows relative to that of the non-Communist world, the less utopian becomes its universal ideological mission, even though its absolute control over its direction and tempo becomes less firm. The development of polycentrism in the Communist orbit, and the evolution of quasi-autonomous Communist movements in non-Communist countries, should not obscure the fact that the Soviet Union remains the central inspiration of all these forces, although it is becoming increasingly less dictatorial in its coordination and direction of the world Communist movement.

Although the Soviet will to transform the world may erode in response to external cohesion and internal fragmentation, it would be a mistake to assume that this erosion is inevitable or will take place automatically. Such an expectation, on the contrary, will virtually ensure the continuing vitality of the Soviet ideological mission rather than encourage its diminution. Only when Soviet power is confronted with a permanent situation in which its security and existence are jeopardized more by keeping its ideological norms wedded to state policy than by permitting their separation will world Communism in Soviet calculations lose its political significance and be disarmed as another unfulfilled universal mission, content to remain a regional civilization.

Since the Soviet leaders recognize power as the magic which converts utopia into reality, the day-to-day diplomacy of the Soviet Union appears to be framed within the traditional canon of power politics: the maximization of its power to realize the fulfillment of state interests. This has led many observers, particularly those versed in traditional diplomacy, to mistakenly assume that Soviet foreign policy was fundamentally indistinguishable from that of any other great imperialistic and aggressively minded power, and that the Soviet state was, in fact, motivated by traditional Russian "national interests," which were somehow timeless in their persistence. According to this view, the extraordinary emphasis which the Soviet Union has placed upon the use of subversion, espionage, mass propaganda, and the direction and manipulation of partisans and organizations in other countries is not really unique, except that these techniques and practices are employed in a cruder, more ruthless and primitive manner by Moscow than by other contemporary Great Powers.

It is neither the character nor the style of its diplomatic instruments that makes Soviet foreign policy unique but the nature and conception of the Soviet "State." "State" interests of the Soviet Union—the Soviet Union is a multinational not a national state—are defined in ideological terms which not only transcend the Western ideological consensus but the idea of the territorial state as well. Whereas in the mid-twentieth century the national interests of most powers, although sometimes framed in inordinately ambitious and extravagantly platitudinous terms, are limited in space, subject to the ravages of time and events, and more or less ideologically vapid, the "State interests" of the Soviet Union continue to be universalist in conception, seemingly immune from the effects of time. Although subject to ideological metamorphoses, they remain stubbornly messianic in their implacability. The Soviet conception of "security" is not territorial or geographical in conception, but ideological, since Soviet leaders persist in the belief that the permanent security of the Soviet social order can be ensured only by the destruction of all competing social systems and by transforming the world into a modified image of itself—that is, they seek to forge a new universal consensus.

Although Khrushchev has declared the Stalinist conception of "capitalist encirclement" obsolete and now boasts that the Soviet Union is immune from capitalist intervention and that capitalist restoration in the Soviet Union is an impossibility, the ideological content of Soviet "State interests" remains unaffected: The security of the Soviet State is inextricably linked with the fate of the ideology of Communism itself, not with the existence of the Soviet State as a distinct and separate entity. As long as rival ideological and power centers are in possession of modern weapons of instantaneous mass destruction, the possibility of seriously damaging the Soviet Union and delaying the Communist millennium is the real fear, not the destruction of the Soviet State or Communism as an ideology, since they are currently considered to be immune from destruction. Soviet leaders consider it possible that the capitalist "ruling classes," in a final desperate effort to stave off the inevitable, may irrationally unleash terrible nuclear destruction and leave only the ruins of civilization to a "victorious" Communism.[2] The "dilemma" which confronts the Kremlin is how to bring about the realization of the Communist millennium without triggering widespread devastation at a time when the class enemy possesses precisely such a capability.[3]

As long as the Western Powers maintain and sustain a retaliatory capacity sufficient to lay waste the Soviet landscape and can convey a credible determination to employ it, Soviet striking power is effectively nullified as a rational instrument for the universalization of its system. But that power becomes transformed into a protective umbrella under which spontaneous and inspired revolutionary changes can take place in various parts of the world without external interference from the Western world. Whether a prolonged period of nuclear stalemate or effective mutual deterrence reacts to the advantage of the West or the Soviet East thus depends upon the direction in which the social equilibrium in various parts of the world happens to be moving. In countries gripped by revolutionary ferment, the nuclear stalemate tends to assure the free development of that revolutionary process; where the status quo is firmly established and accepted, the possibilities of external intervention to impose revolutions by bayonets are considerably reduced. In either instance, direct *armed intervention* on behalf of maintaining the status quo by force or overthrowing it by violence will risk self-destruction for either side.

[2] "The imperialists' intrigues must never be forgotten. Our tremendous successes in building a new life should not lead to complacency, to relaxation of vigilance. . . . As the solidarity of the peoples of the socialist countries grows, the imperialists' hopes for the restoration of capitalist ways and for the degeneration of the socialist countries fade. World reaction therefore becomes more and more oriented toward striking a blow at the socialist states from outside in order through war to achieve the rule of capitalism throughout the world, or at least, to check the development of the countries of socialism. The most rabid imperialists, acting on the principle of 'after us the deluge,' openly voice their desire to undertake a new war venture. The ideologists of imperialism, intimidating the peoples, try to instill a kind of philosophy of hopelessness and desperation. Hysterically they cry: 'Better death under capitalism than life under communism.' . . . Blinded by class hatred, our enemies are ready to doom all mankind to the catastrophe of war. . . . They behave like a feeble and greedy old man whose powers have been exhausted, whose physical capacity has weakened, but whose avid desires remain." Khrushchev's Report to the Twenty-Second Party Congress, *Pravda* (October 18, 1961).
[3] Soviet leaders continue to toy with the notion of "buying off" the capitalists when the jig is up as an alternative to blowing up the world on an irrational impulse. Thus, the new Party Program advises: "It may well be than under conditions of the ever-growing strength of socialism, the consolidation of the working movement and weakening of the position of capitalism in some countries may lead to a situation in which, as foreseen by Marx and Lenin [and also by Stalin, it might be added], it will be profitable for the bourgeoisie to agree to the sale of the basic means of production and for the proletariat to buy them." *Pravda* (July 30, 1931).

II Soviet Deterrent Strategy and Revolution

Deterring Soviet military action, it soon becomes clear—whether nuclear or conventional, limited or unlimited—can only provide the West with a new foundation for policy; it cannot constitute an end in itself as a surrogate for policy, even if permanently sustained. The establishment of mutual deterrence merely shifts the rivalry from the military arena to the social, political, and sub-belligerent levels. Even the achievement of a permanent symmetrical deterrence at every level of external interference from sub-belligerent instruments of subversion, infiltration, and guerrilla warfare to massive nuclear attack cannot frustrate the natural development of social forces and movements operating in individual countries.

A condition of mutual symmetrical deterrence means that the issue of revolution or status quo in individual countries will be determined by the given internal equilibrium of power. In those areas, where the internal forces of the status quo are stronger than the forces of change, external forces cannot be employed to alter the balance of internal power. But it also means that in those countries where the internal forces of revolution are greater than those in support of the existing order, external forces will be precluded from intervening to arrest the developing revolution.

Whether a condition of absolute mutual deterrence between East and West at all levels serves to benefit Soviet foreign policy or that of the West will be determined by the internal social and economic conditions prevailing in the major areas of the world. Thus, while the West seeks deterrence to prevent the Soviet Union from intervening to assist revolution, the Soviet Union pursues it to prevent the United States from intervening to arrest change or support counterrevolution. It should be pointed out, however, that the Soviet Union will persist in its endeavor to assert a position of military supremacy even in the nuclear age, through technological break-throughs of a fundamental character. Whether or not a condition of deterrence exists depends upon the West's willingness and capacity to match or exceed Soviet military technological achievements. A self-executing deterrence does not exist and the permanent, absolute, and symmetrical character of deterrence must be sedulously pursued and sustained.[4]

---

[4] The possibility of achieving a permanent, absolute, and symmetrical mutual deterrence is very remote. Military technology, economic shifts, unexpected or fortuitous occurrences, social movements, etc., are much too fluid, dynamic, and uneven in their development to permit this. Deterrence will always be less than permanent, absolute, and symmetrical. Both sides, and this is absolutely certain in the case of the Soviet Union, will continue to seek a "margin of preponderance" through technological breakthroughs which may provide momentary advantages; the possibility that one side (more likely the United States) may be victimized by a "maginot line" psychology and, through ineptness or unwillingness to sustain financial costs, mistakenly assume that mutual deterrence is a static condition and once achieved, will remain permanent, should not be discounted. Furthermore, it is even more likely that one side may fail to recognize a technological achievement or capacity as altering a hitherto balanced situation. Indications are that

In Soviet calculations, the forces for revolutionary change are spontaneous and inevitable on a universal scale and are likely to develop more intensely in the immediate future; hence, the immediate objective of Khrushchev's foreign policy is to deter the United States as the "gendarme of reaction" from intervening to arrest revolution.[5] American official calculations seem to be based on the assumption that revolutionary currents are Communist inspired and stimulated externally by Soviet action and that their success depends upon some form of outside intervention at various levels.

Under conditions of mutual deterrence, the issue will be decided largely in accordance with that perception and expectation which most closely approximates international social reality. If, indeed, revolutionary movements are externally stimulated by the Soviet Union (or "International Communism") and their ultimate success depends upon some form of outside help, then the exclusion of that help will favor the status quo; if, on the other hand, these forces are indigenous and spontaneous, and Soviet assistance is only catalytic and supplementary, then military deterrence will not be sufficient to meet the challenge of Soviet foreign policy. Consequently, it is of the utmost importance that Western perceptions of international

---

the United States does not fully appreciate the strategic, military, diplomatic, and psychological implications of a Soviet Union unilaterally armed with 50 and 100 megaton nuclear warheads; nor does it seem to appreciate what would happen if the Soviet Union unilaterally acquired a reliable anti-missile system. As long as perfect symmetry and deterrence is not likely, external forces will continue to affect internal social forces in individual countries, and vice versa. This makes it all the more imperative that internal social forces within individual countries and the world at large, for and against the status quo, be precisely calculated in any estimate of the general balance of power.

[5] "Of course, warring classes have always sought to rely on the support of kindred forces from outside. For a long time the bourgeois class had an advantage in this respect. The world bourgeoisie, acting in concert, stamped out centers of revolution everywhere and by every means, including armed intervention. Obviously, even at that time the international proletariat was not indifferent to the struggle of its class brothers, but more often than not it could express its solidarity with them in the form of moral support. Now the situation has changed. The people of this or that country who rise in the struggle will not find themselves engaged in single combat with world imperialism. On their side are powerful international forces, possessing everything necessary to give effective moral and material support. The imperialists, alarmed at the scale of the revolutionary struggle, are not ceasing their attempts to interfere in the internal affairs of peoples and states. This is why they have reserved, in military pacts and agreements, the 'right' to armed intervention in the event of so-called internal unrest, that is, to suppress revolutions, to put down actions by the masses of the people against reactionary regimes. The imperialists charge at every crossroads that the communists export revolution. The imperialist gentlemen need this slander to camouflage in at least some way their claim to the right to export counterrevolution. . . . The communists are against the export of revolution, and this is well known in the West [sic]. But we do not recognize anybody's right to export counterrevolution, to perform the functions of an international gendarme. This too should be well known. The attempts of the imperialists to interfere in the affairs of peoples rising in revolution would constitute nothing less than acts of aggression—a threat to world peace. We must state outright that in the event of imperialist export of counterrevolution the communists will call on the peoples of all countries to rally, to mobilize their forces and, relying on the might of the world socialist system, firmly to repel the enemies of freedom, the enemies of peace." Khrushchev's Report to the Twenty-Second Party Congress, *Pravda* (October 18, 1961).

reality more closely approximate actuality than Soviet perceptions. For, if Soviet perceptions of the fundamental forces affecting international politics and the direction of their movement are more accurate reflections of reality than the perceptions of the West, then correspondingly, its foreign-policy objectives are likely to be achieved more often than those of the West.

III   Soviet Perceptions of International Politics in a Revolutionary World

In analyzing Soviet intentions and behavior in international politics, it is first necessary to understand the multiple and discrete functions which ideology performs for Soviet foreign policy, for it is quickly apparent that a major component of the Soviet challenge is ideological in character. Six discrete functions are performed by Soviet ideology in Soviet policy behavior. It functions as a: (1) Theory of social norms; (2) Theory of knowledge and analysis; (3) Theory or strategy of action; (4) System of social rationalization; (5) Symbol of continuity, authority, and legitimacy; (6) System of communication. Only the first three functions will be discussed at any great length.

The normative goals of Soviet foreign policy have already been amply outlined, and so it is necessary to devote attention at this point to Soviet ideology as a theory of analysis and of action. It should be apparent that to meet the Soviet challenge it is not sufficient merely to dissect, catalogue, and scrutinize Soviet ideological goals and the various strategies and tactics which have been devised to implement Soviet policies.

Typically, Western reaction has been an overwhelming preoccupation with the "strategy and tactics of world Communism," which invariably resolves itself into an unambiguous condemnation of world Communism as a wicked and evil goal to be fervently frustrated, together with exhortations that the West develop "strategies and tactics"—frequently based upon images of Communist strategy and tactics—to prevent the victory of world Communism. This manifests itself in programs designed to improve our propaganda, intelligence, and espionage services; to develop techniques of subversion, infiltration, and guerrilla warfare—all based on the mistaken notion that if we can develop these techniques and instruments more effectively than the Soviet Union, the West will be more likely to achieve its objectives than Moscow. The goal of Western policy thus becomes the obverse of the Soviet's goals—anti-world Communism. Unfortunately, this resolves itself into a "strategy and tactics" for preserving the status quo, whatever and wherever it might be, as long as it is anti-Communist.

If the assumption that Communism is not a universally desired social goal is valid, it can have only limited spontaneous and autonomous appeal throughout the world. Consequently, it must be extended by the power of an external force. A parallel assumption is that an effective response would require the establishment of a permanent and absolute symmetrical deterrence from the lowest levels of sub-belligerence like subversion, infiltration, and guerrilla warfare, through conventional instruments of conflict, on up to the highest levels of nuclear and rocket technology. The first assumption is valid, but the second emphatically is not. Consequently, a policy based upon it will fail to respond effectively to the revolutionary thrust of Soviet foreign policy. It is at this point that we must turn our attention to comparative systems or theories of analysis of the social and political forces operating in international politics. Soviet strategy and tactics do not rest upon the assumption that Communism is a universally desired goal and that the success of world Communism rests upon its immediate attractiveness as a social order; neither does Soviet strategy rest upon the notion that world Communism can be imposed willy nilly by external Soviet power. Rather, Soviet policy rests upon the assumption that in most of the non-Communist world, particularly in Asia, Africa, and Latin America, the existing social orders, that is the status quo, are universally disliked, and that the major spontaneous revolutionary social forces in these regions are directed against the status quo—that is, the same status quo which the West supports against Soviet Communism. Thus, Western policy emerges not only as anti-Soviet or anti-Communist, but also, unwittingly, as opposed to indigenous social revolutionary movements. Since the status quo has a single defender—the West—and two opponents—the Communists and native revolutionary movements—the latter two are forced into a marriage of tactical convenience which manifests itself in many obvious ways. All too frequently, this results in their being lumped together in American foreign-policy calculations.

The strategy of harnessing the energies of native revolutionary movements in underdeveloped areas to the Communist dialectic was established in its broad outlines by Lenin more than four decades ago. In 1920 the founder of the Bolshevik state laid down the principal lines of analysis for exploiting revolutionary movements in underdeveloped countries, even before they had actually appeared, but which, on the basis of Lenin's analysis of imperialism, were inevitable. These ideas have since then been modified, renovated, refined, and adapted to various areas under a variety of circumstances. What is important is that Soviet leaders have had at their disposal a systematically articulated theoretical framework for analyzing and exploiting movements against the status quo for more than forty years. Thus, four decades ago, Lenin observed:

The characteristic feature of imperialism is that the whole world, as we see, is at present divided into a large number of oppressed nations and an insignificant number of oppressing nations possessing colossal wealth and powerful military forces. The overwhelming majority of the population of the world . . . about 70 per cent of the population of the world belongs to the oppressed nations, which are either in a state of direct colonial dependence or belong to the outlying colonial states such as Persia, Turkey and China, or else, after being conquered by the armies of a big imperialist power, have been forced into dependence upon it by treaties. . . . We argued about whether it would be correct, in principle and in theory, to declare that the Communist International and the Communist Parties should support the bourgeois-democratic movement in backward countries. As a result . . . we unanimously decided to speak of the national revolutionary movement instead of the 'bourgeois-democratic' movement. . . . The meaning of this change is that we Communists should, and will, support bourgeois liberation movements in the colonial countries only when these movements are really revolutionary, when the representatives of these movements do not hinder us in training and organizing the peasants and broad masses of the exploited in a revolutionary spirit. Even if these conditions do not exist, the Communists in these countries must fight against the reformist bourgeoisie, among whom we include the heroes of the Second International. Reformist parties already exist in colonial countries, and sometimes their representatives call themselves Social-Democrats and Socialists. . . . There can be no argument about the fact that the proletariat of the advanced countries can and must assist the backward toiling masses, and that the development of the backward countries can emerge from its present stage when the victorious proletariat of the Soviet republics stretches out a helping hand to these masses.[6]

The Soviet objective, thus, is to use non-Communist revolutionary movements against the West and, in the process, establish control over their direction and merge them into the general stream of Communist expansion. Thus, in 1927 Stalin outlined as an accomplishment what was in fact an expectation:

The October Revolution has shaken imperialism not only in the centers of its domination, not only in the 'mother countries.' It has also struck blows at the rear of imperialism, its periphery, having undermined the rule of imperialism in the colonial and dependent countries. . . . The proletariat cannot emancipate itself without emancipating the oppressed nations. . . . The October Revolution has *ushered* in a new era, the era of *colonial* revolutions which are being conducted *in the oppressed countries* of the world in *alliance* with the proletariat and under the *leadership* of the proletariat. . . . The era of undisturbed exploitation and oppression of colonies and dependent countries *has passed away*. . . . The era of revolutions for emancipation in the colonies and dependent countries, the era of its *hegemony* in the revolution, *has begun*.[7]

The more implacable and unyielding the forces of the status quo against these non-Communist revolutionary forces, the more they are impelled in the direction of the Soviet Union, and the more easily they fall under its control. In this way, the Soviet Union emerges as the champion not only of Communism, but also of revolution in general. According to Khrushchev's Report to the Twenty-Second Congress:

Attempts are made to blame us Communists for any action by the masses against their oppressors. When the working people of any capitalist or colonial country rise in struggle, the imperialists begin to cry: 'This is the handiwork of the Communists' or 'the hand of Moscow.' Of course we are glad to have the imperialists ascribe to communists all the good actions of the peoples. By so doing, the imperialists are involuntarily helping the masses to gain a better understanding of communist ideas.[8]

In a world seething with revolutionary ferment and convulsion, the Soviet Union, with its own revolutionary ideology, is thus in a position to exploit most of the opportunities created by the maintenance of a nuclear stalemate. Although the main direction of the revolutionary tide is neither Communist in character nor Communist-

[6] V. I. Lenin, *Selected Works* (International Publishers, 1943), Vol. 10, pp. 239–41.
[7] Stalin, J. V., *Problems of Leninism* (Moscow: 1940), pp. 199–201.
[8] Khrushchev's Report to the Twenty-Second Party Congress, *Pravda* (October 18, 1961).

inspired, it soon becomes Soviet encouraged and supported, since it is directed against the residual bastions of Western paramountcy in the underdeveloped regions of Africa, Latin America, and Asia. The supreme tragedy for the Western world and the United States is not so much that they have been boxed into becoming the most formidable bulwark against the revolutionary tide, but that neither Western statesmen, nor the vast Western public, are consciously aware of this fact. This is particularly true of the United States, where revolutionary verbalism and conservative action have coexisted for so long that a supreme and heroic gesture will be required to leap out of an ever-deepening quagmire of self-deception concerning the social and economic forces which impel revolutionary movements.

The United States is not always aware of its role as the gendarme of the status quo, although the character of the regimes which the United States has supported in the past and at the present time—together with its well-known aversion to socio-economic reforms which transgress the sanctity of private property relationships (no matter where it exists, how it was acquired in the first place, or how venal and corruptive its impact on a given country)—ineluctably stamps the United States as the main bulwark of the status quo in a revolutionary world. Although the image of the United States in most of the world, whether it be Moscow or Peking, New Delhi or Cairo, Accra or Havana, becomes increasingly etched as the mainstay of an old order, there has been a corresponding self-image in the United States of a revitalized and resurgent America leading the forces of freedom and reform against the Communist legions of slavery and reaction. This wide and seemingly incompatible discrepancy between the self-image of the United States as a revolutionary force and that in the revolutionary world as a conservative, sometimes reactionary, force requires critical examination.

During great revolutionary moments in history, when not simply the fate of this or that state, but the destiny of entire ideo-social or civilization systems, is involved, failure to include the various internal social equilibriums between the forces of the status quo and revolution into the calculations of the balance of power can result only in a distorted perception of developing reality. The entire structure of the Soviet image of reality and international politics, the Soviet understanding of power, its manipulation and deterrence, rests upon an awareness of this fundamental truth. The Soviet dialectical method of analysis furnishes Soviet decision-makers not only with dynamic analytical categories, but also with a unique ordering of events, relating them to one another, no matter how widely dispersed in time and space, and coordinating the effects of the various and sundry conflicting forces within individual countries as well as the world as a whole. Thus, according to a recent Soviet scholarly view:

The foreign policy of socialism is based on science and founded on the only correct science of society, the theory of Marxism-Leninism. . . . Marxism is a reliable compass for understanding reality and reconstructing society in a revolutionary manner in accordance with socialist principles. The strength of Marxism-Leninism lies in the fact that it gives the Communist Party and the Soviet State the possibility of discovering the objective laws of the historical process, of steering the correct course in accordance with the internal and external situation, of understanding the inner connection between events and of ascertaining not only how and in what direction events are developing in the present, but also how and in what direction they will develop in the future. . . . However, the mere understanding of the objective laws of social development, and in particular of international relations, is not in itself sufficient to determine the correct course in foreign politics by which major victories can be won. The decisive source of the strength or weakness of foreign policy, of its historical prospects or lack of prospects is the correlation of that policy and social progress; its conformity or non-conformity to the laws of development.[9]

Soviet leaders recognize that social conflicts, tensions, frustrations, and resentments, particularly between classes, conceal tremendous reserves of pent-up social power, which can be detected by dialectical analysis, and then tapped, mobilized, and transmuted into concrete political power subject to the manipulation of Soviet policy. These stored up social energies of a world in ferment and convulsion are released with tremendous force during periods, which Lenin described as "revolutionary situations":

For a Marxist there is no doubt that a revolution is impossible without a revolutionary situation. . . . What are, generally speaking, the characteristics of a revolutionary situation? We can hardly be mistaken when we indicate the following three outstanding signs: (1) it is impossible for the ruling classes to maintain their power unchanged; there is a crisis of the "upper classes" taking one form or another; there is a crisis in the policy of the ruling class; as a result, there appears a crack through which the dissatisfaction and the indignation of the oppressed masses burst forth. If a revolution is to take place, it is usually insufficient that "the lower classes do not wish," but it is necessary that "the upper classes be unable," to continue the old way; (2) the wants and sufferings of the oppressed classes must become more acute than usual; (3) in consequence of the above causes, there is considerable increase in the activity of the masses who in "peacetime" allow themselves to be robbed without protest, but in stormy times are drawn both by the conditions of the crisis and by *the upper classes' themselves* into independent historic action.[10]

In calculating what the Soviets call the international "correlation of forces," or "the relation of forces in the world arena," these internal social factors, and the direction of their movement—for or against the status quo—constitute important elements in the power equation. As a systematic framework for the analysis, mobilization, and manipulation of social and political power under a variety of conditions and circumstances, individually and collectively, separately or simultaneously, Soviet ideology performs an invaluable service for Soviet policy-makers, which is far too often underrated by Western observers.

Soviet ideology is responsible for neither the invention nor discovery of the social "contradictions," nor for the conflicts in international or internal politics upon which Soviet policy thrives. And we can, of course, dispense with the spurious and largely irrelevant claim to "scientific" pretensions made on behalf of Marxism-Leninism

[9] M. Airapetyan and G. Deborin, "Foreign Policy and Social Progress," *International Affairs* (Moscow: 1959), No. 2, pp. 21–22.
[10] V. I. Lenin, *Collected Works* (International Publishers, 1930), Vol. 18, p. 279.

which has diverted virtually an army of scholars and publicists into expending inordinate energy and time in refutations and exposés, in the naive belief that if the "scientific" pretensions of Soviet ideology can be disproven, the entire Soviet ideological edifice will crumble and perhaps the regime and system with it.

What cannot be disproven, however, is that Marxism-Leninism is *a* theory of social reality and, hence, a theory of power, its origins, manifestations, forms, calculations, deterrence, and manipulation; and it is a very powerful and effective theory. Its effectiveness as a guide to action and policy does not rest upon its being "scientific," for it can only be relative in this regard, not absolute, and the only valid measurement of its effectiveness as a theory of analysis and action is to compare it with the effectiveness of corresponding analytic systems employed by Western decision-makers. A true measure of its validity, thus, does not rest upon whether it is indeed "scientific" or not. Its validity is contingent upon its comparison, not with the profusion of theories, models, systems, processes, and games devised by Western scholars, but with comparable theories of analysis employed by Western statesmen as a basis for policy and action, whether they be implicit or explicit, eclectic or synthetic, *ad hoc* or systematic, pragmatic or dogmatic, empirical or *a priori* in character.

Although "contradictions" or conflicts were not discovered by Marxism, the Soviet method of exploiting conflicts to advantage is unique. What distinguishes the Soviet method is that conflicts are viewed in qualitatively different perspective. They are viewed as being in constant flux, as inevitably moving to a foreordained climax and resolution, rather than as being chance or fortuitous occurrences. The Soviet approach to international politics slices deeper than simply the exploitation of state and national interests in conflict (which it recognizes as conflicts between "ruling class" interests). It searches for the more profound, passionate, and explosive animosities and resentments of conflicting social classes and submerged races and nationalities within individual countries, continents, or the world as a whole. The Soviet analytical system provides a scheme for ordering these contradictions and conflicts, establishing priorities, differentiating them into discrete social and power equations, and for manipulating them as the occasion may demand or the opportunity presents itself.

The application of the dialectic to international relations turns up five contradictory equations, each with dynamic formulae, whose values fluctuate in response to changing conditions and opportunities. Each has its decisive moment in history, and each is endowed with its distinctive instruments and forms which can be exploited with maximum effect, singly or in combination. These five general contradictions are:

1. Contradictions between the "bourgeoisie" and the "proletariat" within individual countries, in which the local Communist Party is the chief instrument of exploitation.
2. Contradictions between the "ruling classes" of capitalist states in general for markets, territory, colonies, prestige, and general advantage over the other, which are exploited by economic and political maneuvering by the Soviet Union.

3. Contradictions between the victorious group of capitalist states and the defeated group after the most recent general war, in which the former group seeks to preserve and perpetuate its advantages (status quoism), while the latter group seeks to recoup its former position and plots revenge (revisionism).

4. Contradictions between the capitalist states and the colonial dependencies and former colonial territories which currently receive their greatest exploitation and which promise fruitful results in Latin America, Africa, and Southeast Asia. The chief instrument of exploitation here is "anti-imperialism" or "anti-colonialism," and the "struggle for peace."

5. Finally, the supreme contradiction is that between the capitalist camp and the Communist camp, whose resolution must be delayed until the exploitation of the other contradictions has sapped capitalism of its moral vigor and physical power, rendering it impotent and encircled.

It would be a mistake, therefore, to conclude that Soviet ideology is little more than a manipulative instrument designed to obscure what is in fact an opportunistic exploitation of essentially fortuitous situations and events. This applies only to its theory of action, which is essentially a systematic opportunism, executed within a calculated framework of analysis and devoted to the fulfillment of fixed ideological ends, in accordance with Lenin's admonition "to master the tactics of maneuver, while remaining loyal to the end to principles in the struggle for socialism."

In responding to the Soviet challenge, one of the obvious questions requiring attention is the relative validity and effectiveness of the Western system of analysis, of which its policy must inevitably be an expression. Does the West have as accurate an image of social and political realities in a revolutionary world as the Soviet leaders, or is this image distorted by factors which have not received sufficient attention from scholars? Is the Soviet system of the class analysis of forces and events in the underdeveloped world more or less accurate than the Western basis of analysis, which sedulously avoids referring to classes or class conflict? Are the social and political realities in the underdeveloped world better understood when analyzed in class categories than within the context of impersonal forces like "poverty," "disease," "hunger," "misery"? Is the "class struggle" in underdeveloped countries a more accurate representation of the tensions and conflicts than "democracy versus dictatorship" or "law and order versus violence and chaos"? Do approximations, in varying degrees, of the Marxist conception of a "ruling class" exist in Middle Eastern countries and many Latin American states or is this simply a figment of the Soviet imagination?

A successful response to the challenges posed by Soviet foreign policy will require a courageous and unevasive answer to these vital questions. For, if a class analysis provides better insights as to real events and forces in a revolutionary world, Western policy-makers must devise a strategy that will work with these forces and not rely upon an analysis and strategy that fails to take them into account. A desirable strategy for the West must seek and uncover a common denominator of interests and action between the social status quo in the Western world and the revolutionary forces in the underdeveloped world. Only in this way can the tremendous social and political energies released by revolution in much of the world be tapped to stabilize and preserve the status quo elsewhere against the universalist pretensions of Soviet Communism.

IV Images of the Soviet Challenge

Although Communism, as a social order, has little attraction for revolutionary elites in the underdeveloped world, they are nevertheless impressed with the tremendous advances made by the Soviet Union in the name of achieving a Communist society. What Communism has done for Russia, in a material way, constitutes a concrete challenge which repels the advanced Western countries and strikes fear into the ruling classes of feudal and quasi-feudal societies but which excites revolutionary elites who are interested in quick social transformations.

The Soviet achievement merits careful analysis, for, despite the present success of Soviet efforts, there is still a fundamental hiatus between the ideological goals of Soviet foreign policy and the aims of revolutionary elites. The Soviet system is, first of all, a historical *process* of industrialization and modernization. It rivals that of Western capitalism, whether free and spontaneous or state-directed, as in the cases of Imperial Germany and Japan. Before the advent of the Soviet system, capitalism was the only historical method by means of which states modernized. In its second dimension, it is a *way of life* or *civilization* rival to that of the West.

The original purpose of Marxism was to displace a bourgeois-oriented civilization with one centered on the interests and aspirations of the proletariat. Socialism and Communism were envisaged as systems designed not to compete with Western capitalism as processes of industrialization and change, but to supersede capitalism as a superior and more progressive form of social and economic organization of society—as simultaneously more efficient and equitable. But, because Marxism was adapted to a society for which it was never intended—an underdeveloped rather than an advanced one—it was first converted into a process of industrialization and modernization.

Whenever the Soviet Union has tried to impress its ideological norms upon revolutionary elites, as in Egypt and Iraq, this has resulted in forcing underlying incompatibilities to the surface. From the vantage point of Western policy, the distinction between the Soviet system as a *process of change* and as a *civilization* must always be borne in mind. For just as Moscow and the revolutionary elites are united against the status quo, with respect to the process of change, the West and the same revolutionary elites may find common ground in a determination that the status quo, with respect to some civilized values, will not be supplanted by Communism. This unique triangular relationship not only bears the seeds which may destroy the alliance between the revolutionary nationalist elites and Soviet foreign policy, but it also represents the submerged foundation upon which a durable alliance can be erected between these nationalist movements and the West against Communism as a world system.

The underdeveloped countries are more interested in the process of modernization than in the civilization developed by the Soviet Union, while the Western world is interested in neither (except for substantial sections of the populations in France and Italy, who apparently would welcome some variation of the Communist system). These different perspectives of the Soviet system result in the projection of contradictory images of the Soviet Union and, hence, in varying responses to its foreign policy goals at any given instance. In order to fully appreciate the total charter of the Soviet challenge, it is necessary to reconstruct, as accurately as possible, these different images of the Soviet system and determine what they have in common as well as what separates them.

Nothing could be more subversive than to project unwittingly a single image of the Soviet challenge and to act upon the assumption that it is universally recognized and accepted. The Western view that Soviet Communism represents a despotic regime, born in conspiracy, preserved by violence and terror, extended by military conquest, subversion, espionage, and deception, animated by a wicked doctrine, and governed by venal or misguided rulers, is only one image of the Soviet system and is far from being the most universally accepted. No matter how valid this image may be from the perspective of the West, it is not the image seen by large parts of the world, for it represents, primarily, the image of those societies and social groups who benefit from the status quo the Soviet system is dedicated to annihilating. Thus, it is the image held by a mortal enemy and is ideologically biased, since it is a reflection of the interest perspective of the West. Correspondingly, it is rejected by increasingly larger segments of the underdeveloped world and by those classes and social groups in the West who bear no great enthusiasm for preserving the status quo which Soviet foreign policy seeks to subvert and destroy.

Aside from the Communist image (whether it be the self-image of the Soviet leaders, the image of rivalry held by the Chinese, or the image of patron held by other Communist leaders) of the Soviet Union as the engine of progress, three general images of the Soviet system coexist simultaneously and these images in turn determine the reception accorded to Soviet foreign-policy goals. Each image is shaped largely by the distinctive historical or social experience of a particular community or social group together with the perceived implications and contemplated consequences for a given country or social group if Soviet foreign policy objectives are either partly or wholly fulfilled. These discretely different images of the Soviet system thus represent ideological perceptions of self-interest and the degree to which these self-interests are promoted or retarded by the advance of Soviet power.

THE IMAGE IN THE WEST. The images of the Soviet Union with which the West is most familiar are two variations of the Soviet Union as an aggressive imperialistic power bent upon world domination. These two variants reflect the views of those already subjugated by Soviet power on the one hand and on the other of those who are its contemplated victims. In Eastern Europe, the image of foreign imperialist domination is endemic among the population, and this image is strongly reinforced by historical memories. Russia has traditionally sought to dominate this region and, thus, Soviet Communism appears simply as a more brutish, if technologically more efficient, continuation of Russian imperialism in new garb. With the exception of Yugoslavia and Albania, Communism in Eastern Europe was imposed upon these countries by Soviet conquest and military occupation.[11] The Soviet system never registered any great internal appeal among the population of these countries before their occupation, and the alien regimes imposed from the outside remain highly unpopular in spite of the amelioration of Soviet control since 1956.

The image of the Soviet Union projected to the West is not only of an imperialistic behemoth bent upon world conquest, but also that of a rival world civilization determined to eradicate the spiritual values and social institutions of Western civilization. The West thus represents, in a sense, a former world system in decline, a system whose power and influence have catastrophically shrunk to metropolitan power centers as a consequence of its own internecine and fratricidal conflicts (understandably enough, the two World Wars are viewed by many articulate Asians as essentially European civil wars), the revolutionary pressures released in their colonial empires as a result of these intramural wars, and finally because of the relentless push of the growing might of the Soviet Union. The true meaning of the term "world domination" thus emerges as the dominance of a given set of ideological values and social institutions and relationships in the world at large. In this sense, the struggle between the Soviet world and the West is truly a contest for "world supremacy."

THE IMAGE IN THE UNDERDEVELOPED WORLD. In the underdeveloped countries of the world two images of Soviet power are also to be found. The image among the beneficiaries of the status quo—the ruling classes and landowning groups in Asia and Latin America—is similar to that found in the West, but Soviet power represents a more direct challenge to their ruling position because the image of the Soviet Union among the other sectors of population may be a favorable one. Soviet power, even its very existence, constitutes an important element in the internal equilibriums of feudal and quasi-feudal social orders, because both the ideas of Communism and the example of the Soviet Union serve to mobilize internal opposition to the existing order. The saving virtue here is not so much an overwhelming attitude of revulsion towards Communist ideas, as the ignorance of the masses who are insufficiently educated to understand them; on the other hand, there is the fear on the part of

[11] This undoubtedly serves to explain why it is precisely Yugoslavia and Albania that have dared to defy the authority of the Soviet Party. Both Yugoslavia and Albania do not have frontiers with the Soviet and are relatively inaccessible, but geography alone does not explain the defiance. Like the Chinese Party, they are primarily indigenous in their evolution. Since most of the large Parties outside the Communist Orbit also are basically indigenous, if they come to power, the Communist World is likely to become decentralized even more than it is today. As Yugoslavia, Albania, and China demonstrate, the decentralization need not follow a single ideological heresy but may produce many.

ruling groups that once the masses do understand Communist ideas they may revolt.

The second image of the Soviet Union is to be found among the revolutionary middle-class nationalist elites, whether they have come to power or are seeking it. These emerging elites neither fear nor reject the idea of radical social transformation but, in fact, pursue it; neither do they share in the recognition of the Soviet Union as a neo-colonial empire bent on world conquest. On the contrary, they view the Soviet Union as at least a temporary ally against the status quo and, furthermore, see in the Soviet Union a former underdeveloped country which has made rapid industrial, military, and cultural progress outside the pattern of Western capitalism —in the face of relentless and implacable hostility from the Western world in fact. In the Soviet *process* of modernization and industrialization, revolutionary nationalist elites see an alternative to the capitalist pattern which can be adapted to their own needs and purposes. A brief comparison between the Russia of 1914 and the Soviet Union of the 1960's can perhaps provide us with an insight as to what excites the revolutionary elites about the Soviet system.

In 1914 Russia was militarily weak, having suffered defeat after defeat since 1850, culminating in the humiliating victory of an upstart Japan in 1905. Her rapidly declining military strength was further confirmed by defeat, occupation, and revolution during the First World War. Today, Russia rivals the United States for military paramountcy and in some respects appears to be in the lead.

In 1914 Russia ranked last among the industrial states of the world, but by 1960, the Soviet Union had already outstripped all the great industrial powers of Western Europe (and Japan) in the basic indices of industrial production and is second only to the United States, which it avowedly aims to surpass.

In 1914 Russia had a vast unskilled, uneducated, superstitious, agricultural, and largely demoralized population, 76 per cent illiterate, which had been released from serfdom less than seventy-five years earlier. She produced a few outstanding individual scientists, writers, and composers, but in general Russia lagged far behind the rest of Europe in educational, technological, and scientific achievement. By 1960 the Soviet Union had achieved 98.5 per cent literacy (up from as low as 1 per cent in parts of Central Asia) in a country in which there are nearly twenty-five major languages and linguistic groups, to say nothing of three dozen additional minor ones, all with their own schools, newspapers, and books. Today, the Soviet Union has four times as many students enrolled in institutions of higher education as Great Britain, France, Italy, and West Germany *combined*. Nearly 2,500,000 students are to be found in 766 institutions of higher learning, 3346 technicums, and other specialized secondary schools, as compared with less than 128,000 students enrolled in 1914. The Soviet Union graduates every year nearly four times the number of engineers as the United States and the total number of Soviet citizens with some higher education now totals more than 13,000,000. In many respects, the Soviet Union has established, virtually from scratch, an educational system second to none in the space of a single generation. Furthermore, this was all accomplished during a period when the Soviet population was subjected to unprecedented and unspeakable natural and political calamities, whether it was war, famine, economic dislocation, civil war, terror, purges, foreign occupation, or depredation.

The story is virtually identical in the field of social services, particularly medicine. In 1914 Russian medical science was woefully retarded, and medical care was available only to the very wealthy. The number of physicians and dentists before the Revolution was 28,000 for a population of 159,000,000. By 1960 it was nearly 375,000 for a population of 214,000,000, which gives the Soviet Union today the largest number of doctors in proportion to the population of any country in the world, including the United States and except Israel. Today, every citizen is entitled to free medical care. Life expectancy in Russia has gone up from an average age of 32 before the Revolution to 68 in 1959, which is now among the highest in the world. The number of hospital beds during the same period has increased from 207,300 to nearly 1,500,000.

As in many pre-industrial societies, pre-revolutionary Russia did not provide many opportunities for women. Today in the Soviet Union, 53 per cent of all Soviet citizens with some secondary education are women. Before the Revolution, 10 per cent of all physicians were women; today, they constitute 75 per cent of the total. In the Soviet Union women are to be found in increasingly impressive numbers at all levels of cultural, scientific, and social life—70 per cent of the teachers, 57 per cent of the economists and statisticians, 32 per cent of the lawyers and judges, 30 per cent of the engineers, 39 per cent of the technicians, 36 per cent of Soviet scientific workers, and 20 per cent of the Communist Party are women. Before the Revolution 88 per cent of the women of Russia were illiterate.

These are substantial achievements, and they transcend the issues of ideologies or social systems, for industrial power, military strength, scientific and technological progress, medical care, and emancipation of women are universally desired goals among the new elites. These are the undeniable marks of a modernized, industrialized, and Westernized society. They symbolize power and prestige—dignity and pride for the communities which bear them, whether large or small. The underdeveloped countries are interested in results, for they have no vested interests in dogmas and doctrines, and they are inexorably attracted to that process and system which appears most easily adaptable to their needs and which promises to accelerate their entry into the modern industrial and technological age. In the Soviet experience, they see the concrete fulfillment of the dreams and aspirations of a previously underdeveloped country. This is a fascinating and powerful attraction and its magnetic pull should not be underestimated. What is of singular significance is that the Soviet achievement was not only spectacularly quick, but was virtually a do-it-yourself operation which triumphed over overwhelming odds and in the face of almost universal predictions of failure in the Western world.

In this connection, the fate and progress of the non-Russian nationalities, particularly those in Soviet Central Asia, should be treated separately to see whether the Soviet achievements of the past four decades were reserved only for a ruling European nationality. Progress has been made across the entire spectrum of nationalities, of

Table 1   From Underdevelopment to World Power

Basic Indices of Industrialization and Modernization in the USSR

INDUSTRY		1913	(EST.) 1961	(PROJECTED) 1965	1980
Steel	(mill. tons)	4.2	71	86–91	250
Pig Iron	"	4.2	51	65–70	
Rolled Metal	"	3.5	55	65–70	
Coal	"	29.1	513	600–612	1118–1200
Oil	"	9.2	166	230–240	670–710
Electricity [a]		1.9	327	500–520	2.7–3 trillion
Cement (mill. tons)		1.3	51	75–81	233–235
Machine Tools (thousands)		1.5	175.8	226–236	
Gross Indust. Prod. (bill. rubles)			155		970–1 trillion

EDUCATION, CULTURE, HEALTH	1913	1959
Literacy	24%	98.5%
Higher Education, total	290,000	13,400,000
Students, Higher Ed., current	127,000	2,200,000
All students	10,000,000	55,000,000
Doctors and Dentists	28,000	375,000
Hosp. beds	207,300	1,500,000
Life Expectancy	32 yr	68 yr
Urbanization	15%	49%
Total population	159,000,000	215,000,000

[a] Billion kilowatt hours (KWH).
Sources: *Narodnoye Khozyaistvo SSSR v 1959 Godu* (Moscow, 1960). *Pravda* (October 19, 1961).

which there are more than two dozen, having a total population of at least one million, in the Soviet Union. This is an important point, for if it can be demonstrated that Soviet progress largely left the populations and territories of the non-Russian nationalities untouched, and that they are exploited for the benefit of the ruling nationality, then a charge of Soviet colonialism would be both valid and effective, and the Soviet anti-colonial posture can be exposed as a brazen exercise in hypocrisy. Progress in Soviet Central Asia, however, under the Soviet regime, has been even more dramatic and sweeping than in most parts of the Soviet Union. In the two Caucasian Republics of Georgia and Armenia, the quality of progress has been positively embarrassing, for per capita achievement outstrips even that of the Slavic Republics of the Union.

The Uzbek Republic is the home of the largest and most advanced of the Central Asian Turks, and its progress under Soviet rule provides a good example of Soviet "colonialism." Before the Revolution, only 2 per cent of the population was literate; institutions of higher learning were non-existent; 160 schools were attended by 17,300 children of the privileged land-owning classes. Native engineers or doctors did not exist, nor were there any teachers with higher educational training. In 1960

Table 2   Industrialization and Modernization in Soviet Central Asia 1913–1960

REPUBLIC	STEEL (TONS)	ELECTRICITY (THOUSAND KWH)	COAL (TONS)	OIL (TONS)	TRACTORS
Uzbek					
1913	0	3,300	0	13,000	0
1959	273,000	5,143,100	2,933,000	1,465,000	69,000
Kazakh					
1913	0	1,300	90	118,000	0
1959	287,900	9,583,400	31,674,000	1,544,000	291,000
Kirgiz					
1913	0	0	103	0	0
1959	0	800,000	3,463,000	424,000	16,000
Tadzhik					
1913	0	0	28	0	0
1959	0	1,151,300	817,000	17,000	14,100
Turkmen					
1913	0	2,590	27	129,000	0
1959	680	662,500	0	4,577,000	14,700

EDUCATION, CULTURE, HEALTH

	H. ED. INSTS.	LIBRARIES	BOOKS	DOCTORS	HOSP. BEDS	SCHOOL ENR.
Uzbek						
1913	0	0	118,000	128	1,000	17,300
1959	34	3,099	19,398,000	10,618	42,400	1,431,000
Kazakh						
1913	0	139	4,000	196	1,800	10,500
1959	26	6,126	15,701,000	12,490	60,900	1,631,000
Kirgiz						
1913	0	0	0	15	100	700
1959	9	1,095	3,165,000	2,842	10,100	360,000
Tadzhik						
1913	0	0	0	13	40	400
1959	8	922	3,487,000	2,279	9,800	366,000
Turkmen						
1913	0	0	400	56	300	700
1959	9	1,173	3,301,000	2,631	10,400	260,000

Note: The *non-Asian* proportion of the population in the Central Asian Republics is as follows: Uzbek, 15 per cent; Kazakh, 55 per cent; Kirgiz, 36.8 per cent; Tadzhik, 14.7 per cent; Turkmen, 20 per cent.
Source: *Narodnoye Khozyaistvo SSSR v 1959 Godu* (Moscow, 1960).

the Republic had an Academy of Sciences, an Academy of Agricultural Sciences, 34 institutions of higher learning, 100 technicums, 50 special technical schools, 5800 general ten-year schools, 12 pedagogical institutes, and 1400 kindergartens. Altogether 1,431,000 children are in school, with more than 50 per cent of 80,000 teachers possessing some higher education. The literacy rate in 1959 was over 95 per cent. Before the Revolution, the Republic possessed no libraries; today there are over 3000. The number of books printed in 1913 was 118,000; in 1960 it exceeded 22 million. Of more than 8,000,000 specialists in the national economy of the entire Union who possess a higher or specialized secondary education, Uzbeks accounted for 86,100, while the total number of native Central Asians in this category exceeds 211,000.

Today, the Uzbek Republic follows Japan, China, and India as the fourth most highly industrialized and mechanized state in Asia. In 1913, the region produced only 3.3 kilowatt hours of electricity; in 1959, it was 5,143,100 million kilowatt hours, which means that the Republic produces today five times as much electricity in one day as it did during an entire year in 1913. The Republic alone possesses two and a half times as many electric power stations as all of Russia before the Revolution. In 1960, the Uzbek Republic produced two-thirds of all cotton products in the Soviet Union, three-quarters of the entire Soviet output of spinning machinery, and was the main producer of agricultural machinery for cotton growing and harvesting in the Union. More than 69,000 tractors are to be found on its farms. The Republic has its own chemical industry and a steel industry which produced 275,000 tons of steel and 177,000 tons of rolled metal in 1959, as compared with none in 1913.

Table 3   Higher Education in Soviet Central Asia by Nationalities, 1959

NATIONALITY	SIZE	STUDENTS, HIGHER EDUCATION	SPECIALISTS [a]	SCIENTISTS
Uzbeks	6,004,000	30,500	86,100	3,121
Kazakhs	3,581,000	22,000	68,800	2,057
Kirgiz	974,000	6,500	17,000	528
Tadzhiks	1,397,000	6,800	22,000	749
Turkmen	1,004,000	5,700	17,900	622

[a] With higher education and specialized secondary education, working in the national economy. Source: *Narodnoye Khozyaistvo SSSR v 1959 Godu* (Moscow, 1960).

Although Central Asia has by no means been converted into a biblical paradise, and its achievements are not likely to look impressive to Western Europeans, it is clear that Soviet Central Asia has clearly outstripped its adjacent neighbors in the Middle East and Southeast Asia, whether independent or formerly under colonial rule. It is, therefore, hardly surprising that the Uzbek Republic has been transformed into a showcase for visiting dignitaries from Africa and Asia. Instead of being an example of Soviet colonialism in the eyes of Afro-Asians, the Soviet achievement stands as a monumental tribute to Western hypocrisy, since the standard colonial rationalization has been that generations were required to achieve even modest levels of education and technical training in underdeveloped countries. After nearly 500 years of Portuguese rule, only 1 per cent of the native population in Angola is barely literate, to cite an extreme example. Although the record for low-level literacy has been better in the Belgian Congo, it is notorious that after a century of Belgian rule, hardly a dozen university graduates existed in a country of 13,500,000 in the year of independence, 1960. Although the performance of the British and the French has been much better, and the American record in the Philippines is really extraordinary in comparison, neither can really compare with the Soviet achievement of providing nearly 250,000 native Central Asians (Uzbeks, Kazakhs, Tadzhiks, Turkmen, and Kirgiz) out of a total population of about 13,000,000 with higher or specialized secondary education and of raising the general literacy rate from 1 to 2 to 95 per cent within the span of four decades. These are the comparisons and images which revolutionary elites in underdeveloped countries see. An idea of what might further impress them can be gleaned from information tabulated on Tables 1 and 2.

Conclusion

The Soviet achievement is by no means terminal in character, for during the next two decades, Soviet leaders project even greater accomplishments, with the main objective being no less than to outstrip the United States in major areas of material production and technological attainment. The sustained rapid annual growth of the Soviet economy conveys an impression of tremendous vitality and determination. Even a cursory examination of Soviet target goals for 1980 (an annual production of 250 million tons of steel for example) indicates that Soviet production goals are designed to meet both internal and external-ideological policy of the Soviet Union. The foreign-policy implications of these production goals are quite clear, for the tremendous productive capacity of the Soviet Union in 1980 can be used not only to supply economic and technical assistance to underdeveloped countries, but also to disrupt and shatter the commercial and trade structure of the West.

Aside from the ideological and essentially semantic goals of Communist society, the target goals of 1980 set by the new Program of the Communist Party adopted by the Twenty-Second Party Congress literally stagger the imagination, when measured not only against 1913, but against 1962 as well. Although these are only targets and one can question their feasibility, it must be noted that the Soviet Union has demonstrated a remarkable record in achieving her planned goals. Even if the Soviet targets fall short of fulfillment by 25 per cent, the achievement will remain extraordinary. Furthermore, the steady progression toward these goals during the next decade may itself generate an irreversible psychological shift in the world balance of power, unless the Western world responds with a comparable demonstration. One can hardly quarrel with the anxious warning of the Shah of Iran that "even if this plan [the new Soviet twenty-year plan] is only 50 per cent fulfilled, the world will be faced with a new Communist society," adding that "if we waste our time in countries like mine, time is not going to be on our side." [12]

Soviet Communism thus emerges as a process for the rapid transformation of backward agrarian and semi-feudal states into advanced industrial communities, and although this may be a far cry from the original norms of Marxism (as has been repeatedly demonstrated by various critics), this does not diminish its appeal to the

[12] *The New York Times* (November 5, 1961).

underdeveloped. The Soviet process promises quick transformation of illiterate populations into educated communities, rapid conversion of raw, unskilled peasant hands into skilled technicians and workmen, quick elimination of disease and pestilence, the early emancipation of women, and the promise of a quick improvement in the standard of living. But, above all, it promises the quick acquisition and mobilization of power, influence, and dignity for emerging national communities, whose aspirations currently exceed their capacities.

In short, Soviet Communism offers a seductive and effective way to meet the demands of the "revolution of rising expectations" which is sweeping the underdeveloped lands. After languishing under the long shadow of Western colonialism for many decades, Soviet Communism promises to give the new and the underdeveloped nations a place in the sun. An effective response to this challenge does not lie in denigrating the Soviet achievement or its promise but in providing a more glittering alternative.

The challenge of Soviet foreign policy lies not only in its military might and in its aggressively anti-colonial posture, but also in its formulas for overcoming the poverty, illiteracy, and economic retardation of the underdeveloped countries. These formulas show more promise than anything offered by the West. As protagonists of the status quo, the West is not particularly adept at revolutionary solutions for pressing social and economic problems, frequently forgetting to recall that its own progress was released only after a revolutionary rupture with obsolete and stagnant social systems. These episodes remain only a dim memory, and the mistaken notion has taken root that Western civilization has developed along a gradual, evolutionary, and non-convulsive arc of progress. The Soviet Union, on the other hand, as did revolutionary France more than a century earlier, represents the forces of revolutionary change and, thus, is more likely to manifest greater sympathy for the aspirations and expectations of retarded societies where discontent and dissatisfaction with the existing social order is widespread and endemic.

During the next four decades, the population of the world is expected to rise from 3 to nearly 6.3 billion. According to current scientific opinion, the total resources of the world are sufficiently ample to meet the demands of this explosive population increase, provided they are efficiently exploited, processed, and distributed. The supreme conundrum of the twentieth century is likely to be whether the Soviet system or that of the West can most effectively mobilize the human and natural resources of the world in the interests of social justice. Soviet leaders boast that in the twentieth century all roads lead to Communism, because it has already demonstrated its superiority in this connection. Unless the Western world, led by the United States, is both willing and able to renovate and universalize the values, institutions, and material abundance which it cherishes, and unless it can demonstrate an alternative promising both the material results of Soviet Communism and the freedoms of Western civilization, then Communism or some variant of it is likely to become the universal ideology of revolutionary salvation as the only doctrine that adequately articulates dissatisfaction and protest against the injustices and insufficiencies of the status quo.

11

Communist China's Demands on the World

A. M. Halpern

As the title of this paper suggests, the entire world posture of the People's Republic of China since the accession to power of the present regime has been oriented toward alteration of the international environment. Choosing the right term to describe this alterative posture more narrowly is not simply an exercise in pedantry. To call it the attitude of a "have-not" nation is misleading, at least insofar as there are "have-not" nations whose basic foreign orientation is isolationist. Among these are some neutralist countries whose policies are consistently directed toward maintenance of the contemporary status quo. The term "unsatisfied" implies that the granting of certain claims, most typically territorial claims, will result in a nation's approval of and future protection of a foreseen status quo only slightly different from the existing one. This does not seem applicable to China. Nor does the term "manipulative," implying the preservation or enhancement of one's own position by procuring minor adjustments in the positions of one or more others, quite fit the Chinese posture.

In short, the alteration of the international environment that the Chinese seek is a revolutionary one, and they conceive of the total pattern of international relations as embodying class struggle. In testimony of the general validity of this point, one can cite the standard Chinese formulation of the significance of their revolution. With some variations in detail, the Chinese have consistently described their revolution as a continuation of the Soviet October Revolution and as a major accretion of strength to the Socialist camp. With equal consistency and frequency they have proclaimed that their historic mission is to assist national liberation movements, participate in the struggle against and in the ultimate liquidation of imperialism, and hasten the establishment of Communism as the universal form of human society.

Such sentiments, stated as broadly as has been done here, I take to be not merely ritualistic formulae, but affirmations of consciously recognized predispositions. It is not, however, to be taken for granted that these formulae, as real as their directive effect may be, provide a sufficient statement of Chinese Communist motives so that one can deduce probable behavior from them. This paper is devoted to an attempt to formulate a more detailed statement which, hopefully, will serve that purpose. For lack of intensive studies of Chinese Communist foreign operations, a number of the propositions to be advanced will necessarily be statements of postulates rather than conclusions, and the end result as a whole is designed to guide and be tested by research rather than to enunciate conclusions.

A distinction will be drawn here between the goals (or ends) of Chinese foreign policy and the methods (or means) adopted to pursue those goals. A parallel distinction will be made between strategy and tactics. Though there is no implication that strategy concerns only goals, and tactics only methods, most of the discussion will deal with strategic goals and tactical methods. Regarding goals, the approach is: First, to try to establish a hierarchy of goals; second, to examine the relation of variations in the operational relevance of certain apparent goals to variations in the environment; and third, to examine the relationships, including conflict, between goals and the factors affecting relative priorities as between goals. The treatment of methods necessarily involves the possibility of circular argument. Because of what appears to be a felt need on the part of the leadership for self-conscious direction of its activities, it is often possible to derive a set of goals from official statements and, in a comparatively straightforward manner, review the contemporary tactical pattern for consistency with them. The results on occasion are more interesting than one might expect. In other cases, the goal is inferred from tactical practice and one can only apply the test of coherence to the proposed relationship to avoid falling into circularity. When a given tactical pattern can be more or less reliably identified as a choice among patterns known by precedent to have been employed in comparable contexts of events, the inferred relationship gains plausibility.

I Invariant Goals

Given the basic orientation outlined above, if there are definable goals which the Chinese Communist regime has espoused consistently without reference to environmental changes, these should belong to the highest level of the hierarchy. They would constitute, as it were, the regime's unconditional high strategy. By definition, the constituent goals are very long range, though less than ultimate. Their other defining characteristics are better specified after they have been described.

Of the Chinese demands relating to her position as a separate national entity, two in particular appear to be independent of environmental conditions and to carry great emotional weight. There is nothing in principle that is remarkable about China's insistence on territorial integrity and full sovereignty within what she regards as her legal limits. In some cases China has been willing to barter land for land. In the Sino-Burmese negotiations of 1956, the Chinese defined the factors in the problem as the historical facts, the concrete legal data, and calculations of practical advantage. The final settlement of 1960 had somehow become, at least as represented by the Chinese, an act of grace on their part and a joint political demonstration whose significance transcended its immediate content.

Taiwan and Tibet, particularly, are of more than practical significance to the Chinese. The Tibetan rebellion of 1959 was not simply a revolt against authority, but a "monstrous crime . . . undermining national unity," and its suppression was justified in the name of social revolutionary ideals. Both Taiwan and Tibet are regularly designated as "inalienable" or "inviolable" Chinese territory, and the "liberation" of the former is never mentioned as anything less than a "sacred duty" of the "Chinese people." Full Chinese sovereignty in both areas has been called a question of "great right and great wrong," that is, a matter of principle on which no compromise is possible.

What attracts notice about Chinese irredentism is not that it exists, not even that it is uncompromising or loaded with symbolic meanings, but that its spokesmen think of themselves as servants of destiny. This destiny, furthermore, does not have the same shape as that dreamed of by "bourgeois nationalists."

Similar symbolic values become attached to the Chinese drive toward recognized great-power status. Situations which compromise this status do not often arise, but when they do there is sure to be a reiteration of the Chinese claim that no problem in Asia (latterly, it would appear, in the world) can be settled without Chinese participation. The drive manifests itself in a tendency to issue pronouncements on all world events, of great or small moment. What is more serious, however, is that the Chinese may interpret certain situations as impinging on their world status when to others much less appears at stake. There is not conclusive evidence, but there is sufficient evidence to suggest, for example, that one compelling reason for China's intervention in the Korean War was the conviction that not intervening would be abnegation of the status of a great power.

The Chinese apparently do not regard United Nations membership as a criterion of great-power status but believe it to be a natural perquisite of that status. Although denied access to the United Nations, China occasionally requires an international forum. Therefore, China has promoted the convening of substitute international bodies, such as the Geneva Conference Powers or the Bandung Conference. Success on each such occasion seems to have strengthened Chinese pretensions. In the Chinese view the role of a great power is defined not in terms of diplomatic weight or material power alone. Besides these, a great power displays self-respect, as in the slogan "China has stood up," and demands the respect of others. It also exercises leadership by example. The claim the Chinese make to fulfill this latter role in relation to former colonies is by now well known, though not undisputed.

The Chinese themselves recognize no conflict between their aspirations as a nation and their whole-hearted commitment to the Communist bloc. In spite of the severe disagreements of the past two years concerning middle-run strategy, it remains true that maintenance of bloc solidarity is an overriding consideration in Chinese policy. Much in Sino-Soviet relations remains obscure. It appears, if one accepts the information provided by Crankshaw and Deutscher, that the Chinese Communists came very close to splitting the international movement in December 1960, and that they have not ceased agitation in Party circles since then. But the basic position of the Chinese Communist Party in the recent dispute never involved the possibility of defection from the "Communist camp" to the "imperialist camp." Their dissatisfactions were products, in part, of the fear of a long-term encirclement and, in part, of the fear that the whole of world Communist strategy was tending toward a position that would retard revolutionary processes. Their problem, then, was not whether or not to break from the Communist camp but how to prevent the camp as a whole from drifting away Rightwards from the Chinese position.

In any such intra-bloc dispute, when the Chinese oppose the preferences of the leading power of the bloc, they necessarily speak as a national party and represent the interests of a national entity. To this extent an at least apparent contradiction between national and bloc interests is an ever-present potentiality. The ultimate restraint on the extent to which such contradictions may result in action contrary to collective decisions is probably a matter of expediency. The Chinese seem to realize, despite some brave words about relying on their own resources, that neither their domestic nor their foreign ambitions can be promoted without significant assistance from the Soviet Union and other Communist countries. The same considerations of expediency probably determine their response to signs of independence in the behavior of other Communist countries. But there is, in addition, an emotional quality to the Chinese response which argues that a supra-rational faith in bloc solidarity has been offended.

It is worth recalling that the Chinese condemnation of Imre Nagy's declaration of an intention to withdraw Hungary from the Warsaw Pact in 1956 was clearcut and unhesitant, contrary to some expectations at the time. The position on Hungary, furthermore, was taken at a time when Chinese policy as a whole was in its most moderate phase. The major document stating the position, *More on the Historical Experience of the Dictatorship of the Proletariat,* reaffirmed the special international mission of Communist countries exactly at a time when the declared Chinese line was at the height of emphasis on the common characteristics of China and the non-Communist nations of Asia. The same document is now read by many people as one of the early portents of the later "dogmatist" position taken in the Sino-Soviet controversy of 1959-60.

In a related sequence of events, the Chinese Communist leadership swung sharply to the Left in domestic affairs, partly in reaction to one of the rare displays, in 1957, of public dissent from the regime's foreign policy. This dissent was concerned exactly with overcommitment to the Russian alliance. Internally, the "Great Leap Forward" and the People's Communes were expressions of the trend. In external relations, following the Moscow Declaration of 1957, the Chinese became progressively more militant. One important aspect of this revived militancy was the Chinese attack on Yugoslav revisionism, in the course of which the Chinese developed the doctrine that neutralism on the part of non-Communist countries was progressive but on the part of Communist countries was counterrevolutionary.

If we take the above as some of the fixed principles of Chinese foreign policy, certain of their characteristics deserve noting. They appear as absolutes, as not depending on the contemporary shape of the environment. Although often stated in Chinese declarations, they are not consistently declared but are implicitly constant. They are not, it would appear, to be questioned or discussed among the ranks of the "people." Anyone who does question them loses his standing as a member of the "people." The reaction to any event that appears to threaten these goals is swift, virtually automatic, and expressed in terms of symbolic values.

By the same token, these goals bear only indirectly on those processes of foreign-policy formulation and execution which require decisions to be made. These absolutes are outside the realm to which choice applies. There are, indeed, some other Chinese goals that can be stated in general form and are as absolute as those previously discussed. Such are, for instance, the goals of assuring national security, of maximizing Chinese influence abroad, and of promoting the development of Communist influence and control throughout the world. These are absolutes in the sense that the Chinese would resist, automatically and with emotion, any efforts to impede them. But they are so much, in terms of observable events, tied to environmental conditions and to the making of decisions that they are better dis- cussed at a lower level of strategy.

II Grand Strategic Designs

At the level of middle- to long-run, strategic-policy formulation, the Chinese Com- munist method of operation seems to require, beyond what is necessary for operations, the articulation of a grand design. It is hard to imagine Chou En-lai or Ch'en Yi entertaining for a moment the idea of muddling through. Periodic foreign-policy reports follow a standard form, in which a statement of basic principles (like devotion to world peace) is followed by a description of the state of the world, and this in turn is followed by an outline of current strategic goals. The last is so stated as to appear as a logical derivation from the description of the world.

The description of the world, if judged as an account of facts, is normally distorted to a degree that cannot be accounted for by differences in observational standpoint alone. The Chinese Communist perception of the world has its special character- istics, being ideologically conditioned and displaying a tendency to describe the impending future as the present. Additionally, the Chinese Communists regularly suppress important facts. The outline of the current grand design in Chinese foreign-policy reports often turns out to be a frank statement of intentions.

Since 1949 there have been three major overall patterns of strategy, with some minor variations by way of development or adjustment to new opportunities and setbacks. The dates of major shifts of line can be set, a little arbitrarily, in the sum- mer of 1951 and the autumn of 1957, and the general trend of shift can be desig- nated as from hard to soft (1951) and from soft to hard (1957). Each of these shifts can be correlated with important changes in Chinese estimates of the total world (not the local) balance of power. Other Communist parties concurrently revised their perspectives at about the same times, but our interest here is in the Chinese shifts, which have not always been consonant with those of other Communist parties.

The components of the grand design, then, are not absolutes. The included strategic goals are those consciously decided on as appropriate to the overall "correlation of international forces" as it is supposed to exist or as it is foreseen to take shape so long as the perceived dominant characteristics of the period last. These strategic goals, then, are chosen, not given. They are consequently open to discussion, either among members of the bloc or within China, and are potential occasions for ideological deviation.

For the Chinese, the distribution of world power is unavoidably bipolar. The problem of designing an operating strategy is to make the effective (or "correct") determination of goals and methods for achieving desired changes in this balance.

Between 1949 and 1951, the balance seems to have been apperceived in simple, categoric terms. The West had military strength in the material sense, but the prospects for revolutionary seizure of power, especially in Asia, were favorable. The bipolar conflict was seen as clear-cut. The chosen strategy was to support exclusively orthodox revolutionary movements and to attack all others. There was, then, no room for neutrality or for third powers. This perspective, in part, reflected the neophyte status of Communist China on the world scene and, in part, reflected the limits of China's capabilities for exerting influence. In terms of major tactical patterns directly related to the chosen goals and perspective, propaganda in this phase occupied an especially important place. There appears to have been great faith in its efficacy. This evaluation of propaganda persisted into the following period, but after the bacteriological-warfare propaganda campaign of 1952, it was significantly devalued and has never since played quite the same role.

The soft line of 1951–57 developed not as a dramatic break with past strategy, but as a sort of gradual retooling process. Throughout the period, the bipolar power balance was seen as unfavorable from the Communist viewpoint. In effect, the Communist camp was deterred and the Western camp was not. The main variation in this perspective was that in its earlier half the Communist disadvantage was seen as increasing, in its latter half as decreasing. The strategic goal of the period shifted from undermining Western strength by revolutionary take-over of peoples and territories to preventing the extension of Western strength into the peripheries of China and decreasing its potential where it could not be denied access—in short, the strategy of denial, of the "area of collective peace."

Prestige, as an objective, acquired new importance. Gradually, the Chinese attitude toward neutralism developed from grudging acceptance to enthusiastic endorsement, so that the promotion of the foreign-policy objectives of Asian neutrals became a declared Chinese strategic goal. In the course of time, however, this strategy turned back on itself by freeing Asian neutralism from bondage to its own fears. With the easing of tension in the area as a whole, the altruistic-preventive motive pattern of Asian neutralism lost its relevance. Energies could be redirected to domestic tasks, and in the international sphere the neutralists increasingly came to prefer the role of bridge to that of buffer. In the succeeding period, with the return to a hard line, the improved prospects for the emergence of a third force playing an independent role came once more to constitute a strategic problem in connection with which China had to arrive at new decisions. The Chinese, it appears, still prefer a tight bipolar world.

The post-1957 phase of Chinese strategy was initiated dramatically by the revelation of the Soviet breakthrough in missiles. For the Chinese, an entirely new balance-of-power pattern seemed to come into existence. The pre-1951 balance had been more or less equal as between different types of power—political versus military. The 1951–57 situation was one of unbalance which, however, could be contained. With the advent of nuclear parity, that is to say a balance in respect to the ultimate resort, with both sides possessing comparable resources of the same types —military versus military, the Chinese reading of the situation was that the deterrence positions were dramatically reversed.

Besides the radically new pattern of resources affecting the power balance, China's internal development, her world status, and the established pattern of her foreign relations were all of a different order from 1949. There could not be a complete reversion to the pre-1951 strategy, but the new situation permitted a re-examination of the strategic goals of the soft line. In many respects the Chinese, if it were within their power to decide, would apparently want to revive the pre-1951 strategy in all its essentials—direct confrontation with the West, support of orthodox revolutionary movements, denial of the legitimacy of the "third road," the full pattern of the strategy of revolutionary advance, and this time with the added advantage on their side of deterrent capability.

The present situation does not, however, lend itself any longer to such simplistic strategies. The environment has not been static. In the Asian periphery of China, there are many sources of instability, but no longer the crying weakness of 1949. Chou En-lai in 1954 apparently counted on the ultimate development of an imbalance of economic, military, and political power as between China and her periphery which would secure her dominance in the area. This imbalance, despite the revolutionary optimism of China's native radical leadership, has not arrived at the point hoped for. The soft line produced some successes, and there probably is a wing of the Chinese leadership that has a vested interest in living with this legacy. Above all, whereas the earlier grand designs were almost wholly in consonance with contemporary Soviet strategy, since 1957 discrepancies in the respective analyses of the "correlation of international forces" and in respect to middle-run goals and methods have been obvious.

Two ironies have been born. In an era when the Chinese believe that a "decisive shift" in the world balance of power has occurred, Chinese strategy has not been clear and confident but has vacillated, expressed itself in abortive actions, and retreated from untenable demands made on some target countries at the cost of conciliatory gestures made toward other target countries—not, it must be admitted, a very high price in most cases. The differential handling by the Chinese of the Indian and the Burmese border problems serves as a case in point. The outcome of this backing and filling seems for the immediate future to be an agreement with the Soviet Union to restrict the application of the hard-line strategy to the United States base system and those countries which play host to it. The second irony is that the Soviet Union has found it necessary to intervene directly in areas where Chinese interests are significantly involved. Soviet intervention has been on the diplomatic level, as in Khrushchev's tour of South Asia in 1960, and through physical presence, as in Laos. Thus, the accretion of power to the Soviet camp has brought about a restriction not only of China's range, but of her freedom of maneuver—subject to protest.

III The Topography of Goals and Methods

Strategic goals and, even more, the patterns of tactics developed for reaching recognized goals depend not only on estimates of relative capability, but on the way power is perceived to be distributed in space. Here is the most obscure facet of Chinese strategic thinking. One of the few judgments one can make with any confidence is that the Chinese regime has consistently regarded itself as encircled. Both its hard and its soft strategies can be read as approaches to the breaking out of an encirclement. It is probable also that in both hard and soft strategies, Korea and Vietnam occupy the position of primary security zones. The difference appears in the Chinese willingness to refrain from demanding an end to partition in the soft-line period and their almost automatic resort to demands for unification in hard-line periods. It is not lightly to be concluded that China demands armament equal to the highest world level either as a permanent goal or as a goal of especial saliency in the hard-line period. The regime has for years accepted a military structure which does not admit it to the ranks of powers capable of waging strategic war. There is evidence that the adequacy of this structure has been the subject of controversy inside the regime, perhaps of such dimensions that the proponents of an "incorrect" line qualify as deviationists. One can also suspect a parallel controversy on whether the regime's posture should be basically offensive or defensive.

It is implied in what has been said above that any Chinese grand design, whether hard or soft, requires China to move given target countries in ways that they might not move of their own accord. The Chinese policy-maker, then, must estimate the real-world feasibility both of the results he intends to produce and of the primary tactical patterns he is to employ. There is great difficulty in estimating the amount and kind of information on which decisions are based. In a few rare instances as, for example, when the Chinese publish a detailed statement concerning the fire-power of the Japanese Self-Defense Forces or of Japan's capacity for future production of missiles, or when a Japanese military commentator returning from China specifically states that the Chinese carefully read and analyze everything printed in Japan, we get a hint of the depth of the information available. But this does not provide assurance that the Chinese Foreign Ministry achieves the same depth or detail in regard to all countries. There have also been startling revelations of basic ignorance on the part of both high-ranking leaders and Foreign-Ministry technicians.

The full impact of internal revolutionary history on Chinese images of target countries is also difficult to analyze. There are a few most interesting points of detail which are somewhat indicative. In statements over the past year, Chinese spokesmen, by an obscure method of calculation, arrived at the statement that 90 per cent of the world's population favored the cause of the Socialist camp. The origin of the figure is probably indicated by the publication that appeared at about the same time of Volume IV of the works of Mao Tse-tung. In these writings, by a similar process of calculation, Mao had concluded that at the end of the Second World War, exactly the same proportion of the Chinese population, notwithstanding appearances, favored the cause of the Chinese Communist Party. Coincidences of this sort, and there have been several, justify the conclusion that domestic example predisposes the Chinese leadership to interpret events abroad in stereotyped ways. This predisposition, however, conflicts with a self-imposed requirement for factual knowledge and objective analysis. The result is a persistent ambivalence in China's demands on the world.

The Chinese policy-maker's dilemma rests in his uncertainty as to whether any country outside the Communist bloc can be relied on coupled with the certain knowledge that allies must be made and kept. The permanent enemy is of course the "imperialist camp," or, more specifically and concretely, the United States. Whether any Asian country is treated as a friend or an enemy depends less on that country's posture than on the requirements of Chinese strategy.

In the phase of the simplistic hard line, up to 1951, there was no problem. The division between the two worlds was taken as absolute, and all who were not for the Socialist camp were against it. With the initiation of the soft line came the search for friends and allies. The methods used were developed step by step over several years. The relative emphasis given by the Chinese to various kinds of allies serves to define secondary strategic phases.

At the beginning, allies were defined as social strata within various Asian countries, rather than as national entities. While maintaining a cool attitude toward constituted governments, the Chinese sought their allies in the ranks of Asian labor organizations, the intelligentsia, and non-Communist Left-Wing political organizations in opposition to their governments. The term "people's diplomacy" is an apt one. A kind of bargain was struck whereby China supported Left-Wing social and political protest in other countries in return for the support of "people's" organizations for China's national demands. This created a capability on the part of the Chinese to manipulate the internal politics of other countries in a more diversified way than could be done through dogmatic support of orthodox revolutionary groups alone, but it was hardly the road to international amity.

The transition from "people's diplomacy" to a more normal style of conducting international relations on the state-to-state level came after the Korean armistice and the 1954 Geneva conference on Indochina. The latter was particularly important in that it ratified China's great-power status and made state-to-state dealings possible without compromising Chinese dignity. The conference, and its consequences for the pattern of Asian relations, has never been sufficiently studied in the West. Its repercussions went very deep and considerably modified the international orientations and domestic positions of political bodies throughout the area. The final step, for the Chinese, was achieved at Bandung. Reduced to the essentials, it was here that the Chinese completed the transfer from identifying their national interests with those of the political opposition in other Asian countries to identifying with the international demands of incumbent regimes. In short, China now tried to ally herself not only with the neutralists of Asia, but with neutral Asian states, and raised the possibility of mutually profitable dealings even with states which were only potentially neutral. Concerning the exact content of neutralism, no questions were asked.

In the course of elaborating successive patterns of strategic methods, the Chinese did not wholly abandon any lines of communication but tried to keep them all open. The activities of local Communist parties were de-emphasized. There is, however, no accurate measurement of the extent to which the Chinese exerted themselves to preserve Communist cadres against future need. Slow and patient subversion is not easy to identify on the basis of normal public information. In some countries —Thailand and the Philippines, for instance—the Chinese, through lack of opportunity, have never gotten much beyond the tactics of "people's diplomacy" except by way of verbal gestures. In others, of which Japan is the best example, secondary hard and soft phases in China's approach depend on the contemporary location of power in the target country. There is an observable rhythm in China's dealings with Japan whereby, when a narrow conservative coalition, like the Yoshida or Kishi cabinets, is in power, the Chinese act in the way best calculated to promote polarization of local politics; when a broad conservative coalition, like the Hatoyama cabinet, is in power, the Chinese try to find points of negotiation. Manipulation of the target country's internal political balance is a more prominent aspect of China's approach to Japan than to other countries but is observable in dealings with all. The rhythm just described is, furthermore, not mechanically dictated by the nature of China's grand design, but represents an adjustment which may occur in hard as well as soft periods.

Apart from calculations of the payoff to China of a particular pattern of strategy, there are certain sources of ambivalence affecting the Chinese policy-maker. In regard to Japan, the Chinese seem to vacillate between the hope that Japan can be induced to reverse her alliances and the fear that she will necessarily become a dangerous competitor. Japanese expectations regarding China are similarly ambivalent and even more diverse, adding to China's uncertainty. In regard to the Asian neutrals, China's ambivalent judgment of the reliability of the "national bourgeoisie" is a case of projection. The Chinese regard two-facedness as an attribute of the object rather than as a facet of their own process of perception, and do not perceive those attributes which are objectively present.

In both hard and soft periods, the Chinese policy-maker believes in avoiding conflict on two fronts at once. This self-imposed requirement, besides being articulated in standard ideological statements, can be inferred from Chinese actions. There is also affirmative evidence of its operational relevance. Given the distribution of military strength in Asia, the "direction of the main blow" for the Chinese policy-maker is of necessity to the East. Correlatively, on the alternative front, which happens to be in the South, the strategy and tactics of "neutralizing" and "winning over" are indicated.

In the post-1957 hard-line period, appropriate changes in operating strategy and tactics were initiated. From an early point in this period, the distinction between "peoples" and incumbent governments and the "vanguard" role of the "proletariat" regained something close to their former prominence in Chinese formulations of the state of the world. With the renewed feeling of strength, the negative side of ambivalent views of others again emerged. Japan could be openly dealt with as an enemy. Suppressed hostility to the "national bourgeoisie" again came out into the open. All measures designed to make positive use of the initiative, including resort to war, regained their attractiveness.

Revival of the perspective of revolutionary advance, however, created self-frustrating real-world obstacles. The rest of the Communist world, especially the Russians, did not concur in the "correctness" of the new Chinese hard line, but developed a different hard line conflicting at specific points. The details of the resulting dispute have been analyzed by several students, and a fairly clear picture has emerged of the points of conflict and some of the resolutions thereof.

What is not so often stressed is that by the time the ideological dispute emerged into the open, Chinese operating strategy had lost internal consistency and appropriateness to real-world problems. China made demands, for example, for the unification of Korea, took provocative actions, such as the 1958 bombardment of Quemoy, and uttered threats against the SEATO countries; all of these actions were abortive in the end. The Chinese did nothing to mitigate the development of negative images of China in other Asian countries but, on the contrary, acted in such a way as to antagonize the Asian neutrals beyond any apparent need and for no compensating advantage. As noted earlier, there was a legacy of success as well as failure from the soft line. If the failures could not be expunged by apology, neither did it make sense to abandon the successes, as the "native radical" leadership seemed prepared to do. Confusion developed concerning the "direction of the main blow," partly because the leadership designated too many enemies and partly because of rising apprehensions on the part of the leadership that the distribution of military power in Asia was proceeding toward the creation of an enlarged threat from more than one direction—the so-called "three-pronged attack." Thus, Chinese operations during 1959 followed an aberrant, excessively offensive course. It required all of 1960 to readjust China's posture.

In the course of this readjustment, as earlier noted, the pattern of identification of allies and enemies was once more redrawn. The source of insecurity in the present design is relatively restricted and follows a different topographic concept. It is defined not as a continuous geographic area, but in relation to the United States base system. The Chinese stick to the distinction between peoples and governments and have even apparently achieved some acceptance of their recommended united-front policy. Since the points of conflict have apparently not been fully resolved, one cannot accurately estimate what China has gained or lost. A partial cost to the Chinese has been some loss of freedom of maneuver, to some extent offsetting the growth of a polycentric pattern of intra-bloc relations.

IV Simple Tactics

The focus of attention of this paper has been so much on Chinese high policy as to create the impression that all China's foreign operations fit into and serve a coherent pattern of middle- to long-run goals. There are, of course, some operations and some aspects of Chinese methods which are purely tactical. Furthermore, some aspects of the operating pattern have strategic significance in one phase and only tactical significance in another.

As noted earlier, propaganda was a strategic instrument in the early simplistic hard-line period and subsequently declined in significance if not in volume. In the nuclear parity hard-line phase, especially as directed toward Africa, it appears to have reacquired some strategic import. Prestige as an Asian nation was a strategic goal in the soft-line period but yielded in importance to the necessity for adopting a clear position on the Hungarian incident. The sacrifice of the favorable image of China in Indian and other eyes at the time of the Tibetan incident may or may not have been deliberate. Such incidents, however, indicate that to the Chinese, prestige is, on the whole, of merely tactical value, though a sacrifice of prestige may at times create issues which compromise strategic success.

Certain groups, treated as instruments of Chinese policy, tend to be handled as expendable. As long as local Communist parties, front groups, and sympathizers exist, the Chinese will use them, often as a matter of routine. But the Chinese, no less than the Russians, will sacrifice the local interests of such groups, with apparently little compunction, for their own advantage. What is more surprising is that the Chinese Communists handle the overseas Chinese as if they were an expendable commodity.

With some reservations—the writer being ignorant in the economic field—trade and financial operations outside the Communist bloc, in spite of the prominence given them in propaganda, are here regarded as, for the most part, tactical operations. Allowing for a few exceptional cases, such as the cutting off of economic exchange with Japan in 1958, China's foreign economic activities (where not straight commercial activities) involve the casual practice of economic warfare and much personal intrigue, neither of which appears to serve directly the high priority goals of the contemporary grand design. Perhaps the same can be said of economic aid outside the Communist bloc.

Publicly, the most obvious manifestation of Chinese diplomacy is the state visit. A trip abroad by Chou En-lai or Ch'en Yi is likely to be undertaken only for serious substantive purposes, and the traveler is always well briefed, even though stops en route sometimes are included apparently only for reasons of protocol. The visits of foreign dignitaries to China are similarly carefully prepared and, in a high proportion of cases, seem to be carried off with insight and to great effect, insofar as incidental details are concerned. This attentiveness applies surprisingly far down on the prestige ladder, though not down to the level of the semi-permanent resident, such as lower-ranking foreign diplomatic personnel and students. The joint communiqués and ceremonial speeches which usually emerge in the course of a state visit would repay study. Contrary to the fanfare and display of amity and harmony trumpeted by the Chinese press, comparison of statements often reveals most surprising discrepancies between the accounts from either side of what the harmony is about.

V Summary

The attempt has been made in this paper to identify goals and methods of Chinese foreign policy insofar as there is evidence to justify the identification. It is argued that there is a hierarchy of goals and that the methods in practice at a given time are consciously chosen as means to statable ends; that is to say, that the methods tend to form patterns whose variations through time correlate with changes in the goals pursued.

Within the limits of, and ultimately determined by, a basic revolutionary drive, there are certain goals which are invariant and independent of the shape of the environment. It is asserted that these goals are, within China, outside the realm of discussion, that they are, in anthropological terminology, sacred values. Dissent in respect to them would disqualify an individual from membership in "the people." These are Communist China's high strategic goals.

At a lower level, but still belonging to the sphere of strategy, are those goals which are formulated by a process of conscious decision. In terms of time, they apply to the middle or long run. They derive from an analysis of the shape of the environment. The true form of this analysis is presented, but incompletely, in periodic statements. The goals are intended to remain valid for the duration of the world situation in consideration of which they are formulated. These goals are discussable, but are part of the official line, so that open dissent from them may constitute ideological deviation.

For any given period, strategic goals of the order just described, together with a pattern of methods selected primarily for the purpose of promoting the attainment of these goals, constitute a grand strategic design. It is observed that Chinese Communist leadership apparently requires a high degree of consciousness and of self-guidance in terms of declared policy for satisfactory conduct of operations. The grand design at any given time is also part of the official line, and dissent may be treated as deviation.

Major changes in the grand design since 1949 have occurred twice—in 1951 and 1957—from hard to soft and back to hard. The controlling factor in such shifts has been the perception of the world distribution of power. The Chinese Communists view the distribution of power basically as bipolar. Depending on their analysis of the bipolar power balance, their grand design may identify only enemies outside the

Communist bloc or may identify some non-Communist countries as potential temporary allies; ultimately, however, it does not tolerate an independent third power factor.

Within a major period, the grand design is adjusted to exploit opportunities or accommodate setbacks provided by the environment, resulting in varying identifications of enemies and potential allies and in new decisions, both strategic and tactical. A number of variables, including China's international status, the degree of international tension, and the local topography of power in the Asian area, affect these decisions. Furthermore, the information available to the decision-maker is probably not uniform in quality and quantity, and his estimate of others is likely to be affected by his own ambivalence regarding them.

Within a major period there can be phases. Historically, some of them are derived from environmental developments which permitted the elaboration of the pattern of operations in a consistent direction, the incorporation of new patterns of operation and the change of emphasis on patterns already being employed. In the present period, there was an aberrant phase in which there may have been differences of view within China concerning the correct strategic goals, and in which counterproductive actions, or actions conflicting with normal operating principles, occurred. It appears that these aberrant tendencies have been corrected. The current grand design seems to have been brought into a state of stability, but it may not entirely satisfy the demands of the Chinese.

Certain patterns of tactics seem to vary within the limits of, or without being determined by, the grand design. In some cases there is a tactical rhythm corresponding to events occurring within a single country. Other tactical operations are carried on for their own sake, apparently at a low level of priority. A pattern of operations may in one phase or period be strategically significant, in another only tactically significant. Tactical operations are characteristically short run and intended for limited effect. Mistakes made in conducting them are not ideological deviations.

The propositions advanced here do not necessarily constitute a method of analysis applicable in its entirety to any specific sequence of events. It is the author's hope that they indicate the shape of a frame of reference within which the questions appropriate to such analyses can be formulated. Some of the propositions may, hopefully, turn out to have predictive value, but not directly in relation to problems— which may be of considerable practical import—for whose understanding a much more refined analysis is necessary.

What has been advanced here is intended as a general schema for the determination of what it is the Chinese Communists are trying to achieve in their relations with the non-Communist world. Beyond this loom the questions of how likely they are to succeed, at what points their efforts impinge on the aspirations of others, and of what events within the range from conflict to conciliation are foreseeable or desirable as various patterns of international relations develop. It has been implied here that certain goals of Chinese foreign policy are so heavily endowed with symbolic meanings that they probably are not subject to lasting settlement through bargaining on the basis of expediency, at least until the present Chinese leadership is succeeded by men of very different backgrounds and predispositions.

But Chinese goals and values within the limits of discussability—or, otherwise stated, problems in connection with which choices between alternative decisions are made on the conscious level—include those by which the operating grand strategic design is constituted. Twice in the soft-line period the Chinese accepted realistic negotiated solutions of dangerous military conflicts—in Korea and in Indochina. In the current hard-line period they have adjusted to reality in connection with the incidents at Quemoy and in Laos. Their choices between conflict and conciliation appear to depend, as happens with others, on an interplay between stereotyped thinking and informed judgments of actuality. These choices are thus subject to influence by the information supplied and the disposition of resources undertaken by others. There is, then, no simple way of dealing with Communist China's demands on the world; but there are ways of analyzing them.

●

V

Problems of International
Order in a Revolutionary Age

12

Bipolarity in a Revolutionary Age

Morton A. Kaplan

There is a considerable difference between the real world and the model of an international system. Models are merely starting points from which analysis must be carried forward if it is to have policy relevance. A model is designed to explore selected aspects of reality, and simplifying assumptions are used for this purpose. Moreover, for reasons of theoretical convenience, a model is concerned with conditions making for stability. Although such models can be adapted to circumstances or conditions which are inconsistent with stability, or which lower the probability of stability, these conditions would not be included in the initial statement of the model. To understand how bipolarity may operate in a revolutionary world, it will help first to contrast briefly the model of a "balance of power" system with that of a bipolar system. We can then discuss the features of the present revolutionary age to which the model of a loose bipolar system must be adapted and attempt to explore what their consequences might be.

I The "Balance of Power" Model

A "balance of power" model, as contrasted with a loose bipolar model, has only nation states or national actors as members. The "balance of power," as a system, is characterized by short-term alignments based on relatively immediate security objectives. States are motivated to limit the gains of war—and war itself—for security considerations. A reasonably large minimum number of nation states is neccessary to provide enough potential future coalition partners—or even disinterested neutrals—to prevent dismemberment or total defeat. Thus, the prospect of increasing a nation's gains in victorious war is outweighed by the need to maintain the independence even of present enemies as potential future coalition partners in order to guard against future dismemberment by still other coalitions. Even stronger considerations motivate states to prevent still other states from engaging in other than limited wars.

For these reasons, measures which tend to maintain the existence and independence of nation states or to increase the number of strong states are supported within the system. Coalitions tend to form against states striving for predominance. States captured by supranationally oriented political organizations tend to be opposed, for such organizations are inconsistent with the flexibility of alignment that maintains the stability of the "balance of power" system and that protects the interests of the member states. Members of the system tend to oppose interference in the domestic affairs of other states or premature recognition of and support for revolutionary groups, for such actions would also be inconsistent with the flexibility of alignment necessary to the stability of the system and to their interests.

II The Loose Bipolar Model

The loose bipolar model contains, in addition to nation states, blocs like NATO and the Communist bloc and universal organizations like the United Nations. The blocs are organized on the basis of long-term interests to which many short-term interests are sacrificed. They thus provide a striking contrast to the "balance of power" system with its flexibility of alignment. Alignments on specific issues, none-theless, may cross bloc lines. Although a member of the democratic Western bloc may support the Soviet Union on a particular issue (the Soviet bloc maintains unity on almost all issues *vis-à-vis* the West), this is unlikely to occur on vital issues. And on many other issues, support for the bloc is forthcoming, despite clashes between short-term issues of the individual nations in the bloc and the interests of the bloc.

In the absence of flexibility of alignment, the non-intervention and recognition norms of the "balance of power" system lack strong support. There is no common interest in preventing long-term alignments and thus no strong common interest in supporting the independence of non-aligned states. Indeed, each of the blocs has an interest in subverting the other bloc. The uncommitted nations have an interest in supporting the established norms concerning non-interference in internal affairs in order to protect their independence; and the blocs, in order to obtain the support of the uncommitted nations, at least have to act circumspectly with respect to these norms.

Both within and without a universal organization like the United Nations, the uncommitted states would play a major role for stability in a loose bipolar system. Efforts by the two blocs to obtain the support of the uncommitted states would force the blocs to phrase their demands upon each other in ways more consonant with universalistic standards than if the blocs were in an unmediated face-to-face relation-ship. In addition, the existence of such uncommitted nations permits the blocs to accede to the conciliatory efforts of the uncommitted states—a procedure that is more politically acceptable than accession to the demands of the opposing bloc and that is less likely to give rise to new demands. By influencing the expectations of the blocs in a way to be discussed in more detail later, the uncommitted states might permit the blocs to coordinate on mutually satisfactory criteria for the settlement of disputes, whereas in the absence of such an uncommitted participant, inability to coordinate on such criteria might increase the probability of nuclear war.

III The Loose Bipolar System—From Model to Reality

Under the best conditions, a bipolar system cannot be expected to possess the inherent stability of a "balance of power" international system. However, the model of bipolarity described above includes few of the historic features that particularize real-world situations. The uncommitted states of the model of the loose bipolar system could be similar to the modern developed states of Europe; indeed the model could be expected to operate with greater stability if they were. That these states, for the most part, are instead new and undeveloped, that they remember a colonial past they resent—whether for adequate or inadequate reasons—that they differ in color from the colonial nations, that they suffered from social and racial prejudice and in turn have their own prejudices, and that the ex-colonial nations are all Western nations, allied to the United States, are historic facts.

These facts provide the experience which helps to mold the uncommitted states, to shape their picture of the world, and to determine their attitudes to other nations. That these new nations, for the most part, are revolutionary, not merely in the sense of wanting independence, but also in the sense of wanting political and social changes, that they are suspicious, determined, and in haste, are facts that affect the stability of the bipolar system and that weight the clash between the United States and the Soviet Union.

The transition from "balance of power" to bipolarity, from a reasonably stable to a less stable form of international organization, occurs at a time when revolutionary changes are occurring in the number of nations participating in international politics, in the geographic areas they represent, in the military technology at their disposal, in the scale of economic organization, in the position of the nation state in relation to supranational organization, and in the social movements that are springing up within nations and that spread across national frontiers. Radical changes in habits of life and of expectations concerning the future are familiar aspects of our time. In terms of sociological, political, and economic organization—that is, in terms of its abstract role patterns—and in terms of the goals that motivate men and nations, the world is changing radically and all these changes are occurring at the same time.

Such kaleidoscopic changes are not easy to understand; and it is even more difficult to project their future path. There is at present no social or political theory adequate to this purpose. We can analyze selected aspects of the process individually and treat them more or less adequately in terms of theoretical or propositional knowledge. But, when we ask how all these events and processes interact, we can only attempt to indicate some of the more important factors that influence the stability of the contemporary bipolar system and to assess as well as we can the possible import of the changes that are apparent in the present revolutionary age.

IV The NATO Bloc

Let us look inside the blocs for a moment to see how they function in a revolutionary age. In a bipolar system the main obstacle to predominance on the part of one bloc lies in the cohesion, will to action, and military effectiveness of the other bloc. Unlike the situation in the "balance of power" system, there are no "third" nations to redress the "balance" should one of the blocs be defeated in war. The awful power of nuclear weapons does constitute an element operating for stability, but, in general, a shift toward predominance on the part of one of the blocs may well initiate an almost inevitable and irreversible chain of events. Thus the bipolar system is fragile and lacks resilience. Its stability rests largely upon nuclear deterrence.

The NATO bloc in particular hardly could be expected to function in a thoroughly cohesive manner. In the first place, cooperation among the nations of the West must be mediated through regimes based on party systems—virtually all of a democratic nature—that are structured differently, that have different kinds of audiences, and that hardly can be linked through trans- or supranational party organizations. Although the short-term interests of the nation may be subordinated to long-term considerations in formulating international policy, it would be going too far to expect the requirements for holding political office consistently to be subordinated to such considerations.

And, of course, within limits varying from nation to nation, opposition to bloc-oriented foreign policy becomes "fair game" for the political opposition. Terms of military service, contributions to NATO bases, consultation on nuclear policy, attitudes toward China, and so forth, become involved in the vagaries of national politics; and the cohesion of bloc policy suffers accordingly. This is particularly true with respect to threats of a military nature that fall outside the defined competence of the bloc. Although the overt nature of the danger and the rapid and unilateral involvement of the United States mitigated this somewhat during the Korean War—at least during its early stages—recent events in Laos reveal the extent to which the bloc is a checkrein on, rather than a support of, American policy.

Another factor complicating the cohesion of NATO stems from the fact that almost all the members of NATO except the United States were colonial powers. The United States might have supported a vigorous anti-colonial policy at the close of the Second World War—there were strong indications that Roosevelt desired to—when the European nations were weak, when they required American support desperately, and when the Soviet Union was incapacitated and could not have intervened to create chaos. With the recovery both of Europe and of Russia, however, this kind of policy lacked plausibility.

Although in terms of its own heritage the United States is an anti-colonial power and sympathizes with measures leading to independence, and although its interests in wooing the new and uncommitted nations would lead it in similar directions, it was unable to lead its NATO partners to such objectives against their resistance and had to reckon with the consequences of Russian intervention. Of course, the drive to independence occurred with the support of some of the European nations and perhaps, on some occasions, may have been conveyed too soon and with too little preparation. But there were sufficient exceptions to make the issue a hot one. The tragic case of Algeria, where moderate concessions as late as 1954 might have prevented rebellion, is indicative of the difficulties stemming from conflicting American interests in maintaining bloc cohesion and in not alienating the new and uncommitted nations.

The development of nuclear weapons as a potential factor in inter-bloc warfare also has affected NATO cohesion. The idea of conventional armed defense against the Russians, particularly while the United States possessed a nuclear monopoly, was quite appealing to the Europeans. A Russian drive into Europe would threaten all the Western European nations. Europe had become too small in the age of the jet plane and fast tank for nations to defend themselves individually. Moreover, if they waited for allied military commands to be set up after war had broken out, events would overwhelm them. Conventional defense, through NATO, was preferable to Russian conquest. And massive retaliation did not threaten them while the United States had a nuclear monopoly. NATO served as a guarantee of the interest of the European members of NATO and committed them to little that would not have been required, in any event, if Russia attacked. Moreover, the existence of NATO and the American commitment made Russian attack quite unlikely, whereas in the absence of these arrangements the possibility could not safely be discounted.

Russian possession of nuclear weapons, however, poses a threat of an entirely different nature. Annihilation is not necessarily preferable to Russian conquest to many Europeans. And, in any event, should nuclear war develop, they may desire to shift its locus from their own territory. Russian possession of a large nuclear arsenal may make missile bases seem undesirable, since such bases in national territory might well draw nuclear attack during war. Some nations may not desire to risk attacks even in self-defense. Yet, if these bases are under American control, the United States may hesitate to use them at the cost of nuclear reprisal against the United States. Thus, bases controlled by the United States might draw Russian fire and still not be used to defend the nations in whose territory they were erected. On the other hand, if each nation controlled the bases in its own territory, it might set off nuclear war in support of objectives not acceptable to the other NATO nations. A joint NATO system, designed to operate under specified conditions, has been proposed as at least a partial solution to the problem. Until, however, NATO has adopted some proposal of this sort, the capability of the bloc to take decisive action may well be arrested; and even after adoption, the fear of nuclear war will likely have sufficient impact on democratic governments to retard vigorous bloc policies.

Other factors also retard vigorous policy in the West. Western societies are no longer politically vigorous. Large segments of the public are complacent and desire to preserve what they have rather than to lead crusades that will transform the world. Their attitudes are largely defensive and even the protests against these attitudes are fed more by a gnawing discontent or by impotent anger than by a vision of the future. The bright hopes of the past are transformed into disillusion and bitterness.

There was a day—not too far in the history of the world—when political democratization held forth to most the hopes of redress of past grievances. It was thought that democracy shattered the chains of tradition, made man master of his fate, vanquished ignorance and poverty, and permitted a race of Prometheans to rule the world. Vain hope! It is not that democracy is worse than other forms of government. Indeed, it is better. However futile the hope of self-government and thus of individual dignity, democracy comes closer to reaching these goals than any other form of government. It is consistent with economic vigor, with a standard of living and health higher than any the world has ever known, and with the freedom of man to pursue his own future as he wills rather than as the state dictates. The disillusion does not lie in the comparative lack of achievement of democracy as contrasted with other forms of government. The disillusion stems from the gap between the ideals of the democratic creed and the performance of democratic government.

We have explored the possibilities of democracy and we know that there are limitations on its ability to transform the world. It takes tremendous self-discipline to recognize these limitations as inherent in human organization and to work for limited but possible improvements. For most people, there is a tendency to become complacent about the achievements of democracy and to value personal satisfactions. Such people do not want to sacrifice in the name of an ideal that cannot be achieved. Others find their mission in fighting injustice in some abstract sense. These fasten onto the past and present "sins" of democracy; and, in their desire to punish democracy for its shortcomings, they ignore the immensely larger evils of a creed that still promises abstract justice at some future time if only it can conquer the world.

The essential difficulty of the democratic position is that it seems to deny to many, in democratic nations as well as to those elsewhere, goods that are legitimized by the democratic creed. Any political system must suffer defects. No system can be consistently true to its own ideals. Democracy is challenged in the present age in terms of its own ideals. Its inability to satisfy this challenge by present performance— and sometimes its indifference to real and pressing injustices—creates an internal opposition which cannot be suppressed consistently with the institutions and values it espouses.

Thus, within the democratic nations, there are articulate groups, with some political effectiveness, that are essentially disaffected and that are motivated to inhibit effective political action designed to maintain the security of the NATO bloc. These groups are at basis recriminatory, they are more inclined to view Western policy with suspicion because of its "sins" than they are to view Soviet policy with suspicion. They have a mistrust of capital, which they feel has alienated and exploited man, of military leaders whom they suspect of warlike aims, and of politicians who they believe desire to suppress movements for national freedom and independence. Because many of the articulate intelligentsia belong to these movements, they have a political effect disproportionate to their numerical strength. And, because they are citizens of democracies, their arguments convince many in other nations of the injustice of the democratic nations.

In addition to democratic and idealistic protest movements within Western democracies, there are organized Communist movements in some large democracies and highly organized, if small, Communist Parties and vigorous "front groups," organized or captured by the Communists but containing many political innocents, in others. In France and Italy particularly, political life is precarious because of the size of the Communist Parties and, in Italy, also of the formerly fellow-traveling Socialist Party. This provides a political opposition oriented to the political requirements of the opposite bloc and therefore inconsistent with national security even in a "balance of power" system, let alone a bipolar system. It also provides an organization adaptable to espionage, sabotage, and other measures incompatible with effective political and military security.

An analysis of the complexity of Western bloc structure is beyond the scope of this paper. In addition to NATO, there is the European Common Market, the Free Trade Zone, and other organizational forms. The memberships of the various groupings overlap, although the Common Market and Free Trade Zone in particular have exclusive memberships. There is, no doubt, some conflict of interest among the various groupings. On the other hand, the multiplicity of functional organization may be more consistent with national needs than a more unified bloc structure. And, to the extent this is true, despite the conflicts of interest, bloc cohesion may be greater because of the flexibility of structure. On the other hand, NATO may prove quite fragile unless political and economic arrangements supplement the military ones. For we may enter a period when military dangers may tend to fragment NATO unless there are strong common interests, other than military, to solidify group identification.

V   The Communist Bloc

The Communist bloc is not without its own problems but there are more factors working for it than against it. In terms of organization, bloc ties are informal in a supranational sense, rather than formal as in NATO. Much of the integration of activity is carried on through the Communist Party rather than through the formal governmental apparatus. Although there is no evidence that the Cominform ever had the same functions as the Comintern—and it has since been dissolved by Khrushchev—the Soviet Party took over the functions of the Comintern long before the dissolution of that organization in 1943.

We do not have a good working insight into how the directive powers of the Soviet Party are implemented through the Communist bloc, although we have some evidence with which to speculate. We know the connections exist, for we can follow the purges implemented by Stalin in the postwar period in the satellite nations and the repercussions of the killing of Beria and the removal of Malenkov.

Part of the explanation lies in the fact that the parties in the satellites are genuinely Communist Parties—despite the illusiveness of the concept in terms of the original Marxist principles—and that, at least until the advent of Communist China as a strong and revolutionary Communist nation, heresy would have meant isolation in a non-Communist world and separation from the base of power that gives Communist Parties much of their appeal to their members.

Some of the power of the Soviet Party probably stemmed from the fact that the satellite parties were divided into factions—in particular, the factions that were in the resistance or in exile in the democracies and the factions that were in the Soviet Union during the war. The ability of the Soviet leader to play one faction off against the other, and the possibility that relatively uncommitted members of the Party rallied to that faction favored by Stalin, either for ideological or power reasons, may have played roles here. The presence of the Soviet Army was also not without importance. The lack of factionalism and the absence of the Russian armed forces may have been the major factors permitting Tito's Yugoslavia to break with the Kremlin.

Also, the fact that the Eastern European satellites are minority parties dependent on Soviet power to remain viable plays a considerable role. There is considerable evidence, at least with respect to Hungary, Poland, and East Germany, that the satellite regimes could not maintain themselves except for the threat of Russian intervention. It is interesting that the only satellite in Europe not having a common frontier with the Soviet Union or another satellite (Albania) is also the only satellite to support the Chinese position in the ideological dispute of 1960–61.

At least some of the factors that cause the Communists difficulty within their bloc—public apathy or dissatisfaction—also increase the cohesion of the Communist regimes. They face a hostile world both internally and externally and must unite for mutual support. The Hungarian revolt, and the underlying public antipathy revealed by it, will not soon be forgot. The China question, however, somewhat mars the unity of the bloc by providing a potential alternate center for leadership. Much has been made, since 1949, of congresses and groupings that seemed to indicate Chinese assumption of Communist leadership in Asia. Evidence from Cuba and elsewhere in Latin America and Africa also illustrates efforts by the Chinese to play a stronger revolutionary role in these areas. Whatever the potential ability of China to play such a role, however, it would be unwise to overstress this role presently.

China undoubtedly has co-opted one role for itself that previously was exclusively Russian. It is a fount of doctrinal interpretation—and thus potentially of alternate, if not heretical, doctrinal interpretation. As a geographically vast nation, with the world's largest population, China undoubtedly can serve ideological needs of the other satellites in a way that once only the Soviet Union could serve. The fact that Mao Tse-tung has at least temporal precedence over Khrushchev, or any other living leader of the Soviet Union, as the ruler of a Communist nation, reinforces this function. And the belief, whether well founded or not, that China could survive a nuclear war better than the Soviet Union is not without importance, for it confers a sort of subjective permanence on China. The dialectic of history, after all, cannot work itself out in a devastated nation, and Russia's vulnerability, not to conquest, but to annihilating nuclear attack, is an uncomfortable idea that is difficult to reconcile to an ideology based on an immutable historic providence.

The previous considerations are not unimportant. But other factors should be noted before China is promoted to a joint role with the Soviet Union in the Communist bloc. Although China has engaged in some economic aid activities, its possibilities along these lines are distinctly more limited than those of the Soviet Union. Capital exported by China also is desperately needed for internal development. Even more important, the European satellites depend for their existence on the capacity for military intervention of the Soviet Union.

If the existence of a Communist China increases the bargaining power of the European satellites with the Soviet Union, it does not eliminate their dependence on that nation in military, political, and economic senses. It may be that a decline in the degree of Soviet control over the satellites will have long-term effects on the form of control and the cohesiveness of the bloc. But this is an area about which we know very little. If there is some reason to doubt that the Russian ambassadors can transmit orders to Eastern European satellite nations—as occasionally happened in the past—there is good reason to believe that Russia still exercises substantial control through world party congresses and party interrelationships.

The Communist bloc still faces the world as a cohesive and hostile grouping, unified in its determination to change the face of the world. Indeed, at the present time, it would be wise not to overestimate the extent of the disagreement between the Soviet Union and Communist China. Stories of Russian missiles pointed toward the Chinese heartland make good reading in the popular press; and possibly they are true, although the direction of missile bases is not fixed, as was that of the cannon at Singapore. Khrushchev may possibly be worried about Chinese possession of nuclear missiles, but we are not about to see a re-alignment in which Russia and the United States jointly defend the West against the yellow East.

If one believed that national interests remained identical through regime changes and changes in the international system, we might well see a re-alignment involving Russia, China, and the United States. In this case, however, China, as the weaker juxtaposed power, might seek an alliance with the United States against the Soviet Union—although conceivably in another fifty years, the situation might be reversed. But it is important to understand that both Russia and China are sincerely dedicated Communist nations. They may not mean by Communism exactly what Karl Marx meant and there may be vigorous disagreements between the two concerning the true interpretation of orthodoxy. They may disagree over whether the communes are a leap toward or a retreat from Communism, whether revolutions elsewhere are to be encouraged if the probability of nuclear war is high, and whether pay differentials ought or ought not to exist. Indeed the disagreements here may not be ideological in their basis. The Chinese may need to compress pay differentials in order to carry out their plans under Chinese conditions, while differentials may be necessary to keep production high in a Russia where consumer production is important for political reasons. But both believe in centralized planning; and both are opposed to political liberalism and multi-party systems (despite the formal continuance of appendage parties in China and some of the Eastern European satellites). Both believe in state ownership of industry and both believe in something called Communist morality. In addition, the security of either would be weakened in a world in which the other did not exist (provided the United States continued as a strong military power). China, in particular, is dependent upon the military strength of the Soviet Union.

The Chinese-Russian partnership may be an uneasy one. Possibly, two major Communist powers, ruled according to the principle of democratic centralism, cannot coexist indefinitely in a bloc organized according to looser principles of rule. They may not learn how to behave in situations of this kind. Constant conspiracies to seize bloc control or the efforts of one to impose on the other its particular view of orthodoxy may in the end cause an irreparable rift. These things are possible. It is also possible that as China masters some of her internal problems, the largely internal needs that set her in opposition to the Soviet Union may diminish. And it may come about that Russian leadership is re-established, that Chinese leadership replaces it, or that a formalized bloc government is established. Whichever direction change takes—and social science is not presently sufficiently powerful to predict this—contemporary evidence indicates that the Communist bloc will maintain itself in a hostile world.

There is one important element on which the Chinese and Russians will agree. They both aspire to exploiting the desires within colonial areas and the new nations to be independent, modern industrial nations. Any developments, even developments that bring temporarily anti-Communist elements into power, are desirable if they lessen the ties of the area to the democratic West. The two leading Communist regimes may disagree on the risks to be run in exploiting these developments, the pace at which they are to be forced, or the extent to which local anti-Communist measures will be tolerated. But despite such disagreements, there is a wider and more important range of agreement. The new nations desire change, and China and Russia support them in achieving it. True, Russia may really prefer chaos to genuine independence, as her behavior during the Congo Crisis indicates. It may prefer conditions that ripen the area for Communism. But these are not immediate matters of concern to at least some of the leaders of these ex-colonial areas. To them, the major problem is not the future threat of Communism but the immediate problem of independence, national unification, and economic development. And here Russia and China have interests that converge despite differences about timing and measures of implementation. They are unencumbered by the past; they can and do support every revolutionary demand, every move to the Left, and any development that produces instability.

VI The Uncommitted Nations

The dissatisfactions, protests, and desires for revolutionary change of influential groups in the new and uncommitted nations have already been mentioned. The more conservative political and economic leadership in these areas usually emerged during the colonial period. Such leadership is identified with the transitional period toward freedom and thus—despite its own efforts to bring about independence—may be identified with the colonial past. Unless this relationship is repudiated by radical measures, there is a danger of replacement by groups further to the Left. The rising counterelites seemingly have no direction in which to go except the Left.

In addition, the old elites associated with conservatism and the colonial government are more closely related to the tribalist past and thus have less of a political base from which to support modern national identification. They must break in most cases with their traditional base of support if they are to achieve modern nationhood. This is a difficult type of decision to make and, if made successfully, may force these old elites into a revolutionary position to consolidate their new bases of political strength.

The forced economic development generally believed necessary by the elites of the new nations, if these new uncommitted nations are to enter the modern world, also seems to require state control of the economy and one-party politics. If these one-party systems are mass parties rather than elite parties, such as the Communist Party, they still differ radically from Western parties, and the political systems in which they operate may have more in common with authoritarian systems than with Western representative democracy.

The demands of the new elites in the new and uncommitted areas are more congruent with Communist practice than with that of the West. Even if capitalism would permit them to develop faster—and they do not believe this—capitalism is associated with foreign control, exploitation, and the siphoning off of profits. Thus, even when Western leaders shout that colonialism is dead, leaders of the new nations are fearful of economic control. And as unreasonable as these fears may be, they are not entirely incomprehensible, for on the American border in Canada similar fears are openly expressed by politicians, business leaders, intellectuals, and segments of the public.

Indeed the one major factor operating against the Communist bloc is the fear of the new nations that they might be subjected to a new imperialism. Africa, for instance, in the opinions of the new leaders of that continent is for Africans and not for Russians or Chinese any more than for Europeans. It is exactly here that the seeming split or disagreement between China and Russia is of greatest danger for the West. For, by seeming to indicate that a nation may go Communist and maintain its independence, it reduces the threat of Communism in the minds of the leaders of the new nations. From this standpoint, they may fear Communism, not so much as a curb on their independence, but as a factor that would thrust them into the Cold War, that would increase the dangers for them of hot nuclear war, and that would diminish their ability to bargain off East against West in order to speed their economic development.

The picture presented is an oversimplification, of course, and requires more qualification than we can present here. India, for instance, is presently committed to democratic domestic procedures, although it accepts the Socialist myth and sympathizes more with the Soviet foreign-policy line than with the American. The former French colonies in Africa, with the exception of Guinea and Mali, although inclined to Socialist doctrine, apply it moderately and are inclined to cooperate with the West in many matters of foreign policy. Yet, even here, a vigorous counter-elite sympathizes with the more radical policies of Guinea and Mali.

Among the ex-British colonies, Nigeria is by far the most moderate. Ghana seems committed to far more radical policies nationally and internationally. Egypt is the most radical of the Arab nations, although Morocco, for reasons of internal politics, seems to be swinging to a radical line internationally while maintaining a moderate policy domestically. The South-African situation, however, may worsen the situation in Africa to the point where only radical policies can prevail. Most Latin American states seem committed to democratic evolution, although Castro's influence with the dispossessed is growing and Jacobin tendencies hitherto absent in Latin America are beginning to manifest themselves. Many of the details of these developments are subject to some dispute and we cannot here attempt to duplicate the efforts of the area papers to explicate these situations.

VII   The Uncommitted Nations and Bipolarity

We can now sketch the ways in which the new and revolutionary nations may affect developments in the contemporary bipolar world. The inherent stability of a bipolar system is precarious, and the reinforcement arising from the nuclear weapons systems is an important factor in maintaining its stability. The mediatory functions performed by the uncommitted nations both within and without the United Nations organization are very important to the stability of the system. These two factors go together, for in a bipolar system with nuclear-weapons systems confined to the blocs, the uncommitted states may help to define the criteria according to which decisions are reached short of war.

If we project to a time when both Russia and the United States possess second-strike systems, that is, systems which, even after absorbing a surprise attack, could devastate the enemy, the military situation is peculiarly different from that ever existing previously. (And even where this is not the case, the fear that it is the case, or that in any event unacceptable damage may be produced by nuclear war, may well produce the same result.) Either bloc can impose the most drastic possible penalty on the other for refusing to accept an offered solution. But they are symmetrical in this respect, that is, each can devastate the other. Clearly, mutual destruction would normally be considered worse than some bargain between the two. Yet to agree either on bargains, or the criteria according to which bargains are to be reached, is difficult in a changing world. There are differences of valuation, of interpretations of situations and of motivations, differences in estimation of situational advantage, and so forth. Moreover, as the political world changes, and as Russia and the United States are forced into political, economic, or military intervention or commitment to protect existing interests or to support goals of foreign policy, the potentiality for disagreement is heightened.

The bargaining situation involved has been examined extensively with respect to simpler cases of the same general type. It is one in which situational advantages and the psychologies of the contestants play major roles in determining the outcome of a bargain or whether a bargain will be made. The game in which two individuals can divide a sum of money if they can agree on the division but get nothing if they disagree has some analogies to the nuclear situation. Either Russia or the United States can enforce the "no bargain" (nothing-nothing) solution by setting in operation a train of events leading to nuclear destruction.

A Hitler possessed of an invulnerable nuclear system and willing to destroy his own nation if he cannot rule the world can force others to choose between slavery and death. Short of this extreme case, however, we enter the realm where agreements are possible but the principles of agreement uncertain. Situational factors may enter in. We might feel, for instance, that China has a legitimate claim, if not a right, to off-coastal islands such as Quemoy and Matsu, and we might thus be less willing to risk nuclear war to defend them than to prevent the seizure of Bornholm in the Baltic. Another consideration may also enter here; since the Soviet Union in some sense has a less legitimate claim to Bornholm—indeed no claim at all—than China has to its coastal islands, an attack on Bornholm may be viewed as an undesirable precedent. But this is related to the problem of the criteria, for it is the legitimacy of the claim that reduces the precedential value of the act. The nearness of the action to the border, the importance of the prize sought, whether one side wants it more than the other, the ambiguity of the move (whether, for instance, it was possible to find a group ready to revolt in order to join China), the amount of force involved, and so forth, might constitute criteria.

Now the criteria may be imbedded in some way in nature—it is a fact of nature that Quemoy and Matsu are within China's coastal waters—but nature alone does not determine the expectations that are held. The fact that China has, or at least thinks she has, a legitimate claim to the islands and, therefore, that China can be expected to attempt to secure them makes others less willing to risk nuclear war in order to prevent her from obtaining them. The fact that she knows that others expect her to be willing to take greater risks to obtain the islands than others are willing to take to prevent this gives China a bargaining advantage, or at least would give her a bargaining advantage were she a nuclear power.

The coordination of expectations plays a decisive role in bargaining situations in the nuclear game. The nations involved must coordinate their expectations short of nuclear war or risk mutual destruction. The nation that can make the other nation expect it to hold out for a particular solution and can prevent the other from establishing a similar expectation concerning its alternate solution or criterion for solution has the bargaining advantage. Criteria that have been accepted in the past are known to produce expectations and therefore play a considerable role in the coordination of expectations.

In the Quemoy-Matsu case, the criterion accepted in the past operates to the benefit of a Communist nation. Generally, however, established criteria favor the United States, for they are generally consonant with stability. Established criteria have still further basis for support. An established criterion is reasonably definite and can be singled out; it is easier to coordinate on it than to choose from among alternate competing criteria. Thus, an established criterion increases the bargaining strength of a nation that advocates its application by increasing the probability that the nation will expect a settlement in accordance with it. The probability of coordinating on an alternate criterion is lower and, therefore, the possibility of nuclear war looms larger if the established criterion is not accepted.

The preceding remarks give some insight into the way in which the coordination of expectations plays a major role in reaching bargains or in establishing the criteria that are to govern bargains in a nuclear age. They do not explain the role of the uncommitted states in determining bargains or criteria governing bargains, but the step is now easy to make. The interjection of a third-party opinion changes the expectations that parties to a bargain have of the willingness of each to accept a particular criterion. Provided only that the criterion enunciated by the outside party is not clearly unreasonable, one bargainer sees that the other has external support for his arguments and is likely to reason that the other bargainer therefore expects him to give in. The other bargainer knows that the first reasons this way, and this increases the incentive of the second to hold out for the "arbitrated" solution. The mere fact that the external intervention changes the view of each as to what the other expects and expects him to expect alters the situation to the advantage of one and to the disadvantage of the other. The greater the number of third parties intervening, and the more disinterested they appear, the more true this is (unless they differ with one another). Therefore, the uncommitted states as external mediators, interveners, and so forth gain substantial power to affect bargaining between the United States and the Soviet Union—a power that may be greater than their military weight or than their value as allies or opponents on future issues, although these elements also enter into the determination.

As we mentioned earlier, the uncommitted states would have some interest in maintaining most of the norms of the "balance of power" system since these would be most consistent with their independence. And this would be favorable to American interests; indeed it would be opposed to Russian interests only to the extent that Russia was dissatisfied with the status quo. Particularly since colonialism—at least in the nineteenth-century sense—is a thing of the past, and since existing colonies can expect to gain their freedom in the foreseeable future, one might under these assumptions visualize a reasonably stable bipolar world with a large number of independent and uncommitted states. That the large number of military alliances pursued under the Eisenhower-Dulles policies in non-European areas might not exist might even be viewed as favorable to American interests considering the important role played in maintaining the stability of the system by the uncommitted states.

However, the uncommitted states are also opposed to the status quo; in that fact may lie an important element of instability in the contemporary bipolar system. So far, the disagreements among the uncommitted states have prevented this factor from producing rapid instability; these states have merely been ineffective in reinforcing stability. Yet a cursory glance at the ways in which uncommitted states have already helped to increase the ambiguity of existing norms or have exerted pressure to change the norms (or the criteria of division) may help to indicate the potential instabilities involved in the process.

One example occurs in the Congo dispute. Whatever grounds there may have been for considering Lumumba legal premier of the Congo after dismissal—and such grounds were quite slim if not non-existent—there was no ground under existing international law for regarding Gizenga as the premier of the Belgian Congo. Under some conditions belligerency might have been conceded, but even so the right to intervene in support of him would have been dubious. The direct intervention of Ghana, Egypt, and Guinea—along with the Soviet Union—in support of Gizenga helped to make ambiguous the legitimacy of the Kasavubu regime and to a greater extent of the established norms of recognition, along with their consequences. By recognizing Gizenga and by making ambiguous the norms of recognition, a precedent—which hopefully may not prove important—was set which may effect the expectations of the United States and the Soviet Union in ways upsetting to the status quo. Previous efforts of this kind by the Union and China in Laos, which won some support from India, have similar effect.

These destabilizing actions were not inconsistent with previous positions of the uncommitted nations. Clearly, the United Arab Republic is willing to intervene with military force, politically and economically in the Middle East and Africa, in support of revolutionary movements. Ghana and Guinea have manifested similar aims. India's actions with respect to Laos may have had different motivations but similar consequences. Most of these nations mentioned desire to legitimize intervention in behalf of radical movements but not in behalf of conservative movements. Perhaps this distinction can be maintained; but even so it is open to some doubt whether the results of such intervention may not trigger off uncontrollable unstabilizing tendencies. Castro's activities in Latin America are of the same order. And the South African situation is potentially explosive.

Similar considerations may affect disarmament, arms control, and testing policies. The matter is too complex to be discussed in terms of its merits here, but pressure from the uncommitted states may force the United States into a bargaining situation where the concessions to the Soviet Union will permit Soviet exploitation of revolutionary possibilities present in the international system.

The problem of choosing a successor to Hammerskjold as Secretary General of the United Nations now arises as a consequence of his tragic death. No Secretary General could have represented the interests of the uncommitted nations with greater fairness; some might indeed have accused him of appeasement of the uncommitted nations. His permanent successor, if agreement can be reached on anyone, will be dependent on support from uncommitted nations for his effectiveness. Although the uncommitted nations have so far been unwilling to accept the radical proposals offered by Khrushchev with respect to the office of the Secretary General, there is increasing evidence that a large number of them will be unwilling to support a Secretary General who is not even more responsive to their revolutionary demands than was Hammerskjold. Considering the role played by the Secretariat in stabilizing a number of international situations, this may play havoc with the ability of the United Nations organization to help to maintain bipolar stability.

The indifference of the uncommitted nations to Soviet depredations in Europe may interfere with efforts to take effective action in Europe for preserving the status quo either within or outside of the United Nations. The pressure exerted on members of NATO by uncommitted nations that claim Commonwealth status may have similar deleterious results. We could continue examples but they would only reinforce our earlier statements. Many of the revolutionary uncommitted nations are playing quite risky games from the standpoint of their own independence and ability to profit from bipolarity. Although they might play a role that is important in reinforcing stability, a number of them have forsaken this role for more revolutionary objectives. Should some of them come into possession of nuclear weapons, the dangers involved might be extremely great.

When we consider, in addition, the lack of cohesiveness in the NATO bloc, the internal strains that serve to undermine unity, the effectiveness of policy, and the ability of the Soviet bloc to act in a unified fashion, bipolar stability looks even more precarious. Since the Soviet Union also makes demands and appears more ready to resort to force in favor of changes in the status quo, other bargaining considerations are advantageous to it. Nations fearful of war put pressure not on the nation making threats but on the nation that appears more amenable to compromise. Trouble is postponed even though it may loom larger later. Moreover, the expectation is reinforced that it is legitimate for the status quo to be changed in only one way—that is, in a way favorable to revolutionary developments.

The general picture then is one of quite tenuous stability—of a bipolar system shifting in ways unfavorable to the West, both in terms of international alignments and in terms of domestic regimes. The historical actuality is thus considerably different from the abstract model of the loose bipolar system.

13

Dynamic Environment and Static System: Revolutionary Regimes in the United Nations*

Ernst B. Haas

> So many worlds, so much to do,
> So little done, such things to be.

The words were written by Tennyson. Today they not only represent Kwame Nkrumah's *leitmotif,* but they seem to have become the theme of all contemporary revolutionary leaders. Many of us see, in the crest of violent and impatient doctrines which flood the scene, persuasive evidence of anxiety everywhere. Outcroppings of fear and hatred in politics are paired with distasteful self-awareness and self-loathing. Revolutionary politics and the politics of despair are often coupled in one syndrome. Political extremism and personal insecurity appear as inseparable twins. But to argue thus is to introduce a non-political consideration into the dissection of a decidedly political phenomenon.

No doubt the revolutionary leader violently rejects the present world, but the content of his dogma exudes self-confidence rather than self-fear—the assurance of security rather than the ambiguity of perpetual anxiety. The revolutionary leader is impelled by a vision which, despite its violence and destructiveness, is invariably geared to a utopia which is held to be attainable by rational political means, means which include the systematic dissemination of fear. Far from sharing the nihilism of the mere terrorist or the verbally precocious Beat, extremism in words and deeds is part of a political program, and politics implies structure, order, and formal relations —if only for playing out conflicts. The revolutionary leader does not want to abolish politics; his aim is the same as any other political leader: to fashion and maintain the kind of order which is consonant with his values. In what way, then, can the revolutionary leader and his state be distinguished from any state which participates in the life of the United Nations?

I

Revolutionary regimes, for our purposes, possess two central attributes. They are committed to the complete reordering of their own societies, to the creation of a

* I gratefully acknowledge the support of the Rockefeller Foundation, the research assistance of Suzanne Angelucci and the editorial services of Francine di Palma in the preparation of this paper.

new order or the restoration of an old order radically different from the present. Dogmatic modernism and fanatical nativism are equally acceptable as criteria. Furthermore, a revolutionary regime typically sees itself as struggling against some kind of international "conspiracy" or fighting a global "historic force"; this implies an external dimension in the revolution, since the regime must cooperate with kindred movements in other countries. A few examples will illustrate this combination.

In the words of two students of modern Africa, revolutionary leadership "being exclusivist . . . lives in a world of friends and enemies. Moreover it finds itself uneasy in negotiating on other than on its own terms." It seeks to "combine the skills and talents of a community and mobilize them for a wholesale assault on the problems that lie ahead." While this state of mind suggests a rigid ideological commitment, ideology is no more than the servant of task-oriented expediency.

The immediate tasks of the day, whether to build a dam, change the tax structure or modify the political arrangements in government, will be put in the context of ideological slogans as a form of communication, but opportunism is more compelling than ideology.[1]

At the same time, a peculiar variety of charismatic leadership is often associated with this type of regime. While its local cultural attributes may differ and while the institutionalization of revolutionary progress may attenuate its features, the Latin American admiration for a personalist *jefe* who is also a *macho* (male) is widely repeated, a leader who

. . . is expected to show sexual prowess, zest for action, including verbal 'action,' daring, and, above all, absolute self-confidence. . . . In politics, a man is not commonly elected or acclaimed to office because he represents the social, economic and political position of his followers, but because he embodies in his own personality those inner qualities that they feel in themselves and they would like to manifest, had they but the talent to do so, in their own actions.[2]

If Fidel Castro fits this bill, so do Kwame Nkrumah, Sukarno, Sékou Touré, and Gamal Abdul Nasser.

Perhaps the most direct way to spell out the external aspect of revolutionary leadership is to furnish an example of post-colonial statecraft which self-consciously eschews pan-Africanism. As Félix Houphouet-Boigny put it just one year before the Ivory Coast became independent:

Why do we not demand independence? To answer this question I can only ask another: What is independence? Industrial and technical revolutions are making peoples more and more dependent on one another. . . . Indeed, the countries of Europe . . . are prepared to relinquish a part of their sovereignty. . . . Why, if not to bring about, by association and mutual aid, a more fully elaborated form of civilization which is more

[1] David E. Apter and Carl G. Rosberg, "Nationalism and Models of Political Change in Africa," The National Institute of Social and Behavioral Science, Symposia Studies Series No. 1 (Washington, D.C.: December 1959), pp. 8–9.
[2] John P. Gillin, "Some Aspects for Policy," in *Social Change in Latin America Today* (New York: Harper, 1960), p. 31.

advantageous for their peoples and which transcends a nationalism that is too cramped, too dogmatic and by now out of date? [3]

Note in contrast, Kwame Nkrumah's thoughts on revolutionary statecraft:

My first advice to you who are struggling to be free is to aim for the attainment of the Political Kingdom—that is to say, the complete independence and self-determination of your territories. When you have achieved the Political Kingdom all else will follow. Only with the acquisition of political power—real power through the attainment of sovereign independence—will you be in a position to reshape your lives and destiny, only then will you be able to resolve the vexatious problems which harass our Continent.[4]

To what use should the Political Kingdom be put? It should consolidate freedom, create unity and community among African states, and finally, achieve the economic and social "reconstruction" of Africa by undoing the damage wrought by colonialism and tribalism. Pan-Africanism is an integral part of the program because only through African unity can the "African Personality" be called to life. Political boundaries and tribal divisions are the hallmarks of reaction; an African Personality able to demonstrate the black man's cultural equality with other races will arise only with their suppression. Cultural renaissance, economic progress, territorial revisionism, strong political leadership, and the Political Kingdom are one and inseparable.[5]

So much for the syndrome of factors making up the substance of the doctrine. They necessarily presuppose totalitarian national institutions, in embryo or in full bloom. In the Soviet case and in Cuba such institutions are clearly flowering; in Ghana and Guinea the buds are shooting out. If Egypt, Indonesia, and Bolivia appear merely as one-party or no-party states, it is because their authoritarian way has not advanced to full totalitarianism for reasons associated with underdevelopment rather than from lack of intent.

But it is important *not* to equate revolutionary regimes with a number of closely related categories. Not every totalitarian state is also a revolutionary state, as shown by modern Spain, Portugal, and Yugoslavia. Policies of imperialism may well be pursued in the modern world without being linked to an intention to transform society. Thus, Egypt followed a pan-Arab course, often interpreted as simple Egyptian imperialism, under Farouk as well as under Nasser.[6] But this does not make

[3] Félix Houphouet-Boigny, "Black Africa and the French Union," *Foreign Affairs* (July 1957), p. 594.
[4] Speech by the Prime Minister of Ghana at the Opening Session, December 8, 1958, All-African People's Conference, Accra. The same point was made by the Tunisian delegate to the first Conference of Independent African States, Accra, April 22, 1958.
[5] *Ibid.*, for this train of thought. See also the similar remarks of Sékou Touré as reported in *Afro-Asian Bulletin*, Monthly Journal of the Permanent Secretariat of Afro-Asian Solidarity (Cairo: October–November, 1959), p. 6. The argument that "national" independence of single ex-colonial territories whose boundaries were fixed by Europeans is meaningless as long as any colonial situations survive is common to pan-African thought in English-speaking West Africa and the Cameroons. See George Padmore, *A Guide to Pan-African Socialism*. The same doctrine is expressed unblushingly in the Constitution of the Convention People's Party. See K. Nkrumah, *Ghana* (New York: Thomas Nelson and Sons, 1957), pp. 289–90.
[6] See Farouk's use of the Arab League and of the caliphate in Elie Kedourie "Pan-Arabism and British Policy," in W. Laqueur (ed.), *The Middle East in Transition* (New York: Praeger, 1958),

the pre-1952 oligarchical regime a revolutionary one. Nor is every nationalist regime specifically revolutionary. Indian or Burmese nationalism is not revolutionary because it has no articulate external referents. But Ghana's nationalism is identifiable as revolutionary because of the pan-African strain; Indonesia's is equally so because it holds

. . . that God Almighty created the map of the world in such a fashion that even a child can tell that the British Isles are one entity . . . and that a child can see that the Indonesian Archipelago is a single entity, stretching between the Pacific and Indian oceans and the Asian and Australian continents, from the north tip of Sumatra to Papua.[7]

A further refinement in the application of this definition of revolutionary status is imperative. Having linked contemporary revolutionary pressures with totalitarian political institutions, we automatically exclude from our purview such international revisionist dogmas as may be associated with oriental despotisms, mercantilist imperialisms, and early capitalist assertions. This is *not* to argue, as some contemporary commentators do, that revolutionary conduct in our era is purely a non-Western and anti-Western phenomenon which ought to be linked to cultural differences between the Western creators of international law and its Asian challengers. After all, the impetus underlying such attacks on the international status quo as were hurled from Moscow and Berlin during the thirties can hardly be shrugged off as "non-Western." The international politics and legal doctrines of sixteenth-century Spain, the seventeenth-century Dutch Republic, and the fledgling American Republic showed definite evidence of a "new" state's impatience with certain aspects of the status quo and resulted in the advocacy of international legal norms which were regarded as "revolutionary" in the context of their times. However, they are not "revolutionary" for our purposes because the element of drastic *internal* revolutionary zeal was lacking in the case of three examples adduced: There was no overwhelming commitment to remake Spanish, Dutch, or American society, and the refinements of totalitarian control remained to be invented.

Soviet behavior offers a still finer point. While the Soviet Union is clearly a revolutionary state whose foreign policy fits the requirements of our purpose, it does not follow that every Soviet move is part of a "necessary" and "planned" revolutionary behavior pattern. One careful study, for instance, casts doubt on the "inevitable" character of the communist *coup* in Czechoslovakia.[8] We are, therefore, concerned with the attitudes and poses, the demands and expectations, the style and doctrines, of totally revolutionary regimes rather than with every detail of their foreign policy moves.

Our concern can be pinpointed in another way. If we ask what type of political *system* constrains and limits a policy of self-assertion abroad, because the enunciation of such a course encounters well-entrenched domestic opposition or runs afoul of

pp. 102–103. On Nasser's pan-Arab nationalism see Jean Vigneau, "The Ideology of the Egyptian Revolution," in *ibid.,* pp. 136–38.
[7] Quoted in R. Emerson, "Paradoxes of Asian Nationalism," *Far Eastern Quarterly,* Vol. 13, No. 2 (February 1954), p. 132.
[8] Morton A. Kaplan, *The Communist Coup in Czechoslovakia,* Princeton: (Center of International Studies January 1960).

domestic weakness and disorganization, we come across a number of types which cannot be revolutionary in our sense. To use the typology of Edward Shils, political democracies, traditional and traditionalistic oligarchies do not fit;[9] modernizing oligarchies may, and totalitarian oligarchies, as well as tutelary democracies, most certainly do. The picture becomes clearer if we ask what type of domestic policy requires a foreign policy of self-assertion; or, under what circumstances a domestic policy aiming at the creation of a new society becomes revolutionary in the outside world as well? Put in these terms, we arrive at two varieties of revolutionary regimes, without having to commit ourselves to a specific typology of systems.

A revolutionary elite which is committed to a doctrine of historical struggle represents the first variety. It includes, of course, the major countries of the Communist bloc. The foreign policies of China and the Soviet Union may be interpreted merely as the international application of the inevitable rise to power of the proletariat through the establishment of Socialism and eventually Communism, first in certain countries and finally everywhere. While this implies neither commitment to the notion that war is inevitable, nor to the proposition that all Soviet-bloc moves are part of a "Communist conspiracy," it does locate the Communist bloc within a revolutionary syndrome based on class struggle. In it, the security and survival of Communist states is the minimal, but only the minimal, motive of a foreign policy organizationally and doctrinally linked to drastic domestic change. In the mind of Fidel Castro, this class struggle is "nationalized" in the sense that underdeveloped countries living at the mercy of monopoly imperialism become the equivalent of the proletariat. The international class struggle now is identical with the struggle for freedom and progress on the part of all underdeveloped countries.[10] Agrarian reform in Cuba, for example, is held out as an internationally valid example of inevitable revolutionary transformation. It is hardly surprising, therefore, that Cuba had identified herself publicly with Egypt, Guinea, and Ghana.

Africa, however, offers a different example of thinking along lines of an international revolutionary struggle. As our examples of pan-African doctrines have shown, the creation of the African Personality ranks high among the goals of the revolutionary leaders. Class is here replaced by race. The fight against the racism of the imperialists includes the new self-assertion of "the African," suspicious, if not impatient, of all white institutions and practices. The salvation of Africa becomes the redemption of the black man, with the practical international consequence of giving a reverse racist character to the foreign policy of Ghana and Guinea. To sum up: the Soviet Union, Cuba, Ghana, and Guinea represent a variety of revolutionary leadership in which international policy follows from a "historical strug-

[9] As cited in G. A. Almond and J. S. Coleman (eds.), *The Politics of the Developing Areas* (Princeton: Princeton University Press, 1960), pp. 52–55.
[10] For Castro's views see the revealing marathon speech delivered to the United Nations General Assembly, September 26, 1960. A similar doctrine was developed as early as 1918 by Sultan Galiev. See A. Bennigsen, "Sultan Galiev," in Laqueur, *op. cit.,* pp. 398 ff. Peronista nationalism and policy often used the same arguments and conformed to similar social pressures. See John J. Johnson, *Political Change in Latin America* (Stanford: Stanford University Press, 1958), Chap. 6.

gle" doctrine which is initially and predominantly applied to the domestic plans of these nations.

No similar central theme is present in the variety of revolutionary leadership displayed by contemporary Indonesia, Egypt, Bolivia, and perhaps Iraq or Morocco. To be sure, the internal reformist emphasis is present here too, but it is by no means simply or dialectically translated into foreign policy. Instead, the linkage occurs through the strains and tensions set up by the dissociation between modernizing and traditional political structures and policies, by the vagaries of the so-called non-Western political process. At the simplest level of explanation, self-assertion and even aggressive attitudes on foreign policy are related to the familiar scapegoat, or displacement, device.

When the *raison d'être* of nationalism—the attainment of political independence—has no longer existed, leaders have endeavored in various ways to perpetuate nationalism as an active and unifying force: by demanding a positive role for their new state in world affairs, by creating new external enemies or threats, and by dramatizing the vision of a new society through monumental public works and other such symbols.[11]

Opposition groups have found it easiest to challenge authoritarian-reformist governments by merging their specific grievances with a global appeal for drastic external and internal change, a challenge the government leaders then tend to take up by making equally sweeping demands.

But aggressive foreign policy attitudes in these countries may well serve a more fundamental functional role than scapegoating. The achievement of independence often causes rifts in the national movement. In Indonesia, segments of the urbanized Indonesian bourgeoisie, in alliance with segments of the nobility, had no interest in turning the political revolution into a social upheaval. Hence, they try to divert the continuing revolutionary fervor into external channels, whether directed at the Chinese or the Europeans. At the same time, as rural discontent grows and the demand for further socio-economic reform continues, the fight for change is seen by rural leaders as a continuation of the struggle for political freedom, especially if the obvious "monopolist-imperialist" targets are also foreign corporations, aid-missions, plantation owners, and the like. The struggle for industrialization thus acquires a xenophobic quality despite, or perhaps because of, its dependence on the foreigner. No wonder that the Indonesian Army was able to use the West Irian issue as a device to channel and direct mass discontent in the direction of seizing control over Dutch property.[12] In addition, xenophobic nationalism has the functional role of

[11] James S. Coleman, in Almond and Coleman, *op. cit.,* p. 554. See the similar points made by Lucian W. Pye, "The Non-Western Political Process," *The Journal of Politics,* Vol. 29 (1958), pp. 473, 480. For the identification of such tensions in an African setting involving the danger of disintegration on the part of a pyramidal social structure, merging notions of legitimacy, kinship, religion, land ownership, and chieftaincy (Ashanti), see David E. Apter, "The Role of Traditionalism in the Political Modernization of Ghana and Uganda," *World Politics,* Vol. 13, No. 1 (October 1960).

[12] This thesis is developed by W. F. Wertheim, *Indonesian Society in Transition* (The Hague: W. Van Hoeve, 1959), pp. 327–34.

taking the place of traditional religion. It is suggestive that in Indonesia the Panja Sila are often put forward as a secular-universal reformist creed and that Indonesians tend to invoke the hallowed principles of Bandung far more frequently as an international doctrine than do other Asian nations.[13] Much the same applies in contemporary Bolivia, in which the dispossessed urban middle class and the ascendant Indian peasantry vie with each other in aggressive anti-American sentiments, with the Indians seeking to maximize an only partly successful economic upheaval and the middle class anxious to undo it.

Nor is scapegoating a complete explanation of Nasser's self-assertive foreign policy. The policy is clearly revolutionary since it claims a "civilizing mission" for Egypt in Black Africa and is committed to pan-Arabism. It is linked to domestic reform in Nasser's explicit recognition that the social and the political revolutions are proceeding simultaneously and that it is the duty of the Army to advance both.[14] But it appears that this doctrinal commitment was put to the test of policy in 1955, when the domestic revolution ran into difficulties. It then acquired substance in what appears as a self-conscious effort to divert public attention from domestic failure. But it is also true that the turn to foreign adventure coincided with restlessness in the Army, with the ambitious Aswan Dam project and with the announcement, in 1957, of the plan to create a "socialist, democratic and cooperative society, free from political, social and economic exploitation." [15] A reinvigoration of the program to remake Egyptian society under the tutelary auspices of the National Union and the Army would imply an intensification of the tensions common to non-Western contexts. A glorious role in international affairs would thus serve the same function as in Indonesia.

To sum up again: Certain revolutionary regimes are compelled by the tension and crisis-ridden nature of their internal reform programs, suffering from the hiatus between modernizing and traditional political processes, to turn to foreign poses of self-assertion. The changes they thus come to demand in the international scene are every bit as revolutionary as their domestic aims, and often dovetail neatly with those advanced by revolutionary regimes impelled by doctrines of class and race.

So far we have concerned ourselves only with the substance of policy pursued by revolutionary regimes. But shoe-thumping, name-calling, unbearably long harangues by bearded heroes dressed in green fatigues, uncompromising language, appeals to some universal brotherhood—whether of the black, the downtrodden, or the victims of various conspiracies, are aspects of style rather than of policy. Because of the danger of confusing substance with style, and the possibility that unconventionality of style is not necessarily and always perfectly correlated with an inherently ag-

---

[13] See Guy J. Pauker, "Indonesian Images of their National Self," Rand Corporation Report No. P-1452-RC (August 1, 1958).

[14] Gamal Abdul Nasser, Egypt's Liberation: The Philosophy of the Revolution (Washington, D.C.: Public Affairs Press, 1955), pp. 43–44, 69–71, 84–85, 110–14. Anwar El. Sadat, Revolt on the Nile (London: Wingate, 1957). And especially, Morroe Berger, Military Elite and Social Change: Egypt since Napoleon (Princeton: Center of International Studies, February 1, 1960).

[15] Keith Wheelock, Nasser's New Egypt (New York: Praeger, 1960), pp. 51, 69–70, 134.

gressive policy, an effort will now be made to isolate certain recurring stylistic aspects in the international behavior of revolutionary regimes.

It is a commonplace that the more rationally oriented among revolutionary regimes, that is, Communist regimes, rigorously subordinate means to the achievement of postulated ends. Hence, conventional and perverse styles of behavior alternate freely, depending on the immediate definition of ends. In the case of Fascist regimes the case is otherwise. Here the means themselves reflect certain end values, such as the glorification of violence. Hence, their international style is less flexible than the Communists' and more consistently at odds with the canons of "bourgeois" diplomacy. All revolutionary regimes share an affinity for "dual" diplomacy: the simultaneous conduct of their foreign policy through the medium of conventional channels, with their rules and decorum, and through various non-official channels. The search for allies among "the people," "the peace partisans," or "the freedom fighters" among the citizens of enemy states leads to the widespread use of revolutionary political parties and movements, front organizations, and other "progressive" elements as carriers of the revolutionary regime's policy. Since these non-official allies can be mobilized and disbanded at will, can be made to dovetail with conventional gambits, or can be deemphasized completely, they are aspects of revolutionary style rather than inherent attributes of doctrine or policy.[16]

Revolutionary style thrives on apocalyptic language, immoderate threats, and manufactured international crises. But it would be a mistake to dismiss these manifestations as evidences of infantilism or of irresponsibility. Like the practice of scapegoating, such techniques may well possess a functional role in the political processes of non-Western countries. The scarcity of stable, representative, and functionally specific interest groups and of well-organized political parties aggregating their demands, results in national policies being divorced from any sort of structured upward flow of communication. National leaders tend to act in isolation from popular concerns simply because they do not always know what important segments of the public may wish, and consequently feel compelled to appeal in vague and total terms to an undifferentiated public. At the same time, the very absence of specific policy impulses from below enables the leadership to take more clearly defined positions in the international than in the domestic field. To the extent that such positions, couched in the most undiplomatic terms of a Nasser, a Sukarno, and a Castro, reflect an apocalyptic vision, they may be aimed at unifying their own divided societies while staking out a claim for it in the United Nations.[17]

Immoderate style tends to carry with it an impatience for traditional, legal, as well as diplomatic, techniques. Modes of dealing with international conflict by

[16] This judgment is not accepted by all observers. Michael Lindsay, for example, found that the Chinese Communists see no contradiction in professed allegiance to the *Panch Shila* and the simultaneous commitment to intervention in other countries through the medium of national liberation movements. If Lindsay is correct, the dualistic commitment is not a matter of style, but of doctrine. See his "China and Her Neighbors," in *The Challenge of Communist China*, (Proceedings of a Conference held at the University of Minnesota, April 4 and 5, 1960), pp. 21–22.
[17] This point is developed in detail in Pye, *op. cit.,* pp. 480, 482, 484, and in Almond and Coleman, *op. cit.,* p. 150 ff.

peaceful means frequently imply the open or tacit acceptance of certain principles of law. Revolutionary leaders are always impelled, at least initially, to deny the legitimacy of aspects of international law, in the evolution of which they had no part but which hinder their aims. The practical reasons for this attitude are obvious. It may be suggested, however, that the very qualities of charismatic leadership which are a recurring feature in revolutionary regimes are connected with this impatience. In many non-Western countries the advent of the urban-industrial society implies the erosion of the uprooted villager's reliance on the rural *patrón,* or the tribal chief. In the unfamiliar urban environment he turns to a demagogic national leader as a substitute, identifies with him, relies on him, supports him unthinkingly.[18] The leader, thus supported, feels free to indulge his freedom of maneuver so as to make claims upon and embarrass foreign countries, and to indulge his charismatic role by denying the validity of international law and diplomatic protocol.

Clearly, the nationalism of revolutionary countries is always integral in character. It brooks no qualifications, no nuances, and no considerations which would destroy the image, however unreal upon inspection, of an organically unified people yearning for "justice." Integral nationalism is as much a part of the revolutionary international style as neutralism is a minimal foreign policy attitude. Certainly, as Robert A. Scalapino has demonstrated, a rational basis for neutralism can be found in the realities of contemporary world politics; there is no doubt that it also represents a curious mixture of ambivalence, distrust, and disinterested tolerance for the competing Western doctrines of Marxism and Liberal Democracy.[19] But a neutralist pose also serves the functional role of confident self-assertion for the impatient and emergent charismatic leader in legitimating his own arrival upon the world scene and effectively juxtaposing himself to the "vested interests"—barricaded behind power politics and traditional international law—of the older successful nations.[20] The new regimes, whether in Africa, Latin America, or Asia, represent the advent to power of social groupings not conspicuously successful in terms of wealth and prestige as long as the countries in question were under Western rule or influence. There is no reason now to expect the new classes to display any great respect or affection for Western policy or its international tradition. The very eclecticism offered by a neutralist pose is a much more convincing way of demonstrating self-confidence.

[18] In the case of Brazil, this relationship is developed with respect to Vargas by Charles Wagley, in *Social Change in Latin America Today, op. cit.,* p. 220 ff. A similar point is made by David Apter in his *The Gold Coast in Transition.*

[19] Robert A. Scalapino, " 'Neutralism' in Asia," *American Political Science Review,* Vol. 68, No. 1 (March 1954).

[20] On this point, the particular form of "active neutralism" sponsored by Egypt should be kept in mind. As distinguished from the Indian prototype, this attitude frankly equates the advancing of pan-Arab interests with the organization of a neutralist bloc which would maneuver permanently between the two military camps and thereby compel them to inaction, without expecting necessarily to dismantle them or to eliminate the Cold War, though this eventuality would be welcomed. Since the United States has the reputation of opposing pan-Arab aims, with the Soviet Union at least neutral on this point, "active neutralism" in practice is bound to work itself out in a pro-Soviet direction. For Egyptian thought on this subject see the literature analyzed by Leonard Binder, "Nasserism: The Protest Movement in the Middle East," in this symposium.

Having thus pinpointed the characteristics of revolutionary regimes, in domestic politics, in substantive foreign policy, and in international style, we must put this force into the context of institutionalized world politics—the United Nations. And we must ask ourselves whether the success and multiplication of such regimes makes doubtful the survival of the kind of international system represented by it.

II

In assessing the responsiveness of revolutionary leaders to influences emanating from the international scene, we must posit the characteristics of the central international institution, the United Nations. In doing this, care must be taken to avoid the analytical extremes of assuming a completely structured and fully deterministic UN "system" or of complete freedom of the will for national actors to fashion a cooperative international commonwealth. Abstraction from reality is certainly a necessity, but the system we abstract must remain faithful to what we know to be true in the conduct of the actors. Hence, the recurring patterns and the structured relationships of UN life must be thrown into relief without reification, without sinning on the side of determinism to the extent of not being able to accommodate the organizational evolution, which is not "instability," we know to have taken place. The "system" must permit the "free will" of the national actors to impinge on the totality of relations while retaining the necessarily deterministic properties of any system.

Hence, the category called the "loose bipolar system," made popular by Morton Kaplan, cannot be used as our point of reference. We sacrifice aesthetic neatness by not using this type of system and no claim for an equally cleanly structured approach can be advanced.[21] The desire to remain close to the data saddles us with a more ragged scheme which does not assume as regularly applicable to the UN the systemic rules abstracted by Kaplan. Furthermore, the kind of "systems" approach, here used deliberately, avoids the unnecessary and misleading "balance" and "structure" hypotheses offered by some social psychologists.[22]

But it is equally easy to sin on the side of free will. Some of the ablest commentators on the UN interpret the world organization as an attempt at international institutionalization of Western parliamentary deliberation based "upon the conviction of the reality of freedom of man in the social universe." [23] International organizations are held to fall squarely into the liberal-thought pattern, in the sense that they presuppose sufficient freedom of the will for statesmen to alter the international

[21] Morton A. Kaplan, *System and Process in International Politics* (New York: John Wiley and Sons, 1957), pp. 36–43, 56–64, 83–85, 117–20.

[22] For an example of a nonsensical systems approach to international relations, derived in simplistic fashion from Freudian theory, see Frank Harary, "A Structural Analysis of the Situation in the Middle East in 1956," *Journal of Conflict Resolution,* Vol. 5, No. 2 (June 1961).

[23] Inis L. Claude, *Swords Into Plowshares,* 2nd ed. (New York: Random House, 1959), p. 15. This work is the most incisive in treating the United Nations from this vantage point, as well as the most judicious.

environment by means of rational discussion, negotiation, and voting. Since the institutions of most of the founding states are held to conform to this view of things, the UN could be expected to reflect these influences and thereby gradually "civilize" international politics, if not reform the national political processes of new states. Gradually, a concept of "universal public interest" will come to inform UN deliberations.[24] It is unfortunate for this approach that we already possess convincing evidence from the mouths of Western statesmen that the UN has come under the anti-parliamentary influences of the non-Western world, as the membership has grown more universal; the changing environment has influenced the system more than the liberal school is able to concede and it makes little sense to speak of the UN as a "Western system." [25] A universal public interest could be demonstrated only if members of the UN consistently practiced the kind of "wise statesmanship" which Arnold Wolfers advocated in his reconciliation between determinism and free will, his prescription for following the minimal national interest of self-preservation in such a way as to retain a maximum fidelity to universal values.[26] In the absence of such a demonstration, recourse to the liberal yardstick would saddle us with an approach too hortatory and too effervescent to yield more than disappointment.

Comparative historical-sociological analysis, as in Stanley Hoffmann's study of the Concert of Europe, the League of Nations, and the United Nations comes close to an appropriate system. Assessments are made on the basis of typologies of conflict situations correlated with the characteristics of the states which were prominent participants. And the conclusion:

> With respect to relations among the big powers, the record of the three organizations is this: when solidarity existed the organizations were unnecessary. When it did not exist, they were powerless. The remedy cannot be found in the formal association of these states, whose nature makes a real association impossible. In relations among the great powers, decisive for the maintenance of world peace, international organizations stand exposed to perpetual defeat.[27]

Although Hoffmann grants that in disputes among a minor power not allied with a great power, the methods of collective security have worked and, although he

[24] This idea is developed in some detail by Arthur N. Holcombe, "The United Nations and American Foreign Policy," University of Illinois *Bulletin* (October 1957). See also the reports of the Commission to Study the Organization of Peace for specific proposals for strengthening the UN in line with this conceptual commitment.

[25] See the blunt statement on this score by P. H. Spaak, "The Experiment of Collective Security," Carnegie Endowment for International Peace, *Perspectives on Peace, 1910–1960* (New York: Praeger, 1960), p. 85. Further evidence for increasing disappointment with the liberal-parliamentary aspect of the UN can be found in the Carnegie Endowment's series *National Studies on International Organization*, notably the volumes on Belgium, Australia, Canada, Sweden, and Britain. George Modelski treats the UN as a "western universal system" in *The Communist International System* (Princeton: Center of International Studies, December 1, 1960).

[26] Arnold Wolfers and Laurence Martin (eds.), *The Anglo-American Tradition in Foreign Affairs* (New Haven: Yale University Press, 1956), pp. xxvi–xxvii.

[27] Stanley Hoffmann, *Organisations Internationales et Pouvoirs Politiques des Etats* (Paris: Armand Colin, 1954), p. 412.

credits the League with advancing a concept of international legitimacy in compelling discussion of national aggressive designs, no fundamental change in international relations should be attributed to these trends. My own interpretation of history differs in that it does not assume the category of "great power" to possess the same implications at all times. Put another way, the application of trend analysis to international *systems* requires equal, if not more, attention to the various *environments* in which they operate. Patterned relationships between demands and policies in international systems compel attention to the source of the demands. These remain rooted in the national aims of member states, but, as the advent of revolutionary regimes makes plain, these aims constantly change to produce a variety of environments. Hence, historical conclusions making no allowance for shifting environmental influences are not convincing.

Therefore, the United Nations must be described as a multi-phase system, whose characteristics and evolutionary potential must be specified in terms of the changing environment in which it operates. Environments, in turn, are made up of the totality of policies, aims, expectations, fears, hopes, and hatreds funneled into the institutional structure and its political processes, the "system" proper. If the policies of the United Nations can be demonstrated to change the environment, including the part contributed by the revolutionary regimes, perhaps systemic growth at the expense of the member units can be established. It is important here to distinguish between a "static" system and a "dynamic" one. In a static system the actors channel policies and demands through it and use it as a medium of communication as well as a forum for resolving some conflicts, but they do not necessarily increase the powers and functions of the system in so doing. No growth then takes place. In a dynamic setting, however, some of these efforts carry with them an accretion of new functions and powers for the system, implying the kind of growth we wish to examine in connection with the demands provided by revolutionary regimes.[28]

The variety of demands contributed by member states can be easily grouped along the recurrent lines of discussion which prevail in the UN. They entail (1) collective security, including both enforcement and pacific settlement functions; (2) peaceful change, including the substantive aspects of such areas as the dissolution of colonial empires and disarmament, and the procedural concern with perfecting mediatory and arbitral methods; (3) economic development, technical assistance, and world economic policy; (4) the definition and implementation of human rights. General, as well as highly specific, issues arise in each meeting of UN bodies under each of these headings. But the manner of resolving the issues differs in each phase of the UN system and no issue has so far ever been settled in principle and in perpetuity.

Why is this the case? Formal as well as informal resolutions of issues always take place on the basis of bloc politics; member states never yield a position in its entirety and usually compromise their differences—at various levels of meaningfulness—by a mixture of negotiation and voting. But issues are rarely discussed with sole reference to the category in which a functionally specific analysis would place them.

[28] For the distinction between static and dynamic systems see Kenneth E. Boulding, "Organization and Conflict," *Journal of Conflict Resolution*, Vol. 1 (1957), pp. 122–23.

Foreign policy being a web of interlocking aims, the totality of state objectives is fed into the UN system, resulting in a pattern of decisions featuring inter-functional as well as inter-bloc compromise. The character of the environment seems to determine the nature of this compromise, and the environment is unstable with reference to the predominance of this or that aim. A further environmental instability is introduced by the enlargement of the membership and the resultant quantitative change in the relations among the blocs.

During the first phase of the UN system (1945–47), the honeymoon period among the great powers prevented these strains from impinging on one another. Collective security was the dominant concern and it hinged around skirmishing in the Security Council, and at times it looked as if the Churchillian notion of the postwar status quo might achieve institutionalization by virtue of the UN. But the real onset of the Cold War proved this suspicion wrong, and by 1948 the second phase of the system got under way, characterized by the dominance of the United States and its successful enlisting of the UN on its behalf.

During the second phase, the dominant *motif* was the identification of collective security with the military-political aims of the Western bloc, successfully asserted in Korea and in the Uniting for Peace Resolution. Demands for a world economic policy and far more ambitious economic-aid measures than actively championed by the West were put forward by Afro-Asian and Latin American states but were not implemented in full. Discussion of human rights was initiated and championed by the West so long as it fitted in with Cold-War policy, though non-Western blocs advanced demands in this area for quite different reasons. Peaceful change was demanded in a variety of anti-colonial claims but found implementation only in the case of the former Italian colonies. While the Soviet bloc placed itself in a non-bargaining position by completely disputing the legitimacy of all UN discussion and steps not in line with Soviet policy, the Western bloc dominated the system by successfully obtaining the support of the Latin American and part of the Afro-Asian blocs on collective security issues and "paying" for this by occasional concessions in the economic and colonial fields.

By 1954 the second phase came to its end with important changes in the environment. The number of Afro-Asian members increased, especially after 1955. The European members of the Western bloc grew disenchanted with a policy of collective security which seemed too close to general warfare. The colonial and human-rights issues were linked ever more closely in the demands of the Latin American and Afro-Asian blocs, and the crescendo of economic demands rose as the American security policy grew more and more dependent on general support. And most importantly, Joseph Stalin died. With his demise the role of the Soviet Union in international organizations underwent such an important—if tactical—change as to destroy the environment of the second phase.

Since that time, the third phase has prevailed, involving institutionalized inter-regional and inter-functional bargaining in a setting in which the colonial and human-rights issues have furnished the dominant *motif,* and the practice of collective security has been increasingly subordinated to it in terms of the kind of support forthcoming for Western-bloc demands. Peaceful change, of sorts, has prevailed along with intensified international economic development efforts, in the relatively amicable way in which colonial empires have dissolved under UN prodding. Neutralism has come into its own, quantitatively, and the "balancing" pattern of collective security holds sway, featuring conciliation rather than enforcement.

Shortly, however, a fourth phase will arise. Functionally, it will be marked by the end of the colonial issue as a dominant theme. The human-rights issue well may be eliminated from the demands of the very Afro-Asian and Latin American states which have featured it in connection with their anti-colonial campaign and may reacquire value for Western nations freed from a variety of skeletons in their closets. Economic demands will increase, and collective security aims by the West will have to be paid for exclusively in this area now. Further, if the alliance between the Soviet and certain underdeveloped nations continues, the Soviet bloc may funnel its particular variety of collective security into the UN, and may be expected to pay for it in economic aid. Whatever the precise outline of the pattern of inter-functional and inter-bloc politics may be, a behavior pattern discerned for the revolutionary regimes during the second and third phases cannot a priori be expected to continue with the sharp change in the environment introduced by the end of colonialism.

The UN system is hyperdependent on its environment. Precedents set in one phase, therefore, do not necessarily predetermine action in the next. Unless a great deal of "internalization" of "rules" can be demonstrated, the very multiphase character of the system militates against substantial growth. All issues are resolved ad hoc, stable alliances among interests cannot develop, compromises and related communication patterns among participants can generate no fixed institutional characteristics. Even the "non-resolution consequences" of UN activity display no cumulative pattern. [29] Substituting debate and voting for fighting, in the sense of using the UN as a litmus paper for determining the strength of the opponent, wanes with the change in functional preoccupation. While communication among members may narrow differences in the perception of reality, in one phase, the process may have to start all over in the next. There is evidence that the United States has "learned" the lesson of Korea in no longer expecting the kind of collective-security operation which it mounted in 1950 and is now seeking security through balancing; but there is less evidence that Nasser and Nkrumah have learned the same thing.[30]

How can we assess the impact of a multi-phase system on its environment? Granting the variation in demands and the changes in the political process which convert them into United Nations policy, how do we relate the policy pattern to the environment to determine whether the United Nations is having any kind of influence? One way of assessing the impact is merely to study the behavior pattern of the member states, specifically the revolutionary states. Do they respond to UN resolutions? To what kind of resolutions, in what functional contexts? In other

[29] Chadwick F. Alger, "Non-Resolution Consequences of the United Nations and Their Effect on International Conflict," ibid., Vol. 5, No. 2 (June 1961).
[30] For such evidence see Arnold Wolfers (ed.), Alliance Policy in the Cold War (Baltimore: Johns Hopkins Press, 1959).

words, does the *authority* of the UN system increase as determined by the fidelity of its revolutionary members in carrying out resolutions? Does the *legitimacy* of the system increase as revolutionary states invoke the Charter and past resolutions to link these with an increase in the institutional power and autonomy of the organization?

Another way of obtaining answers is to study the system itself rather than the effects on the conduct of its members. Here it would be tempting to profit from general-organization theory, if this discipline were not so dependent on hierarchical models with firm boundaries and predisposed toward identifying rationality with functionally oriented behavior. In terms of such standards the UN system is not an "organization" at all. "The prevalence of bargaining," say March and Simon, "is a symptom *either* that goals are not operational or that they are not shared." [31] In the case of UN decision-making, they are neither one nor the other; operational goals are not rationally contrasted in policy making, there is no hierarchy, and problem solving does not predominate as a technique of deciding issues. This has been true in all phases of the system, which would come close to being identified as almost entirely dysfunctional in its behavior. Yet the system has survived, and if membership, finance, and scope of operations are the yardsticks of evaluation, even prospered. Hence, formal-organization theory is unlikely to yield answers to our question.

In fact, it must be stressed that in a different focus the UN is a successful, if phase-ridden and politics-dominated, international institution. It has served to channel aspects of national foreign policy never before submitted to any collective scrutiny. It has tamed and civilized national policies by serving as an approximation to an institutionalized process of interest politics, and thereby containing the interests. If the Western political process be conceived, not as dispassionate debate, capped by voting and subject to judicial review, but as the articulate defense of rival group interests in permanent confrontation and subject to cumulative compromises, the UN process is not so very different. The study of policies during the various phases of the system could thus become a study of the methods used to achieve various types of compromises. Systemic development or growth could be evaluated by the role of the organization itself, as distinguished from components contributed by the environment, in advancing compromises.

We already possess a good deal of evidence permitting such evaluations for the period 1945–55.[32] It permits the conclusion that the system did *not* increase the *legitimacy* it enjoys in the eyes of its members. Demands for UN action and invocation of its Charter were *not* accompanied by cumulative claims for a greater autonomous institutional role for the system. This was true for revolutionary as well as non-revolutionary states. However, the *authority* of the system *did* increase for all types of member states, in the sense that many of them increasingly heeded resolu-

[31] James G. March and Herbert A. Simon, *Organizations* (New York: John Wiley and Sons, 1958), p. 196 (italics in original).
[32] See the seven-volume study of the Brookings Institution, published between 1956 and 1958, as well as the twenty-odd volumes which make up the study of the Carnegie Endowment for International Peace, previously cited.

tions and decisions addressed to them.[33] In fact, authority tended to increase as many of the member states grew more and more dissatisfied with the style of debate and the quality of the decisions. Growing dissatisfaction, then, did not engender loss of authority. Whether a similar picture obtains more in recent years and whether it will be true in the next phase of the UN's life remains to be investigated.

Clearly, then, an effort must be made to assess changes produced on the environment, as reflected in the policies and attitudes of member states. But an effort must also be made to specify possible systemic changes after 1955; and the attitudes of revolutionary states with reference to accretions of autonomous UN powers is here a particularly sensitive yardstick.

Relationships developed in resolving conflicts peacefully also furnish a useful index at the level of the system itself. They may hinge around the degree to which member states have internalized the purposes and procedures used to resolve one conflict, and are then prepared to apply them to new ones. Since this would vary with the importance attached to the conflict, with the satisfaction derived from the solution, the adequacy of the attendant communications network and the number of roles served by the relationship, different patterns most likely can be found during various phases. An overall increase in involvement, irrespective of phase and type of state involved would provide excellent evidence of systemic growth.[34] But Robert North, the author of this approach, also cautions that the extent to which a member state relies on the notion of the external and internal "enemy" to resolve or channel domestic conflict, is likely to determine his responsiveness to the international modes of resolving conflicts. Dependence on "enemies" is a typical feature of revolutionary regimes; but would this imply declining responsiveness to the peaceful solution of conflicts in the next phase of the UN's life? It should be remembered that the history of the League of Nations and of the nineteenth-century Concert of Europe indicates that revolutionary regimes are insensitive to the pressures of the international environment in their preoccupation with domestic change. In contrast to conservative and status-quo oriented regimes, external regulative mechanisms were not accepted in the value systems of revolutionary elites and therefore had to be imposed by the use or the threat of force.

Dag Hammerskjold once described the UN as an "institutional system of coexistence" which might evolve toward a federative social system with its own public law if it is entrusted with new tasks which it alone can carry out, and if new environmental challenges are met by growing autonomy and delegated power, including the revitalization of portions of the Charter which have not yet been used.[35] One way of testing the evolutionary strength of the UN is to apply these yardsticks of development to the portion of the environment contributed by revolutionary

[33] This argument is developed in detail in E. B. Haas, "The Comparative Study of the United Nations," World Politics, Vol. 12, No. 2 (January 1960).

[34] Robert G. North, Howard E. Koch, Jr., and Dina A. Zinnes, "The Integrative Functions of Conflict," Journal of Conflict Resolution, Vol. 4, No. 3 (September 1960), p. 366.

[35] Dag Hammerskjold, "Towards a Constitutional Order," in Perspectives on Peace, op. cit., pp. 66–75.

regimes. If they prove responsive to the system's stimulus, growth is likely. The
alternatives might be stated thus:

1. Successful institutionalization of interest politics will enhance the authority
of the UN system and transform the environment by toning down the international
aspects of the revolutionary behavior of certain member states. A growth in legitimacy would also follow.

2. The growing number and extreme demands of revolutionary member states
will substantially change the system during its next phase and perhaps destroy it.

3. New functional relationships will have the result of transforming the environment in toning down aspects of revolutionary behavior without concurrently contributing to the authority and legitimacy of the system itself.

III

Revolutionary states were exposed to the influence of international organization
since 1919. If the revolutionary state simply withdraws from the system when
national aims are in danger of being blunted by its rule, the problem of the system's
transforming the environment can be simply dismissed. This, indeed, is what occurred in the League of Nations in relation to Japan, Italy, and Germany. Each
pursued aims inconsistent with the rules of the system, and upon being stigmatized
—however ineffectually—simply pursued the same aims outside the system. Withdrawal barely caused any soul-searching; the ideology and style of the revolutionary
leadership in question was inconsistent with "international cooperation" in any case
because of its insistence on national strength and self-sufficiency. The League's impact
on the revolutionary environment was nil.

The same is true of the Soviet Union even though its role in the League was
far more complex. Dallin interprets the Soviet role in Geneva as a species of popular
front diplomacy designed to dovetail with the concomitant anti-Fascist work of the
Comintern and aimed at maximizing Soviet security. While it certainly involved
no doctrinal commitment to the rules of the Covenant, Soviet participation had
the incidental consequence of seeking to strengthen the universal system. Not only
did Moscow carry out the sanctions voted against Italy and Paraguay, but it actually
sought to strengthen the legal powers of the League in the field of enforcement.[36]
When contrasted with the earlier sweeping Russian denunciations of the League as
"an alliance of world bandits against the proletariat," the Soviets then, as now,
seemed to demonstrate a fine appreciation of systemic possibilities in *one* set of
environmental circumstances. But the events of 1939 demonstrate that no internalization of rules was involved.

[36] Alexander Dallin, *The Soviet View of the United Nations* (Cambridge: MIT Center for
International Studies, August 1959), pp. 10–12, 18–19. Elliott Goodman, *The Soviet Design for
a World State* (New York: Columbia University Press, 1960), pp. 383–85. Kathryn Davis, *The
Soviets at Geneva* (Geneva: Librairie Kundig, 1934), p. 21.

Since 1945 the international environment has undergone such drastic changes that a more functionally complex analysis is required to do it justice. The field of collective security will be examined first as a source of revolutionary initiatives, including the enforcement as well as the pacific settlement aspects.

Neutralism, not a specific revolutionary content, is responsible for the policy expectations regarding collective security put forth by Indonesia, Egypt, and Ghana. The monarchist regime in Egypt entertained great expectations of UN mediatory and armed help in its struggles with Britain and Israel, until it realized that the great-power balance in the Security Council would give its policy little solace. At that point it turned to neutralism even before the advent of the Nasser regime and denounced UN collective security as "unjust power politics." [37] Whenever the East-West conflict dominates, these regimes seek to conciliate Moscow and Washington, and failing in this, abstain from endorsing any kind of collective action. Indonesia and Egypt gave no assistance to UN forces in Korea, opposed the crossing of the 38th parallel, and abstained on votes concerned with alleged atrocities by UN forces in Korea. Both abstained in the vote on the Assembly's critical report on Hungary, even though Indonesia had supported the creation of the Special Commission on Hungary. "The problem we have to solve here now," said the Indonesian delegate, "is how to diminish and if possible how to dissipate the distrust that exists among the opposing parties." But Indonesia was active in persuading Syria and Turkey not to press their differences to a vote in the Assembly in 1957. In Cold-War disputes, collective security implies exclusive dedication to conciliation by uncommitted powers and abstinence from any enforcement or investigatory action which would favor one side or the other. In disputes involving the colonial issue, however, energetic action is advocated, provided it can be carried out in such a way as to exclude the East-West conflict. The full panoply of UN techniques is then to be thrown into the fray, including troops and neutralization agreements negotiated under the auspices of the General Assembly, as indicated by Ghana's role in the settlement of the Lebanese-Jordanian crisis of 1958. The prejudice against armed action or energetic peaceful settlement, in short, does not apply to the type of dispute which concerns revolutionary nations most intimately.[38]

[37] *Egypt and the United Nations,* Report of a Study Group Set up by the Egyptian Society of International Law (New York: Manhattan Publishing Company, 1957). However, the passage to "active" or "positive" neutralism was an innovation of the military regime. While no doubt produced by the internal needs for status and prestige of Nasser, both in Egypt and in the Arab world, this concept implies an enhanced role for the UN in collective security and in disarmament negotiations as a means to prevent superpower summitry and to institutionalize the balancing role of uncommitted nations. For an explicit argument along these lines see Clovis Maqsud, *The Meaning of Positive Neutrality* (in Arabic) (Beirut: 1960), pp. 128, 135, 137, as quoted in Binder, *op. cit.* Possible relationships between African neutralism and anomic conceptions of authority in new nations are explored by Francis X. Sutton, "Authority and Authoritarianism in the New Africa," *Journal of International Affairs,* Vol. 15, No. 1 (1961).

[38] Jan F. Triska and Howard E. Koch, "The Asian-African Nations and International Organization," *The Review of Politics,* Vol. 21, No. 2 (April 1959), pp. 450–51. Sydney D. Bailey, *The General Assembly* (New York: Praeger, 1960), p. 155. Consulate of Indonesia (San Francisco), *Indonesia's*

Soviet policy in the UN conforms more closely to specifically revolutionary expectations. In the early years of the UN the Soviet regime still regarded the Charter and its rules as legitimating the postwar status quo of big-power dominance, institutionalized through a concert in which each major power wielded a veto and collective security was to be practiced at the expense of smaller powers. Even though the Soviet Union took a very conservative position with respect to the powers of the UN and the absolute sway of the principle of national sovereignty, it relaxed these opinions in practice to permit the peaceful solution of the Corfu Channel and Iranian disputes in such a manner as to strengthen the authority of UN organs. The system seemed to assert itself even over revolutionary members.

This trend was reversed with the announcement in 1948 of the "two camps" doctrine. No concessions to systemic authority were permitted in the Greek, Korean, Berlin, and satellite peace-treaty cases. The UN became a holding operation in which the Soviets sought merely to protect the position of the "Socialist camp" by blocking American action and by propaganda attacks, buttressed with constitutional arguments opposing majority decision-making, functional expansion, and neutrality in administration. But the exceptions are vital: Whenever the interests of the Soviet Union happened to converge with those of the West (as in Palestine, Kashmir, Indonesia), the *ad hoc* concert produced by the international environment resulted in UN mediatory and enforcement action in which the Soviets ignored their own opposition to third-party intercession, commissions of investigation, Secretariat participation, and teams of military observers. But the outbreak of the Korean War proves that this pragmatic attitude of the Soviet Union involved no acceptance of the intrinsic legitimacy of the norms of the Charter.[39]

There are those who insist that the more recent active participation of the post-Stalinist Soviet leadership in the UN marks merely a tactical shift and no change in ultimate objectives: Weakness forced Stalin into an isolationist position toward the universal system, while strength and self-confidence propel Khrushchev into using the UN as a vehicle for actively advancing revolutionary aims.[40] While this may be true, it is not of direct importance to the problem of assessing a systemic impact on the environment; an upgrading of the UN in Soviet policy may bring with it unexpected consequences which must be accepted even by a revolutionary leadership if more basic Soviet aims are to be advanced. In any case, the settlement of the Korean crisis demonstrated for the first time Soviet responsiveness to the balancing efforts of the uncommitted Afro-Asian bloc, to be followed soon by the scrapping of the "two camps" theory. By granting the existence of an uncommitted bloc, a "zone of

---

Voting Record in the United Nations. Kwame Nkrumah, "African Prospect," *Foreign Affairs,* Vol. 37, No. 1 (October 1958), pp. 49–50.

[39] On this period see Alexander W. Rudzinski, "The Influence of the United Nations on Soviet Policy," *International Organization,* Vol. 5, No. 2 (May 1951), and Rupert Emerson and Inis L. Claude, "The Soviet Union and the United Nations," *ibid.,* Vol. 6, No. 1 (February 1952). Subsequent events have done nothing to change the validity of these interpretations.

[40] Especially, Goodman, *op. cit.,* pp. 128–52.

peace" was now interposed between East and West which had to be wooed in non-aggressive ways in order to assure the demise of capitalism without setting off nuclear war. In the process the UN was found useful for the propagation of the doctrine of competitive peaceful coexistence. In instances of outright challenge to the Soviet bloc, as in Hungary, the Stalinist tactics are revived; but in all other situations the new assessment has produced a thoroughly expediential attitude with respect to collective security in which balancing operations, involving conciliation, armed forces recruited from neutrals, and the intercession of the Secretary-General, are tolerated, even if not lauded. Korovin aptly summed up the current attitude with its invocation of the Charter on behalf of the new Soviet world view:

> . . . the constant growth of Soviet economic and defensive might, of the moral authority of the USSR, of the merger of the entire socialist camp on the basis of proletarian internationalism and its growing strength, the support of its international policy by the partisans of peace throughout the world vividly testify to the fact that the realization of the democratic principles of the UN Charter becomes increasingly the unanimous demand of all peaceloving humanity.[41]

It is in this vein that the invocation of UN principles by the revolutionary government of Cuba must be understood. Its appeals to the Security Council and the General Assembly are devices of the Cold War, to equate the policies of the United States with colonialism, and to rally the "democratic principles of the UN Charter" to the side of Socialist and anti-colonial revolt. Although the revolutionary government of Bolivia has supported the Western conception of collective security, the growing link between Havana and Moscow has been accompanied by a Cuban attitude toward collective security which is identical with the Soviet position. The change in the international environment, which was ratified by the package deal on admission to UN membership in 1955, has been a source of self-confidence to the Communist bloc, inducing it to use UN institutions as a means for exacting recognition from the West of the legitimacy of the new status quo. In disputes not immediately invested with the aura of the Cold War, at least this change in the environment has facilitated continuation of balancing as a mode of maintaining collective security, at the expense of concerted big-power action and of permissive enforcement by one of them.

Policy aims in the context of collective security test the capacity of the UN system to deal with violent challenges to its norms. More commonly, however, demands for a change in international relations correspond to national policies falling short of recourse to war. Another test of the system's capacity, then, lies in its ability to facilitate peaceful change, especially the drastic demands put forward by revolutionary member states. Peaceful change, as distinguished from collective security, is any successful adjustment in the international status quo brought about before a specific

---

[41] Quoted in Dallin, op. cit., p. 43. My interpretation owes much to Dallin's analysis of the post-1955 period. Dallin offers convincing evidence that the Soviet leadership made a reasoned decision in 1955 to profit from the tripolarization of power in the UN to upgrade the organization as a vehicle of national policy.

"dispute" involving force or the threat of it arises; this adjustment is always made at the expense of certain reluctant member states and is due to pressure organized through the medium of parliamentary diplomacy.[42] Peaceful change so defined does not imply the complete absence of violence; it merely covers situations in which no formal interstate hostilities take place, but in which the bone of contention does arouse competing state postures.

The contrast between Suez and the Congo provides an example. In the Suez case, previously unsuccessful efforts to change the status quo non-violently (Nasser's unwillingness to satisfy France on Algeria and Britain on the continued neutrality of the Canal) resulted in an act of war, followed by pacific settlement and threatened enforcement measures voted and implemented by the General Assembly, thus restoring the *status quo ante bellum* by means of a balancing operation. The Congo, on the other hand, is an example of "preventive diplomacy," in which the UN, acting through the Secretary-General, sought to anticipate interstate rivalry by insulating the troublespot, and in so doing, "peacefully changing" the bubbling cauldron into a gently seething potion.[43]

This definition of peaceful change corresponds to the actual experience of international organizations and thus conflicts with generally held legal conceptions. It takes for granted that there is no international judicial order which can induce major political change by legal techniques. As Brierly put it:

When a state claims . . . something which is not its legal right, something even which it knows it can have only by an alteration of the legal position, it is useless to suggest that it should submit the determination of its claim to legal decision. It knows beforehand that the answer of the law will be adverse; and that answer is precisely what it claims to have altered.[44]

Nor does it assume the existence of an international legislative order which might give substance to Article 14 of the UN Charter. Legislating territorial change would imply the willingness of the drafters of the Charter to forego the very status quo they wished to institutionalize in writing the norms. Only when the territorial change corresponds to a new generally held consensus, or when it follows from a previous decision by the large powers to wash their hands of an unresolvable issue not vital to them, can the UN successfully perform a legislative task. This happened only in the case of the Italian colonies.[45]

[42] I follow the definition of parliamentary diplomacy invented by Dean Rusk and applied by Philip C. Jessup in "Parliamentary Diplomacy: An Examination of the Legal Quality of the Rules of Procedure of Organs of the United Nations," *Recueil des Cours,* Vol. 89 (Leyden: Académie de Droit International, 1956).

[43] The difference is well developed by Inis L. Claude, "The United Nations and the Use of Force," *International Conciliation,* No. 532 (March 1961), p. 383.

[44] As quoted in Lincoln Bloomfield, "Law, Politics and International Disputes," *ibid.,* No. 516 (January 1958), p. 284.

[45] For interesting information concerning the lack of success of attempted UN legislative change in the peaceful reunification of Korea prior to 1950, see Leon Gordenker, *The United Nations and the Peaceful Unification of Korea* (The Hague: Martinus Nijhoff, 1959). The same conclusion could be drawn from efforts "legislatively" to solve the Palestine issue prior to the outbreak of

So defined, the most conspicuously successful area of peaceful change has been the disengagement of the western powers from colonial responsibilities. The shrinking number of trust territories, the ever more intense examination by the General Assembly of colonial policy in other dependent areas, and the instituting of colonial reform by Britain, France, Holland, the United States, and New Zealand in anticipation of UN criticism are a matter of record. Belgium and Portugal, less responsive in the past to parliamentary diplomacy, are now being subjected to its possibilities. In general, all Afro-Asian, Soviet-bloc and most Latin American countries have made up the UN majorities providing the necessary pressure, whether the regimes were revolutionary or not. Yet it is instructive to single out certain countries and the Congo crisis in order to discover whether anti-colonial demands emanating from revolutionary regimes were exceptionally extreme.

The Soviets have taken the most extreme position in consistently putting forward measures aiming at immediate independence for all dependent territories and blaming the Western powers for failing to cooperate. They have used the debates of the Trusteeship Council for this purpose alone; they justify their acceptance of the principle of trusteeship only because it "contributes to the struggle of the colonial peoples for freedom," and continue to stand "for the revolutionary method of solving the national-colonial question." [46] The African and Asian revolutionary regimes sympathize, as do Cuba and Mexico, but they are willing to tone down specific resolutions on concrete issues to permit gradualist compromises. Nkrumah is candid about his disregard for the legitimacy of the boundaries of UN trust territories when these stand in the way of pan-African aims. He and other revolutionary African leaders only invoke the principles of the Charter in support of specific demands for ejecting European influence but play them down when it comes to future programs. For the coming years they stress sealing off the African continent and creating a regional system of pacific settlement, non-intervention and economic development. [47] In the meantime they argue in favor of strengthening all conceivable agencies of the UN system which might bring closer the day when colonies will cease to exist: the constant use of UN-supervised plebiscites, UN inspections of progress toward independence, more UN follow-up on petitions, strengthening the Committee on Non-Self-Governing Territories, and requiring more and more detailed reports from the

---

hostilities since the resolution recommending partition was never implemented in its official form. But it should be noted that unwillingness to agree to peaceful change is not the exclusive privilege of revolutionary regimes. The Egyptian monarchy initiated the policy of closing the Suez Canal to Israel-bound ships. See Leo Gross, "Passage through the Suez Canal of Israel-Bound Cargo and Israel Ships," *American Journal of International Law*, Vol. 51, No. 3 (July 1957).

[46] B. M. Shurshalov, as quoted in Dallin, *op. cit.*, p. 60.

[47] K. Nkrumah, *Ghana* (New York: Thomas Nelson, 1957), pp. 258 and 261. See also Nkrumah's speech and the final *Declaration* of the Conference of Independent African States, Accra, April 22, 1958, especially Resolutions 1 and 5. All revolutionary regimes sought to influence the plebiscite in British Cameroons so as to result in union with a radical independent Cameroons rather than with a moderate Nigeria. They also favored the attainment of independence by French Cameroons under such conditions as to strengthen the outlawed opposition groups.

colonial powers under Article 73e of the Charter. Interestingly enough, this integrative aspect of the anti-colonial demands is supported by the Soviet Union, which otherwise opposes the creation of new UN institutions. It also has more support from Bolivia, Mexico, and Cuba than from traditional Latin American regimes.

The history of the Congo imbroglio, however, demonstrates the selectivity observed by revolutionary regimes in seeking to obtain satisfaction for national policy through UN action. The extreme of unilateralism is represented by the Soviet bloc. The Communist nations supported UN intervention, as long as such action unambiguously opposed Belgium and seemed to aid Lumumba. Soviet opposition to UN operations, which culminated in the attacks on the person and the institution of the Secretary-General, did not formally arise until the balance had shifted to Kasavubu. But approval of the early UN action had never precluded unilateral Soviet assistance to Congo factions. After the death of Lumumba, Moscow considered the Stanleyville regime of Antoine Gizenga as the only legitimate Congo government, even though the Leopoldville delegation had been seated in New York; drastic action against Belgium, the autonomous Katanga regime, and the Mobutu "mercenaries" were demanded. The failure of the UN to adopt sufficiently stringent resolutions was met by a Soviet refusal to participate in the financing of the Congo Operation. At the end of the fifteenth Session of the General Assembly, the Soviet bloc, alone among the revolutionary regimes, opposed the creation of the second Conciliation Commission, which, unlike the first, was to include European and American representatives; the Soviets also opposed the prompt convening of the Congo Parliament under UN protection and the UN-aided inter-factional negotiations leading to a shoring up of the Kasavubu government.

Of the other revolutionary regimes, only Cuba and Guinea supported the Soviet extreme at all times. But up to March 1961, Ghana, Mali, Indonesia, Morocco, and the United Arab Republic had taken the same qualified position in favor of UN intervention: They went along with it as long at it seemed to serve the pan-African end of creating a united Congo under Lumumbist rule and opposed it when the balance swung to the Kasavubu forces. At that point these leaders withdrew their contingents from the Congo or resigned from the first Conciliation Commission, thus demonstrating their displeasure with the policy of the Secretary-General. The United Arab Republic gave unilateral support to Gizenga, and Ghana openly intrigued against Mobutu.

Second thoughts seemed to arise among these governments when Hammerskjold continued to take an uncompromising position in favor of following a patient policy of supporting whatever regime in the Congo seemed to offer the greatest promise of unifying the country in such a manner as to exclude Cold-War rivalries. Despite its threats, Ghana never withdrew its sizeable forces and the United Arab Republic sought to act as a conciliator (together with Ceylon) in the Security Council debate between the United States and the Soviet Union. As the fifteenth Session drew to its close, all the non-Communist revolutionary regimes went along with the creation of the second Conciliation Commission—which they no longer control—and thus separated themselves publicly from Soviet Congo policy.[48] The peculiar international role played by Guinea, Mali, Ghana, and the United Arab Republic in the deliberations of the UN concerning the Congo and the three Cameroons suggests that the utilization of these potentially integrative techniques remained, at first, rigidly subordinated to the achievement of pan-African goals.[49] But when the dangers of such a course became apparent, they supported the continuation of the UN effort even when hopes for achieving the maximal program had to be abandoned.

Disarmament negotiations exemplify attempts at peacefully changing a serious international irritant which have so far been unsuccessful. Most of the recent substantive negotiations have been carried on outside the UN framework, with General Assembly debate merely creating a "moral climate" and concentrating on procedural aspects. The superpowers themselves have sharply narrowed the areas of difference between them, but this must be attributed to the nature and perception of warfare, rather than to any specific systemic impulse which can be credited to the UN.[50] On the procedural question of whether the Soviet or the Western proposals for various disarmament commissions should be followed, the bulk of the revolutionary states has sided with the Soviet Union or abstained. Bolivia, however, regularly supports the United States; Mexico seeks to mediate, and the Cuban position shifted in 1960 from unswerving support for the West to equally fervid alignment with Moscow. All revolutionary states greeted Khrushchev's general disarmament plan with favor, whereas in previous years they had studiously avoided taking sides on the merits of rival proposals and had merely prodded the superpowers to continue negotiating, though Ghana, Morocco, Mali, and the United Arab Republic moderated their stance by stressing the mediation of uncommitted nations. Again, on the matter of suspending nuclear tests, in general, and preventing the French from going ahead with their plans, in particular, most revolutionary states espoused the extreme disarmament position also taken by the Soviet Union. To the extent that disarmament negotiations are at all influenced by the process of parliamentary diplomacy, the

[48] This summary is based on the debates concerning the following resolutions: S/4369, S/4383, S/4386, S/4404, S/4426, S/4425, S/4453, S/4494, S/4519, S/4523, S/4525, A/L.292/rev 1, A/L.294, A/L.293, A/L.319 Rev 2, A/L.322 Rev 1, S/4578, S/4579, A/L.331 Rev 1, A/L.332, S/4625, S/4741, S/4733 Rev 1, S/4740. I have also drawn heavily on the Secretary-General's statement of December 7, 1960, embodying his comments on docs. S/4573 and S/4571.

[49] See Immanuel Wallerstein, "Pan-Africanism as Protest," in this symposium, for the explanation of how territorial pan-African goals fit into the revolutionary ideology of negritude and independent national modernization. However, the "conservative" new states of the Brazzaville grouping, though not uniformly in sympathy with pan-African principles, followed a course in the UN's handling of the Congo which was every bit as expediential in motivation as was the attitude of the "revolutionary" Casablanca grouping. When UN intervention seemed to protect a confederal solution to the Congo crisis they praised the organization; when, however, the intent of the intervention seemed to be the shoring up of Lumumba, the Brazzaville nations denounced UN action as interference with national sovereignty. See the excellent analysis by Robert C. Good, "Congo Crisis: The Role of the New States," *Neutralism* (Washington, D.C.: Washington Center of Foreign Policy Research, 1961), pp. 1–46.

[50] For a thoughtful analysis of the growth of agreement, see Philip E. Jacob, "The Disarmament Consensus," *International Organization*, Vol. 14, No. 2 (Spring 1960). My summary of UN discussions is based on General Assembly disarmament debates since 1955.

pressure of the revolutionary countries bolsters any proposal which looks promising even if the inspection provisions do not meet with Washington's approval. An eventual softening of the Western position on this point is likely, without implying an accretion of new powers of inspection and supervision to the UN.

The UN may gain nothing from disarmament, and it will soon lose the field of action represented by the dissolution of colonial empires. What areas for potential peaceful change through the medium of parliamentary diplomacy remain which may prevent the system from losing its scope? Controls in outer space, supervision of space exploration, sovereignty over the moon, or at least, the preparation of legal rules for national space activity are obvious examples, even though little progress has been made so far. The preparation of an international investment code and a multipartite system for protecting foreign property in newly independent territories come to mind. The permanent neutralization and administration of inclement but vital territories, such as Antarctica, is such an activity. Whenever a common sense of danger or uncertainty inhibits national action, the systemic ground rules of UN diplomacy are given the environmental scope for introducing change. Science and technology are more likely to furnish the stimulus in the future than are national self-determination and boundary disputes.[51]

Multilateral action for technical assistance and economic development comes closest to meeting rigorous criteria for a general UN "consensus," as constituting a recognized "universal interest." It has not always been so. Prior to the period of Afro-Asian ascendancy in the UN, the economic development issue had split the membership into three blocs; but by 1955 a cumulative train of events had been unleashed which resulted in ever growing accretions of institutional and financial authority in UN hands. Expansion of the system's task was due to the fact that the Western-developed nations gave in, up to a point, to the demands of the under-developed nations and that the Soviet bloc dropped its absolute condemnation of UN assistance.

Yet, with the exception of changing Soviet policy, little can be demonstrated about specific concerns of revolutionary regimes in policy aims relating to economic development. All underdeveloped member states stood for a maximum of multilateral aid, free from strings, and dispensed by international agencies which would be dominated by their votes. Revolutionary, as well as traditional, oligarchies, socialist and conservative regimes, called for the Expanded Program of Technical Assistance, SUNFED, the International Finance Corporation, and the Special Fund. Indeed, the striking feature is the willingness of revolutionary regimes to give up certain cherished aims in the process of finding compromises acceptable to the developed nations.[52]

[51] Examples for fields of action offering opportunities for peaceful change by quasi-legislative action are given in C. Wilfred Jenks, *The Common Law of Mankind* (London: Stevens, 1958), Chaps. 7, 8, and 9. Commission to Study the Organization of Peace *Developing the United Nations,* 13th Report (January 1961), pp. 35–40. Lincoln Bloomfield, *The United Nations and U.S. Foreign Policy* (Boston: Little, Brown, 1960), pp. 157–86.

[52] Benjamin Higgins and Guy Pauker, "Economic Aspects of the Asian-African Conference and its Aftermath," *Ekonomi dan Keuanqan Indonesia* (Nos. 5–6, 1955), pp. 16–17. Oscar Lewis, "Mexico

Mexico, despite its intense nationalist suspicion of foreign capital, strongly supported IFC. The same is true of Egypt, Indonesia, and Bolivia. These revolutionary nations took the initiative in proposing the creation of the Special Fund and expressed their willingness to subordinate themselves to a strong managing director and a qualified majority voting formula in the Governing Council.[53]

Soviet conduct is more complex. Until 1954 the policy of the Soviet Union in UN economic agencies was entirely negative: It blamed underdevelopment on imperialism and opposed multilateral aid as a camouflaged device for perpetuating colonial dependence, insisting instead on the wholesale application of socialist techniques; Soviet speeches and resolutions were confined to attacking Western economic moves, especially the strategic embargo, and to make propaganda charges. Stalin's death changed all this. With the offer of Soviet contributions to EPTA came the recognition of the propriety of multilateral aid. Suggestions for the creation of a new universal trade organization were made while some of the satellites offered to join GATT. Soviet participation in the work of the economic commissions for Europe and for Asia and the Far East grew cooperative, so much so that the Soviet Union offered to contribute to the Mekong River Project. Consistent with this change, Moscow then proceeded to support the creation of SUNFED, IFC, and the Special Fund. In procedural and administrative disputes with the Technical Assistance Board and the Secretariat over the degree of bilateralism to be permitted in the distribution of the Soviet contributions to these agencies, the Soviet position was invariably overruled—and yet the Soviet Union continued to participate on a modest scale. Bilateral aid is also offered by the Soviets within the confines of UN discussions and some commentators suspect that it is the long-range policy of Moscow to maneuver the UN aid effort into a universal bilateralist scheme. But in failing to achieve this, the Soviets as well as other revolutionary regimes have so far accommodated themselves to the evolving rules of the UN system.[54]

Aspirations concerning economic development are common to all types of regimes and even revolutionary governments will swallow aspects of international control in this realm which would otherwise be an anathema. Hence, it is instructive to contrast the policy aims of revolutionary regimes in the field of the international protection of human rights with economic development. The Soviet Union, prior to

Since Cardenas," in *Social Change in Latin America Today, op. cit.*, pp. 306–307. B. E. Matecki, "Establishment of the International Finance Corporation: A Case Study," *International Organization*, Vol. 10, No. 2 (May 1956). Robert E. Elder and Forrest D. Murden, "Economic Co-Operation: Special United Nations Fund for Economic Development" (New York: Woodrow Wilson Foundation, 1954).

[53] See the revealing case study on SUNFED and the Special Fund in John G. Hadwen and Johan Kaufmann, *How United Nations Decisions Are Made* (Leyden: A. W. Sythoff, 1960), pp. 85–122.

[54] Dallin, *op. cit.*, p. 63. Alvin Z. Rubinstein, "Soviet Policy Toward Underdeveloped Areas in the Economic and Social Council," *International Organization*, Vol. 9, No. 2 (May 1955); "Soviet Policy in ECAFE: A Case Study of Soviet Behavior in International Economic Organizations," *ibid.*, Vol. 12, No. 4 (Autumn 1958). R. L. Allen, "United Nations Technical Assistance: Soviet and East European Participation," *ibid.*, Vol. 11, No. 4 (Autumn 1957). Harold K. Jacobson, "The Soviet Union, the UN and World Trade," *Western Political Quarterly*, Vol. 11, No. 3 (September 1958).

1953, strongly supported all general declarations and specific legal texts affirming and defining human rights, especially the rights to national self-determination and protection of natural resources against alien control. But it equally strongly opposed all efforts to provide even a minimal UN machinery for enforcing these rights or reporting on their implementation. A subtle change crept into this position after 1953: Soviet delegates proved quite willing to approve the creation of commissions of inquiry to probe into situations damaging to the West but continued to oppose these when they were to deal with allegations relating to the Soviet bloc. The mellowing of opposition to UN institutional competence in the human-rights field went hand in hand with some disagreement among Soviet jurists as to the degree of jurisdiction international judicial bodies might enjoy over national sovereignty. At the same time the Soviet Union consented to participation in several efforts by the International Labor Organization to probe the existence of trade-union rights in Russia.[55]

Other revolutionary nations show little evidence of an increasing willingness to submit to UN jurisdiction. To be sure, they all espouse the Universal Declaration of Human Rights and have supported the drafting of some of the most far-reaching clauses of the two Covenants. Yet the emphasis is uniformly not on civil and political rights of individuals, but on the collective right of national self-determination, in its political and economic aspects. The African states use the Declaration to legitimize *national* freedom but ignore its provisions when it comes to the rights of *tribal* groups. Universal rights are invoked against present colonialism but untrammeled national sovereignty or regional cohesion is held out for future developments. UN commissions are created to inquire into the colonial aspect, but the revolutionary states vote against the establishment of commissions to define terms carefully, to investigate conditions of national development, or to protect tribal populations living within metropolitan territories. The very intensification of the attachment to non-intervention implies a hardening of opposition among revolutionary nations to international supervision of private and group rights, while the economic and social programs of these regimes make respect for such rights a matter of considerable doubt. When, in 1959, the General Assembly voted to condemn the Peking regime for a violation of the Universal Declaration of Human Rights in Tibet, the bulk of the revolutionary states abstained; the Soviet Union voted "no"; Indonesia opposed the inclusion of the item on the agenda; but Bolivia, Mexico, and Cuba voted in the affirmative.[56] While policy expectations of the UN system correspond to permanent

[55] E. R. Goodman, "The Cry of National Liberation: Recent Soviet Attitudes Toward National Self-Determination," *International Organization,* Vol. 14, No. 1 (Winter 1960). J. A. Armstrong, "The Soviet Attitude Toward UNESCO," *ibid.,* Vol. 8, No. 2 (May 1954). Dallin, *op. cit.,* pp. 45–47. Dallin and Armstrong suggest that the post-1953 Soviet interest in human rights and international intellectual contacts is connected with the Soviet hope of turning all UN agencies into a pro-Communist front organization.

[56] See the resolutions of the All-African People's Conference, Accra, *op. cit.,* for the contrast between domestic exclusiveness and UN legitimacy for anti-colonialism alone. A similar case for Latin America is made by Martin Travis, "The Political and Social Basis for the Latin American Doctrine of Non-Intervention," *Proceedings of the American Society of International Law,* Vol. 53

national aims in the field of economic development, they merely mirror a temporary concern in the area of human rights, thus being only an aspect of the current phase in the history of the system.

This survey of the policy aims of revolutionary states has demonstrated only that their demands are neither rigid nor uniform, that they respond to the give-and-take of parliamentary diplomacy, and that many of their aspirations do not differ from those of conservative regimes. Therefore, the emergence of new common interests in the realms of outer space and in the prevention of limited wars among uncommitted states may yet give the UN new tasks in the next phase of its life, which may facilitate a balancing process involving different functions and different balancers than in the current phase.

IV

The present phase in the life of the UN system, which began in 1955, is earmarked by an inter-regional and inter-functional balancing process. The policies of the sysetm were produced as a result of continuous compromises among regional blocs which differ in internal cohesion with respect to specific UN functions. Functional differentiation, in turn, explains how the mediating role can be assumed by varying balancers and how stalemates can be avoided by shifting majorities. In some situations the mediating role is played so well and national aims are so interrelated that significant policy measures can be produced by almost unanimous votes. Compromises involve not only concessions by one bloc to another, but also feature bargaining on the basis of concessions among functions: increasing economic assistance and support for decolonization efforts are demanded in return for support on questions relating to collective security and peaceful change. Typical policies of the current phase, then, have included the cumulative creation of new UN economic aid institutions and procedures, a growing commitment to peaceful decolonization, and the protection of human rights in Africa and Asia, as well as institutionalized balancing through conciliation, police forces, and Secretariat intercession in crises involving an immediate threat to peace.

Policy aims contributed by revolutionary regimes in this pattern were examined above. While the imperatives of symmetry would be neatly satisfied if all the non-Communist revolutionary regimes were to be grouped as "balancing" states, this is obviously not the situation. If the Western bloc represents the "thesis" of the status quo and the Soviets the "antithesis" of change, revolutionary regimes may be found on both dialectical extremes as well as in the neutralist "synthesizing" force. We must now assess the impact of the system's policies on the revolutionary environment but we must let the chips fall where they belong. Our question is simply: Has the balancing process resulted in a change in the demands and expectations of revolu-

(1959). The Tibetan case is discussed in Bailey, *op. cit.,* p. 248 ff. The fact that a number of western democracies and Latin American oligarchical regimes with minority and human rights problems also abstained suggests that many members were unwilling to set a precedent.

tionary states so as to demonstrate responsiveness to the system? If so, a revolutionary environment clearly need not destroy an institutionally static system based on imperfectly internalized norms.

Soviet conduct in relation to the collective-security issue illustrates this conclusion. It is impossible to demonstrate that the basic Soviet policy of advancing a gradual world revolution toward an international Socialist and Communist society has been abandoned; therefore, the UN has not influenced the substance of Moscow's policy aims. On the contrary, a careful study of Soviet attitudes toward international relations and systems makes clear that a policy of peaceful but competitive coexistence, conceived as a means of combat, has always been favored at least by some of Russia's leaders. Soviet participation in a variety of international systems, some of them hostile to Soviet aims, was always considered feasible in an international environment felt to be transitional on the road to Socialist internationalism.[57]

Membership in the UN system, however, has definitely influenced the tactical manner in which the Soviet Union participates in world affairs. All the early pronouncements concerning the sacrosanct nature of national sovereignty, big power unanimity and the dominance of the Security Council have been downgraded during the current phase of UN life. Despite Soviet hostility to international police and enforcement measures, the Soviet delegate merely abstained on votes creating such forces for Suez and the Congo; even though the veto is still cherished, little effort was made to protest the Security Council's brushing aside of the double veto cast in the Laotian crisis of 1959; when it suited the Soviet purpose, the delegation was quite willing to make use of the General Assembly and the Secretariat; finally, whenever the immediate military security of the Soviet bloc itself was not at stake, the Soviet Union seemed eager to mobilize the UN for collective security operations.[58]

There has been no internalization of norms. The quality of Soviet UN diplomacy has become more sophisticated and self-reliant; its style of participation, far from being defensive, is now self-confident. To that extent, the rigid rejection of institutional evolution has been abandoned and a tactical responsiveness to systemic forces is evident now. But this has been true of a period when the peaceful coexistence phase of Soviet thought happens to coincide with the decolonization phase of the UN. Certainly, a responsiveness to systemic influences is suggested by the continued membership of the Soviet Union in the UN even during the height of the phase of American dominance, though Zhdanov and his supporters seem to have advocated withdrawal.[59] Reciprocal converging interests with the West and with the uncom-

---

[57] Julian Towster, "The Dogma of Communist Victory," *Current History* (November 1959). For a collection of statements supporting this conclusion see also *Khrushchev on the Shifting Balance of World Forces,* U.S. Senate, 86th Congress, 1st Session, Doc. No. 57 (September 1959).

[58] On Laos see Leo Gross in *American Journal of International Law,* Vol. 53, No. 1 (January 1960), pp. 118–30. The other examples are discussed in Dallin, *op. cit.,* pp. 49–51, 84, 90–94, 99–100. But it should be noted that the Soviet Union refused to contribute to the maintenance of these forces. Other revolutionary regimes declining to support UNEF include Bolivia, Cuba, Iraq, Mexico, and Egypt. All the other African and Asian revolutionary regimes have faithfully paid their contributions. Details in Bailey, *op. cit.,* p. 216 ff.

[59] Dallin, *op. cit.,* pp. 33–38.

mitted nations have clearly been experienced, thus explaining the continued stability of the system during the current phase. But the evaporation of the convergences may also imply a passing of the phase. As long as systemic rules have not been internalized, but merely "learned" for short-range tactical purposes, the revolutionary environment remains as volatile as before.

Ghana, Indonesia, and Morocco have shown themselves to be far more responsive to systemic influences on matters connected with peace and security. Even Egypt has complied with the bulk of the UN decisions connected with the liquidation of the Suez crisis, though not without hard bargaining and at little cost to itself. They have appreciated that collective security operations conducted by balancing states can stop local wars and confine the East-West conflict. Again, we cannot claim that long-range objectives have been abandoned, but short-range responsiveness to systemic pressure is pronounced enough to promise its outliving the current phase.

The difference in responsiveness between Communist and non-Communist revolutionary regimes is equally patent in activities relating to peaceful change. Soviet policy has been unflinching in opposing all formal procedural steps for strengthening the executive, legislative or judicial competence of the UN in providing centralized, third-party dominated solutions. Verbal demands for UN measures in South Africa or Spain have not been accompanied with institutional suggestions. Operations in the Congo were denounced as soon as they turned against the Soviet-sponsored regime. UN activities in the realms of disarmament, outer space, and other "frontier" areas of possibly converging interests were never supported unless the Soviet substantive position was also accepted. In short, there has been no increasing responsiveness to the possibilities of peaceful change offered by the UN system.

Other revolutionary regimes have been perfectly willing to respond to and initiate measures of peaceful change in problem areas in which they had as yet no direct interest. With respect to disarmament and UN controls in space roadblocks, international agreement came from the nations with an established interest or policy, but not from Asia, Africa, or Latin America. But it should be noted that much less responsiveness was in evidence in the efforts of the International Atomic Energy Agency to establish rules for inspecting the utilization by revolutionary regimes of fissile materials. Here, after all, is an area in which even underdeveloped nations have already acquired a rudimentary vested interest. If systemic expansion through peaceful change is to take place in these frontier fields the current phase must be exploited before a changed international environment will make task expansion impossible here too.

Decolonization, it would appear at first blush, is the prime field of peaceful change commanding the responsiveness of revolutionary regimes. This is an accurate impression insofar as they invoke the phrases of the Charter and of the Universal Declaration of Human Rights to dislodge the colonial powers and to make use of international debate and supervision to implement the provisions of the trusteeship system. But the manipulative inspiration of this attitude stands revealed in the limelight of the Congo crisis, leading to the conclusion that the dominance of instrumental motives has led to no internalization of systemic rules. Ghana, for example, joined the other African revolutionary regimes in threatening, at the Casablanca Conference, to take "appropriate action" unilaterally unless the UN supported the Lumumbist forces. Nkrumah softened this position later to the extent of seeking to channel the same demands through the UN Operation, provided the Congo were made an all-African responsibility, with the independent African states acting as the "agent" of the UN, much as the United States did in Korea.[60] This still implied a reduction in the powers of the Secretary-General and an indirect endorsement of the Soviet position with respect to supporting the Gizenga regime. Far from acting as neutral balancers, the Casablanca powers made themselves the mouthpiece, under "African" auspices, of the Soviet extreme position; Liberia, Tunisia, and Ceylon— none of them revolutionary nations—acted as the classical balancers. If the search for an African Personality persuaded Guinea, Ghana, Mali, and Morocco to sub-ordinate the processes of the world organization to their specific aims, Ghana at least did not carry its regional focus to the extreme of withdrawing its forces from the Congo. Nasser's United Arab Republic, however, did precisely that, while under-taking unilateral assistance to Gizenga. Egyptian support for UN operations aiming at peaceful change was strictly calculated on the basis of its convergence with Cairo's policy of penetrating Africa. Nasser was far less inclined to assume a balanc-ing role in the Congo, as compared to Nkrumah, and has shown no interest in maximizing the peaceful-change capacity of the UN. The policy of revolutionary Egypt in relation to international institutions is as inconsistently imperialistic as its general foreign policy.[61]

Clearly, not all revolutionary regimes are equally unresponsive to the possibilities of institutionalized peaceful change procedures. Few of them approach the extreme of the Soviet Union, as even Indonesia might accept a temporary trusteeship status for West Irian. But, as we can demonstrate no change in national policy, respon-siveness is an *ad hoc* phenomenon which has not predictably stabilized the environ-ment.

While expediential considerations have imposed a certain amount of responsive-ness upon most revolutionary regimes in the realms of collective security and peaceful change, the impact of the UN is much more striking when we deal with economic development. There the very conditions of the revolutionary environment, when impinging upon one another in the context of multi-functional demands, have produced a massive systemic response in which almost all member states have acquiesced, even the Soviet bloc. The impropriety of indefinitely and irrevocably opposing demands for dealing with the revolution of rising expectations has been recognized by all types of nations at the UN, with the result that parliamentary diplomacy has here produced a genuine new consensus, with an expanded organiza-

---

[60] On the Casablanca Conference see Conference of Heads of African States, Casablanca, January 3–7, 1961, "Declaration Concerning the Situation in the Congo." Also Kwame Nkrumah, speech at General Assembly session, March 7, 1961. When the Osagyefo took the oath of office as Presi-dent of Ghana, he swore "that the union of Africa should be striven for by every lawful means and, when attained, should be faithfully preserved . . ." *External Affairs* (September 1960), p. 221.
[61] My assessment of UAR foreign policy objectives and their "inconsistent imperialism," is based on Wheelock, *op. cit.*, especially pp. 223–57, 270–82.

tional task. To judge by the policy of Bolivia, Egypt, and Indonesia, new nations find it much easier to respond to "capitalistic" development concepts when advanced by international agencies than under other auspices, and consequently tone down earlier policy aims in the field of development. The impact on the Soviet Union, though less marked, is still considerable if we keep in mind the unqualified insistence on "socialism" as recently as 1953.

If we are to believe speeches and conference declarations, the devotion to the universal protection of human rights felt by revolutionary regimes is much greater than such devotion elsewhere. The context in which such sentiments are expressed was explored above; here responsiveness and internalization of the procedures and values involved are under scrutiny. The Soviet Union has flatly asserted that the rights envisaged in the Covenants exist already on its territory so that no special enforcement machinery is necessary. Guinea's Constitution endorses the Universal Declaration by name and enumerates, as binding on herself, the rights there defined. Apparently, this example is followed only by those African territories which owe their status to UN action, but not by Ghana, Mali, or Morocco.[62] Dedication to the UN as the instrument for effectively enforcing human rights cannot be assumed any more than devotion to institutionalized processes of peaceful change controlled by third parties. Mere repetition of verbal sincerity has had no discernible impact on the environment.

As far as the international style of revolutionary regimes is concerned, the balancing politics of the UN's third phase can hardly be credited with having toned down manifestations of truculence and impatience. The fifteenth session of the General Assembly would seem to represent a high point in overt instances of revolutionary style. But to view the systemic impact on style purely in terms of parliamentary behavior is to miss another possible pattern of responsiveness to institutionalized diplomacy, the attitude toward international law as a means of peaceful change.[63] Assuming, at least for the sake of argument, that the Western powers—as the representatives of the international status quo—took the provisions of the Charter with respect to legal means of peacefully changing the norms of the international system literally in 1945, it is easy to demonstrate that certain key revolutionary regimes did not. Communist unwillingness to submit to any kind of UN judicial process is well known, an attitude shared quite obviously by Nasser.[64]

But just as the Western powers, in their inability to mobilize the law consistently

[62] For details see Egon Schwelb, "The Influence of the Universal Declaration of Human Rights on International and National Law," *Proceedings* . . . , *op. cit.,* pp. 223–28. Court decisions citing the Declaration were handed down in West Germany, Belgium, Italy, United States, and the Philippines.

[63] Attitudes toward international law are deliberately treated as aspects of "style" rather than as a rubric of peaceful change because of the predominantly verbal role of UN legal discussion. Thus far, at any rate, judicial considerations have figured more as an aspect of propaganda inputs than as a constituent of an institutionalized pattern of outputs.

[64] Nasser, when asked why he did not wait until 1956 for the natural expiration of the 1936 treaty on the Suez Canal, maintained: "We are quite aware that this treaty wouldn't just expire. The British would take it before some international tribunal and obtain permission for prolonging it.

in support of the old status quo, have displayed a more and more instrumental attitude toward UN judicial institutions, the doctrinal opposition of revolutionary
regimes to this aspect of the system has weakened.[65] This is especially true of the
Soviets. The sharp contrast between Communist and Western attitudes toward international law, which is so often pointed out, applies only if we compare *Soviet practice*
with *Western doctrine,* a facile and meaningless juxtaposition. If Soviet practice is
compared with that of the West, the differences are much less pronounced. The
"law habit" of the West—in international relations—is not much better developed
than the Soviets': Both sides observe and violate their treaty and customary obligations when it suits their policy purposes. More striking still, when we examine lower-
level legal habits with reference to very specific fields, rather than focus on central
points of legal doctrine, the Soviet practice has increasingly approached that of most
states in the last decade.[66]

Differences are narrowed further if we compare *Soviet doctrine* with *Western
practice.* The early Soviet insistence on the role of treaties as the sole source of international obligations has given way to an instrumentally motivated recognition of
custom and general principles of law as sometimes useful, just as the West has increasingly turned to treaties: By now both postures have met somewhere between
these extremes. Western legal doctrine is increasingly moving in the direction of a
less absolute and more instrumentally oriented view of the origin and purpose of
norms.[67] And as William Welch has shown in an admirable survey of Soviet legal
doctrine concerning the position of regional arrangements, these are viewed essentially as the West interprets its military pacts: Both postures are explicable easily on
the basis of the search for immediate military security and the desire to manipulate
the rules of the UN Charter so as to sanctify one's own treaties and castigate the
opponent's. In the process, the arguments have become very much alike.[68] To the
extent, then, that revolutionary and status-quo powers have turned to the UN to

---

We smaller nations haven't much confidence in these tribunals, which we know full well to be
nothing more than courts run by and for the big nations." J. and S. Lacouture, *Egypt in Transition* (London: Methuen, 1958), p. 459.

[65] The limited role of the International Court of Justice is reviewed and explained by Shabtai
Rosenne, *The International Court of Justice* (New York: Central Book Company, 1957) and Max
Sørensen, "The International Court of Justice: Its Role in Contemporary International Relations,"
International Organization, Vol. 14, No. 2 (Spring 1960).

[66] On this point see the articles by Oliver J. Lissitzyn and John N. Hazard, in *Proceedings . . . ,
op. cit.*

[67] On the evolution of Soviet thought on the sources of international law, see Jan F. Triska and
Robert M. Slusser, "Treaties and Other Sources of Order in International Relations: The Soviet
View," *American Journal of International Law,* Vol. 52, No. 4 (October 1958), especially pp.
724–26. An Egyptian lawyer has argued that the revolutionary regime in Cairo has abandoned the
doctrine of the two *dars* in Islamic legal thought, including the concept of the *jihad,* and thus
reapproached a universal law which recognizes an identity of norms governing the relations among
Muslims and non-Muslims. Saba Habachy, in *Proceedings, op. cit.,* p. 61. The Western position on
the reorientation of international law is prominently represented by Myres McDougal and his
associates.

[68] William Welch, "Soviet Commitments to Collective Action," in A. Wolfers (ed.), *Alliance
Policy in the Cold War* (Baltimore: Johns Hopkins, 1959).

legitimate their national policies, they have responded to the systemic forces they invoke by relaxing their earlier legal styles.

Observations of the impact of the system on the revolutionary environment and assessments of changes in revolutionary style do not exhaust the analytic means at our disposal for determining whether the universal system is mastering its impatient members or whether they are destroying the system. The evidence is uneven with respect to the moderation of revolutionary demands, and it may be doubted that the rapprochement of legal styles is of permanent significance. But if we can establish that the system itself has grown in the legitimacy it enjoys in the eyes of its members and in the authority it exercises over them then the inconsistent impact of UN decisions on member state expectations is not a fatal blow to the survival of the organization.

We may conclude that the system proper has increased in importance, at the expense of the states which make up the environment, if cumulative institutional decisions continue to be regarded as "legitimate" even by revolutionary regimes. The criterion of legitimacy is the regular invocation of UN Charter principles in advocacy and debate by those holding out for more UN action as well as by those who seek to block such action (the balancer and the aggressor both invoke the Charter regularly), *plus* the demonstrated willingness to expand the UN's task in order to implement the Charter principles put forward. What is especially significant here, of course, is the willingness of states to support eventually new organizational tasks which they had initially opposed. "Authority," by contrast, implies no acceptance of the rightness of specific organizational action. The "authority" of the system might be said to increase if member states carry out decisions even if they did not advocate them, if they continue to oppose them in principle, and if they do not link the continued exercise of the task to the invocation of Charter principles.

The growth in legitimacy enjoyed by the UN should be observable in the utterances of prominent statesmen associated with the Afro-Asian Solidarity Conference, a grouping particularly useful for the study of revolutionary leadership since it tends to serve as an international front organization for the United Arab Republic as well as for the Communist bloc. Indeed there seems to have been a considerable amount of tugging between Cairo and Moscow as to who should manipulate the Conference.[69] Typical causes which the Conference espouses, apart from a general condemnation of "imperialism" and "colonialism" in terms which conform to the Communist line, include the banning of nuclear weapons testing in Africa, complete disarmament, the Stockholm World Peace Council, the Japanese drive against the United States Security Treaty, the return of Okinawa to Japan, the elimination of all foreign military bases everywhere, Castro's Cuba, and the complete rejection of any Western influence whatsoever in recently "liberated" countries, including economic and military ties voluntarily accepted by the new governments. Indeed, the Conference shows a marked consistency in serving as the mouthpiece of the most extreme anti-Western strands of opinions to be found in Africa and Asia: the UPC in the Cameroons as opposed to the Ahidjo government, the FIN in Algeria, the

[69] Wheelock, *op. cit.,* pp. 266–68.

opposition parties in Somalia against the Somali Youth League government, Lumumba against Kasavubu, etc.[70]

Legitimacy appears to receive a strong prop when the demands of states and of independence movements invoke the phraseology of the Charter in connection with the drive against colonialism. To be sure, such invocations are heard *ad nauseam* when they are useful in supporting the argument for independence. But the Charter principles are held to be violated unless "freedom" conforms to the international revolutionary *mystique:*

A nation cannot attain real independence if there are foreign troops stationed in its independent territory and if it is a member of an organization controlled by an imperialist State if it joins military pacts within imperialist power. [sic] [71]

Therefore, the ligitimacy of the UN operation in the Congo was vehemently denied when it appeared that the "unlawful activity of Mr. Hammerskjold" [sic] proved unsuccessful in bolstering Lumumba.[72] On the occasion of the fifteenth anniversary of the UN, the Conference Secretariat again "hails all the efforts aiming at the application of the principles of the Charter, such as for example, those of the neutralist and Afro-Asian countries," but also noted that "the enchantment vanished. The cases are in fact very rare when the UN served the cause of peace and the liberty of peoples." [73] One African spokesman flatly asserted that whenever the pan-African variety of nationalism fails to win endorsement in New York, the American imperialists succeed in subverting the organization and its Secretary-General. He also argued that multilateral economic aid under UN auspices is to be resisted in such circumstances because "this would only help perpetuating economical neo-colonialism [sic]." [74] Yet it should be noted that the Conference Secretary-General, Youssef El Sebai, urged that:

. . . because of the pressing need for the United Nations in the present circumstances, Afro-Asian peoples are determined to see that the World Organization does not collapse. It is our duty to consolidate it by every possible means, and to endeavour to enable it to play its great role in World affairs, uninfluenced by pressure or intimidation, for the sole benefit of all peoples of the world, for Justice and for Peace.[75]

Clearly, the failure to achieve full endorsement for revolutionary objectives in New York is reflected in a continued overt denial of legitimacy. But the ambivalence of El Sebai's statement and the support Ghana still gives the UN in the Congo warrant the conclusion that eventual legitimacy may still develop either because the UN is a useful Soviet front in some future crisis, or because it still offers the safest way out of a dangerous situation. But it should be noted that the second part of the

[70] For a complete survey of such causes see *Afro-Asian Bulletin*, Vol. 2, Nos. 11–12 (September–October, 1960).
[71] *Ibid.*, p. 32.
[72] *Ibid.*, p. 60.
[73] *Ibid.*, p. 61.
[74] Osende Afana, "Consolidating Afro-Asian Solidarity," *ibid.*, p. 7.
[75] Youssef El Sebai, "Afro-Asian Solidarity Marches On," *ibid.*, pp. 4–5.

criterion of legitimacy, consent to an expanded UN task, has been lacking as far as the Soviet bloc and several African revolutionary regimes are concerned.

Some precision is needed at this point. The two criteria of legitimacy have clearly been satisfied in the case of the expanded UN task in economic development. Charter invocation, equally clearly, has not been accompanied by task expansion with respect to collective security, human rights, and most aspects of peaceful change. Decolonization, however, has conferred increasing legitimacy on the UN even if the reservations explicit in the activities of the Afro-Asian Solidarity Conference are borne in mind. Plebiscites have been held and their results implemented; Trusteeship Council and General Assembly injunctions concerning steps for achieving self-government and independence have been carried out; groups and individuals persecuted by the colonial administrations have achieved respectability and even power as a result of UN intervention. While the Soviet Union, Cuba, Guinea, and Mali have denied the UN full legitimacy over the Congo, they have acquiesced in it with respect to other colonial episodes, thus altering an earlier, more intransigent position. But even if decolonization has conferred increasing legitimacy on the world organization, the passing of the colonial phase makes it doubtful that this acquisition will be readily transferred to new tasks.

Growth in authority, rather than in legitimacy, is the most striking aspect of UN history in its current phase—even at the expense of certain revolutionary regimes. This growth is demonstrable by observing the accretions of power of certain UN institutions and the implementation of their decisions by revolutionary member nations in the face of declared indifference or opposition, following the adoption of appropriate resolutions in the Security Council or the General Assembly.

Even though a general consensus embracing almost the entire membership has developed with respect to the increased institutional role of the UN system in economic development, the revolutionary states had been among those who were most anxious to retain a maximum of national freedom of action in the preparation and execution of development projects. The Soviet Union, in fact, had made a fetish of the need for absolute national autonomy in economic planning. Notwithstanding these commitments of principle, the evolution of UN techniques shows a growth of power on the part of international officials and a willingness of revolutionary regimes to carry out their proposals. The Special Fund exercises much more detailed supervision over national development projects enjoying UN support than did the Technical Assistance Board in earlier years, and the TAB is now adopting more stringent measures. The recommendations of survey teams and inspectors dispatched by the International Bank for Reconstruction and Development are readily implemented by borrowing nations, despite the "Wall Street connections" of that institution. Bolivia has agreed to comply with the drastic deflationary "recommendations" of the International Monetary Fund as a price for receiving further loans in the face of strong domestic resentment. The mediating role of the Bank, when sweetened with appropriate financial sugar, has been a significant one in resolving such crises as restitution to the Universal Suez Canal Company and development of the Indus River Basin. The most capitalistic of aid-giving institutions receives cooperation from revolutionary (but non-Communist) nations when systematic economic development is at stake.[76]

A similar conclusion is made possible by the experience of the rapidly growing system of UN Resident Representatives in aid-receiving countries, an institution not initially proposed by the underdeveloped nations. Almost fifty such officials now reside in member states receiving technical assistance, proposing and channelling projects, coordinating and supervising their execution. On their impact, one UN official writes:

> It is an administrative maxim that power should equal responsibility. The role of resident representative violates the precept; its responsibilities are endless, its powers nil. The resident representative knows that in whatever direction he looks—at the [Technical Assistance] Board, the participating organizations, the government, or the experts—he can order no one. For the essence of the post is that the person holding it achieves results not by commanding and ordering, but by persuasion and giving good counsel.[77]

Obviously, the actual influence of these officials varies from country to country. But since, increasingly, the flow of new grants, loans, experts, and fellowships depends in no small measure on the confidential reports submitted by the resident representatives to authorities at UN headquarters and to specialized agencies, their counsel on the spot is unlikely to be disregarded. Guinea was anxious to receive assistance in this form and turned to the Soviet bloc only when the UN was unprepared to meet hurried requests; Bolivia accommodated itself to it despite a nationalist revolution.[78]

[76] On Egypt's relations with the TAB and specialized agency programs see Walter R. Sharp, The United Nations System in Egypt," *International Organization*, Vol. 10, No. 2 (May 1956). On the Special Fund see Hadwen and Kaufmann, *op. cit.*, and UN Special Fund, Doc. SF 1 (January 1, 1959). On the Bank see Eugene Black, "The Indus: Moral for Nations," *New York Times Magazine*, December 11, 1960, p. 51. Wheelock, *op. cit.*, pp. 190–97. Conditions imposed by the IMF in Bolivia were widely disregarded in 1957–58, but a new IMF effort in 1960 was apparently accompanied by firm assurances on the part of the Bolivian regime. The Left-Wing of the MNR continued to oppose cooperation with the IMF and equated UN "imperialism" with that of the International Cooperation Administration. For details see, Robert J. Alexander, *The Bolivian National Revolution* (New Brunswick: Rutgers University Press, 1958), Chap. 13. Richard W. Patch, "Bolivia: Decision or Debacle," *American Universities Field Staff*, Latin America (Bolivia) RWP-3-'59 (April 18, 1959).

[77] C. Hart Schaaf, "The Role of Resident Representatives of the UN Technical Assistance Board," *International Organization*, Vol. 14, No. 4 (Autumn 1960), p. 556.

[78] See Alexander, *op. cit.*, pp. 245–46. Carter Goodrich, *The Economic Transformation of Bolivia* (Ithaca: Cornell University Press, 1955). Albert Lepawsky, "The Bolivian Operation," *International Conciliation*, No. 479 (March 1952). This, of course, is not to deny that many governments—though not necessarily revolutionary ones—disregard the advice tendered by technical assistance personnel and that resident representatives vary a good deal in the measure of their influence in proportion to their own personalities. While some, in effect, act as key advisers on economic development plans to governments, others are content to play a modest "clearing house" role. For a wealth of information on the degree of control exercised on behalf of the UN system by field personnel and headquarters review procedure, see Walter R. Sharp, *Field Administration in the United Nations System* (New York: Praeger, 1961), especially pp. 376–401, 406–17, 449–63, 494–

Undoubtedly the most convincing item in an argument stressing the growth of UN authority is the development of the office of the Secretary-General. Compared to the ineffectual groping for autonomous influence displayed by Trygve Lie, Dag Hammerskjold had some right to claim that his stand on actual or emerging conflicts "to the extent that such stands can be firmly based on the Charter and its principles . . . thus express what may be called the *independent judgment of the Organization*." [79] The Secretary-General, thus, can speak and act as if he, rather than the member states, represents the system *if* he is able to practice "quiet diplomacy" and enjoy the support of governments as a truly independent agent. If these conditions are not met, admitted Hammerskjold, "he must be prepared to see his future value as a negotiator endangered or even lost. In the latter case, he ought, naturally, to resign from his post." [80] To what extent, then, has this claim to a new autonomous status withstood the test of international politics?

One aspect of the Secretary-General's quiet diplomacy has unfolded in efforts to warn, and encourage the major powers with respect to disarmament negotiations, test bans, and protection against surprise attack. This, of course, implies direct intervention in a Cold-War issue, and the results are common knowledge. Although this type of effort has contributed little to strengthening the authority of the System, another type of quiet diplomacy has prevailed in Hammerskjold's attempts to maintain peace in regions at the periphery of the Cold War. In fact, the major justification advanced for intervening in Arab-Israeli crises, in Suez, the Congo, and Laos has been the exclusion of these trouble spots from the Cold War. In these cases the Secretary-General undertook personal mediation, appointed UN personnel to take charge of specific jobs, such as establishing and supervising cease-fire agreements and clearing the Suez Canal, or created a "UN presence" in the person of delegates to watch and report on implementations of earlier agreements. Success was rarely complete. Israeli-Arab tensions flared up despite mediation and the Laotian crisis was not stabilized; it is too early to predict the attainment of the economic and military objectives of the Congo Operation. Yet, quiet diplomacy did, apparently, succeed in liquidating the Suez Crisis and in stabilizing the relations between the United Arab Republic on the one hand and Jordan and Lebanon on the other. What is the explanation for the differences in impact? [81]

Quiet diplomacy, far from being separable from parliamentary diplomacy, functions best as an arm of some consensus, however limited temporally or functionally among the member governments. This consensus must include the major revolutionary regimes, if only because most of the tensions have arisen in their areas of the

---

503. On the discreet controls exercised by international financial institutions see Henry Bloch, "The Fiscal Advisory Functions of United Nations Technical Assistance," *International Organization* (Spring 1957). International Bank for Reconstruction and Development, *The World Bank: Policies and Operations* (Washington, D.C., 1957). R. G. A. Jackson, *The Case for an International Development Authority* (Syracuse: Syracuse University Press, 1959).

[79] Address in Copenhagen, UN Doc. SG/812 (May 1, 1959), p. 9. (Italics mine.)

[80] *Ibid.*

[81] The major instances in which the Secretary-General intervened are enumerated, but not evaluated and analyzed, in Bailey, *op. cit.*, pp. 22–25.

world.[82] In the Arab-Israeli and Laotian crises this condition was not met, since mediation was not preceded by unambiguous Security Council and General Assembly resolutions and *ad hoc* meetings of the mind. But in the Suez Canal crisis, the General Assembly did furnish the Secretary-General with explicit authorization born from the process of parliamentary diplomacy, and in the resolution of the Lebanese-Jordanian civil war of 1958 the governments again welcomed a balancing operation which would free the area from the danger of American, Soviet, and Egyptian armed action. In all these situations the Soviet Union and the UAR, as the major revolutionary regimes concerned, deferred to UN authority even though they did not welcome or advocate it. Whether the same principle is established by the example of the Congo Operation is still uncertain. To be sure, a consensus produced by parliamentary diplomacy accompanied the actions of the Secretary-General in recruiting and deploying armed forces and in running the Congo economy; but the consensus proved to be ephemeral and had to be bolstered by repeated threats on the part of Hammerskjold to tender his resignation. While the endorsement given to the Secretary-General's authority in the Congo in the resolution of April 15, 1961 was a sweeping one, the revolutionary regimes did not join in it. [83] In the Suez Crisis, the General Assembly created an Advisory Committee on the UN Emergency Force which functioned peacefully, without voting, in backing up the Secretary-General.[84] In the Congo Crisis, the Advisory Committee created for similar purposes lead to a less harmonious existence. The success of the Secretary-General in asserting the authority of the system depends on the mobilization of a majority of member states —including the revolutionary governments—in favor of a balancing operation for the maintenance of peace. It remains linked to the environment and has not yet attained the force of an autonomous agency superimposed over it.

However subtle its manifestations and inconsistent its public assertions, there has been an increase in systemic authority during the third phase of the UN's life. But this increase has not been accompanied by an equal growth in the acceptance as right and proper of these manifestations; there has been no parallel growth in the system's legitimacy. Member states, and especially the revolutionary regimes among them, acquiesce very reluctantly in the assertions of systemic autonomy. They do so

[82] The success of the Beck-Friis Mission in mediating the border dispute between Thailand and Cambodia is an exception. It was a very minor affair which remained outside the policy aims of all other member states.

[83] Conclusions were drawn from the debate and vote on the 17-power resolution A/L.340 and Adds. 1–4, Add. 3/Corr. 1, as well as draft amendments A/L.348 and A/L.342. The overall tenor of the resolution was to "balance" various Congo factions while strengthening the authority of the Secretary-General and of UN conciliation in stabilizing the broadened Leopoldville regime. It was sponsored by non-revolutionary Afro-Asian states. The unsuccessful amendments seeking to limit the UN role were introduced by Guinea. On the final vote, the Soviet bloc and some of the French Community African states voted in opposition; all the other revolutionary regimes (except Bolivia) abstained. *United Nations Review*, Vol. 8, No. 5 (May 1961), pp. 35–37.

[84] Details on the Committee in Bailey, *op. cit.*, p. 25. A judicious evaluation of the independent role of the Secretary-General and of ways of reducing the impact of some kind of "troika" system on the Secretariat can be found in Michel Virally, "Vers Une Réforme du Secrétariat des Nations Unies?," *International Organization*, Vol. 15, No. 2 (Spring 1961).

only because policy aims of primary importance to them cannot be satisfied in any other way without grave danger to their hopes for peace, independence, and economic modernization. But their acquiescence is thus generated by the environment and is not yet based on an internalization of systemic rules. As long as this is the case, the current phase determines behavior patterns. With a shift in national policy and a reorientation of national expectations, the current environmental phase will come to an end, and with it the newly triumphant authority of the system may pass into history. *Systemic growth at the expense of a fluid environment demands concurrent growth of authority and legitimacy. With one but without the other the survival of a stable system into the next phase of its life is all that can be expected.*

This, as yet non-existent, unity of authority and legitimacy can also be regarded as the global *consensus* which must inhere in any system which is supreme over its environment. It is at this level that those who speak of an international public interest can make a conceptually meaningful contribution. The objective existence of such an "interest," some basic values, and associated policies experienced in common by the membership, could be demonstrated if there were a reliable substantive consensus in the organization. To be sure, each phase in the system's history exhibited substantive areas of agreement among and within many of the blocs: But a shift in environment caused this substantive agreement to be dissipated. A pervasive substantive consensus, an agreement on an interest of mankind transcending short periods of almost accidental convergences of national demands, has emerged neither with respect to the imperative of preserving peace, nor with reference to peaceful and orderly changes in troublesome conditions, nor yet on the issue of exalting and protecting the individual as a subject of international law. But substantive consensus, so defined, has come about with reference to meeting the revolution of rising expectations. Furthermore, it is extremely unlikely that this would have happened without the political pressures and avenues of accommodation opened up by the UN system. And so the Marxist, as well as the Liberal, who fashions policy on the basis of some kind of economic determination has come into his own in the machinery of international organizations. His efforts, not those of the direct advocate of peace, order, and human rights, have carried the day in fashioning a genuine international interest.[85]

But there is also a procedural dimension to consensus, the dimension held basic to the life of democratic systems. If procedural uniformities transcending the phases of the UN's history can be isolated, systemic growth could again be demonstrated to have occurred. The role of majoritarian as against unanimous voting, provided whatever trend exists outlives a given phase, would furnish an indicator here. Thus we find that voting in the Security Council has in effect been gradually emancipated from

[85] Francis Canavan, S.J., in "The Levels of Consensus," unpublished paper read at the American Political Science Association Convention, September 8–10, 1960, argued that "consensus" in a democratic society can never mean more than pragmatic, mundane, task-oriented agreement that certain governmental functions of a non-controversial character should be carried out. While he also suggests that this kind of consensus is probably inadequate to legitimate the activities of a strong welfare state, his formulation goes a long way toward accurately identifying the international consensus.

dependence on an absolute unanimity rule on substantive matters, and that this development has not been obliterated by changes in national policy. The admission that abstention by a permanent member does not constitute a veto originated in the early "honeymoon" phase of the system; but it has survived. More striking still, the "consensus" procedure of issuing directives or recommendations without formal vote and the liberalization of the rules regarding the participation of the Secretary-General in Council meetings evolved during the Western-dominated second phase; not only did the Soviet Union acquiesce, but the procedure has been carried over into the third phase in situations not requiring a new basic decision of the Security Council.

Yet no such conclusion can be stated for the General Assembly. The rules of procedure are notoriously permissive and presiding officers are very inconsistent in holding member governments to them. Permanent agreement has not emerged as to whether votes on certain questions involving decolonization demand a simple or a two-thirds majority; the First Committee makes all its decisions on a two-thirds vote even though some of the issues before it could be considered as "unimportant" under the Charter and the Rules of Procedure. No discernible evolution seems to have occurred.[86] And so consensus remains as changeable as the environment which it might stabilize.

V

Let us assume that within the next two or three years the current phase of inter-regional and inter-functional balancing will come to an end—at least in its present form. This will occur because the policy aims uniting the Afro-Asians will begin to diverge as the colonial issue ceases to be relevant. Even now the internal cohesion of the Afro-Asian caucusing groups, like that of the Latin American caucus, is among the weakest of any of the Assembly groups.[87] The elimination of the colonial issues will probably imply the further splitting of both groups, who will remain united only on questions of economic development. As concerns human rights, the revolutionary states in all regions will factor themselves out from status-quo powers in opposing an expansion of the systemic task. Hence, it will become much more difficult for the Western and Soviet blocs to attract uncommitted and underdeveloped nations to their respective positions on collective security because the

[86] I do not mean to suggest, in my analysis of voting rules, that "voting" should be considered as *the* supreme integrative device which explains consensus in the sense of telling us why minorities submit to majorities. Demonstrably, consensus comes about in certain situations without voting and may fare better if voting is avoided. But the history of decision-making on certain issues in the UN also suggests that cumulative votes do create a new consensus, though this consensus does *not* carry over to other functional contexts. I would argue as a general proposition, however, that voting is an integral constituent of the process of parliamentary diplomacy—which is basic to UN decision-making—and that an evolution of voting rules is a meaningful indicator of systemic development.

[87] See Table 1.

fields in which concessions can be offered will shrink in scope. Under these circumstances it is difficult to predict whether the Latin American and Afro-Asian nations
will unite on the issue of mediating in the Cold War, or will begin to choose sides
in that conflict to a greater extent than heretofore.

In any case if the current phase, with its great opportunities for bargaining, has
been unable to transform the UN system into an organization in which institution-
alized-interest politics brings about increasing consensus, authority, and legitimacy,
a future phase which reduces the scope for bargaining is unlikely to succeed. Hence,
we cannot predict that the system will increasingly control that portion of the
environment which is due to the aims of revolutionary regimes. But the opposite
conclusion, that the revolutionary environment will destroy the system, is equally
unlikely. Legitimate authority, if we argue on the analogy of administrative behavior in democratic states, *follows* the successful coordination of separate group and
institutional efforts achieved by means of continuous bargaining, which results in a
revolution of attitudes—a "breakthrough." In the UN we have merely had compromises based on quantitative bargaining and rigid insistence on concessions of
equal value, with a failure to yield "integration" in the sense of the visualization by
the parties of new alternatives for common action in which no state "gives up" anything.[88] But we have had continuous bargaining in which the revolutionary states
have fully participated. There is no reason for thinking that even an environment
offering fewer opportunities for the exchange of concessions will eliminate the
incentives for retaining such stability as the system now possesses. And if the UN
task does expand to the "new frontier" of space and science, the level of negotiation
which results in integration may yet be achieved during the next phase.

We thus arrive at the conclusion that revolutionary regimes may be deterred into
truculent inactivity by their participation in the United Nations, but not thereby be
socialized into the gentle arts of accommodation, leading to ever higher planes of
universal progress under the benevolent aegis of the hundred-odd flags displayed at
the East River. "We tend to identify peace, stability, and the quiescence of conflict
with notions like trust, good faith, and mutual respect," wrote T. C. Schelling.

To the extent that this point of view actually encourages trust and respect it is good.
But where trust and good faith do not exist and cannot be made to by our acting as
though they did, we may wish to solicit advice from the underworld, or from ancient
despotisms, on how to make agreements work when trust and good faith are lacking and
there is no legal recourse for breach of contract. The ancients exchanged hostages, drank
wine from the same glass to demonstrate the absence of poison, met in public places to
inhibit the massacre of one by the other, and even deliberately exchanged spies to facilitate
transmittal of authentic information.[89]

If we add that participation in the politics of the UN acts as a channel for the transmission of blackmail threats, even if it be multilateral and multifunctional blackmail,
the civilizing impact of the United Nations system on the revolutionary component

[88] The distinction between accommodation based on "compromise" and "integration" is elaborated
in North, Koch, and Zinnes, *op. cit.*, pp. 370–73. They, in turn, draw heavily on the definitions
of Lasswell, Mary Follett, and Chester Barnard.

[89] T. C. Schelling, *The Strategy of Conflict* (Cambridge: Harvard University Press, 1961), p. 20.

of its environment will have been established. The environment is changed even if the system itself sustains no growth in task and receives no shining new mantle of legitimate authority.

This relationship bears a marked—if grim—resemblance to the notion of "mutual recognition" of the limit on violence in the theory of limited war. The Yalu River was so perceived by the belligerents, but

. . . not as something that we and the Chinese recognized unilaterally and simultaneously. . . . We recognized that they recognized it, they recognized that we recognized it, we recognized that they recognized that we recognized it, and so on. . . . In that sense, limits and precedents and traditions of this kind have an authority that is not exactly granted to them voluntarily by the participants in a conflict; they acquire a magnetism or focal power of their own.[90]

Likewise, in United Nations bodies, debates and votes, without directly and self-consciously motivating those who debate and vote to behave differently than they rationally wish to do, deter them just the same.

Table 1 Cohesion of Regional Caucus Groups in the United Nations General Assembly, 1945–1958

Cohesion of Member State

CAUCUS	BEFORE CREATION OF CAUCUS %			AFTER CREATION OF CAUCUS %			DURING THE WHOLE PERIOD % *		
	Iden-tical	Soli-darity	Divided	Iden-tical	Soli-darity	Divided	Iden-tical	Soli-darity	Divided
African **	—	—	—	46.7	33.3	20.0			
Western European	65.0	23.8	11.2	82.4	11.0	6.6			
Asian-African	11.4	36.4	53.9	34.4	42.2	23.4			
Benelux							77.5	17.0	5.5
Scandinavian							68.3	23.9	7.8
Commonwealth							13.0	27.7	59.3
Arab							63.4	27.2	9.4
Latin American							28.8	33.2	38.0
Soviet							96.0	3.9	0.1

Source: Thomas Hovet, Jr., *Bloc Politics in the United Nations* (Cambridge: MIT, Center for International Studies, 1958), pp. 64–65, 86, 98, 111, 121–122, 131, 155, 172, 187.
* The caucusing groups listed for "the whole period" were formed before or at the time of the first meeting of the General Assembly.
** The African Caucus had functioned for only two sessions at the time these computations were made, thus precluding firm conclusions. Prior to the formation of the Caucus there were not enough African member states to create a meaningful statistical pattern.

Hovet's study is based on the counting of an "adjusted gross" number of roll-call votes. For the meaning of this device, see Hovet, pp. 239 ff. On an "identical" vote the frequency of members voting the same way, not considering abstentions, is counted; on a "solidarity" vote, the frequency of members of a caucusing group abstaining rather than voting against their colleagues is determined; a "divided" vote covers the situations of direct opposition among members of a group.

[90] T. C. Schelling, "Toward a General Theory of Conflict Applicable to International Relations," *Midwest Journal of Political Science*, Vol. 4, No. 2, pp. 136–37.

14

Revolutionary Nations and the Quality of International Legal Order

Richard A. Falk

The tone of world politics today is being set by powerful revolutionary nations. A revolutionary nation is a state in which the government has sought or is seeking to reconstitute a national society in opposition to an established social order. Frequently, a revolutionary nation is the outcome of a successful revolutionary movement that has gained control of the governmental machinery by illegal means. Occasionally, as with Hitler's Germany, a revolutionary elite is voted into power by constitutional means. The Soviet Union is designated as the oldest existing revolutionary nation; Communist China, the United Arab Republic, and Cuba are others. The existence of these revolutionary nations is responsible for an extremely unstable pattern of international relations.

This essay examines the effect of this instability upon the current role of law in world affairs. There is a parallel need to study the international behavior of revolutionary nations during earlier historical periods.[1] For instance, one thinks of the liberal democratic revolutions that took place in France and the United States late in the eighteenth century. How did these revolutionary nations respond to the claims of the existing international legal order? Does the ideological character of the revolution control international participation in the post-revolutionary period? Or is the external conduct of the revolutionary nation primarily a consequence of the prevailing international political system? A historical study of the behavior of revolutionary nations would help us to distinguish between the unique and the repetitive aspects of the present world situation. It would, as well, increase our ability to isolate the variables that seem most responsible for the pattern of behavior chosen by the revolutionary nation. And finally, this improved knowledge might help us to formulate strategies to moderate the destabilizing impact of the newly emerging revolutionary nations.

* It gives me pleasure to thank Professor Roland J. Stanger of the Ohio State University College of Law for helping me so generously with this essay. I wish also to thank Professor Myres McDougal for his careful reading that led to suggestions for improvement that I have tried to incorporate in this final version.

[1] The general idea of this paragraph was suggested to me by Professor Wesley L. Gould of Purdue University.

The sequence of presentation in this study will be: first, a description of the manner in which international law is today conditioned by the dominance of revolutionary politics; second, the impact of this conditioning upon legal norms governing the use of coercion across national boundaries; third, an indication of the bearing of representative norms of international law upon the specific phenomenon of internal revolution.

It is evident that the international atmosphere is composed of many elements only one of which is law. Economic, social, psychological, military, and cultural factors all interact to generate stability or instability. Law is a relatively *dependent* variable, significantly useful in a stable social system, dramatically marginal in an unstable social system. By itself, legal technique cannot introduce stability. It is deceptive to rely upon international law as an independent variable. This explains why we should not isolate the study of international law from concern with the broad social and political conditions prevailing in the world. International law can contribute to world order only in *conjunction with* other stabilizing forces.

I

A central aspect of the revolutionary spirit is a refusal to accept the limits of permissible behavior as developed by the established order, especially its legal limits. Law is identified with the status quo, and it is the status quo that is the target of revolutionary energy. Law thus bears a problematic relevance to the politics of revolution.[2]

Nevertheless, certain other extra-legal factors give law, particularly international law, a potential importance for current world affairs. Law provides a convenient way for political rivals to specify limits of permissible behavior. If the consequence of unrestrained conflict is mutually destructive then it is rational to seek common limits that will prevent such unrestrained conflict from taking place. For instance, in the Korean War supply centers behind the Yalu and in Japan were both exempted from military attack.[3] The development of nuclear weapons has made unrestrained

[2] It is relevant to observe that the Draft Program of the Soviet Communist Party for the Twenty-Second Party Congress fails to make a single reference to international law in the course of an elaborate reformulation of Soviet foreign policy and aspiration. Even in the extended discussion of the relations between the Soviet Union and other members of the Communist bloc there is little tangible indication of a willingness to overcome national rivalries by the promotion of supranational political and legal integration. There is not even an expressed desire for regional institutions of an extent comparable to those developing in Western Europe. See full text of the Draft Program, New York *Times* (August 1, 1961), pp. 13–20. For negative accounts of the Soviet attitude towards international law see Marek S. Korowicz, *Introduction to International Law* (The Hague: M. Nijhoff, 1959), pp. 108–56; Leon Lipson, *Outer Space and International Law* (Rand Paper P-1434, 1959), pp. 12–17. For an affirmative account see Grigory I. Tunkin, "Co-Existence and International Law," *Recueil des Cours,* Academie de Droit International, Vol. 95 (1958).

[3] Throughout this essay it is important to take account of the particular character of the legal norm. The range of norms includes rules of the game and very specific provisions in international

conflict mutually destructive and the establishment of a legal regime mutually beneficial. There exists an urgent need to use suitable legal techniques to contain struggles for world power within safe boundaries. Thus, despite the existence of the revolutionary nations, international law is peculiarly relevant to contemporary politics because never before has it been so generally felt that legal means must be found to prevent the outbreak of major war between political rivals. The tension between the pressure for unrestraint generated by revolutionary energies and the pressure for restraint generated by the fear of nuclear war is central to an understanding of the contemporary relevance of international law.

This tension is made dangerously taut by the inability of the world community to legislate peaceful changes.[4] Oppressive elites in control of national societies yield only to coercion. The character of reactionary oppression is such that external aid is often needed by the internal protest movement if it is to succeed in its struggle for control of the national society. Two comments follow from this: First, internal social change in oppressive societies must come about by lawless coercion; the oppressive elite will otherwise tend to refuse the internal demands for social change, even when these demands have the support of the world community. The Union of South Africa is an instructive instance. Second, internal revolutionary situations can easily become the scenes of Cold-War conflict as a result of opposing Soviet and American interventions. Thus, internal social change can neither be achieved peacefully, nor can it be kept separate from the Cold War. Traditional international law is ill-conditioned to control such political phenomena since it is premised upon the irrelevance of internal coercion to the maintenance of world order. One way to emphasize the contemporary problem posed for international law by revolutionary nations is to insist upon the current fundamental relevance of internal coercion to international stability. The role of the United Nations in the Congo is at least partly [5] an acknowledgment of

agreements. My preference is to extend the characterization "law" to any "norm" that appears to standardize international behavior. This acknowledges the decentralized character of the international system and emphasizes its deficient norm-producing procedures and institutions. The text example from the Korean War suffers from its specificity in time and place. We usually think of law as providing standards of more general application. Here again, however, the *ad hoc* nature of international regimes is part of the quality of contemporary world order. This feature of specificity serves to remind us of the primitive character of international law. However, it is important to use an inclusive image of law for international affairs so as to perceive all existing ordering possibilities. In contrast, a strict image of law, as developed by Austinian positivism, may usefully focus the task of the jurist in an orderly and advanced social system.

It is essential also to examine the manner in which cultural tradition bears upon normative behavior and expectation. For instance, the deeply enbedded Asian experience with relations of subordination and superordination influence their perception of what constitutes "law." It appears to inhibit commitment to a horizontal legal order—such as the international legal system—that lays stress upon considerations of reciprocity to restrain behavior within limits set by legal norms. This point derives from a comment on an earlier version of this study made by Professor John Lindbeck of Harvard University.

[4] Perceptively foreshadowed in Herbert A Smith, *The Crisis in the Law of Nations* (London: Stevens, 1947).

[5] The United Nations initially was requested to send military assistance to the government of the Congo to permit it to repel "the present external aggression" charged to Belgium as a result of

this relevance. Recognition of this relevance leads to a repudiation of the traditional characterization of internal coercion as a matter of domestic concern.[6]

These introductory comments seek to convey a sense of the texture of world affairs as it relates to the contemporary role of international law. Countless other correlative extra-legal developments are important law-conditioning factors: the growing participation in world affairs of Afro-Asian countries, the development of economic and military regionalism, the growth of specialized and general supra-national institutions, the ideological commitments in the current struggle for power, the impacts of shifting military strategies (the gradual replacement of bombers by missiles), the vitality and impatience of movements for national independence and social innovation in the newly developing portions of the world, and the bipolar-ization of the international political structure.

Revolutionary nations generate instability that challenges the role of international law. For one thing, a revolutionary nation is often evangelical in spirit, exemplary for nascent revolutionary movements in neighboring nations and interventionary in practice;[7] there is a strong tendency, hardened into an ideology of world revolution in Communist countries, to export the revolution to status-quo states.[8] The new Draft Program of the Soviet Communist Party puts this explicitly when it accepts the "duty to support the sacred struggle of the oppressed people and their just anti-

---

"the despatch to the Congo of metropolitan Belgian troops in violation of the Treaty of Friend-ship" between the two countries. However, it was evident that the Security Council responded to Lumumba's request primarily because, as it stated in its Resolution of July 22, 1960, "the complete restoration of law and order in the Republic of the Congo would effectively con-tribute to the maintenance of international peace and security." See generally E. M. Miller, "Legal Aspects of U.N. Action in the Congo," 55 *Amer. J. Int'l Law*, No. 1 (1961).

[6] Traditional international law, as developed before nuclear weapons, emphasized the territorial state as a sovereign minimum unit in world affairs. Territorial jurisdiction was absolute except for the duty to respect the rights of alien residents. Otherwise, international law exempted internal phenomena, even when it crossed the threshold of violence. This exemption was accelerated in the twentieth century by the gospel of self-determination given initial impetus by Woodrow Wilson. With nuclear weapons, the Cold War political stability for the world rests progressively upon the control of internal violence. A sensitive study of the bearing of the new military technology upon the old political system is John H. Herz, *International Politics in the Atomic Age* (New York: Columbia University Press, 1959).

[7] Cuba exemplified this pattern by a series of futile interventions through Central America. The power used was so inadequate (a handful of men with an armful of light weapons) to the ends pursued (the overthrow of a well-organized government) that the revolutionary zeal of the Castro forces seemed like a bad comedy. For a brief description of these 1959 Cuban interven-tions see Richard P. Stebbins, *The United States in World Affairs 1959* (New York and London: Harpers, 1960), pp. 353–57.

[8] It is probably useful to point to phases in the post-revolutionary period. At first, the revolu-tionary government consolidates its internal position and seeks primarily to reconstitute its domestic society along the lines promised by the revolutionary program. External participation is marginal, limited to gestures of sympathy or token participation in foreign-protest movements. However, if the revolutionary government is successful and strong, then this emphasis is inverted. Internal policy becomes "conservative" (that is, conserving the character of the revolutionary society and moving slowly ahead along the same lines), while external policy becomes significantly interventionary. These comments refer to behavioral tendencies rather than to invariable patterns.

imperialist wars of liberation." [9] The revolutionary nations of Africa and the Middle East are eager to sponsor revolutions that aim to overthrow reactionary elites and replace them by revolutionary elites committed to radical internal social change. The missionary zeal of these revolutionary nations induces the status-quo nations to use their influence to resist the spread of the destabilizing gospel. The United States, as the dominant status-quo nation,[10] feels especially threatened by the revolutionary pressures generated by the Communist movement. It resists the spread of Communism by recourse to every available means short of initiating a general war. This reflects the animosity that arises from ideological antagonisms between rival leaders in the Cold War. It is partly also a competitive struggle for world domination. One effect is to compel the liberal democracies to support anti-democratic governments to resist a radical elite that has become identified with the Communist movement; United States relations with China since 1930 express fully this dilemma. It also leads the status-quo nations to sponsor counterrevolutionary internal movements. The rules of international law are today very ineffective to assure national governments their customary control over internal affairs.

Beyond this, the success of a revolution is often accompanied by a repudiation of those norms of international law which restrict the freedom of a state to shape its internal society. The revolutionary nation is usually committed to a program of rapid social change. This leads it to take control over internal capital and to relieve itself of external commitments, like bonded indebtedness. The Soviet Union, as a revolutionary nation, typified this pattern. It expropriated all property that it could reach without providing any suitable compensation and repudiated the debts of predecessor Russian governments. One effect of widespread revolution is thus to weaken the legal support given to international investment. For, in addition to the actual losses incurred, investors tend to withdraw capital or avoid further commitments when the prospects for revolution grow strong. The security of American investment throughout Latin America is at least part of the explanation for our preoccupation with Castroism. The rules of international law were developed to support the interests of the capitalist nations of Western Europe during their expansionist phases of development. This is very vividly perceived by the revolutionary nations, especially those equipped with a coherent radical ideology. International law, in general, is viewed by orthodox Marxist thought as one way by which the

[9] New York *Times* (August 1, 1961), p. 16, Col. 4; see also W. W. Rostow, *"Guerrilla Warfare in the Underveloped Areas,"* Vol. 45, *Dept. State Bull.* (1958), pp. 233, 234.

[10] The designation of the United States as a status-quo nation has important disadvantages. It overlooks the support given by the United States for moderate change. The United States favors the gradual termination of colonial administration and a moderate program of internal social reform. Nevertheless, the United States is called a status-quo nation here to contrast its posture towards change with the indiscriminate radicalism of the Communist bloc. Of course, as the Hungarian uprising of 1956 so vividly revealed, the Soviet Union is hostile to adverse changes taking place within its own bloc. Thus, the contrast between "revolutionary" and "status quo" is useful only when it makes reference to differing attitudes towards the pace of social change in underdeveloped countries.

bourgeoisie perpetuates its favored position in the world. This produces a basic disrespect for international law by the leadership of the revolutionary state.

Such disrespect is extended by the internal revolutionary experience. The revolutionary movement has necessarily flaunted the law to gain power and it has probably been subject to a variety of legal attempts by the former government to suppress its activities. Thus, "the law" tends to be identified with "the enemy" by the revolutionary elite.

In addition, the revolutionary nation is not sensitive to the dangers, even to itself, of external instability. In its early years it fails to perceive the advantages for its own internal development that would result from a reliable minimum world order. Red China continues to take a highly cavalier posture towards external instability.

These considerations lead one to be very skeptical about the impact of international law upon the conduct of revolutionary nations. However, a revolutionary nation, if it survives, comes to appreciate some of the advantages offered by an effective legal order. With the success of the revolution, a passionate insistence upon internal stability emerges to frustrate counterrevolutionary tendencies. This may lead to the moderation of interventionary external practices in tacit exchange for reciprocal deference to its own internal order. The Communist nations have always, in their formal participation in world affairs, emphasized the sanctity of the most conservative aspect of international law—that is, a broad, unrestricted doctrine of national sovereignty. The Soviet advocacy of an absolute position on sovereign immunity is an obvious matter of self-interest. State ownership combined with sovereign immunity would exempt Socialist nations from legal duties in their commercial dealing in capitalist nations without depriving them of legal rights.

The experience of a successful revolutionary nation may in other ways lead it toward conservative participation in world affairs. It may regard war as a genuine danger to its future, and seek to use law to reduce the risk. The Soviet Union often seems to be moving in this direction and is perhaps encouraged by its belief that there are safe ways to increase its relative position in the struggle with the West for world power; it is necessary to distinguish between conservative revolutionary nations (Soviet Union) and radical revolutionary nations (China). The radical revolutionary nation poses the most direct challenge to the maintenance of minimum legal order in international relations. The early experience of a revolutionary government tends to emphasize the negative tasks of eliminating the old order. But the experience of reconstituting the internal society along orderly lines makes the leadership dependent upon legal technique.[11] The revolutionary nation may be isolated in its early years of existence, but when it has consolidated its internal position, then it is likely to seek at least minimal external contacts. This leads to an appreciation for the convenience of legal standards to regulate routine contacts across national boundaries.

[11] See an analysis that suggests general tendencies of social systems to develop an orientation favorable to the application of legal rules, Roger Fisher, "Bringing Law To Bear on Governments," *Harvard Law Rev.* Vol. 74 (1961), pp. 1130–40; Roger Fisher, "Should We Veto the Troika?" *The New Republic* (August 21, 1961), pp. 11–14.

The early hostility to international law tends to dissolve and is replaced by a rather pragmatic attitude toward the rule of law. Soviet leadership has been particularly adept at improvising *ad hoc* invocations of international legal norms to promote its political policies. Thus, it stresses very much the doctrine of non-intervention in relation to Western efforts to transmit hostile propaganda to Eastern Europe [12] and behaves in a very interventionary manner in the dependent parts of the world, particularly in a non-European country controlled by a European imperialistic elite.

Revolutionary nations, then, are very likely to be lawless and hostile to law in their early years of power. Later this attitude is likely to grow more flexible and is expressed by a pragmatic use of the legal norms provided by international law. The nature of revolutionary ideology leads to a special burden upon the legal rules designed to preserve the independence of nations; interventionary policy generates counterintervention and creates conflict situations of high intensity. This is especially true when direct conflict is precluded by the obsolescence of recourse to war as a means of waging a struggle for world power. Status-quo nations, which today include the liberal democracies, also seem to regard international legal norms from a pragmatic angle that accords priority to Cold-War considerations. The significance of revolutionary nations then is to reduce the relevance of law to international politics for all national actors (including non-revolutionary nations).

The distinctive quality of international law as a legal system adds to the difficulty of achieving stability in a world community that includes revolutionary nations.[13] Compared with domestic legal orders, the formulation, interpretation and implementation of legal norms is very decentralized in international society. The principal ordering device is reciprocity.[14] This requires communication and a basic confidence between leading national actors, since adherence to legal norms, except in marginal contacts, is voluntary. Fairness results from self-restraint. The incentive for conformity is supplied by the mutual advantages to all states that result from fair and reliable legal standards. Such a predominantly horizontal legal order, working effectively without a hierarchy of legal institutions or centralized organs for consistent enforcement, achieves fair and predictable legal behavior in stable societies;[15] this pattern is suggested by the legal order prevailing in numerous primitive societies.[16] It depends, however, on a community commitment to stability and to a common base

[12] See the second Khrushchev Message to President Kennedy protesting United States intervention in April 1961 in Cuba, "Mr. Khrushchev to President Kennedy" (unofficial translation of message dated April 22, 1961), reprinted in 44 *Dept. State Bull.* (1961), 664.

[13] M. Kaplan and N. Katzenbach, *The Political Foundations of International Law* (New York: John Wiley and Sons, 1961), pp. 30–55.

[14] See Myres McDougal, *Studies in World Public Order* (New Haven: Yale University Press, 1960).

[15] This depiction is developed in some detail in Richard A. Falk, "International Jurisdiction: Horizontal and Vertical Conceptions of Legal Order," 32 *Temple Law Quarterly,* pp. 295–320, Vol. 32 No. 3 (1959).

[16] See *e.g.,* Bronislaw Malinowski, *Crime and Custom in Savage Society* (New York: Harcourt, Brace and Co., 1932). Max Gluckman, *The Judicial Process among the Barotze of Northern Rhodesia* (Manchester: Manchester University Press, 1955).

of shared values. International law, as it emerged from the natural-law tradition of Western Europe, fulfilled this need so long as world affairs were dominated by Western European actors.[17] But with the significant world participation of non-Western European nations, the divergent cultural backgrounds placed burdens on the horizontal structures of international law; effective communication depends greatly upon the shared experience of a common culture. Distrust and misunderstanding of alien tradition is a universal phenomenon.

This basic tendency to destabilize the common base of understanding needed for a legal order that relies heavily on reciprocity has been accentuated by the emergence of powerful revolutionary actors. For the revolutionary energy is often directed against the restraints and standards that are urged by status-quo nations. The revolutionary nation emerges in a situation of internal instability often confronted by hostile status-quo nations. The status-quo nations fear infiltration and subversion by the revolutionary nation; the revolutionary nation fears counterrevolutionary or interventionary pressure by the status-quo nations. Thus, instability is introduced at the core of the international legal order, undermining the kind of trust needed for the communication that must accompany the reciprocal patterns of practice. Unless nations believe that there is a mutual desire for stability in their relations with one another, instability will result. The dominance of a reciprocal threat to national security induces leading nations to subordinate common standards of legal restraint to political and military goals. The U-2 incident and the April 1961 interventions in Cuba by the United States contrast with the rhetorical pleas of our statesmen for the rule of law in world affairs.[18] Thus, the presence of revolutionary nations generates a destabilizing response by status-quo nations thereby reducing the opportunities for horizontal legal order. And by the same circumstance, states are reluctant to transfer important legal authority to vertical, international institutions; the Connally Reservation instances extreme legal inhibition by the leading status-quo nation. With such diffidence exhibited by status-quo nations—the states responsible for the development of international law—it is hardly surprising that revolutionary nations are reluctant to participate at all in international judicial proceedings, and refuse, for example, to settle disputes in the World Court. For the instability occasioned by the rivalry between status-quo and revolutionary nations is even more detrimental to the growth of the vertical forms of international law than it is to the horizontal forms.

Another way to state this consequence of fundamental distrust is to emphasize the decentralized power of decision entrusted to nations in relation to norms of international law. A state has been allowed great discretion by international-law to characterize its behavior in a self-serving manner. The notion of consent as the basis of international obligation and deference to sovereign prerogative is expressed with

[17] Cp. C. Wilfred Jenks, *The Common Law of Mankind* (New York: Praeger, 1958), pp. 63–172; Filmer Stuart Cuckow, Northrop, *The Taming of Nations* (New York: Macmillan, 1952).

[18] For a collection of statements by important recent political figures in the United States ranging from Robert Taft to Adlai Stevenson agreeing on the urgency of extending the international rule of law see A.B.A., Special Committee on World Peace Through Law, *Compilation of Quotations* (1960); Cp. also William W. Bishop, "The International Rule of Law," 59 *Michigan Law Rev.* 553 (1961).

celebrated clarity in the *Lotus* case.[19] This decentralization does not mean that international law is a futile pretense, but it does mean that the effectiveness of the rule is dependent upon the mutual commitment of nations to minimal standards of legal order. So long as stability is *perceived* as mutually beneficial for all major states, the horizontality of international society is not a disadvantage. The capacity of states to attribute legality to their own contested conduct, without being forced to submit their description to third-party judgment, makes it very important to look at the social reality behind the norms and doctrines of international law. The meaning of the legal norm must be comprehended by an inquiry into the process by which it is translated into behavior.

Independent of the revolutionary situation, skepticism about the role of international law is generated by the refusal of contending states to commit themselves to a procedure that includes impartial characterization. Legal norms exist in complementary sets of opposed prescriptions, thus providing a national actor on every occasion with a lawful explanation of his conduct.[20] Centralizations of authority to characterize legal conduct often produce a more significant growth in international law than do the elaborate codifications of legal norms in law-making treaties like the Geneva Conventions on the Law of the Sea. In this regard the *Nottebohm*[21] and *Asylum*[22] cases have immense juridical importance. For in *Nottebohm* the World Court asserted a vertical test for nationality, rejecting the self-serving characterization made by Lichtenstein, and in the *Asylum* case the majority judgment denied Colombia the right to determine unilaterally whether Haya de la Torre was entitled to diplomatic asylum. Acceptance of vertical characterization is essential to the growth of legal standards in a world composed of states that rarely trust one another. This constructive movement gains momentum as more nations can be made to feel that the risk of an unfavorable vertical characterization is more desirable than the disorder produced by two contradictory decentralized characterizations. Revolutionary nations in the early years of their existence are too jealous of their power, too distrustful of their adversary, too eager for unrestrained expansion to give important legal competence to international decision-makers.

Many discount the meaning of non-intervention pledges or renunciations of the use of force because the nations have not established an impartial procedure for determining when contested behavior falls within the prohibition of the legal rule. Legal rules, standing by themselves, do no more than frame diplomatic debate. The challenged nation invokes one group of legal norms to justify its conduct, and the complaining nation invokes the complementary set of legal norms. The United States condemns the Soviet Union for its "armed intervention" in the internal affairs of Hungary in 1956; the Soviet Union defends its conduct as a response to a request

[19] *S. S. Lotus, PCIJ.*, Ser. A, No. 10 (1927).
[20] Cp. Excellent study by Myres S. McDougal and Florentino P. Feliciano, "Legal Regulation of Resort to International Coercion: Aggression and Self-Defense in Policy Perspective, 68 *Yale Law Journal* 1057 (1959) discussion of complementary prescriptions is clearly stated on pp. 1059–63).
[21] Friedrich Nottebohm [*Lichtenstein v. Guatemala*] (1955), *I.C.J.* Rep. 4.
[22] Colombia Peruvian Asylum Case (1950), *I.C.J.* Rep. 266.

by the "legitimate" (Kadar) government for help in restoring internal order in a time of lawless civil strife. The invocation pattern is reversed if one examines reactions to the entry of American military forces into Lebanon in 1958. Impartial characterization of behavior is needed to assure the relevance of legal norms to patterns of conduct. Actors mutually committed to stability may be expected normally to restrain their conduct in accord with impartial characterizations.[23] It is common to find domestic courts, for instance, determining a controversy brought before it by deference to the national interests of another state. The doctrines of Act of State and sovereign immunity, as well as the solution of international choice of laws problems, reveal areas in which impartial legal standards of self-enforcement operate successfully because of the prevalent acceptance of the criteria of reciprocity. Expansions of this mode of legal order into central areas of contention such as, for instance, non-intervention is precluded by the revolutionary postulate. Political rivalry is given priority over legal moderation, especially where coercion is used by a bloc leader in the Cold War to increase or preserve its relative power. The dominant political instability makes it impossible to render an impartial decision. Each rival views a determination adverse to its national interest as biased and is unlikely to entrust the power of decision to any third-party procedure that did not institutionalize its political ideology. The relative willingness of the United States to fight Cold-War issues within the United Nations is less attributable to its preference for the rule of law than it is to its political assurance of voting majorities on most controversial issues. In this respect even status-quo nations have not displayed a willingness to accept legal limits when vital national interests were involved. Political considerations in Kashmir quickly revealed the scope of India's commitment to the rule of law, and the Suez campaign in 1956 illustrated the willingness of even extreme status-quo nations to override the limits of law.

Despite the fact that complementary norms give nations a "legal" explanation for "illegal" conduct, the consensus of world sentiment tends to provide an independent judgment. This can result in conforming behavior to the legal norm if both superpowers happen to agree with the majority judgment; the effective response of the United Nations to the Suez invasion by France, England, and Israel provides a leading illustration. Even when the superpowers disagree, the vote in the General Assembly provides a weak form of objective characterization that has law-inducing consequences. The growing strength of world opinion, especially as expressed in the United Nations, gives to resolutions of censure the status of an inchoate sanction. It is relevant to compare the prominent ordering role played by ridicule in primitive societies. The Soviet Union has not been unmindful of its international prestige. The

---

[23] It is well to observe that national actors have never operated in conditions of "normalcy" where vital matters were involved. Prior to our revolutionary age, the egoistic pursuit of national interest led states to refuse to accept comprehensive legal standards. For an excellent treatment of the earlier politicization of world affairs along these lines see Charles de Visscher, *Theory and Reality in Public International Law* (Princeton: Princeton University Press, 1957), pp. 71–129. Perhaps the advent of nuclear weapons during the European stage of world history might have produced an effective world legal order. A common cultural heritage might have overcome political differences in the face of the threat of mutual extermination.

prospect of censure, with a resulting crystallization of world opinion, seems to influence, if not restrain, national actions; it acts as a marginal factor to discourage repetitions of Budapest, and it may yet spare Castro an invasion by the United States marines.

One hopes that the passage of time will transform the outlook of the revolutionary nations in the direction of the status-quo nations.[24] The process is cumulative, as when the status-quo nations perceive the waning of the revolutionary zeal they will, in turn, also rely more upon stabilities of law and less upon stabilities of force. The nuclear risks encourage both types of nations to hasten a willingness to strengthen legal order.

II

The effort of post-Medieval Europe to restrict the right of a state to wage war to those instances in which it had "a just cause" ended in failure. Despite the moralizing rhetoric of the *bellum justum* doctrine, drawn by jurists from the corpus of natural law, it became evident that most nations were unwilling to adhere to legal limits when they had sufficient power to attain national goals by conquest. It was the wisdom of the nineteenth century to shift the emphasis from a delineation of the occasions when it was legitimate to wage war to a system of shifting alliances between the leading European states designed to make it impossible for a nation to mobilize superior force against its political rivals. Thus, stability was not a matter of enforcing rules restricting the use of force, but rather the control of force depended upon the existence of countervailing force. Political mechanisms of stability were more successful than the earlier attempt to establish stability by positing clear rules. Law thus became virtually irrelevant to the use of war to promote national interests, although law made important contributions to the effort to restrict the scope of war by the doctrine of neutrality and to regularize the conduct of hostilities to eliminate superfluous horror. The decision to use force, however, was not subject to third-party characterization, and a state was in a position to legitimate recourse to war by giving its own explanation.

The First World War marked the end of the balance of power system. The destructivity of war in the twentieth century gave solemn urgency to the endeavor to control the use of force. The League of Nations was created to provide collective machinery for the determination of unlawful uses of force, thus internationalizing the characterization of war and aggregating the counter force of the world community. However, the unanimity principle, the non-participation of the United

[24] A liberalization of the internal regime tends to encourage the pressure for external accommodation. Such a tendency is transformed by some into a presupposition; that is, legal arrangements with totalitarian nations are a trap for liberal democracies. Thus, we must not expect to develop a universal legal order until there has been decisive internal liberalization in the Communist states. This position is developed by Myres S. McDougal and Harold D. Lasswell in "The Identification and Appraisal of Diverse Systems of Public Order" *Studies in World Public Order* (New Haven: Yale University Press (1960), pp. 3–10.

States, and the unwillingness of nations to act on behalf of world community interests made the League unable to cope with flagrantly aggressive recourses to force by Germany, Italy, and Japan. Widespread efforts were made to persuade nations to renounce the use of force in international relations, culminating in the solemn pledge of the Pact of Paris in 1928 to restrict recourse to force to situations of self-defense. One could question the seriousness of the legal commitment in view of the failure to provide definitions of aggressive war or self-defense and the absence of a mechanism for an impartial characterization of conduct alleged to be in violation of the pledge. With neither a standard nor an agency for third-party interpretation and enforcement, the legal commitment to renounce the aggressive use of force proved to be ineffectual, except possibly as sedation for status-quo nations. Legal rules, without the backing of available and sufficient force, seem unable to discourage recourse to international violence. This observation continues to pertain to the present world situation. The United Nations Charter restricts the lawful use of force to "the inherent right of individual or collective self-defense" in Article 51 and expresses in Article 2(4) a commitment by members to refrain from the use or threat of force in international relations. The prohibition of aggressive war was implicit in the Nuremberg Judgment and received the unanimous support of the General Assembly in a resolution adopting the Nuremberg Principles. Thus, recourse to unlawful war, if unsuccessful, might well result in criminal responsibility for the leaders of the defeated nation. But no serious progress has been made to outlaw war as a way to promote national interests. An authoritative definition of aggression is needed to establish a legal standard that could guide states and suggest the outer limits of permissible coercion. However, one notes with regret, that the United Nations has failed in its attempts to formulate an acceptable definition of aggression; [25] instead reliance is placed upon an *ad hoc* political determination by the Security Council in the unlikely event of agreement among the permanent members or by a two-thirds vote of the General Assembly. Major states do not seem willing to entrust the determination of and control over recourses to force to a non-political commission operating with an advance definition and empowered to compel police action.[26] It is exceedingly problematic to rely upon the indubitable "norm" of international law proscribing aggressive war. For without an effective process for implementing the definition, could it be agreed upon, it is unlikely to govern the behavior of expanding states in their pursuit of national goals. The mere "norm" of international law positing a standard of behavior does not deserve the status of "law" unless it is accompanied by a process of implementation. However, it is not essential that the process be supplied by a central or supranational ("vertical") institution; it may bring about the desired behavioral results by decentralized or national ("horizontal") regularities. For instance, the modest success of the neutrality system in confining the scope of war was based upon the horizontal interplay of self-interested belligerent and neutral nations. Horizontal efforts to control aggressive war reveal more promise. Thus, Cold-War

[25] See Quincy Wright, "The Prevention of Aggression," 50 *Amer. J. Int'l Law*, pp. 514, 517 (1956); Louis Sohn, "The Definition of Aggression," 45 *Virginia Law Rev.* (1959) 697.
[26] Julius Stone, *Aggression and World Order* (Berkeley: University of California Press, 1958).

rivals are intimidated by the probable fulfillment of collective self-defense commitments and the fear of a retaliation that includes nuclear devastation. Such deterrent threats seem to have discouraged the cruder and more central exertions of coercion in the Cold War; the Korean conflict is a special instance because the boundary crossed was not "international," and the United States had been publicly ambivalent about undertaking an advance commitment to defend South Korea. When border-crossing occurs outside the main context of the Cold War, as in Suez in 1956, then the collective machinery of the United Nations increasingly provides effective community response.

Thus, the prohibition of aggressive war seems to be an effective contemporary legal doctrine if the concept of aggression is very crudely defined. However, subtle forms of coercion, even across borders, are not brought under legal control. The United Nations would not respond to the complaints by Israel of episodic Egyptian border-crossings for purposes of terrorizing inhabitants of Israeli territory; such coercive conduct fell short of "an armed attack," and Israel was not entitled to act in self-defense. The absence of control over subtle forms of coercion imposes an immense burden upon a nation that is expected to refrain from the use of "aggressive" force. It is on these grounds that Julius Stone defends the Sinai campaign in 1956.[27] The background threat of nuclear war is so overwhelming that the clear minimum standards of identifying coercion as border-crossing of sustained magnitude must be upheld, even though it may have been very unfair to expect Israel in 1956 to suffer continuing harassment at the hands of Egyptian terrorists.

The instabilities of the era, combining the expansive energies of the Communistic bloc and the eruptive energies of the various Afro-Asian, Latin American revolutionary elites, have not been expressed in conventional war. Nuclear deterrence makes it highly irrational to promote national interests by recourse to war. Thus, the legal norm is backed by political reality. However, the cost of "law enforcement" is exceedingly high, involving the immense outlay of resources needed to ensure a crippling second strike capacity and the horrible risk of accidental war in one of its several forms.[28] It is characteristic of revolutionary politics to maintain order by a reliance upon terror, and it is this frightful condition that appears to be an integral aspect of the current situation. For the very presence of revolutionary impetus in the world particularly rigidifies the distrust of the status-quo nations, especially when the pendulum starts to swing against them, so as to make it impossible to transfer the struggle onto a level where the stakes are less ultimate. Consequently, legal arrangements to banish nuclear weapons and to give to an international organization the force needed to discourage non-nuclear "aggressive war" have small hope for significant adoption even though the dynamics of the actual conflict would remain unchanged. That is, the Communist bloc would continue to support internal revolutionary movements in the less developed parts of the world, and the Western nations would counter that support by helping the presently constituted governments.

[27] Ibid., pp. 99–103.
[28] See John Phelps et al., "Accidental War: Some Dangers in the 1960's" (Mershon National Security Program Research Paper, 1960).

This is a crisis of confidence and imagination which must be overcome if law is to contribute its techniques to enable the conflict to be waged without endangering human survival. For the horizontal system of deterrence based upon a reasonable consensus as to the nature of "aggression" may break down if one side finds itself losing the Cold War. The dysfunctional rigidity of the American response to Castro is an alarming sign of such a possibility. The accumulation of such signs may lead to the triggering of nuclear war and, thus, to a further fulfillment of Samson's last testament.

The tendency of revolutionary nations to export their ideological impetus rarely requires a direct use of force, much less recourse to a full-scale aggressive war. The expansion by the revolutionary nations is carried on by subtler forms of coercion than are entailed by the concept of "armed attack." In addition, the revolutionary spirit in the twentieth century is based upon an anti-imperialist ideology which stresses the urgency of radical internal social and economic changes. Despite the empire-building patterns of the Soviet Union, and now China, the revolutionary mission is primarily the sponsor of nationalist eruptions in the status-quo nations. Subordinate revolutionary energies in the Arab and African worlds stress racial unification on a political level; one supposes that Nasser and Nkrumah envision themselves as eventual heads of sprawling resurgent racial empires. The basic revolutionary appeal, however, is directed to the oppressed classes who are urged to seize control, redistribute wealth, and provide the state with a wide capital base that will support rapid industrial development.

Subtler forms of coercion, often called "indirect aggression," are difficult to regulate, partly because of the special status conferred upon nation-states by international law. The classical formulations of international law underscore the dominance of states in world affairs. It is a historical fact that national governments consolidated internal power to permit effective participation in external ventures of discovery, settlement, and trade. This led to affirmations of the exclusivity of the authority of a state within its own borders and to marginal restrictions upon the capacity of a state to act in world affairs. Thus, there arose considerable doctrinal support for the independence of a state and the implied right of a national society to be free from external interference. Participation in world affairs was confined to the leading monarchies of Europe. Each sought to maximize its power at the expense of the others but had no particular impulse to interfere with the internal affairs of its rival. If conflict was unavoidable by balance of power calculations then war settled the issue—preferably fought on some colonial land far from the home country; war represented a conflict of professional armies and was not nearly so likely to require the total support of the internal population. However, the success of the American and French revolutions changed the character of world affairs. From the Congress of Vienna onwards, the continental monarchies perceived the democratic objectives of revolutionary movements as a contagious disease to be stamped out wherever it appeared. Prussia, Russia, and Austria adopted a responsive interventionary policy in defense of the principle of legitimacy. Armed interventions restored monarchies in Naples, Piedmont, and Spain. For Spain, the avowal of intentions to recapture control over her revolting colonies led to the Monroe Doctrine in 1823, with its insistence that European nations refrain from intervention in the Western hemisphere. It is well known how the shield became a sword as the century progressed. Although Europe was kept out, the United States intervened to restore internal order or to protect American economic interests. The details of the story are no longer important, as a series of twentieth-century hemispheric agreements incorporated an absolute renunciation of the right of unilateral intervention in the internal affairs of a sovereign state.[29] However, the internal events in another state were not sealed off from international concern. The adoption of the principle of collective self-defense in Article 3 of the Inter-American Treaty of Reciprocal Assistance was supplemented by the Declaration of Solidarity at Caracas in 1954, with its condemnation of the interventionary character of the internationalist Communist movement and an *a priori* commitment to view its appearance in any part of the hemisphere as "a threat to the sovereignty and political independence of the American states" that called for collective action. In effect, the formal claim was to revive the concept of protective intervention implicit in the experience of the Monroe Doctrine in order to set limits upon the expansionist tendencies of the Communist movement.

The development of American policy was influenced by events leading up to the Second World War that suggested political limits to the legal commitment to non-intervention. The end of the First World War had led to strong sentiment, most dramatically attributed to Wilson, favoring policies of self-determination and non-intervention. The costly war was itself seen to be, in part, an outgrowth of colonial greed. The reaction led to a widespread endorsement of the right of a people to control their own political destiny. It was also felt that if non-interference prevailed, conflict could be localized. Gradually this induced the status-quo powers to give up interventionary practices and adhere to their pledges of non-intervention. Such a pattern of commitment was part of the atmosphere favorable to the aggressions of Nazi Germany. A combination of subversive intervention by Germany and non-intervention by other European nations facilitated the increases in national power won so easily by Hitler in the years leading up to the Second World War. The acme of non-intervention by the Western democracies took place during the Spanish Civil War and was paralleled by the full-scale intervention of the Fascist nations on the side of Franco and the Soviet Union on the Loyalist side. It became evident that intervention short of armed attack was an effective way to increase national power, at least assuring a friendly government. Furthermore, it was demonstrated that a potential aggressor becomes much more dangerous if it can consolidate its power by maximum use of interventionary tactics prior to recourse to war. The implication of non-intervention is to watch while a potential enemy grows strong through a series of successful interventions. When the occasion to resist arises for the "law-abiding" state, then it may be too late, or at least it is more arduous than it would have been at a stage when the aggressor was weaker. Certainly Hitler was

[29] Comprehensive review found in Doris A. Graber, *Crisis Diplomacy* (Washington: Public Affairs Press, 1959); Aaron J. Thomas, Jr. and Ann Van Wynen Thomas, *Non-Intervention: The Law and Its Import in the Americas* (Dallas: Southern Methodist University Press, 1956).

more difficult to defeat because the liberal democracies did not regard his earlier manifestations of aggressiveness as an occasion for counteraction. Non-intervention is a system that brings stability only if all states powerful enough to intervene refrain from using their power. As soon as one state embarks on an interventionary policy then the legal standards used to measure the duties of non-intervention are a trap for status-quo nations and a shield for an aggressor nation. Thus, in the years leading up to the Second World War, non-intervention was deference to aggression rather than to self-determination. Hence, protective and preventive intervention may be essential to resist the pressure of expansion. This insight has been at the basis of United States policy in the Cold War, accounting for American interventions in Iran, Guatemala, Lebanon, and now, abortively, Cuba and Laos.

Revolutionary internal action necessarily invites intervention [30] under modern circumstances. The dominant elite in control of the national government can often suppress a purely domestic revolutionary movement. However, the internal revolutionary group, especially if it is situated near the periphery of Communist influence, can receive external help; such intervention transforms the domestic revolution into an arena for Cold-War conflict, subordinating the welfare of the inhabitants to the global struggle for power. This was the sad experience of Korea, Indochina, and Laos. Cold-War rivalry can also be used by the successful nationalist revolution to obtain significant external economic aid to allow rapid internal capital development to take place. Nasser discovered this way to exploit the revolutionary situation of world affairs without endangering national independence. Castro, gaining control of a strategically situated nation, has tried the same tactic; but American property interests in Cuba, and the widespread fear that Castroism is a spreading cancer, led to intervention.[31] The United States acted to prevent the successful revolutionary leader from taking advantage of the Cold War to achieve internal material gains.

The historical-political pattern of the revolutionary era conditions the legal norms prohibiting intervention in very comprehensive terms. Article 15 of the Charter of Bogota is typical of the broad doctrinal commitment to non-intervention:

No State or group of States has the right to intervene, directly or indirectly for any reason whatsoever, in the internal or external affairs of any other State. The foregoing principle prohibits not only armed force, but also any other form of interference against the personality of the State or against its political, economic, and cultural elements.

The Draft Code of Offenses against the Peace and Security of Mankind even proposes individual criminal responsibility for promoting intervention in the political affairs of another country. But here, unlike with aggression, there is no horizontal

[30] It is useful to keep in mind the distinction between the *facts* of intervention and the *legal determination*. The process by which a factual pattern of interference is characterized as "intervention" is a significant aspect of the international system deserving of separate, detailed statement. One might experiment with the use of "interference" to describe the events and "intervention" to designate the actual or probable response of an authoritative decision-maker.

[31] For analysis of Cuban intervention see Richard A. Falk, *"United States Participation in the Cuban Invasion and the Rule of Law"* (1961) *Ohio State Law* Jl 546 (1961).

implementation of the broad prohibitive legal commitment.[32] The superpowers do not think that an intervention will provoke a massive retaliation by their rival. In fact, the obsolescence of recourse to war shifts the international struggle for power into a series of interventionary settings. The United Arab Republic has found that intervention by hostile propaganda, subversion, and other means more subtle than so-called "dictatorial interference" in internal affairs is an economical and effective way to expand its influence across national boundaries by sponsoring internal revolutions in neighboring conservative countries. It is ordinarily true that intervention in Africa and Asia is a progressive force for social change unless it leads to an armed clash in the context of the Cold War; it provides the oppressed peoples with an external lever or power that can often enable the revolution to overcome internal weakness. If the occasion for intervention is to prevent a defection by a Cold-War bloc member, then the danger of major nuclear conflict tends to discourage counter-intervention. This certainly seems to be evident for the United States intervention in Guatemala in 1954 and in Cuba in 1961, and for the Soviet intervention in Hungary in 1956.

Political factors take consistent precedence over legal considerations with regard to interventionary phenomena. The legal rules are quite clear, but the urgencies of revolutionary energy in the midst of the Cold-War rivalry give them little more than a rhetorical relevance. That is, especially the United States seeks to veil its interventionary practices by legalistic devices. Thus, the Eisenhower Doctrine stressed the consent of the constituted government to justify action taken to suppress internal revolutionary pressures, and President Kennedy emphasized the absence of direct military intervention to defend America's role in staging the 1961 counter-revolution against Castro. Such concern with legality is significant so far as it actually influences American decisions to resort to military intervention or to refrain from sending troops into a foreign country when the head of state has not requested their presence. In this sense the phenomena of intervention can be confined or enlarged by the broad relevance of reciprocity to the behavior of the leading actors in the Cold War. Thus, the way the United States intervenes in Cuba may influence the way in which the Soviet Union intervenes in Laos. But from the viewpoint of the smaller status-quo nations in Latin America and elsewhere, reliance upon such legalistic factors does not disguise the defeat of the legal principle, and its embodied policy, that one state is not entitled to use its coercive influence to control the internal affairs of another state. For conformity to a technical interpretation of a norm matters far less than the fulfillment of the guiding policy of the rule by finding behavioral ways to unite power with prescriptive imperatives.

The Soviet Union has consistently abetted internal revolutions in the non-Socialist parts of the world by following an openly interventionary policy.[33] In the context of colonialism, the principle of self-determination is given precedence over norms of non-intervention. But when a Socialist country is the target of intervention, then the

<hr />

[32] Domestic (horizontal) implementation of non-intervention policy is technically fulfilled by the provisions of the United States Neutrality Laws. See 22 USCA § § 441–65, No. 18 USCA § 960.
[33] Premier Khrushchev has publicly promised Soviet support for internal wars of liberation.

Soviet Union strongly stresses notions of domestic concern and non-interventionism. For instance, Premier Khrushchev's April 22, 1961 Message to President Kennedy on the American role in financing, training, and administering the rebel attack on Cuba relied heavily and piously upon the norm of international law proscribing intervention:

> What standards of law can be invoked to justify these interventions? . . . If such methods were to become predominant in the relations among states, there would be no place left for law. Its place would be taken by lawlessness and arbitrariness.

And later in his Message Khrushchev says:

> We are for the peaceful coexistence of all states and noninterference in the internal affairs of other countries. . . . We consider that any interference by one state in the affairs of another, especially armed interference is a violation of all international laws.[34]

It is accurate to attribute a schizophrenic quality to the American endorsement of non-interventionism. At the same time that we revive, like Lazarus, the Monroe Doctrine to justify intervention in Cuba, alleging our action to be in accord with the Caracas Declaration of Solidarity, we continue to celebrate Captive Nations Week each July by a unanimous Resolution of Congress despite its frankly interventionary tenor.[35] It is evident that the distinction between intervention and non-intervention is manipulated by the Cold-War leaders to justify their preferred political solution to a given situation. There is no adherence to a common standard, although Khrushchev's Message on Cuba emphasizes the destabilizing effect of the reciprocal acceptance by the Soviet Union of military security as a basis for intervention in states like Pakistan and Turkey that have American bases on the geographical border of Russia. This is an important consideration, as the degree of restraint in an unstable world is based more on reciprocal patterns of practice than it is upon abstract norms of legal control. Revolutionary nations, as their position grows strong, may shift from lawlessness to gradual patterns of reciprocal adherence to common standards. This may be one way to discern the transformation of a revolutionary nation into a status-quo nation.

The policy of non-intervention is closely allied to legal rules about territorial soverignty, equality and independence of states, and domestic jurisdiction. The fundamental policy objective is to affirm the internal supremacy of the national government; however, generally, international law is not concerned with coercive *internal* movements, including revolutions, that threaten to overthrow the existing government. External states may give aid to the constituted government if the civil strife is characterized as "insurgency" but must remain neutral if it is regarded as "belligerency"; some regard the duty of non-interference to include a refusal to give the established government help regardless of the stage of civil strife. Despite contrary claims, no interventionary right ordinarily arises as a result of civil strife. Thus, under the Charter civil strife is a matter "essentially within domestic jurisdiction"

---

[34] *New York Times* (April 23, 1961).
[35] Quincy Wright, "Subversive Intervention," 54 *Amer. J. Int'l Law*, No. 521 (1960), pp. 521–35.

unless it constitutes a threat to the peace. That is, the duty of the United Nations is to maintain *international,* not *internal* peace; but the expanding tendencies of civil strife under revolutionary world conditions very quickly transforms an internal war into an international conflict situation. This certainly accounts for the presence and the immense difficulty encountered by the United Nations in its effort to establish order in the Congo in 1960–61. The Congo conflict combines the Cold War and the battle against colonialism with intense internal struggles for power. The factions are not susceptible, it has seemed, to reconciliation; the establishment of order requires the United Nations to make choices for and against the contending factions, thereby identifying itself with one side in the global rivalry and alienating the opposed side. The United Nations has met this fate in the Congo operation, and yet it is not easy to conceive how else it might have acted to carry out its decision to intervene. The emergence of revolutionary nations—of the Left and of the Right— tends to subordinate actual implementation of centralized interventionary decisions to the urgencies of the Cold War. This was curiously manifest in a recent study of intervention from the perspective of diplomatic history:

> Intervention is legal when it is used to protect vital national or international interests which are in imminent jeopardy and which cannot be protected by other means. When it is undertaken to safeguard lesser stakes, or when peril is not pressing, or when other means are available, or when it violates contractual obligation, intervention is illegal.[36]

In a decentralized legal order this makes law into an appeal to conscience; there are no criteria given whereby patterns of reciprocal behavior can establish reasonable limits to interventionary policy. This is a regressive approach to the relation between law and politics, as it confirms the primacy of political considerations. It is recommended that the motive for interference should not govern the legality of the interference unless it is carried out under mandate of the United Nations. The illegality of intervention is preferably viewed as a series of coordinates ranging from the manifest illegality of armed interference in internal affairs to the subtle legality of a prolonged withholding of recognition from a hostile government; as a second set of coordinates ranging from the illegality of unilateral interventions to the legality of world community intervention; and as a third set of coordinates that expresses the extent of coercive impact. Such a system of normative classification would help us to understand the legal quality of interventionary practice.

A second level of analysis could then relate a particular intervention to the dynamics of the revolutionary situation of the Cold War. From such a perspective we can distinguish the Indian interventions in Kashmir and Hyderabad from the Soviet interventions in Czechoslovakia and Hungary and the American interventions in Guatemala and Cuba. In this connection it is useful to emphasize the spatial relation between the target state and the intervening Cold-War actor; compare, for instance, the American response to the Chinese intervention in Tibet with the alleged Soviet intervention in Cuba on behalf of Castro. Part of the variation here is based upon the feasibility of counterintervention. We find, as well, a minimal stability that results

[36] Graber, *op. cit.,* p. 361.

from reciprocal deference by the leading Cold-War rivals to a region of acknowledged hegemony;[37] here it is useful to compare the verbal "counterintervention" with military counterintervention—for instance, United States–Soviet responses to Guatemala in 1954, Hungary in 1956, and Laos in 1961.

Thus, the interventionary policy of a revolutionary political era takes precedence over the norms of non-intervention present in international law. However, the aging of major revolutionary nations, the threat of war arising out of interventionary clashes, and the growth of regional and international institutions suggests that, possibly, legal claims will be given greater weight in the future. Certainly adequate norms and implementing processes relevant to non-intervention are a prerequisite of a successful shift from instability to stability in world politics.

III

The relevance of norms of international law to the specific phenomenon of an internal revolution is evident. The Communist governments of the Soviet Union and mainland China attained power by successfully staged revolutions. The main way in which the leading revolutionary nations seek to expand their influence, and this includes a non-Communist nation like the United Arab Republic, is to sponsor revolutionary movements in status-quo nations. Techniques of infiltration, subversion, and espionage have been perfected as instruments of indirect aggression without exposing the actor to the immense hazard of direct attack. The bearing of legal norms upon the phenomenon of revolution is a crucial aspect of the relation between a revolutionary nation and international law. The effort to export revolutions is, of course, prohibited by the norms of non-intervention; subversion, infiltration, and propaganda, designed to foment a foreign revolution is a maximum instance of an effort to influence the internal affairs of a sovereign state. In addition to this central notion of non-intervention, international law provides other norms which are more compatible with the interests of the revolutionary nation in instability. For instance, there is the positive legal duty to remain aloof from civil strife, thus legitimating the normal interest of revolutionary nations in denying external relief to the constituted government in its struggle to suppress the revolutionary movement. The non-intervention system of the liberal democracies contributed to the triumph of the Rightist revolution of Franco in Spain. Once a revolutionary government attains control of its national territory, it frequently expropriates the private property and public assets of its predecessor government. The legal rules of Act of State and sovereign immunity in the domestic courts of foreign status-quo states tend to facilitate this process. Municipal courts may, however, seek to interfere with expropriation of property, especially if it is located outside the revolutionary nation. In fact, if a large portion of the assets of revolutionary nations are located in foreign status-quo nations, refusals to give effect to nationalization decrees can seriously interfere with

[37] See perceptive analyses, Georg Schwarzenberger, "Hegemonial Intervention," *The Year Book of World Affairs* (London: Stephens and Sons, 1955), pp. 236–65.

the social program of the revolutionary nations. This is an indecisive area of law with many divergent decisions;[38] considerable disagreement among commentators exists as to the wisdom and effectiveness of using such invalidating legal norms as a weapon in the battle against revolutionary nations. Such partisan use of horizontal institutions of the world legal order (domestic courts) can undermine that portion of international law dependent upon reciprocity.

In addition, status-quo nations can withhold diplomatic recognition from and resist the admission to the United Nations of a revolutionary nation, thereby restricting its participation in world affairs. This politicizes the recognition process making it depend upon the attitude of the status-quo nation to the revolutionary government, rather than making it depend upon the legal (objective) standard of factual control over land, territory, and institutions. Such politicization of legal norms enhances instability in international affairs and seems to have a dubious impact upon the target nation. American non-recognition policy directed first at the Soviet Union, now at China, seems to be dubious politics, as well as weakening the appeal of our plea to other nations to adhere to the rule of law in world affairs. It also tends to legitimate resort to premature recognition by the revolutionary nations. The right to give political fugitives diplomatic asylum within the territory of a foreign state also has an obvious relation to revolutionary activity. Here again, however, the instability generated by the existence of revolutionary nations makes the institution of asylum also selectively valuable to status-quo nations. One thinks, for instance, of the grant of asylum to Cardinal Mindszenty by the United States.

This brief discussion intends only to illustrate how international law bears upon the specific phenomenon of internal revolution. The legal problems raised here are very diverse and complex. They generate controversial solutions and require fuller consideration to permit an adequate appreciation of the relevance of norms of international law to revolutionary activity.

Conclusion

The advent of revolutionary nations has accentuated the tendency of nations to pursue selfish ends by coercive means in world politics. Military strategy and latent internal instability in the newly developing portions of the world have shaped the patterns of coercion used by Cold-War rivals. Legal norms serve to restrain behavior only when they accord with a powerful nation's perception of its national security. Thus, the current relevance of legal norms to world affairs depends upon a careful comprehension of the bearing of social, economic, military, and political variables.

The dominance and pervasity of the Cold War makes manifest the fact that the nations of the globe do not compose a world community. Divergent ideologies and cultures stress the absence of the kind of social cohesiveness propitious to the growth of law. The starkness of this social split is highlighted by the growing interdependence

[38] Decisions are interestingly represented in Milton Katz and Kingman Brewster, *International Transactions and Relations* (Brooklyn: Foundation Press, 1960) pp. 299–398.

of nations. Nuclear testing, for instance, radiates a locus of concern far wider than the physical locus of action. Growing interdependence in a condition of intensifying hostility short of war is one way to summarize the contemporary crisis in world order. As the need for solutions grows more essential, the social basis for agreement continues to diminish to the vanishing point.

And yet we find a continued emphasis by our leaders upon the need to replace the reign of force by the rule of law. President Eisenhower put this very well at New Delhi in 1959: "The time has come for mankind to make the rule of law in international affairs as normal as it is now in domestic affairs." The sincerity of this sentiment makes especially ironic an emerging American pattern of departure from a law-oriented approach to world affairs. Such a departure has been highlighted by the U-2 incident, retention of the Connally Reservation, prolonged non-recognition of Communist China, and intervention in the internal affairs of Castro's Cuba.

This distance between authoritative rhetoric and conduct is more than cynical opportunism by national leaders. It reflects the trap that seems to have been set for status-quo nations by the instabilities generated by the aggressive revolutionary nations. We are caught between the irreconcilable aspiration for a just international order and the necessity to meet force with force to assure our survival. The atmosphere is made particularly tense by the frightful dangers of nuclear conflagration. It is my feeling that this apparent crisis is partly a consequence of a failure of intellect and will. There appears to be a growing awareness that power politics is now more like Russian roulette than a game played for rational gain. But there is at the same time considerable official reticence to acknowledge the implications of this perception. Nevertheless I am led to hope, perhaps naively, that an awareness of the futility of a game will encourage its eventual abandonment.[39] If such an instrumental consensus can assert itself—called recently a "community of fear"—then the task of just ordering assigned to law is clear. But it will be a task that is less concerned with the formulation of "norms" and "doctrine" than with the implementation of rules in action by the development of strong procedures, processes, and institutions for making certain that the word becomes flesh. This desideratum suggests a whole direction for a contextual rethinking of the role of international law in world affairs.

[39] This line of thinking is somewhat suggested by Anatol Rapoport, *Fights, Games and Debates* (1960); and see H. S. Hughes, "The Strategy of Deterrence," *Commentary*, Vol. 31, No. 3 (1961) pp. 185–92.

15

The Arms Race and World Order*

Herman Kahn

Many sober people believe that the current international order, with its emphasis on anarchy, national egoism, and deterrence, is not going to last to the year 2000; that it will not, in fact, last more than a decade or two. One can hold this estimate even after recognizing that many successful adjustments have already been made to modern technology, and that the current arms race is not as uncontrolled as it would be if narrow military, technological, and economic factors were the sole determinants of military research, development, procurement, and operations.

Actually, as compared to the inherent technological possibilities, the current arms race is more of a walk than a race. It is rather severely limited by political, social, moral, economic, and doctrinal constraints on the participants. These constraints and adjustments doubtless "buy time," but many believe that they do not buy enough time for the system to adjust satisfactorily by gradual evolution. It still seems likely *either* that the system must be changed drastically in the near future, *or* that it will "blow up"—that is, change itself in a violent explosive manner. It is the main purpose of this paper to discuss the implications of this either-or view for the revolution in world politics.

If a blowup does occur, it is somewhat unlikely, perhaps most unlikely, that it will result in an "end of history." More likely it will be a very serious crisis that will produce major structural changes in the international scene. It may be a "small" thermonuclear war followed by a viable peace; it may even be a large thermonuclear war, but not an Armageddon. At least in the 60's, it is difficult to visualize a likely sequence of events that would set back either the population or the wealth of the world by more than a generation or so. This would be catastrophic, but it would not be "an end to history" nor even, necessarily, an end to modern civilization. We should make every effort to avoid such a catastrophe but, if this proves impossible, we should be prepared to prevent a second and more serious catastrophe that might mean an end to history or, alternatively, to modern civilization.

It is also possible that even the above rather cautious (as opposed to the apocalyptic or millennial) either-or viewpoint will be wrong, that the international order will

* I would like to acknowledge my indebtedness to Morton Halperin, Morton Kaplan, and Max Singer for the many suggestions that have influenced or modified this paper and my appreciation to the Princeton University Press for allowing me to use some material from my book *On Thermonuclear War* (abbreviated *OTW* in the text).

not change dramatically at all—even though we experience both war and crisis—or conversely, that it will change gradually and develop in such a way that the system will never be subjected to the strains which so many are predicting.

The no-change position can almost surely be ruled out. This 500-year old system which has by and large been very satisfactory and has seen an almost incredible amount of progress now seems obsolete. Indeed, even those "conservatives" who believe that relatively small changes and slow evolution will be sufficient to prevent a blowup also still tend to believe that the advent of nuclear weapons and modern technology will cause changes greater in their effect on the current social and international order than the introduction of cavalry, printing, and longbow, artillery, steam engine, rifles, telegraphy, etc., did in their respective eras. Indeed, it is most likely that the changes produced by modern nuclear technology will come on an accelerated time scale. Although the last fifteen years have set the stage, few believe that the necessary adjustments have been made.

This kind of either-or thinking, or even the more extreme kind which equates every kind of a blowup with an end of history, could and maybe even should lead to hysteria. However, it has been accepted with amazing calmness in the recent past, except by fringe groups. This calmness may not continue in the future. There is now a growing awareness and concern about the implications of the current and future arms race. This concern is expressed dramatically through the activities of the informal and formal "peace," "arms-control," and "international-order" groups. It also has a major impact on both policy and practical politics here and abroad. In addition to the spontaneous (and often perfectly proper) pressures that are building up, there is a good deal of evidence that the Soviet Union has in the past, and hopes even more in the future, to use that widespread fear of arms and the arms race to manipulate the West for purposes of its own. It is, therefore, of the utmost value to examine the different varieties of either-or thinking in some detail and with some care.

It may be helpful to start with a rather extreme example of either-or thinking. The following excerpt is from a well-known speech by Sir Charles Snow,[1] which attracted much favorable comment and little or no unfavorable comment:

We are faced with an either-or, and we haven't much time. The *either* is acceptance of a restriction of nuclear armaments. This is going to begin, just as a token, with an agreement on the stopping of nuclear tests. The United States is not going to get the 99.9 per cent 'security' that it has been asking for. This is unobtainable, though there are other bargains that the United States could probably secure. I am not going to conceal from you that this course involves certain risks. They are quite obvious, and no honest man is going to blink them. That is the *either*. The *or* is not a risk but a certainty. It is this. There is no agreement on tests. The nuclear arms race between the United States and the U.S.S.R. not only continues but accelerates. Other countries join in. Within, at the most, six years, China and several other states have a stock of nuclear bombs. Within, at the most, ten years, some of those bombs are going off. I am saying this as responsibly as I can. That is the certainty. On the one side, therefore, we have a finite risk. On the

[1] C. P. Snow, "The Moral Un-Neutrality of Science," *Science* (January 27, 1961).

other side, we have a certainty of disaster. Between a risk and a certainty, a sane man does not hesitate.

In spite of the rather widespread acclaim with which the preceding statement was received, and in spite of the fact that the author has achieved distinction in both science and letters, the statement is neither accurate nor responsible. The United States is *not* asking for 99.9 per cent security via the arms control routes. In fact, we seem to be willing to accept agreements of a much lower reliability than almost anybody (even the passionate arms controllers) would have been willing to accept a few years ago when they did not know how difficult it was to get reliably enforceable and controllable agreements. Much more important, the "or" described above is not a certainty. Unless Sir Charles Snow has information denied to the rest of us, he cannot know that within ten years some of these bombs are going off. And more important, he cannot know that if some of these bombs go off there is a *certainty* of disaster. Whether any more bombs will go off depends on the situations and the decisions that are made.

It is likely that the reason for the rather widespread acceptance of the attitude expressed by Sir Charles is given in his last sentence. It would be nice indeed if all we had to do was to choose between a certainty and a risk of disaster. In that case, a sane man need not hesitate. Unfortunately for the peace of mind of responsible decision-makers, it is by no means clear on which side the certainties and the risks lie. It might be true that there is a certainty of disaster. It is even conceivable that a detached observer, say from Mars, with infinite wisdom would conclude that it was impossible for us poor creatures on earth to get out of the difficulties we are in; we have discovered weapons of mass destruction and sooner or later we are going to use them—and maybe more than once—until the peace of utter destruction prevents us from using them any more. On the other hand, it might be true that a number of different policies are possible and that these may give rise to varying degrees of risk and different historical outcomes. The latter position seems much more reasonable. The choices open to the human race would also be so unfortunate if the former view were correct, that it is impossible to imagine it as being the basis of policy.

In discussing policy alternatives it is crucial to recognize that the balancing of risks is a difficult job. It cannot be done rigorously, though analysis should help. It will involve, at best, judicious guesses, informed acts of faith, and careful steps in the dark; it is essential to recognize them for what they are. Some new and appealing paths might be even more risky than the perilous one we are now trodding.

In summary, one reason why people like to believe that the current system must inevitably end in total annihilation is that they want to stop thinking. They want to make the choice one between a risk and the certainty of disaster. If they can simplify the choices in this way, as moral men, they need no longer hesitate. Unfortunately, intelligent men cannot pose the problem in that fashion. A moderate form of the either-or position would seem preferable—more moderate in that it does not hold categorically that there really is an either-or situation, and more moderate in that it does not assign quite the same cataclysmic quality to a failure on the "or" side. But although the failure could clearly be catastrophic enough, it need not be so catastrophic as to mean that we ought to be willing to give up all other values to arrest it assuming—almost undoubtedly inaccurately—that such a choice could realistically be made.

It would be helpful at this point to discuss a "hypothetical" situation. What might the world look like in the year 2000 if current technological trends were to continue without any startling change in the international, social, and political order? It is the purpose of this exercise to make plausible the modified either-or view that an extrapolation of the current international order is simply incompatible with plausible technological developments. If one is convinced that the strains on the system are large enough to force large changes, whether one wishes them or not, then one is intellectually and psychologically prepared to think hard about the next set of problems—when and how these changes are likely to occur;[2] what we can do to guide them; and so on. It is a startling experience to examine the literature and find that, until recently, relatively little thought has been given to proposals concerning such problems. Most of this recent thought has been directed to relatively narrow and technical arms control and "legalistic" world government proposals.

Let us start by extrapolating one aspect of this current order. There are about twenty-five nations today which spend between a hundred million and a billion dollars a year on national defense. One can certainly believe, if current growth rates and attitudes toward national defense continue, that before the twentieth century ends, there will be something like fifty nations spending between a hundred million and a billion a year on national defense. Since progress in both the weaponry and the technical ability of these nations would accompany this increase in the number of nations, there would be at least half a hundred "small" nations able, within only a fraction of their customary defense budget, to acquire rather impressive strategic forces.[3] It is most unlikely that these forces would be comparable to the capabilities

---

[2] In fact it seems likely that technological progress, almost by itself, would make the situation critical much before the year 2000, unless there are compensating controls or other changes. However, by picking the year 2000 as a sort of outermost limit for the viability of the current system, almost all of the objections of more conservative colleagues are eliminated.

[3] Although current ICBM's are expensive to procure and maintain, it is quite likely that future models will be much less expensive. This is obvious from looking at the technology of the very next generation of solid-fueled or storable-propellant missiles. There is another reason why some models of ICBM's may reverse the normal trend of weapons systems to greater complexity and cost. Looking at the history of bombers, for example, one notes that the early bombers had inadequate performance, even for the minimum mission—improvements in speed, range, and altitude were of the greatest importance. This meant that technological improvements were applied to solving these problems with a consequent increase in cost. In the absence (and possibly in the presence) of active and passive defense, even the "model T" ICBM has a very impressive performance. This means that technological improvements may be used to reduce the procurement and operating costs, rather than to improve the performance. If one accepts this last remark, then one can almost confidently predict that, in the next few decades, it will be possible for advanced nations to maintain large forces of some models of ICBM's for systems costs of less than $1,000,000 a year per missile and for less advanced nations to fabricate and maintain a force for systems costs less than five times this figure. In addition to being able to get simple strategic systems, many nations will be able to procure systems capable of disguised warfare, either because the weapons are fired from hidden sites (from seaborne or spaceborne platforms, for example) or because the

of the larger powers, and they might or might not serve effectively as "second strike" forces, but they are still likely to be potentially very destructive.

Many of these nations will also have the capability to procure weapons systems that, in the absence of adequate control, can launch missiles anonymously. The delivery vehicle could be, for example, a space platform in outer space, or more likely, a Polaris-type submarine. If the nation has good internal security, it can use even simpler techniques such as unmarked planes or "suitcase" bombs delivered clandestinely.

In addition to the twenty-five nations which today spend between a hundred million and a billion dollars annually on national defense, there are about ten nations spending over a billion dollars a year. By the year 2000, there could be about twenty nations spending more than a billion dollars a year on defense. It is, therefore, quite possible that there will be about twenty or more nations capable of achieving more than a modest strategic capability. These could obtain more than a few Polaris-type submarines or space-bombardment platforms in addition to military systems based in their national territories. By amortizing the cost over ten years, any of these nations will be able to build a nuclear doomsday machine, or its near equivalent, within its regular defense budget. (A near-doomsday machine can be defined as a device or a set of devices which when exploded will destroy all unprotected life in an area of at least continental proportions and also have major world-wide effects.)

The "strategic theory" of such machines has been discussed in *On Thermonuclear War*.[4] The conclusion reached at that time was that although it was most unlikely that any nation would build such devices in the next ten to twenty years, there were circumstances in which a nation might wish it had built such a device. If such circumstances occur often enough, then at least one or two nations may actually construct such machines. It is perhaps as likely as not that such devices will be built in the next thirty or forty years—if one assumes a continuation of the current anarchy. Of course, even if doomsday machines are built, it is unlikely that they will be used. However, almost all agree that the mere existence of a doomsday machine is a vast and totally unacceptable danger. If the present anarchy were to continue for a century or so, then, even though the probability that a doomsday machine will be constructed and used is unknown and unknowable, it seems (or should seem) too high to even the most optimistic prophets.

It is most likely that the international order will change before a doomsday machine is built. It will change partly because of the general and specific political impact of the advancing military and non-military technology, partly as a continuation of current political, legal, and moral trends (the revolution in world politics), and partly as a direct result of the actual or potential diffusion of "normal" weapons. It

---

weapon is so subtle either in its effect or its operation that the attacked nation is not aware—perhaps until too late—that it is being attacked. For example, the possibility of using some concealed form of bacteriological or chemical warfare to debilitate a nation's population over some years, to reduce its competitive capabilities, should not be out of the question by the year 2000 or perhaps earlier.
[4] Pp. 144–51.

is difficult to believe that the world will go unchanged if there are fifty independent, sovereign, small and medium nations with the capability to acquire small amounts of reasonably destructive modern weapon systems and ten or twenty nations with the capability to acquire large amounts. This is true even if many of these nations are not strongly motivated to acquire such systems. Even a weak motivation is likely to be motivation enough—particularly in an unstable competitive situation.

Many nations may obtain nuclear weapons systems without producing cataclysmic instability. For example, the situation might turn out to be similar to that of the old American West. In these societies many people went armed; every now and then a quarrel broke out and somebody was either wounded or killed, but life went on.

The situation might turn out to be even more peaceful than the dueling analogy would suggest. Even before dueling became outlawed, there was a strong tendency in some of the dueling societies to minimize the role of duels. Individuals learned that force was not a proper way of settling personal disputes. And it might indeed turn out that the war system will wither away by itself.

Both of the preceding possibilities, a viable dueling system or an evolutionary withering away of the war system without any "special controls," seem somewhat remote. There are [5] ten problems which would either occur, or be greatly aggravated if there were a widespread diffusion of nuclear weapons. That list is repeated here and each of the problems is discussed very briefly.

1. *Greater Opportunities for Blackmail, Revenge, Terrorism, and Other Mischief-Making.* In a world armed to its teeth in nuclear weapons, every time there is a quarrel or a difference of opinion, there will always be, in the background, a possibility of violence of a kind and degree and speed that is quite different from what is possible today. This could occur even in relatively innocuous quarrels, for example, over fishing rights, as well as over obvious trouble-making irredentist movements or quarrels over prestige. There will be pressures not only to threaten all-out war, but also to use single nuclear weapons to show resolve, to commit oneself irrevocably, or to demonstrate recklessness. In other words, there is likely to be both encouragement and opportunity for playing the game of chicken. This is particularly true because of the previously mentioned possibility for the anonymous delivery of weapons.

2. *Greater Proneness to Inadvertent War.* An inadvertent (unpremeditated) war is one which occurs without the considered intention of any of the governments that wage it. The possibility of inadvertent war could go up not only because there are many more weapons and missiles around, but also because—and even more important—there will be many more organizations around, each with a different standard of training, organization, and operational code. An inadvertent war could be caused by accidents such as a switch failing, a false radar return, or some other statistically possible event. It could also occur because of an unauthorized behavior, irresponsible behavior, a misunderstanding of orders, a generally lax discipline, or any one of a thousand ways in which something can go wrong. It is not inevitable

[5] See Herman Kahn, *Thinking About the Unthinkable* (New York: Horizon Press, 1962).

that any particular provocation or accident will set off a large-scale chain reaction. However, every time there is a small war or accident, there will be great pressure to reform the system. This is, in fact, one likely mechanism for the creation of a crisis which causes a relatively peaceful evolution out of the current system of relative anarchy. Nations will refuse to live with a situation in which nuclear accidents actually do occur. If at all possible, they will do something to correct a system which makes such things likely or inevitable.

3. *Increased Capabilities for "Local" Munichs, Pearl Harbors, and Blitzkriegs.* The tendency to play the game of chicken has already been mentioned. A slightly more reckless, irresponsible, desperate, or decisive decision-maker might simply go ahead and attack another nation, saying, in effect, to the other nations, "what will you do about it?" Even if the attacked nation has a nuclear capability, in many cases it may not have much effective second-strike capability. The other nations, on the other hand, are going to be loath to start a nuclear war to avenge a *fait accompli.* The attacker might even use the attacked nation as a hostage to prevent effective reprisals.

The aggressor may not actually need to launch his attack. He might merely threaten to do so with explicit ultimatums, thus forcing the other side either to back down, or to attack with all the political and military dangers such an attack might bring. In other words, in a situation where there are opportunities for large payoffs through extremely aggressive behavior, we should not be surprised if some nations indulge in such behavior. There are golden opportunities here for both paranoiacs and megalomaniacs.

4. *Pressures to Pre-empt Because of Points One, Two, and Three.* To the extent that the behavior described above actually occurs, as opposed to being an academic possibility, one could expect decision-makers to note that it could happen to them and, therefore, to note also the importance of doing it first. Although few wish to be either executioners or victims, many would prefer the first role to the second if they believed they must choose. A world in which "reciprocal fear of surprise attack" is everpresent is a world which is going to be very unstable. There will also be pressure toward psychological and political pre-emption. In any situation in which there is an important gain to be made by saying something like, "One of us has to be responsible, and since it isn't going to be me, it has to be you," there is a tendency to overuse committal strategies—to say it first and firmly.

5. *Tendency to Neglect Conventional Military Capabilities.* Because of an over-reliance on one's own nuclear capabilities, or fear of the other side's nuclear capabilities, it is likely to be extremely difficult for most nations to take the concept of limited conventional war seriously enough actually to allocate money, manpower, thought, and other scarce commodities into conventional or other limited capabilities. It will be difficult for them to do this, even though they realize abstractly that in a crisis they may find themselves unwilling to rely on their nuclear capabilities. This is likely to create all kinds of instabilities and opportunities for bluff, counterbluff, or actual attack that result in either defeat or escalation.

6. *Internal (Civil War, Coup d'Etat, Irresponsibility, etc.) and External (Arms*

Race, Fear of Fear, etc.) *Political Problems.* It is difficult to believe that in a world as armed to the teeth and as dangerous looking as the one just pictured there will not be both responsible and irresponsible peace and accommodation movements. If every time a difficult decision is being made a major portion of the country is being risked; if every time a country's diplomats walk into a hostile conference room every woman and child feels threatened; if every time a nation stands firm against aggressive probes panic seizes the hearts of many of its citizens, then many citizens will simply adopt an attitude of denial or apathetic fatalism while others call for "peace" with great intensity. The trouble with this kind of political situation is that it is not likely, to put it mildly, to produce thoughtful and considered decisions or programs. In any case, as a result of a combination of apathy, denial, and hysteria, responsible political life is likely to suffer disastrously. And this may encourage or alternatively force other nations to play the game of "chicken."

If some of these "peace" movements are accompanied by violence, or even large-scale illegal non-violence, organized political life in the nation may be threatened even more gravely. In addition, the necessity for reliable internal control of nuclear weapons could force or encourage many governments to practice a rigid authoritarianism or despotism to prevent even small military or political groups from obtaining and using weapons for protest or revolutionary purposes. And eventually, the best of safeguards will occasionally fail.

7. Facilitate Diffusion of Nuclear Weapons to Really Irresponsible Organizations. To the extent that advanced nuclear weapons or components are treated as articles of commerce (perhaps for peaceful uses as in the Plowshare program), their cost will be well within the resources available to many large organizations. In fact, if we get them down to $100,000 or so, and this is not at all implausible, they are, in some sense, available to any dedicated middle-income individual who is willing to save a major fraction of his income for ten or twenty years. Exactly what this could mean is hard to picture without detailed consideration of the various "scenarios" that are possible; but, somehow, few will feel comfortable in a world in which the Malayan guerrillas, Cuban rebels, Algerian terrorists (or the Right-Wing counterterrorists), the Puerto Rican Independence Party, or even gangsters could have access to nuclear weapons or other means of mass destruction. It should be realized that even if nuclear weapons and their delivery systems are not articles of commerce, almost all of their components will have peaceable "relatives." These will be articles of commerce. Thus, only a few special parts or assemblies will have to be manufactured by those organizations or individuals who wish to obtain some sort of weapons capability.

8. Complicates Future Problems of Control. If weapons are diffused widely, then even if an incident or a crisis occurs and even if such an event increases the willingness of most nations to control the situation, such control is likely to be more difficult to achieve because the small powers are now being asked to accept a reduction in their current capability rather than to abstain from the acquisition of weapons. Of course, if the control measures that are envisaged are sufficiently thorough-going and complete, all nations may be treated equally. Even then, it is going to be difficult, if not impossible, to get all of them to junk their nuclear-weapons systems peacefully and not just acquiesce to controls that prevent them from acquiring such systems, though, as France has shown, the last may be difficult.

9. *Creates and Intensifies Agent-Provocateur Problems.* It should be clear that one restraint on the behavior of "respectable" large nations in this super-armed world —and perhaps in any world—is that they do not want a reputation for being blatantly aggressive. Therefore, when a nation does want to be aggressive, it often needs an excuse to make its aggression seem defensive, or at least very special and limited. In the absence of a special situation (such as Berlin), it may be difficult to do this. It is usually almost impossible for a small power to be made to look so provocative against a large power to justify, for example, nuclear retaliation by the large power. But if the small power happens to have nuclear weapons, then many kinds of "accidental" incidents or provocations could be arranged or made use of. They could be used to justify all kinds of ultimatums or actual reprisals up to and including the forcible disarming of the small power which showed itself to be irresponsible enough to nearly cause a holocaust.

10. *Catalytic War or Escalation.* The widespread diffusion of nuclear weapons could give many nations the capability, and in some cases, would also create a pressure, to aggravate an on-going crisis or even to touch off a war between two other powers for purposes of their own. Here again the situation is so complicated that one must think through many scenarios to get a feeling for the possibilities. However, in advance of such systematic exploration, and without discussing our present knowledge of the problem, it should be clear that there are many possibilities for mischief-making by third parties.

The preceding comments should make it plausible that the diffusion of nuclear and other modern weapons can and probably will result in the creation of many more ways in which things can go wrong, and that under current programs, this increase in possibilities is unlikely to be compensated for. Therefore, there should be an automatic increase in the probability that things will go wrong. In short, the diffusion of nuclear weapons will probably increase the number of misunderstandings or crises, their seriousness, and their grim potentialities. This will tend to increase enormously the importance of having responsible and competent governments everywhere. It is likely that some governments will fail inadvertently to take the proper precautions, and that others will deliberately try to exploit the common dangers for unilateral advantages. These "failures" will probably occur too frequently for the system to exist unchanged.

This last statement is likely to be true even if the situation looks superficially stable. The widespread possession of nuclear weapons and delivery systems is likely to be similar to a situation that the physicist would describe as "quasi-stable equilibrium." Imagine, for example, a ball balanced on top of a small cup so that small movements of the ball can be tolerated, but not large ones. If this ball and the cup are isolated, it might sit on top of its cup forever; but if it is submitted to the vagaries and chances of a sufficiently uncontrolled environment, one can guarantee that sooner or later it will fall. This can be true even though every "reasonable" analysis of the situation looking at probable or plausible disturbances shows that the forces are in close enough balance so that the ball should stay where it is. It takes an improbable and implausible force to topple the ball. But some improbable and implausible events will occur. Barring a secular change in the situation, they will occur almost with certainty, and the ball will eventually fall. However, depending on the relationship of the degree of stability to the frequency and violence of the perturbing force, the metastable state might be expected to last for only seconds, or for centuries. My own admittedly undocumented estimate is that a nuclear war is likely to be avoided only for a few decades. After all, it is most unlikely that all the actors in the international scene will be cautious, prosperous, bourgeois nations. In fact, as Kaplan states in his introduction, many will be "conscious antagonists of a system of domestic and international order they regard as bad or immoral." When they get weapons, they may seek to change this bad and immoral international system for one more to their liking.

Although the ball and cup analogy may simultaneously be both apt and misleading, many who have thought about this problem have come to the conclusion that reliable stability can come only through an international agency with an effective monopoly of force, total disarmament, or a permanent stabilization of something like the current system with two or three main blocs and with most non-bloc powers not having modern weapons systems. This last is likely to be stable only if the blocs are both monolithic in their external relations, cooperate on most issues, and act with a great deal of restraint when competitive. (See Kaplan's paper on bipolar system models.) In the long run (or perhaps in the medium run), only some variant of "world government" seems plausible to this writer. Both the bloc solution and total disarmament seem too unstable in the presence of disturbances or the absence of saints in the role of decision-makers.

If this attitude toward the future availability of nuclear weapons, their delivery systems (from the technological and economic points of view), and the instability that would ensue if these technological and economic factors were exploited to the point where there was a widespread diffusion of those weapons is accepted, then the only questions remaining are the following: Under current and future conditions, how much motivation will there be to acquire these systems? If there is enough to create a problem, then how much change is required to handle the situation? How will these changes come about? Can we do much to influence these changes, or will most of them occur in a natural and unguided (but not necessarily peaceful) fashion?

It might be worthwhile at this point to comment on why it might take as long as thirty or forty years before the current system would reach the breaking point. One reason is obvious: Nations like the United States, the Soviet Union, members of the Western European Union, and so on, are extremely cautious about resorting to the use of modern arms or formal threats to do so. In addition to being cautious themselves, they restrain those who are not. In other words, deterrence is likely to work on at least 99.99 per cent of the days (which would imply that with average luck, it would work for about thirty years). The only trouble is that even one failure is likely to be very destructive and might be catastrophic. However, the unsatisfactoriness of a world system based on current deterrence concepts, with their ever present possibility of failure, is no reason for us unwisely to weaken our deterrence. We can easily worsen the situation, not only as judged from a narrow national point of view, but also as judged from the viewpoint of developing a satisfactory world order.

The other important reasons for believing that the current deterrent system will probably be more stable than a superficial examination would indicate have already been mentioned. There are all kinds of constraints on the arms race and military postures and operations. For example, imagine that this paper had been written about five years ago and that there was convincing evidence that the Communist Chinese would openly prepare to test nuclear weapons at some point in the early sixties. (Many people now seem to believe that this is likely.) It would have seemed quite reasonable under those circumstances to assume that the Japanese and Indians would be working hard on their own bombs by now. Since these nations had (and probably still have) an intrinsically greater independent capability for achieving a nuclear explosion than have the Chinese, it would have seemed likely that the early 60's would see three Asian nuclear powers. In fact, one might easily have imagined four or five.

Well, it doesn't seem to be like that. As far as is generally known, neither the Indians nor the Japanese have programs for developing nuclear weapons. Although both Nehru and Bhabba (head of the Indian AEC) have stated that India could have nuclear weapons within two years after a decision to produce them, they have also stated that India will not make that decision. Citizens and leaders of India and other Asian nations now seem (though they may change their minds) to believe that the Chinese will use self-restraint, or that the Americans or Soviets or other nations will protect them from the Chinese; or they have some sophisticated (and probably incorrect) reason for not worrying. Some, of course, just refuse to face the problem.

A similar situation exists in Europe. Five years ago many would have assumed that once the French had achieved a nuclear explosion, the Germans, the Italians, and even the Swiss and the Swedes would also try to procure nuclear weapons. Well, once more, it isn't like that. The last two countries, it is true, have authorized their departments of defense to look into the problem of obtaining nuclear weapons, but in both cases, the legislatures have refused to appropriate substantial sums for this activity. These two nations have merely tried to establish the principle that they are entitled to get nuclear weapons if they want them, but they are not taking any serious actions in a direction that might rock the boat.

Similarly, in the late 40's, it would have seemed reasonable to many technologists that by 1965, or even 1960, some nation such as South Africa would have a gaseous diffusion plant of its own, designed and financed by Europeans, whose major output would be fuel for reactors, but which, as a by-product, would sell uranium to countries which might divert the material to bombs. One could have imagined such a munitions maker engaging in the manufacture and sale of bombs to "carefully" selected customers. It is true that there would be much pressure exerted on the South Africans not to do this, but they are already receiving much criticism and might feel that they could afford to ignore additional criticism. It is also true that South Africa, intensely hated for its Apartheid policies, should, above all other nations, be interested in controlling the diffusion of nuclear weapons to small countries or clandestine groups. However, they might not realize that the sale of weapons to medium and advanced countries could speed the day when revolutionists, blackmailers, or neighboring countries would get nuclear weapons. They could also feel (and possibly correctly) that if they did not engage in this business other nations would, and that, by engaging in the nuclear weapons business, they could exert some control over the distribution in addition to making some profits.

None of these things has occurred or seems likely to occur in the near future. Because of technological and economic reasons, the development of power reactors (another source of fissionable material) has been much slower than expected. Another potential cause of the diffusion of weapons, the AEC's project Plowshare (peaceful uses of nuclear explosives), is being fiercely opposed—mainly because it may facilitate such diffusion. Furthermore, there seems to have been very little interest in some of the latest developments (such as the ultra high-speed centrifuge) which could be used even by small nations to acquire nuclear fuel for weapons.

There are grave constraints on other research and development programs in the United States and, we rather suspect, in the Soviet Union as well. We need only notice how little work has been done on bacteriological and chemical warfare in the United States, both during the Second World War and in the subsequent fifteen years. Although there is now great interest in these subjects, much or almost all of this interest is directed toward incapacitating agents rather than killing agents. By and large, scientists have been unwilling to work in this area, and the government has been loath to appropriate funds. Similar statements can be made about other areas of research or production that might cause—or that might be thought to cause—an undue or undesirable acceleration in the arms race. Fear of the arms race, rather than budgetary considerations or inadequate effectiveness, is probably the main reason for the current neglect of civil defense and de-emphasis on active defense. (See *OTW*, pp. 515–18 for the kinds of civil defense and other programs we might have with a "modest" increase in defense expenditures. "Modest" here implies allocating, 14 per cent or even less of the GNP to national security as we did in the immediate post-Korea years.) In addition, if public discussion is any guide, the emphasis in our nuclear-weapons laboratories has recently been on smaller and cleaner, rather than larger and dirtier weapons. And, finally, one of the reasons for the interest in mobile systems is that they seem to be able to achieve certain kinds of deterrence with many times smaller total yield deployed than is true of the systems available today.

Not only in the United States, but throughout the world, there are important unilateral constraints on the arms race. In addition, there are outlets for both energies and competition in economic development, in the propaganda and political war, and even in technological progress (for example, the space race). These constraints and "peaceful" alternatives may succeed in deferring the day of reckoning for some years, or possibly even for decades. But it is hard for members of even the moderate either-or school to believe that it will be deferred for more than a very few decades. Even if the arms race is controlled, both modern technology and modern morality create pressures and capabilities for a new world order. And if the arms race is not controlled, then any day may see a spectacular and revolutionary weapons development to make all nations equal in potential for violence in much the same way that the six gun became the great equalizer in the American West. Differences in skill, morality, nerve, and recklessness could still be decisive, but mere physical size or wealth could become either irrelevant or a handicap.[6]

Although the breakdown of the current world order by a war or crisis need not lead to an end of history, it could be the most momentous catastrophe to occur in historical time. We would all, of course, prefer to escape from this situation peacefully. How can we go about this?

First of all, we can try to buy time by increasing the safety of the current system while encouraging natural developments. Perhaps we can aid these natural developments by negotiation on *relatively* simple and apolitical [7] technical matters such as a nuclear-test ban or control of surprise attack. Such action would be taken in the hope that the "war system" would gradually wither away to be replaced by another system, perhaps by a more or less satisfactory world government, or, perhaps by some other more sophisticated arrangement whose character is not now clear.

We might try to facilitate the peaceful evolution of the new system by trying to negotiate major structural changes in the international order. There seem to be few significant feasible suggestions, though one will be mentioned later—(a condominium between the United States and the Soviet Union on the use of nuclear weapons). Many experts believe that it is almost impossible to negotiate a comprehensive arms-control agreement without a general political settlement, except as a reaction to a very dramatic event (such as a war or a crisis which is intense enough to have resulted in the evacuation of cities). Yet, in the absence of war or crisis, a general political settlement seems most unlikely. One can hope that the above will turn out to be a self defeating prophecy, but it may not. One can, of course, accept the preceding view and still be willing to negotiate—partly because there are many political and social reasons for going through the motions of negotiating and partly because one's judgment may be wrong. The negotiations may succeed.

There is another possibly overwhelming reason for the study and preliminary negotiation of comprehensive agreements. It is precisely the point of the preceding argument that if one does not believe in a relatively peaceful evolution, then one believes that a war or crisis will occur and that presumably we should be prepared to exploit whatever constructive things could be obtained from the event. Such a war

---

[6] See Chaps. 9 and 10 of *OTW* for a reasonably detailed description of the current arms race.
[7] Simple and apolitical as compared to agreements on important changes in the structure of the present international system. Some of the seemingly apolitical measures, however, may involve presently unforeseen political complications of a structural nature. If sufficiently unforeseen or long range the prospect of such change may not handicap the negotiations excessively.

or crisis is much more likely to result in a satisfactory comprehensive agreement if there are political and military plans and preparations to exploit them—in particular, if an agreement exists ready to be initialled, or there is enough common understanding of what is needed to make it easy to arrive at agreement under pressure.

Consider some of the preceding possibilities. The simplest and perhaps the most important available short-term actions are unilateral measures. To take a most important example, we can make our command and control system so reliable that the possibility of an accident, unauthorized behavior, or miscalculation is very small. We can make our strategic forces so invulnerable that we do not have to respond to an accident or a small attack by launching a major nuclear counterattack.[8] If we carry through both of these measures we are unlikely to be the victim of an accident or even of a deliberate attempt by a third party to set off a war. We will be able and prepared to wait and to analyze what happened rather than react hastily and wrongly. A nation that has invulnerable forces with adequate command and control deters the enemy from attacking *and* minimizes such specially dangerous situations as "reciprocal fear of surprise attack," [9] "self-fulfilling prophecy," [10] and "catalytic war." [11] We need such measures even if they are costly or handicap the operations of our forces. In addition, we must, on our own, design our strategic systems to be able to accept whatever implicit or explicit arrangements can be made; in particular, we must neither develop nor procure systems that needlessly accelerate or exacerbate the arms race. This last is not just a formal remark without content. In many influential quarters the most pertinent question that can be asked about a new weapons system is, "How will its procurement affect the arms race?"

The preceding question is sometimes allowed to dominate the issue to the point where analysts and others have refused to consider otherwise reasonable active and passive defense measures for fear of touching off an offense-defense race. Although an undue degree of unilateral disarmament seems inadvisable, there is much to be said for the concept of the limited use of unilateral measures, both in the hope of influencing others to do likewise and even more because there are limits to what we are willing to do in order to protect ourselves and further our policies. The following chart may help to clarify this point:

Where Do *You* Draw the Line?

1. Insecticides
2. Eating meat

[8] For a detailed discussion of the problems see Chaps. 4, 5, and 6 of *OTW*. I mention there that I expect both the Soviets and Americans to procure such stable systems that under normal circumstances even a number of ICBM's landing and exploding would not touch off an all-out war—though the system is not likely to be so reliable that either side would deliberately test it.

[9] A crisis in which the enemy fears that we will feel so insecure as to be trigger-happy and that he must therefore preempt our possible attack.

[10] Signals being generated by defensive actions by one side, which touch off actions by the other side, which in turn generate signals that cause the first side to take additional precautions, and so on.

[11] An attempt by a third nation to try to touch off a mutually undesired war between the two largest powers for purposes of its own.

3. Any violence
4. Police force
5. Conventional warfare
6. Kiloton weapons
7. Megaton weapons
8. Begaton weapons
9. Doomsday machines
10. Galaxy destroying machines

It is the purpose of the chart to make it clear to both the pacifist, who generally draws the line somewhere between (3) and (5), and the more resolute militarist, who draws the line somewhere between (7) and (9), that they both believe in some degree of unilateral disarmament, and that there are things neither would procure nor plan to do, no matter what military risk might result from their failure to act.

Of course, we have to worry about the Soviets. Will they exercise similar restraint? It has been suggested that we might give them the knowledge and even the tools for decreasing their own vulnerability and for improving their safety practices. Bizarre as it seems today, the idea is not inconceivable; something like this may happen. There is, however, a possible asymmetry between us and the Soviets. Many Marxists seem to be dedicated to a deterministic theory of history in which the so-called permanent operating and other basic factors play the major role. It may be difficult for them to believe that a switch's failing or a fuse's melting could change the course of history. Most Americans have no great difficulty in believing this, since we tend to have a fairly shallow view of history. On the other hand, the Soviets worry a great deal about unauthorized behavior. As a result, in many cases, they will take the same precautions we do, though with different motivation.

It is also possible that the Soviets will systematically exploit the fear of the arms race to corrode the will of the West. They may see only opportunities where we see dangers. However, it is likely that the Soviets will recognize at least the need for highly protected, slow reacting, reliable forces and will procure them almost irrespective of their other policies.

The next thing we can do to stabilize the situation is to negotiate those technical agreements that have little or no political effect but may do much to decrease the immediate risk of war. For example, one might install communication systems between the Soviet and United States headquarters. Then, if any unexpected events occur, the two countries can communicate directly with each other. There is a possibility (though nobody seems to have made any practical proposals) [12] that we can arrange not only to pass information on to the enemy, but also to establish reliable

[12] The problem is that if the crisis is so serious that we are really concerned that the enemy might attack, then we are likely to be unwilling to initiate any kind of unilateral disarmament of other than the strictly offensive forces. By and large, the practical measures that can be taken seem to be almost negligible in their effect on the offensive forces unless they also seriously weaken the defensive forces. The point needs further research, but a superficial initial look has not turned up promising ideas. However, see Thomas C. Schelling, "Arms Control: A Proposal for a Special Surveillance Force," World Politics, Vol. 13 (October 1960), pp. 1–18, for some possibilities.

procedures that would allow him to verify its validity. If a complicated accident occurred, or if there were a crisis, each nation could then explain its view of what was happening and try to reassure the other that it was not in danger from a surprise attack or from other aggressive moves. Even if the verification procedures cannot be worked out, just being able to transmit information and proposals quickly and reliably may be valuable.

Another possibility is the systematic (probably for free rather than on a *quid pro quo* basis) exchange of information in peacetime to reassure each other of the safety of our operating practice; in that way each side would understand the nature of certain types of operations and not erroneously think of them as threatening. This exchange of information could be done formally or informally, explicitly or implicitly, officially or unofficially, openly or surreptitiously. There are many possibilities, and we ought to study systematically how to exploit them. We might even exchange observers to facilitate, on a controlled basis, this exchange of information.

One could also imagine operating warning networks jointly, particularly in outer space, or making agreements to prevent the tracking of mobile Polaris weapons (or, conversely, agreements which facilitate the tracking of third-power Polaris submarines), the spoofing and jamming of warning networks, the shooting down of satellites, and so forth. We may even be willing to cooperate in the operation of a world-wide monitoring and control system designed to prevent anonymous attacks by third powers.

The next class of measures could be implicit rather than explicit or, even if explicit, they could be negotiated on an informal basis, without having the binding character of the usual treaty. For example, we could simply tell the Soviets that if they don't shoot down our reconnaissance satellites, we will not shoot down theirs. Or that if they do not build an AICBM system, we will not build one. Similarly, for civil defense.[13] In all of these and in many other cases, detection is very simple. The projects are either so large that it is impossible to conceal them, or the nature of the acts themselves makes concealment most unlikely.

[13] It is often said that we have today an implicit agreement not to initiate large-scale civil-defense programs. There may be some operational content to this belief. If the United States Government ever seriously considered spending, say, five billion dollars annually on civil defense, one of the most persuasive arguments that would be brought against the proposal would be the high probability of touching off an offense-defense arms race. That is, not only would the Soviets be stimulated into considering such civil defense programs for themselves, but they would also consider buying more and larger missiles, etc. While we might be able to "win" this arms race in the sense of increasing our objective military position *vis à vis* the Soviets, the resulting increase over the next five to ten years in the number and quality of weapons on both sides might represent an increase in the mutual danger that could swamp the competitive aspects. Insofar as the above considerations are both correct and symmetrical, one can say that we have an implicit agreement not to go into civil defense. I believe that they can be exaggerated. In particular, I do not believe that small civil-defense programs—say, of the billion-dollar-a-year level—have such an impact on the arms race. In any case, the Soviets seem to have such a small program, and we do not. Even the effect of large programs can be exaggerated. After all, the ability to kill millions of people, to destroy hundreds of billions of dollars of property, and to leave the environment more hostile to human life might be almost as deterring as the ability to kill tens or hundreds of millions of people.

If the agreements are implicit, there may be some ambiguity. For example, is a warning radar part of an AICBM system? What about an advanced Nike-Hercules designed against antiaircraft, but which has some small capability against missiles? Is the construction of basements that might be used as shelters, or the decentralization of industry for "managerial purposes," the initial phase of a civil-defense program? The ambiguity is not likely to be very important, and in many cases, some ambiguity may be a valuable asset in facilitating agreement and in keeping the agreement flexible. Such implicit agreements between nations are actually traditional; they were almost common in the nineteenth century. They have gone out of fashion in recent years. Reinstituting them could be one of those simple measures that has vast importance for controlling current and future possibilities. Although particularly important as short-term interim measures, they may also have much direct influence on the medium- and long-term situations, particularly if age and custom tend to legitimate them.

It is often relatively easy to reach implicit agreements precisely because there is less difficulty in breaking them—at least in the short term. Neither nation is committed if it changes its mind. If time or experience modifies a country's views about the seriousness, consequences, or asymmetries of the agreement, it can simply inform its opponent that it has changed its mind. In most cases, there should be only the mildest exacerbation of tensions on the resumption of the forbidden practice or project.

Of course, such agreements have dangers. The policies involved in implementing implicit agreements must be examined carefully. These policies may tend in varying degrees to weaken our resolve. They also may discourage our friends and encourage our enemies in the satellite nations. They may have a similar effect on our allies. This last is especially likely to occur if the actions constituting the implicit agreements cause critics or anxious observers to believe that we are thinking of repudiating or modifying our more onerous obligations or that we are planning a private deal in which our allies' interests will not be fully recognized. By decreasing the risk of United States nuclear reaction, some implicit agreements could actually create or increase the opportunity for Soviet or Chinese nuclear blackmail. There can also be deleterious effects on the neutrals. Finally, there is the possibility that wishful thinking may cause us to slight control and inspection in such agreements—the recent moratorium on nuclear tests was, to put it mildly, inadequately inspected. And even if, as seems likely, the Soviets did not cheat by clandestine testing, they certainly used the agreement to slow our program down while pursuing a vigorous theoretical and practical pre-test program that seems to have been definitely aimed at procuring a lead by putting them in a position maximally to exploit their ending of the agreement. It is also worth noting that, although implicit agreements are not as binding as explicit treaties, at least as far as the West is concerned, the longer the agreement is kept in force, the harder it is to break the precedents and customs that have been established.

Even if all of the above general shortcomings are admitted, each proposal should be examined on its merits. Unless their costs are immoderately high, possible implicit agreements ought not to be dismissed out of hand. Almost any constructive action involves costs. Even doing nothing can bring fearful risks. It may even be worthwhile to accept small competitive losses now, not only to increase stability, but also to head off the catastrophic loss in the morale of the West that is likely to occur should an increasingly dangerous arms race ever make our weapons seem more dangerous than an undue accommodation or a surrender.

As part and parcel of such a program, we could institute informal but regular confidential and open dialogues between the Soviets and the Americans to the end that we will understand each other and our problems better. Our ambassador or military attachés, for instance, might ask their opposite numbers such questions as "What do you think your country would do if my country did so and so?" Such dialogues would have to be held in complete confidence and would not commit either government. There are also possibilities for more open dialogues—for example, the recent proposals by D. G. Brennan or R. Leghorn for bilateral or multilateral "World Security Institutes." One could even make more ambitious proposals for international or multi-national research and study that could play an important role in generating and improving the efficiency of the dialogue.

The next type of agreement, the explicitly negotiated binding treaty on other than a minor technical issue, will almost inevitably have major political impact of far-reaching consequences. For this reason, such agreements are much less likely to be negotiated—unless there is at least a partial political settlement. However, they provide some of the major possibilities for big changes and so must be considered even in the absence of such a settlement. The proposed agreement for a nuclear-test suspension is a case in point. It also may be typical of the way in which we are likely to run into all kinds of unexpected difficulties and to find out, in a very costly fashion, that we had not considered the consequences of the agreement until late in the game.

However, it still seems desirable to sign such an agreement on roughly the terms that are currently being considered if no better alternatives can be worked out. Conceding all of the uncertainties and risks, not signing the agreement, if the Soviets are willing to sign, probably would be an enormous step backward. It is hard to see how we can turn our attention and energies to the control of the development and diffusion of nuclear weapons in other nations, if the three major powers cannot agree on self-restraint among themselves. There are other benefits that can be derived from such an agreement. For one thing, we can test future Soviet "sincerity" and the ability of the two countries to work together in the construction and operation of a control system. We shall educate both ourselves and the Soviets in the setting up and operation of one class of arms-control agreements. If nothing else, this should create in both the Soviet Union and the United States a bureaucracy with a vested interest in understanding and maybe even in promoting arms control agreements. We may even build up pressures—hopefully in both countries—for additional measures. And although the consequences of Soviet or Chinese cheating could be much more serious than many proponents of the treaty are willing to concede, it seems—perhaps wrongly—that this is one of those uncalculated "calculated risks" that is worth accepting.

Of course, since the negotiations in Geneva have failed, perhaps we should turn our attention to acceptable "substitutes" that might be even better. One possible alternative (or complement) that probably would be of great importance, is the negotiation of a "Hague" convention against the use of nuclear weapons in warfare. This convention could simply set up a condominium on world affairs between the United States and the Soviet Union to the effect that they will refrain from the first military use of nuclear weapons under any circumstances and, in addition, that they will jointly constrain any third power which uses nuclear weapons in a military operation.[14] Other nations should be encouraged to adhere to the convention, thus making it a truly international accord. If effective, such a convention might be more useful than a test suspension in discouraging the diffusion and in controlling the use of nuclear weapons. It also would be a major precedent for the creation of a very limited but possibly adequate "world government."

In any case, the search for a solution less makeshift than the current one must go on. The time available probably is to be measured in one or two decades, rather than one or two centuries. This seems to indicate that our old concepts of national sovereignty are either obsolete or soon will be. To many this last remark implies that we should be unwilling to risk or fight a war solely to preserve the nation state as an independent sovereign entity. That seems reasonable. But it does not mean that we should not be willing to risk or fight a war to influence or to vote on the system which replaces national sovereignty and independence. However, it is difficult to decide what one should be willing to risk unless the alternatives are spelled out.

It would, therefore, be useful to touch on the most important possibility of all, the comprehensive agreement. Included in this are many of the suggestions for international police forces, world governments, and near world governments.

Probably the most detailed and comprehensive proposal has been worked out by Grenville Clark and Louis B. Sohn.[15] It is difficult for practical politicians, hard-headed statesmen, or professional planners to take such proposals seriously—except as manifestations or symptoms of the impracticality of the "do-gooders." As a result, such studies are rarely read by critics except from the viewpoint of content analysis; their substantive audience tends to be restricted to "friends and relatives." As a result, the Clark-Sohn proposals have not had the benefit of as much hostile informed criticism as they deserve. This is singularly unfortunate because their book is not only an extraordinarily worthwhile basis for continued work but it also may succeed in influencing history, even in its current, relatively unfinished state.

Consider, for example, the following hypothetical scenario of what could happen. The United States and the Soviet Union are today each supposed to have a handful of missiles. Imagine some of these missiles being shot off accidentally. Imagine also that this accident touches off a reprisal by the other side and, possibly, further exchanges on both sides until most or all of the ready and reliable missiles are launched.

[14] See *OTW*, pp. 240–43, for some discussion of this suggestion. Although many will believe it favors the Soviets more than us, in the medium and long run the joint benefits probably outweigh any asymmetries.

[15] *World Peace Through World Law* (Cambridge: Harvard University Press, 1958).

Imagine further that the accidental nature of the strike is soon discovered (since there is no immediate follow-up bomber attack and since the pattern and timing of the missile launchings do not conform to a reasonable surprise attack, this should become clear to both sides quite rapidly). Imagine finally that communications between the two countries are established soon enough so that both sides (today miraculously) succeed in calling off or preventing massive bomber strikes.

With current missile forces, it is most likely that at this point in history possibly five or ten or even more cities on one side or the other, or both, might have been destroyed. But both countries would survive this blow. One could confidently predict that the morning after this event there would be a deeply felt conviction among all the nations, but particularly the two antagonists, that deterrence and anarchy were not a good way to run affairs, that we simply could not go back to the old precarious balance of terror and assume the same risks over again. Under these circumstances, it would not be at all surprising to find the United States and the Soviet Union ready to sign something resembling the Clark-Sohn proposals within a few days. It would be realized that unless an agreement were made within days, that is, before the dead were buried, one side or the other would quite likely try to exploit the common danger for unilateral advantage. In this case the negotiations would probably degenerate into the usual unproductive Cold-War jockeying.

The proposals of Professors Clark and Sohn are enormously valuable. They constitute an alternative preferable to the current arms race. However, their proposals do seem to have serious defects. Therefore, in the absence of an immediate war or crisis, they have given us only a foundation on which to work. Much better proposals can be devised. But the improvement will come about only if hard-headed and realistic people take such proposals seriously and either work on them, or criticize the labor of others. Although much is being done now, more can be done. This is one place where the lone scholar, working without either an inter-disciplinary team or access to classified information, can hope to make a major contribution. However, the big inter-disciplinary studies will also play an important role. Let us, therefore, make a conscious attempt to encourage the design and analysis of "utopias" or other alternatives that might be brought about through the agency of a war or crisis. Bleak as this prospect is, a war or crisis is the most likely route by which we shall achieve a more stable international order.

VI

Problems for Policy
in a Revolutionary Age

IV

16

Economic Development, Political Strategies, and American Aid

Bert F. Hoselitz and Ann R. Willner

It has been well over a decade since American aid was first advanced and promoted as a major means to help save new nations from the inroads of Communism. In the course of that decade, aid to underdeveloped countries has become a firm, if recurrently and hotly debated, part of American foreign policy. As increasing quantities of men, money, and equipment are supplied to increasing numbers of countries emerging from colonial rule, the problem of how to design a more effective aid policy for countries characterized by latent or chronic revolutionary activity becomes increasingly important.

Those who originally framed the outlines of an American aid policy hardly expected, as many critics of aid seem to have done, that loans, grants, technicians, and advisors injected at one end of a funnel would rapidly produce economic development and political democracy at its other end. But they did set up a model that seemed logically to link American aid through a sequence of means or intermediate instrumental goals to the ultimate goal of the maintenance of American political security. Briefly summarized, the model postulated a catalytic flow from programs of economic aid and technical assistance to economic growth in underdeveloped countries, leading in turn to the political stability of these underdeveloped nations and the strengthening of newly created democratic institutions, and resulting in the decline of the internal threat posed by the appeal Communism holds for the hungry.

Subsequent developments have failed to demonstrate the predictive value of this model and have called into question the cause-effect relationships it implied. A decade of experience in Asia, for example, has made it dramatically apparent that the outcomes anticipated as a consequence of American aid are far from their realization. Indeed, the gap has widened between the aspirations of American policy toward the achievement of specified conditions in underdeveloped countries and the actual situations prevailing in them. As a result, coals of criticism have been heaped on the heads of those Americans charged with the formulation and implementation of aid programs.

It is not difficult, on the level of abstraction, to outline a guide to effective policy-making and policy implementation. First, the goals, ends, or desired outcomes are specified in some sequential or hierarchical order so that intermediate goals can be seen as means consistent with and contributing to the ultimate, overriding goal. Then instrumentalities are selected on the basis of their capabilities to take the actions most likely to bring about the desired outcomes. Finally, strategies are employed that maximize the likelihood of success in the situational contexts of these actions.

In reality, those involved in the process of formulating and implementing the specifics of policy are frequently faced with dilemmas of choice. Intermediate goals may be conflicting rather than complementary, so that one can only be obtained at the sacrifice of the other. And predictions must be hazarded as to which is most likely to contribute to the attainment of the ultimate objective. Goals that appear to be equally instrumental to that end may compete for allocation of limited means. When further specified in concrete terms at any level, alternatives increase and dilemmas of choice multiply.

There is little doubt that the history of American aid to Asian countries over the past decade is studded with examples of the failures of those who have made and executed American policy to take action consistent with the ostensible goals of that policy. When faced with dilemmas of choice between alternative intermediate goals, alternative instrumentalities, and alternative strategies, they have too often not resolved these dilemmas in favor of those alternatives most likely to yield optimal results. When the choice has been between progress toward a long-range goal or immediate satisfaction of a short-run objective, they have too frequently given priority to the latter. And short-run gains have resulted in long-run losses when actions taken to secure these short-run objectives have obscured the long-range target and deflected energies and resources away from it.

But in defense of those whose errors and oversights are most easily demonstrable after the fact and by the evidence of history, one must point to the risks of making decisions for policies planned in one country to produce results in another. Predictability of the relative values of alternatives is low for policy-makers who have only limited control over the execution of their plans. Many of those who most strongly decry the failures of foreign-aid programs fall into the fallacy of assuming that the actions of Americans are the major determinant of the direction of history elsewhere. They tend to forget that when we speak of the goals of foreign aid, we envisage outcomes that we hope or expect to take place in other countries.

The measures taken by Americans involved in the planning and administration of foreign aid constitute only one set of variables intervening between the outcomes we desire and the probabilities of their attainment. Far more determining factors are the decisions made and the actions taken by the counterparts of the American decision-makers in the recipient countries. These counterparts, whether as individuals, groups, or institutions, serve as the instrumentalities through which part of the design of foreign aid is shaped and much of it flows. Americans may make assumptions and hazard predictions concerning the behavior of these counterparts in various types of circumstances. We cannot dictate this behavior or control its consequences.

The American model for development in underdeveloped countries was based upon some rather ethnocentric concepts of relations between policy-makers and populations. Its underlying hypotheses were predicated upon the patterns of values, decisions, actions, and responses conditioning political and economic processes in Western European and American environments. But within the realities of their political, economic, and social contexts, policy-makers in the countries receiving aid evolved their own objectives. Even when they understood and shared the goals of the American model, they did not necessarily select the means or employ the strategies that might have helped to put such a model into operation. Often, when their allocation preferences were congruent with ours, they were not in a position, when faced with dilemmas of choice, to make the requisite decisions and/or take the requisite actions.

The problem then becomes one of how to minimize the operational risks of a policy whose ultimate effectiveness depends on the choices made by others as well as those made by us. Can the choices that foreign counterparts are likely to make under various sets of circumstances and the consequences likely to result from these choices be foreseen? Can predictions concerning them be sufficiently reliable to serve as adequate guideposts for further decisions to be made by Americans? In short, can there be framed an operational model which will incorporate conditions, choices, and outcomes in other countries as data to serve as the basis for sounder decision-making from among the alternative choices confronting American policy-makers?

We suggest that a first step is a re-examination of the political realities and economic necessities that have confronted policy-makers in these countries. How have they viewed their problems and how have they faced them? Have their solutions served to advance the goals envisaged by foreign aid?

I Political Realities and the Dilemmas of Choice

The original model for American aid was based upon the expectation that external assistance could be the major catalytic agent in the mobilization of resources, capital, and human energies in the newly independent countries. This expectation was partly derived from the history of economic aid to Europe under the Marshall Plan and from the history of foreign investment in the earlier American economy. Its major fallacy was the failure to recognize that economic development and the growth of democratic political institutions are closely associated with a total process of modernization, necessitating innovations in cultural and social values and behavior patterns.

Underlying this expectation were implicit assumptions concerning the leadership of new nations, the bulk of their populations, and the relationship believed to exist between them. Revolutionary leaders had exhibited a unity of outlook and goals in their nationalist struggles for independence. Therefore, it was anticipated that they would continue to share a unity of outlook on the post-revolutionary goals of maximization and distribution of the benefits to accrue from national independence. These nationalist elites had aroused their followers to political activity with slogans of modernization and economic uplift, and they continued to reiterate these on the level of rhetoric. Therefore, they were assumed to be as strongly motivated to their attainment on levels of decision and action as well.

The masses of these countries were seen as sunk in poverty, illiteracy, and village- and tradition-oriented provincialism. But they were assumed to be uniformly desirous to modernize and to improve their circumstances once shown the way and given the means to do so. And the leaders were viewed as being able to exert the same charismatic influence upon their followers in stimulating behavior appropriate to change as had served to arouse them to political action for national independence. In short, a certain stable relationship was believed to exist between the powerholders on the national governmental level and the populations such that aid given through the former to the latter would have a positive impact.

But in most of the South and Southeast Asian countries, the post-independence period has been no less one of latent or chronic revolutionary ferment than that preceding independence. Political independence only temporarily stilled demands, protests, and resentments directed at central government authorities. What has changed in the main between the pre- and post-independence periods are the goals, the protagonists, their alignments, and their patterns of relationships.

In the late colonial period, political independence served as the single dominant goal to unify the many diverse groups whose nominal political unity had been brought about by a colonial power which administered them as a single unit. Now the goal for all groups became that of obtaining the benefits held out to them by the nationalist revolutionary leaders as the inevitable outcome of successful anti-colonialism.

But for different groups these benefits may take different forms in concrete and symbolic terms. It is no accident that the objectives rhetorically advanced by Asian leaders have so often been couched in what seems to us to be rather vague and general language. For it is easier to obtain support from a diverse following on the basis of general and abstract principles than on the basis of a concrete program that all may not agree with. Nevertheless, these abstract principles are interpreted by specific groups as specific goals. Ethnic and linguistic minority groups tend to view them as mandates to reassert and strengthen their traditional sub-cultures. Peasants see in them hope for more land, or higher income for market crops, or exemptions from the burden of taxation. Tenant farmers look for redistribution of land and plots for themselves. Workers and artisans look for higher wages or more purchasing power from their wages. Small entrepreneurs anticipate loans, subsidies, and protection from foreign and non-indigenous internal competitors. Petty bureaucrats expect increases in status and power in the expanding civil bureaucracy. Whether in the form of concrete items of consumption, aids to production, educational opportunities presumably providing mobility, increased status, or simply more egalitarian treatment by those above them, expectations were aroused among those awakened to join the struggle for independence by slogans predicting democratic equality and economic opportunity. And those who were not initially aroused have subsequently been stimulated through the activities of political parties and other organizations that have begun to penetrate even the remote villages.

In the struggles for independence of the late colonial period, the main protagonists were divided into two camps: (1) the nationalist leaders and their followers and (2) the non-indigenous ruling group. The former generally acted as a unit making, in effect, a single demand—political independence—upon the latter.

As of the last decade, the protagonists on the political scene can be viewed as a hierarchy of units ranged along a vertical axis that is intersected at several points on its lower level by parallel horizontal axes along which other units are ranged.

At the top of the vertical axis are those who comprise the dominant central or national ruling elite. Below them are the intermediary leaders or intervening elites. These may be regional or provincial leaders or recognized representatives of specific ethnic groups who impinge on the national stage but do not play dominant roles on it. Below them are the local leaders, such as village heads, traditional religious figures, and heads of family or kin groups that long have dominated a locality. At the bottom is the bulk of the population which, for some countries, may in turn be divided into urban and semi-urban elements on the one hand and rural elements on the other. At this level, and at the levels of local and regional leadership, the horizontal intersecting axes reflect the particular break-down of religious, ethnic, linguistic, caste, and occupational group affiliations in the society.

Depending upon the particular social structure of any one country, and the particular problems and issues that arose in its political arena in the last decade, there have been alignments and realignments among these groups. In most instances, however, the patterns of alignment and realignment expressed little more than a struggle for power among the membership of the national elite, which was in turn reflected by the members of the intermediate elites seeking entry into the national elites. This was especially true of the early post-independence years in Pakistan and Indonesia where urgent problems were almost ignored in the internecine battles for control within these elites. Many of these conflicts may have been motivated more by personal political ambitions than by basic ideological differences, by the desire to obtain or retain roles on the national scene replete with prestige and material emoluments. But whether in parliament, through the press, or at mass meetings they were always publicly waged in the name of some benefit for the people at large or for some specific group of the population.

The newly independent governments initially assumed the formal trappings of democracy with the establishment, at least on the level of form, of such institutions as parliaments, political parties, and elections. Governmental and party leaders also established and encouraged the formation of such organizations as labor unions, peasant associations, and student leagues both in order to modernize in the image of the countries they looked to as models and to transfer loyalties from traditional authorities to themselves.

It is true that the establishment of nominally democratic government among peoples with little experience in expressing preferences, making political choices, and exercising initiative did not lead to notable success. In several instances, notably those of Pakistan and Indonesia, the democratic forms achieved such little workable substance that they were abandoned. Admittedly, parties and parliaments most often served the ends of the national elites which dominated them. And the new mass organizations served primarily as vehicles of power for ambitious secondary leaders. Nevertheless, they began to provide public outlets for the masses to make themselves felt in the political arena.

Before this period, the significant units for an analysis of the governmental process, whether on the national or the local levels in these countries, were two: the government or rulers and the people or the ruled. Governments were traditionally quasi-feudal or colonial bureaucracies with authority and command flowing down from the top and obedience expected and obtained from below. With the change from non-indigenous rulers to those of national origin, this has become less true, although it is still the prevalent pattern in some areas.

The mobilization of peoples in mass actions against the colonial elites had the effect of loosening the norms of authoritarian rule in many areas of developing nations. Coming after this, the organization of potential action groups among large segments of the masses served to transform them into potentially active agents in the political process. Even the most traditionally oriented elements are being drawn out of passivity into some form of activity. For to protect their interests against the groups which see them as impediments to modernization, traditional leaders have also resorted to mobilization of their followers in formally organized associations.

No longer could those on the upper levels expect that the flow of authority downward would automatically engender a response of acquiescence upward. Nor could they be certain that opposition would be expressed by nothing stronger than the traditional passive resistance. The easy exercise of authority has been supplanted by the need to obtain consensus. The flow has become somewhat reciprocal as leaders on each level must seek increasingly to satisfy or pacify politically aware followers in order to retain a following and maintain leadership.

Thus, the early years of independence were characterized by the development and increasing articulation of a profusion of particularistic goals representing the different orientations of the pluralistic societies of these countries. Ethnic, linguistic, religious, and other sub-cultural differences found expression in movements that repeatedly threatened national unity. In Burma, the Shans, Kachins, Chins, and especially the Karens would only maintain union with the Burmese under guarantees of considerable regional autonomy. And the Arakanese and Mons have, in turn, agitated for separate statehood. India's recent political history has been plagued by demands for the organization of its component states on a linguistic basis. In Indonesia, the Achinese, Menadonese, and Macassarese, to mention just a few of the groups of the outer islands, have at best tolerated and often rebelled against the rule of the dominant Javanese. Ceylonese politics have largely centered around clashes between the Sinhalese and Tamils.

Americans have often tended to underestimate the importance of these differences because this country is also composed of people of diverse backgrounds and traditions. However, it must be recognized that at the time we attained independence, our population was largely of Anglo-Saxon origin. Our ethnic variety has been derived from subsequent waves of immigrants whose descendants rapidly assimilated and adapted to the Anglo-Saxon traditions which constituted a solid core of unity amidst the diversity.

But in countries composed of competitive sub-societies with few commonly held values and forms of social organization below the level of the national elites, the elites are constantly faced with the dilemmas inherent in framing programs for the society at large. Even the measures that would appear to benefit all groups of the society provoke tension and dissent in their application. Thus, education is a universal goal in underdeveloped countries. The desire to eradicate illiteracy and educate the largest number as rapidly as possible has led to an expansion of educational facilities on all levels. But then comes the problem of the language in which education is to be offered. The advantage of a single national language of instruction that will also serve as a unifying force has often been sacrificed to demands for education in local languages. Yet those groups who have most successfully clamored for the latter exhibit resentment when their members do not have easy access to posts and occupations that demand fluency in the dominant national language.

This is but one example of the many conflicting and often internally inconsistent demands voiced to the center by the increasingly organized populations, either directly in the form of demonstrations, or through intermediary leaders. At the same time, the institutional structures were insufficiently developed to reconcile these claims fully and transform them into policy and performance in the national interest.

Attempts to satisfy one particularistic set of claims ran the risk of producing accusations against the center of discrimination in favor of the group advancing them. At minimum, they were succeeded by demands from other groups, possibly feeling themselves disadvantaged, for satisfaction of their needs. Intermediary leaders could not easily resist pressing these demands even when they could recognize that these were contrary to an overriding general interest. For their claims to leadership depended upon their obtaining gains from the government. The groups they led could not easily conceive of the possibilities of satisfying needs through other channels than the government and their leaders.

One of the most deeply ingrained traditions in Asian countries, and one which will probably die the hardest, is that of looking toward government and leadership for benefits rather than toward one's own efforts. He who is a ruler or leader is expected to confer gains upon or secure favors for followers. Yet side by side with this traditional expectation is a more modern lack of reluctance to unseat those in power. The weapons the nationalist elites taught their followers to use against the colonial rulers can be used against them. Resistance and revolution, having become historical facts, are recognized as alternatives to frustration and become future possibilities.

What does a ruling group do when beset by pressures on all sides? Three alternatives are open to it, each with its advantages, disadvantages, and probable consequences. One is to inhibit the development of these pressures from below and to close off or repress the outlets for their expression and further dissemination. This is especially attractive to tradition-based elites intent on preserving the structures that have given them their power positions. But the cost of maintaining repressive mechanisms increases as the difficulties of insulating all elements of the population from modernizing pressures increase. The increasing costs are frequently met by diminishing the returns heretofore accorded the population. Ultimately, when repressive measures go too far, and frustration is felt at some point in the society, explosive situations develop which lead, in turn, to overt revolution.

A second alternative is to permit or encourage minimal transformations by satisfying the most strongly felt and expressed demands. This has the advantage of draining off some of the revolutionary potential, but it only delays the inevitable outcome. It is a choice frequently made by a compromising elite which sustains its power by giving in at points of maximum pressure. Yet in long-range terms, these elites are in a position analogous to that of their colonial predecessors who placed their faith in welfare measures. They ultimately face a replication of the situations that confronted these colonial rulers. For even the minimal modernization permitted in a field such as education, for example, will produce potential rival leaders. These will view the existing leaders as a stumbling block to the promotion of changes which are necessary to satisfy their new goals and aspirations, many of which are a product either of their training directly, or of their new status as members of the elite.

The third alternative is a genuine attempt to satisfy the rising and ever-widening circles of wants. But here again, satisfactions are likely to result in further increasing pressures upon the center. As articulated wants impinge in accelerated fashion upon the limited resources of developing countries, satisfactions cannot continue to be provided simply by dividing the existing pie even on the most equitable basis. What is required is to increase the size of the pie as rapidly—or almost as rapidly—as wants increase. The only long-range defense compatible with accelerating demands lies in stimulating the sorts of basic structural modifications conducive to increasing supplies on a similarly accelerated basis. The genuinely modernizing elite, which recognizes this necessity and directs all efforts toward plans, programs, and measures of implementation in conformity with it, stands the best chance of maintaining stability and retaining its leadership.

We have outlined above an abbreviated model of the process that has occurred over time in Asian countries. With slight variations, this model may be similarly applicable to other new nations. Before describing the strategies adopted by leaders forced to cope with the dilemmas inherent in this process, we wish to make a few distinctions: One distinction exists between the goals on the level of national leadership and the goals on the lower levels of the vertical axis; another exists between different types of follower demand and their implications for revolutionary activity.

We will assume, somewhat optimistically, that the concern of the national elites with the maintenance of power and that of the sub-elites for the attainment of power are primarily directed toward the achievement of national or sub-group ends. For in some instances, they may represent little more than the desire for the material, social, status, and prestige perquisites to which power gives access. However, even if in both cases power is seen instrumentally as a means to further group rather than personal ends, these objectives will contradict rather than complement each other. For the goals that national leadership sets for the country at large are essentially long-range goals. Those that the sub-elites advance on behalf of their followers are generally immediate and short-run. To attain the former necessitates the maintenance of a high degree of centralized power and direction. Yet to prevent the latter from serving as means through which intermediary leaders can unseat the central elites, these elites are forced to diffuse power and weaken their potential for achieving the long-range objectives.

What we have earlier called *demand* can be further broken down into *expectation* and *aspiration*. These are differently derived and generally have different intensities. Expectations are a manifestation of the prevailing norms set by the immediate social and cultural environment. Whether expressed in economic or social terms, the basis upon which the individual forms his expectations is the sense of what is rightfully owed to him. The source of that sense of rightness may be what his ancestors have enjoyed, what he has had in the past, what tradition ascribes to him, and his position in relation to that of others in the society. Aspirations, on the other hand, represent that which he would like to have but has not necessarily had or considered his due. Aspirations are hopes of future gains.

Unrealized aspirations produce feelings of disappointment, but unrealized expectations result in feelings of deprivation. Disappointment is generally tolerable; deprivation is often intolerable. The deprived individual feels impelled to remedy, by whatever means are available, the material and psychic frustrations produced in him. Whereas disappointment may breed the seeds of incipient revolution, deprivation serves as a catalyst for revolutionary action.

The point of this distinction is to lay stress on the fact that the leaders of the new nations were not able to satisfy many of the immediate expectations of their populations, much less their aspirations for the future. In countries such as Burma, Viet Nam, and Indonesia wartime occupation and subsequent military activities in the independence struggles disrupted and destroyed a part of the prewar productive apparatus and installations. Reconstruction needs absorbed much of the available capital resources and foreign-aid contributions. Additional problems of absorbing refugees, as in India, Pakistan, South Korea, and South Viet Nam made further demands upon limited resources. At the same time, the replacement on many levels of the bureaucracy of skilled or relatively skilled administrators by unskilled ones, especially where political reliability and party and faction loyalty were the criteria of appointment, meant that pre-independence norms of governmental performance became even more difficult to restore.

Coercive measures to force further sacrifices for development upon populations whose normal expectations could be satisfied only with difficulty were incompatible with the newly achieved "democracy." India was in the position of having unexpended sterling balances from her use as an Allied base in the Second World War which mitigated the problem somewhat. Other countries succeeded in staving off serious trouble for a few years as a result of windfalls from the Korean War. But as aspirations were internalized and became turned into expectations that could not be realized, the incumbent elites, with a few exceptions, resorted to one or another or a combination of three strategies to maintain their power and retain the confidence of their followers.

The first might be termed the *scapegoat* strategy. Failures were attributed to external circumstances and/or projected upon external agents. The external circumstances might have been the need to protect the country against an outside threat, as in Korea or Viet Nam, or to incorporate as yet unincorporated parts of the new national domain, as Kashmir for India and Pakistan and Irian for Indonesia. The external agent may have been the ex-colonial power, as the Netherlands in the case of Indonesia, or the British, with their insistence upon the maintenance of a base, in Ceylon. We do not wish to imply that there may not have been some basis of reality in these explanations. But, insofar as they provided the rationale for the allocation of resources to the defense sector, resources for consumption and investment in normal development projects were lessened. They served as scapegoat mechanisms by repeatedly focusing public attention on a particular sore spot to which, by implication, all current ills were attributed. Thus, they deflected frustration away from the immediate economic ills, the maladministration and corruption within the bureaucracy, the growing disparity between the groups favored by special privileges through access to government officials, and those groups on whom the special privileges of others placed greater burdens.

This strategy had the double advantage of building upon an already existing nationalism which it was easy to whip up to greater heights while it provided an almost invulnerable defense for the national elite. Its symbolic content was such that other potential leaders dared disagree only at the risk of being accused of harboring unpatriotic, pro-colonial, and pro-enemy sentiments. It therefore served as a unifying element for diversely oriented and potentially conflicting intermediary leaders.

Another advantage was that a number of secondary effects were associated with this policy. Criticisms that resources were not being allocated to meet consumer needs could be defended on the grounds that maximum resource allocation was needed toward an objective of foreign policy designed to preserve or enhance national prestige. The objective need not even be seen as being near attainment. For the subsequent argument could be advanced that the task was now so difficult that more sacrifices were necessary. In Indonesia, for example, Sukarno's political opponents were wont to remark privately "Prices have gone up again. It's about time for Bung Karno to give another speech about Irian." But they could not afford such statements in public.

The second strategy might be termed *satisfaction of expectations on the symbolic level*. This is, in effect, the rechanneling of what are fundamentally economic frustrations into seemingly meaningful, goal-directed, zeal-inspiring, energy-absorbing activities. The encouragement of the formation of associations, clubs, and groups, such as unions, cooperatives, and cultural organizations was an example of this. Movements for the exclusive use of one language on the national level or in education could be seen as serving this function. In actuality, such organizations only realized, in a very limited sense, the objectives they were set up to promote. Nevertheless, they gave the members a sense of participation and achievement, without commensurate power, and an expectation of future gain. In one sense, this was the internal equivalent of the first strategy, for it set up an attainment of rather artificial goals as a prerequisite to the dispersal of economic gains.

This strategy had disadvantages, however, for the central elite. The encouragement of particularistic movements led to their being used as vehicles of greater mobility and power by the leaders of these movements and groups. Many of the leaders of these special institutions were enabled to strive through them for a role on the national stage. And since the demands presented by them were frequently incompatible, some could only be satisfied by frustrating others, giving the leaders of the latter ammunition to attack the national elite, or putting them in a position to demand entry into the elite grouping as a price for keeping their followers in line. What may have begun, therefore, as a national elite with fairly homogeneous outlooks and goals became diversified as a result of compromises with conflicting and competing sub-elite members.

Both these strategies are essentially drain-off processes with only short-run possibilities of success. There comes a point at which the rate of support diminishes in comparison to the growth and consolidation of opposition. Some groups reach the point of refusing to accept the reasons given for the frustration of their long-delayed expectations and take action. Thus, external dangers and the internal violence in South Viet Nam did not prevent the attempted *coup* against the center in 1960. Rather, accusations that these dangers were not being effectively coped with were offered by the opposition in defense of the launching of the *coup*. The major campaign by the largely Javanese central Indonesian elite against the Dutch on behalf of the Irian objective did not deflect or prevent the already-developing insurrections of the economically deprived outlying provinces.

An easier situation, in terms of maintenance of power for the central elite, exists when some economic progress does take place and economic and social gains do accrue to the population at large. Here there tends to be more solidarity on the vertical level between the national elite and the leaders of the next rank. The latter both participate in the benefits and disseminate them. And they, in turn, solidify their leadership positions among their followers by sharing the credit for the benefits obtained. This is best illustrated in India where sub-national Congress leaders have long derived power from and returned support to the central leadership.

However, although relatively successful in the short run, this too has its long-range drawbacks. For with increasing gains come increasing expectations. What once were aspirations become firm and specific expectations, as the rise of education, literacy, income levels, and the growth of urbanization extend the awareness of alternative possibilities not originally envisaged. Even limited mobility shatters traditional views of the necessary state of things and breeds impulses to further gains and further mobility.

When there is a level of overall progress, the benefits do not flow evenly to all the groups and all the particularist sectors. The struggle to maintain the rate of growth is constantly disturbed by a struggle for the distribution of the spoils, as different leaders are forced by the pressures of their followers to contend on their behalf for larger respective slices of the pie. If the central elite is pushed into the position of making concessions at points of maximum pressure, regardless of the rationality of demands, its ability to sustain growth is minimized. If these pressures result in intra-elite struggles at the center, this frequently leads to administrative paralysis and to further frustrations on levels below it.

The center can retain its power, despite such tensions, through the charismatic influence of a dominant leader, such as Nehru in India, or U Nu in Burma; or it can be forced into an alliance with the major instrument of coercion, the military, as has happened in Indonesia, when dissatisfactions portend or produce outright rebellion; or the military elite takes control temporarily, or at least ostensibly for an interregnum, in order to restore failing central direction, as occurred in Pakistan and Burma.

It must also be pointed out that the political tensions that inhibit the development of political stability and the opportunities for economic growth in underdeveloped countries come not only from the revolutionary or quasi-revolutionary movements on the Left, but also from traditionalistic or nativistic or near-totalitarian movements on the Right. These movements often rely on the support of the more traditional leaders, many of whom may have close personal relations with the modernizing elites who thus find it difficult to dispel their influence.

Depending upon the type of assistance provided, the direction in which it flows, and the groups which most clearly benefit from it, American assistance can and has served in many instances to worsen these political tensions rather than allay them. The most obvious examples are the cases in which funds, supplies, and equipment have been diverted at the recipient end into private channels for private gain. This helps to accentuate the differences in levels of living between the members of urban elites who profit from their official positions or access to officialdom and the growing urban proletariats whose leaders are not unaware of the sources of sudden wealth on the part of corrupt leaders. Resistance on the recipient level to audit of counterpart funds, as in South Viet Nam, may be based on more than the administrative difficulties involved. Counterpart financing through the sales of imported commodities, although of benefit to many consumers, can threaten local consumer industries, causing resentment both among local entrepreneurs and among those who are forced out of business or employment.

A less obvious example is provided by the unanticipated side-effects of American-conceived and -sponsored training programs designed to provide better and more knowledgeable administrators for the bureaucracies of these countries. These trainees return to their countries sparked by the desire to put into effect their new notions of rational organization and their new techniques. They expect to be assigned more demanding, responsible positions for which this training has equipped them. What frequently happens, however, is that they become a threat to their seniors in the bureaucracy, who either look with suspicion on their desires to innovate, or see them as rivals. In self-defense, they shunt them off to positions and areas of minimum effectiveness. This, in turn, creates disillusionment and resentment among these officials, and they too form a potentially revolutionary element.

We have outlined above just a few of the political variables that intervene between our goals and their possibility of realization. Also to be considered are the dilemmas of choice affecting the pattern and rate of economic development.

II Economic Development Programming and the Dilemmas of Choice

As in the case of many of the political dilemmas we have discussed in the preceding sections, those which confront decision-makers in the economic realm have not been clearly understood. There have been two naive interpretations representing ideologically extreme positions. On the one hand, there was the theory that imitation of the technological, organizational, and possible value patterns of Western societies would lead to the same result as in the Western world. If only well-functioning markets, free enterprise, motivation for private profit, and a liberal nineteenth-century-style government could be instituted, capital formation, investment, and, hence, economic growth would automatically ensue. This position was held not only by the protagonists of free enterprise in the developed countries, but was shared also by a small number of persons in Asia and other developing regions.

The opposite position was that of the planners. They looked toward the Soviet Union as the model which had achieved a rapid rate of economic growth. The socio-political details of the reality in the Soviet Union were overlooked, perhaps a bit too comfortably, and primary attention was paid to planning. The drawing up of an internally consistent plan was regarded as the major prerequisite for rapid growth. The private sector was accused of having failed, of having misallocated resources, and of having put investment in useless or even socially detrimental structures—such as luxury housing or night clubs for the rich—and the argument was advanced that a rigorous plan was the main and, in fact, only effective instrumentality through which economic advancement could be insured.

This feeling was especially strong in some countries, such as India, and Indian economic intelligence missions were sent to Communist China in order to investigate the techniques and results of economic planning in a developing country exhibiting a level of economic performance roughly commensurate with that of India. The delegations returned and wrote accounts of their visit. In glowing terms the success of Chinese planning was described, and the reports ended in the almost unanimous recommendation that India's salvation lay in adopting similarly comprehensive plans to those of China.

This bias in favor of planning led to some ludicrous interpretations. For example, in one case, Chinese planning was considered responsible for the higher per-acre yields in Chinese rice culture as compared with Indian rice culture. It was overlooked that even in the 1920's—long before a Communist movement of any note existed in China—the differential between Chinese and Indian yields in certain agricultural products was of approximately the same magnitude as that found by the visiting delegation.

This dichotomy between reliance upon free enterprise and upon planning as the major economic instrumentality leading to rapid economic growth sets up the first dilemma. In many developing countries, certain entrepreneurs have proven themselves to be hardy, inventive, stubborn, and successful in pushing their enterprises and, hence, their industries forward; others have been unresponsive, inclined to abuse monopoly power, and dependent upon special privilege or subsidies. Similarly, we find instances in which rational planning has led to generally favorable ends, and others in which it has failed miserably and resulted in a waste of resources that a developing country can ill afford.

One way out of this dilemma was the adoption of a mixed economy. Certain sectors of the economy seemed of such strategic importance as to be fit only for governmental control and, hence, for full-scale planning. Other sectors were left in private hands. But the boundaries between controlled and uncontrolled areas of economic activity have been fluid and changing, and any comprehensive rational "theory of mixed economies" has hardly been elaborated. Governments, therefore, proceed in semi-darkness, are torn between interventionism and a hands-off policy, and alter the scope and pattern of their programming not only from plan to plan, but even in mid-stream.

It has been one of the weaknesses of American aid programs that the United States also had no "theory" to offer. Ideologically the United States has favored free enterprise, but without the ability to show that this would really be the best policy for developing countries with few developed resources, widespread mass poverty, and political impotence of a large sector of the population. At the same time, the United States has acquiesced in and even supported certain overall plans, and in some instances has done so uncritically, presumably because it was felt that any criticism of these plans would lead to political antagonism. This approach has been interpreted by some as vacillation between a principled and a purely pragmatic position and has contributed to the confusion called forth by uncertainties about the proper degree of interventionism.

But this dilemma was relatively mild as compared with two others which confronted the economic decision-makers in developing countries and which are ultimately attributable to the conflicting demands made by short-run and long-run objectives. Here, as in the political field, the inadequacy of resources to meet short-run objectives reasonably fully, without doing irreparable damage to the possibility of achieving long-run ends, has been at the source of the dilemma. In simple and non-technical terms, the two dilemmas called forth by this situation can be designated as the consumption-versus-investment dilemma and the growth-versus-employment dilemma. They are closely related, and it is difficult in actual policy-making to keep them strictly apart. This should be borne in mind even if in an abstract discussion they are being treated independently of one another.

The first conflict is provoked because of the different expectations of a development program by the elite and the popular masses. The former look at development as contributing to the overall aims of national aggrandizement and political independence, to the strengthening of the military posture of the nation and to the inauguration of a period of economic self-sufficiency and higher production. It is true that welfare considerations, such as raising the living standards of the masses, also are desired. But this objective is much less important than the others, although the leaders of the elite, for quite understandable reasons, especially emphasize the objective of rising living standards in their public statements. Basically—and this perhaps explains the predilection that some economic leaders in developing countries have for Soviet-style planning—the overriding objectives of development programs consist in the build-up of capital-goods industries at the expense of rapid expansion of consumption levels in the short-run.

The objectives of the popular masses are the opposite. They have lived for a long time in conditions of misery and deprivation. They remember the promises of their leaders that independence would bring greater economic benefits, and they want some new consumption goods which would make their lives more pleasant and more agreeable. As we have shown, there are second-level elites and leaders of various particularistic organizations who represent these demands in the political arena and who can often muster enough popular support to press these demands strongly with the central elite. Hence, some responsiveness to these demands must be shown, and the great problem becomes to determine the extent to which well-thought-out investment programs shall be modified in order to meet the most urgent of these demands for enlarged current mass consumption.

Much of the incessant debate on efforts to increase agricultural output versus support of rapid industrialization, on the extent to which social overhead investments need be made, on the controls to be imposed on certain imports, and on the capacity of private entrepreneurs to make their own production decisions free from government regulation, have their ultimate *raison d'être* in this dilemma between more consumption goods and less capital accumulation versus its opposite.

This dilemma is clearly not soluble on the economic level alone. It is basically a political problem, though in discussion it is often represented as a question of optimum resource allocation or effectiveness of programs for economic growth. It has been, again, one of the failures of American aid programs to have supported this interpretation and to have clothed the consumption-versus-investment conflict in the sterile garb of a purely technical economic problem. The reason for this appears understandable. It permitted American aid administrators to appear "neutral" with respect to the domestic politics of the developing country. But, ultimately, such a policy of burying one's head in the sand is not conducive to fruitful outcomes.

Closely related to the consumption-investment dilemma is the conflict between growth and employment objectives. This dilemma is most clearly visible in densely populated countries, such as Java, India, Egypt, or Haiti. There the benefits of public health programs and of the massive application of certain measures of preventive medicine have led to an unprecedented multiplication of the population, with the result that increasing numbers of persons enter the ranks of the labor force seeking work. The natural inclination would be to look for productive patterns which are heavily labor-intensive and which use the scarce capital available in these poor countries only sparingly. But many of the installations which tend to bring the most rapid advancements in productivity are capital-intensive and labor-saving. They were elaborated in a technological environment in which labor was relatively costly, and these technologies are now offered freely to developing countries in which the relative prices of capital and labor are the very reverse of what they are in economically and technologically advanced countries.

First, it should be pointed out that although this dilemma is most acute in the densely populated countries, it is not entirely absent in many of those developing nations where there still appears to be much more room. For there, also, population is growing at a high rate, and in many instances similar needs to find more employment opportunities arise, though admittedly with less intensity than in the densely populated countries.

Second, it should be noted that many of the solutions to this problem actually proposed and even implemented are only apparent solutions. For, on the whole, the employment-versus-growth dilemma is met by providing, on the one hand, for highly capital-intensive plants and, on the other, by subsidizing the unemployed and unemployable members of the society by doles in various open or disguised forms. It is clear that this is at best a temporary solution. The reservoir of unemployed persons tends to deepen as time goes on and tends to embrace individuals with higher and higher levels of actual or potential skills.

The problem of the "urban unemployed" is acute in many developing countries already, and among these urban unemployed are found persons with some education whose expectations are far beyond the levels of support with which a dole can provide them. Hence, they tend to join various protest movements inaugurated by all sorts of local "Messianic" leaders. The more high-sounding and, indeed, irresponsible the promises of these leaders, the more likely will they be to gather a following. Even if such an association is only temporary, it may result in widespread instability and sometimes even violence.

It need not be specially stressed that all this contributes powerfully to political instability, especially in many of the urban areas of the new nations. And it must be said again that American aid programs have done little to help resolve this dilemma. Instead of urging new technological solutions which would combine labor-intensive devices with modern design, the foreign-aid personnel, on the whole, know only how to explain the functioning and proper use of American or other technologically highly advanced devices. Moreover, since, of all forms of productive activity, agriculture was the one which tended to absorb the relatively largest share of the working force in developing countries, emphasis has been placed on programs of agricultural improvement. There is no doubt but that such a policy can be defended rationally. With growing numbers, more food must be produced lest scarce foreign exchange be used to import it. But, in terms of the aspirations of the elite and the popular masses alike in developing countries, this concentration on an art, which they thought they knew perfectly well, led to stresses and disappointments. The dynamic sector of the economy was not supported sufficiently, and the more stable and staid branches of production were given the lion's share of technical and economic aid.

It is clear from what has been said that such dilemmas can be mitigated or resolved only by measures designed to lead to rapid economic growth. Although the actual achievement of this rapid growth would not guarantee an end to instability and eliminate the appeal to all sectors of the population of revolutionary action, the absence of real growth will insure their continued existence and probably even their becoming more insistent.

III   The Dilemmas of Choice and the Direction of Aid

In the light of the political realities and the economic necessities outlined in the preceding section, we return to the problem of some guidelines for an effective American foreign-aid policy. This problem can briefly be stated in terms of three questions: What policies and programs in developing countries does the United States favor in terms of its ultimate objective, that is, the ultimate goal of American foreign policy, as a guiding principle? With whom should we work? In what terms and how do we work with these persons?

From what has been said earlier, it is apparent that our ultimate goal is best advanced in the less-developed countries by stress on the speediest possible development, consistent with the satisfaction of current demand and sufficient to maintain stability and to dissipate revolutionary tensions as far as possible. Phrased somewhat differently, it is our objective to channel revolutionary fervor into economically constructive rather than politically destructive directions. This requires what we may call programs of ultimate impact and the harnessing of the efforts of populations in developing countries toward their achievement.

If the problem is stated in this fashion, it first poses the question of economic versus military aid. This dichotomy is acute at present, chiefly in Southeast Asia, but it may become equally acute in Latin America and in Africa. The dilemma between economic and military aid is often posed by saying that before economic development can begin, a country threatened from abroad must be made safe against outside attack. As the experience in Laos and especially in South Viet Nam shows, the problem is less one of outside attack than one of infiltration. If the domestic population is fully behind a development effort sponsored by its own government, tactics of infiltration are much less likely to succeed than if the government does little towards the actual implementation of a policy of growth. In other words, the dilemma between military security and economic aid is largely false. The military security of countries threatened by Communist neighbors must principally be maintained by overall international diplomacy and joint action. Once an actual invasion danger is over, economic policies must take precedence; only the full harnessing of productive efforts will produce attitudes and beliefs in a population which will make it relatively immune to infiltration from a Communist-dominated camp. This is a lesson which can be learned by comparing the situation in Malaya with that in Viet Nam. It would be highly desirable if those guiding the fate of Cambodia and Thailand were to take note of the economic and political tendencies set in motion in the countries near them. In sum, therefore, we may say that after provision for a reasonable degree of security, to be prepared against a sudden surprise attack, the major emphasis should be placed on economic development and aid to further this development.

The type of national leadership required to effect this is what might generally be characterized as a "dynamic modernizing elite." More specifically, its characteristics would include: recognition of the need to focus on the development of long-range economic and social programs on a genuine and not a rhetorical level; ability to plan in realistic terms, i.e., to relate short-term resource allocations to long-term requirements, to mobilize requisite resources, and to organize efforts toward implementation; administrative ability, or the recognition of the importance of efficient administration and the acceptance of sound achievement criteria for the selection of personnel in the bureaucratic apparatus in preference to other criteria.

No less important is the ability to mobilize mass support within a pluralistic society. This means that the national leaders must have the knowledge and be prepared to use techniques which will arouse the imagination of different sub-groups with different social and even cultural values and enlist them in a joint effort toward common goals. These leaders should be intent upon modernizing the economic, political, and administrative structures of their societies. But they must also be able to negotiate within and manipulate the symbols of traditional culture. Working within the existent cultural framework, they must establish linkages between traditional values and behavior needed to serve developmental ends.

The skill to move within the framework of traditional symbolism must be superimposed upon a capacity to introduce more modern and rational methods of production. Whether we like it or not the transition to a more modern economy is likely to be slow and will certainly extend over more than a generation. The older people are not likely to change very much; the youngest are certainly going to change a good deal more. But even the young people—except those in full revolt against their society—will tend to maintain certain traditional forms of behavior and certainly will continue to be influenced by traditional patterns of thought. Hence, the process of modernization in both socio-political and economic spheres cannot be regarded as a full-fledged transformation that happens overnight. It proceeds gradually and unevenly. Until underlying values are basically changed, many of the symbols will contain enough vitality to make them important vehicles of communication. The art of genuinely effective national leadership in this transitional phase consists of a skillful blending of the old and the new to form a workable synthesis.

A few brief examples will serve to illustrate this point. Nehru, perhaps more than most Indian leaders, has a rational outlook, a thoroughly Western education and a modern orientation. Yet, he does not hesitate to make use of *darshan,* the traditional means by which Indians derive sustenance from the presence of their leader as an instrument of solidifying popular support, to communicate his ideas directly to the people. In the villages, for example, the traditional veneration for cattle could conceivably be employed to encourage measures that lead to improved animal husbandry. Some Indian leaders have recognized this and similar forms of appeal and are using them. For example, in some Punjab villages, irrigation schemes were supported by relating them to the life of Krishna and to legends derived from the Mahabharata. Similarly, in Indonesia, Muhammad Hatta, before his disagreement with Sukarno, was active in encouraging the formation of producers' cooperatives in terms of the traditional institution of village cooperation, *gotong rojong*.

In many developing countries, the elites most realistically oriented to the needs and goals of economic development are the Socialist or Socialist-oriented elites. Although in some instances Socialists have shown an inability to gain mass support, as in Indonesia, there are among them, generally, persons who can combine the qualities which we have described. Unfortunately, our policy-makers in the past too often have feared the Socialist label and preferred to deal with those purely nationalist parties and groups who have been unwilling or unable to do more than reiterate time-worn nationalist symbols primarily as a means of retaining power.

In evaluating the effectiveness of a national leadership, one much carefully distinguish between a real capacity to implement policy and mere rhetoric. There is a large amount of the latter in all developing countries. It is, admittedly, not easy to distinguish rhetoric from genuine action, since even action often results only after some years. Moreover, rhetoric is strongly built into the systems of political action in general and into those of the South and Southeast Asian countries in particular.

During the struggles for independence, political rhetoric served when success was lacking. For decades political leaders arose largely on the ability to harangue followers and promise them the cessation of misery and destitution. When independence was finally gained, programs of social reform and economic prosperity were widely publicized and legislative acts converting these programs into laws of the land were solemnly enacted. Yet reality did not easily yield to the dreams, and more words were evoked to cover the gap between promise and achievement.

It was easy to blame the former colonialists, the imperialists, and the losses suffered in the war. For leaders in all countries continued the political habits and styles to which they had become accustomed and feared to face the new and awful responsibilities thrust upon them by independence. They reiterated the promises which they had made and continued to predict that shortly they would become reality. The energies devoted to political rhetoric served to absolve the political elites from engaging their energies in the much more difficult tasks of actually undertaking effective development programs.

Even if we can define the type of central elite which has motivation and ability and can gain the mass support needed to push through what we have termed an ultimate-impact approach, we are still faced, on the practical level, with the problem of whom we shall deal with. The United States has little say in placing regimes in power elsewhere. We are often faced with the dilemma of having to work through existing governments who are either unwilling or unable to take action requisite to the goals enunciated. A plethora of lofty goals have been stated in all countries. The question here resolves itself into the choice of working with the group in power and viewing, with neutral detachment, its inability to effect reforms, or trying to promote our objectives and work in ways that might result in the accusation by the regime that we are intervening in domestic affairs.

Too often in the past we have chosen the first alternative. We have allowed ourselves to be detracted from our long-range goal by efforts to help a regime stay in power in order to secure limited stability or in order to be liked. We have allowed ourselves to be politely blackmailed by leaders who hold up to us the "Communist menace" as a means of prying out aid for particularistic and relatively unproductive purposes. We have mistaken the receptions accorded our visiting officials and other dignitaries and demonstrations organized to impress them as indicators of the popularity of these regimes and of our popularity.

The fallacy of seeming to give whole-hearted support to unpopular regimes because they are the officially constituted governments has been amply demonstrated in Cuba and Korea. Admittedly we must deal with these elites; it is unnecessary to hug them to our breasts. For we cannot confuse official friendship and good will expressed on the parts of other governments with the social, political, and economic developments which are the real objectives of our aid policy. To the extent to which we must work through these regimes, we must utilize whatever influence we possess toward inducing them to take the measures necessary to advance our objective. We can suggest, for example, that pivotal posts in the administrative hierarchy be filled by persons who have our trust and who are able to take the requisite steps to accomplish the aims of our aid programs.

We do not mean to present a "great hero" theory of history. For we are fully aware that individual action may often be thwarted because individuals are subject to the pressures of the environment, no matter what their intentions and their personal qualities of energy and integrity. But we must not forget that we are dealing with short-run situations; and in the short run the "right man in the right spot" may influence events in a far-reaching manner. It is not suggested, moreover, that we should try to designate who should lead a developing country. But in these countries the topmost political figures are often most skilled in manipulating symbols and masses. The actual business of government is performed by high-level administrators and bureaucrats. Hence, pressure to appoint men who can perform the required tasks in these positions and to insure that they get the necessary support from political leaders would be a useful means to support our ultimate goals. In instances such as South Viet Nam and South Korea, where the governments are dependent for much of their yearly budgets upon American economic assistance, we undoubtedly have a position of strength to negotiate from, provided we are willing to use it.

It need not bear repeating that this should not be done too publicly lest it provide grist for the mills of those who delight in accusing the United States of intervention. But it is clear that whatever action we take—from providing advisors to providing cash and to participating in decisions involving the creation of new projects or the appointment of new personnel—we are in a very real sense intervening to affect in some way the status quo. Of course, one may quibble about the precise meaning of the term "intervention." It is obvious that we do not use it here in the sense in which it is employed in the technical language of international law.

That a foreign-aid policy is intervention in a very real sense cannot be denied, if we consider the case of a strictly "neutralist" country, such as India. Would anyone deny that it makes a tremendous difference to the Indian population at large whether or not we supply the means to India to meet foreign-exchange deficits, whether or not we provide India with extensive P.L. 480 grain shipments to stabilize domestic food prices and help to halt wage increases and inflation, and whether or not we supply the technical and financial resources to build a large-scale irrigation project rather than a steel factory? Each of these aid measures has an impact upon the level of employment, prices, and overall income in the recipient country and, what is more important, has a differential impact on social groups and classes.

In such ways foreign aid—its amount, timing, and "real" composition—affects the domestic affairs of the country receiving the aid. One cannot but conclude that foreign-aid operations, even if entered into with predominantly humanitarian objectives, have interventionist results. The choice then is for which goal and on whose behalf we intervene. Intervention in the form of attaching so-called "strings," designed to ensure that the aid we provide is expended on needed projects and by people who attempt to promote development and general welfare in a coherent and organized fashion, can be justified in terms of our goals and in terms of the interests of the people who are intended to be the ultimate recipients of this aid.

It is more realistic to regard foreign-aid policy in this light than to pretend that it is a purely neutral instrument. We do not really believe this ourselves. The number of instances in which leaders of this country have urged that aid to a certain country must be granted precisely because it might make the crucial difference between that country's resistance to Communist subversion and its falling a victim to Communist attack is evidence of this. Let us remember that the Marshall Plan for Europe was justified in these very same terms. When it was pointed out that the overall amounts of American aid constituted only a small fraction of the total resources which became available, it was pointed out—and we believe correctly—that what mattered was not the amount, but the kind and timing of the aid. Similarly, we have justified other aid programs with equally strong emphasis on their interventionist character.

Nor are the recipients of American aid unaware of its interventionist character. In face, a theory of the "new imperialism" has been developed in some countries of Asia and Africa. The theoreticians maintain that, whereas under traditional colonialism or imperialism foreign powers governed them directly, now they are being controlled through foreign aid. Therefore, they argue, the former colonies have gained only a pseudo-independence. Although not openly administered by officials from advanced metropolitan countries as before, since they need developmental aid, they are indirectly subject to the countries that extend it. It is further maintained that this "new imperialism" is harsher than the "old colonialism" which was often mitigated by the welfare orientation of the colonial powers that protected the colonial populations through various forms of legislation. The only consideration governing foreign aid, it is claimed, is the self-interest of the donor power.

It would indeed be easy to expose many of the fallacies underlying such reasoning. Here, however, we are not so much concerned with analyzing the theory as with the fact that it should have gained currency and thus imposed caution on American dispensers of aid. Admittedly, it is an outflow of Communist propaganda that has been accepted and is being reiterated by many who are non-Communists. And what there is of "new imperialism" is practiced far more openly by the Soviet Union than by the United States or by European countries. But because the bulk of aid has thus far come from the latter, they are accused, far more than the Soviet Union, of practicing hidden intervention.

We have paid far too much attention to this factor and to the "images" that the rhetoric employed in the recipient countries suggest concerning the attitudes held toward us. Admittedly, within narrow limits this rhetoric may be an interim indicator of the fluctuations of feeling in some quarters toward this country. But its significance has been greatly exaggerated in the United States, especially by some politicians and, even more, by the popular press. Yet it should be recognized that good will, friendship, and our "national image" are of little importance, or at best of peripheral value, in selecting the means and pressing their use upon those persons in developing countries instrumental to the fulfillment of our objectives. It should not, indeed, surprise us if and when the leadership of some developing countries finds it useful and, in extreme cases, even necessary, to use the United States as the official whipping boy for action that might be necessary but unpopular among the masses, so long as they are willing to take that action. For it is often difficult to convey to an uneducated and illiterate population the necessity of present sacrifices designed to effectuate ultimate gains; outright compulsion or the claim that these sacrifices are imposed by some outside force are sometimes the only effective means of attaining cooperation from the populace.

Here again we must not be too dogmatic, since the image which the people in developing countries have of the United States, does matter, if not in a positive then certainly in a negative way. That is, although it may not be important whether the United States is liked for its relations with developing countries and because of the effective implementation of policies designed to meet United-States objectives in these countries, widespread dislike of the United States may be used by Communist or nativistic groups as an element employed to strengthen the appeal of their propaganda. Hence, the degree of significance of the anti-American sentiment must be judged from case to case, and though it may usually not be a cause for alarm, it may have important consequences in some limiting cases. Yet, it should be realized that in many instances the expression of anti-American sentiment is part of the political rhetoric so common in developing countries. It is born out of a feeling of inferiority rather than out of genuine opposition to our policies. Above all, we must not lose sight of the fact that our long-run objective is the creation of conditions tending to countermand the appeal of Communism. It makes no difference whether our popularity rises or falls in the interim.

The problem of selecting and evaluating the personalities and institutions we work with and the strategies we employ is of importance from the top policy level down to the man in the field working on community development and rural agricultural programs. Very specifically it resolves itself into questions of choice, such as the examples we cite: In the selection of a project and the negotiation of the agreement for it, does one agree to a dam or a road project in a particular spot or region because our counterparts in the developing nation demand it for largely non-economic reasons? Or does one exert all patience and tact, while maintaining a firm line, to insure its placement at a point of maximum utility? In the selection of trainees for study in this country, does one insist upon the maintenance of minimal standards or accept the Minister's nephew who is obviously non-qualified? If a village council is clearly controlled by one group or a single official to the obvious exclusion of others from a particular project, does one accept the assurance that those excluded are not important? Or does one continue to negotiate with the constituted authorities, while unofficially ascertaining the needs and points of view of these others?

What we are suggesting here is that there are sophisticated strategies for dealing with apparent stumbling blocks, strategies which enable us to go far toward promoting our objectives while preserving the face of those who only reluctantly will acquiesce in them. This is perhaps a more realistic alternative than one which is usually termed realistic, but which we would rather call fatalistic, of accepting the stumbling blocks and hoping that somehow some good will result out of an *ad hoc* approach, provided it is consistently followed up.

This should not be interpreted to mean that our approach with respect to development aid must not be thoroughly pragmatic. Unlike the Communists, who have a rigid theory of economic development, we do not have one. Their theory proposes a repetition of the steps taken by the Soviet Union in its own drive toward industrialization, regardless of how well this sequence fits the actual needs and possibilities of a country's economy. India is an instance in which priorities for economic growth were derived from this model; and the difficulties into which the Second Five-Year Plan has run are common knowledge. The result was a substantial modification of targets in the Third Five-Year Plan.

The Communists also have a political model which is not based on the experience of the Soviet Union but on Lenin's doctrine of colonial revolution. It calls for an initial collaboration with indigenous nationalism and "bourgeois" interests only to overthrow these non-Communist leaders at a later stage. Though the realities of each situation have required the Soviet Union and its satellites to alter these policies in various minor ways and to adapt them more effectively to existing contingencies, the model has provided the principal basis on which Soviet aid policy is framed. For the policy-makers in Moscow and Peking, and for the administrators in the field, such a model provides an easy and comfortable means of developing and judging aid policies.

The non-Communist world does not have an alternative model. Though progress is being made in the development of a general theory of economic growth, a simple and relatively easily applied set of rules is not available. The operational demands and possibilities of aid must be judged independently in each case. This requires two things: (1) extensive information on the actual economic, social, and political conditions in all countries to which aid is extended, and (2) the willingness to develop a flexible policy which combines a long-range involvement on the one hand, with highly decentralized execution wherever necessary on the other. Arguments in favor of our gaining much better information than we had in the past, and even than we have now on the actual social, economic, and political conditions in the countries we aid, are obvious. Much of our past information was assembled from relatively superficial sources. Often, we were much better informed about a small section of a country's capital than about the remaining 99 per cent of the nation, especially its rural areas. These defects in our knowledge are slowly being remedied. But in view of the great variety exhibited by the many developing countries, this is, by necessity, a slow process; and it is likely that a number of blunders will be made in the future, not because of misguided intentions but because of inadequate information on local situations.

The need for long-range involvement has just recently begun to be recognized, although it should have been obvious from the beginning. We have already pointed out that the major rationale of American aid is the development of programs of ultimate impact—those that assist in creating structural changes that require sustained effort and whose results are only visible after a long period. Aid of the one-shot type is more often a miss than a hit. Aid programs other than assistance in emergencies resulting from catastrophes require the build-up and continuity that only long-range commitment can insure.

The need for greater decentralization in the administration of aid programs has been less clearly recognized, except by the frustrated men in the field who chafe at the delays and the frequently senseless directives they receive. Yet, this aspect of foreign aid is as necessary as the others mentioned. If long-range involvement prevents the inception of hit-or-miss projects in sudden crises, and the curtailment or reduction of promising ones because of uncertainty of funds, decentralization in the administration of programs gives them a certain flexibility. Flexibility is frequently an imperative because of the complexity of the societies to which aid is given and because of the changing conditions under which projects are carried out. Centralized and remote control has been far too common in American practice. The need for approval from Washington for what are often details has unnecessarily hampered missions in the field. Not only has it delayed vital decisions, but it also has often put programs in strait-jackets when administrators in Washington could not understand the specific needs requiring local tailoring.

Admittedly, overall planning and coordination are required as well as a measure of control and supervision from the center. But many decisions could best be made locally by the men in the field, especially if they are properly selected and given sufficient advance training. It is obvious that the selection process should require more of successful candidates than mere technical competence, although there are instances where even that has been waived. But beyond competence, what must be sought are political skills, independence of mind, imagination, resourcefulness, and cultural adaptability. Admittedly, it is not easy to set out criteria by which these can be measured and by which someone's response to strange climes, customs, and working conditions can be predicted in advance.

Quite often the most standard criteria for personnel selection turn out to be least useful for overseas personnel. Those whose success in this country has been derived from following prescribed and approved career paths may turn out to be too dependent upon familiar institutional supports to work effectively in unfamiliar situations where improvisation is required. Americans whose personalities are "best adjusted" to the norms of our society frequently suffer more intense "culture shock" when faced with the stress of overseas living than those whose adjustment would be considered marginal by our psychologists.

Nevertheless, methods can be evolved to pretest the potential adjustability of overseas personnel to the specific conditions of work in a given country and their psychological adaptability to the cultural characteristics of its population. As far back as the Second World War, candidates for some of the intelligence services were put through tests simulating the conditions they were likely to encounter before they were accepted. Simulation studies have advanced considerably since then and could be a useful tool in the recruitment and assignment of aid personnel.

No less important is the advance specialized training to be given foreign-aid personnel assigned to missions abroad. Up to the present, what is called "briefing" has been little more than a farce. Despite considerable discussion among administrators, anthropologists, politicians, and journalists on the need for adequate training and preparation, little has been done to develop programs to equip personnel with more than the sparsest information on the countries to which they are assigned. As a result of considerable publicity and Congressional pressure, there is now considerably more training in local languages than formerly. But of what use is it if a man uses the right words and the correct pronunciation to say the wrong thing to the wrong person out of ignorance of the culture and the power constellation? For not one adequate handbook has as yet been produced on the areas to which we send aid missions.

Often, not until a new member of a field team arrives at his point of destination is he likely to get operationally useful information; then it is mainly through word of mouth from those who are already there. By the time he learns something about the best means of communication within the local culture and begins to understand the subtleties of its politics and learns to differentiate between those with whom he must nominally deal and those who can and will forward his program, his period of assignment is almost over. Moreover, the experiences of past personnel are rarely drawn upon except through the "grapevine." They are not systematically "debriefed" nor are their reports systematically used to compile analytical and operationally useful studies and summaries for their successors. Yet, it may well be that the success of some projects or the difference between barely approximating their targets and hitting them squarely may depend upon this sort of information.

In summary, we have suggested that clarity and consistency in aligning our policy with our ultimate objective and courage, tact, and patience in taking the actions needed to implement this policy are urgently called for. Also required are the recruitment and selection of personnel sufficiently committed to such a policy and sufficiently sophisticated and trained to employ the strategies needed to implement it. If we cannot promote our objectives in this way, we should not be surprised when dynamic but frustrated leaders and desperate masses are driven to political extremes because they believe that they have no other place to go.

17

Defense and Development in Less-Developed Countries

Charles Wolf, Jr. *

I

One of the distinguishing, but relatively neglected, characteristics of many of the new underdeveloped countries is the large size and important role of the defense establishments which they maintain—usually with substantial external assistance. As Table 1 shows, for many of the principal new countries, the defense effort is consequential relative to the national product and large relative to any of the other usual measures of the national economic scale: for example, total government expenditures, gross investment, or public investment. Table 2 shows the ratio between defense expenditures and each of the four other measures for seven countries over a two-year period; the median proportion between defense and GNP is 5.2 per cent; between defense and gross investment 34.3 per cent; between defense and government expenditures 53.3 per cent; and between defense and government investment 81.7 per cent.

The reasons for these strikingly large percentages are fairly evident, likely to persist for some time, and intimately related to the revolution in world politics represented by the post Second World War emergence of newly independent countries in Asia, Africa, and the Middle East. New countries tend to be zealous about protecting their independence and sometimes even militant about projecting it on to their weaker neighbors. The Sino-Indian border situation is illustrative of both points. New countries are also likely to have internal security problems of considerable proportions as a result both of their own initial weakness and of the stimulus provided to factionalism and dissidence by the achievement of independence itself. When neighboring countries are Communist countries, the defense requirements for internal security will be multiplied by the external threat. Divided Korea and Viet Nam are the most obvious examples.

* The views expressed in this paper are those of the writer. They should not be interpreted as reflecting the views of The RAND Corporation or the official opinion or policy of any of its governmental or private research sponsors. I am indebted to Paul Clark, who was co-leader of the research project summarized in Sect. II of the paper. I also wish to thank colleagues who commented on the paper in an earlier draft.

Table 1   Defense Expenditures, National Product, Government Expenditures, and Investment in Certain Underdeveloped Countries (1958, 1959)
(in millions of dollars)

	GNP		GROSS IN- VESTMENT (I)		GOVERNMENT EXPENDITURES (G)		GOVERNMENT INVESTMENT (Gᵢ)		DEFENSE EXPENDI- TURES (Gₐ)	
	1958	1959	1958	1959	1958	1959	1958	1959	1958	1959
Burma	1,090	1,125	217	212	275	299	66	70	112	113
India	30,700	32,900	4,200	4,400	3,976	4,089	1,520	1,630	656	630
Indonesia	5,150	7,720	249	—	785	895	121	222	281	356
Korea	2,225	2,415	300	—	545	529	257	181	170	187
Pakistan	5,710	5,600	445	485	819	722	314	273	273	223
Philippines	5,230	5,370	535	—	618	583	197	247	90	85
Viet Nam	1,920	2,010	200	217	448	449	44	—	172	175

Source: International Cooperation Administration, Office of Statistics and Reports, Washington, D.C. (1960.) The usual *caveats* about GNP and gross investment statistics in this area should be noted. In all cases, figures are shown in current prices. Budgetary data for 1959 were the most recently available estimates of central- and state-government expenditures. Dollar figures are converted at official exchange rates. No attempt has been made to correct for possible overvaluations.

Table 2   Comparison between Defense Expenditures, National Product, Government Expenditures, and Investment
(in per cent)

	(1) Gₐ/GNP		(2) Gₐ/G		(3) Gₐ/I		(4) Gₐ/Gᵢ	
	1958	1959	1958	1959	1958	1959	1958	1959
Burma	10.3	10.0	40.7	37.8	51.6	53.3	169.7	161.4
India	2.1	1.9	16.5	15.4	15.6	14.3	43.2	38.7
Indonesia	5.5	4.6	35.8	39.8	112.9	—	232.2	160.4
Korea	7.6	7.7	31.2	35.3	56.7	—	66.1	103.3
Pakistan	4.8	4.0	33.3	30.9	61.3	46.0	86.9	81.7
Philippines	1.7	1.6	14.6	14.6	16.8	—	45.7	34.4
Viet Nam	9.0	8.7	38.4	39.0	86.0	80.6	390.9	—
	$\bar{X} = 5.7$		$\bar{X} = 30.2$		$\bar{X} = 54.1$		$\bar{X} = 124.2$	
	Med = 5.2		Med = 34.3		Med = 53.3		Med = 81.7	

Source: See Table 1.
G_d = defense expenditures
G = government expenditures
G_i = government investment
I = gross investment

Although the pervasive conflict between the Communist bloc and the free world, and the military aid provided by each, often plays a prominent role in determining the scope and impact of these various pressures toward large defense budgets, sometimes the role is facilitative rather than causal. Long-standing animosities may simply be rejuvenated by the heady wine of independence from foreign rule, as in the case of Afghanistan and Pakistan and of Cambodia's fears of both Thailand and Viet Nam. In these cases, the defense budget is due less to Cold-War considerations, or to conflict among the great powers, than to traditional hostility.

But besides explaining the large defense budgets in the new countries, there is the possibly more fruitful question of how to evaluate the political and economic significance of these defense efforts. There has been a fair amount of discussion of the political significance of the military in underdeveloped countries,[1] with particular reference to prototypes like Ayub in Pakistan, Ne Win in Burma, Sarit in Thailand, and more recently Pak in Korea. Relatively less analytical attention has been given to the economic and political significance of the United States and Soviet military-assistance programs in the underdeveloped countries and of the defense establishments which these programs sustain. The purpose of this paper is to consider some of the economic and, to a lesser extent, the political side-effects of United States military assistance to the defense establishments of underdeveloped countries. More precisely, I want to describe in a severely abbreviated way the method and principal findings of research that has gone on at RAND over the past several years concerning the evaluation of military assistance in underdeveloped countries.

II

Basically, this research was concerned with developing a methodology, and attempting to apply it, to answer the following question: How can military assistance and the structure of defense forces and budgets in the underdeveloped countries be modified to yield about equivalent military effectiveness and yet generate substantially improved economic and political side-effects? Underlying the question as formulated was the notion that comparing and evaluating alternative military programs—both military-aid programs and domestic defense programs in the underdeveloped countries—requires a multidimensional set of performance measures: economic and political, as well as military. For the military performance measures we relied on war games, comparing outcomes in terms of area occupied in a stipulated time period, or the time required to occupy or defend a stipulated area, casualties, and matériel and property damage. For the economic performance measures, we compared the effects of alternative military programs on *operating costs* of the defense establishment, on public *capital formation,* and on *skill formation* through technical military-training programs. And for the political performance measures, we used more or less informed judgment and conjecture concerning the

[1] See, for example, John J. Johnson (ed.), *The Role of the Military in Underdeveloped Countries,* Princeton: Princeton University Press.

likely reactions of key political groups and of the public, in the countries under study, to various program alternatives. Here we quite frankly relied on the area "expert" for our primary performance measures—a by-no-means riskless procedure.

Focusing on United States military assistance programs, the method we developed had five separate steps:

1. We first drew up alternative programs for spending the same hypothetical military aid dollar budget, the amount of the budget being roughly based on recent experience in the particular underdeveloped countries for which the case studies were conducted—Viet Nam and Iran. The programs were designed to be of equal cost, but they were significantly different in their content. One program, which we might call the "A" program, generally stressed fairly large, conventionally armed and trained forces, following pretty closely the lines of recent military aid programs and force structures in the major underdeveloped recipient countries. The other program, which we may call "B," consisted of smaller, more lightly armed forces, with the dollar savings resulting from these reductions used, hypothetically, for expanding internal security forces, increasing ground and air mobility, providing additional ground and airfield installations intended to facilitate effective intervention by free-world forces, if this should be necessary and, finally, expanding the technical training of military manpower.

2. The second step consisted of formulating a more or less credible range of threats, covering differing levels of violence, from a major insurrection to invasion by a minor neighbor, with only marginal support from one of the large Communist powers and, finally, a larger scale invasion with overt participation by one of the latter powers. The threats were sketched out in game scenarios which gave the game players a set of initial conditions to start from, as well as a plausible sequence of hypothetical events through which these conditions might have evolved.

3. Next, the research group, consisting of two teams of senior retired military officers, and a CONTROL team, conducted the game operations, using the military resources available to them to try to achieve objectives specified in the game scenarios, which were then played *seriatim*. The free-world or "Blue" team used, in sequence, the two different force-and-facilities packages represented by the "A" and "B" programs, while the enemy team used his "best" strategy against each of the Blue alternatives.

4. In the fourth step, we evaluated military performance of the alternative packages primarily in terms of the time, area, and casualty measures I mentioned before. Occasionally, we also evaluated military performance in terms of the bargaining position of the respective teams when game hostilities were terminated and the relative probability that a particular contingency (an insurrection) would have broken out at all, depending on whether "A" or "B" had been implemented in the pre-game years.

I should stress here that in the evaluation we were less concerned with the *absolute* outcomes (who "won" or "lost," and by how much?), than we were with *comparative* outcomes (how did program "A" perform compared to program "B"?).

For reasons that should be intuitively clear, one can have more confidence in the comparative outcomes than in the absolute outcomes of an exercise of this sort, because gross estimating errors in evaluating outcomes are likely to be correlated between the two programs.

5. Finally, independent of the war games, we conducted a separate evaluation of the economic and political side-effects of the two different, but equal costing programs, "A" and "B". Here, as I mentioned earlier, we tried to keep the economic comparisons relatively simple, concentrating on the differing operating costs and, hence, differing budgetary implications of the alternative programs, the differences in their relative contributions to joint-use military-civil capital facilities in the intervening pre-game period and, finally, the numbers of skilled technicians trained under the two differing programs. For the political comparisons, as previously noted, we relied on the best judgment we could get.

Now, what did we find out in this comparison? Let me first consider the general nature of our findings with respect to comparative military performance. First, we found that, between the two fairly sharply contrasting, but still technically tenable, programs, the differences in military effectiveness were neither large nor uniform. In the three-by-two matrix (each of the two programs in each of the three differing levels of violence) which summarized our military outcomes for Viet Nam and Iran, it turned out that one program produced somewhat better military performance in one contingency at one level of violence, while the other program did somewhat better in another contingency. But, more important, the magnitude of these differences did not appear to be very large in any case. In the aggregate, given a reasonably responsible and informed formulation of the contrasting alternatives, factors which were not affected by the program changes which we made (such as the terrain, the size of the existing road net, the distance of a major road junction from the border, the loyalty of the indigenous population, etc.) seemed to dominate most of the factors which *were affected* by the program changes (the size and equipment of forces and the types of facilities).

Let me emphasize the point that this latter generalization applies only to the stated assumption that we were comparing alternatives which, though sharply contrasting, still represented responsible and technically tenable changes. I am not saying that changes in forces and facilities don't matter; but rather that, if these changes are judiciously designed, they seem to trade off against each other at fairly reasonable rates, leaving military performance somewhat better in some contingencies, somewhat worse in others, but not drastically different in any. In this sense, the factors which weren't affected by the program changes tended to have a dominant and pervasive effect that made the overall results more similar than different.

Second, we found that the general technique of trying to design a package of forces and facilities to meet a *range* of threats, rather than a single most-likely threat, appeared to make considerable sense. The military posture which performed most effectively in one contingency, for example, in the major invasion contingency, did not prove to be most effective in the lower violence contingencies.

Third, we found that, while sharp improvements in military effectiveness do not seem possible within existing budget levels, there appear to be opportunities for realizing modest improvements by some specific changes in the force-facilities mix in the underdeveloped countries situated on the Communist periphery. Such specific changes related to internal security forces, mobility, reconnaissance, and at least some of the illustrative "infrastructures."

With this brief summary of the military performance and evaluation, what can be said about the economic and political side-effects of the program alternatives? Not surprisingly, the so-called "B" programs (which sacrificed large ground forces in favor of smaller, more mobile, technically trained forces with additional supporting facilities like roads, airfields, harbor and communication facilities) showed clear dominance over the "A" program from an economic point of view. Operating costs and, hence, budgetary requirements were lowered, thereby freeing resources for developmental purposes—at least in principle. Contributions to "social overhead" capital were enhanced under the "B" program. And finally, the output of trained manpower was increased because of the additional allowance of military-aid funds for this purpose. The significance of these economic findings is clearly enhanced by the fact that the military comparison did *not* exhibit dominance for either program alternative. In this, as in many other decision-making problems, it seems to make sense to base choice on secondary criteria, when the primary criteria, in this case, military effectiveness, do not show clear dominance for a particular alternative.

As to the political side-effects, these were both less definite and less dominant than the economic side-effects. In general, it seemed to us that moving in the direction of the "B" program would be likely to evoke support from some of the principal political elites and to create a more healthy public image of the role of the national military establishment, as well as of United States military assistance programs, than has typically existed in the past.

III

With this severely abbreviated description of both the method and the principal findings of our study of military-assistance programs in less-developed countries, let us, finally, consider its relevance to the general theme of this book: the revolution in world politics.

One, if not *the,* major characteristic of the revolution we are discussing is the number of new nations which have appeared on the world scene and the quality, or "mood," accompanying their appearance. The last fifteen years have produced more "sovereign" nations by a factor of two or three than any similar period in history. The quality of their revolutionary appearance is complex, hard to categorize, and fluid. The notion of "protest" against Western societies, which has been stressed in a number of the papers for this symposium, is certainly part of the quality of the revolutionary outburst: protest particularly against foreign rule, privilege, and arrogance. (But I am not at all sure that it is accurate to put the adjective "Western" before each of these nouns, as is usually done. Korea's protest against Japanese rule, privilege, and arrogance, for example, is qualitatively identical to that of the new Asian and African countries against their former Western rulers.)

In trying to use, direct, and channelize the energy embodied in this elan of protest, the new countries are faced with a massive array of difficult and often conflicting problems—external and internal, military and non-military. Many of the new countries of the "free world" face real and serious external military threats to their survival. If they concentrate on meeting and deterring the *external* military threat and allocate their resources accordingly, they may become vulnerable to internal *immobilisme,* stagnation, discontent, and eventual armed dissidence. Viet Nam and Korea both exemplify this vulnerability.

The internal and non-military problems which they face are no less, and often are more, hazardous for the survival and propitiation of the new countries: investment and technical constraints, population overabundance, natural-resource poverty, traditional and cultural inertia, and so on. If, on the other hand, the new countries concentrate their energy and resources on the internal problems, they can become vulnerable to overt military pressure. India's invitingly weak military posture may be cited as a case in point. And, needless to say, there are various combinations of internal and external vulnerability which can be exploited, as the precarious predicament of Laos suggests. How to maintain a judicious and dynamic balance between offsets to the external and the internal threats, with a view toward survival and vitality, is a dilemma that is especially pertinent in the emergence of those new countries on the Sino-Soviet periphery.

As if this dilemma were not enough, the new countries are often hindered in their attempt to reach such a balance by nationalistic and emotional residues. These residues may either make an obviously efficient technique appear to be a great national question mark (as in the case of Korea's resumption of diplomatic and economic relations with Japan), or may make an obviously quixotic, windmill-tilting adventure seem to be a matter of high national priority (as in the case of Indonesia's fanfare over West Irian).

There is no easy or formulary answer to finding the proper balance between measures to counter internal and external vulnerabilities; or, within the former category, between measures to counter internal *military* and *non-military* vulnerabilities, namely, the vulnerability to armed guerrillas and the vulnerability to frustration and hopelessness. But part of the analytical technique for finding better answers and modifying them as the environment changes is suggested by the kind of multidimensional systems analysis which we applied in the military assistance evaluation study. In analyzing how to meet *military* vulnerabilities and threats, decisions and allocations can be improved by explicitly considering the differential *non-military* effects of various alternatives. If this concept is applied, it should become possible to derive consequential economic and social benefits from military aid programs, forces, and facilities—benefits which many of the principal new countries critically need.

18

On Stability in Deterrent Races

Malcolm W. Hoag *

I

In modern strategy no distinction has been labored more than that between deterrence and defense. Everyone now knows that to avert war is not the same as to protect the nation or win if war occurs. But what everyone knows vaguely, few may know well, and what the distinction implies for the mixture of military forces the nation should buy, still fewer may perceive. For deterrence and defense as military objectives overlap as well as diverge, complement as well as compete, so that a simple distinction can become complicated. Of special contemporary relevance, moreover, what is alleged to strengthen deterrence in the short run may jeopardize it in the long run. About our military preparations, few queries are more important than "How will they influence the nature and intensity of the arms race and, therefore, the prospects for arms control?"

The simplest way to illustrate these points is to move indirectly from the pure concepts to their policy implications via hypothetical situations or models. By doing so the clutter of secondarily relevant detail is avoided. This overriding merit of abstraction is not shared by either of the customary alternatives—careful examination of historical instances or direct comparison of the probable performance of alternative, modern military postures—for all their other virtues. Accordingly, most discussion of policy is deferred until the last section of this paper. As the economist moves from such concepts as "pure competition" to mixed examples in practice—from fundamentals to application—so we try to move to strategy and politics.

Given the freedom to generate the most convenient hypothetical situations, we choose an initial one *circa* 1900. That, among other things, gets rid of airpower but not deterrence. To eliminate seapower, consider the situation of a landlocked country —say, Ruritania. Doctrines of airpower, landpower, or seapower tend to confuse the central issues more than clarify them, not to mention the passions they arouse. Finally, to make our situation as simple as possible, let us suppose that there is only one potential enemy on the land frontier, and that this enemy has roughly compa-

* I am indebted to many colleagues at the National War College in 1959–60. That persons so senior, informed, and intelligent about these matters could nonetheless profit from a re-examination of fundamentals motivated this article. My own understanding owes so much to current associates that acknowledgment in detail is unfortunately impossible.

rable resources. In short, we contrive initially to make military planning as easy as possible.

Let us assume that Ruritania's Defense Minister gets the following instructions as political guidelines: "We want to deter our threatening neighbor from attacking us and to protect our country from invasion if he does attack." A realistic response from a defense planner, grateful for such comparative succinctness, moderation, and clarity, would stop at "Yes, sir." Any bureaucrat would dismiss as a hopelessly niggling philosopher a Defense Minister who, in so ideal a situation, would query: "But what comparative values do you assign to the objectives of deterrence and defense?" It would, in principle, be a legitimate question, but it would be unnecessarily disruptive. It would be very difficult to answer and, whatever the answer, it would have little effect on policy.

It would not be the similarity of the two goals, but the near-identity of military preparations directed toward either of them, that would render the distinction academic. An army is required. If one that is good enough and big enough is provided, Ruritania will be confident that any attack by her neighbor can be stopped. The same prospect should be evident to the neighbor, whose low confidence in the success of any attack should roughly mirror Ruritania's high confidence in successful defense. Therefore, the neighbor should be deterred. How strongly he is deterred by any given balance of opposed armies depends also, of course, upon his bellicosity and recklessness. Deterrence, in the final analysis, always rests upon a state of mind, which raises the age-old issue of whether defense planning should be based upon enemy capabilities or intent.

We assume in this case that a Ruritanian planner, following the classically conservative precept, places primary emphasis upon estimated enemy capabilities. About enemy intent he assumes not the worst, for that would be to assume an enemy so bent upon aggression that he is unmoved by any rational calculations of excessive risk. But he assumes almost the worst: specifically, an enemy who will attack if his military prospects, soberly calculated, are promising. By assuming a malevolent if rational foe, he will generate military requirements that will perhaps provide excessive protection against a neighbor more peaceably inclined. Any excess protection, however, will insure against any precarious misreading of future enemy intent as peaceable.

It will be possible to provide defense here, moreover, in a way that should not make a hitherto peaceable enemy suspiciously hostile. Ruritanian defense measures to strengthen deterrence need not incite an arms race and so, in part, negate themselves. This conclusion follows if we add a special assumption, in this case the empirically founded one that attacking armies require, other things being equal, a considerable numerical superiority to prevail over defending armies.[1] Then Ruritania can meet its stated military goals with lesser forces than its neighbor and,

---

[1] See B. H. Liddell Hart, *Deterrent or Defense* (London: Stevens, 1960), especially Chap. 10. That both sides would have recognized the superiority of prepared defenses in 1900, when most nations were ignoring rather than profiting from the lessons of the United States Civil War, is unlikely, but we presume them unusually enlightened.

provided both sides share this assumption of defense advantage, pose no aggressive threat. Passing over all the complex details of the area to be defended, terrain, equipment, and so forth, suppose that Ruritanian army planners conclude that the old rule of thumb is applicable and that a minimum of ten divisions can hold against the thirty divisions that the enemy is expected to have. Suppose further that they prudently multiply this minimum estimate by two, and that a resultant force goal of twenty divisions is accepted by the government over the protests of a reluctant Finance Ministry. To its neighbor, this force will still fall far short of the numbers required if Ruritania is to be a successful aggressor. Why should it be troubled unless, indeed, it had contemplated attack? How could such explicitly defensive measures provoke enemy attack unless their announcement prior to implementation crystallized previously existing aggressive intentions, that is, moved the enemy to seize an opportunity before it vanished? Barring either of these possibilities, Ruritania's defense measures are consistent with international tranquillity; and, barring only the second, they increase the probability of peace. In short, they lead not merely to deterrence, but to stable deterrence in the dual sense that neither an attack nor an explosive arms race is triggered.

That no such arms race need result follows from the assumption that Ruritania can meet her defense goals with forces numerically inferior to her neighbor's. Any further increase in enemy forces can then be countered by a lesser Ruritanian increase within the range of one-third to two-thirds as much, leaving the enemy to bear higher costs for greater force increases without any gain in prospective performance as an aggressor. This penalty of higher costs for the enemy just to stay even can be expected to damp his ardor for the race, and to do so automatically. This damping effect makes for stability, rather than instability, in an arms competition. That is, if we look not merely at the first reaction of one side to a change, however caused, in the strength of the other, but at the entire sequence of actions, reactions, counterreactions, etc., we get a series of increases of progressively diminishing size. Suppose that an initial increase of a division by the enemy is motivated by prestige, fear of a different neighbor, or whatever, but that it will respond only defensively by simply matching any subsequent increase in Ruritanian strength. Then, if Ruritania responds initially, say, by increasing its army by one-half of a division, and the enemy matches this increase, with Ruritania in turn then offsetting by half of that or an additional one-fourth, and so on, we get an especially simple progression which leads to a total of only one added division for Ruritania. No arms race ever progresses so mechanically or simply, but the illustrated point of whether a non-self-aggravating, or damped, competition occurs, remains crucial.

Because this aspect of arms races is of crucial importance, we shall refer often to military "exchange rates," which measure the effort that would be required by one side to restore any stipulated balance of forces after a given effort by the opposition. Where effort can be illustrated in kind, two equivalent divisions for one, the rate of exchange will be so expressed, although invariably in practice more complex measures of national cost or effort are required. The policy application is direct. It is not enough to find a military preparation efficacious against a fixed estimate of the enemy. It should be appraised also in terms of his likely reactions: Does it impose adverse rates of exchange upon him as he responds, or even, ideally, impossible ones? Some things may be worth doing even when they do not impose such rates, but they must be so valuable for special reasons that they can bear the onus of participating in and possibly provoking a losing arms race.

To recapitulate, Ruritania poses two goals—deterrence and defense—which can be met by the same military measures. Therefore, any conflicts in goals can be overlooked. Military planning, simple both in itself and in terms of broader foreign policy, can legitimately proceed on the basis of "military considerations only." The first-order questions that are always posed by deterrence are easily answered: (1) From what is the enemy to be deterred? (2) By fear of what consequences? (3) How are these consequences to be inflicted? (4) How is the threat of these consequences to be made credible?

In this case, it is invasion by the enemy that is deterred through his fear of failure, with a Ruritanian army the means to promise failure. That the army would be used if deterrence failed is inherently credible, for its use to frustrate the enemy would be synonymous with protection of the homeland. In this case, deterrence, which typically rests upon threatening dire consequences to an opponent unless he is deterred, does not conflict with defense, which seeks to alleviate the consequences to one's self if the enemy is not deterred. By virtue of the happy coincidence of frustration for the enemy and protection for Ruritania if deterrence fails, an army fulfills all requirements. It could be provided, moreover, at favorable rates of exchange, even when planned conservatively on the basis of enemy capabilities rather than intent. To complete the idyllic picture, military planning could proceed with little risk of any troubling foreign-policy by-products. Except for the special case of an enemy already so close to aggressive decision that announcements of strengthened future defenses would trigger attack, Ruritanian defense measures would not be provocative; neither would an explosive arms race be generated.

II

A situation like this enables broad military issues to be put at their simplest and so be more easily viewed as a whole. To do so is relevant because fundamentally the military questions have not changed, just their answers; nor have the issues, just their complexity. But the complexities have grown so formidable that the fundamentals can easily be obscured. More particularly, old lessons are remembered more easily than their rationale. Precepts can be drilled into all—assess enemy capability, not intent; or, more broadly, to defend is to deter and not to provoke—and at their grandest can be elevated into principles of war. What we need, however, is not a group of precepts, but their rationale; not which precept, but which combination, and why.

In short, we must discriminate, for circumstances do alter cases. The hypothetical circumstances in our example were rigged to generate convenient and comforting simplifications. The nuclear revolution, naturally, is mainly responsible for changing typical military circumstances markedly from those in our contrived case, but it is by no means solely responsible. Without moving our example forward into the nuclear age, the picture can be changed by altering our assumptions about the military means, objectives, or both.

This can be vividly illustrated if we convert our example momentarily from land to old naval warfare. Suppose Ruritania to be an island, concentrating upon seapower: The principal effect upon our example would be to invalidate the assumption that a defender enjoys great numerical advantages by virtue of his role. The open seas provide no opportunity for a defender to benefit from dug-in positions on terrain mainly of his own choosing. The fleets of aggressor and defender start virtually even, with superior position in battle dependent upon tactics rather than nature. Moreover, because the firepower of numerically superior fleets may all be brought to bear simultaneously, while the inferior opposition is forced to divide its fire among too many targets, any advantage in numbers should be multiplied in battle effectiveness. The expected relative losses mount not merely in proportion to the relative numbers engaged, but, qualifications aside, to their square.[2] For example, if Ruritania faced five enemy ships with five of equal quality, the outcome would be a fifty-fifty proposition, dependent upon luck and superior seamanship. But if the enemy fleet were increased to seven ships, Ruritania's expected losses in an engagement relative to the enemy would mount in proportion to $(7)^2 : (5)^2$, or nearly twice those of the enemy. Against firepower so disadvantageous, a tremendous load would be placed on good fortune and possible superior performance per ship. Consequently, a great penalty is attached to falling behind in such an arms race, and a correspondingly great premium to being ahead.

The arms race in dreadnoughts before the First World War is a case in point.[3] This kind of competition, unlike that in our army illustration, is not inherently self-damping. At best, precarious equilibrium results when each side is content with matching and a balance is somehow obtained. Then and only then no self-exacerbating series of retaliatory increases is generated. It takes only one side to generate such a series by seeking superiority, even if the other is content with matching. If Ruritania insists upon being one or more battleships ahead, while her opponent is firmly resolved not to fall behind, there is no natural limit. Either the race explodes into war or one side is priced out of the competition. The arithmetic of such an arms race is distressing, which places a much greater burden upon political accommodation.

Our earlier statement of Ruritanian defense objectives was restricted to deterrence

---

[2] The classic development of this finding is in F. W. Lanchester, *Aircraft in Warfare* (London: Constable and Co., 1916).

[3] For a valuable historical account of these and other examples, and some intriguing, if controversial, conclusions, see Samuel P. Huntington, "Arms Races: Prerequisites and Results," in C. J. Friedrich and S. E. Harris, eds., *Public Policy* (Cambridge: Harvard University Press, 1958), pp. 41–86. For a more general and abstract treatment of arms races, see Anatol Rapoport, *Fights, Games, and Debates* (Ann Arbor: University of Michigan Press, 1960).

and defense. If we add, "and *win* if the enemy does attack," we move beyond the acceptability of stalemate and get the more familiar trio of deterrence, defense, and victory. Then the arms race issues, or more generally the issues of provocation, are posed more sharply. These more ambitious aims, when coupled with our switch to a naval setting, obviously contain the seeds of an explosive international competition of the sort illustrated above. With a great premium upon concentration in battle to secure the "firepower-squared" advantages, massed fleets might well meet in one decisive engagement. When the outcome might thus be settled overnight early in the war, little reliance could be placed upon wartime production of such long lead-time items as battleships. The arms race would, therefore, focus upon fleets-in-being. In these vital respects, if not in technology, the situation would anticipate modern aerospace competition.

If we revert to Ruritania as a land power, the addition of victory as an objective would also heighten international tension, but less so. Those who fear her always retain the option of adequate defensive counters that fall short of matching her force increases. Self-damping still characterizes the mechanics of the arms race. The race, moreover, would not depend as sensitively upon forces-in-being, because apprehensions about the possibility of overnight defeat would be lessened. Blitzes are still possible, but much less likely. Greater reliance can be placed by both sides upon mobilization potentials, especially of reserve forces. If, at best, one side knows that the other is not mobilizing, it is reassured; at worst, massive mobilization gives it warning. A defender must take care, of course, that it can neither be greatly overwhelmed in ultimate amount nor outpaced in speed by enemy mobilization. As with armies in being, however, these requirements need not call for matching man for man, and accordingly are less disruptive.

Our digression into naval aspects, to sum up, illustrates how unstable, trigger-happy arms competition can arise, and the lessons are especially pertinent in a nuclear age. The naval example serves especially to emphasize the adverse impact upon international stability of adding victory as a military goal. But whether the naval or land warfare example be used, with their somewhat different impact upon stability, the direct impact upon military planning is only quantitative. In the hypothetical situation, the same kind of forces meet the goals either of deterrence, defense, or victory. This crucial simplification, having served its purpose, must now be removed.

III

The conflict among kinds of military preparations can be put at its starkest if we leap to a missile age. Suppose that Ruritania can buy thermonuclear-tipped ballistic missiles as well as army divisions, that the missiles can be guided fairly accurately to any point in her neighbor's territory, and that they are, by any previous standard, phenomenally cheap per unit of promised destruction, although very expensive per complete installation. If we further assume a Ruritanian monopoly on this option, we get a different kind of classic simplicity in military planning. A missile force by itself can fulfill all military requirements if Ruritania is willing to gamble in one respect; and it can fulfill most requirements even if Ruritania is not willing.

The gamble in question is whether to rely solely upon the influence of an awesome missile threat upon enemy intent. Ruritania can choose to rely completely on nuclear intimidation before and also during any war. To deter, she can threaten to destroy one or many enemy cities if she is attacked; to defend, she can threaten to destroy other cities in order to compel the enemy to withdraw or even disarm; to win, she can perhaps use similar threats even to compel surrender. Given such a policy, which would dispense with an army, the enemy retains a capability to invade. Therefore, Ruritania must not plan to send all her missiles at one blow if she is to defend after war starts as well as deter. What she needs is some combination of residual striking power linked to valuable remaining enemy targets in their vital role as hostages. The policy, in short, is dependent upon intra-war as well as pre-war threats and amounts to pure nuclear intimidation.

Alternative policies would mix missile and army capabilities in various proportions. One possibility would be a defensive army shield much as before, but with a sizably diminished mobilization potential because missile strikes were counted upon to reduce enemy potential. This policy, with its virtually complete insurance against enemy capability, deserves special mention as a natural outgrowth of old plans and doctrine. Incidentally, it would also be consistent with an all-out, single-strike philosophy for missile employment, however imprudent, though conveniently simple, such a philosophy might be.

The nuclear monopoly case is nostalgically interesting, but too easy. The interactions among military goals become lively only when both sides have nuclear striking (missile) opportunities. To examine the implications, it is convenient to suppose that both sides have the same technological options, and these we restrict, unrealistically, to a very few in order to avoid complicated calculations. Suppose the missiles are to be based in clusters of, say, ten missiles apiece, in order to share common facilities and so greatly reduce costs per missile. However, the missiles can be separated enough within a cluster so that, if placed in hardened shelters underground, each becomes a separate target. To complete the list of drastic simplifications, suppose that future progress in technology is expected to lead to superior hardening so in step with increases in missile performance (yield, accuracy, and reliability) that the vulnerability of a missile remains constant. Specifically, we assume that the single-shot kill probability of a missile is one-half against either a single hardened missile, or an unhardened cluster of ten missiles, and that, in the latter case, it applies to air-burst tactics.

Now we can generate simple arms races again, of which the most horrendous arises if both sides seek soft missiles systems—say, ten clusters or a hundred missiles apiece as a beginning. In this situation the balance of terror is obviously precarious. If there is a missile war, whoever strikes first is decisively ahead. If the attacker reserves fifty missiles for intra-war threats and fires fifty (five at each enemy cluster), the probability of any particular cluster surviving is reduced to 3%. The probability that at least one cluster out of the ten will survive is, of course, higher, but it is only about one chance in four. The attacker, moreover, can hedge against the unfavorable outcome that the one chance in four occurs by threats of city attacks that may induce the defender not to retaliate. The attacker has a much greater residual missile force than the defender but, especially given air-burst tactics which minimize fallout, still retains most of the defender's population and industry as hostages. In terms of hostages, the bargaining power of the two sides is virtually even; but in terms of remaining striking power, greatly and perhaps decisively uneven. Nothing can assure the attacker that he will get off scot-free and victorious, but his chances are very good.

Lack of certainty of a favorable outcome may be enough to deter an attack, but that it will be enough requires more stringent conditions than believers in near-automatic nuclear deterrence sometimes realize. Our model incorporates not merely meager retaliatory power, but the disruptive feature of "the reciprocal fear of surprise attack." [4] A high probability of peace requires more than that each side prefers peace even to victory, when victory implies the risk of one chance in four of small but appreciable retaliatory power that might be used. The choices open to each are only two—attack or do not attack; but the possible results are three—attack, peace, or be attacked. If the third occurs, it is much worse than the first. Yet this worst result can be eliminated only by attacking, which rules out also the second result.

So it is not enough that each side prefers peace to war. Each must so much prefer peace to war even on advantageous terms, and be somehow so sure that its opponent will continue to do likewise, that it is willing to live with the risk of catastrophe.[5] To do so may be easy when international tensions are minor, but difficult

[4] See T. C. Schelling, *The Strategy of Conflict* (Cambridge: Harvard University Press, 1960), especially Chap. 9.

[5] To illustrate the principle, once again we can calculate oversimply and precisely where policy-makers never can calculate precisely, even when they can face the calculation psychologically. Suppose a country estimates that its feared enemy is unlikely to attack, but may, with the probability in any single year of 0.05. If it expects this probability to remain the same per year, and decides that it will never attack, the cumulative probability of peace over a decade is, barring accidents, about three chances in five. Assuming arbitrary value weights, we can get this situation:

State	Probability of Occurrence	Utility Score if It Occurs	Expected Value
Attack	0	5	0
Peace	0.6	6	3.6
Defend	0.4	1	0.4
Total			4.0

Here our country prefers peace to overwhelmingly victorious war 6 to 5, but victorious war over disastrous war 5 to 1, so that it can improve its expected "score" from 4 to 5 by rejecting deterrence in favor of "preventive" war.

Yet, this illustration merely sets the stage for a compounding of reciprocal fears of attack. If the enemy estimates that you will estimate as above, clearly his incentive to pre-empt soars. This means that your original estimate of the probability of his attack was wildly optimistic, as his must have been of your intent, and so on in an explosively interacting sequence.

otherwise. Mutual deterrence here does not rest upon a solid foundation in objective conditions that promise to make victorious war nearly as disastrous to the attacker as losing war. It rests mainly instead upon subjective confidence in mutual benign intent, which international conflicts serve precisely to undermine. Wherever such conflicts generate a brinkman's cycle of bluff and counterbluff, originating perhaps in very minor and implicit threats but spiraling to an uncertain outcome, the incentive is strong to forestall the worst outcome by attacking. Each side is so driven, not least because it realizes that its enemy is equally tempted by fear of pre-emptive attack. This interacting sequence of reciprocating fears breeds war. Mutual deterrence that rests upon this shaky base can easily be converted to mutual incitement of the very event that one hopes to avoid.

Nobody finds such a situation tolerable and, hence, the quest for stable deterrence firmly rooted in greatly reduced vulnerability of retaliatory power. A much more stable situation results if Ruritania and its neighbor harden their missiles. Then if one side fires fifty missiles at the other, it can expect, given our assumptions, to kill only twenty-five of them. In purely military terms, the attacker loses in the exchange. He is here trading missiles at the adverse rate of two for one, in contrast to the "soft" basing situation in which he could exchange missiles at rates up to nearly five to one in his favor. Such a trade is catastrophically foolish for the attacker unless he enjoys such overwhelming initial superiority that he can override an adverse rate of exchange by brute force of numbers. Such a superiority can be prevented by an opponent who stays in the arms race, but at less cost than matching missile for missile. A defender who buys one additional protected missile for every two bought by the enemy will not fall behind in terms of absolute retaliatory power but will gain as the race proceeds.[6] Our new hypothetical arms race thus permits a damped competition like the army case discussed earlier, not the unstable naval case. Those who seek stable mutual nuclear deterrence find the key in retaliatory forces so well protected that they impose insufficiently rewarding or even adverse exchange rates upon any attacker.

Our example can also illustrate other aspects of comparative stability as a function of kind as well as amount of protection. Suppose the same degree of protection against unambiguous all-out attack could have been provided by warning measures rather than hardening. This alternative would not have implied the same security. Reliance upon warning for protection of soft missiles sites requires speedy launch, and the resultant trigger-happy system becomes more accident prone. It is also an all-or-nothing system in operation. Any missile war becomes total war because missiles cannot be withheld to back intra-war threats or, more generally, to permit a chaotic situation to be clarified, without inordinate risk that they will be destroyed on the ground. In contrast, missiles so hardened or otherwise protected that they

---

[6] The same percentage survival rate applied to a larger force will yield a greater absolute survival. In addition, as the attacker moves from initial parity to pre-attack superiority, he may go beyond the tactic of only one missile aimed at one missile, with resultant lower kills per missile. Higher absolute-force levels, moreover, will make defensive calculations less sensitive to errors in intelligence about enemy capabilities.

can ride out attacks permit these options. They not only protect against surprise attack, but survive it, and are, therefore, consistent with wartime policies either of massive or limited strategic retaliation.

Given a securely hardened missile force equal to her enemy, need Ruritania add other arms? Should it instead try to deter the enemy from invasion as well as missile attack by threats of missile retaliation, forgoing defense in favor of pure deterrence? To do so involves no direct defense against enemy armies, but an indirect defense that, far from making punishment of the enemy in war synonymous with protection of the homeland, implies the worst sort of reciprocal damage. The worst for him does not equal the best for you, but the worst.

Pure nuclear deterrence will accordingly be sharply questioned but may, nonetheless, be sensible. In its favor will be powerful budgetary considerations, plus the paradox that has been elevated into a prime principle of deterrent strategy—"the rationality of irrationality." Viewed in isolation from other events, missile exchanges against an enemy whose retaliatory power is secure are "irrational." Shooting at enemy missiles, given our assumptions, costs you more than the enemy, and is militarily self-defeating. The alternative tactic is to attack civil rather than military targets. Yet, in trading cities with the enemy, surely the loss of one's own far outweighs any gain from enemy losses of comparable size. So it, too, is "irrational." Yet, a policy of which city trading is but one late element in a related sequence may, nonetheless, make sense, for commitment to the sequence as a whole may be the best means of reducing the probability of the "irrational" act to very low and, hopefully, near-zero proportions. Or, to put this central point the other way around, failure to commit yourself to the entire sequence may increase the probability of the feared act or other disastrous consequences. An alternative policy which leads to different sequential decisions, each of which is rational when judged separately, may generate a probability distribution of sequences that is worse.

The obvious case is massive retaliation in kind for attacks upon one's self. To retaliate after being hit may, in a cold-blooded calculation, be worse than to seek to minimize further damage by bargaining from residual strength that is not dissipated in retaliation. To announce beforehand, however, that one will assuredly not retaliate is madness, for it invites attack. The middle course of assuring the enemy that one will retaliate massively whatever the cost, while reserving with all possible secrecy the likely option of non-retaliation, is tempting but is feasible to only a limited extent. Any such policy invites corrosion of the morale as well as the capability of retaliatory forces, and yet evidence of the corrosion must not become apparent. Consequently, the generals emphasize advance commitment to retaliate, with resolve and fortitude as necessary to deterrence as appropriate weapons. They are right, although their good points can be driven too far. When the means to deter differ sharply from the means to mitigate damage if deterrence fails, difficult choices between them cannot validly be avoided simply by neglecting one goal in favor of the other. If a change in military preparations detracts only slightly from deterrence but promises to alleviate damage greatly in war, surely it should be made. The evident sense of such a change illustrates that a nation rarely, if ever, seeks singlemindedly to maximize deterrence but seeks rather to maximize some complicated goal that, as a minimum, combines deterrence and defense.

But how are deterrence and defense to be weighted in this combination? We can rephrase the now-relevant question posed by military planners to political leaders: "How should we value increments to deterrence relative to increments to defense?" Answers now become unnecessary only if military resources are made so plentiful that competing claimants for different kinds of preparations are all satisfied—Ruritania gets all the hardened missiles and divisions she could want, which is hardly a realistic or interesting case. Suppose instead, to look at hard and, therefore, interesting choices, that Ruritania imposes budget constraints that permit only these alternatives: (1) hardened missiles cut from a hundred to twenty-five, plus army divisions cut from two-thirds of enemy divisions to one-half; (2) no army but the full force of a hundred missiles. Now controversy will be rife, not least because inter-service lines will be sharply drawn.

Suppose the first, mixed-force alternative be adopted, in part because policy-makers find persuasive the argument that only twenty missiles delivered on city targets would be "adequate" and that twenty-five protected ones should therefore be more than enough. Critics of the policy will counter with at least two arguments. First, even granting that twenty delivered missiles would be enough, a pre-attack force of but twenty-five gives very little likelihood that enough could survive to meet this test of adequacy. Given the assumptions of our model, an enemy with a hundred missiles could reserve twenty-five, fire three at each one of Ruritania's, and reduce the expected force survival to only three missiles. The numbers, of course, are arbitrary, but our model is realistic in speaking of degrees of vulnerability rather than of approachable but unattainable invulnerability, and so it serves to warn against the excesses of naïve proponents of "minimum" deterrence. Second, would not the missile deterrent to invasion be so weakened as to offset the deterrent value of armies? Would not the very fact of providing an army as an alternative diminish the credibility in enemy eyes of missile response? Would not the credibility be further degraded by superior enemy missile bargaining-power, either pre-attack (100:25) or post-attack (25:3)? In short, with missiles so few, would not too great a load have been placed upon resolve to substitute for, rather than necessarily complement, inadequate strategic forces?

Answers are by no means self-evident. But these are proper questions, as are those that will be asked in return. Even if an army, as an alternative, diminishes the credibility of missile retaliation and diverts resources from retaliatory power, does it not compensate by providing local deterrents to invasion? As for reinforcing the credibility of missile retaliation, is not city trading an inherently incredible response even to enemy occupation? In the final analysis, arms policies have always rested upon the willingness of some fighting men to put honor and the integrity of their country above considerations of personal safety. Now the issue is cruelly changed, for massive strategic retaliation may imply sacrificing one's country. We seek here to explain arms dilemmas, not solve them, and the most personal dilemma is surely that the path of military duty and honor is no longer clear.

IV

Having manipulated models to illustrate some arms fundamentals, we must ask what they have to do with the real world. Far-reaching simplifications have been made. Neglected, for example, are missile impacts upon tactical (army) operations via industrial and other damage in the classic view of the land battle as the payoff. Yet, to trace these impacts would be misleading, as well as tedious. Massive thermonuclear exchanges, if backed by implementable threats of more, will almost certainly dominate and shortly terminate any war in which they occur.[7] Therefore, we should emphasize the use of nuclear intimidation during as well as before war, and we can neglect "broken-back" tactical war. Any current fixation upon one great thermonuclear strike can only be deplored. This holds true whether it be derived as an outmoded legacy from "smash war-industry" philosophies or from wishful thinking that all enemy capabilities would be completely crushed at a blow.

Other simplifications in the models may mislead. The retaliatory systems as a whole were either soft or hard, whereas in the real world they will always be a mixture. The system with no vulnerable places anywhere in the entire complex of retaliation, with respect to all its components, is but an ideal. Some less hard places will always be present, and there may even be an Achilles' heel in the system. Accordingly, there will always be some scope for militarily rewarding counterforce as well as countercity operations—how much scope cannot be answered without looking at particular situations, but that there will be some is itself a useful reminder to those who unrealistically view counterforce strategies as a flat go, no-go proposition (total disarming of the enemy at a blow or not) and so convert a question of degree into one of kind. We have emphasized threat power during as well as before war, and that power, crudely put, is measured by destroyed enemy weapons as well as by preserved enemy hostages and unspent weapons of our own. Counterforce strategies must continually be reappraised, but they are certainly not outmoded.

Perhaps the most serious shortcoming of our model is its restriction to but two possible enemy provocations, with each of them necessarily a clear and massive challenge to an interest traditionally accepted as vital. We have considered only invasion of, or missile attack against, one's own country. Accordingly, we have stacked the cards in favor of those who stress massive retaliation and have ruled out most limited-war questions by assumption. To consider the case for limited-war preparations fairly, one has to go into far murkier and subtler political issues, precisely those that our model neglects. Central issues there turn upon challenges to allies or neutrals where the nature of our interest—let alone how vital it is—is sometimes unclear; where much besides boundary disputes may be an open issue, with who

---

[7] See Bernard Brodie, *Strategy in the Missile Age* (Princeton: Princeton University Press, 1959), especially pp. 160–72. Dissenters have not yet, to my knowledge, provided the calculations, *inter alia*, of protection against radioactive fall-out in combat areas that would be consistent with political and military prosecution of organized war.

provoked whom a pertinent question; and where challenges need not begin at all in overt or massive form. Accordingly, the appropriate role of force is very different.

How biased our models are against any advocacy of limited-war preparations can be shown more concretely by concentrating upon one possible road to general war. Will control of the limits in any local war be maintained? The probability of general war by loss of such control is a product of two linked probabilities—that of getting into the limited war in the first place and of escalation all the way upward in the second. Would-be massive retaliators stress reducing the first probability by awesome threats which, however, increase the second. Would-be limited warriors stress reducing the second probability by observing whatever limits may be mutually apparent and beneficial, the notable example being non-use of nuclear weapons. But they run the risk of emboldening local aggressors and so increasing the first probability. What compounded probabilities of general war will then arise from the alternative policies? No general answer is possible, but our restricted hypothetical situation suggests that a near-zero probability might be reached by Ruritanian concentration upon massive retaliation, that is, upon reduction of the first of the linked probabilities. But other combinations of circumstances might suggest the opposite, although even in our models the merit of exclusive concentration upon missiles is not evident.

Rigged though it is to favor a policy of pure deterrence, the model nonetheless illustrates that there are conflicting choices between deterrence and defense. The first requisite for realism in military discussion is to perceive these conflicts; the second, to recognize that they cannot in practice be resolved by budgets so high that both of these military goals are met in full. Neither 100 per cent deterrence nor 100 per cent protection against the contingency when deterrence fails is now procurable, if they ever were. And even if they could be achieved, for that matter, conflict between them would be sharpened. For who would pay expensive insurance premiums to cover a contingency that could not happen? Or, if 100 per cent defense were the goal instead, who would pay to lessen the likelihood of events against which he was fully protected?

The military professional yearns for a position comparable to that of a physician whose prescriptions supposedly are governed by considerations of health rather than the patient's income, and he frequently employs the analogy. But the doctor is constrained by the knowledge that good medicine and nutrients must not be taken in excess and is comforted because nature will not react malevolently against him in ways that exacerbate the original complaint. Typically, moreover, his prescriptions cost the patient only small parts of his income. When they do not, budgetary constraints may be nonetheless persuasive for being tacitly rather than openly taken into account. Not all of us who could profit from a three months' cruise find one prescribed. And, for that matter, the nation's deplorable lack of good $5 per hour psychoanalysts is reflected in tight rationing of existing services by the purse. The soldier's desire to rise above sordid politics and economics finds little support in the favorite medical analogy or in any other.

We harp on the point for an old but vital reason: Realistic expectations of budget constraints and choices among imperfect military alternatives should influence what one tries to buy, not merely how much. Starting out for "full requirements" in one military area and then cutting back under budgetary pressure may leave us not with one-half of the right sort of capability but with one-half of the wrong. We can illustrate such a development by another modification of our model.

Suppose Ruritania and her enemy can buy anti-missile missiles to defend their cities, but that the unit cost of these missiles matches that of an offensive hardened missile. Then, substituting a defensive for an offensive missile changes, among other things, the type of defense. Direct defense replaces indirect, for a protected offensive weapon defends cities indirectly in two ways: it reduces the likelihood of enemy attack, and it draws enemy fire to itself and away from other targets if there is an attack. This second indirect defense may itself dominate the argument if we assume (1) that anti-missile defenses fall considerably short of the ideal of a kill probability of unity against an incoming missile—say, to a kill probability of 0.3; and (2) that Ruritania is seriously threatened by an enemy who has outpaced her quantitatively in missiles either through higher total budgets or greater concentration of military resources. Suppose, specifically, that the enemy can fire two missiles at each of Ruritania's; can still withhold one missile as a threat against each Ruritanian city; and can expect an 0.8 kill probability against an undefended city. Then, if Ruritania replaces one of its protected offensive missiles with an anti-missile defense of one city, its loss in indirect defense is measured by the two enemy missiles that are freed for city threats. This loss overwhelms the gain in direct defense, for two extra missiles reduce the survival probability of a city more than the anti-missile defense increases it.[8] Such a shift of Ruritanian defense from indirect to direct would, therefore, be a mistake from all points of view, for it would lessen defense as well as deterrence measured by survivable retaliatory power. Protected offensive missiles, on the other hand, would not so dominate over defensive missiles if Ruritanian total military resources rose markedly, relative to those of her enemy. Then the enemy would not have two missiles to be freed by every removal of a counterforce target, and anti-missile defenses would not confront so dismaying a prospect. The issue of anti-missile defenses would then be open. But an ambitious anti-missile or other program that is based on the premise that tolerable balance in other arms would be maintained as a prerequisite can be a disaster if that premise is falsified. To repeat, what one

[8] With the kill probability of defense set at 0.3, 70 per cent of arriving missiles should survive. The kill probability of an undefended city was set at 0.8 to allow for unreliability and inaccuracy. Against a defended city only 70 per cent survival of the 80 per cent that arrive would be expected, yielding a 0.56 single-shot kill probability. The city survival probability would then be 1—0.56, or 0.44, but if two extra missiles were shot at it, this probability would be cubed, falling to 0.085, or appreciably less than the assumed 0.20 single-shot survival probability of an undefended city.

In the interests of simplicity, we here and elsewhere overlook all sophisticated consideration of the added elements of uncertainty in Ruritanian and enemy calculations that would be induced. Our use of expected values makes discussion too simple, but introduces no significant errors for our restricted purposes.

sensibly buys, as well as how much, depends upon the total resources to be made available relative to the enemy.[9]

V

The extreme case of no direct defense, which outrages military doctrine of happier days when defense conflicted much less with deterrence, is the most provocative aspect of a general military policy to which most of our remarks especially apply. That policy, sometimes labeled "finite" or "passive deterrence," is directed, above all, toward stable deterrence of thermonuclear war. It seeks stability, first, in terms of the balance of opposed forces at any moment of time, and, second, by tempering and damping the thermonuclear arms race over time. Hence, it implies a kind of arms-control policy. It tries, in essence, to institutionalize a less precarious balance of terror rather than to supplant it. The goal is stable mutual deterrence, which in practice amounts to playing for a stalemate rather than a win in the grimmest of games should deterrence fail, and so affronts an even deeper military preconception about proper objectives.

The radical version of this policy would be implemented and announced to our enemy something like this:

We shall maintain a retaliatory capability so big, mixed in composition, and securely protected in all ways that we are confident that we could, at the least, smash most of the cities of any nation or coalition of nations that tried to cripple our retaliatory power by any conceivable attack. We expect, in short, to hold most of your industry and people in perpetual hostage, and to this end shall effectively counter by increased offensive power your defensive measures to remove our hostages. We expect that you will do the same. As a joint result, any rational grounds for surprise or pre-emptive mass thermonuclear strikes by either of us should disappear.

The open question is the strategic budgetary scale, and consequent public image of arms intensity and political tension, on which we shall attain this condition. We propose that it be low in our mutual interest. Confident of our ability to protect our retaliatory power against even superior numbers and surprise, we are willing to tolerate rough parity in offensive power; pessimistic about the cost of further reductions in civilian vulnerability (after some first-order measures, perhaps rudimentary fall-out shelters [10]) relative to the costs of offensive improvements that negate them, we are prepared, if you are, to settle

[9] The military reader will recognize the old sound point that some guide to priorities is better than no guide to allocations at all. I have elsewhere tried to move in turn beyond the inadequacies of blunt military priorities to what, in economists' jargon, are income elasticities. See "Some Complexities in Military Planning," *World Politics*, Vol. 11, No. 4 (July 1959), pp. 553–77.

[10] The first-order civil defense measures cannot be detailed here. They might be constrained, however, by these criteria: (1) favorable exchange rates against enemy offensive counters; (2) catching up with, rather than outpacing, enemy civil defenses; (3) consistency with strike-second protection of people when the enemy tries to preserve them as hostages, e.g., shelters in cities that protect against the fall-out from an enemy first-strike against military targets. Each of these constraints limits our program markedly, and surely no resultant civil defenses could be provocative in any major sense.

for cities whose direct defenses are inadequate. If you agree, we must both, of course, be assured that the implied measures of disarmament are taken reciprocally. If they are, we shall by joint action have pledged the safety of our obviously vulnerable peoples to the elimination of general thermonuclear war.

A stable deterrent policy like this is seductive in its very simplicity, not least because it is consistent with past sins of omission. Its advocacy comforts those critics whose analyses have unpardonably overlooked the vulnerability of delivery forces and the consequent genuine grounds for concern about reciprocal fears of surprise attack, and who, therefore, at best prematurely, have presumed a stability in the balance of terror that is far from automatic. Such a policy also rationalizes past neglect in preparations, notably in paltry appropriations for civil defense that were so much at variance with a declaratory policy of massive retaliation against threats to our overseas interests. But these are suspect, if politically potent, reasons for adoption of any such policy. They should not obscure the real promise of reduced probabilities of surprise attack and a visible slowing down in the arms race that so rightly concerns an anxious world.

Any road to effective arms control looks long and uncertain to all but the soft in heart and head. Yet some roads are surely far less dismaying in prospect than others. While we may have little choice about being in an arms race, we may and do exercise great influence over the kind of race it will be. A policy aimed at stable mutual deterrence, for example, can focus initially upon inspection where it is easiest rather than hardest. Rigorous control of nuclear weapons is probably impossible because they are so easily hidden, and control of delivery vehicles is not much more promising when any nominally civilian means of delivery (civilian airliners) may do. But anti-missile defenses of cities should be highly specialized, prominent, and necessarily located near much-traveled places. So they are much easier to detect. Elaborate civil defenses—shelters in cities designed to protect against high blast overpressures—should be still more observable. Protecting fifty or a hundred million people can hardly be as discreet an activity as hiding a few hundred weapons. Satisfactory inspection of hostages, in short, can be an easy if incomplete substitute for inspection of arms.

Another inducement for taking this road to arms control is that the fundamental agreements can be tacit. One implements the policy by doing and proclaiming rather than by agreeing explicitly and, therefore, very slowly and cautiously to terms that will be binding. What one does unilaterally is clear: First, remove or greatly reduce vulnerabilities in the system of thermonuclear retaliation so that the system can not only survive the worst of enemy attacks, but will impose adverse rather than rewarding military rates of exchange upon the enemy in his attack. Convert any extensive enemy counterforce operations, in short, from a winning to a losing game. Second, be prepared to resume, if necessary, the dangerous arms race that seeks to remove one's people but not the enemy's from hostage status. Because nobody can be sure that the enemy will reciprocate in control, such preparedness is a hedge. It is also a means of bargaining pressure to induce reciprocity, which raises the old dilemma that arms measures may either coerce desired arms control or explode into the race one seeks to avoid. Should one "arm to parley," or the reverse? Some compromise answers may hedge this question acceptably. For example, thorough research and development programs for anti-missile and civil defenses—programs that are required in order to reduce lead times later, if the worst arms race is forced upon us—need not provoke this race unless they move into production and implementation phases. So the dilemma may be resolved.

Appealing as such a policy is, it must face several searching questions, of which perhaps the greatest arises when we move from overly simple two-power to many-power considerations. What happens to deterrence of provocations in third areas if the residual fear of general war—otherwise so powerful a control upon whether local aggressions occur and what limits are observed—is deliberately reduced by a policy of stable mutual deterrence? One popular answer is that third-area deterrence will be bolstered by improved limited-war capabilities. This answer is good and very important as far as it goes, but no tactical limited-war capabilities, in themselves, answer threatened or actual nuclear attacks upon an ally's cities, to take the extreme case. Something more is required. It may be the deliberate proliferation of strategic deterrent forces in third areas, as many advocates of "finite deterrence" have suggested, but such a course hardly serves the global cause of arms control.[11]

A third possibility is a policy of limited strategic retaliation—the destruction of a city in the main enemy's homeland as a strategic reprisal for extreme provocations that cannot be met by limited war capabilities.[12] Such a policy suffers from the political defect, but analytic virtue, of explicit bizarreness. Unless one is confident that the prerequisites have been met for stable mutual deterrence, a strike limited to one city is madness. If the prerequisite of secure forces has not been met on the striking side, a serious risk of rational massive retaliation is incurred. If that prerequisite has not been met by the enemy, it is foolish to forgo the great military advantage of a sizable counterforce strike instead, for such a strike can also be made consistent with limited civilian damage if that be desired for bargaining purposes. If the prerequisites are met on both sides, however, a one-city strike, despite expectations of retaliation in kind, may be the best among the poor alternatives that range from appeasement to self-defeating massive retaliation. In any case, a situation of stable mutual deterrence does not rule out all strategic strikes, but only those so sweeping that they destroy the bargaining power of the striker by dissipation of relative military power or valuable hostages. Some residual strategic backing for limited-war capabilities in third areas is still possible.

If we move toward stable mutual deterrence, the choice will be open between controlled counterforce and limited city attacks as the last resort of international bargaining. The choice must be determined, of course, by empirical matters beyond

[11] An alliance-wide collective retaliatory force, notably for NATO, may be a good compromise, depending upon its design and control.
[12] The first systematic account of this policy, to my knowledge, was that of Morton A. Kaplan, *The Strategy of Limited Retaliation*, Policy Memorandum No. 19 (Princeton: Center of International Studies, 1959). See especially Schelling, *op. cit.* and Leo Szilard, "How to Live with the Bomb and Survive," *Bulletin of the Atomic Scientists*, Vol. 16, No. 2 (February 1960), pp. 59–73.

the limited scope of our discussion. It is a merit of our primitive models that they show how relative numbers can still matter. But what the numbers are and will be are the decisive issues. How many and how soft, for example, will be the inevitable vulnerabilities in the opposing retaliatory systems? Other equally crucial issues will depend on more political considerations. If, say, a particular controlled counterforce operation promises to kill no more of the enemy than a one-city strike, but to improve the military balance significantly, although not decisively, will it strengthen the chances of a favorable outcome? Or will it weaken it because a mass strike runs much greater risk of triggering the kind of massive retaliation that is in nobody's interest, because it floods the alarmed enemy with confused intelligence in a fast-moving and catastrophic situation? Questions like these are pertinent, and their answers should determine the blend between controlled counterforce and limited city attacks.

Many will contend that we should not settle in any case for so modest a goal as mutual stability, or, more subtly, they fear that to try to do so will induce lethargy that yields defeat rather than stalemate. They do not predict or espouse strategic symmetry, but project a favorable asymmetry if we are but resolute enough to exploit it, risks and all. Their classic aim, in contrast, is to win, or, its modern euphemism, to prevail. Again our hypothetical illustrations cannot resolve so fundamental a divergence; they can only illustrate aspects of it. Here we merely remind the reader that when our illustrations in Section II added victory as a third major goal to deterrence and defense, the impact was only quantitative. The prescription then became more of the same, with destabilizing repercussions or not upon the arms race dependent upon the type of arms in question. Those who now seek strategic dominance may argue that it will be destabilizing, and therefore risky but promising; or that it will not be destabilizing, and so not risky but militarily less rewarding. This issue will turn, once more, on the scale and rates of exchange that may be expected in strategic counterforce operations. Or they may argue for both reasonable stability and dominance, fundamentally because we outspend or outwit the enemy. Whichever variant is put forward, adding "to prevail" as an objective in thermonuclear war implies much more than quantitative changes. It implies adding different kinds of capabilities, more dramatically and obviously on the defensive side, that limit damage to us so appreciably that striking first and massively, under dire provocation, becomes a credible policy for us when no longer so for our enemy.[13]

The popular compromise between this ambitious goal and stable mutual deterrence is easy to define as an aspiration; namely, strategic capabilities that promise to lessen damage to us in general thermonuclear war, but not so much so that they need alarm the enemy about our willingness to strike and thus weaken deterrence.

---

[13] I should not like the country to adopt as full-fledged and belligerent appearing a central war preparedness as that advocated by Herman Kahn in *On Thermonuclear War* (Princeton: Princeton University Press, 1960), mainly because to go that far toward a "credible first-strike" posture jeopardizes the longer-term prospects for arms control. My policy dissent, however, is coupled with great admiration for the book, which is enthusiastically recommended for, among other things, a much fuller treatment of many of the issues discussed in this article.

The compromisers want to insure against the catastrophe if it occurs, even though their main hopes are pinned upon its avoidance. And what could be more natural? Yet significant insurance can only be purchased at some cost in strengthening reciprocal fears of surprise attack, for it does make resort to thermonuclear war less costly and therefore less incredible. As always, an offsetting effect can be sought by budgetary increases rather than decreases—more protected striking power to strengthen deterrence, while the damage-alleviating measures weaken it. This expedient moves any possibly destabilizing impacts upon strategic equilibrium to the different plane of the arms race, and to a more complex assessment. If the enemy matches us, mutual fears of pre-emptive attack may be calmed, but, with his greater striking power, what happens now to our prospects for alleviating damage? At what rate of exchange and to what extent has his increased power negated the increment to our protection?

We do well to leave these questions open, for again their answers require quantitative specification. To recognize that deterrence, defense, and victory as goals imply very different military prescriptions is not to supply them, although it is an indispensable first step toward good prescriptions. If we buy retaliatory power plus a wide range of capabilities that limit damage in thermonuclear war, the interactions among defense and deterrence will be many and important. Sensible policy will require that they be given fundamental and explicit consideration. On the other hand, if we opt for stable mutual deterrence, and explicitly rationalize the exchange of hostages as the main means of arms control, direct defense against thermonuclear war will be subordinated.

Having begun our discussion by reference to an old situation when the conflict between deterrence and defense did not matter, since achieving one automatically provided the other, we end by noting the possibility of a conflict among these objectives that matters so much that it must be radically settled. For general thermonuclear war, will deterrence definitely prevail over defense, with counterthreats posed to nullify enemy intent rather than capability, and victory forsworn? By turning classic military precepts upside down, do we come full circle to new simplicity, contrived rather than natural, in arms objectives? Finally, if we have not reached this radical situation yet, will we come to it later, more expensively?

VI *

Those who answer these questions with a ringing affirmative proclaim that there has been a revolution in strategy. Consistent with our earlier approach, this asserted revolution can best be illustrated in the extreme case. There its implications for politics are clearest. What national military capabilities would a radical "finite deterrer" aim for, and what would be the associated arms-control and foreign policies?

The quest for stability in the balance of opposed military forces is the key to the

* This section was written a year after the preceding ones.

radical's prescription. To avoid disruptive and possibly explosive arms races, he would moderate national military objectives and give enhanced weight to some preparations at the expense of others. For the contingency of nuclear war, he would give overwhelming weight to deterrence at the expense of direct defense and, still more, of victory. For the contingency of non-nuclear war, presumably at any one of several overseas locations, he would give priority to defense over victory. If these be the objectives, the main means to attain them in the two contingencies will be, respectively, extraordinarily well-protected retaliatory missiles and modern armies. In both cases the hope is that the technical characteristics of the means will combine with the modesty of chosen objectives to deter the enemy from not just one, but two vital things: (1) He will not attack; and (2) he will not try to offset our capabilities in the course of time by greater strength in kind, for he will perceive the folly of accelerating an arms race in which he must spend more than we without gaining a decisive advantage. The radical prescription, thus, is to cultivate those capabilities that promise to create the kind of objective relationship between future opposed forces that was illustrated by our hypothetical Ruritanian army example and to avoid that typified by the old navy example.

Such an approach relies heavily upon tacit mutual avoidance of grim competitions that promise mutual loss. This reliance is both its main political strength and weakness—strength because it translates shared interests among enemies, and deep but otherwise vague yearnings for a less threatening world, into a tangible prescription; weakness because it is dependent upon a degree of cooperation with a hostile enemy who may be fascinated with the temptations of brinkmanship. The weakness must not be overstated, for the approach is not dependent upon enemy benevolence. Deep-seated enmity need not rule out prudence. Still, what will make enemy acquiescence in this sweeping kind of tacit arms control sufficiently prudent for him?

Clearly the enemy must not be stupid, so that he fails to deduce simple implications; he must not be psychopathic, or so blinded by fanaticism that it comes to the same thing; and he must value human life and his civilian accomplishments highly, although not necessarily as highly as we. These are not stringent conditions, and yet, in the perspective of Autumn 1961, who is perfectly confident that they are and will continue to be met? And by how much would our confidence be further shaken if Red China had Russian military capabilities?

There remains, moreover, another requirement. Our enemies must not be too tempted to incur the risks of brinkmanship because, on our side, we fail to meet likewise indispensable conditions. First, of course, we must meet our modest military objectives with unremitting efforts of very high quality. Such efforts must pervade our military establishment, above all in Research and Development and, disagreeable though it may sound, in Intelligence. Everyone's worst nightmare is the magical new weapon that is possessed by the enemy in sufficient quantity before we can counter it, whether it be a near-perfect defense instrument that negates the ability of our retaliatory missiles to reach their targets, or some offensive device that destroys our missiles and planes before launch. We must take adequate safeguards against the possibility that this nightmare arises; the moral for our efforts should be obvious.

· Second, and no less obvious: Resolve must continue to complement our capabilities. It is not enough that the enemy sees that we are capable of the promised response to a provocation, and that such a response promises an adverse outcome for him. He must also calculate that such a response is not too improbable, despite its cost to us. To the extent that the enemy has reason to expect that we will recoil before the brink much more readily than he, the temptation for him to initiate risky provocations is increased. The main penalty attached to a radical tacit arms-control policy arises here. This policy places, of necessity, a great reliance upon what was earlier called "the rationality of irrationality." Alternative policies, although they seek much less bleak consequences if deterrence fails, may nonetheless involve costs that greatly outweigh immediate gains in war. But the vital political difference may be that they do so far less explicitly. If a democracy adopts a radical tacit arms-control policy, the debate about it, especially about the last-resort threat of Limited Strategic Retaliation, will sharpen public awareness of the "irrational" component in the rational sequence of strategy. And if the public is made more aware, it may become more apprehensive. Can a democracy, still more a coalition composed mainly of democracies, nonetheless be so evidently ready to stand up to a test of nerves that enemies will desist from putting us to repeated tests?

One can pile gloom upon gloom by forecasting that the enemy will perceive such temptingly shaky nerves in the West that he will, riskily, make them shakier. His strategic prescription, in the worst case for us, would be compounded as follows: (1) continue the Pavlovian tactics that alternate local scares with soothing reassurances; (2) assert that the underlying strategic equilibrium, far from being stable, is and is becoming more asymmetrically unbalanced in his favor; and (3) act so that his assertions about nuclear war advantages are not palpably absurd. For example, he could intensify secrecy while undertaking vast programs to install anti-ICBM missile defenses and extended civil defenses in and around his cities. So he would hope to sow doubt in the West that his population remained hostage to us. His moves would demand appropriate counters in the West (in, hopefully, whatever offense/defense blend seemed most efficient), and so the arms race would take another spiral upward. Where arresting the race now looks more promising, because inspection of hostages seems so much easier than of weapons, it could be made unpromising. And, perhaps the most fearful prospect of all, these terror tactics could be amplified by a forthright Soviet supply of advanced offensive missiles and warheads to belligerent satellites.

If all these things were done, cruel pressure would be put upon the West, especially upon the allies of the United States. Certainly we would have to reassure them that our countering military moves were adequate, puncture exaggerated Soviet claims about Soviet capabilities, and continue to demonstrate a responsible but determined commitment to the defense of allies. But would these necessary reassurances be enough? Would incentives of allies to possess nuclear retaliatory capabilities not be strengthened?

We cannot cover the "Nth Country" problem here, but one aspect must be mentioned. The very moves by the enemy that might maximize incentives on the part of our allies to acquire independent deterrents are the moves that would maximize the technical difficulties in satisfying them. In a world where Russia and America settled for stable mutual deterrence at low strategic-budget levels and near-naked cities, a small power might be able to achieve, at moderate cost, a sizable retaliatory capability even against one of the giants. A force of small and unsophisticated missiles, if well protected and controlled, might promise to do the job. But against a future super-power armed with elaborate and ever-changing anti-missile defenses, plus big civil defense, how could a small power guarantee sufficient retaliation? Then we should be back to technical demands for retaliatory capabilities that promise to counter tough defenses with some intricate mixture of varied threats, brute force of numbers, big warheads that can accommodate super-bombs or shielding, etc. The cruel dilemma for our friends is clear. Only in a world where the arms race looked least threatening, and independent retaliatory capabilities accordingly least needed by them, do such capabilities look reasonably cheap and, therefore, feasible.

What, then, are they to do, and what are we to do? Surely the most general and satisfying answer is that we must cultivate ever-greater solidarity. To move increasingly from the gnawing doubt, "Will they stand up for us under pressure?" to the still agonizing but lesser imperative, "Will we stand up for us," is to attack the problem at its source. To meet a common threat, we must become increasingly united. Such a course alone meets our deepest shared values, and it coincides with military expediency. Neither a splintering of alliances in an effort to get independent capabilities, despite the noble slogan of "nuclear sharing," nor an attempt to make "tactical" nuclear war attractive to the countries where it might be fought, looks promising.[14]

For policy, we have now sketched the optimist's hopes for a damped nuclear-arms race and contrasted it with the worst possibilities for enemy non-cooperation. If forced to predict, most of us would share an intermediate outlook. In speculations about stabilizing the arms race, we must emphasize that it is not stabilized yet. Still, most of the current rearming is consistent with such a goal. In particular, the main aims of the American rearmament program have been to decrease the vulnerability of our retaliatory system, to control it still better and so reduce any chance of accidental war, and to increase our conventional capabilities so that the "threshold" would be raised beyond which we are driven to use nuclear weapons. Programs to achieve these ends not only enhance our security in virtually all respects, but also lower world risks. Even the decision to initiate significant civil-defense programs, which might appear inconsistent with the goal of stabilized mutual deterrence, will not actually be so unless pushed much farther than has thus far been indicated. In civil defense there are a lot of first-order things to do that should be possible at costs that compare favorably with enemy military counters and that merely try to catch up with the Soviets rather than precipitate an arms race by getting far ahead.

[14] For argument, see my "What Interdependence for NATO?" *World Politics,* Vol. 12 (April 1960), pp. 369–90. For an incisive analysis of independent nuclear prospects, see Albert Wohlstetter, "Nuclear Sharing: NATO and the N + 1 Country," *Foreign Affairs* (April 1961), pp. 355–87.

We can defer worries about de-stabilizing repercussions for the contingency of much bigger and different second-order programs. Above all, our current rearmament program has not initiated programs to put nuclear warheads and modern delivery systems under the unilateral control of other nations. For those who hope for stable mutual deterrence, in short, we can say that we may have made the right signals to the enemy. Whether he reads them correctly and finds the prospects for tacit reciprocity rewarding enough, we shall see in terms of his militancy, programs, and secrecy.

19

Counterguerrilla Warfare in Southeast Asia

R. C. Nairn

I Introduction

Because Communist doctrine and organization extends across national boundaries, it can be put to work within states as a means of extending the power of the Soviet bloc. Guerrilla warfare is an important element in exercising this Communist capability in some states. States with weak economies, with governmental, administrative, and military systems that express real or imagined grievances, and with large tracts of uninhabited and underdeveloped terrain are particularly susceptible to guerrilla attack. The Southeast Asia Peninsula could be described as such an area. All states in the area, with the exception of Thailand, have faced some degree of Communist insurrection. Three states, Burma, Laos, and South Viet Nam have contiguous frontiers with Communist countries. For a foreseeable period, therefore, it is likely that guerrilla warfare will remain one of the threats posed by Communism in the area.

The purpose of this paper is to examine some of the factors upon which a concept of counterguerrilla warfare might be based and to suggest trends of research, development, and methodology in the evolution of such a concept.

II Some Characteristics of War and Insurrection in Southeast Asia

Since 1941 there has been considerable military activity in Southeast Asia. Some of these activities have been orthodox military ventures while others have been essentially guerrilla-type operations. From all of these operations some characteristics have emerged which more or less determine the course that counterguerrilla operations must pursue if they are to be successful. Some of these characteristics have nothing to do with guerrilla warfare per se, but are indigenous to the area and would affect any military operation conducted therein. Other characteristics are intrinsic to guerrilla warfare.

THE DOMINANCE OF TERRAIN AND ENVIRONMENT. Terrain has always played a dominant role in military operations. The particular combination of guerrilla activity and the Southeast Asian terrain, however, produces not just a variation of well-known problems, but virtual war in a new environment. This contention can be illustrated in many ways. In 1943 and 1944, United States and British forces in Burma launched guerrilla campaigns against Japanese rear areas. These enterprises were not related in any way, but both suffered the same consequences. The British force, known as the Chindits, penetrated twice, more than 200 miles behind the Japanese lines, with the object of striking at supply dumps and diverting Japanese forces from the main battle front. The Chindits operated at greater than brigade strength (more than 5000 combat troops), were specially trained, and were backed by an extensive airlift. In spite of their training and support, their extraordinary fighting spirit, and stamina, they failed to cause a major diversion of Japanese forces and the success of their attacks on supply were relatively insignificant considering the forces involved. The force proved to be so difficult to move and fight in an area of jungle, mountain, and river, that only insignificant numbers of troops could be brought to grips with the enemy at any one time; and these, because they were part of a larger whole, could not operate with full effectiveness by themselves. Similarly, the terrain prevented the Japanese from coming to grips with the Chindits. Over all, therefore, an uneasy status quo prevailed, despite the considerable effort that had been expended on the operation.

Much the same pattern evolved with regard to the United States effort. Thus, in spite of some ingenuity and innovation, the terrain prevented what were essentially orthodox military forces from realizing their potential.

These operations were also geared to a time period. Within a period of about two months the Chindits were to have attained all their objectives. This type of planning was in line with proven military practice, but it robbed the Chindits of an essential requirement of irregular operations, namely, to extend the time scale, to slow down the tempo of events, to stop and wait if need be, depending upon the situation. Being linked to theater plans, such flexibility was not forthcoming. The Chindits' logistic resupply was linked with other theater requirements and could not be extended easily. Their objectives were fairly rigidly fixed, and because they had been linked to the activities of major theater forces, the Command was reluctant to extend any freedom of action to the Chindits in this regard. In any case, the organization of the force hampered maneuvers and, thereby, changes in plans. Smaller units would have offered far greater flexibility, but prevailing military concepts did not allow for such units.

The limited capacity of the personnel to maintain themselves in the trying environment placed perhaps the greatest restriction on the Chindits' operations. Although they had had special training which increased their "jungle threshold" well beyond that of ordinary troops, the Chindits expended the bulk of their efforts "behind the lines" on sheer survival. Was this because they were trying to exist as an orthodox formation? Was it beyond the capability of Western soldiers to adapt to jungle conditions? Or had their training been inadequate or insufficient? Without detailed and objective research it would be hard to say, but the likely answer is that it was a combination of all three. Whatever the reason, environmental factors reduced operational capabilities by appreciable margins. The food, the strange surroundings, the sense of isolation, the weather, disease, fear of the enemy, and the consequences of wounds, all exacted their particular toll. The situation the troops found themselves in was, in spite of indoctrination, substantially different from what they were accustomed to and from what they had been trained primarily to operate in. Soldiers who had already proved their adaptability in such widely different areas as Europe, Norway, and North Africa could not adjust to the Burmese "behind-the-lines" environment.

In a hypothetical and negative sense the Japanese campaign against the British in Malaya in 1941–42 again illustrates how Southeast Asian terrain might have dominated a campaign. In December 1941 Japanese forces landed at Singora in the Kra Isthmus and commenced a drive on Singapore almost 700 miles away. For 55 days the Japanese maintained a rate of advance of 12 miles a day and with a land force of five divisions, of which only three saw any real fighting; they not only captured Singapore and the entire Malay Peninsula but also destroyed an army twice their size. This campaign was essentially a battle for the highways. Japanese forces, which had been drawn from Manchuria and had far less contact with the jungle than had their opponents, did use the jungle for minor tactical outflanking operations to good effect, but under no circumstances could the Malayan campaign be described as jungle war. The question which might be posed however, is what would have happened if the defending British forces, or a sizable part of them, had moved off the main communication axis into the jungle and mountains? Various hypothetical strategies could be evolved which would have permitted them to do this, and the overall effect would have been to introduce a new factor which would have changed the entire nature of the campaign. The tempo of operations would have been immediately retarded. The dominating effects of terrain and associated environment would have produced an entirely different type of war.

An examination of any other campaign in Southeast Asia will reveal that the terrain dominated events. In their official report on their successful campaign against the Hukbalahaps, the armed forces of the Philippines described the terrain as being "as bad as the enemy." In Indo China the French never solved the problem of control of the jungle, the ultimate sanctuary and base of operations of the Vietminh. Initially, the French left the jungle entirely to their adversaries but were eventually forced to take some steps to counter the advantage for surprise and for maneuver that the Vietminh then held. This they tried to do by mechanization of their forces. They acquired mobility on the roads and some limited capacity for airborne operations. But the French never mastered the technique of deep and sustained penetration of jungle and mountain and so did not threaten the security of Vietminh forces and rob them of the initiative. Indeed, with their initiative left intact, and operating from secure bases, the Vietminh were able to turn the French mechanized components into new and profitable "target systems." But one French military enterprise did reveal interesting possibilities and was, in addition, particularly successful. The Dinassaut was a heavily armed flotilla of small watercraft which made use of the waterways of the two main delta areas of Viet Nam. This somewhat fortuitous blending of a product of modern technology and an indigenous terrain feature made it possible for the

French to deploy their superior firepower with sufficient rapidity to dominate those areas served by inland waterways. The idea of investigating how much further technology might be employed in providing a mastery over terrain features was, however, not pursued; but the notion was obviously of some significance.

The British in Malaya, in their campaign against the Communist terrorists, slowly evolved a technique which enabled them to master the environmental problem in the fairly limited manner required by their particular operational circumstances. The British indulged in mechanization, as had the French, but in addition to providing for the security of large areas of Malaya by these means, they also moved into the jungle. They used heavy aircraft, some direct jungle support by light aircraft and helicopters superimposed upon a land force specially trained to operate under any terrain or environmental condition. As a consequence, the British became more adept and more effective in the jungle than their adversaries. When operations of this sort became widely practiced, the Communist terrorists, who at one time were close to taking over the entire Malayan Peninsula, became a small hunted cadre bent only on survival.

Terrain and environment are not the only factors to be considered in formulating a concept of counterguerrilla operations, but these factors do exert a pervasive influence on any contemplated operations. All of the military campaigns in Southeast Asia indicate that mastery of terrain and environment is a first essential. It is also clear that orthodox military forces will have difficulty in adapting themselves to what for them is a new medium. On the other hand, both the British and the Philippine forces have demonstrated that, provided guerrilla warfare is recognized not as an extension of orthodox military activity, but as new type of warfare, success can be achieved; at least under the rather favorable conditions that existed in the Philippines and Malaya.

THE "ACTIVE SANCTUARY." Another dominating characteristic of guerrilla warfare in Southeast Asia has been the role of the "active sanctuary." In his analysis of the French-Vietminh conflict, *Street Without Joy,* Bernard Fall described the "active sanctuary" as a "territory contiguous to a rebellious area which, though ostensibly not involved in the conflict, provides the rebel side with shelter, training facilities, equipment, and—if it can get away with it—troops." A contiguous frontier dramatically alters any concept of counterguerrilla operations. It does more than just augment the fighting power of the guerrillas. It makes victory virtually impossible to achieve by the action of the forces in the field. Success in the field will only produce commensurate gain if, as well, political, diplomatic, and basic military pressure is applied against the "active sanctuary" on a scale that will make it "inactive." Thus, a guerrilla war will inevitably involve participation by the United States and the Soviet Union in fields different from and beyond the locus of conflict.

The "active sanctuary" also limits the flexibility of action of the defending nation. It will be difficult for the defending nation to use its orthodox forces in counterguerrilla warfare without weakening its capability to meet an orthodox military threat—still the quickest and most effective way of taking over a country. A vital factor in the success of the British and Filipino campaigns was undoubtedly the absence of an "active sanctuary" on their borders, which gave them the freedom to use the totality of their military force against the guerrillas and which made blows struck against the guerrillas decisive because guerrilla losses could not be made good.

More is required, therefore, than just counterguerrilla forces in campaigns fought along the borders of Communist China, or, in its present state of mind, North Viet Nam. An appropriate "feedback" is required on an international scale the object of which would be to place the maximum restraint on the "active sanctuary." At best, the maximum restraint attainable in Southeast Asia would be to prevent large scale, overt intervention. In the type of terrain existing in the Peninsula, it would be extremely difficult to identify and stop covert aid.

THE INTELLIGENCE REQUIREMENT. Military methods of intelligence collection, selection, and evaluation are inadequate in guerrilla warfare, but intelligence per se is vital. Geared to its primary role of military activity, military intelligence will assess the guerrilla threat in terms of the numbers of fighting soldiers and quantities of weapons, the nature of the supply system, and so on. All of these factors are important, but a good deal more is needed. As guerrilla warfare will affect every aspect of the national life, the intelligence net must embrace every activity of the people. For example, the nature of mountain "swiddens" was one of many intelligence objectives in Malaya. Expert analysis of swiddens will reveal the identity of a racial group— Chinese guerrilla swiddens will be quite different from other groups. Further research, assuming the swiddens were not Chinese, would reveal whether or not the particular racial group concerned, was producing food surplus to its normal requirements—a condition which would only arise if there were some sort of external demand, an unlikely contingency outside of guerrilla requirements. Data of this kind can contribute to an understanding of the pattern of guerrilla activity, especially locations and strengths. Similarly, anthropological data, such as kinship patterns and village organization, can be of immense importance in assessing the alignment of loyalties or a methodology of influencing people.[1] The list can be extended, embracing all aspects of sociology. A military-intelligence organization cannot cope with this kind of assessment, and a requirement exists for a new type of intelligence system which can relate military, political, ecological, economic, and sociological factors relative to specific localities and operations.

GRADUATED MILITARY POWER. Orthodox military forces have a minimum level of power below which they cannot operate. Indeed, the whole objective of military thinking tends to be toward increasing military power. But in counterguerrilla operations, too much force may be a handicap in certain circumstances. A routine task of counterguerrilla forces is to control civil populations, and this may range from the screening of a village to punitive action. Unless military forces have had special training, quite different from normal concepts, they will not only have difficulty in

[1] The fact that the Malay guerrillas were predominantly Chinese, that the Malays dominated the countryside, and that they feared and distrusted the Chinese, aided the British actions. Many Chinese, however, also supported the British.

meeting the coercion requirement, but their actions may be damaging in the extreme. The military force's minimum level of action starts with the automatic weapon or the napalm attack. In Indo China, the Vietminh made a point of entering villages which had been subjected to this form of punitive action as soon as possible after the event. Here was a fertile field for propaganda. The Vietminh could point to the relatively massive destruction and say, "we have been telling you all along that French were barbarians and now you have proof." Thus this sort of punitive action, instead of weaning the people away from the Communist side, had exactly the opposite effect. In most cases, a much lower level of coercive action was required, but this was not within the purview of normal military operations.

Closely allied with the degree of force to be used is the vital factor of decision-making. Who selects the "targets" for punitive action, and who decides what degree of force is to be used? A military commander in the field will tend to "be sure rather than sorry." If one village is a legitimate target and a second is "doubtful," it is probable that both will share the same fate. Both the British and the Filipinos in their respective campaigns quickly realized that selection of targets for punitive action and the methodology of treatment could only be entrusted to specially trained forces, especially at the executive level.

LOGISTICS. Two viewpoints have arisen with regard to the logistic aspects of guerrilla warfare. The first is that guerrillas can exist and fight virtually without logistic backing; the second view is that Western-style forces have unduly lavish requirements in this regard. There is however a "rock bottom" requirement for food and services for every soldier regardless of his nationality, training, or mode of operations. Similarly, ammunition requirements are determined by the duration and intensity of battle, and a guerrilla's requirements are as great as those of any other soldier provided he is made to fight. Indeed, as the guerrilla will always tend to operate at "rock-bottom" levels, he is particularly vulnerable to any action which makes him use up his supplies or which can directly attack his supply system. The availability of an "active sanctuary," the capabilities of our intelligence system to accurately assess guerrilla logistic capabilities, together with our own capability to act against him would determine how profitable his logistic system would be as a target; but overall logistics are probably the guerrilla's weakest point in situations where he faces a determined opponent.

As a corollary to the exaggerated concepts of the guerrilla's ability to exist on a minimum of supply, has been a demand that Western-style formations should do likewise. But a balance must be struck between economical use of logistics and requirements imposed by a weapons system capable of neutralizing the guerrilla threat. To reduce our logistics to the scale of that of the guerrilla would be to fight the enemy on his terms. Our objective must be to do better than this—to fight him on terms favorable to us, even if this means the devising of special measures to meet logistic, and other, problems.

TRAINING, PLANNING, AND CONTROL. Based upon the experience of past campaigns, it is unlikely that our orthodox military formations can be diverted so far from their primary skills as to obtain comparable efficiency in counterguerrilla operations. In any case, even if existing military forces were to be used, the demands for special training to equip them for war in a new environment would not be appreciably less than if a start were made from "scratch." Similarly, the planning of guerrilla operations imposes requirements not within the spectrum of current military education. The intelligence field embraces features beyond normal military requirements, and the selection of objectives and subsequent actions cannot be confined to military considerations. Over all, the characteristics of counterguerrilla operations do not match the type of training, organization, or operational capability of our military forces whose intended role is quite different from counterguerrilla activity in Southeast Asia.

III Some Political Characteristics

THE INTERRELATION OF MILITARY AND POLITICAL FACTORS. Military and political factors are inextricably linked in guerrilla warfare. There are simply not enough "home grown" Communists in any Southeast Asian country to seize power unaided. Realizing this fact better than anyone else, the Communists see as their main task the creation of the "sea" of Mao Tse-tung within which the guerrilla fish can swim. Thus, at this moment, the daily broadcast from Hanoi radio; the distribution of Vietminh tracts and pamphlets; agent activity including terror, ambush, and assassination; and other activities are aimed at the population of South Viet Nam so that they will give their support (or even just acquiescence) to eventual Communist guerrilla operations. Similarly any counterguerrilla activity must interact on the lives of the inhabitants. A balance must be struck between measures aimed at destroying the guerrillas and the maintenance (or creation in some cases) of stable and progressive conditions in the community. No concept of counterguerrilla operations could possibly be successful if it did not take account of this relationship, not only with regard to policies and actions in the field, but also on the level of strategy. For convenience however, some of the more "political" characteristics of counterguerrilla operations have been separated from aspects more military in character.

AIMS AND OBJECTIVES. At the end of the Second World War, the Vietminh captured the nationalist or anti-colonialist revolution. The French failed because of their procrastination and subterfuge to regain the support of the nationalists—in any case all that the French could offer the nationalists was a return to some form of French rule. Thus, even if the French had won all of the important military actions, it is unlikely that they would have won the war. In Malaya, however, the British gained the support of the indigenous people, both Malay and Chinese. Recognizing that colonialism was finished in the area, the British identified the struggle for national independence with the elimination of the Communist guerrillas. Without a political aim in harmony with national aspirations, counterguerrilla activity cannot succeed; neither could the guerrillas succeed unless they espoused desired objectives even though their real but unstated objective is the introduction of a Communist regime.

The general attitude of the West, however, has been to recoil somewhat from the idea of having a specific and easily identifiable aim for a small war. Our overall basic aim of preventing Communist take-overs and of reducing Communist power is, however, well known. But this is not particularly meaningful to a Laotian peasant, even though the attainment of that aim is in his best interests, in that it will help him to do what he wants to do most of all; namely, to hold on to his particular way of life and to change it in accord with his own national peculiarities. Obviously, the Laotian sees his situation only in Laotian terms and not within the framework of an international struggle. Objectives must, therefore, be expressed in a way that he understands. To do this requires a knowledge of the area fairly rare in the West. Furthermore, our ignorance tends to be compounded by the superficiality of knowledge of diplomats and other Western representatives who have spent their time in the area within tiny alien enclaves in the capital, but yet whose accommodations have authority with their home governments by virtue of proximity to the problem. No single factor so prevents the West from formulating its aims and objectives in terms that the indigenous people might understand as does ignorance.

A knowledge of the area is also fundamental in ensuring that we do not underwrite nepotism, corruption, and reaction by supporting a regime which gains favor by "parroting" vague and general anti-Communist slogans. Such a situation not only weakens the posture of the West by robbing it of its chance to propagate popular aims, but also aids the Communists by allowing them to identify the West with reaction.

Formulation of appropriate aims does not by itself solve the problem. These aims must be transmitted to the people and this calls for an articulate and trained cadre; their activities form an essential part of counterguerrilla operations.

THE WILL TO FIGHT. It is common to hear unfavorable reports on the "lack of will to fight" allegedly possessed by some Southeast Asian nations. Such failings, however, can hardly be ascribed to ethnic factors. The detractors of the Royal Laotian Army, for example, will often laud their kinsmen, the Pathet Lao, as people who possess the will to fight. Looked at from a Southeast Asian viewpoint however, the situation looks somewhat different. The Southeast Asian sees himself as a dependent of one of the blocs; a dependent, incidently, who is in the front line. If he is an ally of the West, he is also conscious of another factor. Thanks to geography, the West's ally sees himself as a small weak nation on the edge of a Communist colossus. Unless he is absolutely certain that he will be supported, not in some vague ultimate, but relative to the issues that confront him in Southeast Asia, he will be more conscious of his relative weakness than of the strength of his alliance. Like anyone else, he is extremely sensitive to events that, even though external, relate to his situation. A statement to the effect that "the two and a half million people in West Berlin are not negotiable" was immediately equated with Laos, where negotiation on two and a half million people was actually taking place. Naturally the Southeast Asian asks himself why there should be a difference.

Such an attitude on his part could place an unacceptable restriction on the actions of an ally such as the United States which must assess its actions relative to global and not regional events. But this does not make the Southeast Asian viewpoint go away. If we wish to retain alliances under such conditions, it becomes the responsibility of the leader of the alliance to establish a degree of confidence, relative to his actions, which assures his allies that support is not weakening even though actions in one area may not be the same as in another. Above all, it is the image we give of our will to fight that will most affect his will to fight. If counterguerrilla operations are to succeed in an area, there must be no doubt in the Southeast Asian ally's mind of our strength of purpose.

THE "WHITE FACE" ISSUE. Too often the cry is raised that a "white face" cannot reappear in a military role in Asia without being identified with latent colonialism. But the Western bloc is already linked to Southeast Asia by means of treaty and military- and civil-aid programs. It is likely, therefore, that we will earn opprobrium in any case, if in fact opprobrium is a factor in the situation. The best way of avoiding it is to be able to define our objectives and give at least the appearance of success. The color of our skins is the least of our problems if we can meet these other requirements. The Filipinos gave tremendous support to the invading United States forces in 1944, although the issues in that situation were admittedly clearly defined. In another clearly defined situation, in Korea, the Republic of Korea gave generally sound support to the United States. In the recent campaign in Malaya, the Malays and the Chinese gave excellent support to the British; indeed without such support, the campaign could not have been waged. The issue, therefore, is not so much a handicap imposed by our ethnic origins as it is one of projecting ourselves in a way that appears to be in accord with national aspirations. As the nation that fought the first successful anti-colonial war in the modern era to set a pattern for the revolutionary wave that has spread over most of Asia in this century, the United States should have the least difficulty in appearing in the role of liberator. This is a commonplace statement, but that does not make it any less relevant. Perhaps the potential for leadership acquired at Concord has not been realized to date simply because no one seems to have utilized it.

On a more practical plain, we should also be prepared to take bold steps in forming composite indigenous and Western units, especially field units which are before the public gaze and where language problems are perhaps not so acute as in more complex fields. The pattern of United States and Korean integration in Korea indicates how far and how successfully mixed racial formations might be exploited, especially in counterguerrilla operations where it is practical to employ smaller and, therefore, more intimate groups.

In the minds of most Southeast Asians, the Chinese are feared and are alien. Similarly, ethnic and cultural differences are considerable within the area proper.

The South Vietnamese, for example, have lost much support that might have been gained from the mountain tribes, even though these people gave the strongest possible support to the French, from whom they probably received the fairest treatment in their history. The intrusion of a "third force" might well be a stabilizing and progressive element in this particular situation, if the "third force" were an educated and bipartisan element.

Although the issue can only be proven in the event, it is contended that an "educated" Western intrusion in aid of a Southeast Asian ally has nothing to fear on the "white face" issue, provided that in addition to an understanding of the particular situation, we can show also that we stand for something, mean business, and have prospects of success.

ECONOMIC REFORM. It is a common view that economic reform is the best counter to Communism in Southeast Asia. There are, however, two qualifications to be added to this theme—one practical and the other reflective.

Once guerrilla action has started (or seems to have started), there simply is not time to institute economic reforms and expect that results will be forthcoming on a scale that will curb demands for change. In countries with a proletariat, a wage increase can produce immediate effects. But economic reforms in Southeast Asia are mainly concerned with production methods, education, health, and market opportunities. Visible results in these cases will be slow in maturing, and the question is whether or not the results of such reforms will be demonstrable in time to affect public allegiance.

It is also questionable whether economic reform, even if successful, removes the Communist threat, as the proponents of these measures seem to believe, or merely changes its nature. A prosperous South Viet Nam may have a reduced threat from internal Communism, but the Vietminh intransigence and their army will remain.

Perhaps it appeals to Western liberalism, or to the Western "guilt complex," to offer economic reform to Southeast Asia, or it may appeal as an easy way out—to buy oneself out of trouble. In the long term, some economic aid may produce beneficial results, but economic aid as a substitute for counterguerrilla action would be a failure.

GOVERNMENT CONTROL. One of the greatest single assets possessed by guerrillas in Asia has been the freedom they have been accorded to organize, recruit, train, recuperate, manufacture, and store without hindrance from the central government. This freedom has primarily been due to terrain, but another aspect in many cases, has been the ineffectiveness of the span of control of the government. The guerrillas have had freedom because the government either lacked the will or the resources to maintain effective control of outlying areas. Without such control, the local people are naked to Communist pressures, and by default, the government loses their support. Of equal importance to any other counterguerrilla measure is that of aiding the central government to be effectively represented throughout the countryside.

Again however, there is a danger that such aid will be in the interests of bad rather than good government. Sooner or later we shall have to decide in what way and how far we must influence an indigenous government, assuming that we have sufficient knowledge of internal conditions, at the people's level, to assess the situation. In the past, protestations by governments that they were "democratic" (even to the extent of having a written constitution) seem to have satisfied us that their intentions at least were good. It is questionable, however, whether the political organization of the government is relevant to those national problems which the Communists seize and exploit. The issue we have to pursue, is the substance of government, not its shadow. Do we believe that land should go to the cultivator? Is the peasant getting fair prices and reasonable credit assistance? Should the police be reformed, retrained, and controlled? Is there some equality of opportunity for bright young men who do not have family and other connections?

This is the stuff that revolutions are made of, and unless these and other ills are countered and not underwritten, we shall not only lose the campaign, but, in the minds of others still free, we shall be identified with reaction. Again one can appeal for a greater knowledge of real conditions from our diplomats; for assessments by people who have been in the field rather than the cocktail party.

IV   A Pattern of Counterguerrilla Operations

Based upon the characteristics of guerrilla warfare already discussed, the requirements for a counterguerrilla force will be different from any capability currently held by military or indeed any other sort of organization. Specifically, what sort of military power is required in counterguerrilla operations, and is it necessary to formulate a practical relationship between the military and those economic, sociological, organizational, and administrative factors that intrude on all aspects of guerrilla activity? The following attempts to outine a pattern of counterguerrilla activity which meets the requirement imposed. The four aspects discussed are interrelated; ideally they should be part of one integrated effort.

ACTIVE AND PASSIVE MEASURES. The classic guerrilla pattern in Asia indicates that their activities are sporadic and are regulated to quite a degree by the pressures brought to bear against them. Usually the guerrilla recognizes his own inability to overwhelm even fairly small military forces in pitched battles until that force has been weakened by, (1) dispersion through trying to counter widely spaced guerrilla activity; (2) lack of popular support and difficult inter-communication as a consequence of guerrilla conquest of the countryside, and (3) as a cumulative result of the first two, a weakening of morale. The task facing the defenders, at the outset, is to prevent this accumulation of guerrilla power with a methodology that does not place intolerable burdens on the community and which does not raise force requirements to unattainable levels—a methodology which utilizes in fact, to the greatest degree possible, orthodox military postures to counter the orthodox military threats. The need to maintain these orthodox military postures in the Southeast Asian Peninsula, with its contiguity with an "active sanctuary," is obvious.

The "passive" action suggested would be to establish "keeps," or areas where orthodox military forces are concentrated, in as many regions as possible, subject to the availability of forces and the maintenance of a suitable posture relative to the orthodox threat. As a generalization, most Southeast Asian nations could effect a dispersion of their military forces which would not only aid internal security, but which would strengthen, rather than weaken, their orthodox defensive posture. Superimposed on the "keeps" would be an innovation. It is necessary to create politico-military teams which can actively patrol the areas outside of the "keeps." These teams would require a high mobility, relative to the terrain, vehicles where possible, helicopters, or river craft. They must also have an effective communications system, and the personnel should be able to assess military, political, and sociological situations at a local level. Their purpose would be to counter Communist activity at the village level, to extend the government's authority into areas where it manifests itself but slightly or is non-existent, and to gain intelligence. The teams should be of mixed composition; the indigenous forces must be involved, but they will need assistance from external skills. Besides, the enterprise as a training media for Western personnel could be valuable.

The effect of active patrolling by teams who have the capability of communicating intelligently—not only upwards to the central authority, but also downwards to the people—cannot be overemphasized. As has already been noted, one of the guerrilla's greatest assets has been the freedom left him to move and operate in the countryside, to impress the local people by his "presence," to demonstrate the ineffectiveness of the government by throwing its absence into relief. This can be countered and positive measures instituted as well. But it is also necessary to back the politico-military teams by military power.

COUNTEROPERATIONS. The reaction to a specific guerrilla situation will be the closest approximation to orthodox military action likely to be undertaken. Nevertheless, these operations impose special planning, command, and training problems, as well as the need for more effective weapons; in other words a new weapons system. Aspects of this weapons system will be discussed subsequently, in the section under that title. It should be noted, however, that the creation of a special counterforce does not necessarily negate the use of orthodox military forces. Indeed, one way of making the employment of orthodox military forces against guerrillas effective and possible would be to use a special counterforce to dominate guerrilla activity so that it is forced into terrain suitable for orthodox forces. On a less optimistic note, the backing of orthodox forces will be essential to most counterforce operations not only in operations, but also with supply and organizational matters.

AUTONOMOUS STRIKE. In addition to reacting to guerrilla activity, a counterforce should be able to take the offensive. The purpose of these operations would be to (1) rob the guerrillas of their secure bases, (2) to support anti-Communist factions in enemy occupied territory, and (3) take advantage of dissatisfaction in enemy territories. Details of these forces are discussed subsequently under "Weapons Systems."

RECONSOLIDATION MEASURES. Action taken after military operations have been completed in a particular area are just as important as the military operations themselves. Reconsolidation measures are necessary to counter latent ideas left by the guerrillas; to re-establish confidence in the government; re-establish communications, commerce, and industry; and to exercise the control of potential supply sources such as food and manpower. This is essentially a task of civil government and is perhaps not too different from many measures which are currently being undertaken. The important issue is to be able to integrate reconsolidation measures with the counter-guerrilla program, regardless of who carries out the duties and to be able to back these activities with power.

V   Requirements for a Weapons System

GENERAL CONCEPT. As the submarine evolved as an effective weapon in gaining control of the sea, so too did counter measures until, eventually, an anti-submarine weapons system was created. Unlike other forms of sea warfare in which surface ship was matched by surface ship, submarines were not fought by submarines. Firepower, mobility, field tactics, administration, and so on still have a place as carry-overs from orthodox military operations just as there was a carry-over from the traditional navy into the anti-submarine force. But just as the submarine brought a new dimension into the war at sea so too does the guerrilla, and the environment he operates in, bring a new dimension into the war on land.

In the past we have endeavored to adopt weapons and weapons systems, devised for different purposes, to the requirements of guerrilla warfare. Until recently (if even yet), no attempt has been made to devise a counterguerrilla weapons system against the specific requirements imposed by the task. A need exists for development to proceed along two lines: First, to develop original weapons systems and second, to assess the suitability of existing weapons systems relative to the specific conditions arising from counterguerrilla activity. A methodology for making such assessments is already in being; it sets the pattern for the development of all orthodox weapons. The task is to apply the technique to operations in a new environment.

A weapons system can, therefore, only arise in a specific sense, as a result of detailed research and development, mainly by experts. Trends which this development might follow are suggested subsequently.

MOBILITY AND COMMUNICATIONS. Superior mobility relative to the guerrilla is probably the key factor in giving opposing forces a decisive advantage. The attainment of such superiority will depend upon a variety of factors. The training of personnel will play an important part (see TRAINING below) as will the utilization of indigenous coastline, inland waterway, road, and rail. But in a war where there might not be "fixed fronts," a "spontaneous" mobility capability is necessary for at least part of the force, rather than a mobility aligned to the fixed communications of a specific area (which under most imaginable conditions would be far too slow).

In addition, a requirement exists for deep penetration of difficult terrain. It is possible that current developments in helicopters may permit a solution to this mobility problem. On the other hand, a cheap, short-range, low-performance aircraft might be a better answer. Until field and other research is undertaken, however, it appears fairly obvious that any solution will arise by chance rather than design.

A communications network is a vital adjunct to mobility, as indeed it is to almost every other aspect of operations. But simple radio sets are a thing of the past, even though it is possible to manufacture them easily and cheaply. Again the rule applies: Field research must be undertaken to determine a requirement in line with the specific operational need. It is pointless to locate the latest (or even obsolescent) Army electronic communications in the little villages strung out along the Annamite Cordilleras in South Viet Nam and expect to have inter-communication.

FIREPOWER. The ultimate arbiter in counterguerrilla operations will be firepower. But the firepower system must be mobile relative to the operating conditions, be easy to maintain, resupply in the field, and yet give a high degree of superiority to our forces. High firepower and mobility mean that smaller forces can accomplish a given task. Gas, for example, has been largely discarded in orthodox war concepts, but gas might well be a highly effective tactical and strategic weapon in counterguerrilla situations. It is also worth examining whether the automatic weapon is the best type for use in deep jungle penetration where logistic resupply becomes a critical factor. Ammunition expended in rapid fire must be replaced, and it is debatable whether the undoubted advantage of the automatic weapon is worth the high cost of keeping it effective in the field. It is interesting to speculate; but in response to a specific requirement, something like an air gun firing needles might well be over all a more effective weapon than an automatic rifle, which is at its best alongside a well-developed supply line. Closely allied to force effectiveness, and an important factor in keeping force requirements at a minimum, is the question of detecting guerillas operating beneath a canopy of jungle. Most recently chemicals have been employed in an attempt to remove jungle cover. However, although we have expended considerable resources in seeking methods of detecting submarines under the water, no comparable effort has been made to devise not too dissimilar means of hunting guerrillas.

None of the developments suggested here may be practical. But if an effective counterguerrilla war is to be fought, it will be cheaper in the long run to develop specific weapons to do the job rather than indulge in modification of weapons devised for other situations. Guerrilla wars can be fought with orthodox weapons, but the probability is that very large forces will be required to accomplish what might be done by a lesser number of appropriately equipped personnel.

PERSONNEL AND TRAINING. Che Guevera, in his short hand book on guerrilla operations in Cuba, noted that untrained personnel could be molded into better guerrilla soldiers than could a regular who had spent his life in the army. The British in Malaya also found that the National Serviceman was certainly not inferior to the regular in the jungle and might have been better. Just as it is difficult to adapt some weapons to the conditions of guerrilla warfare, so it is even more difficult to adapt men, especially when they have spent a fair proportion of their lives doing quite different things. No matter whether the regular is used, or raw material, it is probable that the training period will be the same. It would, therefore, be just as economical and probably more effective to recruit counterguerrilla forces on the basis of the formation of a new arm of the military services. Just as the characteristics of the airplane pilot are different from those of the soldier, so too are the characteristics required of the counterguerrilla operator different from those of the soldier.

The attitude of the counterguerrilla operator must be such as to enable him to perform in a totally different "combat environment" from the ordinary soldier. Beside the usual criteria of age, physical fitness, and educability that are normally used, based upon personal experience it is suggested that the following might also be used, especially when assessing leadership potential: The individual should (1) have some understanding of the history, ecology, sociology (especially religion), and economy of the peoples he is operating among; (2) have motivation to travel and live in primitive areas; (3) be able to live on an Asian diet; (4) and be capable of "getting along" with alien and/or primitive people. A language requirement has been deliberately omitted. It is not practicable to train large numbers of people to become proficient in local languages. Nevertheless, any person who meets the preceding criteria will undoubtedly learn enough of a language to gain a "propaganda" effect, and this should not be minimized. It is recognized that the listing of criteria as that given above provokes the strongest antipathy in military circles, although the complications and difficulties involved, for instance, in training personnel to operate such a complex affair as an aircraft carrier, are accepted with equanimity. Perhaps the greatest difficulty will not be in getting the right sort of personnel or in giving them appropriate indoctrination, as it will in having the criteria accepted as a necessary part of a counterguerrilla operator.

There are also major problems to be overcome in adjusting attitudes to quite different training requirements. The devising of suitable military tactics, weapons usage, and so on will not present difficulties, but other aspects will. As one of the first maxims, the soldier is taught to be on the offensive at all times. But in guerrilla situations offensive action should be graduated, employing on many occasions, the minimum force, not the maximum. The counterguerrilla operator is not concerned with battles fought on divisional scales; and the organization of village communities is of more importance to him than a command structure.

In devising an ideal counterguerrilla force, incorporating the non-military element into the force will present the greatest single problem. To meet the ideal requirement, a new type of operator is required, and he will not be forthcoming without considerable changes in attitude.

FORCE COMPOSITION AND ORGANIZATION. Specific composition and organization of a force can only be arrived at after research and some experimentation and after assessing the effects of local conditions at the time. Some broad guide lines can be established, however, assuming that the mobility and communications factors, weapons development, and the personnel training and selection processess can be satisfactorily resolved.

The intelligence and planning organization must be broadened to include consideration of data beyond the scope of the purely military, and these considerations must be undertaken jointly, not by separate entities. Similarly, the planning function, accepting the mission as being not only to destroy Communist power, but also to create conditions where the people will assist the government, must be by an integrated civil and military group. If this integration is not undertaken at a relatively low level, a condition will inevitably arise where military actions either negate or fail to advance political, sociological, or economic objectives. It is not difficult to conceive of intelligence and planning staffs comprising civil and military elements. It is at the command level in the field (where, after all, most of the plans will be put to the test) that a real change in attitude, to say nothing of reorganization, is required. Either we can train suitable military officers to the new techniques, or a political element should be added to the military-command chain. There is no other way of ensuring that actions in the field are in accord with political and other requirements, the implementation of which will spell success or failure. Of the two solutions proposed, the better one is to have a separate political element with overriding authority. Thus if a conflict arises on the political or military values of an issue, it can be resolved on political grounds and some single command can then be held responsible. But the political command must be educated in military matters. At present, the average political officer is quite ignorant of military affairs and, thus, in his work with military people can use his political authority to override military considerations for incorrect reasons. Then, because he is not a soldier, he can go a considerable distance toward disclaiming responsibility for the results.

Assuming that appropriate intelligence, planning, and command relationships can be devised, the next problem would be to determine the nature of the field forces. Two distinct types of field force are required. The politico-military team should be as small as can cover the required spectrum of military, political, and other kinds of research required in a particular area and yet be able to operate autonomously for short periods. The size of teams would vary, but about six to a maximum of twenty personnel would seem to be a reasonable planning figure. The size of the counterforce teams is harder to assess without detailed research. Their degree of mobility relative to the terrain, their firepower, and the flexibility and degree of their logistic support will be key factors. There will be, however, a minimum size below which a force will be ineffective against the enemy. Conversely, there will be a maximum size beyond which the force will be too clumsy to operate, especially in deep jungle operations. The important point is that it is criteria of this sort that should decide the shape, size, and composition of the force, not traditional military organization which is geared to different concepts of operations.

Although a high degree of autonomy should be accorded counterguerrilla forces, without sacrifice of this autonomy, their activities must be allied with orthodox military postures. A considerable amount of their domestic support, logistic backing, and other services could be most easily provided from the "keeps." Their operations should not conflict with plans for the defence of the area against orthodox attack and, above all, the "keep" forces should provide an ultimate military backing either in emergency, or where operations of the counterguerrilla forces are designed to bring orthodox military power to bear on the enemy.

VI Coordination of Guerrilla Operations with Regional and Strategic Postures

FREEDOM OF ACTION. For familiar reasons, our military thinking has become dominated by technology rather than by real situations. We recoil from war in difficult terrain and justify out attitudes by such catch cries as not wanting to fight "the wrong war, in the wrong place, at the wrong time." This presupposes that we have the option of fighting wars at a time and place of our choosing. Obviously the geographic position of the Communist bloc affords them considerable opportunity for initiating conflicts, and no amount of triteness on our part will rob them of that potential. Almost the only way open to us in the foreseeable future of curbing the initiative vested in the Communist bloc is to be able to counter their activities in those areas where hitherto they have had almost complete freedom of action, namely, by being able to fight small wars in underdeveloped countries.

The Communists' ability to probe in Southeast Asia confers another advantage on them. By stepping up small-scale action (or slowing it down), they can choose an area within which they can operate with relative impunity. If our response to guerrilla activity is ineffective and haphazard, and if it can only be effective when the scale of activity has stepped up to the proportions of a major war, Communist activity is likely to be confined to everything short of that which will provoke intervention by major forces. The area in which the Communists would have relative freedom of action could, under these circumstances, be quite large, possibly sufficient to eventually put them in a position where they could effect a takeover.

It is probable, however, that if a situation deteriorated to this stage, rather than abandon an ally we would intervene, even if all our actions up until that point had indicated the contrary; in this case, in effect, we could have encouraged the Communists to the activities that produced our intervention. Intervention under these conditions would probably be an *ad hoc* affair and involve us in a major war, possibly involving China, if we wanted to restore the status quo.

It is theoretically possible, therefore, for the Communists, with relatively insignificant forces, to so dominate events to produce a situation where we either retreat or stumble into a major war which neither side wants and which, even with victory, will only restore a situation which currently exists. Perhaps the situation does not appear grave in a Southeast Asian setting. But much the same pattern can arise in South America, perhaps in the near future. Without the means of countering Communist guerrilla warfare we accord a freedom of action to our enemy which nullifies much of our diplomacy and which ignores our nuclear superiority.

INFLUENCE ON ALLIES. The availability of an effective counterguerrilla force could have a dramatic effect on the will of our Southeast Asian allies to resist Communist pressures. At present our allies are aware that they must endure considerable enemy activity before they can receive any support beyond encouragement from the sidelines. They also realize that a major crisis must develop before we can effectively intervene, and intervention under these circumstances will probably involve them in what is—at least from their standpoint—a major war.

A danger inherent in the capability for swift intervention is that we might underwrite reactionary regimes. This is a danger, but, conversely, our capacity to promote changes in allied governments will also have been enhanced by the ability to intervene. When an ally can hardly keep his head above water because of external pressures, it is difficult and dangerous to force him to mend his ways, so we postpone the matter hoping the Communists will go away. Obviously a capability to neutralize Communist pressure also confers upon us power to influence changes in our ally's domestic actions.

INFLUENCE ON COMMUNIST POLICY. Communist guerrilla activity which fails to evoke a speedy and effective response will be taken as an indication of the debility of the capitalists and as a clear indication that Communist pressure should be increased. This was the pattern in Laos in 1960–61; it was the pattern regarding the erection of the "Wall" in Berlin. On the other hand, our reaction in the off-shore-islands probe in 1959, where we had a force that was effective relative to the situation, was to make the Communists stay their hand. Although it is the simplest and most demonstrable of all post Second World War political facts, namely, that the Communists react in direct response to our capability and will to use power, it is the fact which we are most reluctant to accept and carry through to its logical end. The Communists will, however, continue to operate along these lines. Where they can create a guerrilla capability (a task which imposes many more difficulties for them than perhaps we imagine), they will use it against us knowing that we lack the capacity to react in kind and must depend upon "feedback" from our nuclear power, which in their eyes is now less frightening than it was. If the reports of the Twentieth through the Twenty-Second Communist Congress are to believed, this is certainly the attitude of Communist China. We may be somewhat indifferent about Communist capabilities in Southeast Asia (perhaps wrongly so), but guerrilla campaigns in South America would pose a much more direct threat. The terrain and the economic and social environment offer distinct possibilities to the Communists if only they can solve the logistic issue through the use of a satellite such as Cuba. The creation of a counterguerrilla capability is not necessarily limited to meeting a threat in Southeast Asia but could become a necessary part of global power.

POLITICAL SETTLEMENTS. In negotiating political settlements in Southeast Asia, the tendency has been to assume that a "neutralist" government is a compromise between a Communist regime and one favoring the West. It also appears that a "neutralist" government is considered to be better than dividing a country into Communist and non-Communist portions. We have proof that a neutralist government which does not contain a strong Communist element can be viable. It strains credulity, however, to believe that in a weak peripheral country such as Laos, for example, a genuinely neutral government could be created containing a major Communist element. It might be more "representative" to divide the country. In the segment aligned to the West, orthodox military postures can be adopted freely and measures could be taken to support dissidents who remain behind in Communist-controlled territory. Above all, the possibility remains to win back the country without a major war, through our own guerrilla activity. On the other hand, once a neutralist government has been taken over by its Communist element, open intervention would be the only way in which the Communists could be deposed. If in 1954 Viet Nam had been "unified" under a "representative government," the odds are that Ho Chi Minh would now rule at least all of the territory of former French Indo China. At best we would be trying to support a threatened Thailand, whereas today, in spite of the inroads of the Vietminh guerrillas into the South, the potential exists, if we are vigorous and brave enough, not only to create a stable, pro-Western South Viet Nam, but also to threaten the tenure of the Communists in the North. This potential would not exist had not Viet Nam been divided at Geneva. It is not suggested that the division of countries is a laudable aim, but if the alternative is division or neutralism, division may well represent the best power equation for us.

COST. If the past is any guide, there is no cheap way of suppressing insurrections, whether they be guerrilla or otherwise. The ratio of forces to guerrillas in particular has always been high, although probably no higher than the ratio of police to criminals in a normal community. The costs of developing a counterguerrilla force, especially initial costs, will be considerable. The development of new weapons systems, the probable rearrangement of orthodox military postures in a threatened territory, and the training of indigenous and Western personnel, to say nothing of operations themselves, involves us in a major effort. The ultimate assessment, however, is whether these costs are worth the containment of Communism as a minimum goal and the reduction of Communism as an ultimate goal. Expressed differently, can we afford to face a Communist take-over in South Viet Nam? How do we choose between deserting our protégé or fighting a major war? How also do we cost a situation, where having made a massive investment in orthodox military forces, we are still unable to stop a continuing series of small Communist gains, not only in Southeast Asia but in other areas as well? While the cost in dollars is important, it is the relativity of this cost to our overall effectiveness to use our power that should be the determinant. At present we are spending a lot of money on military forces and aid programs and are still falling short in countering Communism. A little extra spending along the lines indicated, or some readjustment of present programs, might begin to give us some real returns for our years of investment.

Conclusion

Serious studies in counterguerrilla warfare are almost totally lacking in the West. Our efforts in this field are usually a matter of some last minute improvisation by military men who are given the task of stopping a flood where previously there had only been a trickle; to our standard *post mortem* of "too little and too late," we could usually add "and the wrong sort of equipment, techniques, and policies." The guerrilla war and its ultimate form of full-scale revolutionary war could become far more dangerous than nuclear war and, in its nature, far more complex.

Our first task in finding counters is to recognize that guerrilla warfare is a new military situation and not an extension of orthodoxy—that it is not merely a "brush-fire war" which momentarily diverts our forces from their primary tasks. Recognition of this fact is basic to bringing about that change in attitude which will promote research into the problem untrammeled by traditional prejudices. Research must determine what new weapons can be devised and what new techniques can be used along with them to give us a mastery of terrain and environment and rob the guerrilla of his advantage in this area. Political and sociological values have to be incorporated into the weapons system in planning and in the difficult area of command. We must consciously arrange our strategic postures to assist counterguerrilla action wherever possible. And on actual operations, we must be equally conscious of the intimate relationship between our specific actions and the fighting capacity of our ally. To provide "advisers" who talk and instruct but who are not permitted to accompany their proteges into action would seem to be a certain, even though slow, method of eroding the morale of indigenous forces.

This paper does not pretend to determine the composition of a counterguerrilla force. It has attempted to highlight some of the factors which make guerrilla operations unique and suggest some of the areas where research and development might be undertaken with profit. Without a detailed and comprehensive research program, a final answer cannot be given.

Bibliography

It should be noted that there are no references dealing with counterguerrilla operations as a military politico science *per se*. The following references were used as valuable descriptions of warfare in the Southeast Asian area.

Bernard Fall, *Street Without Joy* (Pennsylvania: Stackpole Co., 1961).
George K. Tanham, *Communist Revolutionary Warfare* (New York: Praeger, 1961).
Col. Baclagon, *Lessons from the Huk Campaign in the Philippines* (Manila: M. Colcol, 1960).
Lucien Pye, *Lessons from the Malayan Struggle Against Communism* (Cambridge: Center for International Studies, M.I.T., 1957).

20

United States Foreign Policy
in a Revolutionary Age

Morton A. Kaplan

I Introduction

The following essay is necessarily oversimplified. In the first place, it attempts to deal briefly with many broad-ranging topics of foreign policy. The complexities of the problems involved in American foreign policy can barely be adumbrated. In the second place, the general line of policy recommended represents a striking departure in many respects from general postwar policy as practiced under both the Truman and Eisenhower administrations. The effort to outline the nature of the policy and to relate it to the structural features of contemporary world politics can best be carried out if the policy is presented in its most stark and simple form.

Of course, no policy can be implemented in this simple fashion, for it is not possible to obtain sufficient domestic or allied agreement. In addition, particular features of individual situations almost always require qualification of generalized prescriptions, regardless of the nature of the prescriptions, unless they are so general as to be meaningless or inapplicable. General formulations are better for establishing frameworks of attitudinal responses than for deriving detailed policy. This essay is intended primarily to indicate the changes in attitudes toward foreign policy that are desirable in today's revolutionary world.

There are many difficulties with the pursuit of American foreign policy, and it is, of course, much easier to criticize than to undertake the responsibility for formu lating and executing national policy. If I were to single out, however, two general criticisms, they would be: (1) that the policy of the recent past has been more appropriate to a "balance of power" system than to a bipolar system; and (2) that policy has been more appropriate to an era in which society is static than to one in which there is rapid and revolutionary social change.

II Bipolarity and Revolutionary Change

With respect to the first criticism, that past policy has been more appropriate to a "balance of power" system, several brief observations may be made. The "balance of power" system operates on the basis of short-term alignments of a flexible nature. It is a system in which alignment preferences are based on specific and limited interests. Thus, the enemy of today may be the ally of tomorrow. The nature of regimes and of internal social conditions are indifferent to alignment decisions. And, hence, morality or sentiment, as contrasted with "interest," plays a subordinate role in the decision process. Although the system can tolerate neutrals, neutrals as such do not play an essential role in the system. Indeed, if important states essayed such a role as permanent, their decision might be quite inconsistent with the stability of the system and with their own long-range interests.

The loose bipolar system, on the other hand, depends upon the formation of blocs based upon considerations of long-term interest. The closer the value patterns of the bloc members, the easier it is to maintain the solidarity of the bloc. Clearly democratic nations could not easily function as members of the Soviet bloc. Although the converse proposition has less force, it still has some validity. NATO solidarity is strong because there are many shared values and institutional practices among most members of the organization. In addition, in the bipolar system it is not desirable to have all nations within the bloc structures. The uncommitted nations play a stabilizing role that, in a nuclear age, is of value to the blocs. The United Nations may also play a mediating role that, within limits, merits the support of the blocs.

For the reasons just enumerated, the policy of building blocs has definite limits in a bipolar age. Also, the distinction between "interest" and "sentiment" is not as compelling as in the "balance of power" age. The kinds of nations one aligns with, and the policies one pursues internationally, ought to be more closely oriented to value —or moral—considerations than was the case in the past.

If we take into consideration that the present age is also a revolutionary one in which change sweeps from nation to nation, sometimes without respect to alignment pattern, the preceding conclusion is strengthened. Blocs cannot obtain generalized suport from uncommitted nations, and specific support may very well depend upon what values the bloc stands for and attempts to propagate. The solidarity of the bloc and the willingness of the populace within a nation to take those risks necessary for long-term stability in a nuclear age may depend upon the pursuit of policies that accord with basic ideals.

If we move from the confines of the model of international politics, this conclusion becomes even more compelling. The West, in particular, the United States, is on the defensive. We have become modern Canutes, attempting to hold back the tides, unresponsive to the currents of our time. In an age when new nations have been proliferating and old nations undergoing revolutionary changes, the United States has been implementing a policy designed in general to discourage radical change and to aid governments in power, regardless of the nature of their regimes, provided they are avowedly anti-Communist. The two aspects of the policy, of course, are related, for often the most anti-Communist governments are those which fear radical change at home and which are willing to join American military alliances to receive support that may bolster them against the forces making for internal change. As a consequence, in many areas of the world, the United States seems to represent reaction and a barrier to the hopes and aspirations of large masses of people. It seems to stand for corruption, inefficiency, and maintenance of the status quo. And, at least to many, the alliances it espouses raise the danger of local war for causes not understandable to large masses of the local populations.

The United States has so defined the issues that, for many revolutionary social movements, to pursue what they desire both nationally and internationally is to oppose the United States. This, of course, gives the Soviet Union great leverage. This also makes the bipolar system even more unstable than it otherwise would be. Since, in addition, many Westerners are opposed to the policies that produce these results, it weakens the ability of the United States to counter the Soviet offensive. Coalition problems increase and elements within the United States become disaffected.

The Soviet Union is an active and disturbing foe. Supported by its belief in the historic inevitability of Communism, it challenges the present structure of world politics. It is little inhibited by domestic opinion or by bloc dissidence. It is not associated with colonialism by the new nations and it can support, almost without qualification, actions designed to change the status quo radically. It holds forth the threat of nuclear war and, because it seems impervious to change or to influence, drives those who fear war to put pressure upon the West to make concessions. Along with the threat of war, it advocates disarmament under conditions that are not genuinely acceptable to the West.

Under pressure from the Soviet and Chinese threats, and faced by revolutionary changes in the world, the West retreats. Its alliances become fragile. Compromise and temporization are the order of the day. And, even in the United States, there is difficulty in mobilizing domestic opinion behind policies involving risks. The effort to halt Communism hardly seems worth the risk of nuclear war to many, particularly if a stand must be made in a remote and seemingly unimportant area of the world. It is much easier to postpone risks and to enjoy the luxuries of contemporary American life or to seek scapegoats either on the left or right of the political spectrum. After all, the hard choices can also be avoided by blaming our problems on Communist subversives or on warmongering generals. The witch hunt and the peace march are both symptoms of the breakdown and rejection of political life. They are both symptoms of an essential malaise in the West—of the absence of a unifying political ideal.

To describe what is necessary to rejuvenate American political life may be beyond the powers of any individual. That subject certainly cannot be considered within the scope of this paper. A few aspects of the problem as it affects the conduct of foreign policy can, however, be mentioned. The goals of American foreign policy must be derived from the basic ideals of the nation if they are to obtain sufficient support for a chance of effective implementation. The United States must begin to think not in terms of specific deals or outcomes but in terms of the kind of world in which American democracy can survive. *Realpolitik* and cynicism may once have been effective techniques for the conduct of foreign policy. If they are resorted to today at the highest levels of policy-making, they will corrode the political faith required for an effective American policy and, if necessary, for the resort to force in support of that policy.

If we enunciate policies merely to gain support and not because we are convinced of their rightness, we encourage others to raise the price of their support. If we assume a posture of strength in support of policies we are not really willing to run risks to implement, the Soviet Union is likely soon to call our bluff and expose our irresolution. If we are to act with hope of success, we must find a source of strength not merely in weapons, but also in our values and ideals.

The United States can no longer afford to be a conservative nation. Conservatism is appropriate when change threatens desirable values *and* when these values can be defended best by defensive measures. There must be an ability to weather the storm. It made sense for Franklin Roosevelt to replace "Dr. New Deal" with "Dr. Win the War." But we are no longer faced with a military conflict of relatively short duration. We are confronted with a revolution of world-wide dimensions, a revolution that cannot be halted by military measures or by temporary defeats. The United States cannot—and should not attempt to—halt this revolution. It can attempt to influence the direction this revolution takes and the values that flourish as it progresses.

Although the "Free World-Communist" dichotomy is grossly oversimplified— witness the authoritarian satrapies of the United States, such as Spain—it points to an essential truth about the present world struggle. Imbedded in the American tradition as it has developed is a belief in the right of each individual to find his own truth, provided only that he respect the rights of others to find their truths. Just as the American political process encourages the enunciation and pursuit of any political goal compatible with the maintenance of a political system permitting such a pursuit for all, the American intellectual system permits an experimental attitude toward beliefs—permits the individual to pursue his thought as best he can. There is no official dogma that circumscribes this process, that must be accepted, that cannot be tested or denied. There is a distaste for official or governmental indoctrination, and a belief that the only dignified beliefs worthy of free men are those that can withstand free and public challenge. There is the belief that the proper goal of society is the mature, free man—and that it is the object of society to provide, or at least to permit, the conditions under which such men can flourish.

The democratic system is one that institutionalizes dissent and that encourages criticism, as long as it does not attack the fundamental principle that others also, even if members of a minority, possess this right. These ideals are imbedded, even if imperfectly, in American institutions. But they are not otherwise related to class, race, religion, or nationality. If we believe in these values, we must believe in them for others as well. And, if we are moral people, within the limits of prudence, we shall not hold to these beliefs passively, but we shall encourage and support those who also subscribe to these values in other lands.

Before examining specific problems, we can summarize the three kinds of major problems facing the United States:

1. The uncommitted states are alienated and act in ways that increase the instability of the bipolar age.

2. The West has no positive set of ideals to generate a confident set of foreign policies. NATO is beset by divisions and fears. The individual member nations complacently desire to protect what they have but lack an image of a world they desire that will induce bold and purposeful programs and policies.

3. The Soviet Union and the Communist bloc constitute an active set of foes. They take advantage of the divisions in the West, and of the fears and complacencies of individual Western nations, to increase the pressure on the West and to force concessions disadvantageous to it. The Communist leaders know the kind of world they want to build and are willing to take risks to achieve their goals. Despite some internal quarrels, they achieve reasonable cooperation and are able to induce reasonable domestic support. The United States must learn how to deal with the Soviet challenge and, to the extent possible, increase the problems facing the Soviet bloc both internally and externally.

There are no complete or easy solutions for these problems. But the United States must learn to cope with them in an adequate way if it is to preserve the values that underlie the American experiment.

III   The Uncommitted States and United States Policy

The passion for self-rule, for independence, applies both to groups and to individuals. Colonial existence, no matter how necessary it may seem at some times to promote still further development, is incompatible with human dignity. And although rule by a local dictatorship is far removed from the ideal, it at least extends to the group that which should also be extended to the individual. It is a necessary, if not a sufficient, condition for human dignity, and Americans ought not to be indifferent to the desire for independence, whether that desire be of the black man in Africa, the white man in Eastern Europe, or the yellow man in Asia.

ALLIANCES WITH THE UNCOMMITTED STATES. Most of the new nations are weak and backward. Their leaders remember a period of colonial subjection. They are fearful that their new independence may be compromised and are dedicated to modernizing. The problems of these new nations are enormous, and their leaders desire to insulate them from quarrels they do not recognize as their own. Moreover, they have a genuine interest in attempting to shift the burden of defense against Soviet aggression to others. They will resent any effort to commit them to objectives that divert them from modernizing or that threaten to move them toward the center of the Cold War.

The United States has, fortunately, given up the idea of creating extensive chains of military alliances that depended on the adherence of uncommitted states. This attempt frightened the leaders of many of the new nations. It brought their nations to the center of the Cold War and subjected them to Soviet political attack. The leaders did not desire this—except where internal problems or national divisions, as in Korea or Viet Nam, seemed to necessitate it. Where the populace knew of the commitment, it often misunderstood it. Counterelites opposed to the governments often used the commitments as weapons, as in Iraq. Those who thought the first problem of their nation was development viewed such alliances as a diversion of resources and effort. They much preferred an anticipated insulation from the Cold War and the opportunity to play the East and West off against each other both politically and in terms of access to investment funds.

Where conservative regimes desired alliances to support internal policies, the alliances identified the United States with the policies of these regimes. Where nationalist regimes existed, the attempt to induce them into alliances against their resistance appeared as a threat to their goals, as in Egypt.

In addition, the idea behind these alliances was unsound from the very start. Such nations had little to add in a military sense, although some of them were able to provide bases that temporarily were important. The military aid often unbalanced the economies of these states. In addition, the real and undervalued mediatory role these nations could play when uncommitted was neglected. Where they might have been bulwarks in upholding desirable principles of international law as uncommitted nations, they were instead weak, vulnerable, and temporary members of a Western alliance.

With few exceptions in the present period, military alliances with the new and largely uncommitted states will serve neither their interests nor ours. Alliances or even strong political coalitions are unlikely to work out well. We shall do best if we attempt to commit these nations to the support of universalistic principles of international law or norms of international behavior rather than to specific American interests. Economic aid and the political problems arising therefrom also will constitute an important problem area for American relations with the new and uncommitted nations. This last problem will now be considered.

ECONOMIC DOMINANCE OVER THE UNCOMMITTED STATES. Many of the uncommitted nations believe that the United States, because of its economic power, represents an economic threat to their independence. This fear undoubtedly is greatly exaggerated, but it exists even in our Canadian neighbor to the North. Whatever the economic arguments to the contrary, it would probably make good political sense to encourage at least some other countries, particularly in Latin America, to purchase controlling interests in large local corporations controlled from or owned abroad, especially those which dominate important natural resources such as oil. The United States government should attempt to facilitate the transfer of ownership and control by underwriting it to some extent.[1] This would help to circumvent

---

[1] John Kaplan of the Hudson Institute has suggested that this might be accomplished by eliminating tax credits for entirely owned foreign subsidiaries of United States corporations doing business in underdeveloped countries. Although this might possibly have too extensive an effect, it might well be investigated. American business ought to consider such arrangements voluntarily, as well as those in which their interests could be liquidated after a fixed period of years. Business may be deterred from such arrangements more by ideological than economic considerations.

extremist demands which might force nationalization under conditions that would cause political strains between particular foreign nations and the United States and that would lead to local irrational economic decisions inconsistent with American efforts to support modernization and political liberalism. Moreover, transfers of ownership and control, freely offered, might do much to dampen the entire issue and to forestall extensions of the nationalization principle that would be economically harmful or that would interfere with needed access by developing nations to the American capital market.

SOVIET AID TO THE UNCOMMITTED STATES. The United States has tended to view Soviet aid to uncommitted nations as a calamity, inconsistent with their independence and with American attempts to entice them into political or military alliances or ententes. This has reinforced the auction aspects of American relations with the uncommitted nations and it has debased American generosity. Instead, the United States should welcome Soviet aid as a substitute or complement for American aid even where we may consider the specific forms of aid undesirable. The receiving nations should be depended upon to insist on conditions that preclude major political gains by the Soviet Union. The United States should be prepared to cooperate with such efforts on the part of the uncommitted states. We should insist that the major burden of maintaining independence rest with the uncommitted states; it should not permit these nations to exploit American fears that they might not want to maintain their independence.

American aid offered merely as an alternative to Soviet aid necessarily leads to an auction that cannot be won. The Soviet Union can pick and choose its aid targets. It was always able to breech the wall of aid containment, even at a time when it was relatively weak economically, and was able to force the United States to utilize its aid in ways that were not economically rational. As the Soviet Union grows stronger economically, the problem worsens. If the United States welcomes Soviet aid as an alternative and offers its own aid without regard to securing allies, this vicious cycle can be broken.

PRINCIPLES OF AMERICAN AID—GENERAL. We can now inquire into the principles that ought to govern the extension of American aid to the uncommitted nations. Although the United States may properly give preference to nations that cooperate with it politically and deliberately bail these nations out of political difficulties, it should not attempt to buy outright support and should even discourage such support on the part of those nations where there is no popular local basis for it. In these last cases, failure to follow the suggested principle makes the regimes vulnerable to criticism for forfeiting independence and drives the opposition into an anti-American position. In general, aid should be given because we desire to live in a world where people can look forward to better lives, not because we expect political support, or even because we believe that better conditions will make Communism less likely. Indeed there is little evidence that aid will accomplish these latter objectives.

The United States and the uncommitted states do not have the same community of values or institutions that the United States and Europe have. Except where there are quite specific and compelling common interests—as in the case of South Korea, for instance—we cannot expect the uncommitted states to share our foreign-policy burdens, whatever some abstract ethical system might seem to imply. It would be foolish, therefore, to use aid as a weapon in an attempt to gain foreign-policy support. Within broad limits, aid ought not to be dependent on the external policies of the aided state—unless, of course, that state goes so far as to become a member of the Communist bloc or unless that state acts in a manner consistently disruptive of desirable principles of international order rather than merely in a manner opposed to specific American interests. Attempts to condition aid on foreign-policy support confuse the purpose of the aid, injure the national pride of the aided nations, and eventually undercut the purposes of the aid either by identifying local regimes with the United States in ways that alienate them from their bases of local support, or by driving such regimes into anti-American positions.

However, we should attempt to convince the uncommitted nations that independence and lack of commitment does not imply that they attempt to compromise the differences whenever the United States and the Soviet Union differ. If they really essayed such a role, then it would be strategically advisable for the United States and the Soviet Union to exaggerate their demands and differences; otherwise, the suggested compromises would be disadvantageous to them. And if either failed, or was unable to do this, the other would gain a strategic advantage that might destabilize the international system. The uncommitted nations must be persuaded—but not coerced by aid policy—to the extent possible, to support universalistic normative rules of behavior consistent with the kind of international system in which their own best interests will be protected. It can be argued that opposition to some specific American objectives might be a small price to pay if the uncommitted states could be committed to certain stabilizing norms of international behavior.

In applying its aid, the United States should be concerned with building the kind of world it desires to live in. Modernization, regional cooperation, and democracy undoubtedly are features of the world the United States desires for the future.

SPECIFIC PRINCIPLES OF AID—MODERNIZATION. The leaders of the new nations—in particular the educated elites—desire modernization and independence. These two goals are viewed as inseparable, for it is thought that independence cannot be maintained without modernization and that modernization can be carried out only by independent governments. The existence of dependent colonial areas or of non-modernizing independent states is viewed as a threat to the modernizing regimes. American exhortations to act moderately, responsibly, or democratically seem, to many modernizing leaders, so irrelevant to their difficult tasks that some believe them to be hypocritical.

The disorder in the Congo and the authoritarian regimes in some of the uncommitted states shock American susceptibilities. But we may be judging these nations by the wrong standards. The historical plays of Shakespeare depict situations no better than those of the Congo; Tudor England was hardly democratic; the Spanish women treated Napoleon's soldiers more cruelly than the *Force Publique* behaved in the Congo; and the Nazi and Ustachi villainies are barely two decades old.

The nations of Europe were not built without bloodshed, corruption, villainy, and misery. But at least these nations did not have modern neighbors to set spectacular expectations for them. They could accept slow progress not only in economic development, but also in the development of a national consciousness and of a state apparatus. Their independence was not seemingly threatened by more developed and more powerful states. In the new nations national consciousness does not exist, except perhaps in inchoate form. There is no state in the European sense. Tribal ties, illiteracy, low levels of resources, production, and skills are inconsistent with the entry into the modern world that their educated elites demand. Even though considerable assistance is available to them, their task is much harder than was the task of the European nations.

Most of the European nations had considerable governmental intervention when entering the modern world. Even in England, Tudor intervention preceded Manchesterian capitalism. Many of the new nations believe they require—and in fact they may be correct—more governmental intervention in the economy than seems proper to us. But we must remember that their economic development is dependent upon political and social revolutions that can be carried out only against the resistance of powerful vested interests. In some of these states, territorial loyalties must replace tribal loyalties. In some, land reform is required. In all, agricultural techniques must be modernized. In many, there is no entrepreneurial class and, even if there were, it could not be expected to take the huge risks required to establish industry, transportation, and communication—without which no contemporary state is viewed as modern. In most, the moneyed interests—where such exist—refuse to use their money productively. Education is essential, but only the state can insure an adequate educational program. These considerations could be multiplied, but that would not be profitable. It is necessary only to point out that these new nations cannot repeat the experience of the United States. If they are to succeed in modernizing at all [2]—and this may be in doubt—there must be considerable intervention in the economy by the state.

Economic aid should be related to the ability of the aided area to modernize, to solve its economic problems, and to build a viable and independent nation or areal grouping.

In many of the countries where American aid may be wanted, modernization cannot be carried out without radical social change. This does not mean that existing regimes are always opposed to modernization, any more than were the Shogunate in pre-Meiji Japan or the Nuri as-Said regime in Iraq. But these last two—perhaps unlike the present Thai regime, which is not based on a large landholding class—were unable to carry modernization through without undercutting their bases of

[2] When and if the modernizing elites of some of these countries discover that the attempts to modernize must fail, there may be far-reaching consequences. They may lapse into sloth and corruption. Or, in desperation, they may resort to the most radical of measures.

political support. In these cases, political revolution was probably a necessary if not sufficient condition for modernization. In some of the Latin American nations the requirements for radical social reform by existing regimes are not so formidable but may still be sufficient to deter the regimes from taking political risks in order to modernize.[3] Where this is the case, American aid is likely to be used ineffectively, and the extension of large-scale aid may even identify the United States with anti-modernist goals.

Intervention in internal affairs to induce modernization is a risky business that may well fail or backfire. Intervention should not be resorted to blithely. On the other hand, the failure of existing regimes to modernize may only insure radical and pro-Soviet revolutions. No specific answers to this problem can be attempted here. There will be cases where intervention may work and others where the risks are too great. But the United States must avoid association with anti-modernist goals. It must display sympathy with modernizing regimes even where specific American economic interests may be affected adversely.

SPECIFIC PRINCIPLES OF AID—REGIONAL COOPERATION. Modernization and cultural independence may be aided by regional cooperation or even by regional integration. The Mahgreb, for instance, is possibly an area where cooperation crossing national boundaries may be feasible and desirable from the standpoint of building a new world order consistent with American principles. Oil-pooling in the Arab Middle East might also be encouraged. Although the Iraq claim to Kuwait could hardly be conceded, the defense of the sovereignty of what is essentially a non-viable political unit demonstrated lack of political foresight.[4]

The American government presently proposes to set up regional groups in Latin America and Africa with which aid negotiations would be carried on. Little study, however, has been made of the consequences of such a scheme for Africa, in particular, where the question of which states to include would have profound political effects both within the continent and elsewhere. It is at least worth asking whether the political consequences of region-wide economic planning would moderate the policies of the more forward African states, inflame the more moderate states, increase continental harmony, or make worse continental frictions. The inclusion of the United Arab Republic would, of course, have other consequences for American foreign policy.

The commitment of the United States to the OAS leaves little choice except to encourage some kind of regional cooperation in the use of American aid to Latin America. Yet, the program of the Kennedy administration is tied to land reform

[3] This is an exceptionally serious problem for which no clear solutions are in sight. Few ruling groups are sufficiently disinterested to reform themselves out of power, particularly if the reforms are not guaranteed to be workable. Perhaps some of these groups should be bought out or ways discovered to force others to get out or to cooperate.

[4] The British were undoubtedly concerned to protect their oil interests. But the present situation is quite unstable. Too much of the Middle East is impoverished and there are too many small oil oases disposing of immense riches. Eventually this situation will change, and the change may be preferable if anticipated and encouraged than if opposed.

and to other social and economic reforms. It is doubtful that many of the existing regimes in these countries will, in fact, carry through reforms of a needed radical nature. For this reason, even within the OAS framework, the United States should consider concentrating its aid to those countries that have the desire and ability to modernize themselves. Brazil, Venezuela, Mexico, and Argentina may fall within this category. By committing the major portion of its aid to areas that do modernize economically and socially, the United States would identify itself with such progress. The nations so aided might serve as examples to still others that they need not go the way of the Castro regime in Cuba. On the other hand, by not entirely denying aid to other Latin American countries, the framework of hemispheric solidarity is maintained and American sympathy for the peoples of the hemisphere affirmed. Within this framework, smaller, specific aid programs oriented to other and shorter-term needs could be formulated and carried out. The case for picking and choosing may be even stronger in Africa where the United States lacks historic ties that demand continental solidarity and cooperation. In all cases, major American aid should be conditioned on efforts by the nations involved to help themselves.

The United States should make clear to all that the major purpose of its aid is to help other countries to enter the modern world. Thus, in general, the United States should not commit itself to outworn social or political systems that cannot satisfy aspirations with which it, in terms of its own national values, must strongly sympathize.

SPECIFIC PRINCIPLES OF AID—INTERNAL POLITICS. For reasons specified previously, new nations, in the effort to modernize, must engage in considerable governmental intervention. Efforts to overcome tribalism or to carry through social revolutions necessary for modernization may lead to considerable authoritarianism. The democratic and humane values destroyed in the process may not be properly appreciated by the leaders of the new nations. Many may lack the sophistication of Attaturk, who used authoritarian forms in an effort to create the conditions under which democracy can maintain itself.

Moreover, many of the leaders of the new nations unfortunately have accepted Marxist myths concerning capitalism. Although in fact the socialism of the new states is more pragmatic and accommodates more capitalism than some Americans believe, there is a real danger that the new states may either stifle or fail quickly to create the middle class that stood as a bulwark against governmental despotism in the West (but that took more than a century to develop). Moreover, much of the human misery of the European economic revolution was the consequence of an impersonal market mechanism rather than of a conscious governmental decision. The governments of the new nations, however, largely take responsibility for economic decisions. Resentment, therefore, may crystallize against these governments for the real or seeming failures of governmental policies. And, in their efforts to modernize rapidly and to maintain control of the situation until this is done, the governments may institutionalize repressive mechanisms resistant to change from below although possibly subject to *coup.*

The United States should leave no doubt concerning its sympathy for the efforts of the elites in the new nations to modernize, of its desire to aid them, and of its recognition that modernization cannot be carried through painlessly or according to its own model. On the other hand, we should not be indifferent to the internal politics of the countries that receive economic aid or assistance from it.[5] The effects on American institutions and values, if the United States becomes an isolated island in a totalitarian—even if non-Communist—world, are too complicated to describe here and in any event are moot. But surely Americans prefer not to live in a totalitarian world and even more surely they do not desire to permit their aid to modernizing nations to be diverted toward the maintenance of a totalitarian police state. (Even if the funds are not used directly for this purpose, they permit the diversion of other funds.) If the United States cannot police the world to maintain democracy everywhere—indeed even if it must recognize that the conditions for democracy are not everywhere present or that in some places democracy may be incompatible with modernization—it does not have to close its eyes to the human drama and to resolve political issues in favor of totalitarianism either through a failure of will, or in a fit of absent-mindedness.

In applying a criterion related to the nature of the regime, an effort must be made to make decisions in context rather than in the abstract. Thus, for instance, a distinction can be made between an area where the conditions for some degree of political liberalism are present but repressed by the government and an area where such conditions are not present. For instance, given the cultural and social background of Cuba, it is dubious that most of the totalitarian measures of the Castro regime are necessary for—or even consistent with—rapid modernization, although a mere return to the old constitution might have forfeited the possibilities for social revolution.

The situation is quite different in Ghana and Guinea—which, in any event, are authoritarian and not totalitarian—where tribalism must be overcome to create a national state where one did not properly exist previously. A distinction must also be drawn between a Guinea which has had little experience in government and little time to create liberal institutions and a Spain which has made no effort to create such institutions and which seems determined to maintain a rigidly authoritarian regime indefinitely. Moreover, although Guinea or Ghana may be given the benefit of the doubt, because of their brief existence, it is possible to distinguish between those two cases and Nigeria, which seems more inclined, at present, to develop representative institutions.

African single-party systems which seem to permit debate and consent within the single-party structure must also be differentiated from Communist-type single-party systems which prevent national debate or dissent and which restrict debate to centralized and hierarchical party structures. Thus, whether a nation such as Yugoslavia

[5] Unfortunately, until recently the United States did little to support modernizing democracies, particularly when important economic interests objected to their policies. Venezuela under Betancourt was until recently an unfortunate example of this national myopia.

is aided might be made to depend on whether the party structure is sufficiently loosened to permit genuine and general debate and political alternatives not decided on in advance by the party leadership.

Even if the only two criteria for aid were those previously discussed—modernization and regime character—the applications would be subject to some debate. Spain would clearly be excluded, for it is not modernizing, and it is committed to the maintenance of an authoritarian regime. Cuba would not receive aid because, although it is attempting to modernize, it is now doing so within the framework of a totalitarian regime, which applies terroristic methods in case of dissent. Nigeria and some of the French African states are modernizing, but not rapidly, in an effort to avoid harsh political methods. Even so, many of those French African states are one-party states. At this stage of their development they should probably be given the benefit of the doubt on both counts. Ghana and Guinea are attempting to modernize rapidly, are following foreign policies that are unpalatable to the United States, are probably on balance pro-Soviet, and are employing quite harsh political methods. Even so, they are not totalitarian and, within the framework of African political experience, do permit political alternatives. They should probably receive the present benefit of doubt, but the decision might well be re-evaluated after a reasonable period of time. So also should the Jagan regime in Guiana receive the benefit of the doubt unless it shows signs of becoming totalitarian or of entering the Soviet bloc.

The difficult questions will involve the choice between the rapidly modernizing and less liberal and the more slowly modernizing and more liberal African regimes. No single criterion can be applied here, for policy decisions must rest on prognostications concerning the probable future course of development of these nations. If the judgment is that the more slowly modernizing nations have a reasonable chance to succeed in modernizing with external support, while maintaining relatively liberal institutions, preference should be given to them where emphasis in allocation is made. If, on the other hand, one comes to the conclusion that modern nationhood in any of these areas rests on rapid and forced evolution from tribalized relations to national solidarity or that political demands on the part of the younger educated elite permit no good alternative, then despite dissatisfactions with their external policies and fears concerning their future political development, aid to the more radically modernizing African nations might have higher priority than would otherwise seem desirable.

In any event, although the United States may prefer a particular set of choices for developing nations, based on its own values and prognostications, and may legitimately allocate aid on the basis of these choices, the decisions on modernization affect it only indirectly. Advice may be offered. Attempts to encourage desirable values can and should be made. But in the last analysis, the developing nations must make their own independent choices, for it is their fate that is directly involved. Where the choice that is made involves a destruction of human dignity that offends our most important values and degrades the human beings so manipulated, as in the case of Cuba, we have an obligation to make our opposition clear. But where the differences are based upon tolerable differences in basic values or prognostications concerning the consequences of particular policies, sympathetic understanding would be more appropriate than harsh rejection.

It is inevitable that particular American decisions, even within the framework of clear policy principles, will be misunderstood by some and resented by others. We do not always properly understand or appreciate the actions or intentions of other nations. The new nations require radical change, and the rich United States is not likely to be viewed sympathetically by the harassed leaders and uneducated masses of these nations. Their values, their goals, and their interpretations of policies differ from ours. Popularity is not to be expected. If, however, there is a posture of disinterested support for modernization, social reform, and political liberalism, if American policy is not tied merely to anti-Communism or to attempts to build systems of alliances, there is some hope that American policy will command respect and that it will invite support when it accords with the most important interests of the uncommitted developing nations.

It must be clear that the United States does not seek *direct* political benefits from its aid. Unlike Communism, which, despite its talk of many roads, has a relatively narrow doctrinal content and organizational form, American favoritism for democracy implies little with respect to the content of legislation—apart from support for modernization—and party and governmental structure. It implies support only for organizational forms that permit the institutionalization of dissent and the relatively free play of ideas. Indeed, the democracies do not possess political means by which control can be exercised over other countries, and, as long as the United States does not attempt to force uncommitted nations into pacts for which they are not prepared, it presents no political threat to their independence.

MODE OF AID. The question of whether aid should be given bilaterally or multilaterally is a difficult one to answer. However, proposals to siphon aid through the United Nations according to its normal constitutional procedures would almost surely be unfortunate. As long as the amount of aid handled through the United Nations is small, the temptation to assert the kind of political control that would be inconsistent with the objectives of the aid will be minimal. As soon, however, as large-scale contributions of aid money to be spent by the organization come to be viewed as a tax to be contributed regularly by the richer nations, the kinds of pork-barrel decisions that are often made in the United States Congress will be made in an even more exaggerated form in the United Nations General Assembly. Since economically irrational decisions are also likely to be made at the national level, this compounding of irrationality would be thoroughly inconsistent with the aims of the aid. Multilateral aid, however, might insulate the United States from criticism in the choice of aid recipients. It is true that the history of bilateral aid leaves little room for optimism. But it is at least easier to reform United States aid programs than to reform international political processes.

In sum, therefore, the question of policy, primarily including economic-aid policy, toward the uncommitted states is not susceptible to an easy answer that permits clear applications. The usual reasons given for aid, namely, that it will make friends, produce political stability, and halt Communism, have little evidence to support them. But, in the end, modernization is probably a good thing. It is doubtful if the demands for modernization can be halted in any event. To the extent that modernization is carried through successfully by non-Communist governments, the expansion of the Communist world system will be halted. Political instability is probably inevitable as rising expectations, new organizations, and political counterelites produce accentuated demands on the governments of the underdeveloped nations. The sooner modernization occurs, the fewer the barriers it must overcome, and the more support the West gives to it, the more successful and the less anti-Western it is likely to be. The more the West attempts either to halt modernization, or use it for ulterior purposes, the more radical and the more susceptible to Communist influence modernization is likely to be. The more disinterested the assistance policy of the West, the greater the control of the West over its allocations of resources and the less susceptible the West is to blackmail in various guises.

Undoubtedly, in nations that lack any democratic experience or tradition, some degree of strong political control—even of authoritarianism—will be needed to handle excessive demands on governmental allocations. In others, such as India, the democratic method may be made to work in modernizing the nation and may serve as a model for other nations, if not in the present, then at least with respect to the future. At present, however, democratic values have no appeal for the poor, the backward, the illiterate. They appear to be luxuries or even undesirable. Our best hope is to produce a period of relative stability during which these values can become appreciated. This will not happen until other and prior—even if less important from our viewpoint—values are first achieved. The present period is a crucial one, and the choices made by the West—and primarily by the United States—will play a critical role in determining the shape of world politics for some time to come.

Although specific choices of aid policy or allocations of funds may be responsive to highly particular circumstances, the philosophy that guides the program will be of major importance in determining its effectiveness and acceptability to the aided nations. This guiding spirit in the intermediate run will have more impact on the consciousness of the leaders and peoples of the developing nations than the details of policy. Mistakes will be made and can be overcome with respect to those details. But the failure of the general outlines of policy to accord disinterestedly with the requirement of modernization eventually will lead to major discord between the aims and accomplishments of policy. The aim of the United States must not be popularity or even instrumental alliances. The major aim of American policy must be a structure of world politics in which the most important Western interests can be protected and the democratic form of government survive. The status quo cannot be preserved. The question concerns the shape of the changes to come. It is here precisely that the West and the United States must take their stand as a matter of principle rather than as a matter of expediency.

IV United States General Alliance Policy

The United States should begin to overhaul its alliance system along with its program of aid. Unfortunately, it is not always wise to scrap alliances that it was initially unwise to form. Withdrawal from an alliance may too easily be interpreted as withdrawal from an obligation to defend and, thus, may set in motion other undesirable events. For instance, withdrawal from SEATO might encourage Chinese aggression and might also encourage political deals favorable to Communism by local political elites. Opportunistic political elites, convinced that withdrawal from the alliances signified withdrawal from an interest in the independence of the area, might then begin to make "hedging" internal political deals. Moreover, some areas literally require an overt United States military guarantee to forestall attack. Taiwan is a case in point.

Except, however, in the NATO area, the system of multilateral military pacts has been a failure. NATO, which so far has been relatively successful, is in serious and, likely, increasing trouble. Many Europeans are afraid of the risk involved in the nuclear age: Some fear that the United States will not risk nuclear war to defend them if they remain in NATO and hope that we will come to their aid anyway, even if they do not contribute to or participate in the nuclear military forces of the free world and desire not to become the locus of nuclear attack. If it is urged that a nuclear-armed NATO is a deterrent to attack, they hope that others will bear the burden of that deterrent. Necessary as a nuclear-armed NATO happens to be, the strains within NATO are bound to increase tremendously as long as it remains a purely military organization.

There is a human tendency to discount risks when the alternatives are especially unpleasant. A Russian military move, therefore, is apt to be discounted if the means of preventing it are nuclear, unless there are incentives additional to military ones for taking risks. If the only incentives are the military, the nation that calls attention to the Russian threat is apt to be disliked; such action forces the attention of other nations on unpleasant things—things they would rather deny or ignore.

It would be much better if NATO were a politically organized community with shared interests and values, and if the problem of shifting risks and responsibilities did not arise in the acute form presently apparent. Nationalism, at least in America and Western European nations, has outlived its usefulness. It is no longer a moral inspiration or a generator of efforts of vast magnitude. Europe has already discovered this in a political and economic sense and is making first efforts to develop larger associations in the form of the Common Market and the various European Communities.

The United States, which has encouraged these efforts so far, has remained aloof. This is unfortunate, for we are no longer viable politically as an independent political entity, though a case might still be made for military viability—at least in the foreseeable future. But even more important, the accession of the United States—

and Britain—to the European Community would provide a psychological as well as a material inspiration of the greatest magnitude. A strong case can be made that economic measures, as the least difficult to secure agreement on, should precede political measures in order to prepare the way by establishing practices and habits of joint action. Conceivably, however, the urgency of the situation and the need to capture the imagination of people may require bold political measures, despite the risk that the attempt at this level might forestall action to construct a genuine Atlantic Community. But it is hard to deny the conclusion that the NATO nations soon must face the world as an inseparable unit, dedicated to a common fate, and united by common policies and values.

The building of a viable Atlantic Community is the most important task facing the West. This Community must represent our best hopes and ideals. Present American relationships with Spain and Portugal are inconsistent with these ideals. These nations do not merely lack institutions that would permit them to participate constructively in such a community. The relationship we have with them presently is inconsistent with the appearance we are trying to present to the world.

It might be argued that Portugal is a valuable member of NATO, that the Spanish bases are important to the United States, and that we have cooperated without serious objection with many other authoritarian regimes. There is, however, a fundamental difference between a newly independent nation, such as Pakistan, which is trying to enter the modern world, and old nations, such as Spain and Portugal, whose leaders regard the modern world as evil. Some degree of authoritarianism may be essential in new nations which are desperately trying to modernize and improve the lot of their people. Authoritarianism is much more difficult to justify in old nations that want only to preserve an oligarchic and backward society. The living standards in Spain and Portugal are Asian rather than European. No major efforts are being made to modernize—to improve standards, to educate the people, or to prepare the conditions under which democracy might develop. Instead, Franco and Salazar take pride in their rejection of democracy and have no desire to improve the conditions of their people.

Our bases in these countries may have some importance, but it is quite doubtful that they are worth the political price. Our exhortations to the new nations to choose democracy and our condemnation of totalitarianism in Cuba appear hypocritical. We also make it difficult for ourselves to take our own ideals seriously when we regard them this cheaply. No one desires another prolonged civil war in Spain. But surely Spain and Portugal need not be welcomed as allies and colleagues; surely some pressure can be brought upon the two governments to reform. If they are totally unresponsive, we can support the democrats in exile.

There is a risk that a Castro type of regime might succeed the present regimes if we pursue this course. But a failure to press for democratization and reform may also so discourage the real democrats that the totalitarians have a clear field in advocating change. And, if we oppose the Fascist regimes before they are kicked out, we at least help to legitimize our opposition to a new authoritarianism should such a type of regime succeed the present regimes.

The attempt to institute idealistic principles in the formation of the Atlantic Community undoubtedly will give rise to serious problems: The military services will resist the loss of bases; conservative groups will fear the political effects of the decisions. The alternative political costs, however, would be much greater.

This advice goes against most recognized principles of statecraft. But those principles are designed for stable international systems in which conservative policies are protective of existing interests. We must learn that it is precisely with respect to this issue that the character of our national response must change. We must learn to act in ways that generate support for constructive changes in the shape of world politics in a period when sufficient support cannot be mobilized to preserve the status quo. We must take some of the risks which all revolutionary movements must take or we shall suffer the fate of all systems that fail either to adapt to their environment, or to adapt their environment to them.

V   The United Nations

American policy toward the United Nations also requires drastic revision. American security—and world peace also—undoubtedly rest more on American military power and on the NATO alliance than on the United Nations. If we are ever confronted with a clear-cut, either-or, choice—and, undoubtedly, this would be a tragedy —the United Nations would have to be subordinated to NATO. On the other hand, the United Nations has a real and important role to play in world politics. It would be a serious mistake—unfortunately, we have repeatedly made such mistakes—to attempt to make the United Nations merely an instrument of the Cold War or to attempt to use it to solve problems which it is not and cannot be equipped to solve given the present structure of world politics.

The postwar period has perhaps seen the United Nations misused in two different ways by the United States. The Truman administration attempted to use the United Nations as an instrument of American foreign policy. The Eisenhower administration attempted to use the United Nations as a substitute for American policy. It would be wrong to deny that convincing rationales for either course can be constructed. And, of course, both charges are greatly oversimplified. Yet it is well to weigh the cost both policies have entailed.

It can be pointed out—and rightly so—that the Truman administration faced an intransigent Stalinist regime in Russia which finally supported—and in all probability ordered—the North Korean attempt to unify the Korean peninsula by force. Although an independent American action in Korea probably would have been preferable to the one followed, it was argued with some merit that an American action that bypassed the United Nations would have reduced the organization to impotence. Yet the United Nations' action in Korea did intrude that organization directly into the Cold—and in this case hot—War. The change in the goals of the operation, from defeating aggression to unifying the peninsula by force, clearly placed too great a burden on the organization. It thrust the organization into a war it could not win—at least under the terms the United States was willing to wage it—and made it a direct and continuing party to a dispute rather than a mediatory agency. Moreover, American efforts on many other issues to put the United Nations on record with respect to Cold-War issues alienated many new and uncommitted nations. It again involved the United Nations as a party to Cold-War disputes rather than as a mediator or as an enunciator of universal rules of conduct formulated in advance of and without specific reference to—until application became necessary—specific Cold-War disputes.

General Eisenhower, on the other hand, evidently considered that the United Nations come closer to being a world governmental agency than most other observers of the organization would believe. Even within a national government such as the United States, some have questioned the ability of the government to act effectively in crisis situations without strong leadership from the executive. Nonetheless, General Eisenhower apparently believed that the United Nations was an appropriate deliberative body, with respect to issues involving the use of force, and that support of its decisions by the United States was the method best calculated to build a peaceful world. This, of course, again shifts the function of the United Nations from mediation and places upon it a burden which some may suspect it is ill-prepared to bear. The crisis in the Congo indicated how, despite strong leadership from the Secretary-General, the United Nations can govern only with great difficulty when the interests of the Soviet and American blocs strongly conflict. The present temporary Secretary-General lacks the late Dag Hammerskjold's strength and it is doubtful that any genuinely strong successor can be agreed to.

It is simply a fact of international life that the security of the West—and indeed of much of the uncommitted world—rests upon the military strength of the NATO nations. The United Nations is no substitute for NATO, and primarily military and security problems cannot be relegated now, or in the immediate future, to that organization. It is not prepared to move quickly or strongly where military matters are concerned; consequently, its resolutions, even when not compromises, lack a deterrent effect. It is the threat of American intervention that prevents more direct Soviet intervention in Laos and the Congo, not the possibility of United Nations resolution. Undoubtedly, United Nations actions play a role, indirectly, by creating a political climate in which American intervention becomes politically feasible—because of the reactions of nations whose cooperation is desirable and because of the reactions of the American public. But the two different effects should not be confused.

It is necessary that the United States play a strong leading role in both NATO and the United Nations, but the nature of the leading role ought to differ with the nature and function of the two organizations. The proper function of NATO in a bipolar world is to provide a military deterrent to the Soviet bloc and to present a political image that facilitates unity of action and that at least does not arouse strong opposition from uncommitted nations. The proper function of the United Nations is to mediate in a way that reduces the possibility of thermonuclear war and that facilitates support for desirable and universal rules of international behavior.

With respect to these functions, there can—and will likely—be conflicts between short-term interests of American policy and the interests of the United Nations organization. Such a conflict occurred at the time of the decision to cross the 38th parallel in Korea. That decision could have been justified from the standpoint of United Nations' interests only had the United States been prepared to carry matters with the Soviet bloc to a military decision at that time.

Another conflict arises with respect to the admission of Red China to the United Nations. Red China is a state within the meaning of the Charter; indeed a very important state. At some point, the United States may have to decide whether keeping Red China out of the United Nations (this is not directly related to American recognition of Red China) is of such overriding importance that it is worth the cost in terms of committing the United Nations organization to universalistic rules of international law. And it must be remembered that it is only on the basis of commitment to such universalistic rules of law that we stand much chance of making effective use of the uncommitted nations in international bargaining procedures.

It is, of course, a grave error to fail to differentiate foreign policies according to the arenas in which they are pursued, for this would assume that the context of a policy decision did not affect the consequences of the policy. If the United Nations plays an important role in American objectives, other objectives—at least when pursued in the United Nations and perhaps also at other times—must be modified to take this objective into account. And as long as the mediatory function of the United Nations is important, or as long as the support of other nations who highly value the United Nations is important, American policies in the organization ought to be related to the nature and functions of the organization and not merely to other objectives of American foreign policy. Much of the opposition to past American policies stemmed from a desire of various nations not to get involved in the Cold War—a not inconsiderable factor to be taken into account—rather than from an understanding of the best way in which the United Nations could execute its functions. But this failure of understanding on the part of other nations does not make less grave the failure of the United States to pursue its own best interests in that organization.

In addition to the mediatory functions of the United Nations, the United States may wish to strengthen functions that isolate some areas or functions from the Cold War in a way that is desirable, or at least acceptable, to both the United States and the Soviet Union. Proposals of this kind ought to be strongly supported and presented in ways appealing to the popular understanding. The present Antarctic treaty, for instance, is not inconsistent with eventual United Nations administration, and such administration might serve as precedent for the moon. Such administration ought to be proposed. The Suez crisis might have been avoided had the Western nations had sufficient foresight to turn international waterways over to international management. It may not be too late for such management, although the issue now would be doubtful at best. It is conceivable that the N-country nuclear problem and arms control may be solved by means of an international agency. In the process, some experience for handling the even more difficult problems that may arise in the future could be gained.

This is a far cry from world government. But there are many disadvantages to world government from the standpoint of human freedom and cultural and social diversity—even were such government feasible. Given the inconsistency of Communist and democratic forms of government and this diversity in cultural and economic standards, clearly such government is not feasible at the present time. To attempt it would be harmful, for such attempts would interfere with support for feasible proposals to control pressing problems.

Even the step toward an international police force, although part of avowed American policy, is unwise at present. *Ad hoc* forces secure, within reasonable limits, cease fires between minor belligerents. But we must assume that the kind of police force advocated as a United Nations police force would be considerable in size and permanent in nature. If roughly equivalent to American or Russian forces, it might only be a source of additional instability. If superior to American and/or Russian forces, this force might itself engage in military adventures. Moreover, how could it be possible to agree on the composition and control of such a force? United Nations organs are not representative in a consensual sense.

Surely the United States and the Soviet Union would not agree to a United Nations force responsive to United Nations organs, except possibly under conditions of veto. But this condition would undercut an essential function of such a force, namely, to control disputes among the major nations. Moreover, if such a force were controlled by the minor nations, what guarantee—or even reasonable presumption—is there that it would be used responsibly? If strong American or Russian units participated, we could expect resistance, sabotage, or other clandestine measures that would impair actions that displeased either of them. Reliance upon a force that might be crippled by internal strife might subvert the deterrent effect of national armed forces. Such a force under existing world conditions would increase rather than decrease uncertainties and would, thus, raise rather than lower the probability of war. And particularly if the United Nations force controlled atomic weapons, we would have problems arising from the increase in the number of nuclear powers. The world has enough uncertainties without increasing the number. Surely it is not a recent discovery that abstract constitutionalism is no substitute for political analysis.

The United States, however, should support the development and possible expansion of the *ad hoc* police-force procedures of the United Nations. It should attempt to demonstrate how these procedures enter into the stream of world politics in a manner supportive of existing law or even in a manner that leads to the growth of law. The independent functions of the Secretary-General ought to be supported and the civil-service status of the staff protected. There should be less hesitation to demonstrate the destructive consequences of present Soviet proposals to reorganize the United Nations. And, instead of agreeing to a larger Soviet quota of staff employees, the existence of any Soviet quota in the absence of independent recruitment should be attacked. The United States ought not to act defensively under

Soviet attack. It ought to counterattack with a program designed to improve the level of the law and orderliness in the world.

The present organization of world politics does not provide a desirable level of security. Attempts either to demonstrate the dangers of the present international organization or the need in at least some respects for new modes of organizing consensus and the institutional means of exercising force are desirable. The belief, however, that radical changes can be implemented at the present time is dangerous, for such belief, unaccompanied by a host of other changes, might produce either an unworkable and dangerous constitutional experiment, or an eroding support for the only measures capable of maintaining even the low level of security we possess under present conditions.

The United Nations is also the forum in which the United States can encourage the new and uncommitted states to support universal principles of law and behavior consistent with the kind of world order we desire to encourage. On specific issues this may involve real costs. For instance, the conflict between American policy on China and universal standards for United Nations representation is one area in which costs may have to be paid. But, in general, the United States desires a world in which overt military intervention in foreign nations is minimized, in which the dangers of nuclear war are reduced, in which new nations are permitted to develop in independence, in which problems of outer space are organized appropriately, and so forth. Within limits too complicated to explain here, the new and uncommitted nations may well support such standards as generally—if not always—consistent with their own interests. As the imperialist or colonial issue vanishes and as political boundaries become more stable in the ex-colonial areas, the coincidence of interest should increase rather than decrease. Support, therefore, may well be won in these areas provided that matters are not confused by attempts to win support on specific issues, as opposed to general policy, and provided that military strength is maintained. If, however, we seek support in the form of generalized alliances, because aid will be withheld if support is not forthcoming, or because we are the "good guys," or if we allow our military strength to dissipate, we shall either frighten off or discourage support, and we shall gain victories on specific individual votes rather than on the issues that count in the long run.

Support for a viable United Nations system may also serve as a positive ideal to disaffected groups in the Western nations; it may also appear as a desirable alternative to those who misunderstand the role and function of NATO. Thus, strong support for an expanded *but realistic* United Nations system may be an important implement in mobilizing the West by appealing to idealism, while many are still wrongly and unfortunately associating NATO only with "power politics."

VI Policy Toward the Communist Bloc

If the United States desires to encourage political liberalism in the uncommitted nations, it ought also to assert its belief in democracy as the proper way of life for those behind the iron curtain—not merely those in Eastern Europe, but also those in Russia and China. To this end a reasonably democratic China in Taiwan is an important means. Unless we have as much faith in democracy as the Russians have in Communism, Communism will eventually sweep the world. Although we cannot encourage premature uprisings at times when we are unable or unwilling to extend aid, we must not come to terms with the status quo. No status quo ever endures, and if we recognize only one mode of change—toward Communism and totalitarianism—we determine the fate of the future by that decision.

But there are other and stronger reasons why we must oppose not merely Communist expansion, but Communism itself. The world is an unsafe place in which to live and it is becoming increasingly so. The measures required to control or to minimize the nuclear dangers are inconsistent with the organizational structure of Communism. The insulation of the Communist system from the outside world minimizes moderating influences on Communist leadership. It is relatively unresponsive to popular pressures as they arise spontaneously or as they are influenced by trends of opinion elsewhere in the world. High-ranking Russians who reported to outsiders on events in the Soviet Union—perhaps on the secretion of nuclear weapons after an arms control agreement—would lack the sanctuary within the Soviet state that American citizens would have in the American state under analogous conditions. In the Soviet Union governmental leaks occur rarely and then usually as a consequence of a high-level decision to leak. Decisions to hide weapons or to engage in surprise attack can be made secretly by a small group of men who have no need to mobilize public opinion in favor of their move prior to it; neither is there within Soviet society a belief in a norm obligating them to do so or obligating citizens to inform on and oppose the government if it secretly violates solemn agreements, as there is in the West. As long as the Soviet Union remains the kind of nation it is, the dangers of nuclear war may be much higher than many people are willing to accept.

If we cannot induce major changes in the Soviet system, and if we are unwilling to live with the dangers of nuclear war, we have one other alternative: We can disarm unilaterally—in effect, we can surrender—and pass on to the Soviet Union the task of policing the world. One possible consequence is that the Soviet Union effectively controls the arms race—that it prevents other nations from acquiring nuclear weapons. This contingency cannot be examined in detail, but it is unlikely that Soviet leaders would be able or willing to do this without considerable political interference in other nations. Evasions of Soviet arms regulations would have to be cruelly crushed. And a nation that has transported entire populations within its own territory may exact a tremendous price from other nations in this respect, in addition to exploiting them economically. We would almost surely have to submit to political tyranny. Indeed the immensity of the task would likely insure this. The physical, as well as the political, difficulty of maintaining control might lead to the development and use of behavior-control devices. Even if the worst of these consequences did not occur, life would be difficult and unpleasant.

However, the Soviet Union might not succeed in imposing arms control on the world. We might, as one possibility, enter a world of independent Communist states, many of which controlled effective nuclear systems. This would likely prove a more dangerous world than the present one. Even today there are important strains between Russia and China, for instance. If the threat of the democracies was removed, the strains among the Communists would become much greater. Yet, these would be governments possessing nuclear systems shrouded in secrecy and capable of being employed without advance publicity. (Indeed several hundred millions of excess Chinese might occupy the United States prior to a nuclear war between Red China and Red Russia.) This is a world which might end up both Red and dead.

Moreover, the policy of unilateral disarmament has even graver disadvantages. If implemented, it is, as we saw, bad enough. But there would be much opposition to it. The advocacy of the policy might only produce policy debates, delays, and compromises that weakened the Western posture and encouraged the Soviet Union to take bold steps that only made war more likely. When the West finally resolved to stiffen its position and to make no further concessions, Soviet miscalculations concerning Western intentions might well precipitate a nuclear war. (A strong argument can be made that the peace movement in the 30's made a major contribution to the development of the Second World War.) Thus, surrender to Communism is not likely to constitute an acceptable solution to the grave problems facing the world today. Attempts to change the Soviet system, or at least to mobilize world opinion against that system, would be preferable.

Therefore, the United States must make clear that the great impediment to arms control or disarmament lies in the nature of the Communist political system. So far, most people speak of the concessions that must be made to the Soviet Union because one cannot expect it to change its political system. Unfortunately, the concessions that can be made consistently, with reasonable security, are not sufficient to minimize the present dangers of the nuclear arms race. It has become necessary to emphasize that it is the Soviet system which must change if the world is to have reasonable security in a nuclear age. And it is the Soviet government which must be thrown on the defensive for refusing to make changes consistent with international security. As nuclear technology improves and spreads to other nations, it may become necessary for the powers of the United Nations to be drastically increased. It is important that long before this we have stated the changes necessary in the Soviet system so that everyone will be familiar with the reasons for them.

This cannot be accomplished by shrinking from negotiations with the Russians as we have so often done in the past. It may be that the Russians misuse negotiations in an effort to impede the West from taking needed political measures or in an effort to change the political situation during the course of negotiations. For instance, political negotiations over Berlin might so alarm some people that political events might be set in train to provide the Russians with what they want without the necessity of making counterconcessions.

These possibilities cannot be denied. The Russians are engaged in serious political warfare with us. Khrushchev has stated openly that coexistence means only a willingness to defeat democracy by means other than by military war and not a willingness to live indefinitely in the same world with democracy. Coexistence does not imply the absence of military threats. Khrushchev is a past master at the use of such threats, having learned much from the practices of the late Adolf Hitler. But even if one believes that Khrushchev really will not resort to overt military adventures—and there is no need for him to do so as long as things go so well for him—coexistence on his terms means a struggle, without any real community of interest, in which deceit and subversion play major roles. Indeed, a failure to understand this is a failure to take the Russians seriously.

The answer, however, does not lie in a refusal to negotiate with the Russians; neither does it lie in bargaining as the Russians bargain, for those techniques are not appropriate to democracies and free associations of nations. But the United States can debate the issues on its own terms rather than on Russian terms. There is no reason why Russian demands on Berlin should not be countered by demands for UN-supervised elections in all of Germany—or even in the other satellites. There is no reason why the relationship of the totalitarian Russian system to the dangers of the arms race should not become the focus of debate. If these issues are linked to the broader issues of peace and war and disarmament and arms control that worry the peoples of the world, it may be possible to use them effectively against the Soviet Union.

It would be wrong to pretend that Communism alone is responsible for the troubles of our age. Indeed, in part, it is a response to even deeper problems. But it is legitimate to point out that Communist political organization increases existing dangers tremendously. It is the responsibility of the American government to publicize these dangers and how Communism increases them. The political organization of the Communist states is not merely an internal matter beyond the legitimate concern of other nations.

Apart from the fact that the Communist states themselves do not hesitate to interfere in other states and attempt to produce changes in their forms of political organization—itself reason to have interest in the internal organization of the Communist regimes—Communist political organization poses a security problem for other states; it increases tremendously the danger of nuclear war and of partial or total destruction. No nation can remain indifferent to this threat. The United States must call upon the Soviet Union to provide more freedom for its people, to permit political opposition, and to open up the country to inspection. Whatever merit there may have been to the Soviet fear that a freer society would have made the Soviet Union more vulnerable to external attack, that fear no longer can have any validity. The Soviet Union is now one of the two strongest nations on earth. It boasts that it is no longer encircled by capitalism and may soon encircle capitalism. It no longer has a right to behave like a weak nation and to plead fear, whether of attack or of espionage. And, if after forty years of Communist rule, the Russian people are unfit to govern themselves, surely that is an indictment of the regime and an additional reason to advocate change of the form of government.

We should make it quite clear that our objection to Communism lies not in its form of economic organization—although we may prefer a different form or even fear that centralized state control of the economy may make free government more difficult—but in its political organization. We must make clear that we do not desire to impose our own substantive views on Russia but desire a situation in which the peoples of the Soviet Union can influence Soviet policy and decide questions of political leadership—a situation in which differing points of view can be put forward and receive circulation.

We should no longer view the Soviet leaders as supermen in complete control of their internal environment. The Soviet bloc has its own strains and stresses. We should attempt to increase them. Potential conflicts between the members of the bloc should be encouraged by American policies designed to bring them into prominence. Internal stresses within the nations of the bloc should be increased where this can be done responsibly, although obviously we do not desire to encourage another "Hungary" where we are unwilling to come to the aid of the revolutionaries. And, most important, we should throw the Russians on the ideological defensive.

VII Military Policy

American security must continue to rest upon American and NATO arms, although, of course, a merely military policy is bound to fail. However, combined with a constructive diplomacy, the policy of armed resistance to military attempts to change the political map of the world is a sound one. As we approach a situation, however, in which both East and West possess credible second-strike forces, the policy of massive retaliation loses credibility, although fear of an irrational massive retaliation may still deter military aggression. We might run great risks to deter future aggressions, but massive retaliation under the specified conditions would be suicidal, and, thus, would serve no useful purpose. Moreover, a military machine geared only to massive retaliation would likely grind to a halt if challenged and, thus, might encourage provocatory actions.[6]

The Russians surely would be clever enough in the future, as they have been in the past, to increase the ambiguity of the circumstances in which they acted and to create at least the pretext of legitimacy or legality. We have already seen them maneuver in this fashion in the Congo and Laos in recent years; and they would surely make their demands, each time they made them, relatively moderate. The crisis would be permitted to build slowly, and each time, our allies in Europe and much of the public at home would put pressure on the government to stand firm and inconsistently at the same time to compromise. The Laos incident is a good case in point. The most effective intervention the United States could make would be against North Viet Nam, and for this there is reason in the extent of the Vietminh

---

[6] The strategy of using limited strategic nuclear strikes against the Communist bloc probably will be accepted in the heat of war—if there is a war. It seems unlikely to gain sufficient acceptance in time of peace, although it would be most effective in war if adopted during peace. Thus, although the strategy has much to recommend it, discussions are likely to be confined to esoteric circles.

intervention. There is also strategic reason, for such retaliation would make of intervention something less than a one-way street. Yet clearly, in the present state of opinion, such a measure is not politically feasible.

Unfortunately, despite the inherent incredibility of the policy of massive retaliation, the threat of massive retaliation will have to play a deterrent role in the coming years. However, because of the lessening credibility of the policy, particularly in ambiguous situations, the United States, if it desires an effective foreign policy, will have to be prepared to intervene where necessary with appropriate non-nuclear forces. An inability to so intervene has reduced the bargaining power of the United States in the Laos case. Similar situations may arise elsewhere in Asia or in Africa and Latin America in the future. The lack of trained manpower in Europe, although undesirable, is not quite so dangerous because the tripwire theory, if not the best military doctrine, still possesses considerable deterrent power. Guerrilla warfare and internal subversion are not as effective in industrial Europe as they are in underdeveloped areas. Therefore, ambiguous measures are more difficult to find. A massive Soviet push across a clearly defined border would confront the United States with a head-on challenge that it could not afford to duck.

Reliance, however, upon local resistance forces is at best an uncertain expedient. Despite assertions about the superiority of defense over offense, with respect to non-nuclear forces, such a policy would probably only slow Soviet advances. There have been too many blitzkriegs in modern times to place much reliance in this defensive strategy.[7] The ability of the attacker to choose the place and time of his attack is a considerable advantage. Perhaps, if the policy of non-nuclear defense were combined with a policy of non-nuclear counterattacks at other points of tension, the policy might have more to recommend it. But clearly this combination would meet with more political resistance than any other kind of strategy including limited strategic nuclear reprisals. There is much to be said for building non-nuclear forces that increase the probability that important areas can be held against non-nuclear attacks even without resort to nuclear reprisals, but there is little to be said for a strategy that depends almost entirely upon the workability of this arrangement for its success. It would be as dangerous as a commitment to massive retaliation.

Unfortunately, democracies such as the United States find it politically difficult to develop a coherent and reasonably rational military policy. Regardless of which policy is resorted to, some aspect of it becomes politically infeasible, either through the inability of the United States to carry its allies, or because of domestic opposition within the United States. It is deplorable, not that different strategic doctrines are advocated outside the government, but that various groups place such pressure on government that no coherent doctrine can be adopted. Unfortunately, some vociferous sections of the public cannot distinguish between advice and coercion.

[7] Demonstrations to the contrary do not fully take into account the massing of manpower and armor at the point of the thrust, disruption after the thrust, the response of civilians fleeing the enemy, the ability or lack of ability of defending forces to control these civilians forcibly, fifth-column activities, other political factors, and the character of the threat and promise tactics of the attacking forces.

The United States faces one of the most curious and dreadful dilemmas that could be imposed upon a free people. There can be no doubt that democratic political organization is a severe handicap in the kind of world struggle in which the United States finds itself. Yet, the United States cannot win this struggle in a way consonant with its own values without maintaining democratic forms. It, thus, has the problem of presenting its military policy in ways least likely to arouse opposition while at the same time maintaining at least a minimally satisfactory military capability. At best, the means employed will arouse fears and opposition; for this reason it is essential that public attention be directed to non-military policy goals that arouse widespread enthusiasm. Attention must be diverted from risks to prospects.

It is as difficult to defend an adequate military policy as it was to answer the charges of the late Senator McCarthy. Such charges have the element of simplicity—answers that of complexity and subtlety. This is particularly true in the nuclear age when weapons of mass destruction arouse feelings of both horror and fear. It is tempting to the public to believe that there are easy answers to these problems permitting complete avoidance of the dangers. Military strategies immediately frustrate such hopes. Military systems must envisage the possibility of use. It would be useless and wrong to argue that military systems eliminate the possibility of nuclear war. But to demonstrate that appropriate military systems and strategies minimize the probability of nuclear war—and the loss of other values as well—is impracticable, although the argument is correct; understanding the logic of the argument requires considerable knowledge, expertise, and emotional maturity. As is so often the case, the marketplace of ideas does not necessarily make truth popular. And just as Senator McCarthy was finally beaten, not by rational argument but by a change of public sentiment, the case for an adequate military policy rests with the ability of the government to create a climate of opinion in which its proposals will be given the benefit of doubt.

One of the more difficult problems stems from a misguided fear that the military want war or that war is more likely unless civilian authorities have firm control. Undoubtedly, many military men resent the damper which the Kennedy administration has placed on their public utterances. But this new policy is necessary, for, given public stereotypes, the military are their own worst proponents. Confidence is much more important than clarity, and the new administration seems effectively to be restoring a confidence that was badly lacking.

The same reasons arguing for a foreign policy that would direct public attention from military hazards to constructive tasks are also beginning to argue for the removal of overseas nuclear bases. We are reaching the stage at which the major deterrent to the Soviet Union can be based in the United States, the oceans, and perhaps also in the Australian desert. Although there would still be some advantages in having IRBM bases in Europe to insure accuracy in limited strategic retaliation, these reasons probably will be overbalanced by irrational fears that such bases would draw Soviet nuclear fire. A joint NATO deterrent—desirable for still other reasons—could be based in the seas. Thus, Europe would have less reason to fear that American or NATO nuclear bases in Europe would draw Soviet nuclear fire. On the other hand, non-nuclear bases, at least in Europe, would also reassure Europeans that they would not be abandoned by the United States. Although the question is difficult to answer on the basis of public information, serious consideration should be given to relinquishing bases entailing more political liability than military advantage. Bases in Spain, Cuba, Japan, and elsewhere may fall into this category. I do not want to argue that military considerations are unimportant or should be ignored or to deny that many public reactions to military policy are unwise and unfortunate. But decisions have to be related to the constraints that exist—not to those we would choose.

VIII   Some Specific Trouble Spots

Berlin

We might take a brief look at a few trouble spots in the world. This will force some qualifications in the more generalized guideposts for policy that have been suggested earlier. However, this is inevitable whenever principles must be applied, and the seemingly anti-climactic nature of the discussion is a necessary price that is paid for greater specificity.

Perhaps the most vulnerable spot lies in Berlin. It is exceedingly unlikely that an airlift would overcome blockade today. Moreover, the Russians or their East German satellites are unlikely to try anything so crude as the blockade, for such a move, although non-military, might permit unified Western resistance. The Communists are much more likely to raise transit costs, to restrict transit routes, and to close off and "repair" facilities in such a way that the city is slowly strangled. There are really no good countermoves available to the West. The suggestion to move Berlin is hardly feasible and in any event would constitute a symbolic capitulation.

The Russians clearly have reasons to apply the squeeze in Berlin. Defeat in Berlin —even by means of a face-saving free-city formula—would constitute a tremendous loss in prestige and would affect the credibility of Western protection elsewhere, including areas where feasible protective measures are available. But even were the Russians forebearing enough not to desire to inflict such a loss of prestige upon the West, they would have reason to apply pressure in Berlin. Berlin is in the heart of East Germany. It not only is an area through which skilled workers and professional people had been able to escape to freedom before the new barriers were imposed, but it also provides a direct contrast for East Germans between democracy and total-itarianism, between a life where joy is possible and a life of Communist drabness and puritanism. Even apart from charges that West Berlin is a spy and propaganda center, the existence of a democratic West Berlin subverts Communist tyranny in East Germany. The East Germans will never accept Communism as a permanent fixture in their lives while they can observe, virtually in their midst, the life of free Germany.

If the issue of Berlin is isolated from other issues, or if the West refuses to consider aggressive action, the trumps are with the Communists. They can choose their moment and need only wait in order not to jeopardize other issues on which they desire negotiation with the West. Their strategic superiority is reinforced by the unwillingness of some Europeans—particularly the British—to take risks for the Germans. Yet, this is an issue on which the West cannot safely concede. It would be morally more indefensible than Munich to sell out the West Berliners, and the political and the military consequences might well be disastrous. If the Communists attempt to strangle Berlin, the West might send an armored column there. Or, alternatively, it might support active paramilitary and subversive actions in East Germany that both threaten the existence of the East German regime and involve a substantial risk of major and nuclear war in central Europe. And the Russians should privately be apprised of a decision to employ such measures before they commit themselves irrevocably with respect to West Berlin. Moreover, we should refuse to treat West Berlin as an isolated issue unrelated to freedom in East Berlin or East Germany. On the other hand, some compromise that genuinely protects the freedom of Berlin ought not to be excluded. However, the sooner the risks on action in Berlin are credibly raised for the Russians, the more likely they are to avoid entrapping themselves, and the less likely they are to confront the West with the alternatives of surrender or of policies involving a high risk of war. The issue here, as in China, should be presented clearly as one of human freedom. We may occasionally have to compromise this principle, but if we betray it, we will destroy the moral basis of our policy. In this present dangerous and unstable bipolar world, we will destroy ourselves unless our policy is based on an idealism that can generate support.

China

Another major American problem is, of course, China, with its attendant problems of Taiwan, Quemoy, and Matsu. There may be indirect reasons in the form of alliance and United Nations relationships to consider Chinese Communist membership in the United Nations, but it is difficult to discover any direct reasons, that is, reasons independent of the reactions of third parties, that would establish any American interest in acceding to Chinese Communist representation in the United Nations. There is no substantial evidence that such membership would modify Chinese behavior in any desirable way. It is abundantly clear that such membership would restrict numerous American actions that make life difficult for the Red regime, that bolster non-Communist nations on the periphery, and keep open the possibility of radical change in the regime or of successful revolution.

It is often said that the Communist regime in China is so firmly established that the possibility of successful revolution is, in any event, no longer present. Certainly there is no present reason to predict successful revolution. But it is going much farther than the adequacy of either social science techniques or information warrant categorically to exclude the possibility. On similar grounds, many would have denied the possibility of the Hungarian revolution—certainly successful until the intervention of the Russian army. The Red Chinese regime is indigenous in a sense that the

Hungarian regime was not, and this may make difficult a unified national uprising. Moreover, a small nation, with a single major center of national control, is easier to take in revolutionary action. In a large nation, troops can be stationed far from their home area and may not sympathize with revolutionary forces. Such techniques of troop disposition were employed both under the Czars and the dictators in Soviet Russia. And troops can be shifted to trouble spots before the revolution sweeps the entire nation. On the other hand, the Russians could not hope to intervene as they had in Hungary. China is too large. In the last analysis, the possibility of successful revolution cannot be excluded, and if this possibility is less probable than the alternatives, the consequences for the United States would be at least as desirable as the event is improbable.

The supposed changes in Chinese behavior that would accompany Red Chinese representation in the United Nations are as hypothetical as a Chinese revolution, and it is difficult to imagine any changes in behavior that would be strongly supportive of American interests, even though such changes might have some desirability. It is not inconceivable that Communist China in the United Nations would be more intransigent than Communist China outside the United Nations. Whether with American support or against American opposition, whether with an agreement that kept the Nationalist regime in Taiwan in the United Nations or not, the fact of United Nations recognition would confirm to many the Communist Chinese view of the United States as a paper tiger. It is likely that Red Chinese representation would have grave political and military repercussions through Asia.

There are two striking arguments favoring this, however. One concerns the general qualifications of membership which ought to apply universalistically. It is possible that the United States ought to support Red Chinese entry—at least on conditions of representation for the Taiwan regime also—on the grounds that interest in the norms governing membership outweighs other consequences of such representation.

A second consideration is that many other nations—some for reasons that are legitimate—believe such action appropriate or desirable and resent American efforts to prevent such representation. The arguments, however, that one must "recognize" reality or that membership in the United Nations will produce better behavior on the part of the Chinese Communists are not worth serious discussion.

It must be added that United Nations representation for the Chinese need not be determinative of American recognition policy. Of course, United Nations representation would remove a barrier to recognition and make more difficult the policy of non-recognition, but the problems of different forums are themselves different, and the arguments that might weight a decision with respect to the United Nations need not be determinative of the decision in Washington. There is no point to United States recognition until we have more to gain from such recognition than we have to lose. And it is difficult to see what substantial present advantages would flow from such actions. The opportunity to have diplomatic representation, to observe directly, and to influence does not seem of prime importance and has been much exaggerated in discussion. On those issues that require negotiations with the Chinese, appropriate *ad hoc* means can be found in the future as they have in the past. They will be successful or unsuccessful depending upon the incentive for the Chinese to reach agreement. And at least the *ad hoc* means required by non-recognition avoid the infelicities and dangers of negotiations at the level of either chief of state or government or high cabinet.

The problem of recognition of the Chinese Communists also directly involves American policy toward Taiwan. Much misinformation exists about the situation on Taiwan, and it is difficult to resolve it in short space. However, a few remarks are in order. The regime on Taiwan is not Fascist or totalitarian. Neither is it an exemplary democratic regime. The national, as opposed to the provincial, government is supposed to represent all of China, and Taiwan is represented only as one of the provinces of China. Along with other measures, including the control of the army and police, this preserves the control of the Kuomintang and of Chiang Kai-shek over Taiwan. Opposition and dissent are permitted but not to the point at which they would challenge the stability of the regime. Personal freedom is quite satisfactory. Economic conditions are improving rapidly despite one of the world's highest birthrates. The land reform is one of the best in the world and has produced a class of peasant entrepreneurs who are proud of their achievements and determined to defend them. Whether the Chiang regime would win a majority vote after freely conducted elections is difficult to determine, but it has at least the passive support of the immense majority of the population. There is no significant support on Taiwan for revolutionary action against the Chiang regime or for Communism. Any policy that permitted Communist conquest of Taiwan would constitute a betrayal not merely of the Kuomintang, but also of the ten million people on Taiwan who abhor Communism and all it stands for.

On the other hand, the Kuomintang is not the organization best endowed to exploit revolutionary possibilities on the China mainland. Although it has reformed considerably since its loss of the mainland, its reputation both in China and in other countries, without whose support aid to revolutionary forces would be difficult or impossible, is bad. A belief that successful revolution would succeed only in re-establishing the Kuomintang in control, although almost surely incorrect, would nonetheless inhibit successful development of the revolution. There are dangers involved in dissociating the United States from the Taiwan regime that should not be underestimated. Yet, in some fashion, a transition in support attitudes seems necessary.

The Quemoy and Matsu problems are exceptionally difficult. There is little sympathy in other countries for retention of these islands, and there seems little doubt that eventually they must be given up to the mainland regime. On the other hand, they do have considerable strategic importance. They block off the important ports of Amoy and Minhow, interdict coastal shipping, and make most difficult any move toward the Pescadores or Taiwan proper. They are quite defensible militarily and could be taken only at a most severe cost considering the high morale and military ability of the defending forces. Moreover, loss of these islands would bring the active war much closer to Taiwan and have considerable psychological and political consequences on that island. The situation grows progressively more difficult; yet, there seems little reason for a change of policy at this time. Perhaps as part of a deal regularizing many of the problems in Far Asia, return of the islands to the mainland regime should be considered. However, that seems premature presently.

Japan

The problem of American policy toward Japan also is quite difficult. We have suffered through a period in which the American Embassy cut itself off from the main currents of Japanese opinion and helped to place Japan in a position in which it appeared to have a satellite foreign policy. This has done grave harm to American interests in Japan. American military bases in Japan also do considerable political harm, primarily because their use is misunderstood by most Japanese. Such bases are not designed for offensive operations of either a conventional or nuclear kind. They are important primarily for tactical and logistic reasons. Without these bases, American ability to act rapidly in case of aggression or subversion in important Asian areas would be questionable. The bases also commit America to Japanese defense in a way not possible in their absence. They, thus, deter the use of nuclear threats or blackmail against Japan. There could be no good military reason to use nuclear weapons against these bases without also using them against the United States. Instead, the Japanese wrongly see these bases as increasing the nuclear danger for Japan. It is doubtful, however, whether argument, no matter how correct, will be persuasive on this matter. The United States may have to decide whether the bases are worth the political costs.[8]

Additionally, the United States must encourage Japan to play an independent role in Asia, a difficult proposition because of Japanese unpopularity in much of Asia. But Japanese political frustrations can best be satisfied when Japan has an independent political role that is satisfactory to its dignity as a great and progressive nation. Even though this may mean occasional differences in policy between Japan and the United States, even with respect to a China policy, the improvement of the political situation in Japan ought to be a far more important objective of American foreign policy than the elimination of policy differences. Indeed, it was a fault of American foreign policy under Dulles that we were too fearful of independent foreign policies on the part of associated nations. Since the United States did not have available Communist techniques for coordination of national policies, despite differences in specific interests, this produced dissatisfaction and malaise on the part of governments that felt they were unwisely or inconsistently coerced or on the part of publics that felt their governments lacked the independence of action consonant with pursuit of national interests and dignity.

[8] There are vociferous groups opposed to American bases in England also. But even larger segments of the public and leadership understand that the bases constitute a commitment that deters rather than provokes the Russians. Moreover, there is a history of alliance with the United States and some willingness to run joint risks. This is absent in Japan.

Cuba

The ill-fated invasion of Cuba in April 1961 compounded military and political errors that need not be detailed here. In brief, however, the United States moved against Cuba before it moved against Right-Wing dictators; it supported the wrong elements from among the various anti-Castro groupings. These political errors were most serious, for the United States cannot permit itself to appear to oppose Castro only because of his pro-Communism or to support certain Cuban groups because they will re-establish American economic interests in Cuba. Quite apart from the validity of the charges that would arise from such appearances—and I believe them to be false—the fact of the appearances cuts the United States off from the support it needs in a world in which it is not politically possible to act merely according to the politics of force.

Intervention, as such, was undoubtedly a sound policy, for the present world is not a world in which non-intervention is possible. It is, however, the effectiveness of policy that is important, and it was with respect to this effectiveness that American policy in Cuba failed. Now that intervention has been attempted and has failed, it would be most difficult to resurrect it as a policy in the absence of acute provocation on the part of Cuba. The major American effort must be devoted to reform and modernization in Latin America exclusive of Cuba. This, plus the possible failure of the Cuban revolution to satisfy Cuban expectations concerning modernization, may lead to increased political dissidence and sabotage in Cuba. If the regime can be isolated by the OAS, it may then collapse, or some later intervention may be attempted under more favorable circumstances.

There is another aspect to the problem, however: This concerns the political consequences for the United States of anti-Castro activities on the part of regimes in nations like Mexico and Venezuela which the United States wishes to support. It is possible that too overt an effort by the United States to forge an anti-Castro alignment would produce consequences more undesirable than the ouster of Castro is desirable. Yet, Castro in power does pose a threat to the hemisphere. Moreover, failure to support the anti-Castro forces would constitute betrayal of the best and most democratic elements in Cuba. Thus, it would appear that some form of support for the anti-Castro forces is mandatory. We cannot afford merely to oppose Castro. We must stand for values we can defend to ourselves as well as to others. Otherwise, we shall fail.

Israel

In the dispute between Israel and the Arab states, there is only one honorable course that the United States can take. Contemporary Arab demands on Israel do not have the function of adjusting a wrong; they have the function of destroying Israel. This is particularly true of the repatriation demand. This does not mean that the United States ought not to sympathize with the plight of the Arab refugees, or that it should approve of the more rambunctious actions of the stiff-necked Ben-Gurion. Yet, Israel has a right to exist; the Israelis have as much right to self-government as the Arabs; Israel is a democratic state; and it represents most of the virtues in which America believes. Even if the latter were not true, the United States could hardly connive in efforts to destroy a state that is legitimate according to the standards of international law merely to win the favor of the Arabs.

It is a truism to call the Middle Eastern problem complex. To deny the Arab claims is not to underestimate the depth of Arab feelings or the difficulties Arab politicians would have in trying to make peace with Israel. Neither is it to deny that the existence of Israel imposes costs on the United States that would not exist had there never been an Israel; nor to deny that the venom the Arabs carry toward Israel helps to corrode their own political efforts individually and collectively. But Israel does exist, and one cannot create the conditions that would have existed had there never been an Israel by cooperating in its demise. Arab demands against Israel are of a nature that cannot be compromised and, therefore, they cannot be met in a way satisfactory to the Arabs short of the destruction of Israel. As much as we need to reconcile the uncommitted states, this is an impossible policy for us. This is true not merely for internal political reasons, but primarily because a cold-blooded policy of this nature would corrupt our own decision processes, make the Arabs contemptuous of us rather than friendly to us, increase the demands of those who wish us ill, and destroy the confidence of those who wish us well. We cannot afford a Machiavellian policy. We would only disillusion ourselves if we behaved in that fashion.

The existence of Israel is due primarily to the desires and organizing skills of the Jews of Palestine. United Nations resolutions and American decisions did not create Israel. They only recognized an existing fact which the Arabs did not have the power to change without extensive outside aid. The United States can share neither the credit nor the blame for the existence of the state of Israel, and those in the Department of State who argued "realistically" for a policy opposed to the Israeli state had little genuine understanding of the world in which they lived. If there was any past mistake in American policy, it was in refusing to impose peace while the United States was strong in the Middle East and the Russians weak. Then, compromises of a durable nature might successfully have been imposed on both sides, and sheer duress might have produced adjustment. Clearly, a state of war would have been difficult to re-establish after the formalization of peace treaties. In the meantime, transactions between Israel and the Arab states, beneficial to both and difficult to sever, might have been established. But that opportunity—sacrificed as usual by the "realists"—is past and cannot be recalled. The present situation is most difficult and will remain so almost regardless of what the United States does.

Harsh as it may sound, the United States cannot gain from major efforts to reconcile the Arab states. It must depend upon their self-interest in maintaining independence from the Russians and in continuing the flow of oil. When and if the Arabs ever become ready, the United States ought to cooperate with them in endeavors or projects consonant with American values and Arab interests. Until such time, there is no point in wishing for a world that cannot be.

Conclusion

Any particular policy recommendation may, of course, prove inappropriate on the basis of more careful analysis or more thorough consideration of the relevant factors. But two general considerations emerge from the preceding analysis that, in my opinion, would constitute good guidelines for policy decisions. The United States needs to enunciate foreign-policy goals that are capable of arousing support and enthusiasm both within the United States and among our allies. Indeed, these goals would serve best if they became known behind the iron curtain and had subversive effects there. The status quo will no longer be sufficient for success. We must take our chances with change and attempt to promote those changes harmonious with our own values and with the best interests of peoples everywhere. Time is no longer with us. Holding the line and delaying actions will not do. We are neither rich nor strong enough to be conservative or to ignore or to deny the aspirations of the great masses of mankind. We must choose, and only if we choose rightly can we hope to preserve those values and institutions that we hold dear.

Positive goals must be backed by a sound military and diplomatic posture. Idealism in terms of objectives must not be confused with muddle-headedness in terms of means. We face a strong foe, capable of resorting to military action and willing to employ threats of the most provocative type. This foe will use negotiations and conferences primarily not to reach cooperative agreement but to destroy our institutions and way of life. Unless and until we can force changes in his mode of organization and operation—not necessarily by physical means—we also must regard the situation as a struggle. We must be ceaselessly alert, reasonably confident, and ready to defend what we stand for.

In our relations with our friends and allies, we must recognize that their interests and their goals are not identical with our own. We must expect some disagreements with them and, if we respect their freedom and independence, we shall also respect their right to disagree. Despite the desperate nature of the struggle, we cannot expect to dictate to other nations. We do and ought to expect general support from our friends. But we must earn this support in terms of policies that win their support. Where this is not feasible, and where we are certain that we are right, we must have the courage and moral fortitude to temporarily go it alone, without renouncing our interest in or friendship for other countries.

These are difficult demands to make in a democracy. To repeat what has become trite, but nonetheless remains true, this cannot be accomplished without strong presidential leadership, which takes the people into its confidence and builds the kind of public support, based on trust, that will permit ventures into the untried and the imaginative realms of statecraft. Beneath the layers of selfishness and self-centeredness, the ideals of the United States will still support policies oriented to vision and faith. There is still an American ideal that views democracy and the products of modern civilization as the heritage of all mankind.

Index

Aborigines Rights Protection Society, 141
Act of State, 319, 329
Action Française (Maurras), 72, 73, 76, 80
Afghanistan, 383
Africa, 19, 26, 54, 138, 268, 269, 275, 314, 371, 440, 443, 457
African National Congress, 141
African personality, 101, 269, 271, 297
African Socialism, 148, 149
Afro-Asians, bloc, 285, 307; cooperation, 182; revolutionary elites, 322; states, 34, 181, 279, 280, 301, 313
Afro-Asian Solidarity Conference, 181, 300, 302
agents-provocateur, 340
aggression (aggressiveness), 321, 322, 323, 325, 329, 400
agrovilles, 203, 204
aid, development, 438–440; economic, 205, 355–380, 420, 436; military, 179–180, 383
Alain, 78, 83
Albania, 225, 258
Aldermaston march, 59, 61
Algeria, 71–74, 81, 89, 90, 147, 150, 160, 255, 287, 300, 339
alienation, 14–16, 55, 84, 90, 92, 98, 256; and intellectuals, 4
All-African People's Conference, 147
All-African Trade-Union Federation, 150
All-China Federation of Trade Unions, 92
Allen, George, 183
alliances, military, 435–436. See also listings of separate alliances social and class; separate listings
Almond, Gabriel, 70, 71
Alsop, Joseph, 200
American Colonization Society, 138
American Declaration of Independence, 5

American Revolution, 23, 323
Americanization, 40, 106
Amis, Kingsley, 64
amnesty, 113, 199
Amoy, 462
Anglo-Egyptian Treaty of 1954, 162, 173, 184
Anglo-Iranian Oil Company, 175
Angola, 230
Antarctic Treaty, 450
Antarctica, 291
anti-Americanism, 18, 20, 21, 67, 82, 87, 95, 98, 99, 135–136, 167, 172, 273, 376, 437, 438
anti-capitalism, 11–14, 18, 98, 99
anti-colonialism, 9, 16–17, 19, 20, 56, 147, 222, 232, 254, 288, 289, 358, 419
anti-intercontinental-ballistic-missile systems (A-ICBM), 347, 348, 401, 403, 404, 408
anti-Semitism, 18, 63
apartheid, 59, 63, 343
apathy, 32, 38, 90, 91, 255, 339
appeasement. See war, peaceful settlement
Aprista parties (Latin America), 123, 125, 126, 135
Arab League, 161, 177
Arab Socialism, 156, 163–174, 189
arbitration (arbiter), 185, 264
d'Arboussier, Gabriel, 150
Arendt, Hannah, 34
Argentina, 7, 113, 116, 122, 128, 131, 134, 441
Armenia (USSR), 229
arms control, 333, 339, 344, 388, 402, 403, 406, 408, 450, 453, 454
arm shipments, 179–180
arms race, 342–344, 346, 349, 388, 390, 391, 392–394, 402, 403, 407, 409, 453, 455
Aron, Raymond, 69, 71, 91, 108
Asanuma, 95

Ashida, 96
Asia, 19, 54, 275, 457
Aswan High Dam, 166, 173, 179, 180, 273
Atlantic Charter, 5
Atlantic Community, 447, 448
Atlee, Clement, 49, 53
Atomic Energy Commission, 343
Attaturk, Kemal, 441
Australia, 458
Austria, 185, 323
authoritarianism, 89–90, 117, 133, 339, 438, 441, 447
Ayub, 383

Baghdad Pact, 161, 162, 178, 179, 180, 181, 182
"balance of power" system, 20, 176, 239, 251–252, 253, 276, 320, 431
Bandung Conference, 146, 171, 178, 181, 182, 184, 235, 241, 273
Bank of England, 35
Bao Dai, 194
bargaining, 262, 263, 264, 265, 281, 294, 296, 308, 455
Barrès, Maurice, 81
bases, IRBM, 53, 58, 67, 96, 458; military, 96, 255, 463
Ba'this, 153, 156, 157, 163, 169, 171, 177, 180, 183, 184
Batista, Fulgencio, 113, 115, 117, 118, 119, 121, 123, 126, 130
Bayet, 91
Becker, Carl, 81
behavior control, 326, 436
Belgian Congo, 265
Belgium, 66, 194, 288, 289
belligerency, state of, 265, 327
Ben-Gurion, David, 465
Bergson, Henri, 80
Beria, Lavrenti, 257
Bernstein, Edward, 52
Bevan, Aneuran, 52
Bhabba, 342
Bhandun Conference, 159
bipolarity, 152, 184, 189, 238, 245, 251–266, 313, 431–433. See also chap. 12
blackmail, 27, 199, 308, 348, 374, 445, 463
Black Muslims, 18
Blanco, Capt. Jesus Sosa, 118
blocs, Afro-Asian, 285, 307; communist, 20, 54, 66, 252, 257–260, 265, 286, 289, 294, 322, 438, 452–456; NATO, 254, 255–257, 294

Blum, Léon, 76, 82
Bolivar, Simon, 116
Bolivia, 115, 269, 272, 273, 286, 289, 290, 292, 293, 298, 302, 303
Bolshevik Revolution of 1917, 23, 209, 218, 227, 228, 229, 233
Bonapartists, 21, 22
Boulangisme, 70, 71
Bourdet, Claude, 80
"Bow" Group, 62
Brazil, 128, 131, 441
Brazzaville Conference (Africa), 149, 150
Brennan, D. G., 349
Brierly, 287
Brimi Conference, 182
British Broadcasting Co. (BBC), 42
British Communist Party, 46, 47, 48, 60
British fascists, 63
British Guiana, 149, 443
British Jewish theatre, 64
British Left, 38, 39, 46, 47, 53, 54
British West Africa, 142
Buddha, 17
Buddhism, 105, 194, 211
Burckhardt, Jacob, 3
bureaucratism, 46, 164, 165, 172, 202, 364, 366
Burma, 189, 239, 270, 360, 363, 366, 383, 411, 412

Cabeza de Goliat, 121, 126, 134
Caesar, Julius, 17
Cambodia, 197, 198, 209, 372, 383
Cameroons, 290, 300
Campaign for Nuclear Disarmament (CND), 31, 57, 58, 59, 60, 68
Camus, Albert, 84, 91, 145
Can, Nho Dinh, 195
Canada, 261, 436
Cao Dai, 194, 198
Cape Canaveral, 129
capitalism, 25, 212, 213, 222, 223, 261, 441, 455
capitalist encirclement, 212, 455
Captive Nations Week, 327
Carnegie, Andrew, 13
Carnegie Endowment for International Peace, 13
Casablanca Conference, 149, 150, 181, 187, 297
Castle, Barbara, 55
Castro, Fidel, 7, 106, 113–136, 262, 265, 268, 271, 274, 300, 314, 323, 325, 326, 328, 331, 441, 442, 447. See also chap. 5

Castro, Raul, 120, 132
Catholics, 8, 55, 71, 76, 194, 195, 196, 200, 204, 205
Césaire, Aimé (Martinique), 144
Cespedes, Dr. Carlos Manuel de, 115
Ceylon, 189, 289, 297, 360, 364
Challe, General, 74
charisma (charismatic leaders), 120, 121, 134, 157, 195, 268, 275, 358
Charter of Bogota, Article 15, 325
Chejne, A. G., 161
Chiang Kai-Shek, 462
Chile, 131
"China Boom" (Japan), 107
China, People's Republic of, 26, 53, 92, 100, 106, 107, 178, 179, 211, 230, 233–247, 258–259, 263, 265, 271, 310, 315, 322, 328, 329–331, 342, 348, 367, 407, 415, 419, 446, 450, 452, 453, 454, 460–463. *See also* chap. 11
Chinese Communist Party, 241. *See also* China
Chinese Foreign Ministry, 240
Chou En-Lai, 237, 239, 244
Christianity, 16, 101, 105, 210, 211
Churchill, Winston, 22, 36, 279
Cienfuegos, Major Camilo, 132
Civil Guard (So. Viet Nam), 201
Clark, Grenville, 350
class conflict, 221, 222
Clemenceau, Georges, 140
Cold War, 53, 92, 136, 150, 181, 185, 189, 190, 191, 261, 279, 284, 286, 289, 304, 308, 312, 314, 316, 319, 321, 322, 325, 326, 328, 351, 383, 435, 436, 448–449, 450
Cole, G. D. H., 169
collective security, 238, 280, 284, 295, 296
colonialism, 63, 141, 264, 269, 279, 280, 286, 300, 301, 326, 328, 358, 375, 417
Colombia (S.A.), 113
Columbus, Christopher, 4, 116
Cominform, 257
Comintern, 257, 283
Committee of One Hundred, 59, 61
Committee on Non-Self-Governing Territories, 288
Commonwealth of Nations (British), 34, 54, 66, 67
Commune of Paris (1871), 70
communism, 116, 209–232, 271, 433, 437, 444, 453, 455; Chinese, 233–247; Russian, 14, 26, 27. *See also* chap. 10
"Communist Camp," 252, 257–260. *See also* bloc, Communist
Communist Manifesto, 153, 209

Communist Party of France (PCF), 56, 70, 71, 72, 83, 86, 257
Communist Party of Italy (PCI), 56, 95, 257
Concert of Europe, 277, 282
Confédération Generale du Travail (CGT), 70
Confédération des Petites et Moyennes Entreprises, 70
Conference of Independent African States, 147
Confucianism, 194
Confucius, 17
Congo, 150, 260, 265, 287, 288, 289, 295, 296, 297, 301, 304, 305, 312, 328, 438, 449, 456
Congress of Vienna, 323
Connally Reservation, 317, 331
consciousness, false, 52
consensus, 32, 33, 46, 68, 75, 91, 92, 99, 212, 297, 306–307, 331
Conservative Party (Great Britain), 35, 36, 37, 41, 42, 53, 68
conservativism, 21, 22, 45, 62, 315, 333, 434
Corfu Channel, 285
corruption, 99, 123–124, 135, 166, 205, 364, 366, 418, 439
Costa Rica, 125, 135
Constitution of 1940 (Cuba), 119
contradictions, 220, 224, 236
Cousins, Frank, 51
Crankshaw, 235
Crosland, Anthony, 52, 61
Crossman, Richard, 61
Crozier, Michel, 77, 78, 82, 87
Cuba, 26, 113–136, 189, 258, 269, 271, 286, 288, 289, 290, 293, 300, 302, 310, 317, 325, 326, 327, 328, 331, 339, 374, 424, 428, 441, 442, 443, 459, 464; communist party of, 131, 132; constitution of, 119
Cuban Communist Party, 131, 132
Cuban Revolutionary (Autentico) Party, 119
Cyprus, 55
Czechoslovakia, 132, 182, 270, 328

Dallin, Alexander, 283
Damascus University, 171
Debré, M., 74
debriefing, 379
decentralized decision-making, 77–79, 90, 245, 317–318, 378
Declaration of Solidarity at Caracas, 324, 327
decolonization, 54, 55, 89, 146, 147, 149, 294, 295, 296, 302
defense, 255, 322, 381–387, 388, 401; civil, 343, 403, 404, 408, 409

democracy, 161, 256, 408, 433, 434, 438, 452, 454, 457, 466
Democratic Party or Liberal-Democratic Party (Japan), 93
Democratic Socialist Party (DSP, Japan), 93, 96
depoliticization, 46, 67, 327, 328
deterrence, minimum (finite), 341, 398, 402, 406; nuclear, 214–216, 254, 388–410; stable, 342, 390, 402–403, 404, 409
Deutch, Prof. Karl, 157
Deutscher, 235
development, 17, 18, 172. See also intelligence, military
deviationism, 245, 246
Diagne, Blaise, 140
dialectic, 219, 258
Diaz, Gen. Porfirio, 128
Diem, Pres. Ngo Dinh, 192, 194, 203, 204, 205, 206
Diet, 96
Diop, Alioune, 145
diplomacy, 212, 274, 283, 287, 290, 295, 304, 456; Chinese, 240, 244
disarmament, 58–61, 68, 187, 265, 290, 291, 304, 341, 345, 454
Dissent, 57
dogmatism, 268
Domenach, 91
Dominican Republic, 113, 134
Dom Pedro II, 114
Dorgères movement, 70, 71
Dostoevsky, Fyodor, 106
Douglass, Frederick, 138
Draft Code of Offenses against the Peace and Security of Mankind, 325
Dreyfus case, 73, 91
DuBois, W. E. B., 139, 140, 142, 143
Dulles, John Foster, 53, 179, 264, 463
Duverger, 88, 89

Economic Development Organization, 167, 173
Ecuador, 113
Eden, Sir Anthony, 34, 45
Education Act 1944 (Great Britain), 39, 64
egalitarianism, 11, 24, 50, 358
Egypt, 148, 152–174, 175–191, 223, 262, 265, 269, 271, 272, 273, 284, 292, 296, 297, 298, 305, 322, 369, 436
Eisenhower, Dwight D., 92, 136, 331; Eisenhower Doctrine, 180, 326; Eisenhower-Dulles policies, 294, 431, 448, 449
elites, counter (alternative, rival), 436; modernizing, 39, 226, 361, 372; revolutionary,

172, 210, 223, 226, 271, 310, 311, 315, 322, 357; ruling, 314
embourgeoisement, 23, 108
Emperor's Rescript on Education, 101
empiricism, 33, 44, 404
Engels, Friedrich, 52, 98, 210
Enlightenment, the, 81
entrepreneurs (capitalists), 127, 366, 368, 369, 439, 460
Epicurus, 17
Esprit, 72
Establishment, the, 8, 9–11, 142, 143
Ethiopia, 138
European, the, 63
European Common Market, 257, 446; British entry, 66–67
European Defense Community (EDC), 71, 72, 77, 78
existentialism, 64, 80, 106
Expanded Program of Technical Assistance (EPTA), 291, 292
extraterritoriality, 100

factionalism, 194; lack of, 258
Fall, Bernard, 414
family influence (regime, rule), Arab, 171; South Viet Nam, 194, 195, 196
Farouk, King of Egypt, 166, 177, 269
Federation of French West Africa, 149
Fédération Nationale Catholique, 71
Fertile Crescent, 157, 158
feudalism, 100, 103, 161, 165, 223, 231
Fidelismo (Castroism), 113, 132, 134, 135, 136. See also chap. 5
flexibility of alignment, 252, 359, 432
food supply (diet), 205, 412, 425
Foot, Michael, 50, 56
Fourth Republic, 76, 79
France, 22, 34, 46, 47, 56, 66, 94, 193, 209, 224, 226, 232, 287, 288, 310, 319, 340, 413, 414, 417; protest in, 69–91
Franco, Francisco, 324, 329, 447
Franco, Rafael, 113
Free officers (Egypt), 160, 166, 167
Freetrade Zone, 257
Free World, 178, 181, 217, 235, 238, 241, 434
French Declaration of the Rights of Man, 5
French North Africa, 141, 142, 144, 147, 148
French Resistance Period, 84
French Revolution, 9, 62, 75, 323
"front" groups, 257

Gaikan, Jorge Eliecer, 134
Gaitskell, Hugh, 45, 49, 50, 51, 52, 53, 55, 58, 67
Garvey, Marcus, 140, 142, 143
GATT, 292
de Gaulle, Charles, 71, 72, 74, 76, 88, 149
Geneva Accord, 204
Geneva Conference, 235, 241, 429
geopolitics (Eurasian Heartland), 8
Georgia (USSR), 228
German Social Democratic Party, 52, 66, 95
German-Soviet Non-Aggression Pact of 1939, 47
Germany, 10, 19, 31, 46, 83, 84, 185, 283, 310, 321, 324; Berlin, 68, 459–460; West Berlin, 12, 68, 285, 418, 428, 454, 455; East Germany, 12, 25, 26, 258, 459–460; West Germany, 12, 54, 226
Ghana, 55, 146, 147, 150, 189, 262, 265, 270, 271, 289, 290, 296, 297, 298, 301, 442, 443
Gide, André, 145
Gil, Frederico G., 120
Gillispie, Coulston Charles, 15, 16
Gingeinbre, 70
Giradet, 91
Gizenga, Antoine, 265, 289, 297
Gold Coast, 141, 143
Good Neighbor Policy, 130, 136
Great Britain, 10, 22, 31–68, 83, 177, 179, 226, 284, 287, 288, 319, 364, 412, 413, 414, 415, 419, 424
great-power status, 235, 241
Greece, 128, 285
Guantanamo Bay, 130, 131
Guatemala, 325, 326, 328, 329
guerrillas, 113, 192, 196–201, 206, 387; warfare in S.E. Asia, 411–430
Guevara, Ernesto ("Che"), 120, 132, 424
Guinia, 149, 150, 261, 262, 265, 269, 271, 290, 297, 302, 303, 442, 443

Haiti, 116, 137, 144, 369
Halévy, Daniel, 80
Hammerskjold, Dag, 265, 282, 289, 301, 304, 305, 449
Hapsburg Monarchy, 10, 24
Hatta, Muhammad, 373
Hatoyama, 242
Havana, 114, 121–123, 125, 127, 130, 131, 219, 286
"have not" nations, 233
Hegel, Karl, 170
heresy, 211, 258
Hill, Robert C., 136

Hinduism, 209
Hippocratic Oath, 5
Hitler, Adolf, 7, 10, 13, 25, 263, 310, 324, 455
Hoa Hao, 194, 198
Ho Chi Minh, 194, 198, 200, 429
Hoffmann, Stanley, 277
Holy Alliance, 21
Hong Kong, 25
hostages, 338, 395, 399, 403, 406
Houphouet-Boigny, Félix, 268
Hukbalahaps, 413
human rights, 13, 139, 279, 280, 293, 294, 298, 307
"Hundred Flowers," 49
Hungarian Revolution, 48, 49, 56, 244, 258, 460
Hungary, 26, 201, 236, 258, 284, 286, 318, 326, 328, 329, 456, 461
Husain, King of Jordan, 159, 160, 167, 176
Hyderabad, 328

Ibarra, José Maria Velasco, 113
ideology, 5, 39, 43, 63, 87, 89, 97, 152, 154, 163, 164, 170, 171, 172, 176, 200, 210, 211, 212, 223–225; Soviet, 216–223, 242, 314, 330, 433, 434
Ikki, Kita, 104
immobilism, 8, 89, 177, 387
imperialism, 98, 191, 217, 261, 269, 271, 300, 316; new, 375
"Imperialist Camp" (See Free World)
India, 34, 179, 182, 188, 189, 190, 230, 239, 244, 261, 265, 270, 319, 328, 342, 363, 365, 366, 367, 369, 375, 377, 387
Indo-China, 179, 247, 325, 413, 416
independence, national, 182, 255, 357, 358, 438–440
Indonesia, 22, 179, 182, 189, 209, 270, 272, 273, 284, 292, 293, 296, 297, 298, 359, 360, 363, 364, 365, 366, 373, 387
Indus River Basin, 302
Industrial and Commercial Workers Union (U. of So. Africa), 141
Inejiro, Asanuma, 107
intellectuals, 4, 14–16, 32, 33, 44, 47, 48, 49, 62, 63, 65, 69, 71, 73, 75, 81–82, 84, 87, 89, 90; Arab, 154, 157; Japan, 92, 95, 97, 99, 106, 110; Negro, 138, 256; Viet Nam, 193, 205
intelligence, 13; military, 216, 367, 407, 415
Inter-American Treaty of Reciprocal Assistance, 324

interest, international, 10, 277, 294; national (public), 9, 395, 458
International Atomic Energy Agency, 296
International Bank for Reconstruction and Development, 302
International Finance Corporation, 291, 292
International Labor Organization, 293
International Monetary Fund, 302
internationalism, 295
internment camps, 202
Iran, 190, 285, 325, 384–385; Shah, 231
Iraq, 154, 157, 160, 162, 180, 189, 190, 223, 272, 436, 439, 440
irresponsible organizations, 339
Islam, 163, 173, 210, 211
Israel, 22, 227, 284, 305, 319, 322, 464–465
Italy, 10, 46, 47, 55, 66, 84, 94, 209, 224, 226, 279, 283, 287, 321
Ivory Coast 268

Jagan, Cheddi, 443
Japan, 10, 19, 92–110, 230, 240, 242, 283, 300, 311, 321, 342, 387, 412, 413, 439, 459, 463
Japan Socialist Party, 93, 94, 101, 103, 107
Japan Teachers' Union, 103
Japanese-American Security Treaty, 95, 107
Japanese Self-Defense Forces, 240
Jaurès, Benito, 76, 82
Java, 360, 365, 369
Jeanson, 91
Jews, 9, 17, 18, 64, 178, 465
Jimenez, Antonio Nunez, 120, 126
Jordan, 53, 160, 162, 180, 304, 305
Jouvenal, Robert de, 79
justice, 8, 9, 178; social, 9. *See also* human rights

Kadar, 319
Kaplan, Morton A., 276, 341
Kasavubu, 265, 289, 301
Kashmir, 319, 328, 364
Katanga, 289
Katayama, Tetsu, 96
Kato-Shidehara Cabinet, 102
Kautsky, Karl Johann, 52
Kennedy, John F., 326, 327, 440, 458
Kenya, 33, 141
Kenyatta, Jomo, 142
Kikuya Central Association (Kenya), 141
Kishi, 92, 242
Kissinger, Henry, 185, 186
Korea, 240, 243, 247, 280, 284, 285, 297, 325,

381, 383, 387; South Korea, 363, 364, 374, 419, 436, 438, 448, 449
Korean War, 235, 241, 254, 285, 311, 322, 363, 448
Korovin, 286
Kuomintang, 462
Krushchev, Nikita, 48, 132, 212, 215, 218, 240, 257, 258, 259, 265, 285, 290, 327, 455
Kuwait, 440

labor, 103. *See* separate listings of labor organizations
Labor Party (Great Britain), 34, 35, 36, 37, 42, 45, 47, 48, 50, 51, 53, 54, 56, 57, 60, 63, 66, 95
landlords, 20, 167, 172, 206
Laos, 190–191, 198, 206, 240, 247, 254, 265, 295, 304, 305, 325, 326, 329, 371, 387, 411, 418, 428, 429, 449, 456, 457
Laski, Harold, 169
Latin America, 11, 19, 113–136, 262, 265, 275, 279, 288, 307, 314, 323, 326, 371, 436, 440, 441, 457, 464
Lavon Affair, 178
Lawrence, D. H., 65
League of Empire Loyalists, 63
League of Nations, 7, 277, 282, 283, 320, 321
Lebanese-Jordan crisis 1958, 284, 305
Lebanon, 53, 154, 157, 160, 163, 169, 180, 189, 304, 319, 325
Leghorn, R., 349
Lenin, Vladimir, 12, 13, 25, 217, 220, 222, 377
Liberal Party (Great Britain), 35, 46, 61
Liberalism, 7, 46, 437, 452
liberation movements, 143, 147, 152–174
Liberia, 137, 138, 297
Lichtenstein, 318
Lie, Trygvie, 304
literacy, 226, 228–231. *See also* intellectuals
L'Observateur, 72
Logan, Rayford, 140, 143
logistics, 412, 416
London, City of, 37, 41, 42
London School of Economics, 169
loose bipolar system, 252, 253, 266, 276, 432
lumpenproletariat, 63
Lumumba, Patrice, 150, 265, 289, 297, 301
Luyen, Ngo Dinh, 195

Macdonald, Ramsay, 7
Machado, Gerardo, 115, 116, 117, 118, 121
MacKinder, Halford, 8, 26
Macmillan, Sir Harold, 45, 62

Madagascar, 141
Mahan, Alfred Thayer, 26
Mahgreb (Mohgrib), 148, 157, 440
Majoli, 159
Makarios, Archbishop, 63
Makonnen, 142
Malaya, 33, 199, 206, 339, 372, 413, 414, 415,
    417, 419, 424
Malenkov, G., 257
Mali, 150, 261, 262, 290, 297, 298, 302
Manifesto of the 121, 72
Mantoux, Etienne, 3
Mao Tse-Tung, 11, 192, 241, 258, 417
March, James G., 281
Marshall Plan, 357, 375
Marx, Karl, 14, 55, 169, 259
Marxism, 11, 12, 55, 80, 81, 88, 105, 109, 170,
    210, 223, 231, 258, 314, 346; Marxism-Lenin-
    ism in Cuba, 132, 209, 221
Masaburo, Suzuti, 98
materialism, 24, 98
Matsu, 263, 460, 462
McCarthyism, 48, 458
mechanization of forces, 81
Meiji Era, 98, 99, 101, 107, 439
Mekong River Project, 292
Mendez-France, Pierre, 56, 72, 87
messianic tradition, 5, 8, 210
Metternich, Clemens von, 22
Mexico, 116, 125, 128, 131, 135, 288, 289, 290,
    292, 293, 441, 464
Michio, Takeyama, 105
Middle East Defense Organization, 177
millennium, 213
Milliard, 142
Mills, Wright, 57
military class, 458; Egypt, 164, 165; France,
    89; Japan, 100, 104; Spain, 116, 117, 118;
    Viet Nam, 205
Mindszenty, Cardinal, 330
Minhow, 462
minority groups 17–18
Misr Organization, 167, 173
missiles, nuclear, 239, 336, 350, 351, 393, 394,
    396
mixed economy, 368
Mobutu, 289
models, 210, 251, 355, 377, 388–410; balance
    of power, 251–252; American aid, 356–362
modernization 85, 88, 98–100, 108, 121, 134,
    164, 223, 224, 226–231, 272, 273, 357, 358,
    360, 362, 372, 435, 436, 438–440, 441–444,
    445

monarchy (ies), 88, 323
Monroe Doctrine, 324, 327
Monroe, James, 128
morale, 349
morality, 4–6, 8–9, 10, 17, 24, 55, 73, 81, 84,
    123, 124, 125, 128, 184, 189, 260, 344, 432
Morocco, 147, 150, 160, 189, 262, 272, 290,
    296, 297, 298
Moscow Declaration of 1957 (PR of China),
    236
Mosley, Sir Oswald, 63
Mossadegh, 175, 178
Murdoch, Iris, 64
Mus, 91
Mussolini, Benito, 25

Nabulsi, 159
Naguib, 161
Nagy, Imre, 236
Naples, 323
Napoleon III, 83
Nasr Organization, 167
Nasser, G. A., 154, 158, 268, 269, 273, 274,
    280, 287, 297, 298, 323, 325
Nasserism, 152–174
nation states (states), 253. See also separate list-
    ings for states
National Association for the Advancement of
    Colored People (NAACP), 139, 140
National Congress of British West Africa, 141
National Health Service, 35, 38, 39
National Institute of Agrarian Reform (INRA),
    120, 126
National Planning Commission (Egypt), 173
National Revolutionary Movement (Viet Nam),
    195, 202
National Union (Egypt), 154, 155, 273
nationalism, 4, 9, 10, 11, 98, 141, 153, 154,
    160, 270, 364, 446
nationalization, 51, 329, 437
Nth Country problem, 408, 450
Negritude, 144, 145, 147, 148, 150
Negroes, 17, 18, 19; Pan-Africanism, 137–151
Nehru, Jawaharlal, 187, 342, 366, 372
Nenni, 55
Netherlands, 22, 101, 288, 364, 365
neutralism, 148, 149, 179, 190, 191, 236, 238,
    280, 283, 284, 428–429; activist, 242; Egyp-
    tian, 175–191; positive, 180
neutrality, 175; responsible, 189–191
neutralization, 185, 242
New Deal, 23, 434
New Delhi, 331

Ne Win, 383
New Left (British), 55, 56, 57, 60
New Left Review, 57
New York Group Theatre, 64
New Zealand, 288
Nhu, Madame, 195
Nhu, Ngo Dinh, 195
Niagara Movement, 139
Nigeria, 261, 442, 443
nihilism, 81, 106, 267
Ning-i, Liu, 92
Ninth International Conference of American States, 113
Nkrumah, Kwame, 141, 142, 143, 146, 147, 148, 190, 267, 268, 269, 280, 288, 297, 323
non-intervention, 159, 160, 182, 183, 252, 293, 316, 318, 319, 324, 325, 326, 327, 329
norms, revolutionary, 210, 216
North, Robert, 282
North Atlantic Treaty Organization (NATO), 31, 53, 54, 58, 59, 66, 73, 74, 86, 252; bloc, 254–257, 265, 266, 432, 435, 446, 447, 448, 449, 452, 456, 458
nuclear weapons system, 262, 311, 336, 337, 340, 450; second strike, 262, 336, 456
Nuremberg Judgment, 321

Occupation, U.S. of Japan, 92, 101, 105, 107, 109
occupational and class structure, 39–44, 46–48, 50, 74–75, 85–86, 89, 90, 97, 101, 105, 108–110, 141, 164, 165, 172–173
Okinawa, 300
oligarchy, 20, 42, 91, 99, 270
Ordmez, José, 113
Organization of American States (OAS), 440–441, 464
Orwell, Sir George, 47
Osamu, Dazai, 106
Osborne, John, 64
Ottoman Empire, 163
Oxbridge (Oxford and Cambridge Universities), 42, 56

Pact of Paris 1928, 321
Padmore, 141, 142
Pak, 383
Pakistan, 327, 359, 360, 363, 364, 366, 383, 447
Palestine, 153, 160, 177, 178, 184, 465
Palestine Revolution (29 Nov. 1947), 177, 180
Palma, Tomas Estrada, 115, 129
Pan-African Congress, 140, 142, 144, 146, 147; 1900 London Conference, 140, 141

Pan-Africanism, 137–151, 269, 288, 290. *See also* chap. 6
Pan-Arabism (Arab unity), 101, 152–174, 273
Paraguay, 113, 134, 283
Paris Exposition, 139
Party of the Cuban People (Leftist), 119
Parti Social Français (PSF), 70
Parti Socialiste Unifié (PSU), 56, 70, 71
Peace Preservation Law (Japan), 102
peaceful (pacific) settlement, 286–287
peasants (*dascamisados*), 23; problems (rural), 75, 97, 104, 192–206
Péguy, Charles, 74
Peron, Juan Domingo, 134
Personalismo (personalism), 120, 134, 195
Peru, 125, 134, 135
Pescadores, 462
Philadelphia Exposition 1876, 114
Phillipine Islands, 230, 231, 242, 413, 414, 415, 416, 419
philosophes, 71, 83. *See also* separate listings
Piedmont, 323
Pierson, William W., 120
Pitts, Jesse R., 78, 79
Plattism, 129–130, 131, 132, 133, 136; amendment, 115
Plowshare, 339, 343
Poland, 48, 258
Polanyi, Michael, 5, 7
political system, 25, 46, 83, 89, 91, 209–232, 270–272. *See also* capitalism, communism, monarchies, etc.
polycentrism, 211, 243
Popular Front, 70, 71
population problem, 167, 168, 232, 369–370, 387
populism (populist), 20, 21, 72
Port Said, 153
Portugal, 22, 230, 269, 288, 447
post-independence period, 357, 358, 359–360, 381
Poujadism, 70, 71, 72, 73, 75, 85, 88
power, 19, 91; power balancing (relationships), 20, 240, 287, 294, 307
Price-Mars, Jean, 144, 146
professionalism, 70, 90
progress, 4–5, 220, 224, 227, 356
propaganda, 24, 26, 198, 199, 212, 238, 244, 285, 326, 329, 376, 416
Protagoras, 16
Provisional Government of the Algerian Republic, 150
Prussia, 323

Psychoanalysis, 15, 400
Puerto Rican Independence Party, 339

Quemoy, 243, 247, 263, 460, 462

Rabemananjara, Jacques, 145
RAND Corporation, 383
Rassemblement du Peuple Français (RPF), 70, 72, 77
rationality, economic, 11, 12, 13, 75, 85
reaction, 31, 101, 390, 391
re-armament, German, 72, 89
Reasoner, The, 56, 57
rebels, 31, 33, 46, 125. *See also* guerillas
recognition, of Red China, 107, 330, 331, 460–463
refugees, 464
Renan, Ernest, 77
Resident Representatives, UN, 303
retaliation, limited strategic, 397, 399, 401, 408; massive, 326, 394, 397, 400, 403, 404, 456–457; nuclear, 255, 340, 402, 403, 404
retaliatory systems, 213, 396, 399
revolution, reversibility of, 24, 327
revolutionary movements, 92, 115, 313, 318, 329
Revolutionary Workers Party (Can Lao) (Viet Nam), 195
Richelieu, Armand, Cardinal, 79
Right-Wing Leagues (France), 70, 71, 81
la Rochelle, Drieu, 74
Roman Church. *See* Catholics
Rommel, Erwin, 177
Roosevelt, Franklin Delano, 23, 47, 130, 136, 254, 434
Rosas, Juan Manuel, 123
Rostow, Walt, 98, 169
Rousseau, Jean-Jacques, 7
Roy, Jules, 91
rulers, 193, 267, 268, 274, 361–362
Russell, Bertrand, 31, 57, 59, 60
Russian Civil War, 7. *See also* Bolshevik Revolution
Ryunosuke, Akutagawa, 106

Saburo, Eda, 95
Salazar, Antonio, 447
Salisbury, Lord, 62
Samurai, 98, 99, 100, 101
sanctuary, active, 414, 415, 416, 421
San Martin, Ramon Grau, Dr., 117, 119, 124
Sarit, 383
Sartre, Jean-Paul, 74, 81, 146, 170
satellite nations, 258–259, 408, 459
satellites, 259. *See also* missiles

Saville, John, 48
Scalapino, Robert A., 275
scapegoats, 81, 272, 273, 274, 364, 433
Schelling, T. C., 308
sea power, 26, 388, 392
Sebai, Youssef El, 301
Second Empire 1870, 69
Section Française de L'Internationale Ouvriere (SFIO), 56, 76
Security Treaty, U.S., 300
Seikyo, Gondo, 104
self-defense, 321, 322, 324, 366
self-determination (national), 23, 143, 176, 183, 271, 293, 324, 325, 326
Senegal, 140, 141, 144
Senghor, Léopold-Sédar (Senegal), 144, 145
Shadow Cabinet (Great Britain), 45
Shaw, Bernard, 5
Shepperson, G., 142
Shils, Edward, 271
Shintoism, 105
Showa Restoration, 104
Shumei, Okawa, 104
Shunsuke, Tsurumi, 105
Simon, Herbert A., 281
Simon, P. H., 91
Sinai Campaign, 322. *See also* Suez Campaign
Singapore, 259, 413
Sino-Burmese negotiations of 1956, 234
slavery (slave trade), 137, 138
Snow, Sir Charles P., 43, 333–334
Socarras, Carlos Prio, 115, 117, 124
socialism, 4, 24, 25, 171–172, 373, 441
Social Democratic Federation (Great Britain), 52
social engineering, 33, 221
Socialist Democrats (Italy), 56
Socialist Party (Italy), 55–56, 257
Socrates, 15
Sohn, Louis B. 350, 351
Sodomei, 104
Sohyo (General Council of Trade Unions), 104
Somalia, 301
Somary, Felix, 3
Sophists, 15
Sorel, Jean, 74
Soustelle, Pierre, 73
Southeast Asia Peninsula, 411, 414, 417, 421, 429
South East Asia Treaty Organization (SEATO), 178, 243, 446
sovereignty, 234, 235, 315, 319, 350, 386
Soviet foreign policy, 209–232

Spain, 15, 46, 47, 116, 122, 129, 270, 296, 323, 329, 434, 442, 443, 447, 451
Spanish Civil War, 76, 324
Special Commission on Hungary, 284
Stalin, Josef, 7, 54, 218, 257, 258, 279, 285, 292
Stalinism, 47–48, 448
status quo, 9, 69, 71, 74, 95, 99, 107, 213, 214, 215, 216, 217, 219, 220, 222, 223, 232, 233, 264, 266, 270, 279, 286, 298–299, 311, 314, 317, 327, 329, 330, 331, 412, 433, 445, 453, 466
Stockholm World Peace Council, 300
Stone, Julius, 322
Strachey, Lytton, 170
strategy, 237, 238, 239, 240, 245, 330, 356, 364, 377, 388, 406
subversion, 209, 212, 214, 217, 326, 329
Sudan, 160, 175, 189
Suez Campaign, 1956, 319, 321, 450
Suez Canal, 34, 53, 55, 56, 59, 161, 163, 167, 175, 179, 180, 287, 295, 296, 302, 304, 305
suicide, 19, 58, 456
Sukarno, 268, 274, 364, 373
SUNFED, 291, 292
supranationalism, 236, 251, 254, 257, 313, 321
surprise attack, 262, 304, 338, 344, 345, 347, 351, 372, 395, 397, 403, 406, 453
surrender, 349, 394, 454
Syria, 157, 158, 161, 163, 169, 180, 190, 284
swiddens, 415
Switzerland, 185, 342
Sylvester-Williams, Henry, 139

tacit agreement, 347, 348, 403
tactics, 184, 185, 189, 197, 199, 216, 217, 243, 244–245, 246
Taijyo, Tamura, 106
Taiwan, 234, 235, 446, 453, 460–463
Takamori, Saigo, 99, 101
Taoism, 194
Technical Assistance Board (TAB), 292, 302
technological change, 231, 253
technology, 5, 25, 90, 185, 209, 217, 332, 333, 335, 341, 343, 393, 394, 414, 427
terrain, 411–414, 427
testing, nuclear, 331
Thailand, 242, 372, 383, 429, 439
theory, "scientific," 220–221
Thierry-Maulnier, 91
Third Republic, 73, 76, 80
Thompson, Edward, 48
Thuc, Ngo Dinh, 195

Tibet, rebellion 1959, 234–235, 244, 293, 328
Titmuss, Richard, 56
Tito, Josip, 187
Tocqueville, Alexis de, 3, 9, 77, 80, 82
Tokugawa, 100, 103
Torre, Victor Raul de la, 134
Tory (Conservative) Right (Great Britain), 52, 62, 63, 66
Tory Worker, The, 52
totalitarianism, 21, 25, 26, 114, 269, 442, 447, 453, 455
Touré, Sékou, 268
traditionalism, 46, 164, 192, 361, 372
Trinidad, 139, 142
Trotskyism, British, 49
Trujillo, Rafael Molina, 113, 134
Truman, Harry S., 431, 448
Tunisia, 147, 160, 297
Turkey, 190, 284, 327
Twentieth Congress of the CPSU, 48
Twenty-Second Party Congress, 211, 218, 231

U-2 incident, 317, 331
Ukraine, 10
ultra-Right (Japan), 97, 104, 105
uncommitted (neutral) states, 252, 253, 254, 255, 260–266, 432, 435–445, 452
underdeveloped (undeveloped) nations, 26, 222, 224, 225–231, 232, 271, 280, 355–380; defense and development, 381–387
unilateral action, 453
Unilateralism (nuclear), 52, 61, 345, 454
Union of South Africa, 67, 148, 262, 265, 296, 312, 342, 343
Union of Soviet Socialist Republic (USSR), 14, 23, 24, 25, 26, 47, 53, 84, 100, 106, 114, 189–190, 191, 258, 262, 263, 264, 265, 270, 271, 283, 285, 290, 292, 293, 295, 298, 302, 305, 310, 314, 315, 316, 318, 319, 322, 324, 326, 327, 328, 329, 333, 343, 346, 348, 367–369, 376, 377, 407, 408, 414, 428, 434; aid to uncommitted states, 437, 453, 454, 455, 456, 458, 460–461; Communist Party, Draft Program, 313; deterrent strategy, 214–216; foreign policy, 209–232
United Arab Republic (UAR), 150, 152–174, 175–191, 265, 289, 290, 300, 304, 305, 310, 329, 440; and Israel, 464–465
United Nations, 132, 181, 186, 267–309, 312, 319, 321, 328, 330, 432, 444, 448–452, 460, 461, 465; Charter, Article 2(4), 321, Article 14, 287, Article 51, 321, Article 73e, 289, 296, 302; Conciliation Commission, 289;

Emergency Force, 305; EPTA, 292; GATT, 292; General Assembly, 289, 290, 293, 295, 298, 307, 319, 444; IBRD, 302; IFC, 291, 292; IMF, 302; Secretariat, 188, 265, 292, 295; Secretary General, 282, 287, 289, 297, 301, 304, 305, 307, 449, 451; Security Council, 276, 295, 305, 306; Special Fund, 291, 292; SUNFED, 291, 292; TAB, 292, 302; Trusteeship, 288; World Court, 317, 318

United States of America, 6, 10, 14, 19, 20, 21, 22, 23, 26, 34, 53, 67, 83, 105–108, 128, 137, 176, 194, 219, 254, 255, 262, 263, 264, 288, 305, 310, 314, 317, 318, 319, 321, 324, 325, 326, 328, 330, 334, 343, 346; American aid, 355–380; and the communist bloc, 452–456; Congress of, 444; Department of State, 9, 465; forces in Burma, 408, 412, 414, 419, 432, 433, 444; and General Alliance Policy, 444–448; military policy of, 456–466; and uncommitted states, 435–445; and the UN, 448–452

Uniting for Peace Resolution, 279
Universal Declaration of Human Rights, 293, 296, 298
Union for the New Republic (UAR), 88
Universities and Left Review, The, 56, 57
U Nu (Burma), 366
urbanization, 121, 122, 134, 192, 365
Uruguay, 113, 122, 134
Utley, T. E., 62
utopianism, 13, 23, 84, 210, 212, 351
Uzbek Republic, 228–231

Valla, Lorenzo, 4
values, Western, 7–9, 225
Vargas Getulio, 134
Venezuela, 122, 125, 134, 135, 441, 464
Versailles, 7
Vichy, 83, 86
Victoria, Queen of England, 44, 139, 141
Viet Cong, 192, 196, 197, 198, 199, 202, 206; "families," 202–203
Vietminh, 413, 416, 417, 420, 429, 456
Viet Nam, North, 456
Viet Nam, South, 192–206, 240, 363–366, 371, 372, 381, 383, 384–385, 387, 411, 413, 415, 417, 420, 424, 429, 436
vulnerability, nuclear, 213, 259, 263

Waelder, Robert, 75
Wahl, Nicholas, 88
Walters, Alexander, 139
Walters, Bishop, 139
war, broken-backed, 399; counter-guerrilla, 411–430, 421–424; defensive, 402; guerrilla, 411–430, 457; inadvertant, 337–338; limited, 294, 338, 399, 400; nuclear, 185, 252–255, 311, 312
Wars of Independence, 114
Washington, Booker T., 138
Weber, Max, 120
Welch, William, 299
Welfare State, 35, 36, 37, 39, 51, 56, 62
West African National Secretariat, 143
Westernization, 99, 101, 121, 122, 141, 227
West Indies, 137, 144
West Irian, 297, 364, 365, 387
Williams, Raymond, 61
Wilson, Woodrow, 139
Wolfers, Arnold, 277
Workers' Musical League (Japan), 103
World Congress of Black Writers and Artists, 146, 147
World War I, 100, 101, 102, 176, 226, 320, 324, 392
World War II, 14, 19, 69, 136, 141, 142, 192, 211, 241, 254, 324, 325, 343, 363, 379, 417, 428, 454
Wylie, Laurence, 78

Yalu River, 311
Yi-Ch'en, 237, 244
Yoshida, Shigeru, 242
Yugoslavia, 178, 181, 182, 187, 189, 190, 225, 236, 258, 269, 442

Zaldivar, Fulgencio, 113
Zengakuren, 106
Zenro, 104
Zhdanovisiu, 47, 295
Zionism, 153